the King's, the Queen's English
But what about power, and feminism, the king's and queen's *two* bodies—and AIDS?
THE BODY POLITIC [Davie, Warner, Lee, Scruton, Gilbert, Fisher, Hughes, Grover, Koestenbaum, Callen]

the king's coin
And the way money talks, in advertising, in philanthropy, in careerism, on Wall Street?
MONEY [Chatman, Romaine, Lesser, Lodge, Odean]

England proper
Not what it means by "England proper," but *is* England proper: English rudeness, English manners?
RECTITUDES [Algeo, Thomas]

as distinguished from Ireland
Ah, the United Kingdom: but what does an Irish poet make of English—and of Irish?
ENGLISHES [McGuckian]

standard form
But don't different practices operate or set different standards, and perhaps threaten standards differently: in the law, in politics, in journalism, in universities, in computer technology, and now in the professionalizing of emotional life?
PRACTICES [Garner, Minow, Lutz, Reid, Raphael, Gross, Lurie, Heim, Rogers, Michaels]

etc.
And what else lurks in this *etc.*, set as it is against "the literary or standard form"? For one thing, those language-worlds which are other than literary because they engage arts other than literature: film, show-biz, opera, music—subway graffiti? For another, the language-world which is other than standard because it uses bad language.
ART [Muldoon, Lenti, Bawtree, Botstein, Ong]
RECTITUDES [Harris, Pitt-Kethley, Hasse, Nemrow]

the literary
And the range of the literary—not only in novels, and in poems (and *as* poems), but in letters and in hymns?
ART [Burchfield, Pinsky, Hollander, Goldensohn, Doody]

C.R.
Cambridge, June 1989

❧ THE STATE OF THE LANGUAGE

A CENTENNIAL BOOK

One hundred distinguished books
published between 1990 and 1995
bear this special imprint
of the University of California Press.
We have chosen each Centennial Book
as an exemplar of the Press's great publishing
and bookmaking traditions as we enter
our second century.

UNIVERSITY OF CALIFORNIA PRESS

Founded in 1893

Publication of *The State of the Language*
was supported by a generous grant from
the George Frederick Jewett Foundation

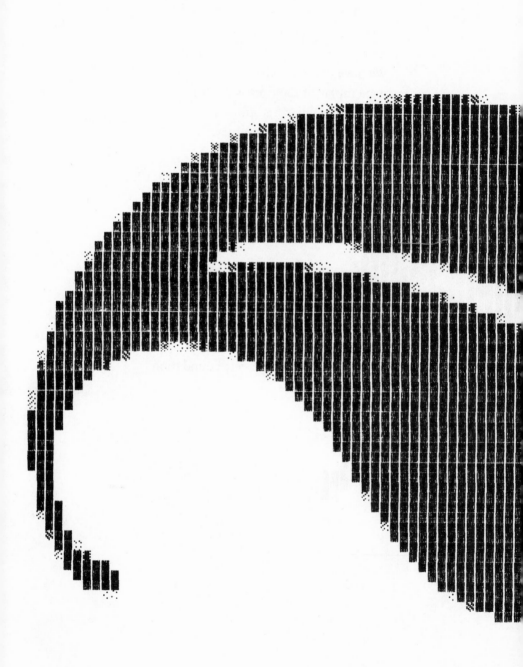

The State of the Language

EDITED BY CHRISTOPHER RICKS
AND LEONARD MICHAELS

Published in association with the
English-Speaking Union,
San Francisco Branch

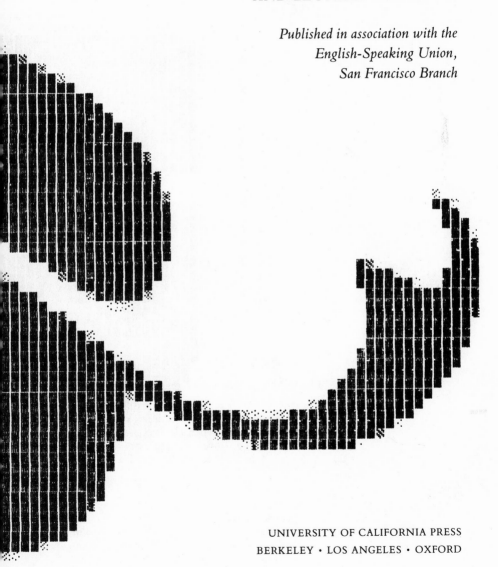

UNIVERSITY OF CALIFORNIA PRESS
BERKELEY · LOS ANGELES · OXFORD

University of California Press
Berkeley and Los Angeles, California

University of California Press, Ltd.
Oxford, England

© 1990 by
The Regents of the University of California

Library of Congress Cataloging-in-Publication Data

The State of the language.
    1. English language—20th century.   I. Ricks,
Christopher B.   II. Michaels, Leonard, 1933–
    PE1087.S69   1990   420′.904   89-4853
            ISBN 0-520-05906-9 (alk. paper)

Printed in the United States of America

1 2 3 4 5 6 7 8 9

The paper used in this publication meets the minimum
requirements of American National Standard for Information Sciences—Permanence of Paper for Printed
Library Materials, ANSI Z39.48-1984. ♾™

❧ CONTENTS

The Body Politic

Money

Practices

Art

Rectitudes

NOTHING IS MORE FRAUGHT WITH CONTENTION and taboo than language. We speak of its armory of "fighting words," and there is the fearful warning, "Watch your language." Jeremy Bentham says, "endless is the confusion, the error, the hostility" to which our delusions regarding language give rise. But simply to speak of language invites hostility, for, in one or another way, the topic raises issues of mystery and faith—how did it begin? where does it exist? what is it? can we ever be so good as not to violate its rules? what are its rules?

Such questions are made more tortuous by Wittgenstein, the great modern philosopher of language. He says, "to *think* one is obeying a rule is not to obey a rule." It isn't easy to know what he means. Perhaps a correct grammarian is to an unself-conscious speaker as a yapping watchdog is to a singing canary, since the bird, obedient to instinctive rules, plays freely in its language. It is the opinion of Octavio Paz that we now give to language the sort of passionate attention we once gave to God, but students of the mystical Kabala have done this for centuries. They believe, says Scholem, "everything that lives is the expression of God's language."

It used to be said that language, "the sign of thought," is what passes back and forth in the air between speakers. Later it was said to be built into the mind, and, since nothing in the mind is inaccessible to the mind, we can hope to know what we don't yet know about lan-

guage. Long ago some philologists believed it exists essentially in literature, but the great majority of languages never had a literature.
Wherever one finally locates language and however it is conceived, it
remains elusive, changing continuously—perhaps every generation—
with the expressive needs of speakers. One language may even change
into another. No less remarkable is how language resembles its speakers, since every word has a biography, perhaps an inner life, or self,
not to mention relatives, enemies, and friends. The witty philosopher
J. L. Austin said words tend to stay in the language insofar as they
sound like other words that have a similar meaning. *Sneer, snicker,
snide* are friendly, nourishing one another. But words, like speakers,
ultimately lose meaning and value, and don't usually come to much
good. Their careers are nevertheless darkly fascinating. Some thinkers
have claimed that language constantly betrays us. Merely to speak, according to Hegel, is a kind of self-betrayal in that we surrender our
innermost being to the mercy of circumstances. He doesn't mean this
happens when we order a hamburger; but more like what happens to
Hamlet:

> . . . I have that within which passes show,
> These but the trappings and the suits of woe.

What he has "within," despite himself, is betrayed in his show of
words, but there is no play and no significant life otherwise.

It is our nature to use language, or, in several senses, to be used by
it. Until recently, it was considered very good luck to be used by English. As a number of essays in this new collection on The State of the
Language tell us, there are now quite a few Englishes, and formerly
colonized people may well prefer to get free of them and be used by
their own language. Other essays speak of pressures from within and
without that oblige English to bethink itself and to change in radical
ways. The new edition of the *OED*, which contains over a quarter
million words, like the language itself, is a miracle of accommodation.

In yet other essays we hear that advertising and popular music are
changing English in the direction of meaninglessness. It's an old complaint that popular music is played so loud you can't hear the lyrics, let
alone detect their meaning. But consider what you do hear in this utterance by the vice president of the United States:

> What a waste it is to lose your mind—or never to have had one. How
> true that is.

One essay notices "doublespeak" everywhere in government and
business. When used deliberately, it is intended not to mean anything,
or else to mean what cannot literally be discovered in the words. In

effect, speakers escape responsibility for whatever you might have imagined them to mean. Through such English, a strange condition prevails. When offered stimulation rather than any substantive communication, listeners somehow produce a feeling of meaning in their minds, though nothing is really there at all. Another essayist tells us that even sophisticated reporters give high praise to speechwriters and speechmakers who can make this happen. This Orwellian phenomenon appears in the academic world where literary theorists argue that the meanings of novels and poems are produced by readers. Still others say there is no such thing as meaning, only a vast illusion of meaning generated by the discourse of society at large. Individual speakers are the media of media. There are really no authors, no originators. Nobody is immediate and we don't even actually communicate, for, like the foamy crest of a wave, our meaning is produced by forces below and all about.

With meaning conceived as evanescent blather, it is strange to find word processors universally available, even being urged upon tiny children in our schools long before they learn there is nothing to say. One essayist tells us these machines are a threat to meaning, or, assuming there isn't any anyway, to the hope of it. He suggests they diminish our ability to distinguish meaning from information, or to understand that meaning is achieved through the difficult work of minds.

Aside from these contentions, the essays here treat English in its present relation to art, manners, sex, feminism, money, obscenity, violence, law, AIDS, religious values, and other matters that suggest its infinite potential to reveal or betray life's infinite variety. The collection includes an essay on the English of *Variety*, and essays on certain unities. For example, the expression *turned on*, very common today, is noticed for its analogy to light switches. One might also notice *turned off*, or, in regard to murder, *offed*. All indicate a unifying current in our thinking which has to do with perceptions of mechanicity. The essays themselves, in their thinking and perceiving, laughter and complaining, indicate we are very different from machines in our language.

We are grateful to the English-Speaking Union, San Francisco Branch, and to its Executive Director, Maryellen Himell, for sponsoring the project and helping in so many ways, to the George Frederick Jewett Foundation for providing funds, and to William J. McClung and Will Sulkin, our editors at the University of California Press and Faber and Faber. Most particularly we thank our project editor, Eileen McWilliam, for her generosity in time and spirit and skill.

L.M.
Berkeley, June 1989

Englishes

If English was good enough for Jesus,
it is good enough for you.

ARKANSAS TOWN SCHOOL SUPERINTENDENT,
refusing request that foreign languages
be taught in high school

✎ DAVID DABYDEEN

On Not Being Milton:
Nigger Talk in England Today

IT'S HARD TO PUT TWO WORDS TOGETHER in creole without swearing. Words are spat out from the mouth like live squibs, not pronounced with elocution. English diction is cut up, and this adds to the abruptness of the language: *what* for instance becomes *wha* (as in *whack*), the splintering making the language more barbaric. Soft vowel sounds are habitually converted: the English tend to be polite in *war*, whereas the creole *warre* produces an appropriate snarling sound; *scorn* becomes *scaan*, *water wata*, and so on.

In 1984 I published a first collection of poems entitled *Slave Song*, written in a Caribbean creole and dealing with the Romance of the Cane, meaning the perverse eroticism of black labor and the fantasy of domination, bondage, and sadomasochism. The British Empire, as the Thistlewood Diaries show, was as much a pornographic as an economic project.[1] The subject demanded a language capable of describing both a lyrical and a corrosive sexuality. The creole language is angry, crude, energetic. The canecutter chopping away at the crop bursts out in a spate of obscene words, a natural gush from the gut.

In the preface to *Slave Song* I speak of the brokenness of the language which reflects the brokenness and suffering of its original users. Its potential as a naturally tragic language is there in its brokenness and rawness, which is like the rawness of a wound. If one has learnt and used Queen's English for some years, the return to creole is painful, almost nauseous, for the language is uncomfortably raw. One has to shed one's protective sheath of abstracts and let the tongue move freely in blood again.

In writing *Slave Song* I had no Caribbean literary models to imitate, since I knew none. Apart from early childhood in Guyana I was brought up in England and no Caribbean literature was taught in schools. So I was wholly ignorant of the creole poetry of Edward Brathwaite or Claude McKay, the latter influenced by the balladry of Burns. What in fact triggered off *Slave Song* were the years spent as an undergraduate at Cambridge reading English literature. There was the discovery of the "gaudy and inane phraseology" of much of eighteenth-century poetry, the wrapping of stark experiences in a napkin of poetic diction. James Grainger's poem *The Sugar Cane*, for instance, in which the toil of plantation life is erased or converted into pastoral. Instead of *overseer* Grainger uses the term "Master Swain"; instead of *slaves*, "assistant planters." The black condition is further embellished by calling the slaves "Afric's sable progeny." Grainger's poem is a classic example in English poetry of the refusal to call a spade a spade. Then there were all those antislavery pieces in a highfalutin Miltonic rhetoric and cadence, in which the poets used the black experience merely as a vehicle for lofty, moral pronouncements on good and evil. Or Coleridge's Greek Ode against slavery, which won him the Browne Gold Medal at Cambridge: the African here is subject to the exercise of classical erudition.

The real discovery, however, was of medieval alliterative verse. Reading *Sir Gawain and the Green Knight* was a startling moment. The sheer naked energy and brutality of the language, its "thew & sinew," reminded me immediately of the creole of my childhood. John of Trevisa, a fourteenth-century translator, described the alliterative poetry of the North of England as "harsh, piercing and formless." This quality of lawlessness and the primarily oral form of delivery bore a curious resemblance to Guyanese creole. I began to see, albeit naively, the ancient divide between north and south in Britain, the Gawain poet standing in opposition to Chaucer in terms of a native idiom versus an educated, relaxed poetic line tending towards the form of the iambic pentameter. The north/south divide is of course evocative of the divide between the so-called Caribbean periphery and the metropolitan center of London. London is supposed to provide the models of standard English, and we in the Caribbean our dialect versions.

The comparison between England and the modern Caribbean is not altogether fanciful, for in a sense we West Indians live in the Middle Ages in terms of rudimentary material resources. The British Empire was after all a feudal structure with robber barons and serfs. Transportation by horse, mule, or canoe, peasant farming, manual labor, villages lying in patches of land encircled by bush in the way that dense forest lay just outside English castle walls, these features and others of Guyana's countryside conjure up medieval life. And if, as Johan Huizinga states in *The Waning of the Middle Ages*, the sound of church bells dominated the air of England, so too in Guyana is religion a vital, noisy force. And out of this matrix of spirit and earth is born a language that is both lyrical and barbaric. But the very unsystematic and unscientific nature of the language which is a source of strength to writers like myself is cause for summary dismissal or parody for others. Peter Porter, for instance, speaks dismissively of the "difficulty" of understanding creole; presumably Porter has no time for Shakespeare or Joyce either. In *Slave Song*, in anticipation of such automatic responses, I clothed the creole poems in an elaborate set of "notes" and "translations" as an act of counterparody, in the way that Eliot had annotated his *Waste Land* supposedly for the benefit of his lazier readers. The more common English response to creole, however, is to be found from Alan Coren's pen. Coren in 1975 published the second volume of the collected thoughts of Idi Amin, which had been appearing in *Punch* magazine for some months. In the introduction Amin is made to reveal the burden of words:

> One trouble wid de bes' seller business: you gittin' boun' to de wheel o' fire. No sooner you dishin' out one giant masterpiece to de gobblin' pubberlic, they comin' round yo' premises an' hammerin' on de door fo' de nex'. "Come on out, John Milton!" de mob yellin', "We know yo' in there! We jus' finishin' de *Parachute Lost* an' we twiddlin' de thums, wot about dis year's jumbo pome you lazy bum?"
>
> It hardly surprisin' E. N. Fleming packin' up de Jane Bond racket an' turnin' to de penicillin business. Dam sight easier scrapin' de mold off bread an' floggin' it up de chemist than bashin' de fingers flat day an' nights on de Olivetti an' wonderin' where yo' nex' plot comin' f'om.
>
> Natcherly, de same happenin' wid de present writer. Las' year, de astoundin' fust book hittin' de shops, an' befo' anyone know wot happenin' de made fans smashin' down de premises o' W. H. Smith an' carryin' de amazin' tomes off by de crate! De pubberlisher rushin' out four impressions in four munce, an' still de cravin' not satisfied. "It no good", de pubberlisher informin' me. "Only one way to shut de slaverin' buggers' gobs, yo' imperial majesty: you havin' to cobble together another great milestone in de history o' literature, how about Wensdy week?"
>
> So here I sittin, shovin' de affairs o' state on one side, an' puttin' together a noo volume o' de famous weekly bulletins f'om downtown Kampala, Hub o' de Universe.

Two ancient images of black people emerge from Coren's pen. First, the sense that they are scientifically illiterate. This idea can be

traced back to seventeenth- and eighteenth-century European writings which describe African societies as being devoid of intellectual
capacities ("No ingenious manufacture amongst them, no arts, no sciences," as David Hume declared). They squat in mud huts and gnaw
bones. They know neither compass nor telescope. European literature
is littered with blacks like Man Friday, who falls to earth to worship
Crusoe's magical gun, or the savage in Conrad's steamship who acted
as fireman:

> He was an improved specimen; he could fire up a vertical boiler. He was
> there below me, and, upon my word, to look at him was as edifying as
> seeing a dog in a parody of breeches and a feather hat, walking on his
> hind-legs. A few months of training had done for that really fine chap.
> He squinted at the steam-gauge and at the water-gauge with an evident
> effort of intrepidity—and he had filed teeth, too, the poor devil, and the
> wool of his pate shaved into queer patterns, and three ornamental scars
> on each of his cheeks. He ought to have been clapping his hands and
> stamping his feet on the bank, instead of which he was hard at work, a
> thrall to strange witchcraft, full of improving knowledge. He was useful
> because he had been instructed; and what he knew was this—that should
> the water in that transparent thing disappear, the evil spirit inside the
> boiler would get angry through the greatness of his thirst, and take a ter-
> rible vengeance. So he sweated and fired up and watched the glass fear-
> fully (with an impromptu charm, made of rags, tied to his arm, and a
> piece of polished bone, as big as a watch, stuck flat-ways through his
> lower lip), while the wooded banks slipped past us slowly, the short
> noise was left behind, the interminable miles of silence—and we crept
> on, towards Kurtz.

Secondly, the sense that they are linguistically illiterate. Just as they
are ignorant of the rules of scientific formulae, so they are ignorant of
the rules of grammar. Their language is mere broken, stupid utterance. Again this view of black expression is firmly entrenched in European conceptualization. In seventeenth-century travel literature and
anthropological writings the bestiality of the natives is reflected in
their language. Sir Thomas Herbert in 1634 suggested that Africans
and apes mated with each other, the evidence for this being that African speech sounded "more like that of Apes than Men . . . their language is rather apishly than articulately founded." Many passages focus on the monstrosity of their organs of speech as well as their organs
of propagation. Whilst John Ogilby (1670) is writing about the "large
propagators" sported by the men of Guinea, and Richard Jobson
(1623) on male Mandingoes being "furnished with such members as
are after a sort burdensome unto them," William Strachey (1612) fo-
cuses on their "great big lips and wide mouths." Thick lips and mon-

strously misshapen mouths, sometimes, as in the case of the anthro-pophagi, located in their chests, indicated an inability to make proper speech. When we find eloquent and civilized blacks in English litera-ture of the period, as in the case of Mrs. Aphra Behn's Oroonoko, their physical features are more European than African: "His mouth, the finest shaped that could be seen; far from those great turn'd lips which are so natural to the rest of the Negroes."

In the eighteenth century, which was the Age of Slavery as well as the Age of the Dictionary, such attitudes to Africans were sustained, the link between barbarism and lack of speech made explicit. *Spectator* No. 389 of May 1712 described Hottentots as "Barbarians, who are in every respect scarce one degree above Brutes, having no language among them but a confused Gabble, which is neither well understood by themselves or others." Given the centrality of the Word in eighteenth-century English civilization (Pope's "What oft was thought, but ne'er so well expressed"; Hogarth's *Conversation Pieces*; Steele's *Tatler*; Johnson's *Dictionary*), the apparent wordlessness of the Africans was deemed to be incontrovertible evidence of their barbarism.

The equation between African and animal, sustained by the issue of language, which gave moral validity to the slave trade, continued in the nineteenth century, the Age of Imperialism and Anthropometrics. Africans' skulls, lips, teeth, and mouths were scrupulously measured by leading white scientists to reveal black cultural and moral primitiv-ism and therefore the necessity of continuing colonial rule. Science underpinned the imperial process. It was also quite obvious, however, that Africans had language, and this posed a problem to white con-ceptualization since language was an undeniable *human* characteristic. Professor Bernth Lindfors illustrates the problem by reference to the case of the San people of South Africa, a group of whom were brought to Britain between 1846 and 1850 to be displayed at circuses and fairgrounds.[2] The speech of the San visitors was their most no-ticeable feature: 70 percent of it consisted of a set of implosive con-sonants, commonly called "clicks," which were absent from the En-glish phonological system. Lindfors states that "the number and variety of these click consonants, complicated still further by subtle vowel colourings and significant variations in tone make it, from the phonetic point of view, among the world's most complex languages." To the Victorians, however, hardly interested in such analysis, San speech merely sounded like animal noises. The *Liverpool Chronicle* re-ported that "the language resembles more the cluck of turkeys than the speech of human beings" (5 December 1846), and the *Era* de-scribed the language as "wholly incomprehensible, for nobody can in-

terpret it. . . . The words are made up of coughs and clucks, such as
a man uses to his nag. Anything more uncivilised can scarcely be conceived" (6 June 1847). Even when admission of the humanity of the
San people was grudgingly conceded, the classics of white literature
were raised against them: the *Observer* wrote that "their distinguishing
characteristic as men is their use of language, but besides that, they
have little in common . . . with that race of beings which boasts of a
Newton and a Milton" (21 June 1847). The science of Newton and the
literature of Milton are sufficient to put black people in their place. Idi
Amin's (Alan Coren's) reference to Milton is not a loose one. Milton's
ornate, highly structured, Latinate expressions, so unattractive to
modern tastes influenced by Eliot and Yeats, are still the exemplars of
English civilization against which the barbaric, broken utterances of
black people are judged.

II

In January 1978 Margaret Thatcher made a speech broadcast on prime-
time television which reinforced the notions of "otherness" so prevalent in British writings on blacks. It was rhetoric which decimated
the neo-fascist National Front party as an electoral force by winning
the far-right of the Tory party:

> If we went on as we are, then by the end of the century there would be
> four million people of the New Commonwealth or Pakistan here. Now
> that is an awful lot and I think it means that people are really rather afraid
> that this country might be swamped by people with a different culture.
> And you know, the British character has done so much for democracy,
> for law, and done so much throughout the world, that if there is a fear
> that it might be swamped, people are going to react and be rather hostile
> to those coming in.

Her pronouncement, however, was very outdated, for the native British some four decades earlier had already exhibited "rather hostile"
(note how the upper-class term "rather" softens the sinisterness of
"hostile" and "afraid") behavior towards fellow black citizens. In September 1948, two months after the first boatload of postwar West Indian immigrants arrived on the *S.S. Empire Windrush*, race riots broke
out in the streets of England. A decade later, in 1958, antiblack riots
erupted in Nottingham and in the Notting Hill area of London, with
gangs of white teenagers engaged in "nigger hunting," the working-
class version of fox-hunting. In the next decade onwards, communal
violence based on Catholic-Protestant/Irish-English hostilities became a daily feature of British life. The killing of civilians, policemen,

soldiers, politicians, and one member of the Royal Family dominated television screens. In the eighties, race riots in Bristol, Liverpool, and London (the old slave ports) led to the police use of plastic bullets for the first time on the British mainland. Today, even Home Office statistics reveal that the number of physical racial attacks on black people runs into the thousands annually, while the nighttime burning down of homes is a routine experience for some immigrant communities. When E. P. Thompson declared that "England is the last colony of the British Empire," it was to such neo-colonial violence and communal strife that he was referring.

One of the many ways in which young British blacks have resisted white domination is in the creation of a patois evolved from the West Indian creole of their parents. The poetry that has emerged from the black communities is expressed in the language of this patois, and one of its greatest exponents is Linton Kwesi Johnson:

> Shock-black bubble-doun-beat bouncing
> rock-wise tumble-doun sound music:
> foot-drop find drum, blood story,
> bass history is a moving
> is a hurting black story.
> ("Reggae Sounds")[3]

Johnson's poetry is recited to music from a reggae band. The paraphernalia of sound systems, amplifiers, speakers, microphones, electric guitars, and the rest which dominates the stage and accompanies what one critic has dismissed as "jungle-talk" is a deliberate "misuse" of white technology. "Sound systems," essential to "dub-poetry," are often homemade contraptions, cannibalized parts of diverse machines reordered for black expression. This de/reconstruction is in itself an assertive statement, a denial of the charge of black incapacity to understand technology. The mass-produced technology is remade for self-use in the way that the patois is a "private" reordering of "standard" English. The deliberate exploitation of high-tech to serve black "jungle-talk" is a reversal of colonial history. Caliban is tearing up the pages of Prospero's magic book and repasting it in his own order, by his own method, and for his own purpose.

A feature of Black British poetry is a sheer delight in the rhythm and sound of language that survives technology, and this joyousness is revealed in poems like Mikey Smith's "R-ooTs" (the line "lawwwwwwd," as Edward Brathwaite says, sounding like the exhaust roar of a motorcycle) or in the writings of Jimi Rand. There is a deliberate celebration of the "primitive" consciousness of sound in Smith's "Nock-Nock":

> Me was fas asleep in me bed
> wen a nok come pun me door,
> bright and early, fore day morning
> before dawn bruk.
> Nock nock—nock nock,
> badoombadoom nock nock
> badoombadoom nock nock
> badoombadoom nock badoom nock.
> Who dat; a who dat nock?[4]

This deliberate wearing of the "primitive" label is even more explicit in his "Nigger Talk" poem:

> Funky talk
> Nitty gritty grass-root talk
> Dat's wha I da talk
> Cause de talk is togedder talk,
> Like right on, out-a-sight, kind-a-too-much.
> Ya hip to it yet?
> Ya dig de funky way to talk
> Talk talk?
> Dis na white talk;
> Na white talk dis.
> It is coon, nignog samba wog talk.[5]

The use of language is inextricably bound up with a sense of being black. Hence John Agard's poem "Listen Mr Oxford Don" is conscious of the way creole suffers from the charge of being surly and indecent ("Mugging de Queen's English"), and Agard links this literary indictment to attitudes in the wide society where blacks are accused of a host of criminal activities:

> Dem accuse me of assault
> on de Oxford dictionary /
> imagine a concise peaceful man like me /
> dem want me serve time
> for inciting rhyme to riot
> so mek dem send one big word after me
> i ent serving no jail sentence
> I slashing suffix in self-defence
> I bashing future wit present tense
> and if necessary
>
> I making de Queen's English accessory / to my offence[6]

Johnson, Agard, and others are reacting against the "rational structure and comprehensible language" which Robert Conquest saw as a distinguishing feature of the Movement poets and which still afflicts contemporary English verse. The charge that Alvarez leveled against the Movement—the disease of gentility—is still relevant today. Andrew Motion, for instance, can visit Anne Frank's room and on emerging conclude that all Anne Frank wanted was to

> leave as simply
> as I do, and walk at ease
> up dusty tree-lined avenues, or watch
> a silent barge come clear of bridges
> settling their reflections in the blue canal.[7]

There is glibness and gentility here, disguised as understatement but really amounting to a kind of obscenity. As Michael Hulse has commented, "to go as a tourist to a house which, like many similar houses in Amsterdam, focussed human hope and suffering, and then to parade the delicacy of one's response, savours somewhat of an opportunism that is slightly obscene." The quiet understatement of Motion's response to human tragedy is as obscene as Conrad's heated, insistent rhetoric ("It was the stillness of an implacable force brooding over an inscrutable intention," etc.): both belong to a tradition of colonizing the experience of others for the gratification of their own literary sensibilities.

The pressure of the same racism that destroyed Anne Frank and encounter with the thuggery that lurks beneath the polite surface of English life and letters force black writers into poetry that is disturbing and passionate. The play of the light of memory upon pine furniture, touching vignettes of domestic life, elegiac recollections of dead relatives, wonderment at the zig-zag fall of an autumnal leaf, none of these typical contemporary English poetic concerns are of special relevance to them. They participate in a West Indian literary tradition which seeks to subvert English canons by the use of lived nigger themes in lived nigger language. Their strategies of "rants, rudeness, and rhymes" look back half a century to the West Indian struggle to establish "black" expression. In March 1931 a new Trinidadian journal, *The Beacon*, attempted to instigate a movement for "local" literature, encouraging writing that was authentic to the West Indian landscape and to the daily speech of its inhabitants. "We fail utterly to understand," an editorial of January/February 1932 commented on the quality of short stories received for publication, "why anyone should want to see Trinidad as a miniature Paradiso, where gravediggers speak like English M.P.'s." Emphasis was placed on the use of creole, and on a realistic description of West Indian life, for political and aesthetic reasons. To write in creole was to validate the experience of black people against the contempt and dehumanizing dismissal by white people. Celebration of blackness necessitated celebration of black language, for how could black writers be true to their blackness using the language of their colonial masters? The aesthetic argument was bound up with this political argument, and involved an appreciation of the energy, vitality, and expressiveness of creole, an argument that Edward Brathwaite has rehearsed in his book *The History of the Voice* (1984). For Brathwaite the challenge to West Indian poets was how to shatter the frame of the iambic pentameter which had prevailed in English poetry from the time of Chaucer onwards. The form of the pentameter is not appropriate to a West Indian environment: "The hurricane does not roar in pentameters. And that's the problem: how do you get a rhythm which approximates the *natural* experience, the *environmental* experience?"[8] The use of creole, or Nation language, as he terms it, involves recognition of the vitality of the oral tradition surviving from Africa, the earthiness of proverbial folk speech, the energy and power of gestures which accompany oral delivery, and the insistence of the drumbeat to which the living voice responds.

England today is the largest West Indian island after Jamaica and Trinidad—there are over half a million of us here—and our generation is confronted by the same issues that Brathwaite and other writers faced in their time. If a writer was to be recognized, the pressure then was to slavishly imitate the expressions of the Mother Country. Hence the vague Miltonic cadence of Walter Mac M. Lawrence, one of our early Guyanese writers, in describing, quite inappropriately, the native thunder of the Kaiteur Falls:

> And falling in splendour sheer down from the heights
> that should gladden the heart of our eagle to scan,
> That lend to the towering forest beside thee the semblance
> of shrubs trimmed and tended by man—
> That viewed from the brink where the vast, amber volume
> that once was a stream cataracts into thee,
> Impart to the foothills surrounding the maelstrom beneath
> thee that rage as this troublous sea.[9]

Brathwaite and others eventually rescued us from this cascade of nonsense sounds. The pressure now is also towards mimicry. Either you drop the epithet "black" and think of yourself as a "writer" (a few of us foolishly embrace this position, desirous of the status of "writing" and knowing that "black" is blighted)—that is, you cease dwelling on the nigger/tribal/nationalistic theme, you cease *folking* up the literature, and you become "universal"—or else you perish in the backwater of small presses, you don't get published by the "quality" presses, and you don't receive the corresponding patronage of media-hype. This is how the threat against us is presented. Alison Daiches, summarizing these issues, puts them in a historical context: the pressure is to become a mulatto and house-nigger (Ariel) rather than stay a field-nigger (Caliban).[10]

I cannot feel or write poetry like a white man, however, much less serve him. And to become mulattos, black people literally have to be fucked (and fucked up) first. Which brings us back to the pornography of Empire. I feel that I am different, not wholly, but sufficiently for me to want to contemplate that which is other in me, that which owes its life to particular rituals of ancestry. I know that the concept of "otherness" is the fuel of white racism and dominates current political discourse, from Enoch Powell's "In these great numbers blacks are, and remain, alien here. With the growth of concentrated numbers, their alienness grows not by choice but by necessity," to Margaret Thatcher's "swamped by people of a different culture." I also know that the concept of "otherness" pervades English literature, from Desdemona's fatal attraction to the body of alien experience in preference to the familiarity of her own culture to Marlow's obsession with the thought that Africans are in one sense alien but in a more terrible sense the very capacities within Europeans for the gratification of indecent pleasures. But these are not my problem. I'm glad to be peculiar, to modify the phrase. I'd prefer to be simply peculiar, and to get on with it, to live and write accordingly, but gladness is a forced response against the weight of insults, a throwing off of white men's burdens.

As to "universality," let Achebe have the last word, even if in the most stylish of English:

> In the nature of things the work of a Western writer is automatically informed by universality. It is only others who must strain to achieve it. So-and-so's work is universal; he has truly arrived! As though universality were some distant bend in the road which you may take if you travel out far enough in the direction of Europe or America, if you put adequate distance between yourself and your home. I should like to see the word "universal" banned altogether from discussion of African literature until such a time as people cease to use it as a synonym for the narrow, self-serving parochialism of Europe, until their horizon extends to include all the world.[11]

Notes

1. Thomas Thistlewood was a small landowner in Western Jamaica during the eighteenth century. He chronicles the daily life around him until his death in 1786. A selection of his writings can be found in *In Miserable Slavery: Thomas Thistlewood in Jamaica, 1750–1786*, ed. Douglas Hall (London, 1988).

2. Bernth Lindfors, "The Hottentot Venus" (paper given at London University's International Conference on the History of Blacks in Britain, 1981).

3. L. K. Johnson, *Dread Beat and Blood* (London, 1975), p. 56.

4. Mikey Smith, *News for Babylon*, ed. James Berry (London, 1984), p. 108.

5. *News for Babylon*, p. 113.

6. J. Agard, *Mangoes and Bullets* (London, 1985), p. 44.

7. A. Motion, *Dangerous Play* (Middlesex, 1985), p. 41.

8. E. Brathwaite, *The History of the Voice* (London, 1984), p. 10.

9. Walter Mac M. Lawrence, cited in M. Gilkes, *Creative Schizophrenia: The Caribbean Cultural Challenge* (University of Warwick, Centre for Caribbean Studies, Third Walter Rodney Memorial Lecture, 1986), p. 3.

10. Alison Daiches, in *Third World Impact*, ed. A. Ali (London, 1988), p. 74.

11. C. Achebe, *Hopes and Impediments* (Oxford, 1988), p. 52.

~ SIDNEY GREENBAUM

Whose English?

IN A ROUSING SPEECH TO THE PATRIOTIC Royal Society of St. George in April 1988, Enoch Powell affirmed the permanent claim of the English to English:

> Others may speak and read English—more or less—but it is our language not theirs. It was made in England by the English and it remains our distinctive property, however widely it is learnt or used.[1]

Powell is a former member of the British Parliament, whose promising political career was destroyed by his vehement expression of views that were widely regarded as violently racist. In the context of a speech that refers to "a gene pool of the English people," he intended to deny privileged status not only to speakers of English from other countries, but also to those born in England who are descended from recent immigrants. At the same time he excluded the other indigenous nations of the United Kingdom (most of whom speak English as their mother tongue), since the Scots, the Welsh, and the Irish would fiercely resent being included among the English.

Powell is a former professor of classics, and he must have given some thought to the relationship between language and national identity. His possessive attitude towards the English language is probably shared by most English people, and indeed by the other ethnic groups that are native to the British Isles. As Janet Whitcut, a lexicographer who is English, remarks, "British people who haven't thought about it believe that the English language belongs to them, in the way Icelandic belongs to the Icelanders; to such an extent that the expression 'British English' may be regarded here, outside professional circles, as a tautology."[2] The attitude reported by Whitcut, and articulated by Powell with a blend of asperity and petulance, derives partly from the use of the same name for the language and for the largest ethnic group in the British Isles, and partly from an awareness that for many centuries the use of English was confined to Great Britain and in particular to England. Among the more thoughtful, it also reflects a protectiveness towards the national language. Others may speak and read it "more or less," says Powell, implying that they may misuse it more or less.

There is a history of disparagement and rejection of non-English competitors of English that extends back to the period in which a standard English began to emerge. The prestige of the distinctive standard of English in Scotland suffered when James VI of Scotland became James I of England and moved to London, and after the Act of Union in 1707 it came to be recognized as a regional dialect rather than an independent standard. From colonial times the divergencies of American English from British English have evoked ridicule in Britain. More recently, ridicule has often given way to fears that Americanisms will permeate the native language of Britain and subvert its national character. A typical instance of objections to the intrusion of Americanisms appears in a letter in the *Sunday Times* (27 March 1988) lambasting the use of *like* in "It wasn't like explained to me"; the letter ends ironically, "It is yet another present from the U.S." British intolerance of American differences still manifests itself two centuries after the American colonists successfully revolted against British domination. A letter in the *Standard* (10 July 1984) complains about "the debasement of the English language by our American cousins," citing as evidence the American use of expressions such as "cookie jars" and the "inevitable farewell" of "have a nice day."

The American colonists initially accepted the standard language of Britain as their standard. But the struggle for political independence was accompanied by a far more protracted struggle for linguistic independence. Those who most vigorously advocated an American standard proclaimed the existence of the American language as an entity distinct from the English language. American writers nurtured the fledgling national standard by incorporating distinctive American usages into dictionaries, grammars, and guides to usage.[3]

Languages characteristically have regional dialects. They also display variation that is related to the status of the speakers—for example, their age, sex, level of education, and social class. Local and group solidarity encourage speakers to recognize that they use distinct geographical and social pronunciations and varieties, while national pride and solidarity induce them to accept that they speak essentially the same national language.

A national language is a symbol of national identity. Noah Webster, that most famous of American lexicographers, expressed the connection that he saw between an independent nation and an independent language in a book published about twelve years after the Declaration of Independence: "As an independent nation, our honor requires us to have a system of our own, in language as well as government."[4] And it was Noah Webster who labored for the establishment of an independent national standard through his writings on grammar, his dictionaries, and his proposals for reforming English spelling, which were inspired in part by his desire that American writing should have a distinctive appearance. Americans were no longer to look to Britain for authority in language. In place of one standard English, there were now two standards—one for Britain and one for the United States.

A relatively few zealots in the United States wanted to go beyond proclaiming an independent national standard of English for their country, among them Webster himself and—in this century—H. L. Mencken. They wanted to convince their fellow citizens that there was an American language distinct from the English language. Indeed, a law enacted in 1923 in the state of Illinois proclaimed that the official language of the state should be known from then on as the American language and not the English language.[5]

There is no obvious measure of linguistic distance that could decide whether two entities are different languages or different varieties of the same language. Danish and Swedish are considered to be distinct languages even though they are mutually intelligible. Speakers on either side of the Dutch-German border can understand each other, but they claim to speak Dutch or German according to their territorial allegiance. Dialect speakers from different parts of the British Isles cannot always understand each other, but they all believe that they speak English. Although Americans do not turn to British authorities for their linguistic norms and some may mock at peculiarities of British speech, they believe that they share a common language with speakers of British English. Conversely, some British speakers may not like the way Americans use the language, but they generally agree that Americans, too, speak English.

The standard language in the United States and Britain is the prestige variety of the language used by those regarded as educated. Neither country has a standard pronunciation associated with educated speakers, though some pronunciations may be liked or valued more than others. Standardization is manifested mostly in grammar and vocabulary (though there may also be some standard regional variations) and in spelling and punctuation. Standard English allows variation according to such dimensions as the medium of communication (spoken versus written) and the relationship between participants in the discourse (the degree of formality). It comes closest to uniformity in the neutral and formal styles of written English.

The process of standardization in the United States and Britain was not controlled by the state or by a government agency or by a self-appointed language academy. In both countries the several attempts by individuals or groups to establish a language academy have failed. The proposals seem to have foundered on the objection voiced by Samuel Johnson in the Preface to his Dictionary (published in 1755) that the establishment of an academy was contrary to the "spirit of English liberty."

The development of the standard language in Britain and the United States was therefore not planned. It emerged from a consensus (in which there remains room for some diversity) of what educated speakers and writers accepted as correct. This consensus was shaped, however, by codifications that generally focused on the written language: dictionaries, grammars, and guides to usage. These works prescribed and still prescribe, whether implicitly or explicitly, the limits of variation in the standard language for spelling, punctuation, forms of words, meanings of words and longer expressions, and the appropriate styles for certain uses of the language. The standard language is maintained by the education system, where it is required at least in writing. It is preserved in printed English by editors, who do not hesitate to query (or to correct silently) the language of their authors; publishers sometimes produce a house guide to usage on disputed matters as well as stipulate that their editors consult a particular dictionary and a particular usage handbook as authoritative for the language.

Despite the absence of a language authority sanctioned by the state, the national standard language in both Britain and the United States remains remarkably uniform and stable, with the conspicuous and inevitable exception that new words and expressions are readily admitted for new things, processes, or concepts. More remarkable still, the differences between the British and American national standards are relatively small. In the last few years, under the pressure of American economic and cultural influence, the British standard is being influenced by the American standard, so that the two national standards are now converging rather than growing apart.

Over the last two centuries Britain and the United States have been the dominant English-speaking countries in population, cultural influence, and economic and military power. It is not surprising that the two national standards have been the major models for foreign learners of English. To a large extent, the two varieties have been extensively investigated to meet the requirements from the education industry for descriptions of the English language that are more accurate and more comprehensive. In some non-English-speaking countries both British English and American English are taught, sometimes in different institutions, sometimes (depending on the teacher) in the same institution. There are even foreign universities that offer courses in each standard, and many others refer to differences between the two. Generally, though, only one of the two national standards is taught, particularly in primary and secondary schools. The choice depends in part on history and geography; for example, on whether the country had been a British or U.S. colony, on its proximity to the United States or Britain, and on which of the two countries has been more influential in its economic, cultural, or technological development. But current political or commercial relations may counterbalance earlier influences.

The two major standards have influenced the national standards that have emerged after other English-speaking colonies achieved independence. Linguistically, Canadian English is closest to American English; for more than a century before the American revolution, Canadians and Americans enjoyed a common culture, and subsequently there have been close cultural and commercial ties between the two countries. But Canadians are apprehensive about intrusions from their powerful neighbor, and the threat that they see to their separate identity is reflected in their exaggeration of the differences between Canadian and American English.[6] Canada, which has also a substantial French-speaking minority, became independent from British rule in 1867 as the Dominion of Canada. Australia, which rivals Canada in the number of its mother-tongue speakers of English, became independent in 1901. Australian English is more closely identified with British English, though like other national varieties it has been considerably influenced by American English since the Second World War. As the countries with the longest history of independence from British rule (excluding the United States), Canada and Australia are particularly prominent in their quest for linguistic separatism, which is reflected in recent decades in the publication of national dictionaries and in research into national usage. At a recent Canadian conference on standard English, one of the speakers declared: "The crucial question for us in Canada is: *Can we be satisfied to accept either British or Amer-*

ican standards?" He cited with approval the answer that went back to the earliest days of the Canadian Linguistic Association: "*NO!*"[7]

There are a number of countries, in addition to Canada and Australia, where the majority of the population are mother-tongue speakers of English—New Zealand and Eire, for example. South Africa has a substantial minority of such speakers. But in none of these English-speaking countries have the standard varieties been investigated to the extent that they have been in Britain and the United States. Most attention has been paid to pronunciation, vocabulary, and some aspects of usage, but the grammars of these national standards have yet to be codified. In the large reference grammar of English that we published in 1985, my coauthors and I were able to refer to numerous instances in which standard American English and standard British English differed, though the differences are relatively minor.[8] We could make only sporadic references to other national standards. For the written language the national standards of all the mother-tongue countries are relatively similar, so that it is reasonable to speak of an international written standard of English with trivial variation in spelling and punctuation and relatively minor variation in grammar. There are more significant differences in vocabulary, partly to cater for differences in the natural and cultural environment.

The English of the United States and the other English-speaking countries I have been discussing derives from the language brought in the first instance by settlers from Britain. Immigrants speaking other languages joined the earlier settlers, but generally their descendants have English as their first language. Quite different is the status of English in other former British colonies such as India, Nigeria, or Ghana, or in the former American possession of the Philippines. These countries were not extensively settled by English speakers. English has always been an additional language for the vast majority of the inhabitants. It has always been acquired largely through lessons at school. After independence, most of the former colonies have retained English in some official capacity for pragmatic reasons: English was an impartial language in countries that were multilingual, where the choice of one native language was opposed by speakers of other native languages, and it was a useful language—the international language needed for modernization and economic development. English was therefore recognized as the sole language or one of the languages approved for use in domains such as the national parliament, the higher courts, the central administration, and higher education. In other words, English is used in these countries for internal communication, indeed primarily for that purpose, and not just for communicating with speakers from other countries. In this respect, the function of

English in India or Nigeria differs from that of English in Germany or Japan. A terminological distinction is often made between English as a second language (in India or Nigeria) and as a foreign language (in Japan or Germany). The distinction is not clear-cut, since some countries (for example, Malaysia) no longer recognize English as an official language but continue to use it internally for certain important functions.

In both cases English is learned at school. The level of English language proficiency reached by students can be quite high in some countries where English is a foreign language—for example, in the Scandinavian countries and in the Netherlands. Such countries have a tradition of well-trained teachers of English who are proficient in the language, their native languages are cognate with English, and students are strongly motivated to learn English. Before their independence, the colonies drew heavily on teachers from Britain or the United States to train their teachers and to teach in their schools and colleges. Since independence, they have had to rely mainly on their own resources. The newly independent countries are generally economically weak, and they are not able to supply adequate funding to train teachers and to develop teaching material. The level of English proficiency of teachers and consequently of students has therefore deteriorated.

Where English is a foreign language, those who speak English look to the standard language of mother-tongue speakers, chiefly standard British English and standard American English, for their norms—though educational systems and their examinations may fail to keep pace with changes in the standard language. French or Japanese speakers may make characteristic mistakes in their use of English, but they would not claim to want to speak French English or Japanese English.

Attitudes are divided, however, as to the norms for English where it is used chiefly for internal communication. Both within and outside countries such as India and Nigeria there are those who not only recognize distinctive national varieties but want to establish varieties used by educated speakers as national standard languages. Others refuse to recognize the existence of such an entity as Indian English: they argue that there is a continuum of competence in English among speakers which reflects their level of study of the language and the competence of their teachers, and that there are considerable differences in the use of the language between speakers from different parts of the country. The compilers of a recent handbook on Indian English, who "do not wish to commit themselves to taking up a position in this controversy," explain: "Since no comprehensive description of this so-called English has ever been made, this [second] group of scholars consider that the term is imprecise and misleading and that it should not be used."[9] The author of a handbook for Nigerian users notes: "the situation in Nigeria at present is a far cry from the stage where it can be said that the norms, generally accepted, of what can be called 'Standard Nigerian English' (spoken and written) have been firmly established; the picture now seems to suggest that any such standard is, at best, in process of evolution."[10] Both handbooks focus on differences between local uses of English and standard British English.

As yet there are no established and acknowledged national standard languages in countries such as India and Nigeria. Some Indians have expressed views on whether it is desirable to have a national standard. Those who oppose the concept of a standard Indian English are worried that to encourage independent local standard varieties will reduce the value of their English for international communication. They advocate retaining standard British or American English as the models for education in their countries. Commenting on proposals for teaching a long-established local variant of English in countries such as Japan and India, a recent article in the *Economist* concludes that it is now clear that even India rejects such proposals: "The English that such countries want is one that enables Indians to communicate not just with each other, but with the English-speaking world. Thank you for your tolerance, they say, but we'd prefer your standard English."[11]

The attitude that the *Economist* reports may not be pervasive, since there is evidence of more favorable attitudes to local models of English among the younger generation of educated users of the language.[12] Local standard varieties are likely to gain increasing acceptance for nationalistic reasons. As in mother-tongue countries, only the educated elite will be fully competent in the standard language. It is this minority who will have most need of English as a written language and as an international language. For their purposes, it is important that the local standard variety not deviate too far from the current international standard English.

Grammarians and lexicographers can play a significant part in ensuring the preservation of the international role of English in their country. Research is needed into the grammar and vocabulary used by educated speakers in countries where English is a second language. On the basis of comprehensive descriptions, linguists should promote variants that have international currency and those that would not lead to misunderstanding in international communication. There are of course some variants among the national standard languages of mother-tongue countries, but it would be a pity to add unnecessarily to their number from the emerging standard languages.

It is easy to deflate Enoch Powell's jingoistic boast: "Others may speak and read English—more or less—but it is our language not theirs." The English too may speak and read English more or less; complaints about the deterioration in the use of the language are voiced frequently in England and in other English mother-tongue countries. And it is difficult to justify England's distinctive claim to English: there are four times as many speakers of English in the United States as in the whole of the United Kingdom, and there are probably more English speakers in second-language countries than there are in mother-tongue countries.

Notes

1. The quotation comes from the text of the speech that appeared in the *Independent* on 23 April 1988.

2. Janet Whitcut, "English, My English?" in *The English Language Today*, ed. Sidney Greenbaum (Oxford, 1985), p. 159.

3. See H. L. Mencken, *The American Language*, 4th ed. (New York, 1936), and the supplements published in 1945; the one-volume abridged edition of Mencken's work by Raven I. McDavid, Jr. (New York, 1963); and D. Simpson, *The Politics of American English, 1776–1850* (New York, 1986).

4. Quoted in Mencken, *The American Language*, 1:10.

5. Mencken, *The American Language*, abridged by McDavid, pp. 93–94.

6. See the discussion in Ian Pringle, "Attitudes to Canadian English," in *The English Language Today*, ed. Greenbaum, pp. 183–205.

7. Quoted in W. C. Lougheed, ed., *In Search of the Standard in Canadian English*, published by the Strathy Language Unit, Queen's University (Ontario, 1986), p. 164.

8. Randolph Quirk, Sidney Greenbaum, Geoffrey Leech, and Jan Svartvik, *A Comprehensive Grammar of the English Language* (London, 1985). John Algeo is preparing a book devoted to the differences between the grammars of British and American English, which will be published by Cambridge University Press.

9. Paroo Nihalani, R. K. Tongue, and Priya Hosali, *Indian and British English: A Handbook of Usage and Pronunciation* (Delhi, 1979), p. 3.

10. Ọbafẹmi Kujọrẹ, *English Usage: Some Notable Nigerian Variations* (Ibadan, 1985), p. 94.

11. "English as she is mis-spoke," *The Economist*, 16 July 1988, p. 18.

12. See Braj B. Kachru, *The Alchemy of English* (Oxford, 1986), chapter 2.

❧ MEDBH MCGUCKIAN

On Hearing an Irish Poem Read in the Linenhall Library

You wake me up with the name
I carry inside me like a first
Language. It becomes needles
On your lips, slightly grey, a waste
Of light I swallow like a syrup.

A tree forks at the level
Of your eyes, it spreads my dark
Diphthong upward like a cup,
I place myself expectantly
Under your open hand.

You talk with your hands
Like two people, you zigzag
Softly from person to person,
Rubbing my names together
As if that was your goal,

Not pushing my thoughts into
The space beneath the bed.
I bring a sentence to your body,
Brimming like an island, I sit
Filled with that, as with a Bible.

❧ AMY TAN

The Language of Discretion

AT A RECENT FAMILY DINNER IN SAN FRANCISCO, my mother whispered to me: "Sau-sau [Brother's Wife] pretends too hard to be polite! Why bother? In the end, she always takes everything."

My mother thinks like a *waixiao*, an expatriate, temporarily away from China since 1949, no longer patient with ritual courtesies. As if to prove her point, she reached across the table to offer my elderly aunt from Beijing the last scallop from the Happy Family seafood dish.

Sau-sau scowled. "*B'yao, zhen b'yao!*" (I don't want it, really I don't!) she cried, patting her plump stomach.

"Take it! Take it!" scolded my mother in Chinese.

"Full, I'm already full," Sau-sau protested weakly, eyeing the beloved scallop.

"Ai!" exclaimed my mother, completely exasperated. "Nobody else wants it. If you don't take it, it will only rot!"

At this point, Sau-sau sighed, acting as if she were doing my mother a big favor by taking the wretched scrap off her hands.

My mother turned to her brother, a high-ranking communist official who was visiting her in California for the first time: "In America a Chinese person could starve to death. If you say you don't want it, they won't ask you again forever."

My uncle nodded and said he understood fully: Americans take things quickly because they have no time to be polite.

. . .

I thought about this misunderstanding again—of social contexts failing in translation—when a friend sent me an article from the *New York Times Magazine* (24 April 1988). The article, on changes in New York's Chinatown, made passing reference to the inherent ambivalence of the Chinese language.

Chinese people are so "discreet and modest," the article stated, there aren't even words for "yes" and "no."

That's not true, I thought, although I can see why an outsider might think that. I continued reading.

If one is Chinese, the article went on to say, "One compromises, one doesn't hazard a loss of face by an overemphatic response."

My throat seized. Why do people keep saying these things? As if we truly were those little dolls sold in Chinatown tourist shops, heads bobbing up and down in complacent agreement to anything said!

I worry about the effect of one-dimensional statements on the unwary and guileless. When they read about this so-called vocabulary deficit, do they also conclude that Chinese people evolved into a mild-mannered lot because the language only allowed them to hobble forth with minced words?

Something enormous is always lost in translation. Something insidious seeps into the gaps, especially when amateur linguists continue to compare, one-for-one, language differences and then put forth notions wide open to misinterpretation: that Chinese people have no direct linguistic means to make decisions, assert or deny, affirm or negate, just say no to drug dealers, or behave properly on the witness stand when told, "Please answer yes or no."

Yet one can argue, with the help of renowned linguists, that the Chinese are indeed up a creek without "yes" and "no." Take any number of variations on the old language-and-reality theory stated years ago by Edward Sapir: "Human beings . . . are very much at the mercy of the particular language which has become the medium for their society. . . . The fact of the matter is that the 'real world' is to a large extent built up on the language habits of the group."[1]

This notion was further bolstered by the famous Sapir-Whorf hypothesis, which roughly states that one's perception of the world and how one functions in it depends a great deal on the language used. As Sapir, Whorf, and new carriers of the banner would have us believe, language shapes our thinking, channels us along certain patterns embedded in words, syntactic structures, and intonation patterns. Language has become the peg and the shelf that enables us to sort out and categorize the world. In English, we see "cats" and "dogs"; what if the language had also specified *glatz*, meaning "animals that leave fur on the sofa," and *glotz*, meaning "animals that leave fur and drool on the sofa"? How would language, the enabler, have changed our perceptions with slight vocabulary variations?

And if this were the case—of language being the master of destined thought—think of the opportunities lost from failure to evolve two little words, *yes* and *no*, the simplest of opposites! Ghenghis Khan could have been sent back to Mongolia. Opium wars might have been averted. The Cultural Revolution could have been sidestepped.

There are still many, from serious linguists to pop psychology cultists, who view language and reality as inextricably tied, one being the consequence of the other. We have traversed the range from the Sapir-Whorf hypothesis to est and neurolinguistic programming, which tell us "you are what you say."

I too have been intrigued by the theories. I can summarize, albeit badly, ages-old empirical evidence: of Eskimos and their infinite ways to say "snow," their ability to *see* the differences in snowflake configurations, thanks to the richness of their vocabulary, while non-Eskimo speakers like myself founder in "snow," "more snow," and "lots more where that came from."

I too have experienced dramatic cognitive awakenings via the word. Once I added "mauve" to my vocabulary I began to see it everywhere. When I learned how to pronounce *prix fixe*, I ate French food at prices better than the easier-to-say *à la carte* choices.

But just how seriously are we supposed to take this?

Sapir said something else about language and reality. It is the part that often gets left behind in the dot-dot-dots of quotes: ". . . No two languages are ever sufficiently similar to be considered as representing the same social reality. The worlds in which different societies live are distinct worlds, not merely the same world with different labels attached."

When I first read this, I thought, Here at last is validity for the dilemmas I felt growing up in a bicultural, bilingual family! As any child of immigrant parents knows, there's a special kind of double bind attached to knowing two languages. My parents, for example, spoke to me in both Chinese and English; I spoke back to them in English.

"Amy-ah!" they'd call to me.

"What?" I'd mumble back.

"Do not question us when we call," they scolded me in Chinese. "It is not respectful."

"What do you mean?"

"Ai! Didn't we just tell you not to question?"

To this day, I wonder which parts of my behavior were shaped by Chinese, which by English. I am tempted to think, for example, that if I am of two minds on some matter it is due to the richness of my linguistic experiences, not to any personal tendencies toward wishy-washiness. But which mind says what?

Was it perhaps patience—developed through years of deciphering my mother's fractured English—that had me listening politely while a woman announced over the phone that I had won one of five valuable prizes? Was it respect—pounded in by the Chinese imperative to accept convoluted explanations—that had me agreeing that I might find it worthwhile to drive seventy-five miles to view a time-share resort? Could I have been at a loss for words when asked, "Wouldn't you like to win a Hawaiian cruise or perhaps a fabulous Star of India designed exclusively by Carter and Van Arpels?"

And when this same woman called back a week later, this time complaining that I had missed my appointment, obviously it was my type A language that kicked into gear and interrupted her. Certainly, my blunt denial—"Frankly I'm not interested"—was as American as apple pie. And when she said, "But it's in Morgan Hill," and I shouted, "Read my lips. I don't care if it's Timbuktu," you can be sure I said it with the precise intonation expressing both cynicism and disgust.

It's dangerous business, this sorting out of language and behavior. Which one is English? Which is Chinese? The categories manifest themselves: passive and aggressive, tentative and assertive, indirect and direct. And I realize they are just variations of the same theme: that Chinese people are discreet and modest.

Reject them all!

If my reaction is overly strident, it is because I cannot come across as too emphatic. I grew up listening to the same lines over and over again, like so many rote expressions repeated in an English phrase-book. And I too almost came to believe them.

Yet if I consider my upbringing more carefully, I find there was nothing discreet about the Chinese language I grew up with. My parents made everything abundantly clear. Nothing wishy-washy in their demands, no compromises accepted: "Of course you will become a famous neurosurgeon," they told me. "And yes, a concert pianist on the side."

In fact, now that I remember, it seems that the more emphatic outbursts always spilled over into Chinese: "Not that way! You must wash rice so not a single grain spills out."

I do not believe that my parents—both immigrants from mainland China—are an exception to the modest-and-discreet rule. I have only to look at the number of Chinese engineering students skewing minority ratios at Berkeley, MIT, and Yale. Certainly they were not raised by passive mothers and fathers who said, "It is up to you, my daughter. Writer, welfare recipient, masseuse, or molecular engineer—you decide."

And my American mind says, See, those engineering students weren't able to say no to their parents' demands. But then my Chinese mind remembers: Ah, but those parents all wanted their sons and daughters to be *pre-med*.

Having listened to both Chinese and English, I also tend to be suspicious of any comparisons between the two languages. Typically, one language—that of the person doing the comparing—is often used as the standard, the benchmark for a logical form of expression. And so the language being compared is always in danger of being judged deficient or superfluous, simplistic or unnecessarily complex, melodious or cacophonous. English speakers point out that Chinese is extremely difficult because it relies on variations in tone barely discernible to the human ear. By the same token, Chinese speakers tell me English is extremely difficult because it is inconsistent, a language of too many broken rules, of Mickey Mice and Donald Ducks.

Even more dangerous to my mind is the temptation to compare both language and behavior *in translation*. To listen to my mother speak English, one might think she has no concept of past or future tense, that she doesn't see the difference between singular and plural, that she is gender blind because she calls my husband "she." If one were not careful, one might also generalize that, based on the way my mother talks, all Chinese people take a circumlocutory route to get to the point. It is, in fact, my mother's idiosyncratic behavior to ramble a bit.

Sapir was right about differences between two languages and their realities. I can illustrate why word-for-word translation is not enough to translate meaning and intent. I once received a letter from China which I read to non-Chinese speaking friends. The letter, originally written in Chinese, had been translated by my brother-in law in Beijing. One portion described the time when my uncle at age ten discovered his widowed mother (my grandmother) had remarried—as a number three concubine, the ultimate disgrace for an honorable family. The translated version of my uncle's letter read in part:

> In 1925, I met my mother in Shanghai. When she came to me, I didn't have greeting to her as if seeing nothing. She pull me to a corner secretly and asked me why didn't have greeting to her. I couldn't control myself and cried, "Ma! Why did you leave us? People told me: one day you ate a beancake yourself. Your sister in-law found it and sweared at you, called your names. So . . . is it true?" She clasped my hand and answered immediately, "It's not true, don't say what like this." After this time, there was a few chance to meet her.

"What!" cried my friends. "Was eating a beancake so terrible?"

Of course not. The beancake was simply a euphemism; a ten-year-old boy did not dare question his mother on something as shocking as concubinage. Eating a beancake was his equivalent for committing this selfish act, something inconsiderate of all family members, hence, my grandmother's despairing response to what seemed like a ludicrous charge of gluttony. And sure enough, she was banished from the family, and my uncle saw her only a few times before her death.

While the above may fuel people's argument that Chinese is indeed a language of extreme discretion, it does not mean that Chinese people speak in secrets and riddles. The contexts are fully understood. It is only to those on the *outside* that the language seems cryptic, the behavior inscrutable.

I am, evidently, one of the outsiders. My nephew in Shanghai, who recently started taking English lessons, has been writing me letters in English. I had told him I was a fiction writer, and so in one letter he wrote, "Congratulate to you on your writing. Perhaps one day I should like to read it." I took it in the same vein as "Perhaps one day we can get together for lunch." I sent back a cheery note. A month went by and another letter arrived from Shanghai. "Last one perhaps I hadn't writing distinctly," he said. "In the future, you'll send a copy of your works for me."

I try to explain to my English-speaking friends that Chinese language use is more *strategic* in manner, whereas English tends to be more direct; an American business executive may say, "Let's make a deal," and the Chinese manager may reply, "Is your son interested in learning about your widget business?" Each to his or her own purpose, each with his or her own linguistic path. But I hesitate to add more to the pile of generalizations, because no matter how many examples I provide and explain, I fear that it appears defensive and only reinforces the image: that Chinese people are "discreet and modest"—and it takes an American to explain what they really mean.

Why am I complaining? The description seems harmless enough (after all, the *New York Times Magazine* writer did not say "slippery and evasive"). It is precisely the bland, easy acceptability of the phrase that worries me.

I worry that the dominant society may see Chinese people from a limited—and limiting—perspective. I worry that seemingly benign stereotypes may be part of the reason there are few Chinese in top management positions, in mainstream political roles. I worry about the power of language: that if one says anything enough times—in *any* language—it might become true.

Could this be why Chinese friends of my parents' generation are willing to accept the generalization?

"Why are you complaining?" one of them said to me. "If people think we are modest and polite, let them think that. Wouldn't Americans be pleased to admit they are thought of as polite?"

And I do believe anyone would take the description as a compliment—at first. But after a while, it annoys, as if the only things that people heard one say were phatic remarks: "I'm so pleased to meet you. I've heard many wonderful things about you. For me? You shouldn't have!"

These remarks are not representative of new ideas, honest emotions, or considered thought. They are what is said from the polite distance of social contexts: of greetings, farewells, wedding thank-you notes, convenient excuses, and the like.

It makes me wonder though. How many anthropologists, how many sociologists, how many travel journalists have documented so-called "natural interactions" in foreign lands, all observed with spiral notebook in hand? How many other cases are there of the long-lost primitive tribe, people who turned out to be sophisticated enough to put on the stone-age show that ethnologists had come to see?

And how many tourists fresh off the bus have wandered into Chinatown expecting the self-effacing shopkeeper to admit under duress that the goods are not worth the price asked? I have witnessed it.

"I don't know," the tourist said to the shopkeeper, a Cantonese woman in her fifties. "It doesn't look genuine to me. I'll give you three dollars."

"You don't like my price, go somewhere else," said the shopkeeper.

"You are not a nice person," cried the shocked tourist, "not a nice person at all!"

"Who say I have to be nice," snapped the shopkeeper.

"So how does one say 'yes' and 'no' in Chinese?" ask my friends a bit warily.

And here I do agree in part with the *New York Times Magazine* article. There is no one word for "yes" or "no"—but not out of necessity to be discreet. If anything, I would say the Chinese equivalent of answering "yes" or "no" is dis*crete*, that is, specific to what is asked.

Ask a Chinese person if he or she has eaten, and he or she might say *chrle* (eaten already) or perhaps *meiyou* (have not).

Ask, "So you had insurance at the time of the accident?" and the response would be *dwei* (correct) or *meiyou* (did not have).

Ask, "Have you stopped beating your wife?" and the answer refers directly to the proposition being asserted or denied: stopped already, still have not, never beat, have no wife.

What could be clearer?

As for those who are still wondering how to translate the language of discretion, I offer this personal example.

My aunt and uncle were about to return to Beijing after a three-month visit to the United States. On their last night I announced I wanted to take them out to dinner.

"Are you hungry?" I asked in Chinese.

"Not hungry," said my uncle promptly, the same response he once gave me ten minutes before he suffered a low-blood-sugar attack.

"Not too hungry," said my aunt. "Perhaps you're hungry?"

"A little," I admitted.

"We can eat, we can eat," they both consented.

"What kind of food?" I asked.

"Oh, doesn't matter. Anything will do. Nothing fancy, just some simple food is fine."

"Do you like Japanese food? We haven't had that yet," I suggested.

They looked at each other.

"We can eat it," said my uncle bravely, this survivor of the Long March.

"We have eaten it before," added my aunt. "Raw fish."

"Oh, you don't like it?" I said. "Don't be polite. We can go somewhere else."

"We are not being polite. We can eat it," my aunt insisted.

So I drove them to Japantown and we walked past several restaurants featuring colorful plastic displays of sushi.

"Not this one, not this one either," I continued to say, as if searching for a Japanese restaurant similar to the last. "Here it is," I finally said, turning into a restaurant famous for its Chinese fish dishes from Shandong.

"Oh, Chinese food!" cried my aunt, obviously relieved.

My uncle patted my arm. "You think Chinese."

"It's your last night here in America," I said. "So don't be polite. Act like an American."

And that night we ate a banquet.

Note

1. Edward Sapir, *Selected Writings*, ed. D. G. Mandelbaum (Berkeley and Los Angeles, 1949).

❧ ROBERT ILSON

British and American English:
Ex Uno Plura?

WHEN ROBERT LOWELL CALLED RANDALL JARRELL "the most heart-breaking English poet of his generation," was Lowell right? Not about Jarrell's heartbreakingness, so readily apparent to anyone with tears to shed, but about Jarrell's being an English poet? Like Lowell, Jarrell was an American who wrote in English. Does writing your poetry in English make you an English poet?

Let us consider two of Jarrell's heartbreaking lines, from the poem "Losses" about American bomber crews during the Second World War:

> In bombers named for girls, we burned
> The cities we had learned about in school—

I asked my British colleagues at the Survey of English Usage whether there was anything in those lines that would identify them as American English rather than British English. Everyone agreed on one such feature. The phrase *named for* was infallibly diagnostic of American provenance. British English uses only *named after*: both *named after* and *named for* are available to Americans, and it is likely that Jarrell made the choice he did for reasons of scansion.

No other feature produced such unanimity. My colleagues could have written *burnt* and *learnt* instead of *burned* and *learned*. They could have pronounced *burned* and *learned* with a final *t* rather than a final *d*.

But no one was willing to claim that *burned* and *learned*, written as Jarrell wrote them, and pronounced, as Jarrell would have pronounced them, with a final *d*, were unambiguously American. And it is remarkable to realize that the two verbs could rhyme; and to realize, more generally, how often American rhymes remain rhymes in a standard British accent and British rhymes in an educated American one.

About the phrase *in school*, opinions differed sharply. Almost everybody at the Survey would have used *at school* (a phrase also available to Americans). But only some of my Survey informants picked out *in school* as a phrase that seemed to them in any way odd, unusual—or American.

Of course, if these lines were read aloud, their pronunciation alone would suffice to establish whether the reader was British or American. But as written texts, Jarrell's lines give a pretty good picture of what the other differences between British and American English amount to in practice. There are some choices available in one variety but not in the other: Americans can choose between *named for* and *named after*, British has *named after* only; British can choose between *learnt* and *learned*, Americans opt for *learned*. There are choices available in both varieties, but with different preferences in one or both: *in school* and *at school* are both available to at least some American people and some British people, but British English seems to prefer *at school* clearly. It is such patterns of choice whose cumulative effect leads us on purely linguistic grounds to infer that a written text came from a British pen or an American one.[1] And we are more likely to make that inference correctly than to be misled by British-American differences into a serious misunderstanding of the text.

Or, as Manfred Görlach says of vocabulary differences between the two varieties, "A look at any good middle-sized dictionary makes it clear that what is characteristic of the difference between the two major world Englishes is not so much the exclusive use of lexemes (neatly organized as translation equivalents), but the fact that individual senses, connotations, stylistic restrictions, frequencies and social/regional currency vary between the two."[2]

Another way of looking at British-American variation in printed texts is to compare the data for the American English of 1961 in the Brown text corpus with those for the British English of 1961 in the Lancaster-Oslo-Bergen text corpus.[3] True, we can find absolute differences of the "translation equivalents" type, such as *windshield* (Brown:6, LOB:0)/*windscreen* (Brown:0, LOB:3) or *aluminum* (Brown:18, LOB:0)/*aluminium* (Brown:0, LOB:50). But we also find preferences in each variety that are clear but not absolute, and that may be stronger in one variety than the other: *toward* (Brown:386,

LOB:14)/*towards* (Brown:65, LOB:318) or *toilet* (Brown:13, LOB:3)/ *lavatory* (Brown:4, LOB:8).

How large do British-American differences loom—or bulk—in the English language as a whole? We are now in possession of a considerable body of appropriate evidence. Since the early 1970s contemporary dictionaries have been published in Britain that were based on American dictionaries, and in America a smaller but growing number of dictionaries have been based on British ones.[4] Thus the Hamlyn *Encyclopedic World Dictionary* of 1971 was based on the *American College Dictionary* published originally in 1947, the British *Longman Dictionary of the English Language* of 1984 was expanded from the American *Webster's* (Eighth) *New Collegiate Dictionary* of 1973, and the *Oxford American Dictionary* of 1980 was expanded from the first edition of the British *Oxford Paperback Dictionary* of 1979. In this important development of mid-Atlantic publishing, no one has played a more important role than Laurence Urdang, and his estimate to me is that in Americanizing a British general-purpose monolingual dictionary or Anglicizing an American one, about 20 percent of the contents must be changed when producing a book of equivalent size. Let us now see what that means in practice.

The British *Longman Active Study Dictionary of English* (LASDE) and the *Longman Dictionary of American English* (LDAE) were both published in 1983. They are both "middle-sized" (or smaller) dictionaries for people learning English as a foreign language, and are both derived from the first edition of the larger *Longman Dictionary of Contemporary English* of 1978. Taking as our sample the entries from *enjoy* to *enter*—roughly one page of each book—and excluding differences of pronunciation, I find the following significant likenesses and unlikenesses. There are no significant differences in the entries for *enlarge, enlighten, enlist, enliven, enmity, enormity* (both *LASDE* and *LDAE* accept the controversial idea that *enormity* can mean "enormousness"), *enormous, enormously, enquire* and *enquiry* (*inquire* and *inquiry* are the main spellings for both *LASDE* and *LDAE*), *enrage, enrapture, enrich, en route, ensconce, ensemble, ensue, entail,* or *entangle*. Nineteen entries are essentially the same.

In ten entries there are significant differences. At *enjoy, LASDE*'s *film* and *cinema* have become *LDAE*'s *movie* and *movies*. At *enjoyable, LASDE*'s *holiday* has become *LDAE*'s *vacation*. At *ennoble, LASDE*'s *honourable* has become *LDAE*'s *honorable*, and, curiously, it is *LDAE* rather than *LASDE* that includes the sense "to make [someone] a nobleman/noblewoman." At *enough: determiner, pronoun, LASDE*'s *hasn't got* has become *LDAE*'s *doesn't have*, and *LDAE* has added, in examples, *money enough* and *food enough*. At *enough: adverb, LASDE*'s "not very but only rather" has become *LDAE*'s "not very, but in an acceptable way" (*rather* may well be stronger in American than in British). *LASDE*'s *very well indeed* has become *LDAE*'s *very well*, and *LASDE*'s *strangely enough* has become *LDAE*'s *strange enough*. Neither dictionary has an example like *They're rich enough that they can retire*. At *enrol(l)*, *LASDE* has *enrol*, *enroll*, and *enrolment*; *LDAE* has *enroll*, *enrol*, and *enrollment*. *LASDE* has a single entry for *ensign*; *LDAE* has two, perhaps for reasons of pronunciation. Only *LDAE* has an entry for *enslave*; its omission from *LASDE* I find totally inexplicable. At *ensure*, *LDAE* shows the alternative American spelling *insure* (the usage note at *insure* itself is much the same in both dictionaries). And at *enter*, *LDAE* has removed *LASDE*'s *enter for* (an exam), which is more British than American, and *LASDE*'s *firm* has become *LDAE*'s *company*.

Another way to judge the extent and importance of British-American differences is to look at their role in a pair of texts longer than two lines of poetry. To the first edition of this book each of its editors, the British Christopher Ricks and the American Leonard Michaels, contributed an essay. It is at least plausible that by comparing the language of these two essays, similar as they are in genre, we can get some idea of the significance of their home varieties for the style that each author has achieved. Unfortunately, however, this sample is skewed. Both essays appeared—as this one now does—in a book prepared for publication in America and subjected to a single set of editorial conventions. As an editor myself, I know how hard it is to prevent a uniform house style from being imposed on the vigorous heterogeneity of the authors'. And it is clear that in *The State of the Language*, American conventions of spelling and punctuation prevailed except in quotations.[5] Thus Ricks is made to write American *humor* and *paralyzed* instead of British *humour* and *paralysed*. Nevertheless, one might expect to find in these comparable essays other differences, of the sort to be found in the comparable dictionaries *LASDE* and *LDAE*.

But in fact one almost doesn't. Punctuation, spelling, and quotations apart, there are in the essays by Ricks and Michaels perhaps four differences between British and American English. Two are deliberate. Ricks glosses *scrape home*: "in American, *scrape by*?—just winning, just safe." Michaels praises a sentence of Martin Luther's: "One might even say, in the desperate contemporary formula, 'I hear you, Luther.'" In the relevant senses, *scrape by* probably is American rather than British, and *I hear you* is probably of American origin. In addition, Ricks asks about clichés, "haven't we got to meet them imaginatively . . . ?," which is perhaps less American than *don't we have to . . . ?*, and

Michaels, surprisingly but understandably, writes of the first sentence of *Pride and Prejudice* that it "marries that single man at the stop," using for its air of finality *stop* to mean "period," a sense of *stop* that *Webster's Ninth New Collegiate Dictionary* of 1983 labels *chiefly Brit*. But it seems that in sentence grammar and choice of words, the differences between British and American English are not great in expository prose: what Geoffrey Nunberg calls "the prose forms that are charged with defining our social and aesthetic values. They include history, biography, reportage and a number of other things" all of which Nunberg collectively refers to "for short" as "the 'critical essay.'"[6]

But however important the critical essay is for us English-users, there is more to English than it. In other genres—poetry, fiction, and of course conversation—the differences between British and American English are greater, as they are also in certain areas of technology and social organization that developed during the nineteenth and early twentieth centuries, between the severance of the overt political links of the U.S. to Britain and the rise of mass intercontinental communication, transport, and travel: in the Brown corpus *railroad* appears forty-seven times and *railway* ten; in LOB *railway* appears fifty-two times and *railroad* once.

In the more informal and personal genres closer to speech, both Brits and Yanks can draw, for local colo(u)r or humorous effect, on their respective regional and social dialects (as Görlach says), and on the resources of those other languages with which they have come into contact as explorers, traders, or conquerors. Thus users of standard American English can (if they wish) say they are *not about to* do something they don't want to do (using a phrase of allegedly Southern provenance), describe a sexy lady as *foxy* (allegedly from American Black vernacular), languish provincially in the *boondocks* (from Pilipino), or call their bosses *honchos* (from Japanese). Brits can, by contrast, use regional *happen* ("perhaps") and *anyroad* ("anyway"), eat *a sarnie* or *a butty* ("a sandwich"; the former a Southern regionalism, the latter a Northern one), or *have a dekko* or *a shufti* ("a look"; *dekko* from Hindi, *shufti* from Arabic). Of striking but perhaps superficial importance for Brits is also Cockney slang, especially of the rhyming sort (which is often truncated, as in *Use your loaf*, where *loaf* is from *loaf of bread* and rhymes with *head* ["brains"]); but rhyming slang is today perhaps cultivated more assiduously in the media than in the East End of London. Nor should we forget the subtle social changes to be rung within British English by moving up and down the scale from the posh U-ness of, say, *drawing-room* to the nervously respectable non-U-ness of *lounge*, with *sitting-room* somewhere in between and essays writable about such other options as *front room*, *parlour*, and *living-*

room. As for American psychobabble and sociobabble, they are now freely available to those Brits who want them—up to and including *I hear you*.[7] But we are now far from the heartland of the "critical essay."

All these microlinguistic differences are fascinating, and when spewed out in great wodges ("dollops") are the stuff of which parody, intentional or unintentional, is made. Thus Lionheart Television's *EastEnders* glossary of 1988 offers Americans this introduction to some of the BBC soap's principal characters:

> Angie thinks Den is nothing but aggro. Den thinks Angie is all mouth and no trousers. Sharon thinks they're both berks. Lofty thinks they're all barmy and wishes they'd just belt up—for once.[8]

And when, in Britain, Jaspistos of the *Spectator* set a competition "to invent an exchange of letters between a Briton and an American in which the differences between the writers' mode of expression and meaning is excruciating and/or crucial," D. B. Jenkinson's winning American parody was a letter asking one Charles Burlington-Burke about holiday accommodation on the Norfolk Broads:

> Hi Chuck,   5/11/87
>   Your Norfolk outfit seems real nice. Just a few inquiries ahead of res-
> ervation finalising [*sic*]: what's else free, side of range produce? Have
> those broads had negative physical checkouts? Do you have something
> neater than regular transportation? Define "near-by access" please on ac-
> count I bathe daily two times. How are you fixed roomwise 8/1/87 thru'
> 8/12/87?
>   Truly yours, T. C. Friche II
>   (3 October 1987)

The glossary seems to be informing Americans of what they do not know about British English, almost as if they were learning a foreign language. The parody seems to be reminding Brits of what they think they already know about American English. The glossary, being a glossary, concentrates on items of vocabulary. The parody, being a parody, embraces not only vocabulary (confusion of American *broads* ["women"] with British *Broads* ["East Anglian bayous"]) but also grammatical constructions (*ahead of reservation finalizing*) and levels of style or formality (*Hi Chuck* to a stranger).

This congeries of British-American differences—sometimes bla-tant, sometimes barely discernible—provokes reactions; and, as Ran-dolph Quirk reminds us, we must in all matters linguistic heed not only use, but also reactions to use. Brits have views and feelings about American English; Yanks, about British English—albeit not so many feelings, nor such strong ones. Lay Yanks tend to play down British-American linguistic differences; lay Brits, to exaggerate them. Even though lay Brits know less about American English than they think they do, they are still likely to know more about American English than lay Americans know about British English. Though in the *Spectator* competition to parody American English "the entries were few," it is hard to imagine an American magazine inviting its readers to parody British English. Nor can one readily imagine an American writing a poem using the style of, say, Tony Harrison or John Betjeman to criticize British English, as in this book's first edition Gavin Ewart used the style of Ogden Nash to criticize American English.

Insofar as Americans think about British English at all, they may, despite *EastEnders*, still associate it, as they have done in the past, with the sort of latter-day Euphuism their college composition textbooks used to call "fine writing":

> An inexperienced writer, attempting to adopt a pretentious style of writing . . . frequently makes the mistake of interlarding his work with foreign expressions or Briticisms. . . . Examples: . . . *garçon, morceau, robe-de-chambre, lift* for *elevator, petrol* for *gasoline* . . .[9]

As Louise Levene points out, Americans may think Brits are pompous for using hard nontechnical words (*prevarication* for *lie*, as it might be), whereas Brits think Yanks are pompous for using technical expressions in nontechnical contexts (*interface*) and for using circumlocutions (*reservation finalizing*).[10] Nannies versus technocrats, as it were. There are also, perhaps, lingering traces of excolonial linguistic insecurity in the U.S., of the sort that made *The Macmillan Handbook of English* of 1948 condemn the Americanism *in back of* ("behind") as "considered undesirable in both speech and writing" and even to say of the Americanism *gotten* that "*Got* is preferred to *gotten* as the past participle."[11] A kind of parallel to such feelings is provided by a recent comparison of British and American writing which concludes that there is a "greater influence of grammatical and stylistic prescriptions in British writing."[12]

Brits may still regard American English as classless, even though that belief would bring a wry smile to the lips of William Labov, Martin Scorsese, or David Mamet. Brits may also admire its exuberant vigor, much as Mencken did. But that vigor may be felt to come from a flaunting of the flouting of prescriptivist conventions, and from a miscegenation of levels of formality amounting to a kind of linguistic atonality (*Hi Chuck* coexisting with *reservation finalizing*). The good side of that, in the style of someone like S. J. Perelman, is what William Scammell calls a "larky prose . . . swooping about among the registers like a thing possessed."[13] But this can cause annoyance in Britain: "one small thing I found slightly irritating is the use of American colloquialisms (an unfortunate feature of many books on Tibetan Buddhism), such as the frequent appearance of the word 'garbage.' "[14]

Or, worse than annoyance, a feeling that American English may be a force for linguistic corruption. In letters critical of the English of the BBC, as David Crystal observes, "feelings about Americanisms can run very deep," even though "as a matter of fact the label 'Americanism' is used less often as a correct description of some word or phrase which comes from the USA and more often as a term of abuse."[15] Such feelings about the dangers of American influence in Britain (cultural, no doubt, as well as linguistic) offer interesting parallels to the fears expressed in other lands (with France perhaps the example *par excellence*) about the deleterious influence of the English language as a whole on other tongues.

Yet all this speculation about British-American differences leaves hardly touched Görlach's "individual senses" and "connotations"— and, more generally still, the cultural differences reflected in the two varieties. All these are epitomized by *robin*. Though British and American robins are both thrushes (or thrushlike), with red (or reddish) breasts, many a "good middle-sized dictionary" will tell you that they are different birds: the American robin the larger *Turdus migratorius*, the British robin the smaller *Erithacus rubecula*. What few if any dictionaries add is what Nancy Salama and Mary Ghali add: that the American robin is a harbinger of spring ("When the red red robin comes bob-bob-bobbin' along") whereas the British robin is a symbol of winter ("And what will the robin do then, poor thing?").[16]

It is in differences of this sort—real-world differences together with their cultural and literary associations—that much of the Americanness of American texts and the Britishness of British texts resides. The American quality of Jarrell's lines lies not just—perhaps not mainly— in the collocations *named for* or *in school*, but in their evocation of bomber crews whose planes have girls' names (unlike the mostly unnamed bombers of the RAF), and for whom the cities of Europe are first and foremost semimythical objects of schoolboy wonder.

Can Randall Jarrell rightly be called an English poet? Speaking strictly, the answer must be no, for the idiom of our language, analogous to that of others, dictates that the phrase *an English poet*, like the sentence *The poet is English*, names the poet's nationality rather than his language. Randall Jarrell's poetry is more American than his passport, and Robert Lowell was being provocative in his form of words. But it may be that those among whom Keats hoped to be after his death, and whom he named in a somehow more hospitable phrase "the English poets," will admit Jarrell to their number too.

Notes

1. See John Algeo, "The Two Streams: British and American English," *Journal of English Linguistics* 19 (1986): 269–85, and "British and American Grammatical Differences," *International Journal of Lexicography* 1 (1988): 1–32.

2. Manfred Görlach, review of *Lexicographic Description of English* and *The BBI Combinatory Dictionary of English* by M. Benson, E. Benson, and R. Ilson, *English World-Wide* 8 (1987): 329.

3. W. Nelson Francis and Henry Kučera, *Frequency Analysis of English Usage: Lexicon and Grammar* (Boston, 1982), and Knut Hofland and Stig Johansson, *Word Frequencies in British and American English* (Bergen, 1982).

4. See Robert Ilson, ed., "British and American Lexicography," in *Lexicography: An Emerging International Profession* (Manchester, 1986), pp. 51–72.

5. For details of spelling, see Sidney Greenbaum, "Spelling Variants in British English," *Journal of English Linguistics* 19 (1986): 269–85.

6. Geoffrey Nunberg, "The Case for Prescriptive Grammar" (paper presented at N-WAVE IX, Ann Arbor, Mich., 1980).

7. On American psychobabble, see David Lodge, "Where It's At: California Language," in *The State of the Language*, ed. Leonard Michaels and Christopher Ricks (Berkeley and Los Angeles, 1980), pp. 503–14.

8. *How to Speak EastEnders: A Brief Glossary of Cockney Expressions* (1988).

9. George S. Wykoff and Harry Shaw, *The Harper Handbook of College Composition*, 3d ed. (New York, 1962), p. 441.

10. Louise Levene, forthcoming Ph.D. thesis on American perceptions of British English (University College London).

11. John H. Kierzek, *The Macmillan Handbook of English*, rev. ed. (New York, 1948), pp. 481, 490.

12. Douglas Biber, "A Textual Comparison of British and American Writing," *American Speech* 62 (1987): 117.

13. William Scammell, "The Story of a Lay Preacher," in *The Spectator* (16 January 1988), p. 28.

14. Stephen Hodge, review of *Introduction to Tantra* by Lama Yeshe, *The Middle Way: Journal of the Buddhist Society* 63 (1988): 45.

15. David Crystal, "Language on the Air—Has It Degenerated?," in *The Listener* (9 July 1981), p. 38.

16. Nancy Salama and Mary Ghali, *American and British Preferences*, research project (Cairo, n.d.).

Talking Black

> For a language acts in divers ways, upon the spirit of a
> people; even as the spirit of a people acts with a creative
> and spiritualizing force upon a language.
> ALEXANDER CRUMMELL, 1860

> A new vision began gradually to replace the dream of
> political power—a powerful movement, the rise
> of another ideal to guide the unguided, another pillar
> of fire by night after a clouded day. It was the ideal of
> "book-learning"; the curiosity, born of compulsory
> ignorance, to know and test the power of the cabalistic
> letters of the white man, the longing to know.
> W. E. B. DU BOIS, 1903

> The knowledge which would teach the white world
> was Greek to his own flesh and blood. . . . and he
> could not articulate the message of another people.
> W. E. B. DU BOIS, 1903

ALEXANDER CRUMMELL, A PIONEERING nineteenth-century Pan-Africanist, statesman, and missionary who spent the bulk of his creative years as an Anglican minister in Liberia, was also a pioneering intellectual and philosopher of language, founding the American Negro Academy in 1897 and serving as the intellectual godfather of W. E. B. Du Bois. For his first annual address as president of the academy, delivered on 28 December 1897, Crummell selected as his topic "The Attitude of the American Mind Toward the Negro Intellect." Given the occasion of the first annual meeting of the great intellectuals of the race, he could not have chosen a more timely or appropriate subject.

Crummell wished to attack, he said, "the denial of intellectuality in the Negro; the assertion that he was not a human being, that he did not belong to the human race." He argued that the desire "to becloud and stamp out the intellect of the Negro" led to the enactment of "laws and Statutes, closing the pages of every book printed to the eyes of Negroes; barring the doors of every school-room against them!" This, he concluded, "was the systematized method of the intellect of the South, to stamp out the brains of the Negro!"—a program that created an "almost Egyptian darkness [which] fell upon the mind of the race, throughout the whole land."

Crummell next shared with his audience a conversation between two Boston lawyers which he had overheard when he was "an errand boy in the Anti-slavery office in New York City" in 1833 or 1834:

> While at the Capitol they happened to dine in the company of the great John C. Calhoun, then senator from South Carolina. It was a period of great ferment upon the question of Slavery, States' Rights, and Nullification; and consequently the Negro was the topic of conversation at the table. One of the utterances of Mr. Calhoun was to this effect—"That if he could find a Negro who knew the Greek syntax, he would then believe that the Negro was a human being and should be treated as a man."

"Just think of the crude asininity," Crummell concluded rather generously, "of even a great man!"[1]

The salient sign of the black person's humanity—indeed, the only sign for Calhoun—would be the mastering of the very essence of Western civilization, of the very foundation of the complex fiction upon which white Western culture had been constructed. It is likely that "Greek syntax," for John C. Calhoun, was merely a hyperbolic figure of speech, a trope of virtual impossibility; he felt driven to the hyperbolic mode, perhaps, because of the long racist tradition in Western letters of demanding that black people *prove* their full humanity. We know this tradition all too well, dotted as it is with the names of great intellectual Western racialists, such as Francis Bacon, David Hume, Immanuel Kant, Thomas Jefferson, and G. W. F. Hegel. Whereas each of these figures demanded that blacks write poetry to prove their humanity, Calhoun—writing in a post-Phillis Wheatley era—took refuge in, yes, Greek syntax.

In typical African-American fashion, a brilliant black intellectual accepted Calhoun's bizarre challenge. The anecdote Crummell shared with his fellow black academicians turned out to be his shaping scene of instruction. For Crummell himself jumped on a boat, sailed to England, and matriculated at Queens' College, Cambridge, where he mastered (naturally enough) the intricacies of Greek syntax. Calhoun, we suspect, was not impressed.

Crummell never stopped believing that mastering the master's tongue was the sole path to civilization, intellectual freedom, and social equality for the black person. It was Western "culture," he insisted, that the black person "must claim as his rightful heritage, as a man—not stinted training, not a caste education, not," he concluded prophetically, "a Negro curriculum."[2] As he argued so passionately in

his speech of 1860, "The English Language in Liberia," the acquisition
of the English language, along with Christianity, is the wonderful sign
of God's providence encoded in the nightmare of African enslavement
in the racist wilderness of the New World. English, for Crummell,
was "the speech of Chaucer and Shakespeare, of Milton and Wordsworth, of Bacon and Burke, of Franklin and Webster," and its potential mastery was "this one item of compensation" that "the Almighty
has bestowed upon us" in exchange for "the exile of our fathers from
their African homes to America." In the English language are embodied " the noblest theories of liberty" and "the grandest ideas of humanity." If black people master the master's tongue, these great and
grand ideas will become African ideas, because "ideas conserve men,
and keep alive the vitality of nations."

In dark contrast to the splendors of the English language, Crummell set the African vernacular languages, which, he wrote, have "definite marks of inferiority connected with them all, which place them
at the widest distances from civilized languages." Any effort to render
the master's discourse in our own black tongue is an egregious error,
for we cannot translate sublime utterances "in[to] broken English—a
miserable caricature of their noble tongue." We must abandon forever
both indigenous African vernacular languages and the neo-African vernacular languages that our people have produced in the New World:

> All low, inferior, and barbarous tongues are, doubtless, but the lees and
> dregs of noble languages, which have gradually, as the soul of a nation
> has died out, sunk down to degradation and ruin. We must not suffer this
> decay on these shores, in this nation. We have been made, providentially,
> the deposit of a noble trust; and we should be proud to show our appre-
> ciation of it. Having come to the heritage of this language we must cher-
> ish its spirit, as well as retain its letter. We must cultivate it among our-
> selves; we must strive to infuse its spirit among our reclaimed and
> aspiring natives.[3]

I cite the examples of John C. Calhoun and Alexander Crummell as
metaphors for the relation between the critic of black writing and the
larger institution of literature. Learning the master's tongue, for our
generation of critics, has been an act of empowerment, whether that
tongue be New Criticism, humanism, structuralism, Marxism, poststructuralism, feminism, new historicism, or any other -*ism*. But even
as Afro-American literature and criticism becomes institutionalized,
our pressing question now becomes this: in what tongue shall we
choose to speak, and write, our own criticisms? What are we now to

do with the enabling masks of empowerment that we have donned as we have practiced one mode of "white" criticism or another?

The Afro-American literary tradition is distinctive in that it evolved in response to allegations that its authors did not, and could not, create literature, a capacity that was considered the signal measure of a race's innate "humanity." The African living in Europe or in the New World seems to have felt compelled to create a literature not only to demonstrate that blacks did indeed possess the intellectual ability to create a written art, but also to indict the several social and economic institutions that delimited the "humanity" of all black people in Western cultures.

So insistent did these racist allegations prove to be, at least from the eighteenth to the early twentieth century, that it is fair to describe the subtext of the history of black letters in terms of the urge to refute them. Even as late as 1911, when J. E. Casely-Hayford published *Ethiopia Unbound* (the "first" African novel), he felt it necessary to address this matter in the first two paragraphs of his text. "At the dawn of the twentieth century," the novel opens, "men of light and leading both in Europe and in America had not yet made up their minds as to what place to assign to the spiritual aspirations of the black man."[4] Few literary traditions have begun with such a complex and curious relation to criticism: allegations of an absence led directly to a presence, a literature often inextricably bound in a dialogue with its harshest critics.

Black literature and its criticism, then, have been put to uses that were not primarily aesthetic: rather, they have formed part of a larger discourse on the nature of the black, and his or her role in the order of things. Even so, a sense of integrity has arisen in the Afro-American tradition, though it has less to do with the formal organicism of the New Critics than with an intuitive notion of "ringing true," or Houston Baker's concept of "sounding." (One of the most frequently used critical judgments in the African-American tradition is "That shit don't sound right," or, as Alice Walker puts it in *The Color Purple*, "Look like to me only a fool would want to talk in a way that feel peculiar to your mind.")[5] That is the sense I am calling on here, understanding how problematic even this can be. Doubleness, alienation, equivocality: since the turn of the century at least, these have been recurrent tropes for the black tradition.

To be sure, this matter of the language of criticism and the integrity of its subject has a long and rather tortured history in all black letters. It was David Hume, after all, who called Francis Williams, the Jamaican poet of Latin verse, "a parrot who merely speaks a few words plainly." Phillis Wheatley, too, has long suffered from the spurious attacks of black and white critics alike for being the *rara avis* of a school of so-called mockingbird poets, whose use of European and American literary conventions has been considered a corruption of a "purer" black expression, found in forms such as the blues, signifying, spirituals, and Afro-American dance. Can we, as critics, escape a "mockingbird" posture?

Only recently have some scholars attempted to convince critics of black literature that we can. Perhaps predictably, a number of these attempts share a concern with that which has been most repressed in the received tradition of Afro-American criticism: close readings of the texts themselves. And so we are learning to read a black text within a black formal cultural matrix. That means reading a literary culture that remains, for the most part, intransigently oral. If the black literary imagination has a privileged medium, it is what Douglass called the "live, calm, grave, clear, pointed, warm, sweet, melodious and powerful human voice." And the salient contribution of black literature may lie in its resolute vocality. But there is no black voice; only voices, diverse and mutable. Familiarly, there's the strut, confidence laced with bitters—

> *I* am a Waiter's Waiter. I know all the moves, all the pretty, fine moves that big book will never teach you. *I* built this railroad with my moves.   (James Alan McPherson, "Solo Song")[6]

Or the boisterous revelator:

> When he was on, Reverend Jones preached his gospel hour in a Texas church that held no more than 250 people, but the way he had the old sisters banging on them bass drums and slapping them tambourines, you'd think that God's Own Philharmonic was carrying on inside that old church where the loudspeaks blasted Jones's message to the thousands who stood outside. At the conclusion of Reverend Jones's sermon, the church didn't need no fire, because it was being warmed by the spirit of the Lord. By the spirit of Jesus. (Ishmael Reed, *The Terrible Threes*)[7]

Yet how tonally remote they are from this cento of Baldwin, a preacher's son for whom King Jamesian inversions were second nature:

> In the case of the Negro the past was taken from him whether he would or no; yet to forswear it was meaningless and availed him nothing, since his shameful history was carried, quite literally, on his brow. Shameful; for he was heathen as well as black and would never have discovered the healing blood of Christ had not we braved the jungles to bring him these glad tidings. . . .

> Where the Negro face appears, a tension is created, the tension of a silence filled with things unutterable.   ("Many Thousands Gone")[8]

Baldwin wrote of "something ironic and violent and perpetually understated in Negro speech," and in this he was describing his own careful, ungentle cadences. Contrast, again, the homeliest intimacies of nuance that Morrison will unexpectedly produce:

> There is a loneliness that can be rocked. Arms crossed, knees drawn up; holding, holding on, this motion, unlike a ship's, smooths and contains the rockers. It's an inside kind—wrapped tight like skin.   (*Beloved*)[9]

There's no hidden continuity or coherence among them. History makes them like beads on a string: there's no necessary resemblance; but then again, no possible separation.

And so we've had to learn to "read black" as a textual effect because the existence of a black canon is a historically contingent phenomenon; it is not inherent in the nature of "blackness," not vouchsafed by the metaphysics of some racial essence. The black tradition exists only insofar as black artists enact it. Only because black writers have read and responded to other black writers with a sense of recognition and acknowledgment can we speak of a black literary inheritance, with all the burdens and privileges that has entailed. Race is a text (an array of discursive practices), not an essence. It must be *read* with painstaking care and suspicion, not imbibed.

The disjunction between the language of criticism and the language of its subject helps defamiliarize the texts of the black tradition: ironically, it is necessary to create distance between reader and texts in order to go beyond reflexive responses and achieve critical insight into and intimacy with their formal workings. I have done this to respect the integrity of these texts, by trying to avoid confusing my experience as an Afro-American with the black act of language that defines a text. This is the challenge of the critic of black literature in the 1980s: not to shy away from white power—that is, a new critical vocabulary—but to translate it into the black idiom, *renaming* principles of criticism where appropriate, but especially naming indigenous black principles of criticism and applying them to our own texts. *Any* tool that enables the critic to explain the complex workings of the language of a text is appropriate here. For it is language, the black language of black texts, that expresses the distinctive quality of our literary tradition. Once it may have seemed that the only critical implements black critics needed were the pom-pom and the twirled baton; in fact, there is no deeper form of literary disrespect. We will not protect the integrity of our tradition by remaining afraid of, or naive about, literary

analysis; rather, we will inflict upon it the violation of reflexive, ste-
reotypical reading—or nonreading. We are the keepers of the black literary tradition. No matter what approach we adopt, we have more in
common with each other than we do with any other critic of any other
literature. We write for each other, and for our own contemporary
writers. This relation is a critical trust.

It is also a *political* trust. How can the demonstration that our texts
sustain ever closer and more sophisticated readings *not* be political at a
time when all sorts of so-called canonical critics mediate their racism
through calls for "purity" of "the tradition," demands as implicitly
racist as anything the Southern Agrarians said? How can the deconstruction of the forms of racism itself not be political? How can the use
of literary analysis to explicate the racist social text in which we still
find ourselves be anything *but* political? To be political, however, does
not mean that I have to write at the level of a Marvel comic book. My
task, as I see it, is to help guarantee that black and so-called Third
World literature is taught to black and Third World and white students
by black and Third World and white professors in heretofore white
mainstream departments of literature, and to train students to think,
to read, and to write clearly, to expose false uses of language, fraud-
ulent claims, and muddled arguments, propaganda, and vicious lies—
from all of which our people have suffered just as surely as we have
from an economic order in which we were zeroes and a metaphysical
order in which we were absences. These are the "values" which should
be transmitted through the languages of cultural and literary study.

In the December 1986 issue of the *Voice Literary Supplement*, in an essay
entitled "Cult-Nats Meet Freaky-Deke," Greg Tate argued cogently
and compellingly that "black aestheticians need to develop a coherent
criticism to communicate the complexities of our culture. There's no
periodical on black cultural phenomena equivalent to *The Village Voice*
or *Artforum*, no publication that provides journalism on black visual
art, philosophy, politics, economics, media, literature, linguistics,
psychology, sexuality, spirituality, and pop culture. Though there are
certainly black editors, journalists, and academics capable of producing such a journal, the disintegration of the black cultural nationalist
movement and the brain-drain of black intellectuals to white institutions have destroyed the vociferous public dialogue that used to exist
between them." While I would argue that *Sage*, *Callaloo*, and *Black
American Literature Forum* are indeed fulfilling that function for academic critics, I am afraid that the truth of Tate's claim is irresistible.

But his most important contribution to the future of black criticism
is to be found in his most damning allegation. "What's unfortunate,"

he writes, "is that while black artists have opened up the entire 'text of blackness' for fun and games, not many black critics have produced writing as fecund, eclectic, and freaky-deke as the art, let alone the culture, itself. . . . For those who prefer exegesis with a polemical bent, just imagine how critics as fluent in black and Western culture as the postliberated artists could strike terror into that bastion of white supremacist thinking, the Western art [and literary] world[s]." To which I can only say, "Amen, Amen."

Tate's challenge is a serious one because neither ideology nor criticism nor blackness can exist as entities of themselves, outside their forms or their texts. This is the central theme of Ralph Ellison's *Invisible Man* and Ishmael Reed's *Mumbo Jumbo*, for example. But how can we write or read the text of "Blackness"? What language(s) do black people use to represent their critical or ideological positions? In what forms of language do we speak or write? Can we derive a valid, integral "black" text of criticism or ideology from borrowed or appropriated forms? Can a black woman's text emerge authentically as borrowed, or "liberated," or revised, from the patriarchal forms of the slave narratives, on the one hand, or from the white matriarchal forms of the sentimental novel, on the other, as Harriet Jacobs and Harriet Wilson attempted to do in *Incidents in the Life of a Slave Girl* (1861) and *Our Nig* (1859)? Where lies the liberation in revision, the ideological integrity of defining freedom in the modes and forms of difference charted so cogently by so many poststructural critics of black literature?

For it is in these spaces of difference that black literature has dwelled. And while it is crucial to read these patterns of difference closely, we should understand as well that the quest was lost, in an important sense, before it had even begun, simply because the terms of our own self-representation have been provided by the master. It is not enough for us to show that refutation, negation, and revision exist, and to define them as satisfactory gestures of ideological independence. Our next concern will be to address the black political signified, that is, the cultural vision and the black critical language that underpin the search through literature and art for a profound reordering and humanizing of everyday existence. We encourage our writers and critics to undertake the fullest and most ironic exploration of the manner and matter, the content and form, the structure and sensibility so familiar and poignant to us in our most sublime form of art, black music, where ideology and art are one, whether we listen to Bessie Smith or to postmodern and poststructural John Coltrane.

Just as we encourage our writers to meet this challenge, we as critics can turn to our own peculiarly black structures of thought and feeling

to develop our own language of criticism. We do so by drawing on the
black vernacular, the language we use to speak to each other when no
white people are around. Unless we look to the vernacular to ground
our modes of reading, we will surely sink in the mire of Nella Larsen's
quicksand, remain alienated in the isolation of Harriet Jacob's garret,
or masked in the received stereotype of the Black Other helping Huck
to return to the raft, singing "China Gate" with Nat King Cole under
the Da Nang moon, or reflecting our balded heads in the shining flash
of Mr. T's signifying gold chains.

We can redefine reading itself from within our own black cultures,
refusing to grant the racist premise that criticism is something that
white people do, so that we are doomed to imitate our white colleagues, like reverse black minstrel critics done up in whiteface. We
should not succumb, as did Alexander Crummell, to the tragic lure of
white power, the mistake of accepting the empowering language of
white criticism as "universal" or as our own language, the mistake of
confusing its enabling mask with our own black faces. Each of us has,
in some literal or figurative manner, boarded a ship and sailed to a metaphorical Cambridge, seeking to master the master's tools. (I myself,
being quite literal-minded, booked passage some fourteen years ago
on the QE2.) Now we can at last don the empowering mask of blackness and talk *that* talk, the language of black difference. While it is true
that we must, as Du Bois said so long ago, "know and test the power
of the cabalistic letters of the white man," we must also know and test
the dark secrets of a black discursive universe that awaits its disclosure
through the black arts of interpretation. The future of our language
and literature may prove black indeed.

Notes

An earlier version of this essay appeared in *Voice Literary Supplement*, November 1988.

1. Alexander Crummell, "The Attitude of the American Mind toward the Negro
Intellect," *The American Negro Academy, Occasional Papers, no. 3* (Washington, D.C.,
1898), pp. 10, 10–11, 11.

2. Crummell, "The Attitude of the American Mind toward the Negro Intellect,"
p. 16.

3. Alexander Crummell, "The English Language in Liberia," in *The Future of Africa*
(New York, 1862), pp. 10, 50.

4. J. E. Caseley-Hayford, *Ethiopia Unbound: Studies in Race Emancipation* (London,
1911), pp. 1–2.

5. Alice Walker, *The Color Purple* (New York, 1982), p. 194.

6. James Alan McPherson, "A Solo Song for Doc," in *Hue and Cry* (Boston, 1969),
p. 43.

7. Ishmael Reed, *The Terrible Threes* (New York, 1989), p. 17.

8. James Baldwin, "Many Thousands Gone," in *Notes of a Native Son* (Boston,
1957), p. 29.

9. Toni Morrison, *Beloved* (New York, 1987), p. 276.

~ NIKKI STILLER

On Jewish Poetry in English

IN A TABLE OF CONTENTS NEAR TENNYSON, Browning, Wordsworth, Shelley, and Keats, the name *Isaac Rosenberg* stands out. Say *Philip Larkin* and one hears the twittering of birds, sees London's postal districts, as Larkin himself puts it, "packed like squares of wheat." For many English poets, the city is only a stone's throw from the greensward; the glade is never far from the English ear. Not that it is all peaceable. The malevolent verse of the current laureate contains pools well-stocked with bloodthirsty pike. But I feel I have to take a course in ecology to read it. *Rosenberg*, on the other hand, suggests a dark shop, a tailor's perhaps, in Golder's Green, which is neither gold nor green; cramped living quarters, immigrant cooking smells, an intense, urban life.

Rosenberg's poems are different, too. They make Wilfred Owen's, his subject the same god-awful war, seem genteel in comparison. Owen's work, slant-rhymed, imagistically daring, is certainly more discordant than Rupert Brooke's, but it refers to a serene pastoral order broken by the war. To Owen, roses and yellow mayflowers and the "kind old sun" make "the pity war distilled" more poignant. To Rosenberg, when a flower does appear, it is the ambiguous, blood-red poppy, already tinged by mortality, "white with the dust." There is no well-wrought urn in Rosenberg's mess kit: his best poems are jagged, unrhymed. Despite his adoration of Keats, beauty per se was not his principal concern. The Jewish poet took it upon himself *l'taken ha olam*, to redeem the world.[1]

To reflect publicly on such matters used to be bad form. I grew up in Connecticut. My father, my mother still boasts, spoke "The King's English," and had forgotten every word of Yiddish. My mother, Russian-born, of Russian-speaking parents, worshipped the English language. My ears were protected from poor grammar and foreign idiom the way other children's were protected from smut. Mrs. Austen, headmistress, had marked me for what I would become: an English teacher, a poet. I loved clapboard houses, rhubarb pie, and my mother tongue. But just as I questioned my relation to the lithograph of Washington crossing the Delaware in every classroom, I was unsure of my connection to the literature that nourished me: Melville, Hawthorne, Dickinson, my parents' beloved Whitman, for all his Biblical cadences, were Not Jewish. I would no more have mentioned this at the Austen School than discussed my parents' sex life.

Later I realized there had been no Jews in England for several hundred years. Why was T. S. Eliot so worried? I used to wonder. The poetic heritage in English *was* goyish: lyrical, pastoral, courtly, or romantic—not to speak of Christian. Beyond Herbert's metaphoric parsonage stood the fellows with the helmets and the spears, pagans to a man. The dissociation of sensibility, that physical-spiritual rift of which Eliot complained, I classified with Original Sin and the Immaculate Conception. Shakespeare, I decided, could have been one of us; Tennyson, never. "The Lady of Shalott" was as gentile as Lenny Bruce's lime jello. In nineteenth-century America, Whitman, the Good Goy, despite his love of million-footed Manahatta, found transcendence in "A spear of summer grass." Moreover, Whitman in his isolation yearned for community; the Jews had had one all along.

The modern era changed this. Eliot and Ezra Pound enabled poets writing in English to be cosmopolitan, dramatic, concrete; to experiment with other languages; to employ diction ranging from that of the urban grid to that of the galaxies. Too bad these great innovators were also great anti-Semites, for the ensuing freedom of expression was good for the Jews, their experience intersecting with modernity in other ways. If gentile Europe was forced to acknowledge its demons during World War I, the Jews had met those demons, in the bloodbath at York or Blois, for example, centuries before. Displacement and exile created not only new minorities but new self-images, among them Joyce's Jewish protagonist Bloom. English itself became an airborne medium of exchange, a cosmic jargon, a lingua franca richer than Esperanto, and the natural means of expression for petty officials in Calcutta, juries in Jerusalem, millions of Jews in a pluralistic America.

This internationalization continues. Thus, while modern English is not Hebrew or Yiddish, to write in it no longer seems an Anglo-Saxon prerogative.

Without a specifically Jewish language, however, what makes a writer or poet Jewish is as complex a question as what makes a person Jewish.[2] In private, chauvinist moments, a Jew may claim any poet whose great-grandmother once strayed into a mikvah. We have been known to boast Rainer Maria Rilke, Mary McCarthy, St. John of the Cross. There are full-blooded Jews who write as if not only they but also their grandfathers were Episcopalians. Others have a basic goyish vocabulary but now and again don certain externals to signify that they have not dismissed their heritage: the Queen Bee wears a yarmulke, the story goes, so everyone will know she is not a Wasp. At the other extreme are poets and writers who appear to have translated their own work from the Yiddish, and the Lulav and Etrog School of Verse: on occasion I feel that if I have to read one more poem about Bubah lighting Sabbath candles I am going to convert. Harold Bloom claims that Jewish poets continue to wrestle with Biblical subject matter, and John Hollander, who writes exquisitely on arcane Jewish subject matter himself, claims there is no such thing.[3]

I will deal only with poets who have proclaimed their Jewishness, but I am looking for something more elusive. I am interested in distinctions such as a character in Philip Roth's *The Counterlife* makes between "the famous Jewish intensity" and "the famous English insouciance"; in what Casals meant when he urged his string quartet to "Play Jewish." If Freud's thought was influenced by that of his Chassidic cousins though he lived at some intellectual remove from them, so, I suspect, the modern Jewish poet's English is influenced by tenets and attitudes originating in the Hebrew Bible, the Talmud, and the Siddur, as well as in the traumas and renewals of the Diaspora.

Neither the world nor the flesh is evil in Jewish thought. Contrary to popular misconception, the Jews are enjoined by their religion to rejoice.[4] There is scarcely any activity over which one cannot say a *brucha*, a blessing, from eating bananas to hearing thunder to washing one's hands or drinking wine. A Jew gives thanks for his functioning veins and arteries before he gives thanks for Torah. This attitude does not lead him to ignore pain or call it good; as prophets and physicians, the Jews have long sought to diagnose and cure. A wonder-working Vilna rabbi to whom emigrating families flocked for a preventive against trachoma would pray over the susceptible parties, give them amulets to wear around their necks, then send them to the best eye doctor in town. This accommodation of reality encourages a freedom of movement between material and spiritual realms, tragic and comic

modes, as modern English allows for a correlative freedom of diction
and tone. God is revealed in historical processes; the Jew is involved
in, rather than alienated from, the world. Human speech is central, as
the Shma, "Hear O Israel," affirms. The Shma, moreover, has a collective point of view. In it, Jews speak as a body, a community of continuous knowledge, experience, and belief. Such a prayer, such a
stance, prohibits the overly self-referential. A Jew joins a minyan to
pray. Private prayer is considered a little dangerous.[5]

I first became aware of the connection between this world view and
the use of English in the work of Delmore Schwartz. Weaned on *The
Waste Land*, I had had a problem with Eliot, his voice "remote," his eye
"a telescope / scanning the circuit of stars / for Good-Good and Evil
Absolute."[6] Prufrock is repelled by the hair on a girl's arms, the
speaker in "The Fire Sermon" by the indelicacy of women: "O the
moon shone bright on Mrs. Porter / And on her daughter / They wash
their feet in soda water." The jingle reveals Eliot's contempt for the
pair of them, never mind their feet. The hyacinth girl is not a creature
but an ideal. "Jerusalem Athens Alexandria / Vienna London" are
"Unreal."[7] Real places, real people, men in shirtsleeves, for instance,
are the degraded objects of Eliot's ironic glance. It is Eliot's disdain for
the sensual that makes him so goyish. Schwartz may be coy about the
interweaving of abstract and concrete, and may display a modish contempt for the colloquial from time to time, yet he insists "Socrates is
mortal."[8] The language of merger, of an eroticized consciousness, is
pervasive. A collection of Schwartz's stories is entitled *The World Is a
Wedding*. And in "Consent, Consent, Consent to Be," his mind's
"Continuous and unreleasing wind . . . Lusts for Paris, Crete and Per-
gamus / Is suddenly off for Paris and Chicago / Judea, San Francisco,
the Midi." A *mind* that *lusts* for places actual and ideal is one for which
the spirit and the flesh are not discrete.

Body and soul are married here, but they certainly have their disputes: Schwartz is a neurotic. The heavy bear of instinct "goes with"
him. Though not identical to him, it poses a threat, "In love with
candy, anger, and sleep." But in "The Beautiful American Word,
Sure" or "A Dog Named Ego, the Snowflakes as Kisses" or "In the
Naked Bed, in Plato's Cave," Schwartz's language expands to accommodate the disparate, the ugly, the ironic, the mechanical. It does not
look down at them from a higher metaphysical perch. His speaker
may be both "Perplexed" and "still wet / With sleep, affectionate,
hungry and cold" at the "mystery of beginning / Again and again."
Schwartz is thus able to sanctify what Wallace Stevens calls "the dreadful sundry of this world." There is no longer a Temple. A Jew prays
wherever he finds himself, with other Jews, if possible. A truly Jewish

music includes both the psalter and the medical textbook: "Manic-depressive Lincoln, national hero!" Schwartz cries, "tricky lawyer full of black despair." In "The Ballad of the Children of the Czar," Aeneas carrying his father on his back is seen as doing "Child labor!" On "this tragic star," Schwartz writes in the same poem, "I eat my baked potato." Does Wallace Stevens eat a baked potato? The closest he comes to it is a bitter aspic. How about Eliot? Prufrock contemplates eating a peach. But a peach is so pastoral. Stevens goes slumming where "the deer and the dachshund are one," that is, in Jersey City, the quotidian. A Jew is enjoined to *daven* there.[9]

This Jewish determination to find meaning not only on Sinai's remote outcropping but in its psychological and historical exfoliations is clear in the work of Allen Ginsberg. Prophet and comedian, prankster, epic narrator, rhapsodist, and yenta, Ginsberg has had a tremendous effect on the American sensibility. Some would say his public persona, rather than his oeuvre, has been his medium, but Ginsberg's poems are intensely social. Crowded with people, they address a crowd. Earthy and ecstatic at once, they scold, praise, issue jeremiads. Ginsberg can be excessive: the work of Jewish poets is subject to all the Jewish diseases—heartburn, diabetes, gas. There is a tendency to dwell on pain, for example, like Charles Reznikov; to be prosaic yet cloying like David Ignatow. Ginsberg can be diagnosed as suffering from flatulence. Yet, at present, when a reviewer rightly compares the work of one establishment darling to decorative wallpaper, Ginsberg's audacity is salubrious.

For anyone to essay a personal Qaddish is indeed chutzpah. Ginsberg's, Hollander contends, neither adheres to—nor consciously breaks with—the traditions of the Jewish one.[10] The Mourners' Qaddish, for example, avoids any reference to death, while Ginsberg's *Kaddish* lyricizes it in a Whitmanesque manner. Both the liturgical Qaddish and Ginsberg's poem, however, celebrate life and affirm faith in the face of great loss. How each does so is another matter. If we are to praise life, Ginsberg insists, it must be the uncut version. Nor is this meditative literature to which the observant bring their own particulars. His mother must be brought to life again. Ginsberg reifies Naomi through that meshing of abstract and concrete, beautiful and ugly, waking and dream which for him constitutes reality: "Strange now to think of you, gone without corsets & eyes, while I walk on the sunny pavement of Greenwich Village," the final edition begins.[11] If the eyes are there, the corset must be there, too. If his mother struggled "toward candy store, first home-made sodas of the century, hand-churned ice cream in backroom on musty brownfloor boards," she also struggled "toward education marriage nervous breakdown, oper-

ation, teaching school, and learning to be mad, in a dream." The concrete and the abstract are bedfellows. "What is this life?" Ginsberg
then asks the reader. Later, he prods us with provocative as well as
evocative imagery: "Farewell / with Communist Party and a broken
stocking / farewell / with six dark hairs on the wen of your breast /
farewell / with your old dress and a long black beard around the vagina." Ginsberg himself may see such an attitude towards experience
and expression as Buddhist. But the language of the Hebrew prophets,
Abraham Heschel writes, "is luminous and explosive, firm and contingent, harsh and compassionate"; like Ginsberg's, "a fusion of
contradictions."[12]

Ginsberg's shifts in diction are occasionally too extreme. "Magnif-
icent, mourned no more, marred of heart, mind behind, married
dreamed, mortal changed," he intones in *Kaddish*, then jolts us with
"Ass and face done with murder." For the most part, he is shrewd and
witty about his breaches of linguistic decorum. Consider "A Supermarket in California," in which Ginsberg finds transcendence in the
"neon fruit" heart of suburbia. "What thoughts I have of you tonight,
Walt Whitman," the poem begins, "for I walked down the sidestreets
under the trees with a headache self-conscious looking at the full
moon." The phrase recalls Whitman's "hankering, gross, mystical,
nude," but being mystical and nude is different from having a
headache.

Not that Ginsberg's humor obviates the lyrical impulse. His lyri-
cism incorporates the comic, and the familial. Jewish poets are fasci-
nated by their relatives, living and dead. Perhaps this has to do with
the Jewish sense of history. For what is genealogy if not a privileged
and private unfolding of God's design in time? In "Aunt Rose," elegy
for an era as well as an individual, political events of the period that
the poem evokes provide metaphoric vehicles of an emotional intensity equal to those of natural processes. The same yearning that
has driven young men into the Abraham Lincoln Brigade drives this
crippled woman named for a flower. Her tears of "sexual frustration"
and acts of loving kindness like powdering the boy's legs with calomine
exist on the same plane as collecting money for her left-wing cause.
The historical *is* personal. "Hitler is dead," the poet informs his departed relative, "Uncle Harry sold his last silk stocking / Claire quit
interpretive dancing school / Buba sits a wrinkled monument in Old /
Ladies Home blinking at new babies," and, in farewell, "the war in
Spain has ended long ago / Aunt Rose." Here all human endeavor is
seen as significant, whether tragic as the Loyalists' defeat, or silly as
Claire's interpretive dancing. Remembering—*zakhor* is a command to
a Jew—dignifies even the old lady's blinking inanity.

For Wallace Stevens, "It is the human that is the alien / The human that has no cousin in the moon." The Jewish poet might retort, "I don't know about the moon, but the human has plenty of cousins on earth." The titles of Irving Feldman's poems—"Assimilation," "The Nurses," "Family History," "Genealogies," "The Human Circle"— bear witness to this.[13] Many of these derive their primary metaphors from our exchanges, inventions, interactions; from our drama and our reckoning. "The Heir," for example, takes place in a hospital room; there are no yellow mayflowers here either. The poet, "a surgeon re-sectioning the heart," struggles over "the very nature of reality" with the corpse that "sits up and shouts at him 'You idiot, / do you know how to do anything right?' " What could be a more painful exchange than the son accepting "his father's dead heart, commonplace, / appalling, and the old man's misery and maiming / return in the son's chest to their brutal beating"? These spiritual engagements mimic social ones: he "who was the doctor / is now the patient"; the son being "Devoted and good, his normality resurrects / in dull parody that bitterness and failure." The violence is man-made, too, the knife and gun: "Unloaded, held to his head, / the catastrophic life clicks repeatedly / in the empty chambers." Doctor and patient, student and teacher, father and son; the insult and the lesson; disavowal and identification animate the lines: "and carried away for a moment, he says, as if / repeating an important lesson, earnestly, / with yearning and with pride, 'Actually, / Dad and I have the same sense of humor.' "

In another of Feldman's poems, "The Pripet Marshes," the color is literally in the people, friends and relatives whom he sets down in a Russian village moments before the Germans arrive: in Frank who has "The hair and yellow skin of a Tartar"; in "blond Lottie"; in "Abbie, whose coloring wants lavender"; in his mother "whose gray eyes are touched with yellow"; in his "brown-eyed son" and "red-haired sisters." Again and again the words evoke character, personality, individuality: one is "good-hearted," the next "coarse and miserable"; one "Sullen," another a "moping melancholy clown." There are the names, Marian and Adele and Munji, of those who engage in sociable activities, "walking the streets, visiting, praying in shul" and "arguing." There is banter and impatience and merriment. The emphasis on dailiness here is not a hand-me-down from Yiddish with its dearth of descriptive natural terms. Rather, the mainstay of this kind of speech is its humane consanguinity, the voice of one separate yet linked with the lives of the rest, of the whole. In "The Pripet Marshes," as the Germans approach on their motorcycles, the speaker cries, "I snatch them all back, / For, when I want to, I can be a god. / No, the Germans won't have one of them! / This is my people, they are mine." But the primordial mist with which he seeks to cover and save his people "clouds" his own mind instead. In the struggle between consciousness and unconsciousness, the individual and the undifferentiated marshland—an inhuman force like fascism itself—the poet gives out, sinking down "as though drugged or beaten." The inhuman and unindividuated has defeated him, except for the act of the poem itself, a kind of Shma which speaks not only for the poet but for the people Israel.

Nor is this vocabulary limited in Feldman's work to poems with overtly Jewish subject matter. *All of Us Here*, as its title indicates, reveals the same insistence on the primary importance of man relating to man, to woman, woman to child, each to each. In "They Say to Us," a family is "passing photos from hand to hand, / the living and the dead, / who mingle here / as nowhere else." To Feldman, "This ritual is profound, / solemn, religious—we feel it, / become weighty ourselves, / judicious, like gods; / even and merciful in judgment, / simple, courteous and worthy."[14] Community *is* communion.

The Jews have been city dwellers for a long time, but the urban condition is now general. Many gentile poets, however, continue to find their language in the shrinking natural world. Even the Song of Songs, with its bleating and skipping lambs, celebrates a wedding. Perhaps it is the essential this-worldliness of Jewish spirituality that permits Jewish poets to transform "the dreadful sundry," to infuse it with life. Geoffrey Hartman, interpreting Auerbach, maintains that the Bible's "truth claim" is "so imperious that reality in its sensuous or *charming* aspect is not dwelt upon."[15] Exposure to this truth claim helps guard the Jewish poet against prettiness. There is nothing pretty about Irene Klepfisc's monkey house as metaphor for the family in *Keeper of Accounts*. Nothing is pretty about Robert Mezey's elegy for Nely Sílvinová, "Theresienstadt Poem," which specifies her camp number and "the red penis of the commandant," its realism more potent than Randall Jarrell's "A Camp in the Prussian Forest."[16] Jewish spirituality includes a horizontal component which looks across—rather than up or down—and has a great deal to do with looking at ourselves. *All of Us Here* begins as a reading of George Segal's sculpture. And in Philip Schultz's "Deep Within the Ravine," its title that of a Hans Hoffman painting, the poet's guardian angel, Stein, warns him against becoming metaphysically imbalanced, and urges him to go refresh himself with Rubens's "'juicy nudes . . . after so much crazy abstraction.'"[17] Humor and perspective.

Humor, that admission of the inevitable failure between longing and accomplishment, in a good marriage, can facilitate peace. At least, it can keep either party from reaching for the meat cleaver. As many Jewish poets are humorous, many popular Jewish comics are poetic.

Some are downright literary: S. J. Perelman, pearl of the *New Yorker* as well as of the Hollywood set; Mel Brooks, pal of Joe Heller; Groucho Marx corresponding with T. S. Eliot. Woody Allen's Zelig, predicting that "In the future, America will be a nation of great doctors and great patients," could be mistaken for Allen Ginsberg. "A spider as big as a Buick" finds its way into Diane Keaton's bathtub in *Annie Hall*. One of Allen's proverbs pronounces, "The Lion shall lie down with the Calf, but the Calf won't get much sleep."[18] Vision, yes, but not at the expense of reality. Nature—that spider—in a social context. The comic poet and the poetic comic overlap. Ginsberg, Feldman, Schwartz are not afraid to be funny. I do not mean playful. Jewish poets do not incline towards play for its own sake. Even a dreidl is marked "Nes gadol haya sham": "A great miracle took place there."

If Jewish poets are at home in the quotidian—Ginsberg cooking broccoli when "The Lion for Real" appears—Jewish prose writers often seem to enter the Inner Sanctum of Poetry as easily as they would their mothers' kitchens: Henry Roth in *Call It Sleep*, for example. Bernard Malamud's narrator steps out of the novel entirely at the end of *The Tenant* to chant for mercy. The center of *The Counterlife* is the Host, which Roth transmutes into a gigantic spud, a Jewish version of a gentile symbol, and we are back to baked potatoes once again. This reification of the sacred, or sanctification of the prosaic, distinguishes the diction of the Jewish writer. Moreover, the Jewish God, to my understanding, prefers a gathering at which it is incumbent upon us to speak up. Robert Frost's buck does not happen to break the silence. We ourselves break the silence: "Hear, O Israel; the Lord is Our God, the Lord is One." The writer, the poet, must keep talking, arguing, pleading with the Other in order to redeem the world. Thus, while John Ashbery considers his self-portrait in a convex mirror, Irving Feldman writes "Teach Me, Dear Sister." Which is better? Who can say? In the past few decades, however, the lyric form has become smaller, narrow, celibate, a vehicle for self-contemplation, divorced from the active life and the passions. Perhaps the future of poetry in this language depends not so much on a little red wheelbarrow but on any group with something to say and the sense of a community to say it to.

Notes

1. See Anthony Rudolf's introduction to the Jewish poets of "England, Scotland, and Wales," in *Voices Within the Ark: The Modern Jewish Poets*, ed. Howard Schwartz and Anthony Rudolf (New York, 1980), pp. 394–400; also, Ian Parsons's introduction to *The Collected Works of Isaac Rosenberg* (New York, 1979).

2. Norman Roth, "*Am Yisrael*—Jews or Judaism?," *Judaism* 37 (Spring 1988), posits

a "continuum" with "room for every kind of Jew, from the most observant to those whose interests are entirely secular" (208). I follow him in this definition here.

3. Harold Bloom before a conference on Hebrew Literature at Yale University in April 1988; John Hollander, "The Question of American Jewish Poetry," *Tikkun* 3 (May/June 1988): 33–37.

4. My source for summaries of mainstream Jewish thought, unless otherwise noted, is Isaac Klein, *A Guide to Jewish Religious Practice* (New York, 1979).

5. Klein, citing various authorities, concludes that "the rabbis clearly preferred public prayer to private prayer." The community, he quotes Dr. Elie Munk as saying, "does not suffer deficiencies. What is lacking in one individual is made up by the other" (pp. 14–15).

6. Emanuel Litvinoff, "To T. S. Eliot," in *Voices Within the Ark*, pp. 715–16.

7. T. S. Eliot, *The Waste Land* (New York, 1962), pp. 37, 44.

8. Delmore Schwartz, "All Clowns Are Masked and All Personae," in *Selected Poems: Summer Knowledge* (New York, 1967). All quotations are from this edition.

9. To *daven* is to pray.

10. Hollander, "The Question of American Jewish Poetry," 34.

11. Allen Ginsberg, *Collected Poems* (New York, 1980), p. 209. All quotations are from this edition.

12. Abraham J. Heschel, *The Prophets: An Introduction* (New York, 1969), p. 7.

13. Irving Feldman, *New and Selected Poems* (New York, 1979). Quotations are from this volume unless otherwise noted.

14. Irving Feldman, *All of Us Here* (New York, 1986), pp. 40–41.

15. Geoffrey Hartman, "The Struggle for the Text," in *Midrash and Literature* (New Haven, 1986), p. 15 (italics mine).

16. The Mezey poem may be found in *Voices Within the Ark*, pp. 550–51.

17. Philip Schultz, *Deep Within the Ravine* (New York, 1984), p. 51.

18. Woody Allen, "The Scrolls," in *Without Feathers* (New York, 1983), p. 28.

❧ ANTHONY HECHT

Naming the Animals

Having commanded Adam to bestow
Names upon all the creatures, God withdrew
To empyrean palaces of blue
That warm and windless morning long ago,
And seemed to take no notice of the vexed
Look on the young man's face as he took thought
Of all the miracles the Lord had wrought,
Now to be labelled, dubbed, yclept, indexed.

Before an addled mind and puddled brow,
The feathered nation and the finny prey
Passed by; there went biped and quadruped.
Adam looked forth with bottomless dismay
Into the tragic eyes of his first cow,
And shyly ventured, "Thou shalt be called 'Fred.'"

❧ HUGH KENNER

Further Thoughts: Little Words

IN "SONG: THE WINDS OF DOWNHILL" (circa 1970) George Oppen tells us we're so impoverished

> the words *would with and* take on substantial
> meaning . . .

And in his "Veritas Sequitur" (circa 1965) we find a tribute to

> The small nouns
> Crying faith
> In this in which the wild deer
> Startle, and stare out.

"In this in which": not a noun in sight in that phrase. The poem's small nouns, in order of occurrence, are "deer," "eyes," "lips," "teeth," "grass," "roots," "mouths," "woods," "paths," "fields," "leaves," "sun." "Sun" is the climax, making everything happen, drawing up water to be shed as rain, nourishing roots and grass and leaves to feed and shelter deer, warming the deer who need the food and shelter. "In this in which the wild deer / startle and stare out": that refers to a forest, enabled by the sun, and says there's more to say about it than even the word *forest* can say. No word says enough. *Forest*—the second noun in the poem—doesn't quite qualify as a small word. And the small words are the ones that say the most.

Then the other Oppen poem, where

> *would with and* take on substantial
> meaning handholds footholds

as we dig in our heels, "sliding"? What about nonsubstantive words like those? *Would* says volition (but conditionally); *with* says alliance; *and* says just conjunction, weaker than *with*. Such little words are always a challenge. Oppen was mesmerized by what they do, though no one thinks to ask. Yet how they throng! In 1918 Godfrey Dewey surveyed 100,000 words of English prose and found that the 14 English words most frequently used were these:

the, of, and, to, a, in, that, it, is, I, for, be, was, as

Reflecting a habit of English, *the* occurs twice as often as anything else. Louis Zukofsky's first longish poem was called "The," and his very longest was called "A." Louis, for whom English had been a second language, enjoyed looking up words like those in any dictionary that offered. The lexicographers who'd expended great pains on such entries had doubtless enjoyed little hope they'd ever be looked up. (The *OED*'s entry for *the* is twelve columns long—nearly 10,000 defining and exemplifying words.)

Dewey's list deserves a more intent look than it's usually gotten:

the, of, and, to, a, in, that, it, is, I, for, be, was, as

The and *a* of course reflect the habit of English nouns, which routinely take "articles." Articles have no direct Latin equivalent. Written Latin—we've no way to know about spoken—said "Equus est bonus" for "The horse is good": no grunt up ahead of "equus." Just north of the Alps, though, as the Empire was disintegrating, they bandied frontier-talk. "Equus" gave way to "caballus," a word for a nondescript frontier horse, a nag. Then it seemed important to specify that you were talking about just one of those, "unus caballus," moreover just *this* one of them, using a form of the demonstrative pronoun *illus*; and after centuries, lo, "Cela, c'est un bon cheval": that there's one fine hoss, pardner. Specifying number, pointing attention in a certain direction: whether in frontier Texas or frontier Gaul these seemed instinctive aids to getting yourself understood. Such worries pertain to wherever, as in New York, you can't rely on a secure culture.

Back to Dewey's list. We've accounted for the articles, and for *that*, and *is* and *was* may go without explanation for now. *Of* is more interesting: so complex a relator the *OED* gives it nineteen columns. Its original sense was "away," "away from"; thus "notions of removal, of separation," senses which involve "the notion of taking, coming, arising or resulting *from*." You can see how far that can lead, though *of* has also come to denote possession. And whereas *of* separates, *and* joins. Junction, disjunction: those are categories of experience.

To and *in*? They seem to connote "direction," hence movement; I go *to* the house and end up *in* it. *For*? Substitution, exchange: when I sue you *for* all you are worth, if you lose it, I'll get it.

Deprivation, movement to and into, substitution: whole plots can be founded on those. Substitution and deprivation: that's the *Iliad*; deprivation and much movement: the *Odyssey*. Homer and Joyce alike based large designs on notions a single syllable can pinpoint. We may be isolating fundamental gestures of the mind. Those three words "The Winds of Downhill" regarded with raised eyebrows are by Dewey's count pretty frequent: *and* is the third most common of all words, *with* the sixteenth, *would* the forty-ninth.

Next, an interesting rule can be gleaned from the *Harvard Concordance to Shakespeare* or the Gabler word index to *Ulysses*: it seems that, in any substantial English sample, just forty small words, forever repeated, repeated, make up fully 40 percent of the text we read. That's the 40–40 rule, and it's arresting. How did it come about? Well, the grammar of the language was not handed down by Jehovah; it consolidates many million interpersonal decisions. What must one person specify so another won't be left guessing? Remember how the French articles, *un* and *le*, arose from the numering *Unus*, the pointing *ille*. That will once have served a purpose: will have helped toward clear-cut understanding. Statistics of "usage" reflect how millions of people, over and over, once kept deciding what needed to be pointed out. (They were—in Oppen's phrase—Being Numerous? Yes, and they'd no choice.) Devising a clean-cut language, a language unredundant, tidy, is a game. It's been played by solo players, from Bishop Wilkins (1667) to C. K. Ogden (1930). But always a catch: that having published his schema, the soloist must sit and wait for anyone else to be interested. Few save cranks ever are. Languages that *work* arise out of numerousness.

And, Darwin's shade would have us observe, any language actually spoken, not excluding English, stays in use because it works: has worked over and over, in many billion transactions. That we Indo-European speakers need those frequent small words the most is a firm law based on millennia of experience. That they're our least-regarded words, also our least definable, deserves pondering. *Define* means, "state the sense in *different* words." *Assegai* you can define in a couple of lines. The *OED* needed 60,000 defining words for *set*: easily the length of a Barbara Cartland novel. Ms. Cartland, like the rest of us, has it easy. Neither she nor we, to get on with our talking, our writing, need think about the sense of *set*, the sense of *sense*.

Note

Hugh Kenner's essay in the 1980 *State of the Language* was entitled "Machinespeak."

❧ ARTHUR DELBRIDGE

Australian English Now

THOUGH "NOW" IN THE TITLE MEANS *NOW*, Australian English has had only a blink of time in which to be, to be known, and to change. It is the mother tongue, now, of about twelve million people, out of the sixteen million who inhabit the world's biggest island, smallest continent. The other four million include the Australian Aborigines— 228,000 in the 1986 Census—who have shared between them some 250 languages (only 5 of which now have more than a thousand speakers, though 25 are reckoned to have a good chance of survival, and some 180 are either extinct or known now only to the older generations), and recent immigrants from Europe, Asia, and the Americas, who have brought with them, as mother tongues, about 140 languages, some of which are now "community languages" in what had earlier been a monolingual country.

When the Commonwealth of Australia was founded in 1901 by the federating of its states, its population was 3,773,801 persons. Of these, 77 percent had been born in Australia, 10 percent in England and Wales, 3 percent in Scotland, 5 percent in Ireland. Australian society was clearly British to a very high degree, and English was its language. To be more precise, Australian English was its language, even though at that time the distinction was not clearly recognized. At best the local variety was felt to be a "pretty crook" approximation to the best British English, and at its worst, "the most brutal maltreatment that has ever been inflicted on the mother-tongue of the great English-speaking nations."[1] By 1900 Australians were already conscious of their distinct ethos, expressed in popular literature and in language. Uneasily conscious, because of what A. A. Phillips in 1966 called "the Cultural Cringe," in its two forms, the Cringe Direct and the Cringe Inverted (in the latter, one's assumed flaws of character and behavior are flaunted): "The core of the difficulty," he wrote, "is the fact that, in the back of the Australian mind, there sits a minatory Englishman."[2]

There had been nothing minatory about the English inhabitants of the first penal settlement of Sydney Town in 1788—except for the English soldiers who guarded them, brutally. The language of the convicts and of the free settlers who followed was dialectically mixed, though it had a strong London phonological component and more than a flash of the "flash" vocabulary of the underworld of petty villains. Not an auspicious start, this, for an emerging national variety of English. It began to emerge early in the 1830s when the number of "currency" children (born in the colony) began to equal and then exceed the number of "sterling" children (born in the British Isles). By this time the vocabulary had already been considerably Australianized by the often ignorant application of British words to the physical novelties of the land, and by the borrowing of Aboriginal words that were inexpertly realized in English speech and reduced haphazardly to writing. But more significant was the appearance among the currency lads and lasses of an Australian accent, with some of its features like Cockney, but others quite unlike, and with a uniformity of phonological structure, wherever it was spoken, that is still a feature of Australian English now in 1990. On this reckoning, then, Australian English is about 160 years old, and is much the same everywhere, now as then. It has had two great peaks of development in that time, with a third one building up now.

The first peak, between the 1880s and 1914, coincided with a new image of a distinctively Australian culture on a national scale. At last the image of Australia created by European settlers and visitors began to be replaced by an image created by Australians themselves. Just as the Australian accent had been born with the demographic ascendance of "currency" children, now an Australian idiom came with the demographic ascendance of the adult native-born Australian in the 1880s and 1890s. And with this shift came a striking development in literature.

Australian popular literature had its roots in the English village and town culture of its early settlers, in the "flash" argot of thieves, and in orally transmitted colonial songs and ballads with themes of isolation, hostility to authority, and mateship in the face of hardship and social wrong in a harsh land. But towards the end of the nineteenth century, Australian society had come to be largely urban, industrialized, and literate. A dual system of education, public and private, had been in operation since midcentury, and the University of Sydney was incorporated in 1850. In these circumstances the oral literature of the colony gave way to a literature of the popular city press. It started with the Sydney *Bulletin*, founded as a weekly in 1880. "It was rude, slangy, smart, happily vulgar, modern in journalistic style, and above all funny—especially in its cartoons."[3] Despite its city location it quickly became the leading image-maker for rural Australians. Radical in its politics, outspoken in its criticism of the convict system which had brought the colony into being, it came to be known as the "bushman's bible." Largely written by its readers in the form of paragraphs, anecdotes, "Aboriginalities" (a *Bulletin* coinage), ballads, and short stories, it was a forum for the discussion (indeed, the glorification) of the language of country trades and country people, people from the outback: the shearer battling for a cut, the ringer (best shearer in the shed), the sundowner with his swag, the squatter on his thoroughbred. Many of the expressions aired in the *Bulletin* are still well settled in the colloquial idiom of Australia: *fair dinkum, larrikin, bonzer, bloody* (still celebrated as "the great Australian adjective"), *offsider, fair cow, battler, bludger,* and so on. The *Bulletin* also displayed what is perhaps an Australian line in phrase-making ("miserable as a bandicoot on a burnt ridge," "better than a poke in the eye with a burnt stick")—wry, self-depreciatory, rough as bags, the sustaining language of the underdog.

But the *Bulletin* held up the mirror to the idiom of the bush, which was uniquely Australian, rather than to the language of the urban majority, with its greater diversity of styles and traditions. It discovered the image of the bushman and made that the image of Australia, soon to be sharpened and idealized by *Bulletin* poets and short story writers who became professional writers and are now figures in the annals of Australian literature: "Banjo" Paterson, the author of "The Man from Snowy River," Henry Lawson, in whose short stories dialogue is for the first time convincingly in the idiom of the bush, and Joseph Furphy, self-educated in the libraries of the Mechanic's Institute, the author of *Such Is Life*, the classic novel of Australian attitudes and experience in the outback.

This first peak of literary nationalism was a mythmaker in language and theme: the losing battle against the hard land, the egalitarian posture of the underdog in the face of social inequalities, the faith in camp-fire philosophies, the wry humor of making the best of things, the pathetic hope of good times ahead. But against this literary image was the reality of a highly structured rural society, and a much more numerous and heterogeneous urban society in which there was a flourishing bourgeoisie, a lively group of flagrantly bohemian Australian-born but European-trained painters creating in impressionist paint the same bush image as the *Bulletin* writers, a public library system in which the works of European and American writers were available, and an intellectual milieu with its roots in European ideologies and assumptions.[4]

It was here in this milieu that the first interest in Australian English as an object for study emerged. In 1898 there appeared the first Australian dictionary, *Austral English*, compiled by Edward E. Morris, an Oxford scholar who had a chair at the University of Melbourne. Morris used the historical principles of the *OED*, and his book is valuable for its collection of citations and his treatment of Australian fauna and flora. But he revealed a colonial attitude when he declared that "Austral English" meant "all the new words and new uses of words that have been added to the English language by reason of the fact that those who speak English have taken up their abode in Australia, Tasmania, and New Zealand." Very different, this, from Webster's declaration, in the first of his *Dissertations on the English Language*:

> As an independent nation our honour requires us to have a system of our own, in language as well as government. Great Britain, whose children we are, and whose language we speak, should no longer be our standard. For the taste of her writers is already corrupted, and her language is on the decline. But if it were not so, she is at too great a distance to be our model and to instruct us in the principles of our tongue.[5]

Nothing like that was to appear for Australian English until the 1940s, when after a period of casting about for a new vision, the second peak emerged.

Like the first, it had a popular face: an Australian Mencken, the journalist Sidney J. Baker wrote a book called *The Australian Language* (1945). It had become clear to Baker "that we need some better starting point than Murray's *Dictionary*. We have to work out the problem from the viewpoint of Australia, not from the viewpoint of England and of the judgments she passed upon our language because she did not know it as well as we do."[6] Sweeping comprehensively through Australian life and times, Baker's book attempts to show that here is a new language, needing a new name. He pushed the argument too hard and was weak on philology, but his discursive presentation of the Australian lexicon, especially at its less formal end, showed that the Aus-

tralian idiom, both for city and country, had its own character, and
was not merely a curiosity of English transported and added to an already adequate English stock.

The other face of the 1940s peak was academic. A. G. Mitchell of
Sydney University initiated a series of studies of the Australian accent
and its historical and social aspect. He took Australian English to be a
national variety of English in its own right, with a phonological structure and phonetic realizations developed out of the British tradition
under the influence of local social forces. He was at pains to compare
it, phonologically and phonetically, with standard British English,
which in the minds of most Australians in the 1940s was the only standard available, and one which threw into sharp relief the horrors of
their own maltreatment of good British vowels and consonants.
Mitchell alarmed Australians by declaring "There is nothing wrong
with Australian speech." Up to this time (1942), the conventional
view was the one expressed in 1926 by S. H. Smith, director of education in New South Wales:

> It is sad to reflect that other people are able to recognise Australians by
> their speech. Most unfortunately our variation from the accepted stan-
> dard is along lines which are harsh, unmusical, and unpleasant to the
> ear. . . . Teachers must do their utmost to check this development away
> from standard English.

So Mitchell's declaration, in spite of his good reputation as a scholar,
had a generally hostile reception. Looking back on the public debates
which followed, he confessed that it had been very hard to get a sympathetic hearing for his defense of the Australian accent: "It was denounced as amounting to no more than a neutral document that whatever is is right, that it tolerated and encouraged what was slovenly and
slipshod. It was even said that it implied a contempt for Australians by
suggesting that any old kind of speech was good enough for them."[7]

But Mitchell's influence was much stronger than he believed, and it
is still prominent among the forces which shape the progress of English in Australia now. His work began the process which brought
Australians, however uneasily, to the point where they could accept
Australian English as the language of their own community, adequate
as any other for making their own contributions to the conversation
of humanity. As an example of this changed attitude let me take radio
broadcasting. There are two broadcasting systems: national radio,
funded entirely by the federal government, and commercial radio. For
the latter the question of language is simple: language is an aspect of
personality, which must express a preconceived station image. But for
national radio the question is more complex.

The Australian Broadcasting Corporation (ABC), created in 1932 as a commission, broadcasts in all states of Australia, its programs reflecting the variety of cultural interests, both high and popular, in the community. Language became an issue very quickly. In 1943 the Sydney branch of the English Association sent a letter to the commissioner expressing the view "that action should be taken . . . to ensure a measure of correctness and uniformity in the use of English as spoken over the broadcast networks." The committee set up for this purpose recommended particular pronunciations to announcers, with (on the whole) a British bent: Daniel Jones's *English Pronouncing Dictionary* was the nominated reference book. W. J. Cleary, chairman of the commission, revealed in 1941 that of 450 applicants for announcing posts "only two could be selected as possible announcers." He declared Australian speech to be "slightly objectionable" in its monotony and in "the throatiness and distortion of its vowels, due to a tendency to speak with the lips and teeth closed." "Every quest for announcers," he said, "has revealed that the number of men most suitable have been Englishmen."[8]

The influence of Professor Mitchell on the committee soon became apparent, however, in its championing and eventual adoption of "educated Australian speech" as the style for national broadcasting. But Mitchell meant something more particular than that phrase itself suggests. In 1940 he had presented a paper to the English Association offering an analysis of Australian speech made mainly on the basis of the pronunciation of certain key vowels (specifically, the vowels in the words *beat, boot, say, so, high,* and *how*). One sort of pronunciation he called Educated, and another sort with a more fronted articulation and wider diphthongs he called Broad. The Educated set was certainly closer phonetically to the vowels of Daniel Jones's "Received Pronunciation" of educated southern English. The ABC, then, was to stick to the Educated vowel range rather than the Broad, which was more demotic—more like the speech of the shearers and drovers who had carried the burden of the nationalist myths of forty years earlier. But Mitchell insisted that both Educated and Broad were good, in their places.

In later research, Mitchell revised the classification of Australian pronunciation: the spectrum of vowel quality now divided three ways, as Cultivated, General, and Broad, with a range of correlations with the gender, education, and socioeconomic background of the subject speakers (some nine thousand high school pupils at the end of their secondary schooling).[9] This more extensive research confirmed the assumption made in the ABC's practice that there is but a single dialect of English in Australia, with no significant regional variation.

But it also encouraged questions about the ABC's insistence on "educated" (now Cultivated) speech in national broadcasting. For in this study Cultivated correlated strongly with gender (nine girls spoke Cultivated for every one boy), superior education (especially in independent, fee-paying schools), and comfortable urban living.[10] Nevertheless most speakers revealed an ability to switch from their usual variety to another whenever a change in style seemed to be called for. The ABC's Standing Committee on Spoken English, as it is now called, has shown a growing concern with these ranges of variation, and with the employment of speakers not so exclusively Cultivated. A Cultivated Australian accent is no longer a primary requisite; since 1983 the Corporation has required only "acceptable styles of educated speech." But now all questions, whether of pronunciation, usage, or style, are referred for a first opinion to an Australian dictionary, not a British one.

The history of lexicography in Australia belongs firmly to the "now" of this essay. Morris's *Austral English* never became a household book, and until recently Australian lexis has been represented only in British and American "international" dictionaries. Typically, *Webster's Third International* glosses *station* (definition 5e) as "*Austral*: RANCH." That, and no more. But in Australian usage *station* is the nucleus of a set of terms which embraces some of the most representative features of Australian rural life: *sheep station, cattle station, out-station, back station, station hand, station manager, station owner*, etc. Their use reminds us that in the convict era settlers in rural areas had the use of convict labor that must be guarded, so that each grazing property was in fact a military outpost—a station. There has long been a need for dictionaries with an Australian focus, in which Australianisms are not treated as oddities to be given regional labels, and words from the common core of world English have their senses defined and arranged so as to reflect the patterns of their Australian usage. The first Australian dictionary to present a comprehensive word list in which all the pronunciations, spellings, and definitions of meaning are taken from the use of English in Australia was published in 1981. It is the *Macquarie Dictionary*, produced at Macquarie University by a group of editors, of whom I was one. We wrote it so that Australians could consult a dictionary that was addressed to them, and that focused on their own language practices.[11] It has become the national dictionary, as well as the basis of comparison with other national varieties of English.

So much has been written about Australian slang that one might begin to believe that all Australian English is slang, and that slang is the real expression of Australian character. But its unforegrounded treatment in the *Macquarie* and an excellent citation-based *Dictionary of Australian Colloquialisms* by G. A. Wilkes have both helped to put the wilder shores of Australian idiom into perspective.[12] A dictionary of Australianisms on historical principles was published by Oxford University Press in 1988.[13] Lexicographical activity of this extent, for a population of barely sixteen million people, is not a direct product of the worldwide renaissance of lexicography in the last twenty years, though it has made use of the same linguistic bases and the same technology. Rather, it is a response, like Webster's so much earlier, to the feeling that as an independent nation we have a language system of our own which needs well-made reference books.

And now, at the bicentenary of the first British settlement in Australia, what are the forces that are changing Australian English? The "accent" is still there: it identifies us, either starkly, at the Broad end of the spectrum, or more subtly at the Cultivated end. But especially under the influence of the multicultural, multilingual aspects of the society, the extremes are now converging on the middle ground of the speech spectrum, and General Australian is more the acceptable norm than merely the next best thing to Cultivated. The strength of British English as a model has dissipated, and we are more open to other influences, especially the American. It would be surprising if 265 million speakers of American English did not have some influence on the language practices of 16 million Australians. But numbers aren't everything: Australians had learnt, especially in school, to take an anti-American stance in language, especially in spelling.

The spelling choices that Noah Webster made were not specifically American choices, for it was open to anyone to have made them. Although Dr. Johnson favored *governour*, for example, its *-or* spelling had been current in England since the fourteenth century and prevailed over Johnson's choice in the nineteenth century. But for about thirty *or/our* words the British have maintained a preference for *-our*, and that has also been the Australian preference until recently. For in Australia as in Canada the two greater national traditions—British and American—meet, and increasingly settle down together more or less happily. In mid-1985 six of Australia's major urban newspapers used *-or* spellings for *colo(u)r*, *hono(u)r*, *favo(u)r*, etc.; five used *-our* spellings. But most book editors choose *-our* and prefer *centre* to *center*, *catalogue* to *catalog*, *travelling* to *traveling*.

Lexical borrowing has reflected the history of race relations, migration, and culture dissemination. The 1985 revised edition of the *Macquarie Dictionary* included a thousand headwords and phrases which had not appeared in the 1981 edition but now clamored for a place, not necessarily because they had not been in English before, but because they now have a local relevance and a density of use that requires their listing in an Australian dictionary. Some have a purely Australian origin, like *koori*, the Aboriginal word by which English-speaking Aborigines are now preferring to be known, and *gub* or *gubba*, their derogatory term for a white man. Others reflect the presence of immigrants from non-English-speaking countries: *tai chi, tandoori, doner kebab, yarmulke, tabouli, bratwurst, mullah*, etc. But most are words of British stock, some local, some borrowed, reflecting changing aspects of local culture: *ageism, bottom-of-the-harbour, bikeway, blended family, double dipping, medifraud, preloved, privatisation, repetitive strain injury, rogaining*, etc. Some are specifically from British English, like the *minis* and *maxis* of *miniskirt, maxiskirt, minibus, maxiyacht, minibudget*; words descriptive of lifestyles (*mod, sloanes, skinhead, punk*); and colloquial words like *loo, knickers, charlie, sod*, and *knackered*.

There have been American words in Australian English since 1850, some now well embedded in the Australian idiom in specifically Australian senses (*digger, block, township, bush, bushranger, squatter*). But the current crop of borrowings has acclimatized less uniformly: new verbs like *to impact, to source, to oversight, to trial*; phrasal verbs like *to psych up, to rip off*; new adjectives like *upfront, on-camera, off-campus*; prefixed verbs like *deescalate, deflate, reflate*; sentence modifiers like *healthwise, hopefully, regrettably*; phrasal nouns like *rip-off, sit-in, teach-in*; and truncated forms like *hi-fi, hi-tech, sitcom*, and *sci-fi. Chips* yields to *French fries*, *biscuits* to *cookies*; *radio* has supplanted *wireless, movies* has displaced *pictures* and *flicks, commercial* gathers strength against *advertisement, lorry* long ago yielded to *truck*, as *garage* has to *service station*.[14]

But purely lexical considerations are yielding in the interests of the wider and more urgent social aspects of language. For the first time, successive recent federal governments have seen the need for a national language policy which will define the relation of Australian English to the "community languages" of migrants from non-English-speaking countries and set guidelines for the teaching of English as a second language, for language maintenance among the children of migrants, and for the development of language tolerance in the Anglo-Celtic majority that has always thought of Australia as monolingual and needing to be nothing more. Governments and corporate institutions have put money into the development of "Plain English" as a communicative medium that should modify or replace the professionalized jargon of lawyers, doctors, politicians, insurers. A language of "equal opportunity" is beginning to replace (though not without dissent) the language of gender bias in newspapers, school lessons, industrial relations, even in dictionaries. And in literature our novelists and short story writers, always in the vanguard of literary social realism, have moderated their preoccupation with the real or invented Australianness of their settings and of the language of their characters. The uniqueness of setting and language is less likely now to be foregrounded, and is made more subservient to the development of character and plot in ways that are pointed, intentional, and relevant. By the year 2000 the Cringe Direct, which made us kiss the minatory rod, and the Cringe Inverted, which made us aggressively Australian, will perhaps not even need to be mentioned.

Notes

1. From a comment by William Churchill, member of the American Philological Society, who visited Australia in 1911.

2. A. A. Phillips, "The Cultural Cringe," *Meanjin* 9 (1950): 299–302.

3. Geoffrey Serle, *From Deserts the Prophets Come* (Melbourne, 1973), p. 60.

4. The so-called Heidelberg school, active in Melbourne and Sydney, dominated Australian painting from 1885 for three decades.

5. Edward E. Morris, *Austral English* (London, 1989), p. xi; Noah Webster, *Dissertations on the English Language* (1789; reprint, 1967).

6. Sidney J. Baker, *The Australian Language* (Sydney, 1945), p. 11.

7. A. G. Mitchell, "The English Language in Australia," in *An Introduction to Australian Literature*, ed., C. D. Narasimhaiah (Brisbane, 1965), p. 134.

8. See G. Leitner, "Australian English or English in Australia—Linguistic Identity or Dependence in Broadcast Language," *English World-Wide* 5.1 (1984): 55–85.

9. A. G. Mitchell and Arthur Delbridge, *The Speech of Australian Adolescents* (Sydney, 1965).

10. This striking contrast between boys' and girls' speech is discussed in A. G. Mitchell and Arthur Delbridge, *The Speech of Australian Adolescents* (Sydney, 1965) pp. 38–41 and 70–74. At the time of the study, coeducational schools were usually to be found only in the state education system, and then only in country towns. Otherwise boys and girls were educated separately, both in independent and in state schools. The effects on pupils' pronunciation of any speech training in the curriculum appear to have been insignificant, except in some independent schools for girls. Since independent schools are fee-paying, the girls and boys attending them come mainly from families with a high socioeconomic standing, with fathers or mothers in the professions or high administrative or business positions. But gender is stronger than either school or family as an influence on speech patterns. The analysis showed that "there is only a fifty to one chance that a boy will come within the Cultivated range of sounds, whatever school he goes to, and that girls in the Cultivated vowel range are to be found in all school systems, though the proportions are greater in the Independent schools than in the State schools" (p. 42). It was quite conceivable that a girl from an independent school might be classifiable as Cultivated while her brother in another independent school turned out to be Broad. There was evidence that "girls care about speech rather more than boys do, even to the extent of improving on nature and convention

in vowel sounds. They use modifications to vowels much as they might use cosmetics, and for the same purposes" (p. 40). But boys seem specially anxious "not to be conspicuous by reason of their speech, and particularly not to expose themselves to the charge of snobbishness associated with distinctive speech" (p. 40).

11. Arthur Delbridge et al., *The Macquarie Dictionary* (Sydney, 1981).

12. G. A. Wilkes, *A Dictionary of Australian Colloquialisms* (Sydney, 1978).

13. W. S. Ramson, *The Australian National Dictionary* (Melbourne, 1988).

14. B. Taylor, "American, British, and Other Foreign Influences," in *Australian English*, ed. P. Collins and D. Blair (St. Lucia, Queensland, 1989), pp. 239–44.

CHRIS WALLACE-CRABBE

The Inheritance

Dunked into life, a squalling brat
aping the role of perfect child,
I let this language buoy me up,
shock troops lightly graduated:
nasty, nice, nectarine, nasturtium, noun.

The stuff was rich as mother's milk.
I couldn't see it didn't fit,
making it do so anyway,
eliding what was grossly wrong.
Origins prove nothing, said William James.

I romped round discourse in my room
only devouring foreign books—
northern, that is—containing heath,
lorries, wolves, bobbies and snow.
The signified was quite inadequate,

a mere Australia. City fathers
had long conspired with Empirespeak
by cancelling native foliage;
so every winter English buds
flashed into fluffy pastel bloom again.

There isn't an Aussie kid won't know
that spring means simultaneously
May and September: Shakespeare's tongue
cranks a *musée imaginaire*
where Xmas comes around in wintertime.

As cunning as a leaning dunny,
this international currency
parades its virtue in old rhymes,
tomb after womb, as death with breath.
We swim along with it. We swim and drown.

RANDOLPH QUIRK

Further Thoughts:
Sound Barriers—Ten Years On

"SOUND BARRIERS AND *GANGBANGSPRACHE*," my title ten years ago, evoked a Mach 1 image: high-speed English creating sonic booms of shocked susceptibilities as we learned to say new things and dared to say old ones. But it might have been used with a less dramatic metaphor in mind: the frontier barriers separating off different communities. Indeed, nearly a quarter of the 1980 *State of the Language* was devoted to a dozen essays on various aspects of language in relation to group identities.

The years between have shown that linguistic separatism continues to have momentum. I'm not just thinking of demands for the use of Spanish in American schools and courts, of English place-names obliterated on Welsh road signs, or of men in the Maze prison learning Irish. These could be readily paralleled in many countries: the continuing tension between French and Dutch in Belgium, the vigor of Basque and Catalonian within Spain, to name a couple of familiar examples in the Western world alone. No, I'm thinking rather of the separatist momentum within a language traditionally regarded as a single unified entity. Here again such fission is not confined to English. Within Spain, one is made increasingly aware of the pressure upon Castilian in the face of demands from Andalusian, Galician, Valencian, even Canarian.

But if English is far from unique, it is at least a striking example.

So dubious have we become about "English" in stark nudity, that we feel we have to cover it with protective adjectives—some rudimentary, some diaphanous, and some of them opaquely woolly. "American English," "British English," "Scientific English," "Literary English," "Ashkenazic English" are far less precise than the confident labeling suggests—and there are shifts in the taxonomic base to contend with as well. And when I come to what Fernando Peñalosa distinguishes as "Anglo English" and "Chicano English," I confess myself stumped.[1] But the discriminations are not without educational impact. Writing a year or so ago in a respected educational journal, a respected educationist professed herself unwilling to teach her New York pupils Standard English because of her conviction that they identify outside school more with the neighboring black children than with the remoter offspring of WASPs: and after all, she added, " 'I don't have none' " shows "a correct use of Black English negation."[2]

Such policies, together with claims for the right of ethnic minorities to be taught (and to fulfill citizenship more generally) in their own languages, have, not surprisingly, provoked some response. In the U.K., the Kingman Report in 1988 reasserted the primacy of Standard English in schools.[3] And in the U.S., referenda on the constitutional entrenchment of English have produced results which suggest that many in the ethnic minorities themselves share the view that English is uniquely important, and indispensable for breaking down barriers to careers and social mobility; in short (as Kingman puts it, in the British context), "more likely to increase the freedom of the individual than diminish it."

But the adjectives dividing up English are by no means confined to Britain, America, and the other countries that we think of as English-speaking. In the linguistic and educational literature, designations like "Indian English," "Nigerian English," and "Filipino English" are freely used, each implying a unitary and reasonably well-established variety of English, specific to the country concerned.[4] The fact that such labels tend to be shunned by those in the media and in governmental authority may call their validity in question, but if the linguists and educationists are right, then we may well be facing a rapid and unpredictable development of new language barriers. What is more, it is timely to wonder whether these barriers are arising through a perfectly understandable sense of national identity that actually *wills* a recognizably different variety of language to match a recognizably different flag and national anthem; or whether (as a linguistic friend of mine put it in a letter from East Africa recently) recognizing a local "variety" is just an effort to put into respectable disguise low levels of English attainment resulting from failures in the education system.

Certainly, anyone traveling in former colonial or quasi-colonial territories anywhere from Ghana to the Philippines repeatedly hears of local perceptions about a downward spiral in English standards, and it would be foolish to write off such opinions—impressionistic though they may be—as the nostalgic moans of old-guard traditionalists among the local elite. If they are well-founded, after all, it could be very serious for the territories concerned, operating with a variety of English that is not merely very different from the English elsewhere but inherently shaky and inadequate. Imagine the British trying to run a ministry or the transport system in what they know of French!

With notable exceptions, however, the weight of responsibility placed on English as a medium for internal communication in such countries as India or Malaysia or Kenya is far less than it was a generation ago, and this brings up a further aspect of the State of the Language. Despite the persistent and glib assumptions in Britain and America, we are witnessing a significant relative decline (perhaps even an absolute decline) in the currency of English worldwide. This may come as a surprise to those who think of English as the medium of high-tech skills, international conferences, and professional journals; here indeed continued growth is doubtless the order of the day. But these are relatively slim and specialized lines of communication.

In the world as a whole, English remains an exotic tongue to perhaps 90 percent of the population—and the percentage is growing. Growing as a matter of demography (where the numbers born to speak Chinese, Hindi, and Spanish—to name but three—far outstrip the numbers for English). But the percentage is also growing as a response to the shifting perceptions of international prestige, individual national consciousness, and the dynamic of local politics. Witness the efforts by the New People's Army in the Philippines to marginalize English and to make it seem the language of the oppressing and privileged few; witness the response by President Aquino's government to give greater currency and higher prestige to the Tagalog-based Pilipino.

We get an analogous perspective from some of the more politically alert novelists and poets. Beside the successes of some African and Asian writers working in English (examples like Wole Soyinka and Raja Rao are often cited), many such writers are acutely aware that English enables them to reach only a small and unrepresentative fraction of their own people—however attractive it is that their work be accessible in Los Angeles and London. Far from recognizing that any "variety" of English is (or can be made to be) indigenous in most ex-colonial countries, Ngugi wa Thiong'o vehemently repudiates the idea of a black African writer addressing black African readers in English.[5] That way, he says, you don't just reach a *small* readership; you reach the *wrong* readership.

    English itself a sound barrier?

Notes

Randolph Quirk's essay "Sound Barriers and *Gangbangsprache*" appeared in the 1980 *State of the Language*.

   1. Fernando Peñalosa, *Chicano Sociolinguistics* (Cambridge, Mass., 1980).

   2. L. M. Goldstein, in *TESOL Quarterly* 21 (1987): 417–36.

   3. *Report of the Committee of Inquiry into the Teaching of English*, Chairman, Sir John Kingman (London, 1988).

   4. See Randolph Quirk, "Separated by a Common Dilemma," *Times Higher Education Supplement* 849 (1989): 15–18; "The Question of Standards in the International Use of English," in *Language Spread and Language Policy*, ed. P. H. Lowenberg (Washington, D.C., 1988).

   5. For example, in a BBC World Service broadcast of November 1988.

~ RICHARD W. BAILEY

English at Its Twilight

In the earlier incarnation of *The State of the Language*, several contributors bewailed imprecision, jargon, slang, and colloquial usage (other than their own). Following Orwell, they regarded it as axiomatic that "most people who bother with the matter at all would admit that the English language is in a bad way."[1] Representative of this threnody for mixed voices was John Simon: "There is, I believe, a morality of language: an obligation to preserve and nurture its niceties, the fine distinctions, that have been handed down to us."[2] Such observations almost always confuse the underbrush with the forest—Simon's certainly do. But words like *obligation* and *morality* evoke other than linguistic values: Duty, Honor, and, inevitably, Empire. As Churchill long ago discerned, the old political empire with its metropolis and colonial outposts has nearly disappeared, replaced by a cultural empire of "English-speaking peoples." For many, this new idea has nearly erased the bad old idea of empire, so much so that the *Economist* recently celebrated, without postcolonial remorse, the alleged "universality" of the English language with the bold headline "The New English Empire."[3]

A decade after its first appearance, *The State of the Language* needs to get beyond moralizing and beyond the traditionally anglophone nations since worldwide the number of people who now learn English as an additional language surpasses those who learn it as a mother tongue. English seems to be everywhere. Those who predict its future, however, almost always presume one of two opposing possibilities (both of which I have suggested by my deliberately ambiguous title): at one extreme, the present twilight is the harbinger of the bright morning of a universal lingua franca; at the other, it presages the gloom that comes at evening, a forecast of another confusion of tongues of the sort that seemed so frightening to the tower-builders at Babel. Perhaps, as this essay is intended to suggest, there is some other likely future for our language—that it will become the language of the powerful few at the expense of the powerless many, neither a universal language nor a dead one.

No one today can ignore the dramatic rise of nationalism and the politics of language that accompany it, but "nationalism" is now more complicated than the nineteenth-century idea of the nation state defined by geographical boundaries. Nowadays, nationalism is a matter of ideology. Islamic fundamentalism, for instance, links people who are citizens of geographically dispersed, politically different, and linguistically various states into the global nation of Islam. Modern multinational capitalism, in many ways parallel to other affiliations built around texts written in a revered language, recapitulates the dominance of the Hanseatic League six hundred years ago; such corporate "nations" bring together people who speak different languages, inhabit different countries, and yet share much the same culture. Like nation states themselves, these movements influence political affiliation, cultural loyalty, and language choice.

The connection between language and nationalism, broadly defined, then, is one that needs to be explored with much greater care than it has hitherto received. The continuing agony of Northern Ireland demonstrates that a common language is not the inevitable predictor of civil tranquility; the continuing stability of Canada and Switzerland shows that multilingualism and national consensus are not incompatible. Political nationality is one cultural force to be reckoned with; linguistic nationality is another and often separate one (and it includes the cohesiveness of discourse communities built around salient varieties of what philologists would regard as "one language"). As a starting point in this exploration, I invite readers to reflect on three political and cultural developments that will shape the use of English in the next decade.

The first is the remarkable rise in multilingualism. (More people than ever before, both numerically and proportionately, now routinely use two or more languages.) As Peter Strevens has pointed out, those who command only one language are at a distinct disadvantage, especially those monolinguals (including English-speaking monolinguals) who seek consent and commerce from language communities richer or more powerful than their own.[4]

A second trend will have even greater impact: far from approaching the status of a universal language, English is diminishing proportionately as explosive birthrates shift the balance of the world's population toward other language communities. No doubt English is the most frequently chosen *additional* language, and it is likely to continue to enjoy that popularity. But even the major centers of the anglophone world (Britain, Canada, the United States, and Australia) are becomming more and more diverse in languages and language varieties. These demographic facts have implications for the future of English and for the kinds of languages we will use in the future.

A third issue that merits our present consideration derives from research in second-language instruction: the attitude of those acquiring a new language is the most influential of the variables that predict the rate and success of learning—more important than aptitude, age, or teaching method. Consequently, attitudes toward English are strong predictors of uses of English that will, in the future, shape its form and purposes.

Most of our histories of English presume a "normal" *evolution*. Language spreads from the center to the periphery; the periphery develops independent "standards" that first compete and then coexist with those of the homeland, and these new standards may in their turn become new centers of radiating influence. Declarations of linguistic independence often precede actual linguistic differentiation. As far as English is concerned, people who declare their political independence often proclaim a "New English" before the larger community has discerned one. (Not until the 1840s did Americans come to be distinguished from Britons, even though Noah Webster and others had proclaimed much earlier a new "American Language.")[5]

This evolutionary model adequately describes language spread from the British Isles to many anglophone nations: the United States, Canada, Australia, and New Zealand. Most Americans no longer have a residual yearning after British norms (except in relatively arcane contexts like productions of Shakespearean drama). The intensity of the yen for England varies in the other countries just named. All Canadians have "repatriated" their constitution from the British Parliament, and the anglophones have "patriated" their English. Australians (especially male Australians) have created a national linguistic mythology that now distinctly spurns the English of the poms and celebrates a ripsnorting English with which parallels are frequently drawn to the more boisterous days of the American West. New Zealanders, too, have very recently come to regard themselves as linguistically independent, parallel to their perceived political distance from Britain (as a consequence of Britain's membership in the EEC) and from the United States (following New Zealand's withdrawal from the ANZUS treaty). If one listens, as I have had the pleasure of doing, to the "phone-in," "talk-back," or "call-up" radio broadcasts in all of these nations the emergence of evolutionary norms is clearly apparent.

The evolutionary model does not, however, explain the emergence of all linguistic variety. We must consider the rather different nature of linguistic *adaptation*, a change that is often planned, managed, and promulgated by those who support a new tongue for new times. Evolution is taken to be a matter of fate; adaptation is a matter of choice.

In literary contexts, adaptation often draws, sometimes quite explicitly, on the Wordsworthian notion that authors should employ "a selection of language really used" by ordinary people.[6] The principal traits of linguistic adaptation are clearly present in the following polemic from Emeka Okeke-Ezigbo:

> The adoption of Nigerian Pidgin for national literature will arrest our writers' flight to English, a difficult foreign language which even a writer of [John] Munonye's standing "doesn't know enough," let alone his less privileged countrymen. Not only is Pidgin a much simpler language, syntactically, but it is also a practical, viable, flexible language distilled in the alembic of our native sensibility and human experience. This lusty language, which transcends our geographical and political boundaries, grows daily before our very eyes. It is our natural, unifying weapon against the divisive forces of English. In West Africa, English splits; Pidgin unites.[7]

Okeke-Ezigbo anticipates in this argument something more than mere evolution. He supports a managed and revolutionary shift from English to something more local, a trend especially apparent both in Nigerian literature (like that associated with Onishta market) and in literature written out of the same spirit, for instance Ken Saro-Wiwa's *Sozaboy* (1985), set in Nigeria; Frances Milloy's *No Mate for the Magpie* (1985), set in Ireland; Keri Hulme's *The Bone People* (1984), set in New Zealand; and Armando B. Rico's *Three Coffins for Nino Lencho* (1987), set in the American southwest and Mexico.[8] These works vary in their intelligibility to outsiders: some far out-Wordsworth Wordsworth; others are more moderate in imitating the "language really used" in the communities they represent. Yet it is not useful, I think, to see these novels as modern recapitulations of American nineteenth-century humorists, regionalists, and local-colorists—mere extinct branches of linguistic evolution. Instead, these modern writers presage further adaptation and a linguistic world of pronounced differences.

Okeke-Ezigbo's desire for a "unifying weapon against the divisive forces of [international] English" is not his alone. Even where English may continue to be used as a result of "the necessity of limited choices" (these words are those of a South African, Njabulo Ndebele), the myth of English as a purely neutral instrument of human expression is dying.[9] Consider this prediction from Ndebele:

> There are many reasons why [English] cannot be considered an innocent language. The problems of society will also be the problems of the predominant language of that society. It is the carrier of its perceptions, its attitudes, and its goals, for through it, the speakers absorb entrenched attitudes. The guilt of English then must be recognized and appreciated before its continued use can be advocated.[10]

A chastened English freed from racism (or other *-isms* alleged to suffuse it) will not result from evolution but from adaptation consciously carried out as part of a broader program of social reform, and not only in South Africa.

Evolution and adaptation are two of the three categories needed for understanding the ideology of linguistic history. The third is *rejection*, usually a decision made silently, or in our case beyond the range of anglophone hearing.

English has sometimes been seen as a language that has taken root wherever it has spread, though such a view leaves out of account its virtual disappearance from Ireland by the end of the sixteenth century. The reasons for the rejection of English in Ireland are significantly bound up with the symbolic values the language carried: Protestantism (versus Catholicism) and foreign domination (versus national autonomy). Only the vigorous and often violent "plantation" of Ireland by English speakers (thrust into the country in successive waves throughout the seventeenth century) led to the restoration of English as the language of the nation.

This example from the past provides a useful direction for looking at present-day English. Symbolic values associated with English have come to include economic prosperity, science and technology, development and modernization, and the attractions of popular culture. But there are other important values that discourage the acquisition and use of English, ones that are closely tied to self-expression and cultural worth. Illustrative of these values—ones often introduced in support of rejection—are the following observations by Bhalchandra Nemade in an essay titled "Against Writing in English: An Indian Point of View":

> Whereas every word in the mother-tongue presents its own geology, the words in a foreign language offer insipid solidarity to the writer's com-

petence. A foreign language thus suppresses the natural originality of Indian writers in English, enforcing upon the whole tribe the fine art of parrotry. It is worth noting in this context that the cases of Indians praising Indians' command over English are more frequent than those of Englishmen making patronising under-statements about Indians' use of English. This smacks of Crusoe-Friday relationship, since an Indian nightingale does not receive even the status of a crow in the history of English literature.[11]

In attacking the use of English in India, Nemade repeats Gandhi's warnings three-quarters of a century ago; the English language, Gandhi often said, had "enslaved" Indians and deprived their languages of the invigorating possibility of intellectual enrichment. If Indian writers can aspire only to be crows among English writers, who could persuade them not to employ their creative talents elsewhere?

No writer has been more articulate in his denunciation of English and the values associated with it than the Kenyan novelist and playwright, Ngugi wa Thiong'o. The focus of his scorn has not been restricted to the Anglo-American audience; he is also concerned with the anglophone elites who dominate the multilingual societies of many African and Asian nations. Here is his brief summary of the argument:

> Language is a carrier of a people's culture. Culture is a carrier of a people's values. Values are a carrier of a people's outlook or consciousness and sense of identity. So by destroying or underdeveloping people's languages, the colonizing nations were deliberately killing or underdeveloping the cultures, values and consciousness of the people. And by imposing their languages, they were also imposing the culture, values and consciousness carried by them. The result was often the creation of a minority who spoke and understood the language of imposition and who, in the process, had internalized the culture of imperialism. Thereafter, this minority would look at the world through the eyeglasses of imperialism. They would become the defenders of imperialist languages, cultures, values and world outlook and, hence, the most avid defenders of the economic and political programs of imperialism—ruthless exploitation and repression of democracy. It is through this minority that imperialism has continued to maintain its economic stranglehold on Africa in a neo-colonial form. The tension generated by the struggles of the African masses against these comprador minority regimes is necessarily a tension between the national democratic assertion and the neo-colonial forces of imperialism.[12]

Getting beyond parlor polemics, Ngugi decided in 1977 to turn his creative energies to his native language, Gikuyu, and to kiSwahili; in 1986 he bade "farewell to English," though hoping to keep in touch with his international audience "through the age old medium of translation."[13] Ngugi's vigorous and articulate presentation of the case against English commands a ready audience far beyond Kenya.

It would not be accurate to attribute the present state of English literature in East Africa to Ngugi's advocacy of indigenous languages. Still, a recent survey of the literary scene by R. N. Ndegwa notes a "consistently low" level of "production" among the creative writers in English in Uganda, Zambia, Malawi, and Tanzania:

> Kenya has been the only country which seemed to have a trickle of worthwhile literary works, but alas! even that seems to be diminishing, leaving only works of very little or no literary value from amateurish authors with no idea of literary style and hardly any skills in writing.[14]

Reports of this kind are hardly good news for the future vitality of English in the region.

Rejection of literary uses of English does not tell the whole story, of course, and the idea of English as an important medium for various aspects of national life still helps to sustain its popularity. Even so, a much diminished use of English for artistic creativity should be disquieting to those who believe that English is on the verge of becoming a universal world language.[15] What is of greatest consequence is that the flight from English arises not from the failure of schools or from blandishments from competing languages of the northern hemisphere but from clearly stated personal principles. Here is one representative opinion from Oceania that finds its echoes in many places:

> The formal educational systems (whether British, New Zealand, Australian, American or French) that were etablished by the colonisers in our islands all had one main feature in common: they were based on the arrogantly-mistaken racist assumption that the cultures of the colonisers were superior (and preferable) to ours. Education was therefore devoted to civilising us, to cutting us away from the roots of our cultures, from what the colonisers viewed as darkness, superstition, barbarism and savagery. . . . If we may not be as yet the most artistically creative region on our spaceship, we possess the potential to become the most artistically creative. There are more than 1,200 indigenous languages, plus English, French, Hindi, Spanish, and various forms of pidgin with which to catch and interpret the void, reinterpret our past, create new historical and sociological visions of Oceania, and compose songs, poems, plays and other oral and written literature.[16]

Writers who heed this call to recreate "the roots of culture" will do so in the languages that seem to them best fitted for the purpose; their work will not inevitably be written (especially where oral literary traditions still prosper), and, if written, by no means inevitably in English.

An instance that seems to run contrary to these trends is that of Singapore, where English is increasing both as a second language and as a mother tongue. Though populated by only 2.6 million citizens, Singapore is emerging as an economic and cultural center for many nations in Southeast Asia. The other mother tongues in the Republic are under seige, both from Putonghua (which has been mandated in schools) and from English.[17] Official government policy has hedged the bet that English will continue to be the international language for the region by supporting Putonghua in case China should grow more important to Singapore's economic interests. A consequence of this policy is that "unrecognized" local languages now enjoy even less government support; two of the four "official languages"—Malay and Tamil—are also diminished by these efforts.[18]

Public dissents from the policy that has promoted English (and Putonghua) in Singapore are uncommon, but present-day Singaporeans do not often enjoy the benefits of unfettered public disputes about political matters:

> English has always been the dominant, privileged language in the country, first as the *lingua franca* of the British Empire and now as part of a developmental Empire that has the same strengths and weaknesses as its ideological model. One exchanges very rapid development and perhaps more than a fledgling fling at guided parliamentary democracy for first, linguistic apartheid masking as bilingualism and finally through the covert suppression of indigenous tongues by declaring the vocabulary inadequate, insufficiently sophisticated, not "ready," or a dialect.[19]

Politically, the unnurtured languages of Singapore may attract the sort of nostalgia and ardor associated with Welsh in Britain, Yiddish in the United States, or Basque in Spain. But these languages of Singapore are not those of tiny minorities but regional languages of important and populous international communities.

Enforced English in Singapore is part of a blunt ideology of outward-looking aspirations in a wealthy nation. The role of English in Bangladesh reflects an ideology of inward-looking patriotism representative of many of the poorest. In 1989, an estimated 112,757,000 people lived in Bangladesh—more than the combined population of Australia, Britain, Canada, Ireland, and New Zealand. With a population density of 2,028 people per square mile, Bangladesh is also among the most crowded nations in the world.

Language choice is particularly important in the recent history of Bangladesh, even though the vast majority of its people speak only Bangla. When it emerged from British colonial rule in 1947 as "East

Pakistan," Bangladesh found itself dominated by political leaders in West Pakistan (even though it contained a majority of the population of the newly partitioned state). In an audacious move to assert the dominance of the western region of the nation, Mohammad Ali Jinna, the Governor-General from West Pakistan, spoke at a rally held at the Dhaka Race Course on 21 March 1948: "Urdu and Urdu only shall be the state language of Pakistan." This policy, affirmed by subsequent government action, stimulated a "Language Movement" in Bangladesh to assert the use of Bangla and the political independence of "East Pakistan." On 21 February 1952 a demonstration on behalf of the Language Movement led to an attack by troops and the death of some of the demonstrators. This event was subsequently seen as the first stage of a political evolution that led to the independence of Bangladesh, and its symbolism gives language policy an enduring significance in national political life. The demonstrators of 1952 are memorialized in the Central Shaheed Minar, the "Language Martyrs Monument," and recalled in the annual observance of "Ekushey February," the 21st of February.

At the celebration of Ekushey February in 1987, President Hussain Muhammad Ershad stated: "I had declared on January 24 in the Jatiya Sangsad that except in communication with foreign countries, in all other spheres in the government and private organisations, all letters and files will have to be maintained in Bangla." He added that the government is providing support for "a master-plan . . . for publication of a large number of books on modern scientific and technological subjects" and called upon "the intellectuals and others [to] come forward to establish Bangla in all institutions."[20] To mark this step in the history of the nation, the president ordered that English-language street signs be replaced with ones in Bangla.

In an editorial written in response to this proposal, *The New Nation*—one of Dhaka's English-language newspapers—provided the following perspective:

> The use of Bangla in the administration is yet to be universalised. If an official directive to conduct official business in Bangla has to be issued periodically (the latest one was issued a few weeks ago) it means that the transition to Bangla is not yet a fait accompli and a section of bureaucrats are slow to reorder their thinking and habits to the demands of an independent nation. While English is still being unjustly retained in the administration, on the other hand, English is being squeezed and weakened in the wrong place, namely schools and colleges and the curricula. The realisation does not seem to be there that a vigorous pursuit of a second language is not only a part of good education but is also in keeping

with the spirit of Ekushe. It is equally painful to contemplate that some
among the countrymen of Salam and Barkat [two of the Language Mar-
tyrs] should demonstrate a contemptible vulnerability to the forces of
anti-culture and decadence. Ekushe symbolised not only the demand for
seeing Bangla as a state language but also one for social and cultural
emancipation of the people. In that broader perspective the vision of Ekushe is as distant as ever. Thirtyfive years after the start of the language
movement, two-thirds of the people cannot read and write and for them
it is immaterial whether the road signs are written in Bangla or in any
other language. The promise of Ekushe is yet to be realised in our cultural life.[21]

Against the idea that "pursuit of a second language is . . . a part of
good education" (which underpins the concern expressed by the editorial writer about the decline of English-teaching in the schools) is
President Ershad's opinion that "one's mother, mother tongue and
motherland are inseparably linked[;] mother and mother tongue are
indivisible and dishonour to one amounts to dishonouring the other."
Whatever the value of English as an international language for foreign
affairs, views like Ershad's emphasize the connection between language and nationhood. Insofar as such opinions are shared within
Bangladesh and elsewhere, they do not bode well for the continued
expansion of English among peoples who seek to assert their independence first and their internationalism afterwards.

   Language politics in Bangladesh is rather more complicated than
the public statements summarized above suggest. English remains the
language of command in the military officer corps, and the urban elite
competes strenuously to provide education in English for their children. Ekushey in 1987 was not the first time a national leader denounced the use of English, nor will it be the last. Yet in August 1988,
President Ershad declared "at a student's gathering in his hometown
in northern Rangpur District" that the time had come to implement
English as a "second compulsory language" for all Bangladeshi school
children.[22] Given the limited pool of English-speaking school teachers, such a massive educational scheme cannot possibly be imple-
mented. One may see in Ershad's contradictory statements his attempt
to conciliate both the postcolonial elite and the masses of people who
may be placated by the idea that English will eventually provide their
salvation. English is of substantial value in a nation that is dependent
on foreign aid from anglophone nations and from Japan, yet neither
that economic condition nor the compradors who manage it are likely
to prevail indefinitely.

   Political arguments linking "mother, mother tongue, and motherland" are often persuasive ones in many countries (including our

own), as are positions that proclaim the need of a nation to be free from outside political domination, to assert its cultural independence, or to declare that not one but many languages will serve democratic or economic goals. Such ideas are to be found around the world, but the climate of belief they represent is expressed in many voices, and only some of those voices, now and in the future, are speaking in English.

Notes

1. "Politics and the English Language" (1946), *The Collected Essays, Journalism and Letters of George Orwell*, ed. Sonia Orwell and Ian Angus (Harmondsworth, Eng., 1970), p. 156.

2. John Simon, "The Corruption of English," in *The State of the Language*, ed. Leonard Michaels and Christopher Ricks (Berkeley and Los Angeles, 1980), p. 38.

3. *The Economist* (28 December 1986–2 January 1987), pp. 127–31. An essay in linguistic politics written for an American audience uses the same metaphors to make its point: "English: Out to Conquer the World," *U.S. News & World Report* (18 February 1985), pp. 49–53.

4. See Peter Strevens, "Language Teaching Contributes to and is Influenced by the Spread of Languages," in *Language Spread and Language Policy: Issues, Implications, and Case Studies*, ed. Peter H. Lowenberg (Washington, D.C., 1988), pp. 320–30.

5. See Allen Walker Read, "The Identification of the Speech of Americans in England" (unpublished paper presented to the Linguistic Society of America, 2 August 1947).

6. William Wordsworth, "Preface to the Second Edition of the *Lyrical Ballads*," reprinted in *Criticism: The Major Texts*, ed. Walter Jackson Bate (New York, 1952), p. 336.

7. Emeka Okeke-Ezigbo, "The Role of the Nigerian Writer in a Carthaginian Society," *Okike* 21 (July 1982): 28–37.

8. Onishta, a major economic center in eastern Nigeria, developed an extensive "pamphlet literature" (including drama and fiction) in the late 1940s. A selection of these works has been anthologized—*Onishta Market Literature*, ed. Emmanuel N. Obiechina (London, 1972)—and some Onishta writers have attracted international attention—for instance, Ogali A. Ogali.

9. So influential a body as the British Council declared in its annual report for 1960–61: "Such an interpretation—that the materials to be used and skills to be taught abroad should be determined by what people wish to learn, and not merely by what we like to teach—reflects a sound educational principle, but involves the concept of English taught as a politically and culturally neutral means of communication. This may seem strange or even faintly alarming to those English-speaking peoples who have for long been accustomed to regard their language as an expression of their own national development" (*The English Language Abroad* [London, 1961], pp. 9–10). What seemed strange at home could not long be believed abroad. Nonetheless, it is still possible for people to declare that English "is as culture-free as calculus" (K. M. Larik, "English as an International Language," *Ariel* [University of Sind, Pakistan] 7 [1981–82]: 78).

10. Njabulo Ndebele, "The English Language and Social Change" (keynote paper delivered to the Jubilee Conference of the English Academy of Southern Africa, Johannesburg, 1986), p. 14. But see also Kelwyn Sole, "Culture, Politics and the Black Writer: A Critical Look at Prevailing Assumptions," *English in Africa* (Grahamstown) 10 (1983): 37–84.

11. Bhalchandra Nemade, *New Quest* (Shivajinagar)·49 (1985): 33.

12. Ngugi wa Thiong'o, "The Tension between National and Imperialist Culture," *World Literature Written in English* 24 (1984): 3–9. See also Hansel Nolumbe Eyoh, Interview with Ngugi wa Thiong'o, *Journal of Commonwealth Literature* 21 (1986): 162–66.

13. Ngugi wa Thiong'o, *Decolonising the Mind: The Politics of Language in African Literature* (London, 1986), p. xiv.

14. R. N. Ndegwa, "Africa: East and Central," *Journal of Commonwealth Literature* 20 (1985): 1–2. Whether Ndegwa employs "production" to describe the quantity or the quality of literary efforts is not clear.

15. Popular journalism in the principal anglophone nations tends to assert that English is already a world language and to adduce as evidence the role of English in transport and trade, in science and technology, and even in the proliferation of franchised food outlets (see note 3 above). The first serious prediction that English would rise to worldwide use was apparently David Hume's; he urged Edward Gibbon to write his historical works in English rather than French. The emergence of English in North America was to him a harbinger of "a superior stability and duration to the English language" (Letter to Edward Gibbon, 24 October 1767, in *The Letters of David Hume*, ed. J. Y. T. Greig [Oxford, 1932; 1969], pp. 170–71).

16. Albert Wendt, "Towards a New Oceania," in *Writers in East-West Encounter: New Cultural Bearings*, ed. Guy Amirthanayagam (London, 1982), pp. 210, 212.

17. Putonghua is "the standard spoken language now in general use throughout the People's Republic of China, based on the northern dialects, esp. that of Peking" (*OED Supplement* [1982]). Since 1950, writers in English have used *Putonghua* in place of the obsolescent term, *Mandarin*.

18. This despite article 152 of Singapore's constitution: "(1) It shall be the responsibility of the Government constantly to care for the interests of the racial and religious minorities of Singapore. (2) The Government shall exercise its functions in such manner as to recognise the special position of the Malays, who are the indigenous people of Singapore, and accordingly it shall be the responsibility of the Government to protect, safeguard, support, foster and promote their political, educational, religious, economic, social and cultural interests in the Malay language" (quoted from Albert P. Blaustein and Dana Blaustein Epstein, *Resolving Language Conflicts: A Study of the World's Constitutions* [Washington, D.C., 1986], p. 91).

19. Jan B. Gordon, "The 'Second Tongue' Myth: English Poetry in Polylingual Singapore," *Ariel* (Singapore) 15 (1984): 63.

20. *The New Nation* (21 February 1987), p. 1.

21. *The New Nation* (21 February 1987), p. 5.

22. *The Bangladesh Observer* (16 August 1988), p. 1.

The Body Politic

A language is a dialect that has an army and a navy.
MAX WEINREICH

The book has somehow to be adopted to the body, and
at a venture one would say that women's books should
be shorter, more concentrated, than those of men.
VIRGINIA WOOLF

No steel can pierce a heart so icily as a period
put in the right place.
ISAAC BABEL

Articulacy. Hints from the Koran.

First lesson: Don't
get ahead of yourself, don't gabble.
For a pell-mell of syllables, is
that what it means to assemble,
as when He assembled our bones
like the articulated members of a saying?

Be sonorous.
                    Like a goose?
When the Writ is goose-like
(which will not be often), honk,
honk like a goose. And when
the text, as you may call it,
is plummy, gorge it with plums,
savour the vowels, give them,
each as it comes, full presence.

Next, imagine yourself
the privileged herald to
your chosen, not
chance-met companions;
with whom there is much that can be
taken for granted, since

they know all that you tell them,
though in an inferior fashion.

When the Writ runs into
consonantal crackle,
cacophonies, crackle with it.
This is the most of music:
thorn-hedges set round orchards.

Next you imagine yourself
the angel Gabriel who
divulges to the privileged
intermediary
what he shall relay.

And this is perilous, as
assuming the Angel is
always perilous. Now you
address a generality
of strangers, and there is
temptation, since you fear them,
to bully, or inveigle.

When Holy Writ quotes writ,
acknowledge the quotation-marks
by a doubled pause and poise,
keeping the voice lifted.

When the sense rides over
the end of a verse, accord it
enough and no more than enough
check, to gather its haunches
before the brush- or water-
obstacle that you,
no steeplechase-rider, will not
accelerate to get over.

Last (this not often attained)
you imagine yourself the Speaker
of what He divulged through angels.
So holy the act of reciting.

These are not prescriptions
on how to wow an audience,
but to diaphragm and pharynx
and parts more inward, how to
give body to the unbodied.

Man imagines his bones shall
not be reassembled.
He wants to be open-ended
as far as he can see:
one discrete happening after
another, all exclamation,
the palm of his hand unaware what his fingers are up to.

But the first, the second, the third
knuckles of every finger
are articulated more
closely than the best
reciter or singer can manage.

The act of reciting, however,
generates faith, done rightly.

Fighting Talk

"STUNNING MAISONETTE" READS THE ESTATE agent's sign. "What a knock-out!" stands in two-inch-high letters above the pinup with the knockers. "We was thinking of doing it just for the crack of it," the gas fitter tells me, of a plan he and his mates at the yard were cooking up to relieve the tedium. (He could have said "for the hell of it," meaning fun, too.) A friend writes a postcard from Korčula, Yugoslavia. "The scenery is ravishing," he says. The playwright tells an interviewer, "The tutors were dead for it, but not the students."[1]

Staggering, knock-out, stunning, smashing, stupendous, cracking, flabbergasting, helluva, dead—they have been in current use as praise, in adjectival or adverbial form, since the late nineteenth century at least; they qualify—with enthusiasm—objects of admiration, desired states like success, moments and conditions of well-being. Some have an upper-class slant: *ripping, cracking,* and the Wodehouse world's *killing,* as in *killing story* or *killingly funny.* Some have a more working-class register: *dead right that is.*

Probably before Catullus spoke of love in terms of excruciating agony, certainly since the medieval mystics borrowed Latin expressions of rapture, Zeus's abductions provided a model of ecstasy. Although the context never proposes that rape and religious ravishment are the same, the imagination seems to falter before the power of the experience and fails to find another way of describing it, beyond the sphere of erotic encounter and assault. At the same time as the statutes warned of the penalties for "Felonious Rapes or Ravishements of Women Maydes Wieves and Damsells" (1576), Thomas Bowes was writing, "This degree of love may be rightly called ravishing, in which the lover is so rapt out of himselfe, that he forgetteth himselfe" (1586).[2]

The vocabulary of pleasure depends on the imagery of pain. Terms of wonder, appreciation, and awe evoke the body dealt a blow, or otherwise assaulted. It becomes difficult, in one semantic zone, to comb out the tangle between feelings that feel nice and feelings that feel nasty. Can widespread masochism be the answer? Is Freud's diagnosis of the death instinct sufficient explanation, or indeed, an explanation at all? In some places where language is born, the twofold drive towards annihilation and bliss may bring forth new images of hurt: some of the drug culture's slang conjures states of recognizable pleasure—*rush, buzz,* or *high.* But much of its imagery sifts the lexicon of hard knocks: phrases like *getting a kick* or *a bang, it blew me away, it took the top of my head off;* words for the dose—the *hit;* and street talk for the drugs themselves—*smack, crack.* Though the gas fitter's *crack* was Irish for fun, for the whackiness, the dizziness, and comes down a different road from the new American drug, it arrives at a similar destination, at the image of splitting, breaking open, with the memory of a whip's passage somewhere behind it. *Flabbergasting,* if one pauses over it for a moment, turns into an ancient-looking word—laying flab to waste?[3] *Thrilling,* one of the oldest ways of describing the shivers and tingling of pleasure, derives from Middle English *thirlen,* to pierce, as in nostrils: nose-thrills or nose holes. With the verb *to pierce,* as well as associated images of penetration and delving, the metaphor of forced entry still remains live, inspiring sympathetic tremors, unlike so many current violent expressions for physical bliss, from which the color and power have faded. Saint Teresa's angel makes himself felt, through the text, when he lifts "a great golden spear . . . and plunged into my heart several times so that it penetrated to my entrails."[4]

Such imagery attempts to communicate the reality of the pleasure, its tone and pitch and volume, by locating it in sensations that familiarly bring the body to the forefront of consciousness. However, just as Elaine Scarry argues that pain is "unspeakable," in that a sufferer cannot express suffering in terms that will convey its intensity and its fullness to another who does not experience the same torment, so language stumbles and falls over the complexity of pleasure, and seeks to make it feel real and strong by invoking experiences that by their very power introduce a dominant note, sweeping aside all other sensations. Scarry writes that the ascetics scourged and otherwise punished themselves not to deny the body but to feel its presence so acutely that they shut out all else: "so emphasizing the body that the contents of the world are cancelled and the path is clear for the entry of an unworldly, contentless force. It is in part this world-ridding, path-clearing logic that explains the obsessive presence of pain in the rituals of large, widely shared religions as well as in the imagery of intensely private visions.[5] The estate agent who declares the maisonette to be stunning wants a prospective buyer to think of nothing else, in the same way as if, were he to fetch his client a stunning blow, he would effectively focus his victim's attention.

Obviously, the effect of exclusion explains only one part of this peculiar language of delight. Another model of relations governs the metaphors: the model of contest. It is not a simple model, however, for it affords different points of entry, which alter the angle of vision and change the meanings produced. From one position, fighting talk identifies pleasure with winning: a person experiencing pleasure is cast in the role of a winner; proves his prowess; enjoys the pleasure of success. As in sports, the feeling is *knock-out* (boxing), it's *smashing* (tennis, or boxing again), the player in question is a *smash hit*. *To make a killing*, meaning success not murder, passes into usage to describe a grand *slam* in the game of bridge. From this aspect, the model of contest represents the pleasured person as active, an agent of experience, a maker and bringer of sensation, a knock-out opponent, a killer player. As Scarry says, "the particular perceptual confusion sponsored by the language of agency is the conflation of pain with power."[6]

The imagery of contest flies towards a simple goal, to narrow the field and bring the whole confusing business of feelings within range. The sports trope helps to do this, because typically it envisages two contestants, who may be champions of single combat, or at most two teams confronting each other; there must be a lone winner, a supremo. Technology searches out the ultimate victor, beyond human faculties' reach, with electronic split-second stopwatches, computerized cameras. As Primo Levi writes in *The Drowned and the Saved*, the crowd loves spectator sports because they divide the issue so simply. Gray areas, margins, mixed feelings, torn loyalties, the "half-tints and complexities" are abolished—or at least banished. The Manichaean tendency "is prone to reduce the river of human occurrences to conflicts, and the conflicts to duels—we and they."[7]

The model of contest contains at least two participants, however, and can be looked at, and entered, from the point of view of the vanquished as well as the victor. Fighting talk, when applied to the pleasures of sex, frequently abolishes the difference between them, and presents sexual conquest as annihilating defeat (locating much pleasure therein). What is significant with respect to stunning pinups and flabbergasting blondes and staggering maisonettes and so forth is that a blow is imagined where there is no blow, where there is sometimes no action, no movement even.

In such a bout, the smash hit has happened in the imagination of only one of the participants. It circulates from its origin therein, traveling to the body that brought about the effect, and is then attributed to that entity, which becomes a smashing girl, a stunning flat. The knock-out lover can be a champion and a victim at once, can see himself, through this duplicity of language, as both knocking and knocked.

At this point, the observation of the lexicographer Jonathon Green becomes important: much adverbial usage of *smashing* and *staggering* and so forth might be euphemistic, especially as such words, many occurring first in the late Victorian period, are tinged with gentility. They may be substituting for stronger intensives expressing pleasure, while retaining the trace of the original thought: *ripping* and *corking* instead of *fucking*. ("A fucking beautiful maisonette.")[8] With the help of this insight we may find that just as the internal switchback—the hypallage—in the epithet *ravishing* transposes the impulse to ravish from the beholder to the beheld, so the girl who is a smash hit at a party may simply be fucking lovely (*a corker*) to the men who behold her. The descriptions of affect, all those invocations of physical stupefaction and exhaustion, of thrust and its climax in victory, of diminished consciousness in order to communicate some state of bliss, of stunning and being stunned, of the conquering hero overcome, of corking and uncorking, amount to the obvious, really. Does it have to be spelled out?

Familiar expressions of pleasure, the vernacular of sought-after sensation, are grown in the experience of sex; and the experience is being regarded from within a male body, envisaged from a man's vantage point. We are outside the territory, passionately invoked by feminists in France like Hélène Cixous and Luce Irigaray, of "writing the body" of woman.

The symbolized body from which many shared terms of pleasure issue forth is not necessarily the only possible male body, or the only body of male experience. But it is one that historically and culturally we have inherited, one we understand to be inhabited by people of the male sex. And the lexical constraints on the concept of maleness seem to be tightening: the circulating vocabulary of masculinity insists upon action, aggression, prowess, and conquest ever more intensely, to the great distress of parents who have sons, and the confusion of those sons themselves, not to speak of the general dismay of women.

It is not always easy to occupy a summit; there is a terrible oppression in being exhorted to be the master sex as well. (And in this case, sympathy isn't wasted, for we are all implicated, men and women alike, in the parceling out of value to gender.)

Taking two mass markets, for instance, with clearly sexually defined targets—toiletries and toys—the buckles of gender roles make themselves felt, and painfully. Eaux de cologne for men are called Polo, Denim, Aramis, and Brut (the last no doubt after champagne, but not ignoring other connotations). The cosmetic companies want to avoid sissy overtones, obviously, so they stress the robust, musketeering, sporty character of their fragrances. (Women's perfumes are brewed in some pretty wild alembics these days: the latest concoctions are named Anaïs, Opium, Poison, as the *odor di femmina* becomes ever more *fatale*.)

Toy manufacturers have an equivalent need to overdetermine the products' gender, in that they do not want small boys to think they are being soppy, playing with dolls. One series of "action figures"—a best selling line—contains the following cast of characters: Budo, a samurai; Muskrat, a swamp warrior; Spearhead, a pointman and Max, his bobcat; Hit & Run, a light infantry man; Lightfoot, an explosives expert; Hardball Multishot, a grenadier; Blizzard, an Arctic attack soldier; Charbroil, a flamethrower, Sneak Peek, advanced reconnaissance; Crazylegs, an assault trooper; Gung-ho, a marine; Tunnel Rat, a sapper; Chuckles, an undercover agent; Falcon, a green beret; Jinx, ninja intelligence; and Dodger, Blocker, Blaster, and Knockdown, who man vehicles and weapons with names like the Eliminator, the Dominator, the X-wing Chopper.[9] As with men's perfumes, the nomenclature of dolls for boys puts down its roots in warfare and sports; but it communicates action and power not only semantically, through the meanings of its images, but aurally too: the names of the warriors and the scents are short; plosives and gutturals appear far in excess of their usual distribution (there is an element of orientalism in this, of harking back to ancient gods whose names begin or include lots of zs and ks and xs too). If a name runs longer than two syllables, it usually ends with a consonant to forestall any impression of yielding or weakness. Girl children, meanwhile, are sold toys with long, meandering names—My Little Pony, Lady Lovelylocks and the Pixie Tails.

Two or three years ago, the Chinese press reported that in Jiangyong county in the province of Hunan a women's language had been discovered.[10] It was very old indeed; so old the script resembled the earliest writing known to the world, the characters on the oracle bones of the Shang. The photograph showed two eighty-year-old women, heads tied in headcloths and inclined together over a paper they both held, where some of the six hundred surviving characters were no doubt inscribed. The *China Daily* reported the findings of the Chinese anthropologist who had uncovered this remnant: the women had kept the language alive amongst themselves while weaving, and songs and poems and fragments of autobiography survive, even though one of the last "seven sisters" who knew the language burned documents in order to preserve its secrecy; the language had also been used in a local goddess's temple where women prayed for good husbands and fertility.

Since the report there has been no more word of the language's character, though a dictionary and edition of the surviving songs and poems were promised. In their absence, the secrecy opens into a wide fair country of dreams: will this prove that place where the muffled voice of women will be raised? Where the opposition male/female will not generate strings of corresponding pairs, strong/weak, above/below, reason/instinct, active/passive, robust/fragile, Marauder Motorcycle Tank/My Little Pony, Brut/Anaïs, and so forth. It's of course much more likely that this is dream, that a language, however secret it's kept, cannot be produced pure, out of the woman's ground of being (whatever that is) without reflection of her social and historical conditions. There exist languages in which women speak differently from men in obvious ways, conferring their gender on their utterances, as in Romance languages' agreement of subject and participle, or in Iroquois, where a phrase like *my house* becomes a word of feminine gender on the lips of a woman, masculine on a man's. But such grammatical conventions yield scanty insights into tradition, history, or psychology.[11]

In English, no rules of grammar follow from the speaker's sex, and the language itself is politely neutral, conferring neither gender nor animation on objects that in French, for instance, are always feminine, like *la bête*, the beast or insect, and *la victime*, the victim. The poet Tom Disch has urged,

> It is a lovely language,
> English. One senses, instinctively, listening
> To it, that it was created, like chromosomes,
> In strict parity by women and by men:
> By Mother Goose and Father Time
> With their long memories, by the quick
> Co-equal wits of Mirabell and Millamant.[12]

But Mother Goose and Father Time have different memories, and English is gendered beyond the rules of grammar, as psychologists and sociologists are discovering. There's a wondrously rich and old vocabulary to describe precisely the different and varied character of female speech (which can be practiced by men, but at their peril). To prattle, chatter (chit-chat), tattle (tittle-tattle), tongue wag, gush, are not manly things; *my gossip* used to mean my friend, spoken by a woman, of a woman; scolds, nags, tongue-lashers, wheedlers, complainers, screechers, railers are, notoriously, women; as many writers before me have pointed out, one man's oratory is a woman's stridency; one man's fluency is a woman's garrulity. Of course English isn't the only language to categorize women's talk so richly. In a carnival mood, the Dutch produced an antisaint, Alwaere ("All-true"), patroness of raucousness and rowdiness, of strife and quarreling, who wears a screeching magpie on her head and rides a braying ass.[13]

The very abundance of words denigrating women's speech tells us not that women kept quiet—hardly—but that they were guilty because they failed, in Emily Dickinson's word, to be "still."[14]

So, if women's disobligingness in the matter of silence rings down the centuries in the insults against their wagging tongues, can the particular language of female affect be found? And if it can, where? Women might buy a stunning maisonette, and like to look ravishing, and respond with excitement to the smashing prices at the supermarket, and so forth. But without being essentialist about women's bodies and universalizing all female sensation, the historical witness of women's writings and other testimony, like the records of trials, reveal an inclination to a different set of blissful blazons, a different way of invoking pleasure, which imagines a woman's body as the site of well-being.

Besides the eye and the genitals, the other organs of sense pass on to women special information of pleasure. In Caroline Walker Bynum's eloquent study of female mystical practice and rhetoric in the high Middle Ages, imagery of nurturance (of mother's milk and the blood of generation, of flesh as food) dominates the visions of Catherine of Siena and her later compatriot, Catherine of Genoa, offering to the reader or hearer's senses—one could say dishing out—a personal eroticism.[15] While unsavory to contemporary taste, this keyed-up language of appetite succeeds in transmitting undreamed-of states of pleasure, felt by women. The divine bridegroom here does not stun the visionary, or even pierce her, so much as offer himself in draughts of milk and blood, often presenting his incarnate body in the image of the visionary's renounced maternity: " 'My beloved,' [Christ] said to her [Catherine of Siena], 'you have now gone through many struggles for my sake . . . I today shall give you a drink that transcends in perfection any that human nature can provide . . .' With that, he tenderly placed his right hand on her neck, and drew her toward the wound in his side. 'Drink, daughter, from my side,' he said, 'and by that draught your soul shall become enraptured with such delight that your very body, which for my sake you have denied, shall be inundated with its overflowing goodness.' "[16]

Fancying a man today, young women still return to the metaphors of the mouth: "Dishy," they say, or "very tasty"; they might find a caress "delicious," a glimpse of tight jeans "juicy." This is not to claim that a man will not speak of a woman in these terms too, but just that in the current vocabulary of pleasure, women incline to metaphors of nourishment, not always of spectacle or violent action. Often, they are not themselves the imagined consumer, but offer themselves for consumption.

In the sixties and seventies, some polemicists were angered by endearments—and curses—turning women into food (sweetiepie, honeybunch) and their sexual parts into fruits (cherry, melons). But it has to be said that women, exploring union from a female somatic viewpoint, have themselves deeply enriched the trope. When the motif of ravishment appears, imagery of engulfment follows in the train of the threat to integrity, and the encounter comes accompanied by images of immersion and incorporation—analogous to the eucharistic union with Christ in the mystics' thought, the oneness with the savior achieved by eating him. To take one example, from the nineteenth century: Emily Dickinson's famous poem, beginning "I started Early," tells of her encounter with the tide, vividly personified in the poem as a pursuer:

> But no Man moved Me—till the Tide
> Went past my simple Shoe—
> And past my Apron—and my Belt
> And past my Bodice—too—
>
> And made as He would eat me up—
> As Wholly as a Dew
> Upon a Dandelion's Sleeve—
> And then—I started—too—
>
> And He—He followed—close behind—
> I felt His Silver Heel
> Upon my Ankle—Then my Shoes
> Would overflow with Pearl—[17]

The water's movement, imagined from the I's viewpoint with startling intimacy, begins by immersing her ("past my Bodice—too"), then swallowing her (like dew drenching a flower), to spilling out of her shoes, in a sequence of metaphors that attribute to her pursuer, coming after her like a man giving chase in a dream, certain engulfing, oceanic, flooding, and devouring characteristics traditionally ascribed to the female body in the act of love. Describing her own state—and the poem conveys vivid, reverberating pleasure—Emily Dickinson pictures the assailing tide in the image of female sexuality, accomplishing a reversal comparable to that of the mystics, who taking Christ's body into their own in the form of the host feel themselves to be incorporated. The highly wrought erotic picture of the shoes, overflowing with pearl, first comes up before the eye as Aphrodite foam, but does not stay there, as specular pleasure. It expands to excite the senses of taste and touch: to place before us cups and chalices brimming.

"Writing is precisely the very possibility of change," writes Hélène Cixous in her rhapsodic manifesto "The Laugh of the Medusa," where she rails at the silencing of women, their difficulty of speech because the dominant language belongs to the lawmakers, the fathers.[18] Though not tongue-tied myself, though able, by privilege of education and profession, to express myself in language, and make myself heard (I think, sometimes), I recognize what Cixous is saying, because I find my voice falters in the site of pleasure, that I have no words for it, that there, I am gagged. The words that circulate don't suit ("That was smashing"? "You're a knock-out"?). And far beyond the personal sphere of well-being and of sensual gratification, in ever widening rings, the language of appreciation is intertwined with metaphors of violence; consider the critics' stock of terms: *impact, force, explosive, searing*. Women don't avoid the imagery either. A fellow novelist, writing about Louise Erdrich, says "*The Beet Queen* imparts its freshness of vision like an electric shock."[19]

Cathérine Clément, Cixous's collaborator on *La Jeune née*, talks of the nervous cough Dora developed because she could not speak her story, and of Rosalie, a singer, who could no longer sing after she had witnessed her uncle's abuses; their pages are filled with so many Procnes and Philomels, the stifled voices of the exemplary heroic hysterics of the past, whom they idealize in the interest of their own impassioned rallying cry.[20]

Sometimes, this kind of desire to hymn women's oppression leads to exaggeration of their enforced silence, and a paradoxical diminishment of women's place in history and in culture; but it seems to me that in this matter, the expression of pleasure, the character of our metaphors shapes the character of those feelings. Is saying something violently saying it well? Is feeling something violently feeling it in the only possible way? Perhaps, if we were to set aside the language of pain, we might find our shoes, too, filling with pearl.

Notes

1. Nigel Swain, in "Ex-Ulster Officer's Terrorism Drama," by David Lister, in *The Independent*, 24 August 1988.

2. *De La Primaudaye's French académie*, trans. Thomas Bowes (London, 1586–94), vol. 2 (1594), p. 294.

3. From the same root as *ghastly*, it turns out: so, literally "terrifying" or "alarming" flab.

4. *The Life of Saint Teresa of Avila*, trans. J. M. Cohen (London, 1957), p. 247.

5. Elaine Scarry, *The Body in Pain: The Making and Unmaking of the World* (Oxford, 1985), p. 34.

6. Scarry, *The Body in Pain*, p. 18.

7. Primo Levi, *The Drowned and the Saved*, trans. Raymond Rosenthal (London, 1988), p. 22.

8. Communicated to the author in conversation, for which much gratitude.

9. Catalogue, *GI JOE: A Real American Hero*, 1987.

10. *China Daily*, 13 May 1986; *Guardian*, 19 May 1986. I am grateful to Frances Wood for this information.

11. See Marina Warner, *Monuments & Maidens: The Allegory of the Female Form* (London, 1986), pp. 64–70.

12. Tom Disch, "On the Use of the Masculine-Preferred," *Times Literary Supplement*, 23 January 1981.

13. See Christine Megan Armstrong, *The Moralizing Prints of Corneliz Anthonisz*. Ph.D. diss., Princeton University, 1985, pp. 64–76.

14. Emily Dickinson, "They shut me up in Prose," in *The Complete Poems*, ed. Thomas H. Johnson (London, 1986), p. 302.

15. Caroline Walker Bynum, *Holy Feast and Holy Fast: The Religious Significance of Food to Medieval Women* (Berkeley, 1987).

16. Raymond of Capua, *Life of Catherine of Siena*, quoted in Bynum, p. 172.

17. Dickinson, *Complete Poems*, p. 254.

18. Hélène Cixous, "The Laugh of the Medusa," trans. Keith Cohen and Paula Cohen, in *New French Feminisms*, ed. Elaine Marks and Isabelle de Courtivron (Brighton, 1981), p. 249.

19. Angela Carter, from the jacket of Louise Erdrich, *The Beet Queen*, Pavanne edition (London, 1986).

20. See Hélène Cixous and Catherine Clément, *The Newly Born Woman*, trans. Betsy Wing (Manchester, 1986), pp. 3–57.

Power: Women and the Word

POWER. MEANINGS: THE ABILITY TO DO SOMETHING, to effect, to act upon. A faculty of body or mind. A force. Political or national strength. Authority or dominion over. Legal authority. A ruler, a state, a prerogative, a celestial body or influence. A body of armed men. The rate at which electrical energy is fed into a system. A measure of magnification. A large amount. Nuclear energy. Power drill, power house, power plant, power politics, black power, power of attorney. Examples: from kings, fathers, patriarchs, princes, bishops, armies, lawyers. (Exceptional cases: the daughter of Jove, Cleopatra.) Quotations: Absolute power corrupts absolutely, thine is the Kingdom, the Power and the Glory, happy men that have the power to die, the balance of power, Him the Almighty Power hurl'd headlong flaming, He that hath power to hurt and will do none, the awful shadow of some unseen power. Etymology: from Middle English *poër*, Old French *poer, poeir, pouoir*. *Pouoir* goes forward into Modern French *pouvoir*, and backwards to *podere*, from late vulgar Latin *potere*, from Latin *posse*, to be able. The present participle of *posse, potent-em*, provides *potentia*, and hence Old French *potence*. Meaning: power, ability, strength, sexual power (male). From this comes *potency*, also potent, potentate, potential, and potentiality.[1]

No wonder, with this pedigree, that the word *power*, derived from the same root as *potency*, is used more often than any other word in feminist discourse to stand for male supremacy. That supremacy is frequently identified as linguistic: naming is power. The word *power* belongs to those who are in power. It follows that the feminist use of the word is extremely ambivalent. *Power* names something which is resented and feared, but which is also desired and aspired to. It is a revealing word in current feminist discourse because it can take opposite meanings. Other key words do not require a context for their value to be expressed. *Creative*, or *pleasure*, or *freedom* is likely to mean well; *rape*, or *humiliation*, is bound to be bad. *Power* is bad when it is identified with male supremacy and the oppression of women, as in Andrea Dworkin's "it is through intercourse that men express and maintain their power and dominance over women," or Kate Millett's "both the courtly and the romantic versions of love are 'grants' which the male concedes out of his total power."[2] *Power* is good when it is identified with female creativity and potential.

In the good sense it is frequently associated with the use of language, as when Adrienne Rich asks women to consider "language as transforming power," or Mary Daly plays with language to release "the complex creative power" of women, or Toril Moi describes Kate Millett's rhetoric as "a powerful fist in the solar plexus of patriarchy."[3] A word that can mean both well and ill is a manipulable word. Adrienne Rich, in an essay called "Power and Danger," gives a feminist history of the word as used against women:

> Powerless, women have been seduced into confusing love with false power—the "power" of mother-love, the "power" of gentle influence, the "power" of nonviolence, the "power" of the meek who are to inherit the earth.[4]

Rich's scorn of a rhetoric which pretends that powerlessness can be a form of power is directed, of course, at male (and especially Christian) rhetoric. But strategic manipulations of the word are not a male prerogative. In the uses to which it is put in current feminist writing, two ways of making over the language can be discerned, the one utopian, the other confrontational. Both are intensely problematic.

If the language is to be reinvented for feminism, the word *power* presents a crucial challenge—and invitation. Can it be transformed, or must it be rejected? Any rewriting of women's history, as in this neutrally informative passage, has to center on the word:

> An understanding of the interdependence of the spheres reveals that women have wielded more power than has been apparent, and that aspects of women's lives which appear to be restrictive may actually be en-

abling. Women's history is concerned to see women, not as victims of
oppression, as passive spectators of the drama of history, but as having
an influence and a history of their own. . . . Historians of women
broaden their conception of power to include subtler forms—informal,
invisible, collective—recognising that "the location of power" is "a
tricky business."[5]

Here the word changes its value through a historical reinterpretation
which makes powerlessness, after all, into a form of power. This
would presumably not suit Adrienne Rich, who argues in "Power and
Danger" that this is what women have always been told, and much
good it has done us. Rich requires more than historical reconsidera-
tion. Like Virginia Woolf in *A Room of One's Own*, inviting women
writers to make use of the special knowledge they have inherited from
their mothers' history of exclusion and silence, Rich wants a history
of powerlessness to issue in a distinctive language (essentially a language of poetry) which will express "that instinct for true power, not
domination, which poets like Barrett Browning, Dickinson, H.D.,
were asserting in their own very different ways and voices."[6] Rich's
phrasing shows what a tricky business it is to give a utopian meaning
to the word *power*. *Power* still has to go with *asserting* (though *asserting*
is an inaccurate description of what Emily Dickinson and H.D. were
doing). Yet *asserting* is contrasted, in a shaky opposition, with *domination*. And *power* itself has to be qualified by *true*, in order to distinguish it from the bad old "false power" (that is, powerlessness) offered
to women by the male oppressors. We are presented, then, somewhat
awkwardly, with a utopian idea of a language of "true power" which
will assert but not dominate. What could such a language actually be?

Feminist revisions of language in the last decade, powerfully influenced by Julia Kristeva's critique of Freud and Lacan, have insisted on
a female language as the expression of *what has been repressed* in the
male sentence. Mary Jacobus defines *écriture féminine* as that which is
"located in the gaps, the absences, the unsayable or unrepresentable of
discourse and representation."[7] Female language is identified, in such
now-legendary texts as Hélène Cixous's "Le Rire de la Méduse" (1975)
and Luce Irigaray's "Ce sexe qui n'en est pas un" (1977), as a playful
revealing of what has been hidden. Language as an eruption of female
sexuality, or *jouissance*, can be a potent alternative discourse. This discourse is indebted to Kristeva's theory that the pre-Oedipal phase of
childhood, in intimate connection with the mother, which precedes
the "entry into signification and the symbolic order," can persist in
"oral and instinctual aspects of language which punctuate, evade, or
disrupt the symbolic order—in prosody, intonation, puns, verbal
slips, even silences."[8] For Irigaray, this means that "woman would

find herself on the side of everything in language that is multiple, duplicitous, unreliable"; her language is "a deranging power."[9]

Utopian polemicists for a female language repeatedly oppose its "deranging power" to the established power systems within which it must operate. So woman must be, and speak, "that which is neither power nor structure."[10] How can this be put into practice? Recommendations vary from the use of myth and fable, diaries and notebooks, gaps on the page, poetical prose and domestic imagery, to, at the most inept, "the vocabulary of menstruation, reproduction or craft work."[11] More specific linguistic programs call for women to coin neologisms, break grammatical rules, and defamiliarize taken-for-granted parts of speech.

If this fabricated language is to express "that which is neither power nor structure," it has to be identified with negatives: amorphousness, evasiveness, splits, darkness, and depth. Here, for instance, a conscientious Americanized version of *écriture féminine* uses strategies of syntactical blurring, fragmentation, exclamation, rhythmic patterns, and an alternative vocabulary to ridicule the culture's mythical respect for male linguistic power:

> But that male body, how IT dominates the culture, the environment, the language. Since 3,000 B.C. in Sumeria, Tiamat's monsters again and again, and every myth an effort to keep the sun rising. Save the sun, everybody, from the watery deeps, the dark underneath it must go—Into—Every night into such dangers, such soft inchoate darkness, what will become of it, will it rise again will it will it rise again? The language of criticism: "lean, dry, terse, powerful, strong, spare, linear, focused, explosive",—god forbid it should be "limp"!! But—"soft, moist, blurred, padded, irregular, going around in circles," and other descriptions of *our* bodies—the very *abyss* of aesthetic judgment, danger, the wasteland for artists! That limp dick—an entire civilization based on it, help the sun rise, watch out for the dark underground, focus focus focus, keep it high, let it soar, let it transcend, let it aspire to Godhead———[12]

This kind of programmatic writing consigns women and their language, all over again (as they have traditionally been consigned by inspired "phallocentric" writers such as Yeats, Whitman, and Lawrence) to the realms of "inchoate darkness," the unconscious, mothering, hysteria, and babble. It is a version of female "powers" which has been emphatically challenged, very often as part of a debate between the Gallic school of psychoanalytical and linguistic feminists, and the Anglo-American school of Marxist/socialist/"materialist" feminists. The latter criticize the essentialist identification of the feminine with "absence, silence, incoherence, even madness" as "a mistaken strategy" which "abandons territory which can and

ought to be defended against masculine imperialism: coherence, rationality, articulateness."[13]

A more socialized, functional attempt at fabricating a female language is currently being made by the American feminist theolo-
gian Mary Daly. In *Gyn/Ecology: The Metaethics of Radical Feminism*
(1978) and *Pure Lust: Elemental Feminist Philosophy* (1984) she makes
determined efforts at "wrenching back some word power."[14] The
phrase refers to her title, *Gyn/Ecology*, which Daly says is meant
to draw attention to the pollution spread by patriarchal myth and
language. Daly's split words and coinages (dis-membering and remembering, a-maze, man/ipulate, O-Zone, Hag-ocracy, the/rapist,
Nag-Gnostics) belong to a self-conscious process of reeducating the
users of the language by "targeting/humiliating the right objects."

> Gynocentric writing means risking. Since the language and style of pa-
> triarchal writing simply cannot contain or carry the energy of women's
> exorcism and ecstasy, in this book I invent, dis-cover, re-member. At
> times I make up words (such as *gynaesthesia* for women's synaesthesia).
> Often I unmask deceptive words by dividing them and employing
> alternate meanings for prefixes (for example, *re-cover* actually says
> "cover again"). I also unmask their hidden reversals, often by using less
> known or "obsolete" meanings (for example, *glamour* as used to name a
> witch's power). Sometimes I simply invite the reader to listen to words
> in a different way (for example, *de-light*). When I play with words I
> do this attentively, deeply, paying attention to etymology, to varied
> dimensions of meaning, to deep Background meanings and subliminal
> associations.[15]

Daly subverts the word *power* by pluralizing it, proposing an opposition between "Elemental Powers of Be-ing" (female, naturally) and
"patriarchal power." The strategy perfectly sums up the utopian feminist desire to reclaim all the "established" meanings of power (potency, control, activity, authority) and change their value:

> Women who are unveiling the Archimage, Realizing active potency, are
> unleashing Archaic powers. To be actively potent is to Realize/release
> that which is most Dreadful to the impotent priests, the prurient patri-
> archs—our participation in Be-ing. . . . It is predictable that priestly
> predators will attempt to use fear-filled women as powers holding down
> Elemental female powers.[16]

Daly's self-conscious, artificial wordplay, bent on reminding us
that language is a construct which can therefore be de- and re-
constructed according to different laws, is liable to disbelief or ridicule. Why? Partly because her educative intention—to alert readers to
the covert or suppressed potential in their language and to make mor-
ibund usages or weakened meanings come back to life—can look too

much like willfulness or whimsicality. (Daly's passion for puns and coy alliterative pairings, and her solemnity about her own playfulness, don't help.) But the problem is not just one of manner. This extreme example of a utopian project to manufacture an alternative language differs from comparable attempts of dialect or minority-language speakers to free themselves from the superimposition of a dominant culture's "standard" language.[17] The aim of such groups is to *write what they speak*: to challenge the power of a mainstream, colonial literary tradition by the force of an oral tradition. But no one speaks, or has ever spoken, a distinctive, alternative female language. If it is to come into being, it must be an entirely fabricated, artificial, written invention.

The danger—the "risking"—of a utopian, alternative female language expressive of "woman's powers" is that it will be felt to fall short of, or evade, the real world's balance of power. In which case, feminists have to find another way of making their words potent.

The confrontational mode of female language mimics or mirrors the enemy's use of the word *power*. Kristeva, in a section called "The terror of power or the power of terrorism" in *Women's Time* (1979), analyzes the tendency of women struggling against the "power structure" to "make of the second sex a counter-society," "a counter-power which necessarily generates . . . its essence as a simulacrum of the combated society or of power." This countersociety is as violent, as paranoid, and as power-hungry, as the system it opposes. Hence, according to this argument, the large number of women in terrorist groups.[18]

Monique Wittig demonstrates a linguistic version of terrorist "counter-power," explaining her use, in *Les Guérillères*, of the pronoun *elles*:

> To succeed textually, I needed to adopt some very draconian measures, such as to eliminate . . . *he* or *they-he*. I had to provide a shock for the reader entering a text in which *elles* by its unique presence constitutes an assault, yes, even for female readers. . . . The adoption of a pronoun as my subject matter dictated the form of the book. Although the theme of the text was total war, led by *elles* on *ils*, in order for this new person to take effect, two-thirds of the text had to be totally inhabited, haunted, by *elles*. Word by word, *elles* establishes itself as a sovereign subject [and] also imposed an epic form, where it is not only the complete subject of the world but its conqueror.[19]

Draconian measures, eliminate, shock, assault, dictated, total war, sovereign subject, imposed, epic, conqueror: the language of power is being not transformed, but turned against the enemy with a vengeance.

The most offensive of these counteroffensives is that of the American polemicist Andrea Dworkin, frequently referred to as a "powerful" voice in the women's movement, whose argument is that the sex act is an act of terrorism against women. There are no exceptions to this rule, since the world according to Dworkin is a constructed male-dominated system of social institutions, sexual practices, and economic relations in which women are silenced, exploited, and damaged. There is ("thus") an essential connection between the foul end—what Dworkin calls "the real shit"—of sexual relations (pornography, rape, wife-battering, incest, prostitution) and the sanctioned end (marriage, love, "so-called" normal intercourse). As much in the legal as in the illegal sphere, "intercourse is political dominance; power as power or power as pleasure." The conspiracy to believe that women like to be hurt is universal. Just as the law allows for unspeakable abuses of women in pornography, so it gives "protective legitimacy" to the ownership of women by men. *Ergo*, "marriage is a legal licence to rape," "fucking is the means by which the male colonializes the female":

> Women are a degraded and terrorized people. Women are degraded and terrorized by men. Rape is terrorism. Wife-beating is terrorism. Medical butchering is terrorism. Sexual abuse in its hundred million forms is terrorism. . . . Women are an occupied people. . . . This fascist ideology of female inferiority is the preeminent ideology on this planet.

Dworkin thinks of, and uses, language as a weapon: "dirty words" and "antifeminist epithets" are the equivalent of physical attacks. "Women live defensively, not just against rape but against the language of the rapist." She provides the clearest and most extreme example in the feminist belief in language as power, since, in her argument, "power determines the meaning of language." It is, noticeably, her most used word, as in "Intercourse consistently expresses illegitimate power, unjust power, wrongful power."[20]

Dworkin's weapons, like those of Kristeva's "counter-society," are simulacrums of the enemy's. So her strategies—generalizations, diktats, exhortations—are those of dictatorship. The objects of her attack are, frequently, horrifyingly convincing. But her totalitarian refusal to allow exceptions ("Men love death"; "Women have to pretend to like men to survive"; "Relationships called love are based on exploitation") makes a desolating language which can only imitate what it opposes. In this language, the meaning of *power* cannot be transformed.

Must it be so? Toril Moi (arguing with Irigaray over the word *power*) writes these heartening words:

> Women's relationship to power is not exclusively one of victimisation.
> Feminism is not simply about rejecting power, but about transforming

the existing power structures—and, in the process, transforming the very *concept* of power itself.[21]

How is the "very *concept*" of power to be transformed? We go back to the beginning again. There are no conclusions, only arguments. But it may be that through the arguments themselves, transformation begins to occur, and *power* takes on its most promising and least hurtful meaning, that of *potential*.

Notes

1. *Oxford English Dictionary, Collins English Dictionary, Oxford Dictionary of Quotations.*

2. Andrea Dworkin, *Right-Wing Women* (New York, 1983), p. 83; Kate Millett, *Sexual Politics* (1969; London, 1977), p. 37.

3. Adrienne Rich, *On Lies, Secrets, and Silences* (New York, 1979; London, 1980, p. 247); Mary Daly, *Gyn/Ecology: The Metaethics of Radical Feminism* (Boston, 1978; London, 1979), p. 79; Toril Moi, *Sexual/Textual Politics* (London, 1985), p. 26.

4. Rich, *On Lies, Secrets, and Silences*, p. 254.

5. Gayle Greene and Coppélia Kahn, eds., *Making a Difference: Feminist Literary Criticism* (London, 1985), p. 17.

6. Rich, *On Lies, Secrets, and Silences*, p. 257.

7. Mary Jacobus, *Reading Woman: Essays in Feminist Criticism* (New York and London, 1986), p. 109.

8. *Reading Woman*, p. 148.

9. *Reading Woman*, p. 65.

10. Josette Féral, "Antigone or *The Irony of the Tribe*," *Diacritics* 8 (1978): 11, quoted by Elizabeth Meese, *Crossing the Double-Cross* (Chapel Hill, 1986), p. 112.

11. Maggie Humm, *Feminist Criticism* (Brighton, 1986), p. 8.

12. Frances Jaffer and Rachel Blau du Plessis, "For the Etruscans: The Debate over a Female Aesthetic," in *Feminist Literary Theory: A Reader*, ed. Mary Eagleton (Oxford, 1986), p. 228.

13. Terry Lovell, "Writing Like a Woman," in *Feminist Literary Theory*, p. 85.

14. Daly, *Gyn/Ecology*, p. 9.

15. Daly, *Gyn/Ecology*, p. 24.

16. Mary Daly, *Pure Lust: Elemental Feminist Philosophy* (London, 1984), pp. 188–89.

17. See the essays on "Identities," especially those by Geneva Smitherman and Monroe K. Spears, in *The State of the Language*, ed. Leonard Michaels and Christopher Ricks (Berkeley and Los Angeles, 1980).

18. Julia Kristeva, "Women's Time" (1979), trans. Alice Jardine and Harry Blake, in *The Kristeva Reader*, ed. Toril Moi (Oxford, 1986), pp. 201–3.

19. Monique Wittig, "The Mark of Gender," in *The Poetics of Gender*, ed. Nancy K. Miller (New York, 1986), p. 70.

20. Andrea Dworkin, *Intercourse* (1987; London, 1988), p. 197; *Letters from a War Zone* (London, 1988), p. 200; *Right-Wing Women*, p. 202; *Intercourse*, p. 201; *Right-Wing Women*, p. 84.

21. Toril Moi, *Sexual/Textual Politics*, p. 148.

~ ROGER SCRUTON

Ideologically Speaking

I CANNOT PREVENT MYSELF FROM FEELING an inner revulsion whenever the word *person* is self-consciously summoned to take the place
once occupied by *man*, or when the flow of a sentence is interrupted
by a distracting use of *he or she* where *he* would once have been man-
datory. Far from serving to remove the "irrelevant" reference to gender from the English language, such practices heighten that reference,
and transform it from a harmless quirk of grammar to a vigilant ideological presence. I resent this ideological intrusion, and its insolent
dealings with our mother (perhaps I should say "parent") tongue. But
like many who share such reactionary sentiments, I find it difficult to
justify them except in ways which are too *ad hoc*, or too *ad feminam*,
to gain a hearing from those who do not already share them. It
seems to me, therefore, that a great service would be done to the dwindling body of linguistic reactionaries if an argument could be found
for their position which is something more than a mere reiteration of
it. In this article I search for that argument—though with a despairing
sense that it lies, in the end, too deep for words, being presupposed in
every word that is used to utter it.

I have mentioned two strategies of "gender elimination": the substitution of *person* for *man*, and of *he or she* for *he*. They are only superficially similar. A moment's reflection tells us that while the second
change is stylistic, the first is also semantic. The word *person* comes to
us from the Latin *persona*—originally meaning "a mask," but tran-

formed by Roman law to designate the bearer of rights and duties, who comes before the law in order that his rights and duties should be determined (or rather, in order that *her* rights and duties should be determined, for *persona*, of course, is feminine). As Sir Ernest Barker beautifully put it: "it is not the natural Ego which enters a court of law. It is a right-and-duty bearing person, created by the law, which appears before the law."[1] The Roman-law conception passed into jurisprudential and philosophical usage, so that already in Boethius the word *persona* is used to denote the human individual, in his quality as rational agent. It is now quite normal among philosophers to assume that "personality" belongs to our essence, and that this puzzling fact is independent not only of law, but of all human institutions. Personality is no longer something bestowed upon himself by man, but something discovered in him, by all who would treat him as he really is. It was from this concept of personality that Kant distilled the Enlightenment morality which has all but replaced the morality of Christendom. And it is the classless, genderless—indeed sexless—morality of Kant whose brilliant rays are dimly reflected in the sermons of the modern feminist.

Not all persons are human. There are corporate persons, such as churches and firms; there are (or may be) divine persons, angels and devils. Moreover, not everything that belongs to our humanity belongs also to our personality. The embodiment of the person in the human organism brings with it a "human condition": a bond by which the free being and the animal are inseparably united, so as to confront the world from the same eyes, and with the same mystifying countenance, and therein to wrestle with each other till death do them part. The human being suffers and dies; he is at one with nature and with the animals, attached to his flesh and to the flesh of others. He rejoices in the sight, sound, smell, and touch of things: of his child, his dog, his horse, and his lover. And all those ineffable experiences are invoked when we refer to him not as *person*, but as *man*. This term returns us to our incarnation, and places the flesh where it should be, in the center of our moral view:

> man, proud man,
> Drest in a little brief authority,
> Most ignorant of what he's most assur'd,
> His glassy essence, like an angry ape,
> Plays such fantastic tricks before high heaven,
> As make the angels weep.

Even if we considered personality to be the most important fact of our condition, this could not lead us to the conclusion that we should refer to ourselves always as persons, or that we do not need a word to designate our incarnation and to locate us not in the hierarchy of angels, but amid the throngs of life. To use the word *person*, where our poets and liturgical writers have chosen *man*, is to deny the need to capture our destiny in words of our own.

But why the word *man*? For does this not imply some preference for the masculine gender, some lingering attachment to the view that, when the chips are down, it is men, and not women, who count? If not *person*, why not some other word which is semantically equivalent to *man* in its generic use, and yet free from every resonance of gender? Slavonic languages have such a word—*chelovek* in Russian, *člověk* in Czech, *człowiek* in Polish—whose etymology has nothing to do with man or woman. Why do we not follow suit, perhaps inventing a word for the purpose?

We could indeed adopt this strategy. But think of the cost. All at once we cease to use the word reserved by our language for the most important of the world's phenomena. More: we begin to treat the word as somehow polluted and unclean, to be avoided in polite society and reserved for onanistic use. Our past literature becomes tainted for us, something to be read or uttered with secret pangs of guilt and naughty titters—something that is no longer part of us, as antiquated and absurd as the Roman toga or the Morris dance. The result would be a massive "deculturation," as we cease to hear the language of Shakespeare and the King James Bible as addressed directly to the modern ear. And, in all probability, the experiment would fail. In a few decades the new word for man would be uttered always in inverted commas, like *citoyen* in post-Restoration France, or *comrade* in the modern communist state.

What is at stake becomes clearer when we consider the other example of "gender elimination": the use of *he or she* where *he* was once the norm. That this usage is inelegant will be freely admitted, even by those who advocate it. One philosopher has even suggested (and used) the alternative device of randomization, so that in neighboring sentences the impersonal pronoun is now masculine, now feminine.[2] The result is a stylistic catastrophe of unprecedented proportions. In such an idiom, neither the well-turned counsel, nor the poignant perception, can find utterance. Others still have advocated the use of *they* as a genderless third-person pronoun—a usage which has a certain popular authority. Dale Spender even argues that this usage was once universal, and that the rule requiring *he* is the invention of "patriarchal" grammarians in the nineteenth century.[3] If that were so, then we should have to thank the Victorians for a considerable stylistic gain: try to use the generic *they* consistently, and observe the confusion of syntax and number that immediately follows. In fact, however, the truth seems (as so often) to be the opposite of what is confidently affirmed by Dale Spender. It is true that there are early instances of the generic use of *they*: "Each of theym sholde make themselfe ready," writes Caxton in *Sonnes of Aymon* (c. 1489), while Shakespeare has "God send everyone their heart's desire" (*As You Like It*, 1598). Nevertheless, some of the first examples of the systematic use of *they* as a generic pronoun are in the polemical works of John Stuart Mill, where the author's usual eloquence is expressly constrained by his feminist principles. Seventeenth- and eighteenth-century English almost invariably seems to use *he* as a generic pronoun, and this is what we find in the works that did most to create the literary English of modernity: the King James Bible and the Book of Common Prayer. As these works abundantly demonstrate, the generic pronoun owes much of its power to the fact that it places before us an image of the human *individual*, but in the *general* condition which defines him. It reminds us that all counsels go unheard, until the individual life is touched by them: "He that findeth his life shall lose it: and he that loseth his life for my sake shall find it" (Matt. 7:39). The occurrence of the generic pronoun in the New Testament is of course influenced by the Greek. But the style of that sentence is the style of the surrounding English language: "He that is too much in any thing, so that he give another occasion of satiety, maketh himself cheap" (Francis Bacon). Consider what would happen to the writings of Addison, Johnson, Arnold, Ruskin, Dickens, or George Eliot, if every generic pronoun were plural, or if it should appear, when singular, always yoked to its feminine partner, struggling against it in a marriage of inconvenience. Even the law, which speaks not of man but of persons, has need of an individualizing generic pronoun, and therefore employs the standard *he*: "The words of a testator's will necessarily refer to facts and circumstances respecting his property and his family and other persons and things . . ."—which impeccably tautologous utterance comes to us with the authority of Halsbury's *Laws of England*.

Logically speaking, the pronoun is the equivalent of the mathematician's variable: it stands "in place of" the noun which fixes its referent. That it should bear a gender of its own is a grammatical fact of no semantic consequence. For semantically, its gender is the gender of the noun for which it stands proxy. The impersonal *he* stands proxy as a rule for *man*: for the general noun which describes us as instances of human life rather than as persons. And once again the complaint will be made that the resonance of gender here involves a reaffirmation of the discredited belief in the precedence of the male sex.

How can such a complaint be answered? First, we should not neglect the fact that linguistic gender distinctions are far from universal.

The Finno-Ugric and Turkic languages provide us with the nearest examples, culturally speaking, of genderlessness, and it is instructive to compare them with the Indo-European languages whose grammar has given so much cause for offense. No doubt there is difficulty in conducting the necessary investigations. But at least the genderless languages give us a point of comparison. And if they tell us anything, it is that the masculine pronoun has little power to oppress the female sex. The historical emancipation of the Finnish woman is part of a wider Scandinavian phenomenon—one welcomed by Ibsen and bitterly complained of by Strindberg. It was neither advanced by the Finnish language, nor retarded by the Swedish and Norwegian. The historical subjection of the Turkish woman was an *Islamic* phenomenon, and her partial emancipation, when it came, was not the result of a "genderless" perspective, but the effect of secularization, and of a quaint old-fashioned belief in modernity. As for the position of Hungarian women, how are we to distinguish it, in general, from the position of women in Bohemia, Moravia, and Austria? Even if we accept the feminist view of traditional Europe as a society based on "patriarchal" oppression, there seems to be little evidence that pronominal gender has done anything either to reinforce or to legitimize the ancestral power of men.

The feminists would, I imagine, be unimpressed by those considerations. The "emancipation" of European women, they will argue, was a matter of local adjustment, whereby the chains of male domination were made to chafe less severely, precisely so that the victim should cease to struggle against them. The true oppression is "structural": it runs through all institutions, not showing itself in overt violence, but maintaining, nevertheless, a persistent and tacit preference for all that belongs to the male. To such a "capillary" oppression language cannot but add its justifying signature, and what better way for women to free themselves than to cancel masculine dominance in this, its longest-standing citadel?

Our language is particularly unfortunate. For gender usually becomes apparent in English only at the pronominal level. In Romance and Slavonic languages, as in Greek, German, Hebrew, and Arabic, gender attaches to every adjective and every noun. The idea that gender has something to do with the sexuality of the thing described is apt to strike the speaker of such a language as faintly ridiculous. Having introduced the moon as *la lune* I must naturally refer to it thereafter as *elle*. But consider some of the vagaries of gender in those languages which are structured by it. In Arabic, for example, all adjectives qualifying plural nouns which refer to nonhuman things must occur in the feminine singular, while the numeral adjectives from three to nine are used in the masculine gender with feminine nouns and in the feminine with masculine nouns. In Czech there are two masculine genders, one for words which describe "animate" objects, and one for words which describe "inanimate" objects; in French the generic pronoun can be either *il* (standing for *quelqu'un*) or *elle* (standing for *une personne*); the Germans refer to girls in the neuter (*das Mädchen*), and agree with the Arabs, French, and Italians in seeing towns as feminine. And so on. All such facts, however interesting in themselves, have not the slightest bearing on sexual politics, and serve only to emphasize the semantic arbitrariness of gender.

In English, however, with a few rare exceptions (such as the personifying *she*), *he* and *she* are used exclusively of things with male or female *sex*. Gender in language is therefore seldom attributed to deep-rooted habits of grammar which are perceptibly beyond the reach of conscious change. It really may seem, to someone faced with the choice of using *he* as opposed to *he or she*, that he is confronting a question of sexual morality, rather than one of conventional usage.

There is an intellectual device that runs through all Marxist and feminist criticism and that is probably the mainstay of radical social analysis in our time. This is the theory of ideology, as adumbrated by Marx and Engels, and the "hermeneutics of suspicion" (to use Paul Ricoeur's apt expression) which derives from it. According to this theory, historical societies have been characterized by distinctive economic structures, by political superstructures which derive therefrom, and by ruling "ideologies." These ideologies arise spontaneously from the social process and render natural and authoritative the prevailing disposition of social and economic power. Ideology includes systems of belief, such as religion, but it is always more than that. It is a form of what Marx called "consciousness," and what current Foucauldian jargon prefers to call "discourse": a mode of systematic representation of the world. This mode of representation may also be systematically false, in the way that lenses can be systematically false—not so much by authorizing this or that erroneous conclusion, but by employing concepts and categories that distort the whole of reality in a direction useful to the prevailing power. Marx believed that there could be a scientific, or unideological, consciousness, and that such a consciousness would be true to reality, in the manner of lensless spectacles. Recent offsprings of the theory have tended to forego that interesting claim, using the theory more as an instrument of criticism than as a prescription for any "correct" understanding of the world. For the Foucauldian, suspicion is all, and power, stark power, lurks behind every discourse, even the discourse which tells us so.

Such a theory has almost unlimited capacity to disestablish existing authorities. Whatever you say, it can penetrate behind your utterance and establish conflagration in your camps. No claim to truth or objectivity can survive its proof that your very *choice of words* is steeped in self-serving falsehood. What matters is not the objective truth-value of a judgment, but the ideological quality of the "discourse" which is employed in it, the implication being that objectivity and truth either have no independent authority, or else are but another "mask." Truth and objectivity are created *within* a given discourse, which are therefore unable to assess it from any point of view that is not its own. "Truth" is but another name for self-serving error. Nietzsche came close to believing this self-refuting proposition. Feminists frequently embrace it in all its absurdity:

> Piercing through to the essence of this debate, Adrienne Rich (1979) summed it up succinctly when she stated that "objectivity" is nothing other than male "subjectivity". The patriarchal order is the produce of male subjectivity and it has been legitimated and made "unquestionable" by conceptualizing it as "objectivity" . . . The meanings encoded under the rubric of psychology, or history, or even biology, for example, have also been political, although not necessarily frankly so. That these meanings have not been open to question, that they have been justified on grounds of "objectivity", is no longer a defence, for "objectivity"—as it has been defined and appropriated by males—is just as much a political act as any feminists are currently engaged in.[4]

This seductive way of thinking does not stand up to a moment's philosophical analysis: if the patriarchal order has been made "unquestionable" by our discourse, how is it that Dale Spender and her colleagues are able to question it? If "objectivity" is another patriarchal mask, what of the theory that tells us so: is it objectively valid, or not? (Neither answer is available; and yet there is no third possibility.) And so on. Nevertheless, ideological criticism seems to offer a method and a goal to the study of literature. In every age critics have recognized that their concern is not with the literal truth or falsehood of a text, but with the values, emotions, and resonances that are conveyed by it. But why are they so concerned? Ideological criticism offers an answer, and one which justifies the critic as no other answer has justified him. Criticism exists, it tells us, precisely to go behind the spurious claims of truth, and to discover the power which is seeking to make use of them. By doing that, we show to be artificial what had been previously perceived as natural, and we expose the reality of choice where choice has been denied. Stripped of ideology, the world becomes a "field of action": the disinterpreted world is *ready for change*.

Ideological criticism has immense charm. For it too can play its part in that "brokerage of power" which it denounces. It promises precisely to *transfer* power, from the one who now possesses it to the one who unmasks him, from the speaker of prevailing discourse to the zealous critic who lays bare the realm of choice. This is why ideological criticism has all but conquered the academic world and become the intellectual center of the humanities. It is the final vindication of the donnish life; the instrument which gives to the teeth-gnashing fantasist his longed-for power over the world of real things. The ideological critic can never stop short at criticism, however. Always he seeks to legislate: to fill the consciousness of men with the ultimate choices that he discerns, and to force open every door against which ordinary humanity has stacked its moral baggage. What is the consequence of this legislative impulse?

When Lenin and his band of bolsheviks took power, they were in the grip of Marxist theory, and sincerely believed that their task would be impeded not only by the bourgeoisie, but also by the Russian language, which had hitherto been steeped in bourgeois ideology. They therefore began to devise a new "discourse," one that would be transparent to the truth of history, and from which the lurking ideology of the "class enemy" would have been expelled. Each thing was to be referred to by its proper (that is, Marxist-Leninist) name. People were divided into "exploiters" and "the proletariat"; references to authority, to the sacred, and to law were either put in inverted commas or else qualified with some pejorative adjective like "bourgeois." "Revolutionary legality," when it came, bore only a superficial resemblance to that "bourgeois legality" which it replaced, just as the newly invented "masses" had no connection with the "common man" of bourgeois thinking. The old language of human relations was also to be purified: "proletarian solidarity" took the place of individual friendship (indeed, friendship between individuals became something like a contradiction in terms); and terms like "peace" and "friendship" were to be applied henceforth not to negotiated relations between those with unequal power, but only to relations of *equality*, in a world in which the "class struggle" had come to an end. (The resulting semantic transformation of the word *peace*—according to which there can be peace only when both parties to it have "accepted socialism"— has had fatal diplomatic consequences.)

It is of no great consequence that the "scientific" theories which inspired the new language are false. Human error has been built into language from time immemorial without destroying man's capacity to correct it: the capacity to say of witches, that there are none; of the Emperor, that he has no clothes; and of patriarchy, that its days are numbered. Of more consequence is the emergence of a phenomenon which is perhaps peculiar to the modern world: the phenomenon which the French and Russians call "wooden language," and which we might call, in honor of Orwell's satire, newspeak. Recent studies by Petr Fidelius and Françoise Thom cast interesting light on the syntax and vocabulary of communist language and both suggest that the revolutionary attempt to *impose* an interpretation on events, by embodying it in discourse, has in fact diverted language from its referential function.[5] It makes no difference that the purpose was to *emancipate*—to reveal the choices that had hitherto been canceled by ideology. Vocabulary, syntax, logic, and style all take on a new purpose, which is not to describe the world, nor even to interpret it, but to *uphold the interpreting power.* The interpretation is no longer understood in relation to the world (the world is of no relevance to the "correct" use of language), but in relation to the political power which decreed it. Linguistic deviations are assessed according to whether they accept or question the tacit claims of power. Hence what matters in any criticism is not its truth or falsehood, but whether it accepts or rejects the legitimizing language.

In Czechoslovakia, for example, you could write that the "fraternal assistance offered by the Soviet Union to the people of Czechoslovakia in 1968 did not lead to effective normalization, and only partially eliminated the counterrevolutionary forces," and the implied criticism would be assigned to some bureaucratic category and ignored. But were you to write "the Soviet invasion of our country conferred the greatest benefit in reestablishing the Leninist system of party dictatorship," you would be arrested at once: not for praising the invasion, but for using language transparent to the thing described. You would have broken the circle of newspeak, whereby words rise free of reality and return always to their dominating purpose, which is to conceal and render "natural" the ruling power. Facts are of secondary importance, and can be amended as linguistic propriety requires. While no party ideologist believes the theories of Marx, all recognize that truth and reference have no serious part in the public discourse of communism. Language is used in another way. Actual events are therefore generally described in abstract terms, as peculiar impersonal processes, contending in a nebulous region of pure power; people are seldom mentioned by name, and actions are assigned to no real personality. Reality appears always as a contest of opposites: "positive" and "negative," "progressive" and "reactionary." But only one thing remains clear: that the power which speaks these terms is "correct," and in no need of criticism from those who are not already absorbed by it.

Here is an example, taken from Mikhail Gorbachev's "new thinking for our country and the world":

Many competent specialists admit that social and economic development in Soviet society can be accelerated and that success in the current drive for restructuring will have positive international consequences. They justly reason that the world community can only stand to gain from the growing well-being of the Soviet people and further progress of democracy. The scope and scale of the social and economic programs undertaken by the Soviet Union bear evidence of, and offer material guarantees for, its peaceful foreign policy. . . . Leaving aside many evaluations and estimates that we see as disputable, we, on the whole, regard this position as realistic and welcome its predominantly constructive orientation.[6]

This passage, chosen at random from a book which proceeds in that vein for 250 pages, could have been written by a party computer; perhaps it was. No people are identified: only "competent specialists," "evaluations," and "estimates"; no events are described: only a vaguely characterized "development," "restructuring," and "further progress in democracy" (further than what?). We are offered a glimpse of "social and economic programmes," and are invited to admire their scope and scale: but what they are, and who is in charge of them, we cannot tell. Everything is bent to the sole task of emphasizing that the Soviet Union is not a threat (it has a "peaceful foreign policy"), and that to recognize this fact is "positive," showing a "predominantly constructive orientation." The passage is succeeded by another, following the Manichaean logic of newspeak, in which those who say that *perestroika* is simply a device to enhance and consolidate the power of the Party are liars and warmongers, propagators of "scares concerning dynamism in domestic and foreign policies," who "hope to cause our people's mistrust towards the leadership." These enemies of the people, we learn, are "ready to use anything to achieve their ends."[7]

The enemy—thus vaguely and abstractly characterized—has no other quality than his determination to speak referentially: he is the one who refuses to enter the charmed circle of newspeak and decides instead to call things by their names. Interestingly enough, Gorbachev concludes his invective by confronting the enemy directly, and in the course of doing so, covertly admits that what the enemy says is true: *perestroika* is indeed another word of newspeak, designed to name and legitimize the Party's monopoly of power:

today members of the Politburo and the Central Committee are unanimous as they have never been before, and there is nothing that can make that unanimity waver. Both in the army, in the State Security Committee (the KGB), and in every other government department, the Party wields the highest authority and has a decisive voice politically. The drive for perestroika has only consolidated the Party's position, adding a new dimension to its moral and political role in society and the state.[8]

The language here is no different from that used by previous leaders, and is as devoid of referential purpose as theirs. But woe betide the person who refuses to speak it, and who, in defiance of the Party, insists on calling a spade a spade.

A student of communist newspeak will be struck by an extraordinary paradox. The attempt to chase ideology from language, to achieve a discourse transparent to social truth, has in fact produced the opposite: a discourse that is *opaque* to truth, precisely because it is devoted to uprooting "class ideology." Such a discourse has *become* an ideology, in the Marxist sense: an instrument for legitimizing power. But it is nothing *else*. As Thom and Fidelius have demonstrated, its referential function has all but "withered away"; so too have the possibilities of deliberation. It is impossible to use such a language to suggest that things might be *fundamentally* changed. It is, moreover, a language in which honest communication is next to impossible, and in which all agreements are canceled in the very act of making them, since neither the subject nor the object of agreement can be defined.

The example returns me to the feminist attempt to expropriate the language of dissent. The feminist, like the Marxist, is deeply suspicious of power—at least, of power in the hands of others—and shares the Marxist conviction that power lurks within the structures of our thought and language and must first be expelled from *there*. Modern English is a "patriarchal" discourse and this, for the feminist, is the most important fact about it. The need arises to expose the underlying patriarchal assumptions, and to offer another language, free from ideology and transparent to social truth. As with Leninism, what is offered is *emancipation*, an opening of the world to previously canceled choices. And, I suspect, the long-term consequences could well be the same as those of Leninism: a complete *ideologization* of language, and a displacement of its primary referential function, so that it ceases to be a medium of rational decision-making, or a means to conversation with one's kind.

Langue de bois emerges only with the seizure of power, and the subsequent emergence of a public discourse of warning. But the way is already prepared for this event by a theory which sees nothing in language *besides* power, and which represents all decisions of style, syntax, and semantics as ultimately reducible to transactions in an ideological "struggle." In this respect, the language of modern feminism can be compared with that of Lenin: a vigilant, depersonalized meditation on a world gripped by hostile powers: "an acute and impassioned *attentiveness* to the ways in which primarily male structures of power are inscribed (or encoded) within our literary inheritance," as one feminist critic has expressed it.[9] The feminist, like the Marxist, wishes to uproot and destroy the power that hides itself in language.

Marxist suspicion was directed towards what Hayek would call the "catallactic" aspects of thought: the aspects which arise "by an invisible hand" and which, while the result of many choices, are themselves never chosen. Like prices in a market, the structures of language are unchosen outcomes of a myriad individual decisions. In this, the follower of Adam Smith might argue, lies their wisdom. They provide solutions to problems that are generated and solved socially. These problems cannot be fully understood by one person, and could never be solved by a plan. Nor can the natural solutions that mankind has hit upon be improved by some steering committee of experts. Such a committee would wish to impose as *law*, and in the teeth of human instinct, a solution which can exist only as a tacit convention. Just as the Leninists ended by displacing the primary functions of discourse and producing a monstrous, all-encompassing version of the very evils that they claimed to fear, so, I suspect, will the feminists produce a new *langue de bois* of their own. The sole study of the user of this language will be to dispose his words and thoughts in accordance with the rules of ideological correctness. Truth, reference, deliberation, and honest feeling: these would take a secondary place, and be recognized, if at all, largely as masks adopted by the patriarchal enemy. When this happens, the writings of English-speaking feminists will be as unreadable as the speeches of Gorbachev.

Notes

1. Sir Ernest Barker, introduction to O. Gierke, *Natural Law and the Theory of Society, 1500–1800*, trans. Barker (Cambridge, 1934), p. lxxi.

2. D. Gauthier, *Morals by Agreement* (Oxford, 1985).

3. Dale Spender, *Man-Made Language*, 2nd ed. (London, 1985), p. 149.

4. Spender, *Man-Made Language*, pp. 61 and 63.

5. Petr Fidelius, *Jazyk a Moc* ("Language and Power") (Munich, 1983), translated by Erika Abrams as *L'Esprit post-totalitaire* (Paris, 1986); Françoise Thom, *La Langue de bois* (Paris, 1987); translated as *Newspeak* (London, 1984).

6. Mikhail Gorbachev, *Perestroika: New Thinking for Our Country and the World* (London, 1987), p. 126.

7. Gorbachev, *Perestroika*, pp. 127, 128.

8. Gorbachev, *Perestroika*, p. 128.

9. Annette Kolodny, "Dancing Through the Minefield: Some Observations on the Theory, Practice and Politics of a Feminist Literary Criticism," in *Feminist Literary Theory: A Reader*, ed. Mary Eagleton (Oxford, 1986), p. 186.

~ SANDRA M. GILBERT

Reflections on a (Feminist) Discourse of Discourse, or, Look, Ma, I'm Talking!

IF, IN A SYNCHRONIC ANALYSIS OF THE PROCESSES of signification through which the (female) subject is constituted, we problematize the intertextual (en)genderings of the signifier, will we foreground the possibility that language itself is always already phallologocentric? In other words, can women talk like women?

My mother would be astounded by the first formulation of this question; she might begin to understand the second one. And these two points "foreground" (you'll pardon the expression) a problem (or perhaps, to be slightly higher brow, a "problematic") that seems to have something to do with the state of the language today. As those of us who are women, feminists, and academics begin increasingly to "deploy" an exclusionary "discourse of theory," what happens to our "status" in a political movement that has long celebrated sisterhood—and motherhood and daughterhood—as both powerful and empowering? If we believe, as some of us do, that we *are* speaking subjects (even if "intertextually" constructed by an elaborate system of "linguistic fields"), to whom do we speak, for whom do we speak, and in what words do we say our say?

In the history of feminism that is now somewhat deprecatingly called "the Anglo-American tradition," women have always tried to write and talk so that lots of other women could understand and be moved by their sentences. The *un*spoken assumption was clearly that "the Movement," so called, should be moving. From Mary Woll-stonecraft's impassioned meditations on the rights and wrongs of womanhood to Margaret Fuller's discussion of "the Great Law Suit" between the sexes, Sojourner Truth's forthright "Ain't I a Woman?," Elizabeth Cady Stanton's sardonic comments on the Bible, and Charlotte Perkins Gilman's frank put-downs of the private home, our tradition has been one of plain speaking. And of course such plain speech persists in the lives and works of a number of otherwise very different contemporary feminists—for instance, Betty Friedan and Andrea Dworkin, Germaine Greer and Gloria Steinem. Yet in the academy, just as (or perhaps because) feminist criticism has come into its own, those of us who spend much of our time, in the words of Mary Ellmann, "thinking about women," are being engulfed in a clamorous tide of "discourses." What do such discourses mean, how might they evaporate meaning, and what might be their consequences for feminism?

Complaining about language—even, to use a newer phrase, putting certain kinds of language "in question"—is, of course, always risky. On the one hand, if you protest vulgarisms or slang, you appear to be a prude. On the other hand, if you dislike specialized or difficult terminology, you seem to be a know-nothing. For second-wave feminists like me, long inured to the sloganeering that inevitably goes with any mass enterprise—"up from the pedestal," "sisterhood is powerful," "off our backs"—the first issue isn't usually either a problem or a problematic. If the political is the personal, so is it also the accessible, the linguistically succinct. But that in itself makes the second issue a real one. Is there any way in which we can reject or revise the language of high theory without being anti-intellectual?

To be sure, such a question might be asked by male as well as female academics, especially literary critics. In the last decades, the old "New Criticism" has been replaced by an array of other *-isms*—structuralism, deconstructionism, Marxism, new historicism—each of which comes *tout ensemble* with its own rarefied "discourse" (or, to put the matter less kindly, its own jargon). And the proliferation of such language has been a godsend for many literary critics, who feel marginal in a culture that by and large scorns poems and novels while revering the arcane knowledge secreted in the technical vocabularies of astrophysics and computer science, brain surgery and market analysis. Privileging and foregrounding, historicizing and defamiliarizing, putting texts *sous rature* or at least in question, manipulating signifier and signified, decontextualizing and interrogating material conditions, the professor of literature is no longer a mere reader, historian, and interpreter. He is both a technician with access to esoteric speech and a kind of philosopher king who lords it over those bodies of language that used to be called "authors." Remember the old joking definition of the literary critic as the guy who cleans up after the authorial elephant? Well, ever since interpretation has been replaced by theory and ordinary language by "discourse," there's no more mopping up after the elephant. The elephant is in fact dead. Long live the erstwhile cleaning man, who marches today at the head of the parade, all decked out in royal robes.

Obviously the strategies of self-certification that can turn cleaners into kings are, and no doubt should be, as available to academic women who do feminist criticism as they are to their male counterparts. But what if such strategies cut us off from many of the readers we need to reach? More, what if adopting the terminology of high theory subtly causes us—in a phrase of Judith Fetterley's—to "identify against ourselves"? That is, what if (to hazard another metaphor) the Empress's new clothes prove merely to be the Emperor's glad rags? It is arguable, after all, that the Emperor can afford to wear odd garments, especially if he only wants to talk to other kings and courtiers, but the feminist Empress presumably wants to make points with ordinary people.

Some current feminist thinkers would claim, however, that the points which most need to be made can *only* be made through the complex discourse of theory. Alice Jardine, herself the author of a difficult and ambitious book entitled *Gynesis*, has summarized this position in wonderfully straightforward language:

> Roughly speaking, *"Anything worth saying can be said simply and clearly"* is our Anglo-American motto par excellence, while much of continental and especially French philosophy and criticism over the past twenty-five years has unveiled the presuppositions of that "simple clarity" with admirable lucidity. To choose an attitude toward interpretation—and therefore toward language—these days is to choose more than just an attitude: it is to choose a *politics* of reading, it is to choose an *ethics* of reading, whose risks and stakes for feminism are what interest me.[1]

In Jardine's formulation, clear and simple language is itself always already contaminated—polluted (though she does not say so here) by a patriarchal context and by a set of unspoken (and therefore primordially powerful) assumptions about origin and authority. And I suspect she would add, in response to any query of mine about "admirable lucidity," that whether or not continental theorists have unveiled such a context and such presuppositions with what most American readers would consider "lucidity," their enterprise has been crucial.

Significantly, Jardine's comment on "our Anglo-American motto" was made at the beginning of an important essay on the Bulgarian-French critic Julia Kristeva, whose *Revolution in Poetic Language* she sees as offering, through "semanalysis," "a non–Cartesian theory of the subject, not dependent on the ideology of language only as a transparent communication system, but as reverberated through the Freudian and Lacanian unconscious." Arguing that Kristeva's "vocabulary was refined and signed" in that work, Jardine exulted that *Revolution* showed us "how semanalyzing poetic language could help us to shed our stubborn Cartesian and Humanist skins—and begin to look beyond the so-called 'message' or 'ethic' of a text to its form, its networks of phantasies; to a sentence's rhythm, articulation, and its style—how it could help us to understand how those elements *are* the message, bound up in a conceptuality that we cannot hope to change only at the level of the utterance."[2]

And no doubt Jardine is right, accurate in her appraisal of the importance and impact that *Revolution in Poetic Language* has had, and right, or at least appealing, in her passionate desire for a way in which women might shed the "stubborn Cartesian and Humanist skins" we have inherited from centuries of patriarchal philosophy. Yet here is part of a passage in which Kristeva (in translation, to be fair) defines "the semiotized body" as "a place of permanent scission," and explains one of her key ideas:

> We view the subject in language as decentering the transcendental ego, cutting through it, and opening it up to a dialectic in which its syntactic and categorical understanding is merely the liminary moment of the process, which is itself always acted upon by the relation to the other dominated [*sic*] by the death drive and its productive reiteration of the "signifier."[3]

What hidebound skins, one wonders, have been shed here—and by what exposed nerves have they been replaced?

To continue being fair: Kristeva is a traditional theorist, a European intellectual who has never, to my knowledge, sought to speak to "the people" or apologized for her participation in the empyrean *Tel Quel* group. Yet even while her descriptive work has been hailed—in the name of linguistic liberation—by a number of American feminists, it has also been (no matter what her own intentions are) closely allied with the *pre*scriptions, rather than *de*scriptions, of such Parisian colleagues as Luce Irigaray and Hélène Cixous. These last two figures, in particular, are the prophetesses of a *parler femme* or an *écriture féminine* in which woman might erotically "come to language" (as Cixous puts it). They are, in other words, the sibyls of a female speech that might be fluid, fluent, multiple, multifarious, and joyful (*jouissant*) in its overturning of the old, rigid, patriarchal "binaries" or "hierarchies." And here is one of Irigaray's celebratory meditations on such language, from her energetically subversive and sophisticated *Speculum*. It is a meditation, as readers will realize, in which—through such stylistic devices as hyphens, slashes, and parentheses as well as through impassioned metaphors—the French theorist practices what she preaches, "disconcerting" language in order to repudiate what she sees as the constraints and coercions of "univocal utterance."

> The (re)productive power of the mother, the sex of the woman, are both at stake in the proliferation of systems, those houses of ill fame for the subject, of fetish-words, sign-objects whose certified truths seek to palliate the risk that values may be recast into/by the other. *But no clear univocal utterance, can in fact, pay off this mortgage since all are already trapped in the same credit structure.* All can be recuperated when issued by the signifying order in place. *It is still better to speak only in riddles, allusions, hints, parables. Even if asked to clarify a few points. Even if people plead that they just don't understand.* After all, they never have understood. So why not double the misprision to the limits of exasperation? Until the ear tunes into another music, the voice starts to sing again, the very gaze stops squinting over the signs of auto-representation, and (re)production no longer inevitably amounts to the same and returns to the same forms, with minor variations.
>
> *This disconcerting of language, though anarchic in its deeds of title, nonetheless demands patient exactitude.*[4]

I quote this passage at such length not only because it is exuberant and anarchic but also because it is prose poetry that is self-consciously aware of the risks it (or its "author") takes through a commitment to "riddles, hints, parables," self-consciously aware of danger, with its weary concession that people may "plead that they just don't understand." But what if people really do plead that they don't understand? What if my mother, and my daughters, and my sisters in "the Movement," *don't* understand? What if they say, *a multiple and anarchic language can't change my life as a woman: it won't pass the ERA, it won't get me a job or an abortion—or child care—and it won't even really help me in graduate school, though it may very well sell books for the "avant-garde."*

Aha: the avant-garde! The avant-garde has "always already" been alienated from "ordinary people," so why shouldn't we feminists "go with the flow"—to descend from the theoretical to the colloquial? No one would pretend, in any case, that literary criticism has anything to do with regular "life." Or would they? I guess, for some of us, in the wake of a major election year, this looks like a serious question. It looks (in our country) as though we ought to wonder whether we should put our energies into an interrogation of clear and simple language or into an effort to *use* clear and simple language, with all its flaws, to change the world (whatever that is).

And speaking of the world, hasn't David Lodge's classically parodic *Small World* already hinted at how, in our solemnity, we revisionary feminist theorists might inadvertently, or advertently, align ourselves with those whose philosophical verities we protest? Readers will perhaps recall that at the end of Lodge's brilliant *commedia d'academia* his erstwhile heroine gives an MLA paper whose excesses seem, at certain points, to exceed even those of the one-time followers of the authorial elephant. "Jacques Derrida has coined the term 'invagination,'" proclaims Angelica, a beautiful theorist of "romance," "to describe the complex relationship between inside and outside in discursive practices. What we think of as the meaning or 'inside' of a text is in fact nothing more than its externality folded in to create a pocket which is both secret and therefore desired and at the same time empty and therefore impossible to possess." But although Angelica discusses Barthes, "climax," "deferred satisfaction," and textual "orgasm" from a determinedly feminist perspective, denouncing Barthes as "overly masculine," "no one . . . in the audience" except for Lodge's naive hero, Persse, seems "to find anything remarkable or disturbing about her presentation." In the *opera buffa* of our profession, the feminist critic can too often, it seems, become a comedienne whose "letter C" (to recall Stevens) evokes little more than, on the one hand, Cooptation, and on the other hand, Cacophony.

I do write here as someone who has argued elsewhere that we women *can* write as women without performing very many linguistic acrobatics. In the final chapter of our recent *The War of the Words*, Susan Gubar and I insisted that language—ordinary language—*is* ours, if for no other reason than that mothers teach daughters how to talk, even when their efforts are mediated, à la Lacan, by patriarchal structures.[5] But the urgency I feel at this moment actually transcends my own theoretical position. At a conference my collaborator and I attended recently, someone punningly suggested to Susan that feminism now occupies a "dying berth" in the academy because it has been so marginalized in "mainstream" culture. We've lost the ERA, George Bush has won the election, who knows what will happen in the Supreme Court, and the so-called Gender Gap didn't do us a bit of good. In humanities departments on university campuses, as I noted earlier, arcane and esoteric vocabularies—those that sound like the language of astrophysics or brain surgery—will always trump clear and simple speech because they will always function to foster self-certification for the marginalized few, who necessarily must define themselves (ourselves) as the fortunate few, the happy few. And given (what one hopes is merely) a temporary faltering of the feminist movement, it may seem to some that such lexical moves are the only ones that might keep us, albeit hermetically, alive.

Yet when Virginia Woolf called for a "woman's sentence," and when she rejoiced that her fictive Mary Carmichael, one of the imaginary heroines of *A Room of One's Own*, had broken "the sequence" of received narrative as well as of patriarchal language, she surely did not think we should be indifferent if people "plead that they just don't understand." In 1974, in an interview that has since been widely reprinted, Julia Kristeva remarked that "In women's writing, language seems to be seen from a foreign land; is it seen from the point of view of an asymbolic, spastic body? Virginia Woolf describes suspended states, subtle sensations, and, above all, colors—green, blue—, but she does not dissect language as Joyce does. Estranged from language, women are visionaries, dancers who suffer as they speak."[6] Throughout *A Room of One's Own*, however, Woolf speaks to, for, and about women: this famous text of hers, in fact, began as "two papers read to the Arts Society at Newnham and the Odtaa at Girton in October 1928."

Always aware of her audience, and of an urgent need to move them, Woolf writes not as an "asymbolic, spastic body" but with an imperative lucidity that seeks to facilitate change. Her prose, in fact, takes for granted the idea that women want to be comprehended by other women, that it would be a bad thing if her listeners and readers said "they just don't understand." Of her radiantly mythic Judith Shakespeare, for example, she argues that "she lives; for great poets do not die . . . they need only the opportunity to walk among us in the flesh. This opportunity, as I think, it is now coming within your power to give her. For my believe is that if we live another century or so . . . then the opportunity will come and the dead poet who was Shakespeare's sister will put on the body which she has so often laid down."[7]

Woolf's romance of a woman writer's linguistic resurrection, then, is really a fierce and hortatory dialogue with an audience which, in her view, *must* understand. And she does not suffer as she speaks; she would suffer if she could not speak. Indeed, were Woolf to "put on the body" that she "laid down" in 1941, she might well wonder what hope there can be for Judith Shakespeare—and for our mothers, sisters, and daughters—if, in our desperate desire to transform a "man's world," we simply buy into some of the equally desperate commodities—the discourses and dialectics, the indeterminacies and idiolects—of that world.

Notes

1. Alice Jardine, "Opaque Texts and Transparent Contexts: The Political Difference of Julia Kristeva," in *The Poetics of Gender*, ed. Nancy K. Miller (New York, 1986), p. 97.

2. Jardine, "Opaque Texts," pp. 107–8.

3. Julia Kristeva, *Revolution in Poetic Language*, trans. Margaret Waller, with an introduction by Leon S. Roudiez (New York, 1984), pp. 27, 30.

4. Luce Irigaray, *Speculum of the Other Woman*, trans. Gillian C. Gill (Ithaca, 1985), p. 143; emphases mine.

5. See chapter five, "Sexual Linguistics," in Sandra Gilbert and Susan Gubar, *No Man's Land: The Place of the Woman Writer in the Twentieth Century*, vol. 1, *The War of the Words* (New Haven, 1988), pp. 227–71.

6. Julia Kristeva, "Oscillation Between Power and Denial," an interview by Xavière Gauthier, trans. Marilyn A. August, in *New French Feminisms*, ed. Elaine Marks and Isabelle de Courtivron (New York, 1981), pp. 117–18.

7. Virginia Woolf, *A Room of One's Own* (New York, 1929), pp. 117–18.

Further Thoughts:
The Correct Spelling of a Secret Word

I AM THINKING ABOUT THE WORD RIDICKLUS, not ridiculous. It's one of my private words, because of its ridiculosity, its complete silliness.

I think I began to use it when I was in boarding school, first about Mrs. Brownley, our housemother. She was a small, dainty, extremely ladylike person, and the ridiculosity in her was because her first job at being a housemother was such a nasty tough one, for her at least: she had to spy on and then break up a ring of hard-core pornographic activity, which went on for about two weeks, every night and often most of every night, after school started in the fall.

My younger sister Anne was one of the willing girls, in a kind of cult or guild that had me a little worried about her, but never enough to tell her so. Of course, I knew all about it but I was never a part of it. From what I remember of those top-lofty years, I may have considered myself above it in some strange way, although all the people concerned with it trusted me and told me everything that went on. This may have been because I was so stupid or naive, but I really do believe that they trusted me because I would never dream of telling on them.

The leader was a girl named Ivy, or Ina perhaps. She left the school in about a month and nobody ever missed her, although she was in complete control of the ring while she lived in the next room to ours. She was overtly in a change in her life when she became completely masculine. Of course, we were all like oysters at that age, so that we could go either way according to the tides and so on. My sister, for instance, was always very female, and was disturbed by the maleness of Ivy/Ina, whereas I recognized the male-girl immediately and never thought any more about it. This recognition was tacit. No words about it were ever spoken between us, but Ivy/Ina knew that I did not worry about her, or myself, or even her partners in the hard-core porn cult, and that my small worry about my sister was of no importance to anyone. I knew that she would survive it and she did.

Ina/Ivy's roommate was a very feminine, exquisite little kid, very sexually aware and alert. It was said that she had been secretly married and had been separated from her lover by her irate and very rich parents and hidden in our prim and private boarding school. She was young, perhaps sixteen, and she ran away in about two weeks. It was interesting, but only I knew about it all apparently, because she escaped one night through our bathroom window to her husband or lover and was never mentioned again.

While she and Ina/Ivy were together they gave a little show late every night on how men and women made love, with Ina/Ivy always on top. I suspect that it was very primitive and simple "missionary" stuff. The girls, though, were even simpler, all of them, so this was an education in a way, and it could have been worse for them.

The night they were raided, I knew it was all arranged, and by then I felt very sorry for Mrs. Brownley, and part of me wanted to warn her about it, but of course I did not. I did not warn the girls either. It went very quickly and discreetly, of course, and there was no talk at all on the surface, and the next night the little girl disappeared with her lover and then two weeks later Ina/Ivy went away too, and my sister Anne went on in her own ways and Mrs. Brownley and I did too, and I don't know who was left feeling the most ridicklus. To me, it was Mrs. Brownley herself, so impossibly ladylike was she and so ridicklusly impregnable was I. Or were we?

Note

M. F. K. Fisher's essay in the 1980 *State of the Language* was entitled "As the Lingo Languishes."

Source

Where did all those tears come from?
Were they the natural spring?
He'd returned, happiness,
He'd won the war. End of the table
Every evening, so bursting with presence
He alarmed his children. What were your tears
Looking for? Something you'd lost? Something
Still hurting? Or
You'd got into a habit,
Maybe during the war, of connecting yourself
To something beyond life, a mourning
That repaired you
And was necessary. You were so happy
Your sisters-in-law lived embittered
With envy of you. Hadn't your tears heard?
The sparrows on the chimney
Cared nothing for God,
Did without the grief-bump,
Tear-ducts, they simply went plop
When your eldest shot them, and dropped backwards
Into the soot-hole. Your sorrowing
Was its own blindness. Or was it

Blinded with tears of the future? Your future,
Fulfilling your most secret prayers, laid wrinkles
Over your face as honours. Your tears didn't care.
They'd come looking for you
Wherever you sat alone. They would find you
(Just as I did
On those thundery, stilled afternoons
Before my schooldays). You would be bowed
In your workroom, over your sewing machine.
They would snuggle against you. You would
Stop the needle and without a word
Begin to weep quietly, like a singing,
With no other care, only to weep
Wholly, deeply, as if at last
You had arrived, as if now at last
You could rest, could relax utterly
Into a luxury of pure weeping—
Could dissolve yourself, me, everything
Into this relief of your strange music.

☙ JAN ZITA GROVER

AIDS: Keywords

IN 1956 RAYMOND WILLIAMS DELIVERED the manuscript of *Culture and Society* to his publisher with a lengthy appendix tracing the shifting meanings of sixty words he considered central to explorations of culture. The publisher demanded a shorter text, and Williams's "keywords" were sacrificed. Twenty years and many additions later, *Keywords: A Vocabulary of Culture and Society* was published. Williams's aim was "to show that some important social and historical processes occur *within* language, in ways which indicate how integral the problems of meanings and of relationships really are."[1]

The words that Williams traced were invented or reimagined at the straining points where old social relationships were giving way to new ones: neologisms (*capitalism*), adaptations or alterations of existing terms (*society* and *individual*), extensions (*interest*) or transfers (*exploitation*) of earlier meanings. Williams read such changes in commonly held meanings as barometers of more widespread shifts in society and culture. He saw them as indicators of "very interesting periods of confusion and contradiction of outcome, latencies in decision, and other processes of a real social history, which can be located rather precisely in this other [that is, linguistic] way, and put alongside more familiar kinds of evidence."[2]

The advent of AIDS as a socially meaningful fact has generated an enormous outpouring of words. Within this immensity of journalistic, political, and medical writing, several terms recur with an uncanny regularity. They cut across these different discourses in a way that might tempt us to conclude that AIDS has brought the worlds of scientist and humanist closer together.

But because of Raymond Williams's work, we might equally—and with greater plausibility—see in their similar usages an indication of shared assumptions already embedded in these discourses.

It was Williams's hope that *Keywords* might open up critical scrutiny of "a crucial area of social and historical discussion" so that the language used to describe our world could be adapted or changed to fit our reality, rather than passively accepted as an already-authorized tradition. Such a critical attention to language is essential to our understanding of and response to AIDS as a social construction.

AIDS is not simply a physical malady; it is also an artifact of social and sexual transgression, violated taboo, fractured identity—political and personal projections. Its keywords, like those identified by Williams, are primarily the property of the powerful. "AIDS: Keywords" is my attempt to identify and contest some of the assumptions underlying our current "knowledge." In this effort I am joined by many AIDS activists, including people living with AIDS.

It is my hope, as it was Williams's, that identification of some of these terms may contribute "not resolution but perhaps, at times, just that extra edge of consciousness. In a social history in which many crucial meanings have been shaped by a dominant class, and by particular professions operating to a large extent within its terms, the sense of edge is accurate. This is not a neutral review of meanings."[3]

Acquired Immunodeficiency Syndrome (AIDS)   As Jacques Leibowitch asks in *A Strange Virus of Unknown Origin* (1985), how do we know when we are faced with a new sickness—something that has not existed before, that cannot be understood and treated under a rubric that already exists.

What is now called AIDS was first pieced together in 1981, when physicians in New York, Los Angeles, and San Francisco, many of whom had noted enlarged lymph nodes (lymphadenopathy) in their gay clients as far back as 1978, began seeing gay men with a very rare pneumonia (PCP) caused by a protozoa, *Pneumocystis carinii*, as well as cases of Kaposi's sarcoma (KS), a cancer of the blood vessels that usually follows a slow and relatively benign course. Previously it had been seen most often among Central Africans and elderly men of Mediterranean origin.

The virulency of PCP and KS among these gay patients pointed to an underlying immune deficiency, since adults with intact immune systems are not normally prey to either disease. Both had been seen, however, in transplant patients with deliberate, drug-induced immunosuppression and in cancer patients whose chemotherapies produced immunosuppression as a by-product of therapy. Initially, the complex of KS/PCP was termed GRID (gay-related immune deficiency), CAID (community-acquired immune deficiency), or AID (acquired immune deficiency). As more symptoms, diseases, and invasive organisms were identified, the complex was further qualified by the medical term, *syndrome*, "a set of symptoms which occur together; the sum of signs of any morbid state; a symptom complex."[4] The syndrome officially became Acquired Immune Deficiency Syndrome, courtesy of the federal Centers for Disease Control, in 1982.

There is a significant distinction to be made between a *syndrome* and a *disease*, one that is not commonly made in the case of AIDS (see below): a *syndrome* is a pattern of symptoms pointing to a "morbid state," which may or may not be caused by infectious agents; a disease, on the other hand, is "any deviation from or interruption of the normal structure or function of any part, organ, or system (or combination thereof) of the body that is manifested by a characteristic set of symptoms or signs and whose etiology, pathology, and prognosis may be known or unknown."[5] In other words, a *syndrome* points to or signifies the underlying disease process(es); a disease, on the other hand, is constituted in and by those processes.

This is not merely a semantic distinction: diseases, if infectious, can be communicated to others; syndromes cannot. What constitutes AIDS is an immune deficiency produced by HIV (the human immunodeficiency virus—see below). A state of severe immune deficiency in the West produces a fairly invariable set of symptoms—in this case, *diseases-as-symptoms*: PCP, KS, severe cytomegalovirus and herpes infections, seemingly ad infinitum. In poor tropical countries, on the other hand, the spectrum and incidence of opportunistic infections are different. In Central Africa, for example, tuberculosis and toxoplasmosis are more common than they are among U.S. patients. In Haiti, PCP is hardly seen at all, but the incidence of cryptosporidiosis and isospora infections is much higher. These differences point to the fact that the immune suppression evincing itself as AIDS works with whatever is already present, though generally quiescent, in an HIV-infected population.

Unlike most infectious diseases, those that commonly afflict people with AIDS are usually incapable of causing overt illness in people with intact immune systems. Many of us have already been exposed to and mildly infected by them. For example, about 50 percent of all adults in the U.S. are infected with cytomegalovirus, a virus that causes blindness among PWAs (people with AIDS; see below).[6] Its devastating pathogenicity occurs only in people with profound immune deficiencies, however; in the otherwise healthy, it may cause a short-term, vague, flulike illness. Similarly, *Toxoplasma gondii*, the protozoan that causes a deadly encephalitis in PWAs, infects about 50 percent of adults in the U.S.[7] In people with noncompromised immune systems, initial infection with these two organisms is followed by latency lasting the life of the host. In people whose immune systems have been severely compromised or destroyed, however, the virus and protozoan are reactivated because the immune system is unable to suppress their emergence as fulminant infections. Because they seize opportunities to cause infection, these diseases are called *opportunistic infections*. They occur only when an opportunity—immune suppression—is present. Within a given medical/cultural setting, these organisms cause the same infections whether a person is immunosuppressed because of a virus like HIV or because of chemotherapy-induced immunosuppression.

The syndrome AIDS, in other words, cannot be communicated, nor can the opportunistic infections that constitute the syndrome be readily communicated to those with healthy immune systems. Mistaking AIDS for a disease is one of our culture's profoundest confusions of a signifier for a sign. We keep pushing the signifying chain toward that ultimate sign—our collective mortality.

AIDS . . . The Disease   The popular press, politicians, and physicians regularly move from speaking of "acquired immunodeficiency syndrome . . . AIDS" to speaking of "AIDS . . . the disease." What are the consequences of this shift?

Diseases, we are taught, are communicable. When AIDS is identified as a disease, many consequences follow—not the least of which is widespread public terror about "catching" AIDS from people in public places or during casual contact.

The communicability of AIDS was fixed in the public and medical memory by early public health reports. AIDS was repeatedly compared to hepatitis B virus (HBV), since both appeared to be blood-borne and sexually transmitted and both were found with great frequency among urban gay men. Before HIV was isolated by the French in 1983, the severity of AIDS and its obvious sexual communicability made the equation of the syndrome with a disease an understandable (if ultimately false) inference. In significant ways, however, the human immunodeficiency virus (HIV) and HBV are not similar at all:

HBV is far more infectious and far smaller, making it more difficult to control (HBV can pass, for example, through natural-membrane condoms, whereas HIV probably cannot).

Because the similarities in HIV's and HBV's most publicized modes of transmission (sex and drugs) are so socially charged, they have obscured HIV's and HBV's equally important differences. The result is that AIDS, a terminal phase of HIV infection, is firmly fixed in people's minds as an HBV-like "disease"—highly infectious, easily spread to the unsuspecting diner or drinker.

AIDS Test   In 1983–84, French and U.S. researchers managed to isolate and culture HIV-infected human T cell-lines, leading to the identification of HIV as the principal causative agent of AIDS. Once HIV could be grown in quantity, it became possible to use protein extracted from inactivated virus as a basis for an HIV antibody test. The enzyme-linked immunosorbent assay (ELISA) was rapidly developed and on the commercial market in March 1985. It has since been used as a screening test for donor blood in U.S. blood banking.

The ELISA reacts to the presence of antibody to HIV in a subject's serum; antibody indicates that the subject's immune system is actively fighting a foreign protein or sugar molecule (in this case, the HIV) that has signaled its presence. There is no unanimity among scientists and physicians on the significance of HIV antibody positivity: it may signal active infection or the body's successful fight against infection. Practically, HIV antibody positivity is taken as a marker of infection with the virus. Antibody positive people are assumed to be infectious (that is, their blood, semen, and breast milk are capable of infecting others).

Like the phrase *AIDS virus* (below), *AIDS test* implies that the invariable outcome of HIV antibody positivity is AIDS—that seropositivity equals AIDS. The phrase is employed regularly in the *New York Times* and *Los Angeles Times*, *Time* and *Newsweek*, the tabloids and television commentary. The practical consequence of this causal and *casual* linkage between antibody positive status and the end-drome, AIDS, has been statutes like the Illinois state law mandating "the AIDS test" as a condition for taking out a marriage license and John Doolittle's California Senate Bill 1001, which the *Los Angeles Times* dutifully reported as a bill (now law) "requir[ing] that the AIDS test be offered . . . to all applicants for marriage licenses." State bills mandating "the AIDS test" for convicted prostitutes, prisoners, and inmates of state mental institutions are under consideration nationwide; the federal government already implements "routine testing" of immigrants, military and other government employees stationed overseas, and federal prisoners.

AIDS Virus   A seemingly ineradicable term, much employed in the popular press but increasingly found in interviews with physicians, scientists, and public health planners as well. The effect of this usage, which conflates HIV (human immunodeficiency virus) infection with a terminal stage of infection—AIDS—is to equate infection with death. It also supposes that the invariable outcome of HIV infection is death, whereas the examples of every other known disease's natural history suggest that a spectrum of outcomes is possible, ranging from quiescent, asymptomatic infection to symptomatic but subacute infection to immune exhaustion and subsequent attack by opportunistic pathogens and neoplasms—what is clinically defined as AIDS.

The only long-term prospective studies of people infected with HIV have documented that approximately half the subjects are diagnosed with AIDS within 8.7 years. Evidence from the San Francisco Gay Men's Health Study, gathered by Nancy Hessol and George Rutherford of the Department of Public Health, San Francisco, uses serum samples gathered and stored since 1978 as part of a hepatitis B study to document infection with HIV and progression among those infected to AIDS.[8]

To date, about 70 percent of the 6,700 men followed have become infected with HIV. Mathematical modeling with the Kaplan-Meier survival curves of these long-infected men suggests that a sizable proportion of them will develop the secondary infections and cancers that are termed AIDS. No data in the study, however, establish the inevitability of death from HIV infection.

The *AIDS virus*, then, remains a term more projective than descriptive. It imposes a mortal sentence on anyone infected with HIV— a projection compounded of fact, hostility, and fear that makes one speak another's death in part to quell one's own anxiety.

AIDSpeak   In his partially fabulous account of AIDS in America, 1980–85, *And the Band Played On: The Politics of AIDS*, Randy Shilts coins the neologism *AIDSpeak*:

> AIDSpeak [is] a new language forged by public health officials, anxious gay politicians, and the burgeoning ranks of "AIDS activists." The linguistic roots of AIDSpeak sprouted not so much from the truth as from what was politically facile and psychologically reassuring. . . . the language went to great lengths never to offend.

AIDSpeak comes by its Orwellian overtones intentionally. For Shilts, the active cooperation that characterized relations between San Francisco's gay male community and the City and County Department of Public Health—as well as the active hostility that characterized relations between New York City's gay male community and city government—are evidence of the threat of politics per se in disrupting the rule of common sense. For Shilts, good bourgeois, his own interpretation of the facts of AIDS is objective, while others are mere propaganda—hence the need to disparage and reduce them. In this, his tactics are fittingly Big Brotherish—war is peace, hate is love.

Shilts introduces this diaphanous concept with an anecdote designed to show the media as tough and public health officials as "behaving like politicians." It is crucial to *And the Band Played On* that the problems with early conceptions of AIDS be laid at the doors of activists and public health officials so that the narrator can stand as one of the lone voices of common sense.

What precisely AIDSpeak consists of is not clear, although Shilts constantly reifies it as if it were ("AIDSpeak was the language of good intentions in the AIDS epidemic; AIDSpeak was a language of death"; "AIDSpeak still dominated public health decision making"; "Under the rules of AIDSpeak . . . AIDS victims could not be called victims"). AIDSpeak appears to be spoken by a strange assortment of characters—characters that his readers might expect to be at odds with one another. This confusion is reflected in Shilts's grammatically and logically contorted proposition that AIDSpeak "allowed *gay political leaders to address and largely determine public health policy in the coming years* because public health officials quickly mastered AIDSpeak, and it was fundamentally a political tongue" (my emphasis). For Shilts, command of a hypothetical language allows "gay political leaders" to determine public policies and to spread the infection of politics to public health, which is not supposed to be a political art. One can only marvel that control of public policy is so easy to come by—and wonder why it is that so many wordsmiths are hiding their political clout under a bushel.

Significantly, Shilts does not condemn the role played by media in producing the discourses he describes with such contempt. Activists' and PWAs' call for an end to terms like *AIDS victim* and *bod(il)y fluids* were aimed at *media*, not at the public health officials and activists that Shilts identifies and condemns.

Bisexual Popular faith in the balkanization of sexual desire being what it is, how to explain the manifest *spread* (see below) of HIV infection into *the general population* (see below)? Enter the epidemic's

1986 model bête noire, the bisexual: only he can account for and absolve the heterosexual majority of any taint of unlawful desire.

The bisexual is seen as a creature of uncontrollable impulses—"their internal denial may make them more dangerous"—whose activities are invariably covert. "Because of their double lives, they may be the most difficult group to reach and counsel," observes Chris Norwood in *Advice for Life: A Woman's Guide to AIDS Risks.*[9] Dr. Art Ulene, the *Today Show*'s resident medic, points to the bisexual as the furtive source of spread: "It also takes only one bisexual man to introduce the AIDS virus [*sic*] into the heterosexual community [see below] . . . the risk is easily hidden when they are having sex with women."[10]

That the dreaded bisexual must find partners within what is otherwise fantasized as the realm of exclusively heterosexual desire and practice is a matter left unexamined in these scapegoating accounts, as is the fundamental identity of heterosexual and homosexual sexual practices. The bisexual is seen as demonically active—the carrier, the source of spread, the sexually insatiable. Such a characterization is necessary to preserve the virtue of his (passive) heterosexual *victims* (see below).

Bod(il)y Fluids   It was not so very long ago that this phrase, drawn from a tradition of imagining the body that goes all the way back to Aristotle, referred to all the "humours" of the body: bile, saliva, blood, urine, semen . . . Everything except fluids peculiar to modern medicine, such as cerebrospinal and interstitial fluids. Originally a specimen of ancient medical theory rather than of verbal prudity, *body fluids* has become a phrase fatally linked to AIDS: will it ever again be possible to think of the phrase save as a code word for transmission routes for HIV?

Today, *body fluids* popularly refers to those human liquids most likely to contain free HIV or the leucocytes that harbor the virus. Although preeminent among these is blood, the phrase resonates most fully as a genteel and unspecific synonym for genitosexual liquids: urine and seminal or vaginal fluid.

The press and networks used the phrase between 1982 and 1987 instead of terms specific enough to be helpful to most people. As a result, AIDS hotlines countrywide received calls from panicked souls worried principally about saliva and sweat. In a miniorgy of self-flagellation, media workers later criticized (and then exonerated) themselves for bowdlerizing transmission information. The U.S. Surgeon General played a large part in setting a standard of bluntness: his belated but useful pamphlet "What Every American Should Know About AIDS" called blood, urine, semen, and the rest by name. So

too have most privately funded AIDS service organizations since
1983.

But using public money to name offending fluids (and practices) has
often been another matter. Here as elsewhere, the political right has set
a disproportionate amount of the agenda by finding such words and
practices as *cum* and *fisting* offensive to their sensibilities and then
holding up the dispersal of education monies to those who don't. The
battle is therefore not only over naming body fluids but over who has
the power to name. Senator Jesse Helms of North Carolina attempted
in 1987–88 to prevent public monies from going to preventive education that might "promote homosexuality" (that is, acknowledge it).
Helms used materials that he found visually and verbally offensive to
argue that federal subsidies to the audiences these materials would
reach were morally indefensible.[11]

Carrier   *Webster's Third* defines the medical meaning of *carrier* as "a
person, animal, or plant that harbors and disseminates the specific mi-
croorganism or other agent causing an infectious disease from which
it has recovered or to which it is immune and that may therefore become a spreader of a disease." The term, as used in media discussions
of AIDS, is accompanied by a faint suggestion of covertness, as if a
carrier had indeed "recovered" or become "immune" to that now invariable accompaniment of *carrier*—"the AIDS virus." The unspoken
model here is Typhoid Mary, asymptomatically infected with typhoid
fever, who in popular fancy *wilfully* continued to work as a food-
handler after her infectious state was made known to her. (That Mary
Mallon was untrained for any other kind of work does not enter into
this fable.)

Randy Shilts's "Patient Zero," a French-Canadian airline steward,
plays this role in *And the Band Played On*. Shilts's treatment of the steward collapses the man's entire life into his sexual practice with an avid-
ity and prurience tailor-made for the use of Jesse Helms and the mass
media. The media in turn dutifully reported the Patient Zero story as
if pointing to this single early case of a person with AIDS symbolically resolved the thorny problem of blame, so central to alleviating
anxiety over the question of who is at risk for HIV infection and to
constructing AIDS as a moral issue.

Condone   In the distinctive public discourse surrounding AIDS, the
verb *condone* is used most frequently by conservative commentators to
obscure and stigmatize practices of which they disapprove: "Provid-
ing/instructing teenagers about condom-use is *condoning* teenage sex";
"To provide condoms to prison inmates is to *condone* homosexual

practices in prison"; "Offering junkies clean needles is *condoning* illegal drug usage"; to write an account of the economic effects of AIDS on a gay couple, as *Money* did in June 1987, is "to *condone* homosexuality," as a California doctor wrote to the magazine in complaint. Here, acknowledgment of empirical fact is deliberately confused with encouragement of controversial social practices.

Significantly, the mass media have not challenged this specious reasoning. To do so would be to open themselves to the same charges leveled by right-wing critics against public health workers: that by raising unpopular issues, they are *condoning* unpopular practices like intravenous-drug use and teenage sexual activity.

The near-universal slippage between transmission modes (for example, shared needles, penetrative sex) and traditionally stigmatized social categories (for example, non-middle-class intravenous-drug users, gay men) in discussions of prevention produces the desired conservative effect: condemnation of social categories and silencing of the opposition (those who would *condone*, that is, acknowledge, their practices). Like Nancy Reagan's "Just say no" strategy for keeping kids off drugs, it treats persons likely to be at risk not as historical subjects operating within specific historical and social formations but as *tabulae rasae* upon which the powerful can write their own cultural scripts.

Family When California state senator John Doolittle sponsored a Senate bill on AIDS and the family in the 1986 legislative session, it passed without a single opposition vote. The bill legalized creation of designated-donor pools to keep donated blood *within families* so as to prevent transmission of HIV from anonymous donors to "the general population." Who, after all, would oppose such a bill? It would be like voting against your mother.

Implicit in the bill, however, was the notion that the family has already cast out its HIV carriers, if indeed it has any. And implicit in this is the belief that those infected with HIV are readily identifiable—visible gay men, street junkies with (shared) needles sticking out of their arms. Righteously cast these out, and the family circle contains only the healthy, those whose blood you would happily share.

Nowhere in Doolittle's bill was there any acknowledgment that families often contain and accept openly gay and lesbian children—and parents—as well as intravenous-drug users (needle-sharing and otherwise). Doolittle's law is written around an idealized and inaccurate notion of the family as a locus of moral and social purity, a zone exempt from conflicts and contagion—or as one that has expelled such problems from its midst. Evidence of how much more problematic real American families are comes from a recent State of Washington study that found directed-donation blood (that is, blood donated by a family member or other designated donor) had a higher rate of HIV infection than randomly assigned donations. So much for the family as bulwark against the coming chaos.

General Population Heterosexual is not a particularly polite word; it's commonly used only in gay circles or in those liberal settings where there are a large number of professed *non*heterosexuals present, where it functions as a self-conscious preface, as in, for example, "Well, I'm heterosexual myself, but . . ." In gatherings where lesbians and gays are not visibly present, the term is seldom needed because the presumed identity of everyone present *is* heterosexual. The term thus plays its differentiating role only in the presence of its implied (or explicit) opposite. This verbal patrolling of the boundaries of normalcy extends to matters other than sexual. Growing awareness of the extent of middle-class intravenous-drug use—particularly of cocaine abuse—produces a similar need to patrol the boundaries and seal off the *not-us*, the *them*, so that the respective turfs remain intact. Hence the usefulness of the phrase, *general population*. As a term, it breathes neither sex nor revolution. Its very opacity guarantees widespread identification—who, after all, would not regard him- or herself as part of the *general population*?

The answer, of course, is that no self-respecting queer, bisexual, or drug user can or should. As a person with AIDS (PWA), James Hurley noted in the 10 August 1987 issue of *Newsweek*, "It hurts me very deeply to read that I'm not part of the general population."

Well, think again. The asexuality, the vagueness of the term, stands in marked contrast to the terms used to describe most PWAs—for example, homosexuals, gays, junkies, intravenous-drug users. The *general population*, according to the term's users (the press, public health officials, politicians) is virtuously going about its business, which is not sexual, not pleasure-seeking (as drugs and gay life are uniformly imagined to be), so AIDS hits its members as an assault by diseased hedonists upon hard-working innocents (see *Victim*). Gary Bauer, former President Reagan's assistant, once explained on *Face the Nation* that Reagan did not even utter the word AIDS publicly before a late 1985 press conference because the Administration had not perceived AIDS as a problem before then: "It hadn't spread into the general population yet." Rather like the Nixon/Agnew phrase *silent majority*, the *general population* becomes the repository of everything that you wish to claim for yourself and deny to others.

Gay/Homosexual Community   If ever a term embodied infinite regression, this one might: the people characterized as the *gay/homosexual community* are too diverse politically, economically, and demographically to be meaningfully described by such a term, whether it's used by spokesmen for said community or by its enemies. (One only has to attempt its opposite, the *heterosexual community*, as a few embattled right-wing politicians have, for the full absurdity of such a term to become clear.) Its convenience is undeniable: one can reduce the troubling diversity of humankind to a single stereotype or scapegoat. Depending on who uses it, *homosexual/gay community* can emphasize human difference ("they're all sick/perverted/sex-crazed") or human similarity ("we're all healthy/normal/under attack"). It fastens upon that which is most frightening and alluring in an other—for example, gay men's (fancied) freedom from sexual and family constraints—and projectively makes them the sole markers of an identity. Like the disembodied "they" of childhood plaints ("All the other kids do it"), the vague "they" of the *homosexual community* gets everything we're denied, both extreme pleasure and extreme pain. Just don't ask who the *they* or the *we* are, or the tent folds in on itself: *they* are those who have already been defined as victims of their own excesses, those-who-have-AIDS.

Heterosexual Community   Embattled conservatives have discovered yet another community that is discriminated against: their own. Though the primacy of heterosexuality in our nation's laws, education, politics, medicine, and culture would seem to sufficiently guarantee the security of man-woman units to make their status unremarkable, the compulsion to define oneself in terms of an other operates with a fine extravagance here.

The modern connotation of *community* comes interestingly into play in the phrase *heterosexual community*. Williams notes in *Keywords* that from the midnineteenth century,

> the sense of immediacy or locality was strongly developed in the context of larger and more complex industrial societies. *Community* was the word normally chosen for experiments in an alternative kind of group-living. . . . *What is most important, perhaps, is that unlike all other terms of social organization . . . it seems never to be used unfavorably, and never to be given any positive opposing or distinguishing term* [my emphasis].[12]

Particularly since the mid-1960s, the noun *community* in the U.S. has been most frequently invoked as an oppositional term to identify a local, ethnic, racial, or political variant to the mainstream.

To find the mainstream identifying itself as a variant, then, is surprising news. The political conservative battling for the *heterosexual community* is clearly not weighing in against social and cultural forces that have shut him or her out. But because the widely hypothesized *homosexual community* must be seen here as a negative and (crucially) aggressive, recruiting community (see *Bisexual* and *Victim*), its opposite—the *heterosexual community*—must be devised as its positive opposite. Viewed from within, the heterosexual majority becomes the mirror of the victimized minority community, besieged from without.

Lesbian   Sexual desire being one of the chief markers of modern identity, the woman whose desire turns toward members of her own sex has been marked out as essentially and socially different from the *general population*. She shares this illicit status with, for example, gay men, blacks, intravenous-drug users. Gay men, blacks, and intravenous-drug users are members of known *risk groups* (see below) for AIDS. Therefore lesbians are also probably at high risk for AIDS. How well does this syllogism play for you?

It's played fine with blood banks and physicians. In 1982–83, local branches of the American Red Cross advised that lesbians should self-defer as volunteer blood-donors, as gay men were being urged to do. In Britain, tainted lesbian blood still occupied space in the pages of the medical journal *The Lancet* in the summer of 1986: "Should 'Lesbians' Give Blood?" (16 and 30 August). In the summer of 1987, the Sonoma County (California) Red Cross turned down a proposal by a group of women's motorcycle clubs to turn a weekend run to the Russian River into a blood drive. Sonoma County didn't want lesbian blood.

It is probably restating the obvious to note that there is a lower incidence of HIV infection among lesbians than any other population group tested (see also *Prostitute*). So the scare about lesbian blood has less to do with rational fears about transmission of HIV than with fear of sexual and social taint, the sort of taint that surfaces obsessively in lesbian vampire fantasies in such films as *Daughters of Darkness* and *The Hunger*.

At the federal Centers for Disease Control, lesbians are people who can be diagnosed with AIDS only through sexual contact with men (intravenous-drug users, bisexuals, hemophiliacs, persons born in some African and Caribbean countries, and so on), transfusions of blood or blood products, treatments for blood disorders, or intravenous-drug use. Like Queen Victoria, the CDC evidently cannot imagine sex between women as a source of infection. In effect, by providing no transmission category for cases of woman-to-woman sexual transmission, they have ensured that such diagnoses will not be made.

Prostitute   Prostitutes have been blamed for breaches in national security, the fall of principalities and mighty men, the desecration of home and hearth.[13] Now they are being blamed in many quarters for the *spread of AIDS* (see below). HIV-infected prostitutes in Florida, Texas, and California have received a great deal of media attention, including one woman in Florida whose sentence included wearing an electronic collar to alert police when she left her house. The medical, public health, political, and media attentions paid to prostitutes as a significant source of infection function primarily as a scapegoating device. They make no distinction between prostitutes who are intravenous-drug users and prostitutes who are not. In this respect, the category *prostitute* is taken as an undifferentiated *risk group* (see below) rather than as an occupational category whose members, for epidemiological purposes, are divided into intravenous-drug users and nonusers, each of whom has significantly different rates of HIV infection.

In the long-term study of sexually active women (professionally and nonprofessionally) conducted by Project AWARE at San Francisco General Hospital, for example, the incidence of HIV infection among non-intravenous-drug-using sex-industry workers was lower than it was among nonprofessional, non-intravenous-drug-using women. The difference is accounted for by prostitutes' widespread demand that clients use condoms, something that most nonprofessional women do not demand of their sexual partners. Other U.S. and European studies that distinguish between prostitutes who use intravenous drugs and those who do not have produced similar findings.

Like lesbians, prostitutes are viewed as embodiments of infectivity less for their actual rate of infecton than for their symbolically and historically tainted status. This is even more sensationally the case when the prostitutes in question are male prostitutes. Women's "frailty" might be forgiven by the fathers, but what of their erring sons? Dr. Art Ulene, in his *Safe Sex in a Dangerous World*, typically reserves his deepest contempt (and fear) for the male prostitutes who "still *dot* the streets of my city" (like the plague? like Kaposi's?), men so lacking in self-respect and restraint that they are lost to all appeals to decency. (That male prostitution, like female prostitution, is primarily an economic formation remains unspoken here.)

PWA (Person with AIDS)   At the second AIDS Forum held in Denver in 1983, a group of men and women with AIDS and AIDS-related complex (ARC) met to form an organization that would speak to their own needs. The Advisory Committee of People with AIDS, forerunner of today's National Association of People with AIDS, issued the following statement: "We condemn attempts to label us as 'victims,' which implies defeat, and we are only occasionally 'patients,' which implies passivity, helplessness and dependence upon the care of others. We are 'people with AIDS.'"

At the 11 October 1987 Lesbian and Gay Rights March on Washington, PWAs from all over the U.S. took the naming of their condition one step further, announcing that they were "people *living* with AIDS (PLWAs)." It is a measure of the press's need—left, center, right—to distance itself from AIDS that few journalists have chosen to employ the term; the commonest usage in the media is *AIDS victim* (see below). Nor is *PWA* widely used by physicians, for whom the PWA is first and foremost a *PT*, *patient*, or *case*. Politicians, particularly on the right, rarely use *any* term to describe people with AIDS: their manifest concern is with those who remain uninfected, the *general population* who must be protected from AIDS. This is probably a prudent move: calling attention to the need for protecting the healthy majority from the (AIDS) victim minority would make its absurdity clear.

More recently, the term PWA has been supplanted in some activists' vocabulary by *PLWA* or *PLA* (person *living* with AIDS). There are subtle shadings of emphasis in these usages that vary from America to Britain. American PWAs deployed the term *PLWA* in order to emphasize the fact of their survival, the living on terms with their diagnosis. This reflected not only personal optimism and group solidarity but also the fact of longer survival. In San Francisco, for example, the average life-expectancy following diagnosis of PCP was 9.8 months in 1986 and over 20 months in April of 1989. *PLWA*, then, countered the popular equation AIDS=DEATH with a corrective image of AIDS as a diagnosis one lives with.

The British usage, *PLA*, on the other hand, also attempted to correct the equation AIDS=SELF—in other words, the collapsing of an entire life into a diagnosis. Employed in the British newsletter *Positively Healthy*, *PLA* emphasizes that AIDS is an addition to a person's identity, not something that supplants it. Such usage reflects the influence of psychoanalytical and poststructuralist theory in contemporary British thinking on gay identity. Writers like Jeffrey Weeks, Simon Watney, and Stuart Marshall (editor of *Positively Healthy* and director of the important 1985 videotape *Bright Eyes*) see identity as fragmented, contradictory, and dynamic. *PLA* is meant to reflect this conviction by making the phrase *living with AIDS* modify the agent himself or herself.

Risk Group   The concept of *risk group* is an epidemiological one; its function is to isolate identifiable characteristics that are predictive of where a disease or condition is likely to appear so as to contain or prevent it. In the case of AIDS, the syndrome was first identified in gay men, leading CDC and other researchers to speculate on the possibility that something they termed "the gay lifestyle" may itself have been responsible for the condition. Among the factors thought possibly responsible were amyl nitrate poppers, rogue genes, sports of common sexually transmitted diseases (STDs), too much sex ("excessive assaults on the immune system"), fast-lane living.

The discovery in late 1981 that Haitians and intravenous-drug users were also acquiring the syndrome did not square with this theory. A virus quickly became the prime suspect, though it would not be identified until spring of 1983. Still, the concept of *risk group* remained useful for public health preventive purposes in the early years of the epidemic: it roughly identified people whose membership in a group by *risk behaviors* was likely to bring them into contact with the virus. What should have followed, however, did not: before 1986, public health officials in the U.S. did not make nationwide, visible efforts to inform people of how the virus was transmitted. Even then, initial efforts were hedged around with euphemisms ("Avoid exchanges of body fluids") and moralisms ("When it comes to preventing AIDS, don't medicine and morality teach the same lessons?" quoth Ronald Reagan to the American College of Physicians in 1987).

Most commonly, in the media and in political debate, the epidemiological category of *risk group* has been imported into public discourse to stereotype and stigmatize people already seen as outside the moral and economic *cordon sanitaire* of "the general population." Jesse Helms's October 1987 success in preventing federal dollars from supporting safer-sex information for gay men, the hardest hit "risk group" in the U.S. (as well as the only one in which new transmission of the virus has declined—to less than 2 percent of new infections in San Francisco in 1987) makes clear the social and political (as opposed to *epidemiological*) functions of the risk-group concept: to isolate and condemn people on the basis of their demographic profile rather than to use it to advise and protect them. Here it functions much like the conservative use of the term *homosexual/gay community* in assuming uniform behavior and beliefs.

Risk Practice   This concept has replaced *risk group* for all but surveillance purposes in the thinking of the National Academy of Sciences. It moves the emphasis away from characterizing and stigmatizing people as members of high-risk groups. The aging of the epidemic has made clear the HIV's indifference to human categories like *drug abuser*, *faggot, innocent victim*, and *cock-sucker*. It doesn't care whether it enters the body of a nurse or a prostitute, a Paul Gann (state senator from California) or a gay man. As heterosexual transmission increases, the only meaningful *risk behaviors* become injection and penetrative sex, both of which are voluntary activities engaged in by people of every sexual persuasion.[14]

The continued emphasis upon *risk groups* rather than *risk practices* in press and political discussions of AIDS masks the evidently unspeakable fact that functionally there *are* no differences in the sexual practices engaged in by gay men and heterosexual men and women.[15] It overinsistently calls attention to the reassuring specter of *sexual difference* as the Scylla protecting heterosexuals.

Spread   Our sense of an unfamiliar illness is constructed largely through the language used to describe it. In the case of AIDS, the terms *carrier* and *spread* are central to popular descriptions of HIV transmission.

AIDS is popularly seen as a disease initially confined to identifiable *risk groups* who were not themselves part of the *general population*. *Spread*, or *leakage*, as it is sometimes termed, suggests the insidious movement of the syndrome, infection, and its carriers as they move outside their "natural" limits. *Spread* and *leakage* share common sexual and pollution connotations embodied in media descriptions of gay male sexual practices and social haunts; the anus (for popular purposes regarded as an exclusively gay-male orifice) becomes a cesspool, an unnatural breeding ground for the "AIDS virus"; bathhouses and bars like the Mine Shaft become the luridly described sewers or *loci* of leakage and spread. Similar usages are employed in discussing prostitutes.

Victims   *Webster's Third* tells us that "*victim* applies to anyone who suffers either as a result of ruthless design or incidentally or accidentally." It is a term that people with AIDS share with others living with terminal illnesses—most particularly cancers and degenerative conditions. Who nominates "victims" of illnesses *as* victims? It would appear that *victim* is a neutral, descriptive term for a person on whom an undeserved ill fate is visited. Hence the cliché: we are all potential victims. A victim is someone like us, someone for whom we have empathy. What, then, is wrong with *victim*?

1) *the fatalism*. Within the many self-support groups founded by people with life-threatening diseases, the term is emphatically rejected. Yet it persists in the media, among healthcare workers, among politicians battling for "victims' rights." Fear and pity are the emotions raised by the victim; these are less than useless emotions for dealing actively with serious issues. Fear and pity are aroused in order ul-

timately to be cathartically disposed of, to enable passive spectators of the AIDS "spectacle" to remain passive, and eventually to distance themselves from the scapegoated object of fear and pity.

Fatalism implies that nothing, or next to nothing, can be done about the cultural, social, and medical crises presented by AIDS. It denies the very possibility of all that is in fact being done by PWAs and those working with them. The opposite of the fatalistic term *victim* is *aggressor, assaulter*—a role too frequently taken by those most determined to see people with AIDS as victims.

2) *the effect of cancellation.* The term functions most obviously as a distancing device, a conceptual and verbal boundary separating *victims* from the rest of us, the (presumably) healthy who can afford to patronize and pity those less fortunate. The need to maintain this safe distance sometimes approaches the hysterical—for example, a student in the "Media(ted) AIDS" class I taught at California Institute of the Arts in the fall of 1987 who called a social services organization to inquire about specific services for people with AIDS was connected to a social worker who immediately corrected his use of the phrase *people with AIDS*. "No," she told him, "They're *AIDS victims.*"

3) *the negative psychological sense.* In a modern "psychological society," we cannot live our fatalism undiluted. Fates are often joined by unconscious wishes, and victims are often seen as in some way complicit with their fate. Victims of rape, for example, must constantly battle the suspicion that they were "asking for it," and women (and gay men) are often equated with a kind of emotional masochism that allows them to be victimized. Victims always end up revealing some tragic character flaw that has invited their tragedy. Current favorites on the pop psych circuit are *internalized homophobia, unhealthy lifestyle, Type A personality.* Despite Susan Sontag's contention in *AIDS and Its Metaphors* that AIDS has yet to be psychologized, that particular frontier has long since receded.

The proof that *victim* is not simply a term applied to the unlucky, to those undeserving of and noncomplicit with their fate, is the frequently employed phrase *innocent victim,* which is not seen as redundant. "The most innocent victims" is *Newsweek*'s caption accompanying two photographs, one of two young parents and an infant, the other of a woman with a small child. The caption implies that other people with AIDS are less innocent. The *Village Voice*'s Nat Hentoff, who has shown considerably more compassion for unborn fetuses than for PWAs, has found the linguistic device that neatly captures the distinction between guilty and innocent victims, replacing the telling redundancy *innocent victims* with one that identifies them instead as "victims of AIDS victims."

A patronage that simultaneously grants "victims" powerlessness and then assigns them blame for that powerlessness is nothing new. It's important to make the connections between the ideological construction of AIDS victimhood and similar concepts visited on the poor, who also suffer the triple curse of objectification, institutionalized powerlessness, and blame for their condition, as well as on people with other mortal conditions. (People with cancer, for example, are frequently exhorted to *search their hearts* for the bad habits, the cancer-inducing behaviors or personalities that provoked their condition.)

War on AIDS   War was defined not so long ago as failed diplomacy or diplomacy *in extremis*; it was waged against other people (reified as *the state* or *sovereign*). More recently, war has been waged against a number of shadow enemies that might more accurately be seen as structural defects in our society: poverty, drugs, pornography, cancer, and now AIDS. "Enemies" are hard to identify in social phenomena as complex as drug-dealing and drug-taking; it's easier to turn pent-up anger against the first displacements available—persons who can be made to *embody* the problem.

This is easy but unproductive. As Admiral James Watkins, appointed Chairperson of the Presidential Commission on the HIV Epidemic, told an interviewer on the Public Broadcasting Services' 1989 *AIDS Quarterly*, "I found I'd been in the military too long . . . the military was a lot easier" than AIDS. The reduction of a complex problem to the figuration of warring sides did not help the Admiral to understand America's HIV epidemic. He rejected the war model for his inquiry after several weeks on the job.

Yet he resurrected it at his surprise press conference in June 1988, the day before the Committee's report was sent to Reagan (a move he is widely believed to have made to ensure that its recommendations would not be buried by the White House; Reagan in fact never did comment directly upon or implement the Committee's recommendations), calling for an all-out war on AIDS. He conspicuously trained his sights against the structural enemies within the epidemic (health-care systems, the Food and Drug Administration, housing, employment, and legal discrimination) rather than on people as enemies. In doing so, he recurred to war metaphors to emphasize the assessment and deployment of resources against common (if uncommonly defined) enemies. This use of war as metaphor emphasizes mobilization of forces, a usage also urged by Mary Catherine Bateson and Richard Goldsby in *Thinking AIDS: Social Responses to the Biological Threat* (1988).

Susan Sontag, on the other hand, has called for an end to all war metaphors, which she sees as invariably reductive and belligerent. But

Sontag does not concern herself in *AIDS and Its Metaphors* with how such metaphors currently play themselves out in policy-making and other cultural practices. Instead, her interest in AIDS is primarily that of the term (and its metaphors) used as a second-order signifier for *fin-de-siècle* doom and gloom. Those instances of military thinking about AIDS that she cites as examples in the here-and-now amount virtually to straw men; it is only when she wields AIDS as a metaphoric displacement for various contemporary malaises that her stake in describing AIDS becomes apparent.

If it is true that we understand our worlds largely through language, then we need to pay closer attention to the words with which we shape our understanding of AIDS. We must make connections, wherever and whenever possible, between the keywords of AIDS and the wider vocabulary of power struggles to which these words are linked.

Notes

An earlier version of this essay appeared in *October* 43, published by the MIT Press. Copyright 1988 by October Magazine Ltd. and MIT.

1. Raymond Williams, "Introduction," *Keywords: A Vocabulary of Culture and Society*, rev. ed. (New York, 1983), p. 22. Williams's account of *Keywords* can be found in the introduction, pp. 11–15, and *Raymond Williams: Politics and Letters* (London, 1981), pp. 175–77.

2. Williams, "Keywords," in *Politics and Letters*, p. 177.

3. Williams, *Keywords*, p. 24.

4. *Dorland's Medical Dictionary*, 26th ed. (Philadelphia, 1985).

5. *Dorland's Medical Dictionary*.

6. H. Stern and S. D. Elek, "The Incidence of Infection with Cytomegalovirus in a Normal Population: A Serological Study in Greater London," *Journal of Hygiene* 63 (1965): 79–87.

7. J. A. Krick and J. S. Remington, "Toxoplasmosis in the Adult—An Overview," *New England Journal of Medicine* 298 (1978): 550–53.

8. Nancy Hessol, George Rutherford, et al., "The Natural History of Human Immunodeficiency Virus Infection in a Cohort of Homosexual and Bisexual Men: A 7-year Prospective Study" (abstract), Third International Conference on Acquired Immunodeficiency Syndrome (AIDS) (Washington, D.C., 1987).

9. Chris Norwood, *Advice for Life: A Woman's Guide to AIDS Risks* (New York, 1987).

10. Art Ulene, *Safe Sex in a Dangerous World: Understanding and Coping with the Threat of AIDS* (New York, 1987).

11. For an account of Helms's maneuvers, see my "Safe Sex Guidelines," *Jump Cut* (Spring 1988), and Douglas Crimp, "How To Have Promiscuity in an Epidemic," *October* 43 (Winter 1987): 256–66.

12. Williams, *Keywords*.

13. See Alan Brandt's *No Magic Bullets* (Oxford, 1985) for an account of the positioning of prostitutes as scapegoats during World Wars I and II.

14. Nursing an infant is another proved mode of transmission, but since it is not

hedged round with the fretwork of hysteria characterizing the concept of *risk groups* (*mothers?*), I only note it here.

15. I say functionally because of course there is a technical difference in anal-penetrative sex when a man rather than a woman is the receptor. Structurally, this is a minor difference—a variation, one might think. Symbolically, however, this hotly contested (male) hole remains, for the heterosexual man, a site of extreme privilege—his pink badge of *virtù*, so to speak.

❧ WAYNE KOESTENBAUM

Speaking in the Shadow of AIDS

—for C., in memory of his brother

BECAUSE I HAVE LIVED TO SPEAK ABOUT AIDS, what I say about it appears relative, fussy, only true to a point. AIDS is not the only crisis that dwarfs language and makes speakers weigh their sentences; but AIDS is exemplary, among contemporary catastrophes, in demanding that we examine the disaster itself as a consequence of words.

From the start, AIDS posed vocabulary difficulties. Should it be called GRID, gay cancer, the plague? Is it caused by the "AIDS virus," by HTLV-III, by the African Swine Fever Virus? These problems in nomenclature disguise the question of who owns AIDS, who has the primary right to speak of it. As cultural capital of escalating value, it has become a contested body, claimed by countries, doctors, writers, politicians, celebrities, and quacks. Because of the number of bidders, speaking about AIDS can seem a usurpation, a demand to be first, a totalitarian and unilateral forging of the terms under which others must live; but nothing I present in the following pages is strictly my own. I want only to give a subjective rendering of widely understood propositions; to manipulate a grammar I did not invent; to observe AIDS coalesce into four themes, without the indulgence of variation, or the rigor of exposition.

Silence

Evasions mark the public debate on emergencies such as poverty or arms control, but elisions have an apparently inevitable, or organic, relation to AIDS. Hence, activists have mobilized against silence itself as the enemy. Inside cash machines, and over the mouths of models advertising diet drinks, members of ACT UP place stickers with the slogan "Silence=Death," as if cash, and "Lite" ads, were part of the fatal conspiracy, linked, through the logic of protest, to the gays slain by Nazis, victims memorialized by the pink triangles that are so ubiquitous and welcome in New York City, where my encounter with AIDS began. Every fragment of public speech that does not directly address AIDS—so these stickers claim—indirectly kills through the agency of omitted words; every dollar is a murderer if it is not spent on AIDS care or research. Although ACT UP suggests that speaking out fully and publicly about AIDS is always beneficial, civil libertarians claim silence is a privilege, and wish to protect the right to keep sexual preference secret, or to withhold results of the HIV antibody test. Disclosure and confidentiality are particularly at war in AIDS obituaries: the wish to conceal the cause of death opposes the need to document the disease's reach.

Even when AIDS is disclosed, it means more than simply a sickness. The word *AIDS* implies sociological categories—a population, an inclination, a failure; a primary affiliation (gay, Haitian, drug user) that is assumed to pave the way to sickness. The word *AIDS* thus becomes an accusation, and an act of housekeeping; it clarifies the caste system of the culture it assaults.

AIDS, as sign, is not so much silent as tentative; ambiguous, it defeats our effort to speak clearly and to understand the meanings of symptoms, physical or linguistic. AIDS poses interpretive problems for which there are not always absolute solutions. What do the test results mean? What is this purple spot on my face? Why am I sweating at night? Is this thrush? Has anyone recovered? Does living with AIDS for five years mean dying for five years? Do I have *Pneumocystic carinii* pneumonia, or do I have AIDS? The notion of "possession" is itself questionable. Does one "have" a disease? Is it a discrete entity to be owned? Rather, AIDS seems a *tendency*—a direction but not a predestination, a likelihood but not a finality. When speaking of AIDS, words cease to offer documentation; words become the markers of fear and hesitation. It is not simple to interpret contradictory data, to phrase each physical sensation, or to calculate the nearness of death.

In response to obfuscation and hysteria, it is impossible to believe the "figures"—neither the forecasted death tolls, nor the public men and women who assemble evidence and put it into words. The gay press entertains conspiracy theories; the common reader, part of the fictitious "general population," trusts that the disease is everywhere and nowhere, a neighbor and a foreigner. AIDS must borrow the rhetorical strategies of the Cold War because it was not born with its own vocabulary. No disease has an intrinsic language; it assumes an identity within a society. Though AIDS, as we know it, is inseparable from the verbal and prejudicial structures that mantle it, it also contains elements of a more archaic, essential dialect: sounds of pain, phrases of regret.

Because a person with AIDS (PWA), facing isolation or eviction, may hide the disease, and because the syndrome first achieved notoriety among gay men, AIDS—as guilty secret—has been linked, like homosexuality itself (the love that dares not speak its name), to unspeakability. In response, activists seize AIDS as a chance to decry silence, to refuse it. And yet protest and protection often take the form of wordless innuendo. Gay men, for example, made a token of seduction out of infancy's safety pin. Like all codes, safety pins close up; they keep their point to themselves. But when unclasped, they draw a drop of blood. All indirections, like this safety pin, promise security and immunity, but possess a sharp point—a moment of reckoning, an instant when, finally, subterfuge is no longer possible. In the era of Silence = Death, sly or shy signs cease to be revolutionary, even if they promise to save lives.

Nervous Public Speech

As Simon Watney, Sandor Gilman, Susan Sontag, Leo Bersani, Douglas Crimp, Cindy Patton, and many others have said (and it needs to be repeated, it is such a difficult lesson), there is no a priori category of experience—and experience's deliquescence—called "AIDS."

Even if, on this subject, Reagan kept his lips strictly, fastidiously, stupidly shut, and neither candidate in the 1988 presidential campaign expressly addressed the issue, AIDS has—everywhere but in these obvious summits of power—provoked nervous, excessive, unregulated speech. It makes news, and requires advertising: four-part stories in the *New York Times*; condom ads on subways, billboards, TV—each directed to a different community, white or Hispanic, gay or straight, drug-using or "clean." Languages and vocabularies describing how to prevent the disease proliferate because it can't yet be cured. Terms are invented and circulated; AIDS operates, in the media, like any event—transformed into a newsworthy situation, and then turned off. AIDS will only be news as long as it feeds a dread that sells. Though AIDS remains closely associated with silence, what is, finally, silent about it? It speeds into print. No customs agent can stop it, and precisely because of its quickness, the syndrome excites vigilance on geographic, linguistic, sexual, racial, and economic borders.

Michel Foucault, who died of AIDS, gave us a theoretical framework to explain how private language and life are webbed by public forces. We may think we control words, as if they were neutral, transparently instrumental, but language is larger than our efforts to wrangle it into reflecting our desires. Think of all the words spent in the name of AIDS—preventing it, fearing it, spreading our ignorance around like music. AIDS may present us with an excuse for declaring our alienation from public language, and yet the suffering and sorrow we have learned to call "AIDS" only shows how our bodies are veined by a coursing power that seems remote but is nearby, and that finds a voice in every fragment of public speech. Public events—newspapers, congresses, sound bites—manipulate and mangle the way we interpret our bodies, our lives, and our deaths. How, then, can we trust that any physical sensation is truly private? Even if we feel aloof from the media, or from governmental utterance, we are implicated by the advertisement's slur, the politician's omission.

Because language is multiple, the word "AIDS" always means more, and differently, than we intend. There is no possibility of an independently elected language; every word is stained by community. Any self, whether founded in nationality, religion, or sexual preference, depends on vocabularies coined by an omniscience sometimes called history. The *AIDS* subjected to celebrity benefits is the same *AIDS* hurled as insult. One disease, one word, appears in a patient's medical chart and in a piece of graffiti ("your butt full of AIDS-tainted cum"). We may wish AIDS to be merely a medical classification, or a private wound, but it has been put to communal uses. It has served as a pretext for loathing. Like glamor and notoriety, purity and filth, it divides the world in two; and we cannot will it, through careful speaking, back into a single, harmless whole.

Confession

Gay liberationists, from the start, have assumed that to be "queer"— or at least to admit it—is political. In elaborating AIDS as a platform in gay politics, activists have relied on the theme of "coming out"; identifying oneself as a PWA, they claim, is emancipatory, a gesture meant to reverberate throughout a community, and to change the conduct of nations.

I agree that private speech may bring public change, that confession means freedom for more than the one who confesses. The privileged speaker, in this case, is the person with AIDS. If anyone fears a PWA's speech, it is because a PWA, confessing, dares to be inappropriate and unpleasant; his or her simplest sentence threatens the political order that neglects AIDS research or impedes the availability of new drugs. By asserting, however, that a PWA cannot help but stir up trouble by talking, I sentimentalize his or her position, and turn revolution into keepsake—as if the political resonance of PWA speech lay only in its truculent pathos, the words quickly becoming posthumous.

These memorials, these private, atomistic uses of language, add up into open outcry. The Names Project Quilt was assembled from pieces of speech, sewn into a fabric of common cause; tapping the techniques of patriotism and of Yankee frugality (the sewn flag, the sampler, the patched, darned garment), as well as a resistant tradition of female quilting, mourners spoke through accumulation, and made multitude itself a message. Piecework formed an instant monument, and signaled the end of solitary speaking. Some tragedies seem intended; they proceed from individual actors whom we can blame. Other emergencies exceed any one catalyst; because disaster is various in its causes, the language opposing it must also be collective and diverse. To speak effectively about AIDS, we must abandon the single author, the myth of redemptive individuality. AIDS is not just another subject demanding sentence production as protest and catharsis. More than an excuse for making statements, for expressing oneself, AIDS exposes the solitary voice in the wilderness as a fiction, inadequate and outmoded. With the demise of the omnipotent "I," a general faith in literary speaking has disintegrated, for literature depends on a gradual, genial handing down of authority from generation to generation. AIDS, killing off young and old at random, disturbs that rhythm, a cycle that endowed even such radical poetic projects as Auden's and Spender's, in the 1930s, with a sense of measure, propulsion, and optimism. Writing their political poems, they could trust that they would outlive Spain's revolution; they could look forward to the melancholy of retraction and recantation. Paul Monette, however, began his AIDS memoir, *Borrowed Time*, by saying, "I don't know if I will live to finish this." Long before AIDS, writers worked with the knowledge of approaching, untimely death; but even after commentators have demystified the syndrome and its social effects, the sense persists that AIDS is a new affliction, and that it has generated different, unprecedented anxieties.

Amidst these fears, the cry "come out" resounds; for AIDS remains associated, unjustly or not, with a need for brave candor that itself has its roots in 1960s confessional politics. The desire to be clear, to sketch

the human profile of AIDS, to decode its name, its past, its likes and
dislikes, stems from our belief that the syndrome has an intrinsic connection to certain communities. Sympathetic as well as hostile parties
wrap rhetorics, vocabularies, and iconographies around the disease
because they want to rationalize and map the way AIDS travels. Describing a disease as a traveler is itself a troubling figure of speech:
travel assumes a place of origin and a crossing of boundaries, whether
legally or illegally, to reach an alien, perhaps desirable elsewhere.

In response to the picture of AIDS as a murky, traveling cloud of
toxins, the language with which the "general population" assures itself of immunity grows explicit and unembarrassed. No longer un-
mentionable, anal and oral sex enter the vocabularies and cosmologies
of doctors, elected officials, the press. However vague and fabular the
origin of AIDS (Africa? the CIA? God?), however uncertain its eventual outcome, its manifestation in language remains garish and explicit. AIDS, like the Kinsey Report, has shown exclusive heterosexuality to be hardly the rule. The erotic structure of our society,
illuminated by this brutally inquisitive disease, is full of unmention-
able affiliations and crossbreedings. The new construction of the "bisexual" as wandering contagion, a viperous chameleon, has led to a
repressive vigilance over the behavior of all men and women. As heterosexual transmission of AIDS gains publicity, and as the dividing
line blurs between straight and gay as *identities* (as opposed to behaviors), baths, bars, and comics become classrooms for the new safe
practices.

AIDS marks language even when no confession is intended, and
when the disease is not directly invoked. No sentence or sentiment
that broaches the sexual is exempt from having some oblique relationship to AIDS. Every kindling of desire becomes a possible reference
to "it"; every orgasm must pass through this censor. AIDS, as unwanted implication, pools voraciously, and "language," as opposed to
"experience," enjoys a savorless triumph. Phone sex and pornography
come of age as legitimate and healthy practices: talking of sex or reading about it is more hygenic than the acts themselves—and hygiene
(fitness, cleanliness) is a contemporary grail. Language, in the form of
the phone lover's voice, acquires iconic status, greater than the unsafe
events it displaces—acts that are no longer possible in their old, pure
form, and that glow like the practices of a golden age.

When dementia sets in, language, the will to speak, the ability to
assemble sentences, breaks down. AIDS sometimes ends in blindness,
incoherence, fragmentation, forgetfulness, as if the quilt (of words, of
cheerfulness, of futurity), the sewn synapses, were to unravel.

Language is always a raft, a connective tissue, but in the case of a disease, like AIDS, that can strike swiftly, small verbal lapses and interruptions, daily ellipses, grow huge. AIDS, for the PWA, for the friend, is full of words tragically missing their mark: the unanswered phone call (when the call is returned, the friend has died, or gone into the hospital for the last time); erased names in private phone books; the difficulty of funeral parlor conversations; the shame I feel using words under tragic circumstances.

Speaking about AIDS, one becomes a citizen of it, and obeys its rules. The first rule: there is no such thing as *outside*. Every word takes place within the syndrome's perimeters. In 1989, in 1990, I can hardly speak of perimeters. Because the word *spread* implies a willed inexorability, a center and origin, such as Patient Zero, where dispersal begins, I will not say that AIDS is spreading, but that there is more dying; and people who speak about it will increasingly find that they are subordinated by what they hope to master and evade. AIDS, a condition that has stolen lives adjacent to mine, is an occasion for reflecting on adjacency itself—the permeability of the membrane between event and emotion, neighbor and myself.

Illiteracy

I have, so far, assumed a singular language. But because AIDS is borderless, it is futile as well as arrogant to consider the disease from a solely English-speaking point of view.

If the first vanity of my endeavor has been the assumption that *language* means English, my second vanity has been to speak solely of the literate. The underclass, in which AIDS makes progressively fiercer encroachments, has an uncertain relation to literacy; AIDS strikes the literate, but it also strikes those for whom writing is an inaccessible power. Without access to written language, it is impossible to read a condom ad, complete a job application, negotiate welfare, or bargain for AZT. AIDS may seem to have little to do with subjects and verbs; but it has everything to do with the acts that depend on language— renting an apartment, hiring a lawyer, voting.

Medicine is not free. Nor is language, which empowers a speaker, or writer, to outguess and recompose a riddling society. I should be discussing money, not words, for money flows or stops according to who talks and who listens. The stock market and the Pentagon are languages. These tongues of power, of duress, underwrite the suffering of the PWA, and of the countries AIDS afflicts. Mapping AIDS, we return to the familiar vocabulary of weapons, ideologies, famine, currencies. The syndrome may not have a will or a mission, but it has been imprinted with the directives and prejudices of the societies where it flourishes; so AIDS, like hunger, like war, is an affair of money and its transport, a matter of unjust circulation.

The motive behind this brief inquiry into AIDS and language has been an attempt, perhaps immodest, to mold words into something stainless. AIDS has made me watch my speech, as if my words were a second, more easily monitored body, less liable than the first to the whimsy of a virus. Writing about AIDS, a subject I avoid *and* take to heart, I try to speak naturally, without guile or prejudice, without my position revealing itself and corrupting what I say. And yet, asserting that language and the body are intrinsically separate, in danger of polluting each other, I make the old mistake of believing flesh's claim to be master over mind, reason, and codes. Bodies have always wanted only one thing, to be aimless: or so I say, knowing that *bodies*, and *always*, and *aimless*, are among the most seductive, and the most outdated, of the several rhetorics I must soon discard.

AIDS: The Linguistic Battlefield

AIDS IS THE MOMENT-TO-MOMENT MANAGEMENT of uncertainty. It's like standing in the middle of the New York Stock Exchange at midday, buzzers and lights flashing, everyone yelling, a million opinions. AIDS is about loss of control—of one's bowels, one's bladder, one's life. And so there is often a ferocious drive by those of us with AIDS to exert at least *some* control over it. When I was diagnosed in 1982, I decided that I'd have to pay close attention to the language of AIDS—to keep my wits about me in order to see beyond the obfuscating medical mumbo-jumbo meant to dazzle me into a deadly passivity.

AIDS is a sprawling topic. War is being waged on many fronts. From the beginning of this epidemic, there have been a number of important battles over how we speak about AIDS which have had subtle but profound effects on how we think about—and respond to—AIDS. These linguistic battles have also affected how those of us diagnosed as having AIDS experience our own illness.

In the early seventies, the gay liberation movement won a smashing victory when it forced the American Psychiatric Association to declassify homosexuality as an illness. But with the creation of a new disease called G.R.I.D., or gay-related immune deficiency, as AIDS was first termed, in an instant, those of us whose primary sexual and affectional attraction is to members of our own sex once again became medicalized and pathologized—only now we were considered literally, as opposed to merely morally, contagious.

Soon, gay-related immune deficiency was discovered in nongay people and a new name for this disease had to be found. All factions were poised for a political battle over the new name. Instinctively, those empowered to create and police the definition of AIDS (and those who would be profoundly affected by it) were aware that the new name would affect how the epidemic would be handled by the federal government and the "general" (meaning, generally, the non-homosexual, non-IV-drug-using, rest-of-you) public.

In the end, a neutral sounding, almost cheerful name was chosen: A.I.D.S. Words can resonate with other words and take on subtle, sympathetic vibrations. AIDS: as in "health and beauty aids" or, to retain some of the sexual connotations of the disease, "marital aids." Or AIDS: as in "aid to the Contras." Or, "now is the time for all good men to come to the aid of their country." "AIDS" sounded like something . . . well, helpful.

My highly trained eye can now spot the letters A-I-D on a page of newsprint at lightning speed. It's amazing how often those three letters appear in headlines: afrAID, mislAID, medicAID, pAID—even bridesmAIDS. Every time I would hear a newscaster say "The president's aide reported today. . . ," I'd be momentarily disoriented by the linkage of "president" and "AIDS."

It's interesting to speculate, by the way, what the public response to AIDS might have been had the name proposed by a group from Boston prevailed: *herpes virus reactivation syndrome*. Prior to AIDS, the American public—general or otherwise—had been barraged by *Time* magazine cover stories about another fearsome, sexually transmitted epidemic: herpes. If those with the power to name the current plague had linked its name to the herpes epidemic, getting the American public to take AIDS seriously might not have been quite so difficult. One important consequence (some would say cause) of the profound immune disturbance we now call *AIDS* is that latent herpes viruses are reactivated, leading to a vicious cycle of immune suppression. Had the name *herpes virus reactivation syndrome*, or *HVRS*, been selected instead of *AIDS*, it might not have taken so long to convince Americans to support research into a disease which, by name at least, everyone was theoretically at risk for. But perhaps because *HVRS*, as an acronym, does not roll tripplingly off the tongue, the more neutral sounding *AIDS* was chosen.

What the "L" Is Going On Here?

The most momentous semantic battle yet fought in the AIDS war concerned the naming of the so-called AIDS virus. The stakes were high; two nations—France and the United States—were at war over who first identified (and therefore had the right to name) the retrovirus presumed to cause AIDS. Hanging in the balance was a Nobel prize and millions of dollars in patent royalties.

U.S. researcher Dr. Robert Gallo had originally proposed that HTLV-I (human T-cell leukemia virus) was the cause of AIDS. Meanwhile, scientists at the Pasteur Institute isolated a novel retrovirus, which they named *LAV*, to stand for "Lymphadenopathy Associated Virus." The U.S. scoffed at French claims, arrogantly asserting that HTLV-I or HTLV-II must be the cause of AIDS. When it became obvious that neither HTLV-I nor II could possibly be the cause, if for no other reason than because Japan (where HTLV-I and II are endemic) was not in the midst of an AIDS epidemic, the U.S. had to find some way to steal both LAV itself as well as the credit for having discovered it first, while covering over the embarrassing fact that they had proposed the wrong virus as "the cause" of AIDS.[1]

What to do? In an election year (1984), it was simply unthinkable that the French could so outshine U.S. medical research. The United States hit upon a brilliant solution. Gallo simply renamed LAV "HTLV-III" and Secretary of Health and Human Services Margaret Heckler staged a preemptive press strike. She declared that another achievement had been added to the long list of U.S. medical breakthroughs: "the probable cause of AIDS has been found—HTLV-III, a variant of a known, human cancer virus . . ."

The ploy was certainly ballsy. And looking back, amazingly successful.

But what was going on here? The *L* in HTLV-I and II stands for leukemia, since it is proposed that HTLV-I and II account for a particular form of leukemia. Unfortunately for the perpetrators of this massive fraud, it just so happens that leukemia is one of the few diseases which is *not* a complication of AIDS. So, in order to retain the symmetry of nomenclature, Gallo quietly proposed that the *L* in HTLV-III and HTLV-IV now stand for *lymphotropic* instead of *leukemia*.

It is now widely acknowledged that HIV is not a member of the HTLV family at all. It is a lentivirus. But the consequences of Gallo's bold attempt at semantic damage control are still with us. The *Index Medicus* listing for AIDS still refers to HTLV-III, not HIV. The legal dispute was eventually settled by the state department; the presidents of the U.S. and France signed an agreement whereby their nations would share credit and royalties, a settlement potentially worth billions. But what was the cost in human lives lost from research delays caused by the willful misclassification of HIV?

"Cause" for Concern

The language of AIDS depends upon many presumptions, piled one upon another like a house of cards. When you happen to doubt a particular presumption often the entire superstructure collapses, making communication difficult if not impossible. Three commonly used terms which betray no evidence of the enormously complex presumptions encoded within them are *the cause*, *the AIDS virus*, and *HIV disease*. When AIDS was first discovered, there was, appropriately, a good deal of speculation as to its possible cause or causes. Was it a drug? Was there something in the lifestyles of those who developed AIDS that might explain it? Was it an old microbe? Was it a newly introduced pathogen? What could explain the differences in opportunistic infections among the "risk groups"? Why, for example, does Kaposi's sarcoma occur as an opportunistic complication of AIDS almost exclusively in gay men?

Great social consequences have followed from the pronouncement that HIV is "the cause" of AIDS—that already socially stigmatized groups are carrying and spreading a lethal, cancer-causing agent, a single contact with which is said to lead, ineluctably, to gruesome death. Houses of HIV-infected children have been burned down. There are people currently in jail—and others on trial—for being HIV antibody positive and having sex without telling their partners. In Cuba, HIV antibody positive individuals are quarantined for life. HIV antibody positive individuals who have bitten police are charged with assault with a deadly weapon. Immigrants are denied admission to the U.S. on the basis of strands of protein formed by the body in response to infection with HIV.

Precisely what do we mean when we refer to HIV as "the cause" of AIDS? What is the evidence, beyond a correlation with AIDS, that HIV causes any illness at all? When, how, and by whom was it decided that this retrovirus was sufficient to explain a disease as complex as AIDS? And what do we mean when we speak of "cause"? Necessary but not sufficient? Necessary and sufficient?

Prior to the announcement of HIV as "the probable cause of AIDS," there were many other interesting explanations, many of which were as "probable" as the HIV single-agent hypothesis. Why did they suddenly become less "probable"? Why has no one ever answered the possibility that HIV itself may be nothing more than a harmless, reactivated opportunistic infection found in those whose immune systems are deficient for other reasons? When and how did an openly skeptical U.S. press drop the adjectives *probable* and *putative* from their reporting on HIV?

I am a member of a small but persistent group of HIV heretics who cling to the belief that HIV—generally referred to as "the AIDS virus"—has not been proven, by any acceptable standards of scientific inquiry, to be "the cause" of AIDS. While I and other HIV skeptics admit that there exists a physical entity which we call variously HIV (1 or 2), LAV (1 or 2), HTLV-III, or ARV, the evidence adduced in support of its having a causal role in making people sick is pretty sketchy. There is a correlation with AIDS; but it used to be admitted in science that correlation was not the same thing as causation.

Because I do not accept HIV as the central deity in the fundamentalist monotheism which passes for scientific objectivity, it becomes difficult to communicate with others. Every time I hear "the AIDS virus," it is like a lash across the tattered flesh of my sanity.

When newspapers say someone has "AIDS," they generally mean that a person has some laboratory evidence of infection with HIV.[2] Media reports and the general public also confuse exposure to HIV with infection with HIV, and further confuse infection with HIV to mean clinically ill with AIDS or ARC. One can be exposed to a pathogen without becoming infected; and certainly one can be infected with HIV without ever getting sick.

Increasingly, one hears the neologism *HIV disease*, which reflects the current momentum to do away with the Centers for Disease Control's admittedly imprecise spectrum: HIV antibody seronegativity; HIV antibody seropositivity; HIV asymptomaticity; lymphadenopathy syndrome; AIDS-Related-Complex; and full-blown, CDC-defined AIDS. This is immensely frustrating to those of us who would like to keep alive the important debate about what is causing AIDS.

The ability to define AIDS rests with the CDC. During a time when there was still lively and important debate about whether HIV was the cause of AIDS, the CDC quietly modified the definition of AIDS to require laboratory evidence of HIV infection for a real diagnosis of AIDS, thus settling a complex theoretical issue by semantic fiat. Now, *as a matter of definition*, you can't have AIDS without HIV.

The debate effectively cut off, the world now puts all its research eggs into the HIV basket. In 1989 2.5 billion federal dollars were earmarked for HIV research.[3] Nearly every AIDS treatment strategy is antiretroviral; and millions are being spent on developing a vaccine based on HIV—despite the fact that antibodies to HIV are *not* thought to be protective. Something has to be done, moreover, about those troublesome cases of unexplained PCP, KS, cryptococcal meningitis, and any of the other two dozen or so opportunistic infections which happen not to be infected with HIV.[4]

Simon Watney and Paula Treichler, aware of the stigma which has resulted from the simplistic notion that socially stigmatized groups are carrying and spreading a killer virus, are driven to semantic contortions. Treichler writes:

> Any characterization of AIDS has a history, it has a vocabulary, origins, and consequences. Even a seemingly innocent and straightforward term like "the AIDS virus"—a term that now permeates technical and general AIDS discourse—is in fact profoundly misleading. . . . [Simon Watney's] point is not that what we call "HIV" is "real," but that [the term HIV positive] is a much more preferable *representation*. What we call "AIDS," he argues, consists of some thirty diverse clinical entities and conditions. Although a virus may initiate the breakdown of the body's immune system, which in turn makes possible the development of one or more of the thirty diseases and conditions, it does not cause "AIDS." Suppose a thief enters your house, ties you up, cuts your phone cord and burglar alarm, steals your silver, and uses your credit cards to catch the next plane to Copenhagen. Because you're still tied up, you can't do anything when the microwave explodes and starts a fire. Is the thief an arsonist?[5]

Well, to belabor Treichler's analogy, yes, HIV is both thief and arsonist: provided that you're sure you've arrested the right thief, and provided the thief has been given a fair trial, and provided the thief/arsonist is convicted on more than circumstantial evidence. If, as Watney and Treichler clearly believe, HIV actually *causes* the underlying immune destruction which leads to death from opportunistic infections, then what's the point of this bizarre refusal to call it "the AIDS virus"? Such semantic hairsplitting sidesteps the important question: does HIV actually "cause" AIDS?

HIV has been anthropomorphized into a voracious, insatiable, lethal killer, stalking the immune system, laying waste to everything in sight. The evidence is quite the contrary. This is a pathetic pathogen—easily killed. By the HIVists own admission, it infects fewer than 1 in 10,000 T-cells even at its most active stage. The body generates more than that number of T-cells in a day. There is simply no way that direct T-cell killing by HIV can account for AIDS.[6] So now there is a mad scramble to explore so-called indirect mechanisms. Since the

HIV/T-cell theory can't explain AIDS, we've recently witnessed the dawning of the age of the macrophage.

However we seek to explain AIDS, we must not allow the relentless repetition of an immensely complex set of unproven presumptions to be concentrated into the disarmingly simplistic phrase *HIV disease*. We must continue to ask this important and central question: is the evidence that HIV is "the cause" of AIDS sufficient to justify our abandonment of other possible explanations?

Who Has the Power to Name?

The question of who has the power to name is an ongoing turf battle between people with AIDS and those who insist on defining us as victims. I was at the founding of the people with AIDS self-empowerment movement in Denver, Colorado, in 1983. When the California contingent insisted that we make part of our manifesto the demand that we be referred to as "people with AIDS" (or the inevitable acronym "PWAs") instead of "AIDS victims," I must confess that I rolled my eyes heavenward. How California, I thought.

But time has proven them right. Americans, whose ability to think has been dessicated by decades of television and its ten-second-sound-bite mentality, think in one-word descriptors. Someone on the TV screen must be labeled: a feminist, a communist, a homosexual, an AIDS victim. The difference between the descriptors *person with AIDS* and *AIDS victim* seems subtle until one watches oneself on re-runs on TV. To see oneself on screen and have the words *AIDS victim* magically flash underneath has a very different feel about it than when the description *person with AIDS* appears. Its very cumbersomeness is startling and makes the viewer ask: "Person? Why person? Of course he's a person . . . " In that moment, we achieve a small but important victory. Viewers are forced to be conscious, if only for a moment, that we *are* people first.

The founding statement of the PWA self-empowerment movement (known as the "Denver Principles") is quite eloquent on this point:

> We condemn attempts to label us as "victims," which implies defeat; and we are only occasionally "patients," which implies passivity, helplessness and dependence upon the care of others. We are "people with AIDS."[7]

This statement was further refined in the founding Mission Statement of the National Association of People with AIDS (NAPWA):

We are people with AIDS and people with AIDS-Related Complex (ARC) who can speak for ourselves to advocate for our own causes and concerns. We are your sons and daughters, your brothers and sisters, your family, friends and lovers. As people now living with AIDS and ARC, we have a unique and essential contribution to make to the dialogue surrounding AIDS and we will actively participate with full and equal credibility to help shape the perception and reality surrounding this disease.

We do not see ourselves as victims. We will not be victimized. We have the right to be treated with respect, dignity, compassion and understanding. We have the right to lead fulfilling, productive lives—to live and die with dignity and compassion.

In a gratuitous aside in his best-selling AIDS epic, *And the Band Played On*, Randy Shilts attacked the right of people with AIDS to choose how they wish to be referred to. Completely twisting the empowering impulse of people with AIDS to wrest some control of our lives, Shilts accused us of attempting to minimize the tragedy of AIDS:

> AIDSpeak, a new language forged by public health officials, anxious gay politicians, and the burgeoning ranks of "AIDS activists." The linguistic roots of AIDSpeak sprouted not so much from the truth as from what was politically facile and psychologically reassuring. Semantics was the major denominator of AIDSpeak jargon, because the language went to great lengths never to offend.
>
> A new lexicon was evolving. Under the rules of AIDSpeak, for example, AIDS victims could not be called victims. Instead, they were to be called People with AIDS, or PWAs, as if contracting this uniquely brutal disease was not a victimizing experience. "Promiscuous" became "sexually active," because gay politicians declared "promiscuous" to be "judgmental," a major cuss word in AIDSpeak. The most-used circumlocution in AIDSpeak was "bodily fluids," an expression that avoided troublesome words like "semen."
>
> . . . Thus, the verbiage tended toward the intransitive. AIDSpeak was rarely empowered to motivate action; rather, it was most articulately pronounced when justifying inertia. Nobody meant any harm by this; quite to the contrary, AIDSpeak was the tongue designed to make everyone content. AIDSpeak was the language of good intentions in the AIDS epidemic; AIDSpeak was a language of death.[8]

Shilts notwithstanding, there is now a movement to further emphasize hope. In some quarters *PLWAs* and *PLWArcs* have entered the language: Persons *Living* With AIDS and Persons *Living* with ARC, respectively. There is also a new movement to organize all individuals suffering from conditions related to immune deficiency. Acronym conscious, its leaders say they are "PISD" (pronounced "pissed"), which stands for "Persons with Immune System Disorders."

The *New York Times*, whose editorial policies influence other newspapers, has been drawn into the battle being waged by people with AIDS to reclaim some small amount of linguistic control over our lives—a battle similar to one being waged by gay people over the *Times*'s intransigent use of *homosexual* instead of *gay*. The following exchange concerns the *Times*'s obituary of the first president of the New York People with AIDS Coalition:

> December 1986
>
> We protest the New York Times' not listing Kenneth Meeks' surviving life-mate of over ten years, Mr. Jack Steinhebel. Upon calling your office, I spoke to "Fred," who told me that it was the policy of the Times "not to include lovers" as survivors. That policy is totally inappropriate in that it lacks sensitivity and basic respect. "Fred" also informed me that in his "six years at the Times and with hundreds of phone calls the policy had not changed" and that we should "not expect it to change in the future." How sad.
>
> Finally, the labeling of People with AIDS as "victims" in Ken's obit was incorrect and more so in light of Ken's extensive work to end such practices. We are greatly disappointed by such journalism.
>
> Sincerely,
> Michael Hirsch
> Executive Director
> People with AIDS Coalition

The *New York Times* responded:

> No slurs were intended, but I can well understand your feelings about Kenneth Meeks's obituary. We are reviewing our obituary conventions regarding mention of intimates other than blood relatives and spouses. I cannot predict what we will decide to do, but think you have contributed to consciousness-raising.
>
> As for the word "victim," I cannot agree that it is pejorative. Along with most of society, we have long written about "stroke victims," "heart attack victims," and "cancer victims." The logic is equally applicable to AIDS, and I am uncomfortable about drying [*sic*] idiom for any cause, no matter how meritorious.
>
> Sincerely,
> Alan M. Siegel
> News Editor
> New York Times[9]

In the ensuing three years, there has been no change in the *Times*'s policy of refusing to acknowledge the status of "intimates other than blood relatives and spouses" (now, there's a mouthful) in the obituaries of lesbian and gay people. If a change of policy so obviously just and easy to accommodate cannot be made by the *Times*, one holds out little hope that they'll ever use a descriptor other than *victim* when referring to PWAs.

An Epidemic of Acronyms

There is a separate, specialist language of the AIDS subculture which must be mastered if one wishes to be considered AIDS literate. And this language contains a great deal of shorthand. To the uninitiated, hearing a conversation among urban gay men is like stumbling into a medical convention and being dazzled and dazed by an explosion of acronyms. Here are just a few one must recognize to be included among the AIDS cognoscenti: Ab+; Ab−; ACTG/ATEU; ARC; ASFV; AZT; CBC; CD4+; CD8+; CDC; CMV; ddA; ddC; ddI; DFMO; DHEA; DHPG; DNCB; DTC; EBV; ELISA; EPO; FDA; GM-CSF; HBLV; HBV; HIV; HIV-1; HIV-2; HSV-1; HSV-2; HTLV-I, II, III, and IV; IL-1 and IL-2; IND; IVDAs or IVDUs; KS; LAS; LAV; MAI; NIAID; NIH; NK; O/I; PCR; PCP; T4; TB; TNF; and WBC.

We're in the midst of an epidemic of acronyms. Whatever else AIDS may be, it is itself an acronym. When first introduced, AIDS used to be clearly identified as an acronym because it always appeared with dots: A.I.D.S. Then, consistent with the American tendency towards elision, reduction, and (over)simplification, AIDS rapidly dropped the periods and became a thing in and of itself. In Britain, except for the curious initial capital *A*, AIDS has lost all sense of ever having been an acronym; it is generally referred to as "Aids." (One never sees *syphilis* or *gonorrhea* with an initial capital.)

The acronym epidemic threatens to get out of hand. We even have acronyms within acronyms, as in AIDS-Related Complex—which stands for Acquired Immune Deficiency Syndrome-Related Complex. It verges on an infinite regress. ARC-related symptoms actually translates: Acquired Immune Deficiency Syndrome Related Complex related symptoms. Another redundancy in common usage is *HIV virus*, which translates into "Human Immunodeficiency Virus Virus." I propose that we insist on referring to "the human immunodeficiency virus" or "the HI virus."

Is there anyone who can talk about AIDS and emerge from the battle unscathed? Probably not. We all want to control AIDS somehow, and at times language seems to be our only weapon. But we must not try to master AIDS by crushing its complexities, mysteries, and terrors into convenient labels that roll trippingly and with false authority off the tongue. We must always speak fully and carefully about AIDS, even if that often requires a mouthful—cumbersome constructions full of words strung together by hyphens—to say precisely what we mean. The stakes are simply too high to do otherwise.

Notes

1. The saga of the competition between U.S. and French AIDS researchers reads like a bad espionage novel. Gallo requested, and the French twice supplied, cultures of LAV. At the time, Gallo claimed that he was not able to grow LAV from these samples. A recent BBC documentary, however, produced evidence of altered documents, suggesting that in fact U.S. researchers had grown LAV from the French cultures. Embarrassingly for Gallo, when he first published on "HTLV-III," he mistakenly provided an electron micrograph photo of "LAV" taken for the French. More damning still, when a DNA-fingerprinting was done on Gallo's HTLV-III and the French's LAV, they were found to be essentially identical.

2. Whether or not an individual referred to by the press as having "AIDS" actually still harbors any HIV, or whether or not he or she is infectious, or whether or not these antibodies are protective, is never clarified.

3. "AIDS," an interview with Dr. Robert Gallo, by Anthony Liversidge, *Spin Magazine*, March 1989.

4. See Michael Callen, "Not Everyone Dies of AIDS," *Village Voice*, 3 May 1988. In a study undertaken by the CDC, a group of long-term survivors originally given a diagnosis of AIDS as the result of KS, PCP, and cryptococcal meningitis had their blood tested. Nearly a third showed no laboratory evidence—antigen or antibody—of infection with "the AIDS virus." The only solution available that would maintain the new definition of AIDS requiring laboratory evidence of HIV was to remove these individuals from the AIDS fraternity. Because they didn't have AIDS in the right way—because they did not have HIV—they were stripped of their right to take pride in the fact that they'd survived an illness which everyone was telling them was 100 percent fatal.

5. Paula A. Treichler, "AIDS, Gender, and Biomedical Discourse," in *AIDS: The Burdens of History*, ed. Elizabeth Fee and Daniel M. Fox (Berkeley and Los Angeles, 1988), pp. 229–32.

6. For a devastating critique of the hypothesis that HIV causes AIDS, see two articles by internationally renowned retrovirologist Peter H. Duesberg: "Retroviruses as Carcinogens and Pathogens: Expectations and Reality," *Cancer Research* 47 (1987): 1199–1220, and "Human Immunodeficiency Virus and Acquired Immunodeficiency Syndrome: Correlation But Not Causation," *Proceedings of the National Academy of Sciences USA* 86 (February 1989): 755–64. See also Joseph Sonnabend, "AIDS: An Explanation for Its Occurrence Among Homosexual Men," in *The Acquired Immune Deficiency Syndrome and Infections of Homosexual Men*, 2d ed., ed. Pearl Ma and Donald Armstrong (Stoneham, Mass., 1989), pp. 449–70.

7. "The Denver Principles," quoted in *Surviving and Thriving with AIDS: Collected Wisdom*, vol. 2, ed. Michael Callen (New York, 1988).

8. Randy Shilts, *And the Band Played On: The Politics of AIDS* (New York, 1987), pp. 314–15.

9. Reprinted in *PWA Coalition Newsletter* 18 (December 1986).

Money

Money speaks sense in a language
all nations understand.
APHRA BEHN

The value of money has been settled by general consent
to express our wants and our property, as letters
were invented to express our ideas; and both these
institutions, by giving more active energy to the
powers and passions of human nature, have
contributed to multiply the objects they were
destined to represent.
EDWARD GIBBON

Money talks.
English proverb

~ SEYMOUR CHATMAN

The Pajama Man:
Idyll Without Words

SAY YOU ARE AN INDUSTRY *MAUDIT*, an industry under a cloud—in short, the tobacco industry. How do you sell your wares? Will people even read your language any more? Probably not: print is too weighty, too legalistic, too *moral* for your compromised invitation. It's best not to compete, verbally, with the Surgeon General for a dying market.[1] So you turn to visual imagery (a medium at once subtler and more elemental than language), to images evoking the nice feelings smokers get from smoking. How? By telling a story, the story of lighthearted folks (like we all used to be) who smoke for the simple pleasure of it, and couldn't care less about official admonitions. Admonitions, of course, always come in dull old language.

For rationality is more likely to break through into discursive language than into storytelling. Stories have always been the best means for obviating reason. Persuasion through words always risks backtalk. "Cigarettes are harmless" prompts the rejoinder "Cigarettes are deadly." But who can fault a story? All that *it* claims is that some folks enjoy smoking. It even allows that the particular folks it portrays are characters, fictions, though it also strongly implies that there are millions very much like them out there. Such a story has "plausible deniability": "We're not claiming anything about the cigarettes beyond the fact that lots of perfectly respectable people smoke them." There is no suggestion that the audience should generalize, inductively, to the population at large. Rather, we are simply invited to join the happy group.

Telling the story purely in pictures, a medium unusually resistant to discursive challenge, blocks potential counterarguments even further. Magazine readers are unlikely to visualize *non*smoking stories: as Baudrillard puts it, "What characterizes the mass media is that they are opposed to mediation, [that they are] intransitive, that they fabricate noncommunication—if one accepts the definition of communication as an exchange, as the reciprocal space of speech and response, and thus of *responsibility*."[2]

So most cigarette advertisers suppress the language—erase it completely, or reduce it to some simple incantation ("For people who like to smoke . . ."). The linguistic bits left are merely captional. They have little to do with persuasion. What really counts is the visible story, which slips under doors firmly locked against expository prose, bypassing the intellect and going directly to our hearts, or what has replaced them, our "pleasure centers."

A past master at telling such stories is the agency that does Benson and Hedges ads. For several years they have presented the message in captionless comic strips, or more properly *fumetti*, since the panels consist of photographs, not drawings. The story is, they contend, a simple one of pleasure, of lighting up and enjoying. (Implication: the pleasure of smoking is visceral, impossible to put into words.) Only pictures can do justice to so happy and communal an experience. For example, the evening-of-cards ad.

In an ad that follows the standard Benson and Hedges two-panel formula, the upper panel shows two smoking couples in sports clothes sitting on colorfully upholstered wrought-iron furniture. One of the men is dealing cards; the others are laughing. Three of the four visible hands hold cigarettes. One couple sit in a loveseat, the woman leaning intimately against the man, whose head is raised in a hearty chuckle. In the lower panel, only they remain in their house. The woman has snuggled up and fallen asleep. His cigarette raised aloft in his left hand, his right arm thrown casually along the arm of the love seat, his leg up on the table, he smiles contentedly into a bright future. The story? Clear as a bell: Friends have come over for an evening of lighthearted cards. (Yuppies do not take cards seriously.) Everybody smokes and has a good time. Afterward, as his wife sleeps, the host, over a fresh cigarette, reflects on the simple pleasures of life.[3] The appeal is modest: all that the ad wants you to do is to feel the characters' pleasure, or something like it. It does not suggest that you light up too. The appeal is metonymic, only an illustration that pleasure lies cheek-by-jowl with cigarettes. In this kind of interchange, the cigarette is not so much a cause as a *sign* of Pleasure. The other objects in the photograph are not intended to mean anything: they are free-floating signifiers. They have no fictional (or interestingly fictional) referents. Rather they evoke, nostalgically, a great good place where we would all rather be—without, of course, denying the illusoriness of that place.

Free-floating signs elicit free-floating Desire. What is signified and hence promoted as object of desire is not smoke or taste but the sense of being—or at least being with—happy, successful, contented people. The cigarette is the sign that we can share with them. The desire elicited is not so much to *have* something as to *be* someone else in a happier somewhere else. Thus, the ad practices Seduction, in Jean Baudrillard's sense: "Seduction is that which extracts meaning from discourse and detracts it from its truth." Seduction lives at the pole opposite that inhabited by interpretive discourses (for example, the discourse of the psychotherapies), which salubriously try to find latent truths behind manifest appearances. Ads of late-stage capitalism purposely blur what interpretive discourse tries so hard to clarify. In seducing, they reconceal the latent behind the manifest. "In seduction . . . it is somehow the manifest discourse, the most 'superficial' aspect of discourse which acts upon the underlying prohibition (conscious or unconscious) in order to nullify it and to substitute for it the charms and traps of appearances."[4] Baudrillard's point is that *all* discourse gets caught up in this subversion. But advertising seems most consciously to pursue it.

Until recently, the Benson and Hedges ads have practiced a seduction of the most banal and transparent sort. But suddenly one appeared which set the advertising world on its ear—the "pajama man" ad.

Here the puffing conviviality—smoking conjoined with a pleasant gathering—is familiar, but suddenly one character has turned problematic. A slim, curly-haired young man, attired only in pajama bottoms, stands with shy impudence at the end of a table littered with the remains of an elegant luncheon. He is not robust. He is no Marlboro man. His tummy protrudes like a small boy's. Even his cigarette is dinky; unlike the long ones flaunted by the ladies, his is short but still erect, tucked between the knuckles of his dangling hand. Two walls are visible: upon each hangs an oil painting. The room is flooded with light. The six diners in business clothes—five attractive young women and a balding middle-aged man—relax over cigarettes. The women laugh pleasantly, presumably over the pajama man. The bald-headed man turns and raises his wineglass to toast him.

In the denouement, the young man stands behind one of the women. He bends over her, his hand on her shoulder; she smiles up at

The "pajama man" ad

him, her arm around his neck. The bald man pats the young man's naked shoulder.

Have the advertisers changed their tactic? Is the mysterious ad some appeal to the discriminatory faculty? Not really. It projects the same audience—one that is open, easy, knowing, sociable, tolerant. Tolerant, especially, to the idea of cigarettes as a facilitator, like drink, of communal good cheer, and, later, as a coal in the afterglow. However odd the young man's attire, we readily join the diners in receiving him (and all smokers) into any room. The reception, indeed, is joyous, celebrating the unflappable and sophisticated good humor of the metropolite. If the ad did nothing more than promote good-natured tolerance of smokers, its sponsors would be content. But clearly they intended—and in fact achieved—more intense response. Magazine readers wanted to know what was *happening* in this ad. *Newsweek* exclaimed:

> Just what's going on here? Who is this guy in his jammies? So many people have asked those questions that Advertising Age magazine was recently compelled to sponsor a "What's Going on Here?" contest. Officials at Wells, Rich, Greene, the cigarette's ad agency, say the picture has prompted a flood of calls and letters. The strategy behind the concept? As it turns out, perhaps none at all. Rob Ramsel, the actor who played the pajama man, says the ad was largely the result of a fluke—and the keen eye of photographer Denis Piel. When Ramsel wandered into the picture from a bathroom setting where another B&H ad was being shot, Piel captured the ambiguous scene on film. "What does the ad mean?" laughs Ramsel. "It means that Robbie gets a check."
>
> Call it ad hoc advertising. At a time when many ads are getting safer and more homogenized, some Madison Avenue firms are finding success in old-fashioned spontaneity. On-the-scene inspiration has helped sell everything from oatmeal to antacids—often with astonishing results.[5]

Oh, sure: "ad hoc." Did Benson and Hedges spend a bundle merely to publish some photographer's *objet trouvé*? The ad doesn't make an abstract collage; like its predecessors, and as *Advertising Age* understood, it purports to tell a story. Or, rather, it stimulates the audience to tell any number of stories that might explain the odd costume. That's hardly an "old-fashioned" or "spontaneous" tactic. Not that the agency has departed from the seductive, empathetic principle; all they have done is to enliven it with a character who must forever remain unexplained—however much the audience is teased into speculation. In other words, we are seduced not only to the usual pleasures of cigarette smoking but also to the creation of stories that perfom such seduction.

We know very well that we shall never learn this guy's identity or the reason for his jammies. Even as our better judgment tells us that he is only a pretext to idle speculation, we cannot help swallowing the bait.[6] A business suit would not cause a problem: a junior executive stands at the head of the table because he has just been promoted. The bald man and the five women toast him at a luncheon party thrown in honor of the occasion. The paintings, the light, the absence of other tables suggest that the room is not in a restaurant. It's a staff luncheon, a catered party in the boardroom.

But what could a man half-clad in pajamas be doing in a board-room? Why is he being toasted? Why all the laying on of hands? People usually wear pajamas at home. Is the young man entertaining this group? But why in deshabille? Perhaps he's eccentric, some kind of artist: the painting behind him looks fashionable. Maybe he is entertaining the owner and salespeople who have come over from the gallery where his successful show has just opened. Or maybe he's a rock star who gets up late and is staring sleepy-eyed at his manager and staff: he has overslept the celebration, but remains the apple of every eye. Or perhaps it's a family matter: he's the son of the older man. The luncheon is not taking place at corporate headquarters but at his father's penthouse apartment. The young man hasn't seen his father in a while. He arrived the night before from out of town, went to sleep not knowing that his father had planned a luncheon for his staff, heard merriment, and just wandered in. Or perhaps it's the favored young woman's apartment, one she shares with the pajama man (lover, husband, brother, roommate?). He didn't know that she had invited her colleagues home to celebrate her promotion. Or, imagine a metatextual possibility: a group of actors hired to do a cigarette ad find their Manhattan studio set invaded by a pajama-clad young man on a cigarette break from another shoot. Seeing the hilarity of the situation, they take their own break, lighting up (now they're *really* smoking, rather than merely acting that they're smoking). The older man raises his fruit juice to toast the handsome young interloper. Accepted so jovially by his colleagues, he hugs one of the actresses, in a purely collegial way, and is hugged in return. Or, perhaps . . .

Cigarettes are distributed handily, of course, but the narrative focus is elsewhere. The story is about "who" a character is and "why" he might be in that room, in those pajama bottoms (quotation marks for red herrings). The advertisers bank on our willingness to create worlds in which events corresponding to these images are feasible. But it's all in fun—there *is* no story, really, and all our attempts to make the story coherent are lightheartedly parried. This is a meta-appeal (or even a meta-meta-appeal), an appeal to our sophistication about the canniness of advertisers. We are seduced not only into smoking but into joining an advertising team that conspires to get us to smoke. From such appeal, the potential trouble of a countervailing discourse is as distant as the moon. We are charmed not only by these happy and prosperous folk at their posh luncheon but by the ingenious and clever ones just offstage who so daringly thought up the joke.

The joke is that no narrator shall ever tell us definitively what is "really" happening, who these people are and why the young man is wearing pajama bottoms. The advertisers have created a narrative which can never come to closure. Why should they close it when they get so much mileage out of keeping it open? They don't really care what interpretation we ultimately hit upon: they are content to watch us busily trying some out. Unlike the appeal of the yuppie cardplayers ad, that of the pajama man ad is duplex. In addition to sharing the joy of the smokers, it invites us to join the mischievous authors. The ad is "self-conscious" ("self-reflexive," "metafictional," "autoreferential"). To the joys of smoking are added the joys of making stories that sell people on smoking. Why? Well, why not? Pleasure is pleasure, and if the audience has reached a decadent late-capitalist phase in which they take as much pleasure in helping compose ads as in responding to them, who is the tobacco industry to argue?[7] Making up ads is as good a response as any other. What could be more heartwarming to advertisers than the spectacle of their audience expending so much imaginative energy on their client's product? If we have arrived at a moment in history when pleasure is *self-acknowledgedly* narcissistic, advertisers are perfectly content to accommodate.

This "open" ad represents no great textual innovation. "Aleatory" or random fiction is one of the well-established self-reflexive forms of postmodern literature. And the pajama man story is just barely aleatory: every interpretation arises bathed in (invisible) tobacco smoke. A range of alternatives is offered, but a cozy range: not *too* many options are available, and each one provides disarming answers to potentially troublesome questions. All promote the cause of enjoying oneself, and doing so with a cigarette. What this ad celebrates is "the brilliant surface of nonsense and all the play that it makes possible."[8]

Benson and Hedges asks little more from us than graceful tolerance. These ads are not aimed at solitary four-pack-a-day addicts but at moderate social smokers or exsmokers who have forgotten (or remember all too well) the fun of it (not too clearly distinguished from the real sources of fun—the sense of companionship). This ad, like Benson and Hedges's usual ones, jovially accepts—indeed, promotes—"reasonable" smoking, convivial smoking. Which is to say, a wishy-washy attitude toward cigarettes, obscuring in a magical cloud of good cheer the threat that everyone understands they pose.

The magic suggests still another theory of the man's identity: who better ministers magic than a presiding demon? Maybe that's who the young man really is—Puck, the tutelary spirit of nicotine, a kindly minor deity, the good genius of the East Side, protecting and reassuring those who wander, innocently seeking pleasure, into his haunts. How *could* he wear street clothes on such an occasion?

Why should it be a cigarette company that first ventures into the bold genre of aleatory narrative? Is it because smoking is—or so the company wants it to seem—a random matter? Is it because the aleatory tale is an analogue to the random act of picking up a cigarette, to "enjoying," instinctively, against all evidence of the deadliness of the habit? "If you're sufficiently knowing to understand the clever open-endedness of this story, dear reader, you also know, in your heart of hearts, that life itself is chancy. Who knows what the future will bring? Smoke, enjoy, forget the Surgeon General and his slogans. This is no time to worry about mere words." Perhaps the industry itself takes a random attitude, since at this stage it has little to lose. With blunter and blunter medical warnings in the offing, the more oblique the innuendo, the better.

As the adage has it, a picture is worth a thousand words. But surely that's a modest figure, applicable only to simple objects—a "cornice," for example, or "subulate leaves," both economically pictured for me in my desk dictionary. For atmospheres, whole realms of feeling, where shall we find, outside of pictures, especially storytelling pictures, a more intimate, yet nebulous evocation? That, at least, is what the tobacco industry is betting on, as it tries to recover the audience of exsmokers, those who remember the feeling of tobacco along their very neural paths. Could even a million words capture the value of feeling good, of hanging out with friends, of the nicotinic spurt?

In such a scenario, words are obsolete, bypassed—not because we are illiterate (though such texts obviously contribute toward that eventuality), but because someone up there believes our values no longer rest on distinctions but on ambience. Read some ads in a magazine or newspaper published a hundred years ago: crude as they are, it is language, not storytelling pictures, that frames their appeal. And discursive language at that. My favorite, from 1888, promotes a masklike device of gutta-percha or plaster that ladies are invited to clamp on their faces to iron out wrinkles during sleep. At the top appears an engraving of the machine, but most of the space is given over to a reasoned argument for the utility of the device. The argument is in the best rhetorical tradition, complete with "firsts" and "seconds," "therefores" and "in conclusions." Of course, it would be naive to say that the author had any great respect for the psychology of ladies. But at least he treated them as an audience that could read and even reason. What has happened to that audience?

Do dialogue-less narrative ads portend The Death of Language? Probably not. The spoken language must continue, at least until a faster and more efficient communicative method is developed, some kind of electronically driven telepathy, perhaps. But the printed word is in trouble. And as it languishes, so does our capacity to articulate and to tolerate the articulate. Visual narratives, which mainline a sense of well-being into our viscera, lead the assault on our dwindling articulative faculty. With our capacity to articulate impaired, how shall we be able to reason?

At issue are matters of greater consequence than cigarette-smoking—for instance, electing a president. The vulnerability of reason to visual storytelling was well demonstrated in the 1988 election campaign. More than ever political appeal followed advertising techniques, especially picture stories that illustrated a candidate's virtue or vice—especially vice—by metonymy, by guilt by association. Nobody actually believes that Dukakis opened those cell doors or personally dumped in Boston Harbor. But many shall never separate him from the aura of those attaching visuals. Just as Benson and Hedges get people to hang out, vicariously, with yuppies and ingratiating pajama men, the Republican Party got people to shun the company of Dukakis. What they practiced was not rhetoric but the subversion of rhetoric. True rhetoric, the only kind of reasoning available to most of us, is being destroyed by the hypertrophy of one of its own figures—metonymy. And as true rhetoric dies, how can public discourse—and perhaps language itself—survive?

Notes

1. Newspapers tell us that the question for the industry is not how to reconstitute the waning market but how to extract revenues from it for as long as possible.

2. Jean Baudrillard, *Selected Writings* (Stanford, 1988), p. 207.

3. What is never seen in any of these ads is smoke. Like butts and ashtrays it is unwanted detritus, here magically eliminated by the photographic process. We are reminded that the industry is currently spending millions to develop "smokeless" cigarettes.

4. Baudrillard, *Selected Writings*, p. 149.

5. *Newsweek*, 2 May 1988, p. 51.

6. Not only idle but distracting: we are distracted from the only real question about cigarettes: why are they still legal?

7. There exists now a whole genre of "brainstorming" ads which are not at all concerned with the product advertised but focus on the production problems facing the admakers in putting their case forward. The appeal is to public fascination with media *as* media.

8. Baudrillard, *Selected Writings*, p. 150.

↜ SUZANNE ROMAINE

Pidgin English Advertising

THERE HAVE RECENTLY BEEN ATTEMPTS to use pidgin English as a medium of advertising in Papua New Guinea, and these have given rise to a number of linguistic and cross-cultural dilemmas. Tok Pisin ("talk pidgin") is an English-based pidgin spoken in Papua New Guinea. Like all pidgin languages, it arose as a lingua franca among speakers of many different languages. It shares with other pidgin languages the characteristic that its lexicon is drawn mainly from one language, in this case English (hence it is referred to as an English-based rather than, say, a French-based pidgin). Its grammar is drawn from another source, in this case, the numerous indigenous languages of Melanesia. This means that even when items derived from English are used to express grammatical categories in pidgin, the syntactic patterning and meanings of them often follow structures found in the indigenous languages. One such instance can be found in the distinction between inclusive and exclusive first person plural pronouns, which is made in Tok Pisin and most, if not all, of the indigenous languages of Melanesia but not in English. Thus, where English has only *we*, Tok Pisin has *yumi* (from English *you + me*), which is inclusive in its reference, and *mipela* (from English *me + fellow*), which is exclusive. One must always distinguish in pidgin between "we" which includes the speaker and addressee(s) and "we" which includes the speaker and others, but not the addressee(s). Although the lexical material used to

make this distinction is clearly drawn from English, the meanings encoded by it can be understood only by reference to grammatical categories present in Melanesian languages. The use of the suffix -*pela*
(from English *fellow*) is another case in point. While *fellow* does not
have any grammatical function in English, it has been taken over into
pidgin as an affix or classifier marking the word class of attributive adjectives. Thus, we have *gutpela man* ("a good man"), *naispela haus* ("a
nice house"), *wanpela meri* ("a/one woman"), and so on. In the pronoun system it appears as a formative in the first and second person
plural, *mipela* ("we" exclusive) and *yupela* ("you" plural).[1]

Tok Pisin is the descendant of a number of varieties of a Pacific Jargon English which was spoken over much of the Pacific during the
nineteenth century and used as a lingua franca between English-
speaking Europeans and Pacific Islanders. This jargon was learned by
Papua New Guineans on plantations in Queensland, Samoa, Fiji, and
in Papua New Guinea itself. The typical pattern of acquisition was for
Melanesian workers to pick up the pidgin or jargon on the plantation
and then bring it back to villages, where it was passed on to younger
boys. Tok Pisin crystallized in a distinctive form in the New Guinea
islands and spread from there to the mainland.

Although Tok Pisin was born in and kept going by colonialization,
it quickly became more than just a means of communication between
the indigenous population and their European colonizers. Since its origin in about 1880, Tok Pisin has become the most important lingua
franca for Papua New Guineans, who, according to one estimate, have
around 750 indigenous languages. Although it was originally learned
as a second language, it is now being acquired by children as their first
language. When this happens in the life cycle of a pidgin language, we
can speak of creolization. In sociolinguistic terms, then, Tok Pisin can
be described as an expanded pidgin which is currently undergoing
creolization. It now has a sizable number of native speakers (about
20,000), and roughly 44 percent of the population claim to speak it.
Indeed, the question of whether Tok Pisin should become the national
language of Papua New Guinea has recently been the subject of much
discussion. At the moment it has official status, along with two other
languages: English, and another pidgin, Hiri Motu, which is based on
Motu, one of the indigenous languages of what was, until independence in 1975, the Territory of Papua. Hiri Motu is, however, region-
ally restricted, and only about 9 percent of the population speak it.
The name Tok Pisin was officially adopted for English-based pidgin in
1981. It had been previously referred to as Neomelanesian, Melanesian
pidgin, *Tok boi* (from English *talk* + *boy*), or just pidgin.[2] It is now,

since independence, the preferred language in the House of Assembly, though English is the official medium of education.

One of the things which happens when a pidgin expands and stabilizes, and possibly then creolizes, is that new linguistic resources have to be created or borrowed to fulfil the new functions to which the language is put. For instance, there is an increase in vocabulary so that new concepts can be expressed: *nesional baset* ("national budget"), *minista bilong edukesan/edukesan minista* ("education minister"). More complicated syntactic structures such as relative clauses emerge, which allow the creation of more sophisticated discourse and stylistic alternatives. Tok Pisin is used now in political debates in the House of Assembly, in media broadcasts, and in journalism.

Tok Pisin has drawn heavily on English in all its new functions. So much English has been borrowed into the language, particularly by urban educated speakers, that many linguists have recognized two separate varieties of the language, urban and rural (or bush) pidgin. Consider this example in which a student being interviewed on a radio broadcast in 1972 said:

> Mi salim eplikeson bilong mi na skul bod [me send application belong me and school board] i konsiderim na bihain ekseptim mi na mi go [consider and behind accept me and me go] long skul long fama [to school of farmer].[3]

"I sent my application to the school board and then they considered and accepted me and I'm going to agricultural school."

Here *eplikeson, skul bod, konsiderim,* and *ekseptim* are all recent loans from English. In some cases there are established pidgin equivalents which could have been used. For example, instead of *ekseptim,* one could say *ol givim orait long dispela* or *long mi* ("they gave the okay for this/to me"). Nowadays students would probably not use the term *skul long fama* but say *agricultural college.* In many cases we can see that borrowing a word in English fills a lexical gap or expresses a concept which is foreign and which could be expressed in pidgin only by means of a lengthy circumlocution. For example, *baset* ("budget") could be paraphrased as *ol man i lukautim mani bilong gavman i raitim daun ol samting bilong mani bilong gavman* ("the people who look after the government's money write down things having to do with the government's money"). The circumlocution is self-explanatory, whereas the borrowing is not. People often do not understand the meanings of very frequently used English borrowings. When the country became independent in 1975, the term *independens* was used, but many people then did not understand what it meant, and still do not. I worked with bush informants in 1986 and 1987 who said they were happy their country was independent because it meant that Australia would help them, when in fact it means just the opposite. In practical terms, increased borrowing from English in urban areas has the effect of making town pidgin unintelligible to rural dwellers. But in other cases, though there are equivalent pidgin words, English is borrowed simply because English has more prestige. For example, pidgin uses the term *askim* (from English *ask*) as both a verb and a noun, but increasingly in urban pidgin a more recently borrowed term, *kwesten* (from English *question*), appears too. Thus, one could say either *Mi gat askim* or *mi gat kwesten* ("I have a question") or *mi laik askim kwesten* ("I want to ask a question"). Another example is *infomesen* (from English *information*) and *toksave* (from Tok Pisin *tok* + *save*, that is, talk know), which means "information, knowledge, advice." Tok Pisin *toksave* can be used as either a noun or a verb, whereas the English *infomesen* can be used only as a noun.[4] There has also been an increase in the use of English plurals ending in -*s*—*ol gels* (from English *girls*), for example, as opposed to *ol meri* ("the girls/ women").

Until the last few decades Tok Pisin was only a spoken language. Now it is written too and more and more literature is published in it. One main vehicle for Tok Pisin as a written language is the weekly newspaper *Wantok*, founded in 1970. (The word *wantok* means "one language" and is used to refer to a person who is part of the same social or kin group, or village.) Written almost entirely in pidgin, Wantok has a circulation of over 10,000 and more than 50,000 readers in Papua New Guinea, and its staff now consists entirely of nationals. Most of the material that appears in it is a translation of news releases from the Department of Information and Extension Services in Port Moresby. It is in Wantok that we find the most extensive use of pidgin in advertising.

Advertising creates special problems for newspapers aimed at a Papua New Guinean public. Most of the products are Australian and geared to western lifestyles, which were originally accessible only to expatriates. Now, increasingly a new market is found in the indigenous urban elite. While products like cars, trucks, and refrigerators are still luxuries for the average Papua New Guinean and therefore advertised largely in English, even in *Wantok*, it is no longer uncommon for Highlanders at the end of the coffee season to come into town and pay cash for a vehicle. Consequently, ads for cars and trucks—for instance, Toyota—are starting to appear occasionally in pidgin. While the names of such products mean something to Australians, they carry no meaning, and correspondingly have no use, for most Papua New

Guineans. Products like Vegemite, Omo, and Pine-O-Cleen are just foreign words. For advertising to be successful, the product has to be not only advertised, but also explained in such a way as to create a need for it. One very simple ad which is effective, at least from the advertiser's point of view, is that used by the Wopa biscuit company. The Wopa ad shows a muscular man holding the product and saying, "Mi kaikai" (I eat). The implication is that the product is good for you because it makes you strong and big. Bread and flour-based products are not part of traditional diets, so they have to be explained and made appealing, whether they are nutritious or not. These products increasingly find their way into every village trade store.

The ad for Sunflower tinned fish, in which the product is clearly illustrated, is effective primarily because of its use of idiomatic Tok Pisin. The slogan says: *Em i bun bilong mi stret* ("it bone belong me straight"), a colloquial expression which means that it is just the thing to serve as the foundation of a good diet. In the literal sense *bun* means "bone" or "skeleton"; one who is *bun nating* (from English *bone + nothing*) would be very skinny.

The ad for Paradise Pineapple Crunch biscuits, however, is probably much less effective because it relies too heavily on English borrowing. The ad boasts of *tropikal fleva insait long bisket* ("tropical flavor inside a biscuit"). The words *tropikal* and *fleva* are new English borrowings and won't be understood by those who do not know English. The Anchor milk company uses a heavily anglicized description of the product, next to which is a photograph of a jug of milk, a cup of coffee, and a can bearing a label in English, "full cream vitamin enriched instant milk powder." To a reader who knows no English, it could as well be an ad for coffee. Most Papua New Guineans have no experience of real milk, let alone powdered milk.

The kinds of clever and catchy advertising slogans typical in Western societies like *drinka pinta milka day, go to work on an egg,* and *if your clothes aren't becoming to you, you should be coming to us* are impossible to translate literally into another language because they rely on linguistic devices like vowel reduction ("*drink a pint of milk a day*"), alliteration, rhyme ("*Beanz meanz Heinz*"), and so on. Although presumably these strategies are available to some degree in most languages, the extent to which they are used and the purposes for which they are used will vary.

There are also other kinds of difficulties in literal translations of slogans, even where special devices like rhyme or punning are not brought into play in the original. For example, the Omo soap company wanted to advertise their product in *Wantok* and say simply that this is the best powdered soap you can buy. But in pidgin two product

names for soap powder have become generic now in the same way as
the brandname Hoover is used in Britain to refer to any vacuum
cleaner or the name Jello is used in the United States for any fruit-
flavored gelatin. (One can even use the name Hoover as a verb, at least
in Britain, where it is more usual to "hoover" a carpet than to "vacuum" it.) Pidgin speakers use both *rinso*, another brandname, and *omo*
to refer to all soap powders, which would lead to an advertisement
that said something like: Omo is the best rinso you can buy, or Rinso
is the best omo you can buy.[5] It would be like saying in English: I've
just bought an Electrolux hoover.

The difference here is that English already has generic terms like
soap powder, detergent, vacuum cleaner, carpet sweeper, and so on,
whereas pidgin did not until it pressed a particular brandname into service. In the case of pidgin omo and rinso, the particular brand provides
the first name for such a substance and thus is synonymous with it.
The status and desirability of brandnames used as generics are debatable. The American Heritage Dictionary includes an entry for example for Kleenex ("a trademark for a soft cleansing tissue") and one for
Jello ("a trademark for a gelatin dessert"). But of course the whole
point of brandnames is to establish uniqueness. One can assume from
the advertising campaign mounted by the Coca Cola Company—
"coke is the real thing" or simply "coke is it"—that it is not unequi-
vocably pleased with the use of Coke as a generic term for a cola
drink. Nevertheless, it can also be advantageous for a company's product to become a "household" word. If Kleenex is synonymous with
tissues, then the consumer may be predisposed to seek this brandname
when buying tissues.

A related problem arises from the lack of specialized terms in pidgin
to refer to foodstuffs which have already undergone a certain degree
of processing and are therefore "table-ready" or "oven-ready." (Traditionally, of course, Papua New Guineans do not sit down at tables
to eat.) The distinction between English "pork" and "pig" and "beef"
and "cow" is of course well known. Interestingly, English has borrowed from French the terms which refer to the edible version of the
animal on the table, while it has used its own native terms to refer to
the animal on the hoof, so to speak. There is a current ad for chicken
which mixes English and pidgin and refers to its product in a confusing way as *Niugini table birds kakaruk* ("New Guinea table birds
chicken"). This is also the company's name. The term *table bird* is a
collocation specific to English referring to the product in a-ready-to-
cook-and-serve state (and possibly even grown for that special purpose). Neither the term nor its concept is known to pidgin speakers.
Presumably the idea is to establish an equation between ready-to-cook

(as opposed to live) chickens and this particular company through invoking the pidgin term *kakaruk*, "chicken."

At the moment there is very little exploitation of linguistic devices like rhyme, alliteration, and punning to achieve catchy slogans in Tok Pisin. I found only one example in an advertisement for eggs, and it plays on the English word *eggs* rather than the Tok Pisin term *kiau* (from Tolai, one of the indigenous languages of Papua New Guinea). It describes eggs as "eggcellent," "eggciting," and "ineggspensive," and then says in pidgin that they are good value for money. A pidgin speaker who does not know English will not of course know what these blends mean. There is plenty of scope for creative advertising slogans drawing on native pidgin terms and devices. For instance, one Australian rice producer has named its product *Trukai* (Tok Pisin *tru + kaikai*—"true food").

Tok Pisin also has a number of named special registers which could provide a productive source for advertisers. *Tok piksa* ("talk picture") is a term for a way of speaking which relies on analogy and similes. *Tok pilai* ("talk play") refers to the jocular use of extended metaphors. *Tok bilas* ("talk decoration") is used to say things which are potentially offensive but can later be denied. *Tok bokis* ("talk box") is a deliberate attempt to disguise meaning by the substitution of familiar words with hidden meanings. There are many others. Advertisers would, however, have to be careful here because some brand names already figure in certain registers. For instance, a common tok piksa term for beer is *spesel Milo* ("special Milo"), and Milo is already a brand name for a chocolate drink. Biscuit advertisers would benefit from knowing that Tok Pisin *switbisket* (from English *sweet biscuit*) and *draibisket* (from English *dry biscuit*) have metaphorical meanings. The former can refer to a sexually attractive woman, and the latter to a woman past her prime.

Some of the advertising techniques used by Western advertisers would simply not work in Papua New Guinea because they would be offensive and/or culturally inappropriate—for example, the innuendo and overt display of sexuality in the sale of perfumes, cars, and other luxury items. *Wantok* newspaper refused an ad from the Gillette company because it showed a European couple in the bathroom nude from the waist up, the woman admiring the face of the smoothly shaven man. Shaving does not interest women in Papua New Guinea, and sexuality would not sell razor blades. On the contrary, it would discourage them.[6]

Conversely, however, many bodily functions do not have the same taboo surrounding them in Papua New Guinea as they do in Western culture, and euphemisms for these things are only just beginning to emerge in Tok Pisin under the influence of western practices. Euphemism is widely used in advertising, even for nontaboo subjects. Take, for instance, the use of "fun-size" for small candy bars. I was amazed when a young schoolgirl I was interviewing used a new euphemistic term, *troimwe excretia* ("to throw away excretia"), for the normal pidgin *pekpek* ("to defecate"), which is used in all contexts. Similarly, *pispis* is the normal term for "urinate," though there is a new Tok Pisin euphemism now: *kapsaitim wara* (from English *capsize + water*). The kind of subtlety and allusion used by Western advertisers to sell toilet tissue (for example, fluffy puppies playing with toilet rolls in gleaming bright bathrooms) and sanitary products (not even advertised until recently in Western media) will be lost on most Papua New Guineans from rural areas who have no experience of modern sanitation facilities. Ads for sanitary napkins, which have just recently begun to appear in *Wantok*, do not explicitly describe or depict the product. Although the language itself is not heavily anglicized and would be intelligible, the advertisers do not explain what the product is or does. Thanks to western taboo, the reader is simply told that Johnson and Johnson have *ol gutpela samting* ("good things"), and shown a picture of a girl daydreaming. The dividing line between euphemism and mystification is very fine in this case. It may well be, however, that this phrase does carry unintended sexual overtone and would therefore offend, because the Tok Pisin term *samting* ("something") is used in *tok bokis* to refer to genitals.

Other familiar Western-style household products are increasingly aimed at Papua New Guineans: for example, Pine-O-Cleen, Mortein, and similar detergents and cleaning agents, and insect sprays. Here it is essential that the product be displayed as well as explained. In these ads an appeal is typically made to the notion of protecting your family against disease. We see here the introduction of Western metaphors into local culture.[7] When such products are advertised in Western media, women are usually portrayed as the protectors of the household, warding off dirt, germs, and other hazards with the right product. Ads for insurance also use the protection metaphor. Then there are also many ads which are used to explain institutions that are culturally alien: banks, taxes, telephones. The effectiveness of the ads depends on how successfully they can render into pidgin the concepts involved. For example, in an ad for PTC (Post and Telecommunication Corporation) the Western metaphor "time is money" (*yu save olsem taim em i mani*—"you know that time is money") is invoked to get people to use the telephone to conduct transactions which would ordinarily be done face-to-face in casual encounters and not by appointment. The concepts "social call" and "business call" are thus introduced.

These are a few of the difficulties presented by advertising in pidgin English. Some of these derive from the problems of the linguistic medium itself, which is in the process of expanding, while others have more to do specifically with the pragmatics of cross-cultural communication. In order to resolve some of the difficulties I have noted here, cooperation between linguists, manufacturing industries, and advertising agencies is essential.

Notes

1. See S. Romaine, *Pidgin and Creole Languages* (London, 1988).

2. This word order pattern in *tok boi* also illustrates the use of English items in compound constructions based on those found in indigenous languages. Compare *kot ren* (from English *coat* + *rain*—"raincoat"), *haus man* (from English *house* + *man*—"men's house"), and so on. The word *boi* was used by Europeans to refer to an indigenous man of any age, particularly in indentured service. It has recently been "reborrowed" in its English sense to refer to young men in order to replace Tok Pisin *mangki* (from English *monkey*).

3. This example is taken from L. R. Healey, "When is a word not a pidgin word?," *Tok Pisin i go we?* (Where is Tok Pisin going?), ed. K. McElhanon, Special Issue of *Kivung* (Linguistic Society of Papua New Guinea, 1975), pp. 36–42.

4. The word *save* is from Spanish/Portuguese (*sabir/saber*—"to know") and is widespread in pidgin and creole languages throughout the world and not just in those of Spanish/Portuguese base. This is one of the few cases where English has borrowed a term from pidgin: that is, *savvy*. Though it can be used only as a noun or adjective in English, in Tok Pisin it can be used as a noun or verb.

5. See the comments of the first editor and founder of *Wantok*, in F. Mihalic, "Interpretation Problems from the Point of View of a Newspaper Editor," in *New Guinea Area Languages and Language Study*, ed. S. A. Wurm, vol. 3 of *Language, Culture, Society and the Modern World* (Canberra, 1977), pp. 1117–26.

6. See Mihalic, "Interpretation Problems," for his discussion of the newspaper's policy.

7. See G. Lakoff and M. Johnson, *Metaphors We Live By* (Chicago, 1980), for their discussion of some of these metaphors.

Thanks, I Suppose

LAST DECEMBER I BEGAN ASKING PEOPLE whether or not they gave money to beggars. This was a question which had not troubled me, at least on a conscious level, for many years. Like most residents of Berkeley (perhaps like most residents of any modern urban area), I had long since developed a slight frown and a quick shake of the head to shrug off all requests for spare change.

What startled me out of this condition, last December, was a brief encounter in a parking lot not far from my home. My little boy and I were crossing from the video rental place to the office supplies store when we were stopped by a heavyset, middle-aged woman. "Excuse me, ma'am, can you spare a quarter?" she said. I did my routine head-shake and hustled on.

"What did that lady want?" asked my two-and-a-half-year-old.

"She wanted money," I said.

"*Why* did she want money?" he persisted.

"Because she's poor."

"What's poor?"

With that, my assumptions were brutally jarred out of their comfortable, long-inhabited positions. What I had just done, I realized, was to teach a small child to be hard-hearted. I was creating a monster of unthinking selfishness—or, alternatively, I was presenting myself as a monster of selfishness in the eyes of an innocent, innately tender-hearted child. Dickensian shame rushed over me.

I immediately undertook an informal survey to determine how other people behaved in similar situations, and why; that is, I asked a few friends whether they gave money to beggars. One California friend, who is in general prone to charitable acts, said he usually tried to give something, though he exercised some discrimination: "For instance, I don't give to the smoking poor." My New York friends, perhaps spurred to a consistency of action by the more profound evidence of need in their city, all seemed to give in one way or another. "If I have any change in my pocket, I give it," said one. "If the request is fairly original, and if it's not aggressive, I generally respond," said another. "I carry five quarters in my pocket whenever I go out, and I give to the first five people who ask that day," said a third. "I carry five one-dollar bills whenever I leave the house, and they're usually gone by the time I get to the corner," said a fourth. (I informed her she was paying over the market rate.)

Finally I asked my husband, "Do you give money to beggars?"

"What is this, a Christmas question?" he growled.

"No, I'm really trying to find out what people do."

"No, I don't give money," he said.

"Why?" I asked.

"Because I was a panhandler once too," he began, "and I know—"

"No," I said. "I mean, what's the philosophical rationale for not giving? I don't give either. But *why* don't we give? What's our justification?"

My husband paused. "Because the government should be doing that, not private citizens," he said.

"Yes," I sighed, relieved at rediscovering the familiar reason.

But my satisfaction didn't last long. A couple of weeks later, this time just before Christmas Day, I was again walking with my little boy on a shopping street near our house when a raggedy, bearded man in a soiled watch cap asked me for money. I snatched at the second chance. "Yes," I said, "just a minute," and I reached into my purse and pulled out two quarters. "Here," I said.

"Thank you, ma'am," he responded—verily, as it seemed to me, tugging on a forelock. "Merry Christmas to you, ma'am. And Merry Christmas to your little boy, too," as he bent down, benignly but still rather frighteningly, over my son.

I felt awful. If anything, I felt worse than when I hadn't given. And that, I realized then, was the impossible situation we had now arrived at. When things get bad enough for some people but not others, when there are poor people in the streets asking you for money, you can't win either way. You can be a malevolent Scrooge or a disgustingly self-congratulatory Lady Bountiful, but you can't remain innocent. No course of behavior is the correct one.

Dickens himself, I think, understood a great deal of this. That's why his philanthropist figures make us so uncomfortable. The Royal Shakespeare Company's 1981 stage production of *Nicholas Nickleby*, for example, tried to stress the enduring social problem over the temporary individual solution by filling the stage with shivering waifs as Nicholas and his family go off to their singularly particular happy ending. A 1987 episode of the television show *The Equalizer* did the same thing: after Robert McCall had saved one homeless family from life in a Times Square flophouse (his self-defined job being merely to protect individual victims), the camera focused its closing shot on a wistful little face, the face of one of the numerous children still left at the drug-ridden hotel. This type of thing is well intentioned, but it assuages even as it means to question. Leaving the theater after *Nicholas Nickleby*, or turning to the (hardly less disturbing) eleven o'clock news after *The Equalizer*, we congratulate ourselves on having achieved the proper perspective on the problem. One philanthropist isn't enough; more needs to be done. We can have our sentimentality and eat it too.

In its original form, Dickens's philanthropy is not so easily digestible; it festers and continues to disturb. Because what Dickens is questioning is not just the amount of good any one philanthropist can do, but the very act of philanthropy itself: the gesture of reaching out to save another by means of one's own relative wealth. Inevitably, that gesture is somewhat creepy. This may not always be easy to see in the early and middle novels. With *Bleak House*, for instance, critics often like to compare the "bad" Mrs. Jellyby (who collects for African relief while neglecting her own family) to the "good" Mr. Jarndyce (who adopts Ada, Richard, and Esther). But in taking this line such critics must be squelching their own instinctive reaction. Isn't there something the least bit squeamish-making about the way Jarndyce coyly approaches his philanthropic role, and something even more obviously nauseating about the way Esther Summerson devotedly renders him eternal gratitude? You might not be prepared to attribute this effect to Dickens; you might want to view it as an unintentional by-product of his salvational plots, a modern perspective superimposed on a Victorian device. But there is *Great Expectations* to contend with, if you try to hold that view.

In his last completed novel, Dickens laid bare the corruption engendered by the most benign kind of philanthropy. The inexplicable trust fund that brings Pip to London and educates him as a "gentle-

man" not only cuts him off from beloved friends of his own class (Joe
and Biddy), but also distorts his relationships with Miss Havisham
(whom he mistakenly believes to be his benefactor, and whom he cra-
venly submits to as a result) and with the benefactor himself. When
Pip discovers that the source of his wealth, education, and new class
status is a transported convict, he is filled with disappointment and resentment; he almost hates the man who made him rich. This is not
class snobbery alone. It's a result of the discrepancy between what he
feels a philanthropist *should* be (a higher type of person, reaching
down to help the low) and what his philanthropist *is* (an even lower
man who allowed Pip to climb to success on his back). In questioning
philanthropy as it affected him, Pip unintentionally casts doubt on the
whole enterprise in its more usual (opposite) form. There is something inherently dishonest and unbalanced about the granting and acceptance of "free" money, because the no-strings-attached grant always turns out to be tied quite tightly to the giver. One incurs a debt—
of gratitude, of respect, of affection-on-demand—by accepting the
gift. In Pip's case, it's possible to contrast the relatively honest exchange at the beginning of the novel (when the convict uses fear to ex-
tort food and equipment from Pip, much as the IRS extorts our taxes
from us) with the much more corrupted exchange that takes place
when the convict subsidizes Pip's whole life. (What the convict gets,
in this exchange, is the satisfaction of having created a gentleman.) In
the first case, the obligations end with the exchange: Pip carries away
his fear, the convict his "wittles" and file. In the second case, the obligations are so large and so irrevocable that they can never be paid off,
by either party to the arrangement. The convict has made Pip's fortune
and ruined, in a sense, his life, while Pip, at first despising his benefactor for not being someone else, can never fully make up for that initial failure of gratitude.

The real problem with philanthropy is that it calls into question the
character of both the donor and the recipient. "Philanthropy is almost
the only virtue which is sufficiently appreciated by mankind," Thoreau noted in the first chapter of *Walden*. "Nay, it is greatly overrated;
and it is our selfishness which overrates it. A robust poor man, one
sunny day here in Concord, praised a fellow-townsman to me, because, as he said, he was kind to the poor; meaning himself." But if
selfish egoism is the flaw exposed in the recipient, something not too
different surfaces in the philanthropist himself, as Thoreau goes on to
point out in the next paragraph: "Under what latitude reside the heathen to whom we would send light? Who is that intemperate and brutal man whom we would redeem? If anything ail a man, so that he
does not perform his functions, if he have a pain in his bowels even,—

for that is the seat of sympathy,—he forthwith sets about reforming—the world." And to this amusing theory, Thoreau appends a wry and typically ironic self-assessment: "I have never dreamed of any enormity greater than I have committed. I never knew, and never shall know, a worse man than myself."[1] Thoreau's confession has the obviously intentional ring of a boast. In his very moment of rejecting philanthropy most deeply, of advocating a tend-your-own-garden technique, he manages (with his habitual Janus-faced approach to meaning) to echo the kind of public avowal of one's own sins that typifies one form of present-day "philanthropist": that is, the TV evangelist.

First published in 1854, *Walden* was written at a time when *philanthropy* still meant something very close to its Greek roots. The first examples given in the *OED*, from the early seventeenth century, show the word being used strictly in the sense of "love of one's fellow man" (or, by extension, love of God to man) and the beneficent acts attached thereunto. This meaning extends up to the middle of the nineteenth century (an 1849 quote, from Wilberforce, refers piously to "the lessons of universal Philanthropy"). But by the late nineteenth century the word had taken on a less spiritual and more pecuniary meaning. "A great philanthropist has astonished the world by giving it large sums of money during his lifetime," runs an 1875 entry in the *OED*; *Harper's Magazine* in 1884 referred to "the head of a great hospital and many philanthropies." This is the sense the word has for us today: it has moved away from a personal and occasionally religious form of giving to a more purely financial one.

If one wanted to speak about giving money during the seventeenth, eighteenth, and early nineteenth centuries, one used instead the word *alms*—or, occasionally, *charity*. *Alms* derives from *eleemosynary*, a word which got its most famous outing (I would venture to say that many people know it only from this context) in the first sentence of Fielding's *Tom Jones*: "An author ought to consider himself, not as a gentleman who gives a private or eleemosynary treat, but rather as one who keeps a public ordinary, at which all persons are welcome for their money." The novelist's mistrust of philanthropy had thus begun by 1749, a good century before Dickens. And the ambivalent feelings attached to charitable giving did not appear only in fiction. Samuel Johnson, in his 1773 Dictionary, defined the word *alms* straightforwardly enough as "What is given gratuitously in relief of the poor." But he then went on to illustrate the word by offering the sentence, "The poor beggar hath a just demand of alms from the rich man; who is guilty of fraud, injustice, and oppression, if he does not afford relief according to his abilities"—which kind of takes the gratuitousness out of "gratuitously." Dr. Johnson also remarked, with his typically digressive sense of the truly interesting, that the word *alms* "has no singular." One cannot give an alm, only alms—again, the subliminal sense of obligation and extension (one quarter is not enough . . .).

In fact, all the words associated with philanthropic giving seem afflicted with comparable grammatical eccentricities. *Philanthropy* itself has no verb form (to philanthropize? to philanthrape?), despite the fact that it currently denotes an action. Perhaps that omission came about partly through its origins as a purely spiritual or attitudinal virtue: Johnson defines it as "love of mankind; good nature," both of which can be possessed without necessarily being demonstrated. *Benefactor* (to which Johnson gives the secondary definition of "he that contributes to some public charity") also has no verb form, only another noun—*benevolence*—to represent the action rather than the actor. In Dr. Johnson's time, *benevolence* had the primary meaning we give it now ("Disposition to do good" is the way he puts it), but it also had the subsidiary meaning of a kind of tax, devised by Edward IV and abolished by Richard III. *Benevolence*, in other words, has gone the opposite direction from its fellow philanthropic words: it once meant money and now means only love. *Benefactor*, Johnson notes, "is used with of, but oftener to, before the person benefited." *To* certainly makes more sense—the money or other benefit is going *from* the benefactor *to* the recipient—but in our own time we've dropped that locution, relying entirely on the connecting *of.* This strange preposition essentially makes the benefactor a product of his recipient: the role of benefactor is conferred on him by his relationship to the person who receives the benefit, and the apparent direction of virtuous flow is thus reversed.

Charity, like *philanthropy*, is a word which used to point toward love and now points toward money. (Note that the Spanish and Italian word *caro* and its English equivalent *dear* still gesture simultaneously in both directions.) In Dr. Johnson's period, the word teetered in the balance: Johnson's first three definitions of *charity* are all allied with the old meanings of *philanthropy* (goodwill, universal love, etc.), while definitions four and five ("liberality to the poor" and "alms") tend toward our modern interpretation of philanthropic activity. *Charity* in the singular can still occasionally retain a religious overtone, a sense of disinterested tenderness, but the plural form has been eaten up by the business of public giving. Roget's Thesaurus evades the problem by giving only the adjectival form, *charitable*, thus restricting the meaning to spiritual values (kind, generous, Christian, and so forth). Oddly enough, my 1958 edition of Roget, billed on the cover as "up-to-date" and "newly written," similarly restricts the meaning of philanthropy ("altruism, humanity . . . good will to men"); that is, this supposedly revised edition ignores the financial meanings that have seeped into the word since 1852, when Mr. Roget first published his listings. These meanings have by now so completely flooded the word *philanthropy* that it has for us an inherent tone of hypocrisy: its philology suggests a personally expressed love for humanity, but its present practice mainly involves relatively impersonal monuments to vast fortunes of celebrated donors. These days, a philanthropist is much more likely to act out of the desire for reflected self-love than out of a disinterested love of mankind. (Thoreau would have me question, though, the extent to which the word *disinterested* could ever apply to a philanthropist, even in his day and earlier.)

Henry James wrote his final novel, *The Golden Bowl*, just as *philanthropy* had shifted permanently from its largely attitudinal to its more financial connotation, and his philanthropist, Adam Verver, is parked squarely in the center of that shift. A "simple," "innocent" American businessman who has somehow managed to accumulate gigantic sums of money (James, no idiot, must have been aware of the irony), Verver goes around Europe collecting "fine" things—old, beautiful, artistic things—for a projected museum to be located in his rough American hometown (shades of J. P. Morgan). Two of the things he collects are an extremely handsome, nobly born Italian son-in-law and a young, beautiful American wife. Both of these purchases—Prince Amerigo and Charlotte—are well aware of the extent to which good money has been paid for them, and they feel correspondingly and somewhat oppressively obliged. The Prince becomes especially conscious of the unremittingness of his situation during a dinner party in which he occasionally catches his father-in-law's eye:

> This directed gaze rested at its ease, but it neither lingered nor penetrated, and was, to the Prince's fancy, much of the same order as any glance directed, for due attention, from the same quarter, to the figure of a check received in the course of business and about to be enclosed to a banker. It made sure of the amount—and just so, from time to time, the amount of the Prince was made sure. He was being thus, in renewed installments, perpetually paid in; he already reposed in the bank as a value, but subject, in this comfortable way, to repeated, to infinite endorsement.

Charlotte, always the quicker of the two to formulate things in words, has confided to the Prince, several pages earlier, a similar realization about her own situation:

"I've got so much, by my marriage"—for she had never for a moment concealed from him how "much" she had felt it and was finding it— "that I should deserve no charity if I stinted my return. Not to do that, to give back on the contrary all one can, are just one's decency and one's honour and one's virtue. These things, henceforth, if you're interested to know, are my rule of life, the absolute little gods of my worship, the holy images set up on the wall. O yes, since I'm not a brute," she had wound up, "you shall see me as I *am!*" Which was therefore as he had seen her—dealing always, from month to month, from day to day and from one occasion to the other, with the duties of a remunerated office.[2]

The language of James's paragraph encompasses all the different senses of philanthropy, even extending to the religious ("the absolute little gods"). And lest we forget that the "charity" Charlotte speaks of involves both love and money, we get James's constant reminder of the compression of the two, in the form of the Prince's frequent address to her, "*cara mia.*" Charlotte is both expensive and beloved—very "dear."

What is disturbing about *The Golden Bowl* (aside from all the other, perhaps more obviously anxiety-producing elements, like the love affair between Verver's son-in-law and Verver's wife) is the way the two kinds of philanthropy—love for the nearest representatives of humanity and gift-giving on a large impersonal scale—both turn out to be riddled with ego. Adam's acquisitiveness seems appropriate on neither front: money seems a sufficient but not, finally, a satisfactory way of acquiring either a spouse or an artistic heritage. Yet James doesn't let us rest with condemning Adam Verver. When you read *The Golden Bowl*, you begin to feel that all love partakes of ownership and all philanthropy of self-glorification. The very possibility and indeed the very value of "disinterestedness" come under fire, especially since the most disinterested character in the novel, Fanny Assingham, is the person largely responsible for landing her friends in their distressing situation. We come back in the end to a viewpoint very much like Thoreau's, but one in which the ante is greatly raised by the move from the isolation of a beanfield to the necessarily complex relations of a social world. One can only remain innocent of the failures and excesses of philanthropy by remaining entirely apart from society, as Thoreau does; but James won't let his characters off that hook, and most of us can't get off it either.

These days, very few of us encounter philanthropists in the flesh (except in the sense I began with, as small alms-givers). For the most part, our experiences with modern philanthropy are experiences with philanthropic organizations. (The *OED Supplement* reflects this transition by recording the word *philanthropoid*, first used in 1949 and defined as "a professional philanthropist, a worker for a charitable or grant-awarding institution.") As a consultant and a project director, I have been on both the giving and receiving ends of these transactions—have been, so to speak, both philanthropoid and philanthropee. Of the two, I found receiving far less painful.

I don't know what things were like in the salad days of organizational philanthropy (or even when those salad days might have been—I would guess the 1950s). But since about 1981, when I entered the picture, philanthropy has become more and more of a business. A foundation may still be handing out "free" money, but it wants to make sure it's getting some kind of bang for its buck. It "evaluates" competing requests; it "measures benefit" (even, sometimes, on a crude cost-per-person basis); and it demands "accountability" from its recipients. These recipients, too, now tend to be organizations rather than individuals. Nobody, for instance, gives money directly to a poor person any more (except, under duress, on the street). Instead, a wealthy organization transfers funds to a "service" organization, which in turn sees that something is done for the poor. The process works similarly when the beneficiaries are medical, educational, arts, or environmental agencies rather than organizations serving the poor: in such cases, the philanthropic justification has to do with "improving the quality of life" rather than strictly spreading the wealth.

Severing the tie between the individual donor and the individual recipient has had both good and bad effects. On the negative side, there is something ludicrous, if not downright offensive, about having a group that serves meals to the homeless (or carries out some other obviously philanthropic service) fill out quarterly reports describing the cost-benefit ratio of the operation. This is *Hard Times* Gradgrindism at its worst. On the other hand, the presence of an intervening organization certainly reduces the degree of forelock-tugging required by the philanthropic relationship. If they don't directly confront their benefactors, the poor needn't act—or even feel—particularly grateful, and that in itself is a great boon.

Ironically enough, philanthropy works best—in the sense of being most painless and least embarrassing to the participating parties—in the area where it is least needed: that is, in the arts. Over the years, both the artists (along with their representative organizations) and the philanthropies have tried to portray arts grants as in some way equivalent, if not identical in nature, to grants that benefit those in dire need. But the brute fact is that art doesn't *need* philanthropy. The artist, a poverty-stricken consumptive, might need a handout; that's a different matter, and in that case he qualifies as a poor person, not an artist. But art itself is something that will either generate and survive or not, regardless of foundation grants. It may be a lot easier for people to *see* the art if philanthropies support art museums and symphony orchestras and theater companies and literary magazines; but that support will not in itself guarantee (or even, I would guess, further) the production of really good art. The best art, of the present as of the past, is independent of subsidy, at least as a causal factor. I'm not saying that artists don't work for money: *Great Expectations* and *The Golden Bowl* might never have been produced if their authors hadn't been able to make a living as writers. But I sincerely doubt that a nineteenth-century MacArthur award, if granted to either Dickens or James, would have led to anything greater than those two novels. The rallying cry of most foundations is that they want to "make a difference"; but in the area of the arts, the flat truth is that they probably don't.

Philanthropic organizations have a sneaking suspicion of this fact. In order to squelch the uncomfortable realization, they often tack on some requirement for "public benefit" in their grants to artists: the writer must give a reading at a public school, the dancer must perform in a prison, and so forth. These requirements imply a belief that pure support of art is not an appropriate function of philanthropy. Such rules also suggest that the artist is somehow outside the bounds of public obligation, and needs to be brought into the fold. But the "public benefit" clause is a foolish way to do this, for the artist—if he can be compromised at all—will already have been compromised by the mere acceptance of the philanthropist's money. That, rather than any spurious public appearances, is what marks his signature on the social contract. Like Pip taking the convict's money, the artist irreversibly acknowledges his bond with society simply by accepting the grant. Depending on his personality, he will then proceed to honor the bond or bite the hand that feeds him. Neither response will determine the quality of the art he produces, and neither will ultimately be caused by his having been given a grant. The renegade artist will be a renegade with or without philanthropic support, and the conformist will be likewise.

On some level, artists suspect all this, which is why they are so irritating for foundation people to deal with. They accept philanthropic support as their unnecessary but nonetheless demanded due; they feel the philanthropies should be grateful for getting to assist *them*. In this belief, history supports them: we can now see that Leonardo da Vinci's and Michelangelo's patrons got a lot more from their artists—in terms of public recognition and spiritual glorification—than those artists ever took from them. And, as James suggested, more recent philanthropists like the fictional Adam Verver and the very real J. P. Morgan actually collected art for the fun of it—to redound to their own material and aesthetic credit—rather than out of the kind of self-sacrificing "love of mankind" that motivated do-gooders like Jane Addams.

Because there is no real bond of obligation or gratitude incurred on either side, philanthropy to the arts is somehow cleaner and clearer than other kinds of giving. This is not at all to say that it's better: I would be sorry indeed if my words were used as an excuse to transfer millions of dollars from Headstart programs and Meals-on-Wheels to the coffers of art museums and opera companies. But giving to the arts lacks some of the inherent inconsistencies that Thoreau discerned in philanthropy. Arts giving, unlike other kinds, doesn't inevitably set up a high/low-status relationship between the two participants in the event. And arts giving, because it really doesn't involve a felt response to human need, cleanly severs the bond between philanthropy and its Greek roots. This kind of giving isn't about love; it's purely about money. That may sound brutal, but it's in fact less disturbing than the curious mixture that remains in the other philanthropic fields.

There's a United Way television commercial that takes various forms, each one showing some grateful recipient of United Way funds acting in a heartwarming manner. At the end of the commercial, the recipient looks out at the anonymous TV audience and says, "I don't know you, but I love you." This is the opposite of the clean break: this is the "phil" in philanthropy taken literally. But the direction of the love has been reversed. Here it's the receiver, and not the giver, who feels impersonal love of his fellow man. And the love is not a disinterested feeling, but a coerced and coercive combination of gratitude and pleading. "Thanks for helping me, and could you please help me some more?" is what the commercial really means. If this is love, then my tortured giving-up of a few coins to a street-person is generosity.

Notes

1. Henry David Thoreau, *Walden and On the Duty of Civil Disobedience* (New York, 1962), pp. 64, 65.

2. Henry James, *The Golden Bowl* (New York, 1905), pp. 230, 225.

From the Novel *Nice Work*

FOR ROBYN AND CHARLES weekends were for work as well as recreation, and the two activities tended to blend into each other at certain interfaces. Was it work or recreation, for instance, to browse through the review pages of the *Observer* and the *Sunday Times*, mentally filing away information about the latest books, plays, films, and even fashion and furniture (for nothing semiotic is alien to the modern academic critic)? A brisk walk in Wellington boots to feed the ducks in the local park was, however, definitely recreation; and after a light lunch (Robyn cooked the omelettes and Charles dressed the salad), they settled down for a few hours' serious work in the congested living-room-study, before it would be time for Charles to drive back to Suffolk. Robyn had a stack of essays to mark, and Charles was reading a book on Deconstruction which he had agreed to review for a scholarly journal. The gas fire hissed and popped in the hearth. A harpsichord concerto by Haydn tinkled quietly on the stereo. Outside, as the light faded from the winter sky, melting snow dripped from the eaves and trickled down the gutters. Robyn, looking up from Marion Russell's overdue assessed essay on *Tess of the D'Urbervilles* (which was actually not at all bad, so perhaps the modelling job was turning out to be a sensible decision), caught Charles' abstracted gaze and smiled.

"Any good?" she enquired, nodding at his book.

"Not bad. Quite good on the de-centring of the subject, actually.

You remember that marvellous bit in Lacan?" Charles read out a quotation: " '*I think where I am not, therefore I am where I think not . . . I am
not, wherever I am the plaything of my thought; I think of what I am wherever I don't think I am thinking.*' "

"Marvellous," Robyn agreed.

"There's quite a good discussion of it in here."

"Isn't that where Lacan says something interesting about realism?"

"Yes: '*This two-faced mystery is linked to the fact that the truth can be
evoked only in that dimension of alibi in which all "realism" in creative works
takes its virtue from metonymy.*' "

Robyn frowned. "What d'you think that *means*, exactly? I mean, is
'truth' being used ironically?"

"Oh, I think so, yes. It's implied by the word 'alibi', surely? There
is no 'truth', in the absolute sense, no transcendental signified. Truth
is just a rhetorical illusion, a tissue of metonymies and metaphors, as
Nietzsche said. It all goes back to Nietzsche, really, as this chap points
out." Charles tapped the book on his lap. "Listen. Lacan goes on: '*It
is likewise linked to this other fact that we accede to meaning only through the
double twist of metaphor when we have the unique key: the signifier and the
signified of the Saussurian formula are not at the same level, and man only
deludes himself when he believes that his true place is at their axis, which is
nowhere.*' "

"But isn't he making a distinction there between 'truth' and 'meaning'? Truth is to meaning as metonymy is to metaphor."

"How?" It was Charles' turn to frown.

"Well, take Pringle's, for example."

"Pringle's?"

"The factory."

"Oh, that. You seem quite obsessed with that place."

"Well, it's uppermost in my mind. You could represent the factory
realistically by a set of metonymies—dirt, noise, heat and so on. But
you can only grasp the *meaning* of the factory by metaphor. The place
is like hell. The trouble with Wilcox is that he can't see that. He has no
metaphorical vision."

"And what about Danny Ram?" said Charles.

"Oh, poor old Danny Ram, I don't suppose he has any metaphorical vision either, otherwise he couldn't stick it. The factory to him is
just another set of metonymies and synecdoches: a lever he pulls, a pair
of greasy overalls he wears, a weekly pay packet. That's the truth of
his existence, but not the meaning of it."

"Which is . . .?"

"I just told you: hell. Alienation, if you want to put it in Marxist
terms."

"But—" said Charles. But he was interrupted by a long peal on the doorbell.

"Who on earth can that be?" Robyn wondered, starting to her feet.

"Not your friend Wilcox, again, I hope," said Charles.

"Why should it be?"

"I don't know. Only you made him sound a bit . . ." Charles, uncharacteristically, couldn't find the epithet he wanted.

"Well, you needn't look so apprehensive," said Robyn, with a grin. "He won't eat you." She went to the window and peeped out at the front porch. "Good Lord!" she exclaimed. "It's Basil!"

"Your brother?"

"Yes, and a girl." Robyn did a hop, skip and jump across the cluttered floor and went to open the front door, while Charles, displeased at the interruption, marked his place in the book and stowed it away in his briefcase. The little he knew about Basil did not suggest that deconstruction was a likely topic of conversation in the next hour or two.

Basil's decision to go into the City, announced to an incredulous family in his last undergraduate year at Oxford, had not been an idle threat. He had joined a merchant bank on graduating and after only three years' employment was already earning more than his father, who had related this fact to Robyn at Christmas with a mixture of pride and resentment. Basil himself had not been at home for Christmas, but skiing in St Moritz. It was in fact some time since Robyn had seen her brother, because, for their parents' sake, they deliberately arranged their visits home to alternate rather than coincide, and they had little desire to meet elsewhere. She was struck by the change in his appearance: his face was fatter, his wavy corn-coloured hair was neatly trimmed, and he seemed to have had his teeth capped—all presumably the results of his new affluence. Everything about him and his girlfriend signified money, from their pastel-pale, luxuriously thick sheepskin coats that seemed to fill the threshold when she opened the front door, to the red C-registration BMW parked at the kerb behind Charles' four-year-old Golf. Underneath the sheepskin coats Basil was wearing an Aquascutum cashmere sports jacket, and his girlfriend, whose name was Debbie, an outfit remarkably like one designed by Katherine Hamnett illustrated in that day's *Sunday Times*. This classy attire was explained partly by the fact that they had been to a hunt ball in Shropshire the previous evening, and had decided on impulse to call in on their way back to London.

"A hunt ball?" Robyn repeated, with a raised eyebrow. "Is this the same man whose idea of a good night out used to be listening to a punk band in a room over a pub?"

"We all have to grow up, Rob," said Basil. "Anyway, it was partly business. I made some useful contacts."

"It was a real lark," said Debbie, a pretty pale-faced girl with blonde hair cut like Princess Diana's, and a figure of almost anorexic slimness. "Held in a sorter castle. Just like a horror film, wonnit?" she said to Basil. "Suits of armour and stuffed animals' heads and everyfink."

At first Robyn thought that Debbie's Cockney accent was some sort of joke, but soon realised that it was authentic. In spite of her Sloaney clothes and hair-do, Debbie was decidedly lower-class. When Basil mentioned that she worked in the same bank as himself, Robyn assumed that she was a secretary or typist, but was quickly corrected by her brother when he followed her out to the kitchen where she was making tea.

"Good Lord, no," he said. "She's a foreign-exchange dealer. Very smart, earns more than I do."

"And how much is that?" Robyn asked.

"Thirty thousand, excluding bonuses," said Basil, his arms folded smugly across his chest.

Robyn stared. "Daddy said you were getting disgustingly rich, but I didn't realise just how disgusting. What do you do to earn that sort of money?"

"I'm in capital markets. I arrange swaps."

"Swaps?" The word reminded her of Basil when he was her kid brother, a gangling boy in scuffed shoes and a stained blazer, sorting conkers or gloating over his stamp collection.

"Yes. Suppose a corporate has borrowed x thousands at a fixed rate of interest. If they think that interest rates are going to fall, they could execute a swap transaction whereby we pay them a fixed rate and they pay us LIBOR, that's the London Interbank Offered Rate, which is variable . . ."

While Basil told Robyn much more than she wanted to know, or could understand, about swaps, she busied herself with the teacups and tried to conceal her boredom. He was anxious to assure her that he was only earning less than Debbie because he had started later. "She didn't go to University, you see."

"No, I thought she probably didn't."

"Not many spot dealers are graduates, actually. They've usually left school at sixteen and gone straight into the bank. Then somebody sees that they've got what it takes and gives them a chance."

Robyn asked what it took.

"The barrow-boy mentality, they call it. Quick wits and an appetite for non-stop dealing. Bonds are different, you have to be patient, spend a long time preparing a package. There are lulls. I couldn't last for half-an-hour in Debbie's dealing room—fifty people with about six telephones in each hand shouting across the room things like '*Six hundred million yen 9th of January!*' All day. It's a madhouse, but Debbie thrives on it. She comes from a family of bookies in Whitechapel."

"Is it serious, then, between you and Debbie?"

"What's serious?" said Basil, showing his capped teeth in a bland smile. "We don't have anybody else, if that's what you mean."

"I mean, are you living together?"

"Not literally. We both have our own houses. It makes sense to have a mortgage each, the way property prices are going up in London. How much did you pay for this place, by the way?"

"Twenty thousand."

"Good God, it would fetch four times that in Stoke Newington. Debbie bought a little terraced house there two years ago, just like this, for forty thousand, it's worth ninety now . . ."

"So property governs sexuality in the City these days?"

"Hasn't it always, according to Saint Karl?"

"That was before women liberated themselves."

"Fact is, we're both too knackered after work to be interested in anything more energetic than a bottle of wine and a hot bath. It's a long day. Twelve hours—sometimes more if things get lively. Debbie is usually at her desk by seven."

"Whatever for?"

"She does a lot of business with Tokyo . . . So we tend to work hard on our own all week and live it up together at the weekend. What about you and Charles? Isn't it time you got hitched?"

"Why d'you say that?" Robyn demanded.

"I was thinking, as we saw you through your front window from the pavement, that you looked just like some comfortably married couple."

"We're not into marriage."

"I say, do people still say 'into' like that, up here in the rust belt?"

"Don't be a metropolitan snob, Basil."

"Sorry," he said, with a smirk that showed he wasn't. "You've been very faithful, anyway."

"We don't have anyone else, if that's what you mean," she said drily.

"And how's the job?"

"In jeopardy," said Robyn, leading the way back to the living-room. Debbie, perched on the arm of Charles' chair, her hair falling over her eyes, was showing him a little gadget like a pocket quartz alarm clock.

"Is Lapsang Suchong all right?" Robyn asked, setting down the tea tray, and thinking to herself that Debbie probably favoured some brand advertised on television by chimps or animated teapots, brewed so strong you could stand the teaspoon up in it.

"Love it," said Debbie. She really was a very difficult person to get right.

"Very interesting," said Charles politely, handing Debbie's gadget back to her. It apparently informed her of the state of the world's principal currencies twenty-four hours a day, but as it only worked within a fifty-mile radius of London its liquid-crystal display was blank.

"I get ever so nervy when I'm outside of the range," she said. "At home I sleep with it under my pillow, so if I wake in the middle of the night I can check on the yen-dollar rate."

"So what's this about your job?" Basil asked Robyn.

Robyn explained briefly her situation, while Charles provided a more emotive gloss. "The irony is that she's easily the brightest person in the Department," he said. "The students know it, Swallow knows it, the other staff know it. But there's nothing anybody can do about it, apparently. That's what this government is doing to the universities: death by a thousand cuts."

"What a shame," said Debbie. "Why doncher try somethink else?"

"Like the money market?" Robyn enquired sardonically, though Debbie seemed to take the suggestion seriously.

"No, love, it's too late, I'm afraid. You're burned out at thirty-five, they reckon, in our game. But there must be something else you could do. Start a little business!"

"A business?" Robyn laughed at the absurdity of the idea.

"Yeah, why not? Basil could arrange the finance, couldn't you darl?"

"No problem."

"And you can get a government grant, forty quid a week and free management training for a year, too," said Debbie. "Friend of mine did it after she was made redundant. Opened a sports shoe boutique in Brixton with a bank loan of five thousand. Sold out two years later for a hundred and fifty grand and went to live in the Algarve. Has a chain of shops out there now, in all them time-share places."

"But I don't want to run a shoe shop or live in the Algarve," said Robyn. "I want to teach women's studies and poststructuralism and the nineteenth-century novel and write books about them."

"How much do you get for doing that?" Basil asked.

"Twelve thousand a year, approximately."

"Good God, is that all?"

"I don't do it for the money."

"No, I can see that."

"Actually," said Charles, "there are a great many people who live on half that."

"I'm sure there are," said Basil, "but I don't happen to know any of them. Do you?"

Charles was silent.

"I do," said Robyn.

"Who?" said Basil. "Tell me one person you know, I mean *know*, not just know of, somebody you talked to in the last week, who earns less than six thousand a year." His expression, both amused and belligerent, reminded Robyn of arguments they used to have when they were younger.

"Danny Ram," said Robyn. She happened to know that he earned a hundred and ten pounds a week, because she had asked Prendergast, the Personnel Director at Pringle's.

"And who's Danny Ram?"

"An Indian factory worker." Robyn derived considerable satisfaction from uttering this phrase, which seemed a very effective putdown of Basil's arrogant cynicism; but of course she then had to explain how she came to be acquainted with Danny Ram.

"Well, well," said Basil, when she had finished a brief account of her experiences at Pringle's, "So you've done your bit to make British industry even less competitive than it is already."

"I've done my bit to bring some social justice to it."

"Not that it will make any difference in the long run," said Basil. "Companies like Pringle's are batting on a losing wicket. Maggie's absolutely right—the future for our economy is in service industries, and perhaps some hi-tech engineering."

"Finance being one of the service industries?" Charles enquired.

"Naturally," said Basil, smiling. "And you ain't seen nothing yet. Wait till the Big Bang."

"What's that?" said Robyn.

Basil and Debbie looked at each other and burst out laughing. "I don't believe it," said Basil. "Don't you read the newspapers?"

"Not the financial pages," said Robyn.

"It's some kind of change in the rules of the Stock Exchange," said Charles, "that will allow people like Basil to make even more money than they do already."

"Or lose it," said Basil. "Don't forget there's an element of risk in our job. Unlike women's studies or critical theory," he added, with a glance at Robyn. "That's what makes it more interesting, of course."

"It's just a glorified form of gambling, isn't it?" said Charles.

"That's right. Debbie gambles with a stake of ten to twenty million pounds every day of the week, don't you my sweet?"

" 'Sright," said Debbie. "Course, it's not like having a flutter on a horse. You don't *see* the money, and it's not yours anyway, it's the bank's."

"But twenty million!" said Charles, visibly shaken. "That's nearly the annual budget of my University."

"You should see Debbie at work, Charles," said Basil. "It would open your eyes. You too, Rob."

"Yeah, why not?" said Debbie. "I could probably fix it."

"It might be interesting," said Charles, rather to Robyn's surprise.

"Not to me, I'm afraid," she said.

Basil glanced at his watch, extending his wrist just long enough to show that it was a Rolex. "Time we were off."

He insisted that they went outside into the slushy street to admire his BMW. It had a sticker in the rear window saying BOND DEALERS DO IT BACK TO BACK. Robyn asked what it meant.

Debbie giggled. "Back to back is like a loan that's made in one currency and set against an equal loan in another."

"Oh, I see, it's a metaphor."

"What?"

"Never mind," said Robyn, hugging herself against the damp chill of the evening.

"It's also a joke," said Basil.

"Yes, I see that a joke is intended," said Robyn. "It must rather pall on people following you down the motorway."

"Nobody stays that close for long," said Basil. "This is a very fast car. Well, goodbye, sister mine."

Robyn submitted to a kiss on the cheek from Basil, then from Debbie. After a moment's hesitation and a little embarrassed laugh, Debbie brushed Charles' cheek with her own, and jumped into the passenger seat of the car. Charles and Basil waved vaguely to each other as they parted.

"You don't really want to visit that bank, do you?" Robyn said to Charles, as they returned to the house.

"I thought it might be interesting," said Charles. "I thought I might write something about it."

"Oh well, that's different," said Robyn, closing the front door and following Charles back into the living room. "Who for?"

"I don't know, *Marxism Today* perhaps. Or the *New Statesman*. I've been thinking lately I might try and supplement my income with a little freelance journalism."

"You've never done anything like that before," said Robyn.

"There's always a first time."

Robyn stepped over the soiled tea things on the floor and crouched by the gasfire to warm herself. "What did you make of Debbie?"

"Rather intriguing."

"Intriguing?"

"Well, so childlike in many ways, but handling millions of pounds every day."

"I'm afraid Mummy will consider Debbie what she calls 'common'—if Basil ever dares take her home."

"You rather gave the impression that you thought her common yourself."

"Me?" said Robyn indignantly.

"You patronised her terribly."

"Nonsense!"

"You may not think so," said Charles calmly. "But you did."

Robyn did not like to be accused of snobbery, but her conscience was not entirely easy. "Well, what can you talk about to people like that," she said defensively. "Money? Holidays? Cars? Basil's just as bad. He's become quite obnoxious, as a matter of fact."

"Mmm."

"Don't let's ever become rich, Charles," said Robyn, suddenly anxious to mend the little breach that had opened up between them.

"I don't think there's any danger of that," Charles said, rather bitterly, Robyn thought.

KATHLEEN ODEAN

Bear Hugs and Bo Dereks
on Wall Street

WHEN THE STOCK MARKET CRASHED on 19 October 1987, before the day was out Wall Streeters had started calling it *Black Monday*. The next day, another frantic one for investors, immediately became *Terrible Tuesday*. In the months that followed, exchange officials sought methods to prevent the market from plummeting again. Wall Streeters soon dubbed the proposed measures *circuit breakers*, a term for the electrical device that temporarily shuts off power in the case of an overload.

Like many occupational groups, brokers and traders have an extensive body of slang, known mainly to those on the Street. As I found when collecting Wall Street slang over several years, the oral nature of the stock market makes it a fertile ground for coining slang words and phrases that describe its people, places, and products.

Despite its widespread use in the financial markets, Wall Street slang has been largely overlooked by students of language, who may have assumed that all business language is dull and bureaucratic. Yet the stock market has a long and rich tradition of creating snappy words and apt images. The *OED* gives citations for *bear* in 1709 and *bull* in 1714 as stock market terms; the slang lexicon has been expanding ever since, in England and the United States.

While slang experts have neglected the stock market, they have given disproportionate attention to the language of the military and of

criminals, including prison slang. All three groups share several characteristics: they are made up primarily of men who spend a lot of time
together in close quarters and whose lives fluctuate between boredom
and great tension—during busy markets or crashes, during war, and
during prison riots or criminal acts. Fluctuating conditions are unusually conducive to slang inventions, but the world of Wall Street,
which encompasses investment businesses throughout the country,
invents it constantly because Wall Streeters talk so much in their work.
Traders shout and chat on exchange floors all day, while brokers spend
their time on telephones trying to make sales. The spoken word
clinches agreements, for the proverb "My word is my bond" is taken
seriously in this milieu. Any newcomer who renegs on an oral promise will be shunned by fellow traders.

In the same spirit, brokers take, buy, and sell orders from their customers on the telephone and execute them before any paperwork is
mailed out. A customer who places an order but later denies it because
the stock price has dropped will have to find a new brokerage firm, if
possible.

While traders work *on the floor*, as the exchanges are called, brokers
work *upstairs*, the term for brokerage offices. There, novice brokers sit
in an open space dubbed the *bullpen* and make cold calls to find new
customers, a practice known as *dialing and smiling* or *dialing for dollars*.
Big producers, brokers who bring in large commissions, occupy individual offices with several telephones.

Because establishing a congenial atmosphere is essential in telephone sales, brokers like to open their conversations with jokes, anecdotes, and colorful slang terms, including nicknames: "Want to buy
some Bo Dereks? or some James Bonds?" *James Bonds* are bonds that
will mature in the year 2007, and *Bo Dereks*, which were issued when
the movie "10" starring Bo Derek was in the theaters, are bonds that
will mature in 2010.

Brokers who serve retail customers often chat first about what's
happening on the Street, bringing up nicknames for prominent Wall
Street figures such as *Icahn the Terrible* for Carl Icahn, *Irv the Liquidator*
for Irwin Jacobs, or *Dr. Gloom* for Henry Kaufman. Hearing the slang
makes the customer feel more "in the know," more like a true Wall
Streeter, a feeling investors relish. At the same time, the esoteric language serves to mystify and impress customers and other outsiders,
who would like to be closer to this realm of money.

Within the expanse of Wall Street exist many subgroups with their
own specialized language, such as the traders on the exchange floors
who create dozens of nicknames for stocks, many of which the brokers upstairs don't know. These nicknames not only serve to identify

members of the group but occasionally form part of an elaborate practical joke reminiscent of a college fraternity hazing. Before computers replaced chalkboards on exchange floors, a new trader would receive an order from the brokerage he worked for to buy a hundred shares of Transatlantic Bridge (or Third Avenue Railroad or Coney Island Sand), although no such stock existed, whereupon his fellow traders would gather around a specialist, one of the exchange members who buy and sell stocks, bidding on Transatlantic Bridge. The specialist would ignore the novice's attempts to bid, and meanwhile the stock price would climb steadily. Finally, when the price had gone way up, the specialist would sell some to the new broker. But as he walked away, the broker would hear the price drop dozens of points—and be convinced that he had failed miserably on one of his first trades.

Many of the nicknames are derived from the stock symbols that appear on the electronic ticker tape and computer screens. Thus, Northwest Airlines' stock symbol NWA becomes *Nawa*, and DMP for Dome Petroleum becomes *Dump*. Traders turn GHO for General Homes into *Ghost*; HUM for Humana into *Hummer*; and MDR for McDermott into *Murder*. They call Dayton Hudson (DH) *Deadhead* and General Instrument (GRL) *Gorilla*.

A trader will approach a specialist and ask for a stock price by saying "How's your *Dynamite*?" for General Dynamic stock or "How's your *Organ*?" for Wurlitzer. Nicknames function as shorthand when they can be said more quickly or clearly than stock symbols, most of which consist of three letters. Speed matters during brisk trading, since the more transactions a trader makes the better. But because mistakes are costly, distinct names are prized over brief ones. Nicknames are also easier to remember than symbols, an important feature for the floor's *two-dollar brokers*, who trade in many stocks and must remember them all.

Besides stock symbols, a corporation's products or the corporate name may provide the basis for nicknames. Kellogg's nickname is *Cornflakes*, Ralston Purina's is *Dog Chow*, and Wrigley's is *Gum*. Traders call stock in Lucky Stores *Unlucky* and stock in Chesebrough-Pond *Cheeseburgers*.

Market inhabitants have been coining nicknames for over a hundred years. In a list compiled in 1895, A. J. Wilson gives eighty "Slang, or Corrupted Names" from the London Exchange. *Marbles* stood for Marbella Iron Ore Shares and *Imps* for Imperial Tobacco Company shares; Aerated Bread Shares were *Breads*, while fractions of these shares were *Bread Crumbs*.

Traders have always enjoyed slang terms with sexual references. In the 1960s, according to magazine articles, Wall Streeters dubbed Simmons Mattress Company *America's Playground* and Italian Development Bonds *Lolas*. Southern Bell Telephone was known as *Scarlett O'Hara* and Continental Can was *Zsa Zsa Gabor*. Traders still talk about the nicknames for two companies that are no longer traded: Welbilt Corporation, *Marilyn Monroe*, and Pittsburgh Screw and Bolt Corporation, *Love 'em and Leave 'em*. Currently heard at the New York Stock Exchange are *Huge Tool* for Hughes Tool and *Dildo* for Snap-On Tool, Inc.

As these examples illustrate, traders refer to many stocks by women's names. Londoners traded *Floras, Berthas, Claras, Clarettes, Coras, Noras*, and *Saras*. In the U.S., Wall Streeters have dealt in stocks named *Becky, Amy, Old Mona, Maggie, Pamela, Jennie Tel, Weeping Mary, Rebecca, Minnie, Alice, Annie*, and *Molly*.

In the late 1800s, Wall Streeters called Erie Railroad the *Scarlet Woman of Wall Street* and the *Harlot of the Rails*, because speculator Daniel Drew had ruined the stock's reputation by repeatedly manipulating its price. A popular stock market proverb also treats stocks as feminine, with some as prostitutes: "When the paddy wagon comes, they take the good girls with the bad"—when the market crashes, strong stocks fall along with weak ones.

Traders may *goose Jennie Tel, ride Pamela*, or *pull out of Becky*. The market also is portrayed as female and subject to sexual maneuvers. Traders *straddle* the market when they execute *spreads*; they perform *in-and-out trading*. Among the orders traders carry out are *touch but don't penetrate* the market and *participate but don't initiate*.

When it comes to describing the market in female terms, the commodity traders interviewed in Bob Tamarkin's 1985 book *The New Gatsbys* use slang familiar outside of Wall Street: "For many traders the market is a 'bitch,' a 'cunt,' a 'whore,' an 'old lady.' . . . If you 'fight' it or 'go up against it,' chances are you'll be 'screwed' by it or maybe 'fucked over.' "

The sexual nature of the language reveals the traders' need to assert their masculinity and cultivate a macho image. Former options trader Nancy Bazelton Goldstone reports that male options traders start their workday by discussing their sexual exploits of the night before. She adds, "Raunchy jokes are the order of the day—the dirtier, the better."

The derogatory aspect of many nicknames for stocks—*Slob* for Schlumberger, *Murder Burgers* for McDonalds, *Bare Ass* for Boeing—is part of the macho, rebellious persona traders cultivate. True to this image, commodity traders in Chicago refer to their work as the *Last Frontier*, as though their lives were as free and rough as a cowboy's. Similarly, high-powered Wall Streeters have been known as *gunslingers* and *hipshooters*.

The recurrent violent images in the slang suggest that Wall Streeters see themselves as fighters in a dangerous financial world. On the exchange floors, the most aggressive traders are lauded as *floor animals*, and after a busy day, observers will comment on "the blood on the floor." The well-known proverb "Don't buy until the blood is running in the streets" advocates buying when others panic.

Even the once proper world of investment banking has adopted a body of slang in the last two decades that portrays corporate takeovers as a fight over female corporations. In the *takeover wars*, *raiders* come to metaphoric blows with *white knights* over attractive corporations that both would like to acquire, known as *sleeping beauties* or *damsels in distress*. The raiders have employed such tactics as *strong bear hugs*, *blitzkreig tender offers*, and *Saturday Night Specials*. These *takeover artists*, who use junk bonds to finance takeovers, meet at the annual conference known as the *Predators' Ball* to learn the latest junk bond techniques.

To ward off raiders, target corporations concoct *poison pills*, also dubbed *cyanide capsules* and *doomsday pills*. They sell off their *crown jewels* and adopt other *scorched-earth policies*. Lawyers and public relations experts known as *hired guns* or *killer bees* try to *bulletproof* the targets against attacks.

The takeover wars require secrecy, which has inspired espionage-like practices. For example, investment bankers who research possible targets for raiders like to refer to these companies by code names. In one takeover, McGraw-Hill was dubbed *Milk and Honey*, while the company they acquired, Monchik-Weber, was *Merry Widow*. In another case the female code name for the target, *Raquel*, from movie star Raquel Welch, conveyed the desirability of the target company Reliance.

Some raiders secretly employ other companies to buy stock for them, in order to hide who is really acquiring the stock. The companies that do the buying are nicknamed *beards*, because they disguise the identity of the purchaser.

The theme running through the slang, whether violent or sexual, is dominance. The image Wall Streeters want to project is one of being in control, winning the war or conquering the female, doubtless because they have so little control over the main force in their world—the market.

The lack of control frequently results in loss of money. Standard wisdom has it that 95 percent of those who trade in commodities, and 80 percent of those in options, lose money. Although the stock market is not considered dangerous, large losses are a frequent occurrence—despite all the methods devised for beating the market. In slang, Wall

Streeters imagine themselves as fighters, thus denying their impotence in the market.

Outside forces in the economy, the government, and the rest of the business world dictate the ups and downs in stock prices. News of President Eisenhower's heart attack in 1955 triggered the biggest market plunge since 1929. When the Federal Reserve Board raised interest rates during the week of 19 February 1989, the Dow Jones Industrial Average—a measure of the market—fell a substantial forty-four points; as they say on Wall Street, "When the party starts to get merry, the Fed takes away the punch bowl." Even unsubstantiated rumors can affect stock prices. When a story circulated after the Chernobyl disaster that mutant sugar beets were growing out of control in the Ukraine, the market in sugar futures soared.

The commodities market has to contend with another unpredictable force: the weather. Because some of the commodities traded are crops, catastrophes such as droughts and floods affect trading, so many commodities firms employ meteorologists to give them weather forecasts.

No Wall Streeter, no matter how shrewd, can consistently predict the market. The great financier J. P. Morgan, when asked for a market forecast, always gave the only certain answer, "It will fluctuate." Big drops in the market, such as the *October Massacres* of 1978, 1979, and 1987, result in layoffs and even firm closings. The precarious nature of jobs, the market's volatility, and the large amounts of money at stake produce widespread anxiety on the Street. Wall Streeters themselves can see the stress they suffer by being in the market, but, one hears, "There's more anxiety caused by being *out* of the market when it is going up than there is being *in* the market when it is going down."

One also hears that "the market climbs a wall of worry," or that the market is a cruel force that *blows out* speculators, *burns* them and *kills* them. In return, traders *hammer* the market, *jackscrew* it, and *dump* stocks on it. They *pound* stocks and *slaughter* them, *fill and kill* orders, and execute *strangles*. But since the market is ultimately unpredictable, it is no wonder that some Wall Streeters try to control it through illegal maneuvers. In the highly publicized cases of *insider trading* during the 1980s, Wall Streeters acquired information about imminent takeovers in order to trade with certainty. Current investigations of the Chicago commodities market have revealed that traders have been illegally securing profits at customers' expense in a maneuver known as *bag trading*. Stories also appear in the news periodically about brokers *churning* customers—depleting their accounts through numerous trades solely to produce commissions for the broker.

Such crimes do immeasurable harm to the image that the public holds of Wall Street by reinforcing the longtime perception of it as shady, the result of many swindles and scandals in the market's history. Although presumably only a small percentage of Wall Streeters are guilty, the reputation of the whole profession suffers, as two jokes, one from the 1960s, the other from the 1980s, illustrate:

> Dear Abby, I've met the most wonderful man. We're engaged and plan to be married, but I have a terrible problem. He doesn't know about my family. My father's in jail, my mother's running a whorehouse, my sister's a prostitute there, and my brother is a stockbroker. Dare I tell him about my brother?

and

> Q: What happens when you cross a Wall Streeter with a pig?
> A: There are some things even a pig won't do.

The public's attitude towards Wall Street is one not just of distrust but of hostility. When the market slumps or crashes, even those who have no investments suffer. As Will Rogers said in 1929, "Let Wall Street have a nightmare and the whole country has to help get them back in bed again." The public bitterly resents it when the stock market harms the general economy.

For their part, brokers have traditionally used slang to vent hostility against customers behind their backs. Disappointed investors rant at their brokers, but brokers who would like to respond in kind must restrain themselves because they rely on their customers' goodwill. At brokerages, as elsewhere, "the customer is always right," but brokers can joke with each other about *churning and burning* customers or *blowing them out after a point*, that is, making trades for the sake of commissions, or selling a *cemetery spread*, a trading combination guaranteed to kill any possible profit.

Slang terms for unsuccessful, gullible investors have proliferated throughout market history, including *suckers, mullets, lilies, barefoot pilgrims, Aunt Janes*, and *widows and orphans*. In the late 1700s in England, a popular term for an investor who suffered large losses was *lame duck*. As William H. Ireland cautioned in 1807,

> If to the Stock Exchange you speed
> To try with bulls and bears your luck
> 'Tis odds you soon from gold are freed
> And waddle forth a limping duck.

Wall Street adopted the term, and added the variation *dead duck* to describe a speculator who had lost everything. (*Lame duck* had gained its political usage by 1863.)

Money itself has a dark side, as stock market slang and general slang reveal. It is associated with dirt, as in *filthy rich*, and losing money is expressed in terms of getting cleaner. A person who *takes a bath*, gets *taken to the cleaners*, or gets *put through the financial wringer* loses money. To be *wiped out* or *cleaned out* leaves the person metaphorically cleaner—and financially worse off. At a stock market *laundry*, victims got swindled out of their money in a maneuver known as the *laundry business*. *Washing the market*, another illegal maneuver, takes money out of the market and puts it in the swindler's pocket. Money obtained illegally seems to be dirtier than other money and needs to be *laundered*, moved through a number of financial channels until it appears to be respectable.

Wealthy people wallow in luxury the way pigs wallow in mud. Freud noted the link between money and feces in dreams and folklore, also found in the old proverb, "Money, like dung, does no good till it is spread." In the same vein, millionaire J. Paul Getty commented in 1967, "Money is like manure. You have to spend it around or it smells."

The ambivalence towards money—which is at once dirty and desirable—is yet another factor that traders cannot control, along with the attractions and anxieties, the dangers and rewards, of Wall Street, long ago christened both the *Street of Sorrows* and the *Golden Canyon*.

Practices

The rights of nations, and of kings, sink into
questions of grammar, if grammarians discuss them.
SAMUEL JOHNSON

Some speak and write as if they wanted to say
something: others as if they had something to say.
ARCHBISHOP WHATELY

Just as the writer, if he truly is one, appears
to "plagiarize" the reader, so today's impertinent
reader seriously believes that he is the true
author and knew it all before.
JOSÉ ORTEGA Y GASSET

The sun shone, having no alternative, on the nothing new.
SAMUEL BECKETT

ᴥ BRYAN A. GARNER

The Missing Common-Law Words

OF THE COMMON-LAW WIFE, LORD DENNING ONCE WROTE that "no such woman was known to the common law."[1] Nor *by* the common law, one might add, for lawyers often personify the law. The common-law wife is certainly well known to Anglo-American lawyers, although the circumstances surrounding the creation of her status vary from jurisdiction to jurisdiction.[2] Notably, the term *common-law husband* occasionally appears but is little known in comparison with its spouse.

That is but one of numberless curiosities in Anglo-American legal language, which has reached a stage in its development similar in some ways to that of the English language in the seventeenth century. The assertion may seem an odd one in this day, when legal writers increasingly attempt in their prose to approximate good idiomatic English. Yet it remains that the legal vocabulary has been imperfectly recorded at best, even in law dictionaries. The legal lexicographer of the late twentieth century finds something akin to what Samuel Johnson found when he undertook his great *Dictionary*: a speech copious without order, and energetic without rules; perplexities to be disentangled, and confusion to be regulated; choices to be made out of boundless variety. One may hope that this has been a "time of rudeness antecedent to perfection," which Johnson, in the famous Preface to his *Dictionary of the English Language* (1755), optimistically attributed to every language. None has yet approached that postulated state of perfection, and legal writers do not even dream of it.

The imperfections in legal language are easily pointed out. What is one to make of a learned profession whose most exalted members, the judges, elevate malapropisms to the level of near-standard idioms? A historical misnomer like *common-law wife* is at worst a venial blunder, at best a convenient neologism. Not so certain other developments, such as the confusion of *testamentary* with *testimonial*. The one has to do with wills, the other with testimony; the first syllable in each of the words is identical in form and etymology, but there the similarities end. Nevertheless, American judges have had difficulty keeping the words straight. Upon first seeing the phrase *documentary and testamentary evidence*, one might call it an unfortunate anomaly. With only a little research, however, one finds a number of examples in published judicial opinions.[3]

The misusage would not occur outside a legal context, and might go unnoticed by a layman anyway. Bungles of this kind seem to be on the rise. Now that Latin is a forgotten as well as a dead language, once established legal phrases such as *corpus delicti* have been transmogrified into erroneous forms. The macabre solecism that often appears today is *corpus delecti*, which is not merely a clever attempt at necrophiliac humor.[4] Similarly, *lex loci delicti*, which refers to "the law of the jurisdiction in which a wrong was committed," has become *lex loci delecti*.[5] The reader with training in Latin might suppose that to be "the law of the jurisdiction where delight occurred." *Delictual*, meaning "tortious," has not yet become *delectual*—a good thing, too, since some readers might further confuse that with *delectable*. Cicero, that great lawyer, would weep at what has become of his language in the hands of modern lawyers.

These are "learned bloopers," so to speak. Judges also partake of the more amusing type of malapropism, the howler that any educated reader recognizes. Thus a federal appellate judge writes, "To overturn the judge's denial of the motion to recuse would be an effrontery to his character." Other legal writers emulate Mrs. Malaprop and Mistress Quickly more closely still; a writer for a law journal states, "The main impotence for recruiting someone who has published is to ensure that he is used to long hours." And then there is the lawyer who requested judgment on his client's "meretricious" claim, noting that several witnesses had vouched for the client's "voracity."

Of course, lexicographers need not account for such freaks of usage, unless, like the misuse of *testamentary*, these begin to gain currency. (*Webster's Third*, after all, notes without comment that *flaunt* is sometimes used for *flout*.) What lexicographers should account for, all would agree, is the growth of the English vocabulary. It is a never-ending task.

Although any dictionary is obsolete to some extent by the time it appears in print, modern lexicographers strive to record linguistic innovations as soon as these prove to be something more than *hapax legomena*. It is a delicate balance, staying current while not giving sway to overnight fads. Delicate though that balance is, currency is what our dictionary-makers seem to pride themselves on most highly. In his preface to the second edition of *The Random House Dictionary of the English Language* (1987), Stuart Berg Flexner writes, "The twin explosions of knowledge and vocabulary from many sources have increased in magnitude during these past twenty-one years." The result, he says, is an expanded English vocabulary,

> not only from such obvious fields as science and technology and new forms and styles in the arts, fashion, and leisure activities, but also from history itself and from such social and cultural movements as concern with [*sic*] the environment, the women's movement, and a new awareness of and respect for ethnic diversity.[6]

When the controversial *Webster's Third* appeared in 1961, its editor, Philip B. Gove, explained in his preface that "the scientific and technical vocabulary has been considerably expanded to keep pace with progress especially in physical science (as in electronics, nuclear physics, statistics, and soil science), in technology (as in rocketry, communications, automation, and synthetics), in medicine, and in the experimental phases of natural science."[7] Similarly, the redoubtable Robert Burchfield stated, in his preface to the second volume of the *OED Supplement*, "The rapid expansion of work in all the sciences has been fully taken into account: anyone interested in the history of scientific words will find much of permanent value in the pages that follow. The terms of the printing industry and the names of plants and animals have continued to yield lexical material of considerable interest."[8] The printing industry—he would be interested in that, wouldn't he?

Amid all this talk of the explosive growth of the English vocabulary, hardly a word is to be found about the language of the law. The reason is not, as one might suppose, that linguistic innovation is rare in law. On the contrary, neologisms abound in modern legal writing, though both writer and reader are often unaware that certain commonplace law words have yet to find a home in English dictionaries. Why is it, for example, that a word like *conclusory*, in its modern legal sense, remains unaccounted for in all the major English-language dictionaries, though it has been used by lawyers since at least 1923? (More about this word in a moment.)

The answer lies in ignorance of legal language, coupled with a strong (however understandable) aversion to it. The pervasive misconception among laymen is that legal language is stranded somewhere between Chaucer and Shakespeare; that legal terminology consists in centuries-old words and phrases that lawyers dare not stray from. Vallins gave voice to this myth when he wrote, in *Good English*:

> The "standard" language, or current usage, has within it or, as it were, around it, all kinds of special languages which have their own constructions, modes of expression, syntax, idiom. Legal language is perhaps the best example. They, like the main standardised language, have their natural changes, though these changes are usually very slow, and sometimes (as in legal language) scarcely exist at all.[9]

Lexical changes occur in legal language far more than "scarcely at all," despite what our best dictionaries would suggest.[10] In truth, legal terminology is a curious mixture of the old and the new; what is new merely tends to be ignored amid all the archaic words.

Lexicographers fail to discover legal neologisms in part because legal writing both intimidates and bores them. They therefore tend to omit it from their research. One sympathizes with the lexicographers here, for who could think of a fate worse than having to read page after page of legalese?[11] Even so, the oversight is a serious one, given the number of meritorious (some might say meretricious) headwords that are excluded purely because the lexicographer has no clue about their frequency in law, or perhaps even about their existence. Besides, readers would find that legalese is gradually fading away; it is not all that difficult nowadays for an educated layman to read, for example, the opinions of the United States Supreme Court.

A less plausible explanation for these oversights we may reject out of hand. Lexicographers do not view legal English as being largely outside their purview, since they include *per stirpes, remittitur, replevin,* and thousands of other purely legal terms in our general unabridged dictionaries.[12] Vallins's reference to a standard language having specialized languages all around it calls to mind the famous statement from the preface to the *Oxford English Dictionary*: "the circle of the English language has a well-defined centre but no discernible circumference." The lexicographer, it is true, "must draw the line somewhere . . . , well knowing that the line which he draws will not satisfy all his critics."[13]

Well, here is one critic dissatisfied with the treatment accorded to legal language in our modern dictionaries, both legal and general. The circle as drawn is no circle at all: it is a pie with a piece missing. To illustrate the reasons for my dissatisfaction, I have collected a number of twentieth-century neologisms that, despite their indisputable currency in law, remain nonwords in the pages of our most highly touted reference works.

Conclusory is perhaps the prime example. The word is included in the *OED* really as nothing but a needless variant of *conclusive*, and is illustrated by three nineteenth-century quotations. One finds no hint in the *OED* of the modern legal sense. *Webster's Second* lists it as "rare" for *conclusive*, and *Webster's Third* leaves it out altogether. The first edition of the *Random House* omitted it; the second edition revived it as a main entry, presumably because its editors began to run across the word in legal contexts, but they misdefined it by following the *OED* and giving *conclusive* as its synonym. Most law dictionaries are equally unavailing; the word appears in no law dictionary other than my own *Dictionary of Modern Legal Usage*, which defines the word as "expressing a mere conclusion of fact without stating the specific facts upon which the conclusion is based." Thus a border-patrol agent's statement, "He is an illegal alien," is conclusory, whereas "I saw him swim across the Rio Grande and, when I questioned him, he admitted he had crossed the border illegally" is not.

An accurate dictionary entry for the word (modeled after *OED* entries) might appear as follows, the modern legal sense being sense (2):

> **conclusory** (kŏn-**klū**-sŏ-rē), *adj.* [f.L. *conclus-* ppl. stem + -*ory*: on L. type **conclūsōri-us*] 1. Relating or tending to a conclusion; conclusive. *Rare.*
>
> **[1846] 1876** *Contemp. Rev.* XXVIII.128
> This conciliatory and conclusory chapter.
>
> 2. *U.S.* Expressing a mere conclusion of fact or a factual inference without stating the underlying facts upon which the conclusion or inference is based.
>
> **1923** *Ringler v. Jetter*, 201 N.Y.S 525, 525 (App. Div.) The motion [is] granted, to the extent of directing the service of an amended complaint, omitting paragraphs 16, 17, and 30, and all conclusory matter of the nature pointed out herein. **1931** *Sprung v. Zalowitz*, 250 N.Y.S. 352, 354 (App. Div.) The description of the threats is conclusory in character. No facts are set out to support this conclusion. **1940** *People v. Hines*, 29 N.E.2d 483, 487 (N.Y.) Facts in detail supporting conclusory statements herein are available in the record. **1954** *Mietlinski v. Hickman*, 136 N.Y.S.2d 321, 325 (App. Div.) A conclusory statement by a layman on such a question is not entitled

to substantial weight as an admission. **1985** *Oregon Dept. of Fish and Wildlife v. Klamath Indian Tribe*, 473 U.S. 753, 787 (Marshall, J., dissenting) Ultimately, this produces a largely insensitive and conclusory historical inquiry that ignores how events almost certainly appeared to the Tribe. **1987** *Senate of Puerto Rico v. U.S. Department of Justice*, 823 F.2d 574, 585 (D.C.Cir.) [I]t is enough to observe that where no factual support is provided for an *essential* element of the claimed privilege or shield, the label 'conclusory' is surely apt. **1988** *United States v. Chaudhry*, 850 F.2d 851, 857 (1st Cir.) [D]efendant relies on the bare, conclusory, and entirely self-serving assertion that such "selective recording [constituted] a violation of his right to due process, confrontation, and a fair trial."

A computer search of American judicial opinions, conducted in April 1988, revealed more than 21,000 cases in which *conclusory* appears.[14] It has been used for more than sixty years in state and federal courts, including the United States Supreme Court. Yet when a justice on the Wyoming Supreme Court felt the need to use the word in 1987, he was troubled by its omission from our collegiate dictionaries: "After painstaking deliberation," he wrote for the court, "we have decided that we like the word *conclusory*, and we are distressed by its omission from the English language. [As if omission from a dictionary equaled omission from the language!] We now proclaim that henceforth *conclusory* is appropriately used in the opinions of this court. . . . Webster's, take heed."[15]

The justice's reaction to the omission is laudable, and unusual. The more frequent reaction is for the dictionary-user to conclude, with exaggerated deference to the dictionary-maker, that the use of such a word is incorrect. Thus in the 1880s, a bill was thrown out of the British Parliament because one of the words used in it was not in "the dictionary"—a reference, naturally, to Johnson's work.[16] Several judges have actually tried to wage a minor battle against *conclusory* on grounds that it has no support in the dictionaries. Hence the lexicographers' oversight has led to confusion among legal writers, who often derive their views about right and wrong in language from dictionaries. (Few modern lexicographers, of course, labor on the assumption that their work will be relied upon in this way.)

When the *New York Times* printed a story on *Modern Legal Usage* shortly after its publication in late 1987, the article suggested that I was "more accommodating" than "lawyer purists and nearly all dictionaries," which were said to "resist" *conclusory*.[17] The statement may be entirely correct about the lawyer purists, but it is quite wrong about the lexicographers, who have simply overlooked much of the linguistic innovation in law.

Among the more than thirty legal neologisms that were first documented in *Modern Legal Usage* are *ancillarity*, *asylee*, *benefitee*, *certworthy*, *condemnee*, *conveyee*, *discriminatee*, *enbancworthy*, *enjoinable*, *litigational*, *nonrefoulement*, *pretextual*, *quashal*, *recusement*, and *veniremember*. To be sure, some of these words are more apt than others, but they have all gained currency in law. Like many other words that receive no mention in our unabridged dictionaries, they are used daily by American judges and lawyers. Would not the editors of, say, the second edition of the *Random House* have seized the opportunity to document these words, if only they had known of their existence and the extent of their use? And would not the users of that dictionary be better served if the words had been documented and defined?

Quashal, the noun corresponding to the verb *to quash*, is a striking example of a legal word that has been neglected in conventional English lexicography. The word dates back to the 1880s, when the Florida Supreme Court seems to have invented it: "Yet the judgment might . . . have been put there *nunc pro tunc* . . . with the effect of removing the ground of quashal."[18] Today this lexicographic ghostword appears frequently (and usefully) in legal contexts.

Because the language of the law has remained largely untraversed by our best lexicographers since the days of Noah Webster (himself a lawyer), abundant inconsistencies have grown up within it. In the absence of authoritative dictionaries to settle questions about standard usages, competing neologisms—often, indeed usually, with no differentiation in sense—have cropped up. The opinions of the United States Supreme Court, for example, contain not just *conclusory*, but *conclusionary* and *conclusional* as well.[19] These two variants sprang up in federal-court opinions in the 1940s; since then, they have been largely ousted by *conclusory* (whose sense they share), though some legal writers persist in using them.

One might proliferate examples of the "choices to be made out of boundless variety." Restitution being a common subject in law, we find any number of examples of *restitutionary* and *restitutional* in law reports, although our unabridged dictionaries give only *restitutive* and *restitutory*. (These last two are little known to American lawyers.) Although our lexicographers keenly picked up *recusal*, a neologism dating from 1950, they are apparently unaware that, in some jurisdictions, *recusement* and *recusation* prevail.[20] The new *Random House* omits both of these. Though its battle for supremacy has certainly been lost to *injunctive*, the adjective *injunctional* might deserve a quick nod with more than 180 uses to its credit. What is the neutral adjective—that is, not *litigious*—corresponding to *litigation*? Even our most authoritative unabridged dictionaries do not tell us whether to use *litigational*, *liti-*

gatory, or *litigation* itself. *Black's Law Dictionary* supplies as little help on these questions as on most others.[21]

Sadly for the lawyer—indeed, for anyone in need of legal-linguistic guidance—English-language dictionary-makers have been far more keen on recording novelties in the vocabulary of scientists and doctors than those in the vocabulary of lawyers, even though the legal word-hoard has been growing at a surprising rate. That is one of the many reasons why the law needs its own unabridged historical dictionary, to be for lawyers what the *OED* is for everyone else. Then lexicographers would no longer "resist" new legal words out of ignorance that they even exist.

Nor would we be mistakenly led to believe that a word like *adversarial* was first used in 1967, or thereabouts. That is what *Webster's Ninth New Collegiate Dictionary*, published in 1983, indicates is "the date of the earliest recorded use in English, as far as it could be determined."[22] A simple computer search of legal databases would have yielded this American example from 1926: "No adversarial interest between parties is intrinsically involved."[23] That same computer search would have provided other specimens in law cases from 1949, 1952, and 1954.[24]

The ability to conduct computer searches has vastly improved our ability to monitor the entry of words into the legal lexicon.[25] Recently, for example, I came across the phrase *chicanerous litigant* in the celebrated treatise on federal practice by Professors Charles Alan Wright and Arthur Miller.[26] Not recognizing the adjective *chicanerous*, though its sense was clear, I turned to the second edition of the *Oxford English Dictionary* (to no avail), and then to *Webster's Third* (again to no avail). A computer search called up several uses of the word in published judicial opinions, the earliest dating from 1969.[27] Who would argue against the merits of having an adjective that corresponds to the noun *chicanery* (or *chicane*)? One wonders, however, whether we shall have to wait half a century before we can verify the word's existence in English-language dictionaries.

When it comes to neologisms, common-law English is, after all, not so very different from the common-law wife. Both live in the shadows, having attained a status of minimal respectability, even though they deserve better. Yet a large segment of the population continues to think that anything unsanctioned by the legislative codes is illicit. (Most people consult dictionaries precisely as if they were legislative codes.) How else can one explain why *common-law wife* is often loosely applied to a concubine or mistress?[28]

In venturing upon the *Oxford Law Dictionary*, of which I have assumed the chief editorship, The University of Texas School of Law and Oxford University Press have done much to address the problem. If legal lexicography has been in a shambles over the past century, this historical law dictionary, following in the path of the *OED*, should go a long way toward rectifying the numerous lexical oversights in law. The fruits of the *Oxford Law Dictionary* should be of value to general English lexicographers. Among the least consequential advantages is that judges will no longer feel compelled to write, out of defensiveness about using a common legal word, "Webster's, take heed!"

Of greater consequence will be the ability of judges, lawyers, and scholars to determine what the old words meant, not what the new ones mean. For the first time, we will be able to determine how certain words were used and understood at specific points in the evolution of Anglo-American jurisprudence. Thus what did *jurisdiction* generally mean in legal texts contemporaneous with the American Constitution? The *Oxford Law Dictionary* promises to rekindle the interpretative debate between those who hold to the original intention of constitutional and statutory framers and those who would give constitutional and statutory words their modern acceptations. The *Oxford Law Dictionary* will supply not just the missing common-law words, but the missing common-law meanings as well.

Notes

1. *Davis v. Johnson* [1979], A.C. 264, 270.
2. See *A Dictionary of Modern Legal Usage* (New York, 1987), s.v. "common-law marriage."
3. For instance, the United States Court of Appeals for the Eighth Circuit has written: "Bankrupts then offered documentary and testamentary evidence to rebut the Government's proof." *Solari Furs v. United States*, 436 F.2d 683, 685 (8th Cir. 1971). Nary a testator nor a beneficiary appears in that case; the writer meant to say *testimonial evidence*. Following is another example: "In the present case the subpoena *duces tecum* called only for non-testamentary [read *nontestimonial*] evidence to which was added an oral option." *United States v. Santucci*, 674 F.2d 624, 628 (7th Cir. 1982). Why *nontestimonial*, even, in place of *documentary*?
4. A search of the American state-court decisions on Westlaw, the on-line database, conducted on 31 October 1988, turned up 260 cases in which the spelling *corpus delecti* appears. For example, "The confession may be used to establish the *corpus delecti*." *Wooldridge v. State*, 653 S.W.2d 811, 816 (Tex. Crim. App. 1983).
5. "At one time Arkansas courts followed the traditional approach of the First Restatement, termed *lex loci delecti* (law of the place of injury)." Note, *Multistate Torts*, 10 U. Ark. Little Rock L.J. 511, 516 (1987–88) (repeatedly spelling the phrase incorrectly). "Most of the numerous inadequacies inherent in *lex loci delicti* also exist in the other traditional *lex loci* rules." *Duncan v. Cessna Aircraft Co.*, 665 S.W.2d 414, 421 (Tex. 1984).

6. Stuart Berg Flexner, Preface, *The Random House Dictionary of the English Language*, 2d ed. (New York, 1987), p. vii.

7. Philip B. Gove, *Webster's Third New International Dictionary* (Springfield, Mass., 1961), p. 4a.

8. Robert W. Burchfield, *A Supplement to the Oxford English Dictionary* (Oxford, 1976) 2:viii.

9. G. H. Vallins, *Good English: How to Write It* (New York, 1952), pp. 2–3. Cf. Bonamy Dobrée's misconceived statement that law and science are "realms in which prose seems to have remained static [from 1934 to 1964]" (*Modern Prose Style*, 2d ed. [Oxford, 1964], p. vii). Even apart from vocabulary development, Dobrée's statement was incorrect; to give an elementary example, in discursive legal prose, as opposed to drafting, syntax came to be less tortuous (on the whole) during this period.

10. Legal scholars have long been aware of terminological changes in law, as this turn-of-the-century statement demonstrates: "As our law develops it becomes more and more important to give definiteness to its phraseology; discriminations multiply, new situations and complications of fact arise, and the old outfit of ideas, discriminations, and phrases has to be carefully revised." James Bradley Thayer, *Preliminary Treatise on Evidence at the Common Law* (Boston, 1898), p. 190.

11. Presumably, also, the outside readers who volunteer to do systematic reading for a work like the *OED* do not ordinarily clamor for the law reports or law reviews.

In the preface to volume 3 of the *OED Supplement*, Burchfield acknowledged that "changes of emphasis or detail here and there" reflected "the research interests of scholars in various subjects, and the vicissitudes of the OED Department and of my own life" (p. v). Similarly, Frederick Mish, the editorial director at Merriam–Webster, has referred to the "strong influence of the editors' interests" on the selection of materials read for Merriam–Webster dictionaries. See John Willinsky, "Cutting English on the Bias: Five Lexicographers in Pursuit of the New," *American Speech* 63 (1988): 44.

12. Of one of the major American dictionary publishers, a scholar has (generously) written: "Though the Merriam Company admits the possibility of sometimes inadequate reading programs (as in mathematics, as noted in the preface to *6,000 Words*, p. 17a), secretarial errors, and/or debatable editorial judgment, their data are generally reliable because of the company's long-time integrity and huge continuing files. . . . While Merriam's bases for inclusion or noninclusion are a bit shadowy, their long experience precludes capricious decisions." Garland Cannon, "Viability: The Death of Recent New Items in English," *Word* 38 (1987): 155, 157.

13. Preface to the *Oxford English Dictionary* (Oxford, 1933).

14. On 25 April 1988, Charles Alan Wright wrote, in a letter to Judge Robert E. Keeton of Boston: "As of this morning the Allfeds database [of Westlaw] shows 12,248 documents in which *conclusory* appears, and the Allstates database has 9,365. This is 389 new federal instances and 681 new state instances in the last eight months."

15. *Greenwood v. Wierdsma*, 741 P.2d 1079, 1086 n. 3 (Wyo. 1987).

16. See H. Whitehall, "The English Language," in *Webster's New World Dictionary* (Springfield, Mass., 1962), p. xxxii.

17. Laura Mansnerus, "Lawyer Talk? You Can Look It Up," *New York Times* (11 December 1987), p. 18.

18. *Adams v. Higgins*, 23 Fla. 13, 1 So. 321, 324 (1887). The reporter for the Texas Supreme Court soon adopted the word: "*Held*, that the court of appeals affirmed the quashal of the distress proceedings." *Brown v. Collins*, 77 Tex. 159, 14 S.W. 173, 173 (1890) (case summary).

19. *Conclusional* is a revival, not a neologism. The *OED* records uses from 1471 and

1695 (in the sense "final"), but nothing more recent. The Supreme Court used the word in 1954: "These conclusional allegations add nothing." *United States v. Employing Plasterers Association*, 347 U.S. 186, 192 (1954). Many other examples appear in American judicial opinions, though *conclusory* outnumbers *conclusional* by a ratio of about ten to one.

20. The second edition of *Random House*, in accordance with its practice for dating the entry of words into the English language, gives 1955–60 as the spread of years within which *recusal* first appeared; the *OED* gives 1958 as the earliest known date of the use of the word. Yet the word appeared at least eight years earlier, in an opinion of the Alabama Supreme Court: "On the 13th of April, Judge Longshore filed an order of *recusal* accompanied by an order vacating his former order." *Methvin v. Haynes*, 46 So. 2d 815, 817 (Ala. 1950).

21. *Black's* actually defines *litigious* as if it were a noun: "Litigious. That which is the subject of a lawsuit or action; that which is contested in a court of law. In another sense, 'litigious' signifies fond of litigation; prone to engage in suits." *Black's Law Dictionary*, 5th ed. (St. Paul, Minn., 1979), p. 841.

22. *Webster's Ninth New Collegiate Dictionary* (Springfield, Mass., 1983), p. 17. *The Second Barnhart Dictionary of New English* (New York, 1980) also gives 1967 as the date of the earliest known use of the word, and erroneously suggests that the word is of British origin.

23. *McWilliams v. Hopkins*, 11 F.2d 793, 795 (S.D. Cal. 1926).

24. For example: "This clearly shows an adversarial element which appears to have been absent in the Rainger case." *Brooks v. United States*, 84 F.Supp. 622, 629 (S.D. Cal. 1949). See also *Sanitary Farm Dairies v. Gammel*, 195 F.2d 106, 115 (8th Cir. 1952), and *Your Food Stores of Sante Fe, Inc. v. AFL*, 124 F. Supp. 697, 700–01 (D.N.M. 1954).

25. See Fred R. Shapiro, "Legal Data Bases and Historical Lexicography," *Legal References Services Quarterly* 3 (1983): 85.

26. "[I]t was believed that a pleading containing inconsistent allegations indicated falsehood on its face and was a sign of a chicanerous litigant seeking to subvert the judicial process." C. A. Wright and A. Miller, *Federal Practice and Procedure* (St. Paul, Minn., 1969) 5:372.

27. See *United States v. Jefferson*, 257 A.2d 225, 226 (D.C. 1969). See also *State v. Kay*, 350 A.2d 336, 337 (N.H. 1975) ("such unfair, deceptive, and chicanerous actions as the defendant is charged with committing").

28. See David M. Walker, *Oxford Companion to Law* (Oxford, 1980), s.v. "common-law marriage."

❧ MARTHA MINOW

The Case of Legal Language

LAWYERS NOTORIOUSLY TALK IN OBSCURE and bulky language.[1] Lawyers use terms that disable nonlawyers from commenting or understanding. These terms simultaneously equip lawyers with a shorthand to summarize and juggle complex ideas. An example is the case name. Under the name of the parties, such as *Brown v. Board of Education*, lawyers in Britain and the United States subsume an entire legal dispute, the arguments of combatting parties, the judge's choice of a governing rule, the rationale for that choice, and the application of the rule to the facts deemed relevant by the judge.[2] This contrasts notably with the practices in other countries. In continental Europe, a concern for privacy leads the courts to use the parties' initials rather than their names in entitling a case, and the courts seldom cite such earlier cases because statutory rather than judge-made law is the central source for legal authority. Celebrated cases become known by the date of their decision, or by the subject matter they raised.

Anglo-American lawyers and judges, however, call cases by the names of the people who were plaintiffs and defendants. Lawyers use these names to argue in summary fashion for particular results in a new controversy: "*Mathews v. Eldridge* controls," or, implying that cases are like tables resting on one another, "this case is on all fours with *Roberts v. Jaycees*."[3] Lawyers cite case names as though they were features of the geography, like mountains or roadways: "*Richardson v.*

Marshall . . . will enable prosecutors to circumvent Bruton [v. United States].'"⁴ Sometimes case names are flags of opposing teams. One side claims the banner of, say, *Fullilove v. Klutznick*, while another marches under the colors of a contrasting case, such as *Wygant v. Jackson Board of Education*.⁵ There is something intimate about the case names, something more personal than the welter of institutional and political factors embodied in a lawsuit and in a judicial decision. There is also something magical, something talismanic, when lawyers talk of case names. The name is something to hang on to; the words in the name represent a rule, a judgment—and a power somehow beyond the human beings who are the parties and the judges.

The name of the case may come to stand for a proposition of law, such as that public schools may not segregate students on the basis of race. The case name, rather than a proposition of law, allows a more supple use of the precedent. By talking of the case by name, lawyers restate and reshape its proposition of law to suit, or to avoid, a new constellation of facts in a fresh controversy. Making salient a factor that was present but not emphasized in the case, an advocate may argue that the sheer fact of racial segregation is what mattered in *Brown*; an opponent can maintain that it was the explicit public law requiring segregation that was critical to *Brown*'s result. Thus the process of case-by-case reasoning flourishes. Opposing parties invoke a given case name, redolent with the atmosphere surrounding the previous contest.

Redolent, maybe, but not fixed: the name of the precedent, set off by itself, may also shake the case free from its full factual and historical context. Stringing together citations of case names, and removing the names from the actual historical contexts of the disputes giving rise to the judicial decisions, may help an advocate evoke a sense of an organic evolution of legal doctrines. An advocate may even treat the precedents as a lineage. A case holding two hunters liable when it was not clear which gun produced the shot wounding the plaintiff is marshalled as ancestor of a case holding a pharmaceutical company liable when it was not clear who manufactured a drug with harmful side effects.⁶ Lawyers' talk implies that the early case bred the later one.

Similarly, an image of organic evolution is evoked with the standard legal technique of grouping together disparate exceptions to a rule. The exceptions name the cases which, for particular reasons, suspended the usual requirement, say, of a warrant before a police search. Out of these exceptions, the legal speaker declares a new principle to house this family of exceptions. Commentators actually talk of the "progeny" of a case, the offspring produced after a significant precedent appears.⁷ Once a court rules, as the Supreme Court did in *Kovacs v. Cooper*, that the first amendment does not protect speech amplified by a sound truck traveling through a residential neighborhood and conveyed to listeners who are "practically helpless to escape," lawyers can serve as midwives for new rules in assertedly analogous situations.[8] Thus, unwilling listeners have been protected—and speech has been restricted—on city buses, in airport ticket lines, and even on the radio airwaves.[9] Later cases cite as a litany the earlier ones, even though some of the descendants bear only a faint resemblance to their progenitor. The discourse of a kinship among cases carries with it an image of the law's natural and necessary development. Altering the line of descent requires extraordinary effort, even at times an act of violence, to cut off, or reverse, a line of legal development. It requires "overturning" or "confining" *Kovacs*, or any important precedent. It means rebelling against the parental authority, or, in the extreme, revolting against the enthroned ruler.

Usually, the device of the case name rules even those whom others would believe to have the power to rule. Judges cite prior cases by name, and attribute to them the power that commands the result in a new case. A judge will announce that it is because of *New York Times Co. v. Sullivan* that this court finds for the defendant in this case; it is because of *World-Wide Volkswagen Corp v. Woodson* that this court concludes it has no power to hear the plaintiff's claims here.[10] The absence of precedent similarly gives judges something outside themselves to point to when they deny a claim.[11] Scholars argue that this attribution of responsibility to the external authority of the precedent has helped judges avoid experiencing their own responsibility for judgments.[12] This is especially odd when a judge describes a case he and his colleagues decided just a year earlier as a ruling by the court whose commands must now be followed. More is at work here than merely summarizing rules in the form of a precedent and then calling precedents by the names of the litigants. The institutional roles of judges and litigants, the substance of legal argument, and the deference to the past are all implicated in the use of case names.

Many contemporary precedents stand for rules so open-ended and so explicit in their call for the balancing of factors and the assessing of individual instances that judges often cannot help acknowledging their own contribution to the decisions they reach. Yet the convention that allows the judge to name a prior authoritative rule and to talk of conflicting values, as though they were either names of ancestors or features of a natural order, helps judges give the impression that they are constrained and passive enforcers of the preordained.

Cases are named for the parties, not the judges, which may make the parties feel more weight than the judges do in the announced rule

of law. Doctors, in contrast, almost always name the diseases they discover after themselves. But lawyers and judges use the names of the
patient, or not-so-patient, parties. When Judge David Bazelon re-
viewed the criminal conviction of Monte Durham, he announced for
his court a new rule for evaluating the sanity of a criminal defendant.[13]
The rule generated considerable controversy both within and beyond
legal circles. No doubt the controversy stemmed from Judge Bazelon's
call for criminal court judges to consider the entire economic and social circumstances along with psychological ones that may have contributed to the defendant's act. Judge Bazelon sought to enlarge the
range of evidence that could justify a finding of no responsibility. This
position, never popular, became increasingly unacceptable as politicians attacked the courts for being soft on crime. In the midst of the
controversy, a rather unusual act of communication occurred. Durham himself wrote a letter to Judge Bazelon. He acknowledged the
notoriety his case had attained, and complained that it made the whole
world associate Monte Durham with the insanity defense. Durham
wrote that instead of calling the case *Durham*, the judge should have
named the case after himself. After all, he pointed out, that's what astronomers do when they discover a star.[14] The name of a case thus carried meanings for the person who inspired it, as well as for others
touched by its shadow.

Ultimately, Judge Bazelon himself grew disillusioned with the *Durham* rule. As he later explained, the mental health experts disappointed
the courts by turning the newly created opportunity to include all
kinds of evidence in the judicial inquiry about criminal responsibility
into yet another occasion for control and manipulation through the
language—the jargon—of expertise.[15] The psychiatrists and psychologists who testified in insanity defense cases insisted on labeling the
defendants as schizophrenic, psychopathic, or some other professional
tag. The experts thus buried the critical societal decisions about criminal culpability inside the labels that the experts themselves controlled.
In response, Judge Bazelon led his court in announcing the reversal of
Durham in a case named *Brawner v. United States*.[16] Ever since, lawyers
have recounted how *Durham*'s short life was terminated by *Brawner*
and a new lineage of precedents emerged.

Judicial cases, as recounted by judges, often are remote from other
versions of the underlying controversy. For example, lawyers cite
Hansberry v. Lee for the proposition that a class action—a device to collect many people together to stand as a party with united interests—
cannot foreclose from a later lawsuit the claims of people whose interests are actually at odds with the initial class.[17] It looks like an abstract proposition, like mathematics: X may speak for Y where X ad-

equately represents Y, but not where X inadequately represents Y. Put the case back in its original context, however, and what do we see?

In a white neighborhood in Chicago, in the 1930s, all of the homeowners included a racially restrictive convenant in the deeds to their homes; they agreed not to sell their houses to nonwhites if ninety-five percent of the other homeowners signed this agreement. And to ensure enforcement, the homeowners had gone successfully to court in a class action claiming to represent all of the homeowners. The class representatives stipulated that ninety-five percent of the homeowners signed the restrictive convenant, and they obtained a judicial declaration that acknowledged and affirmed the racial restriction. Then Hansberry, a black man, purchased a house in the neighborhood. Although Hansberry had found a willing seller, other homeowners came to court to challenge the purchase as a violation of the restrictive covenant. The neighbors argued that the prior decision bound this case.[18] It was then that Hansberry argued he could not be bound, or held, to the prior judicial decision enforcing the restrictive covenant. Hansberry maintained that the homeowners who sought that prior order could not represent his interests. He lost in the Illinois Supreme Court, which ruled that the matter had already been resolved in the prior suit. But Hansberry won in the United States Supreme Court. That highest court reasoned that people have a right to be adequately represented before they can be bound by a class adjudication.

Nowhere in the language of the judicial opinion in the case do the costs of the struggle to Hansberry appear. Those costs, both financial and emotional, so embittered the man that he left the country, lacking money, peace, and hope. This we know from his daughter, who years later wrote to the *New York Times* in response to the paper's editorial disapproving sit-ins and street protests against racial segregation. The newspaper's editorial had argued that more orderly means for challenging the law should be used. Lorraine Hansberry explained her disagreement by describing how her father had devoted his life to the methods of orderly reform advocated by the editorial, and how the case bearing his name was considered "progress" toward racial justice, as declared by the Supreme Court. Those who urged continued reliance on orderly change through law, she argued, paid no attention to such costs "in terms of emotional turmoil, time, and money, which led to my father's early death as a permanently embittered exile in a foreign country when he saw that after such sacrificial efforts the Negroes in Chicago were as ghetto-locked as ever."[19] Like the editorials in the newspaper urging peaceful reform rather than street protests, the language of the courts neglected the impact of the litigation on the lives of Hansberry's family. Hansberry's daughter helped supply the missing words when she recalled for readers of the *New York Times* how "the fight required that our family occupy the disputed property in a hellishly hostile 'white neighborhood' in which, literally, howling mobs surrounded our house. One of their missiles almost took the life of the then eight-year-old signer of this letter. My memories of this 'correct' way of fighting white supremacy in America include being spat at, cursed and pummeled in the daily trek to and from school. And I also remember my desperate and courageous mother, patrolling our house all night with a loaded German luger, doggedly guarding her four children, while my father fought the respectable part of the battle in the Washington court."[20]

Lorraine Hansberry supplied still more words to describe the experience when she wrote her award-winning play, *Raisin in the Sun*.[21] There, with anger and pride, in dialogue and monologue—in language professionally excluded from legal opinions—she depicted the conflicts within a black family fighting to live in a hostile white neighborhood and struggling among themselves over how to define their blackness. Lawyers' skills and commitments induce insensitivities to some forms of pain in order to perform legal surgery. The legal tools press for abstract and universal principles, pushing even the most concrete and immediate terms—like the parties' names—to serve the goals of generalized justice. The law states principles in terms removed from their factual contexts and meanings to the original parties. At the same time, lawyers avoid specifying a norm by calling a case by the name of its parties.

During the time that they have contact with law, people forgo defining for themselves their experiences and even their identities because they must use legal terms. Something changes in the translation. The language of law simplifies matters often by casting people into premade roles. For the lawyer, "the plaintiff," "the witness," even "the judge," and "the agency" identify the perpetual roles, in many ways indifferent to the particular human beings standing in for them. Sometimes these preformed roles come with such heavy costumes that they disguise or distort the people beneath them. The plaintiff who alleges victimization by the defendant, whether resulting in physical injury, racial or sex discrimination, or contractual disadvantage, must portray herself as helpless, powerless, and blameless. The victim who testifies for the state in a criminal trial similarly must seem helpless and blameless—inviting, therefore, strategies by the defense attorney to show how the victim really asked for the crime, or has a blemished past herself and thus does not fit the role.

Sometimes the law gives exclusive salience to one trait or element in a person's effort to secure recovery, exercise a right, or obtain a benefit. Then the person jumps and strains to satisfy the test: I am legally "dependent" and therefore entitled to benefits. The test is particularly circumscribed when legal meanings of such terms, rather than common-sense meanings, control. For example, the Supreme Court concluded that it is constitutional to deny survivors' benefits to illegitimate children, even if they are *economically* dependent, because they fall outside the *statutory* definition of dependency.[22] Even while enforcing social conventions, some common-sense meanings are more generous than legal ones. Some laws define an identity that people then try to claim or assign to others in order to fit a rule: I am a handicapped person as defined under the protective legislation; I am a small businessman and hired that man only as an independent contractor, not as an employee—he is liable, not me, for the injuries he caused while working; I am typical of all the other fishermen injured by this pollutant, so I can represent them in this class action.[23] In each instance, the law invites the individual to seek a name, a label, to obtain desired legal treatment even at the cost of obscuring a more complex reality.

Lawyers address questions that philosophers, historians, and social theorists have asked through the ages. Lawyers, however, reach—or anyway, give—answers where the others continue their debates. Other professions produce their own kinds of closure through their own ground-rules for cutting off some debates, but the lawyers take issues of guilt and innocence, fairness and equality, and produce arguments and judgments to settle, at least temporarily, eternal disputes about the meanings of these ideals. It cannot be that lawyers are smarter or wiser than others. The lawyer's job is to help courts and agencies achieve closure; lawyers supply the devices to make closure plausible, at least for a while. Besides obvious devices, like burden of proof rules that direct which side should prevail in case of doubts about the evidence, lawyers help produce answers through language that simplifies and abstracts. Legal language casts people in roles and removes judges from their own sense of involvement. Legal language implies a natural and necessary evolution from the past and remakes experience and identity so that even those it describes may no longer fully recognize themselves. Lawyers' language provides words for rearranging and reasserting needs and claims. Legal language includes the toeholds for the next argument. It affords guide rails, stringing past debates as a chain of revered precedents. But legal language seldom expresses human dreams, pains, joys, doubts, or whispers. Those parts of human experience await other kinds of language.

Notes

1. See David Mellinkoff, *Legal Writing: Sense and Nonsense* (New York, 1982).
2. *Brown v. Board of Education*, 347 U.S. 483 (1954).

3. See *Lassiter v. Department of Social Services of Durham County*, 452 U.S. 18, 27–32 (1981) (citing Mathews v. Eldridge, 424 U.S. 319 (1976)); and *Board of Directors of Rotary International v. Rotary Club of Durate*, 107 S.Ct. 1940, 1945 (1987) (citing Roberts v. United States Jaycees, 468 U.S. 609 (1984)).

4. Note, "*Richardson v. Marsh*: Codefendant Confessions and the Demise of Confrontation," *Harvard Law Review* 101 (1988): 1877.

5. *Fullilove v. Klutznick*, 448 U.S. 448 (1980) (approving, despite constitutional attack, congressionally specified preferences for minority businesses in contracting and spending programs of the federal government); *Wygant v. Jackson Board of Education*, 476 U.S. 267 (1986) (plurality opinion) (rejecting as unconstitutional a local school board's layoff plan that protected minority teachers, absent proof of governmental discrimination justifying the plan).

6. *Summers v. Tice*, 33 Cal.2d 80, 199 P.2d 1 (1948); *Sindell v. Abbott Laboratories*, 26 Cal. 3d 88, 163 Cal. Rptr. 132, 607 P.2d 924, cert. denied, 449 U.S. 912 (1980).

7. *D'Oench, Duhme & Co. v. Federal Deposit Is. Corp.*, 315 U.S. 447 (1942), for example, discusses progeny of *Swift v. Tyson*.

8. *Kovacs v. Cooper*, 336 U.S. 77, 87 (1949).

9. *Lehman v. City of Shaker Heights*, 418 U.S. 298 (1973); *International Soc'y for Krishna Consciousness, Inc., v. Rochford*, 585 F.2d 263 (7th Cir. 1978), and *Cohen v. California*, 403 U.S. 15 (1971) (captive audience doctrine); *FCC v. Pacifica Foundation*, 438 U.S. 726 (1978) (shielding listeners from offensive language on radio airwaves).

10. *New York Times Co. v. Sullivan*, 376 U.S. 254 (1964) (setting standard for evaluating libel actions brought by public figures); *World-Wide Volkswagen Corp. v. Woodson*, 444 U.S. 286 (1980) (setting limits on state court jurisdiction over out-of-state defendants).

11. See Joseph Singer, "The Reliance Interest in Property," *Stanford Law Review* 40 (1988): 611.

12. See Robert Cover, *Justice Accused* (New Haven, 1975); John Noonan, *Persons and Masks of the Law* (New York, 1976).

13. See *Durham v. United States*, 214 F.2d 862 (D.C.Cir. 1954), overruled, *Brawner v. United States*, 471 F.2d 969 (D.C.Cir 1972) (en banc).

14. Letter on file with Judge David L. Bazelon.

15. David L. Bazelon, *Questioning Authority: Justice and Criminal Law* (New York, 1988), pp. 24–70.

16. *Brawner v. United States*, 471 F.2d 969 (D.C.Cir. 1972) (en banc).

17. *Hansberry v. Lee*, 311 U.S. 32 (1940).

18. Lee, who initiated the suit, claimed to represent other property owners who sought to enforce the racially restrictive covenant.

19. *New York Times* (23 April 1964), reprinted in Lorraine Hansberry, *To Be Young, Gifted and Black*, adapted by Robert Nemiroff (New York, 1969), p. 51.

20. *To Be Young, Gifted and Black*, p. 51.

21. The play opened on Broadway in 1959 and won the New York Drama Circle Critics Award for the best play of the year.

22. *Mathews v. Lucas*, 427 U.S. 495, 507–516 (1976).

23. See *School Board v. Arline*, 107 S.Ct. 1123 (1987) (person with a contagious disease is handicapped for the purposes of Section 504 of the Rehabilitation Act); *Cowan v. Eastern Racing Assn.*, 330 Mass. 135 (1953), Restatement (Second) of Agency sec. 220 (1958); *Pruitt v. Allied Chemical Corp.*, 85 F.R.D. 100 (E.D. Va. 1980) (applying Federal Rule of Civil Procedure 23).

~ WILLIAM LUTZ

The World of Doublespeak

FARMERS NO LONGER HAVE COWS, PIGS, CHICKENS, or other animals on their farms; according to the U.S. Department of Agriculture farmers have "grain-consuming animal units" (which, according to the Tax Reform Act of 1986, are kept in "single-purpose agricultural structures," not pig pens and chicken coops). Attentive observers of the English language also learned recently that the multibillion dollar stock market crash of 1987 was simply a "fourth quarter equity retreat"; that airplanes don't crash, they just have "uncontrolled contact with the ground"; that janitors are really "environmental technicians"; that it was a "diagnostic misadventure of a high magnitude" which caused the death of a patient in a Philadelphia hospital, not medical malpractice; and that President Reagan wasn't really unconscious while he underwent minor surgery, he was just in a "non-decision-making form." In other words, doublespeak continues to spread as the official language of public discourse.

Doublespeak is a blanket term for language which pretends to communicate but doesn't, language which makes the bad seem good, the negative appear positive, the unpleasant attractive, or at least tolerable. It is language which avoids, shifts, or denies responsibility, language which is at variance with its real or its purported meaning. It is language which conceals or prevents thought. Basic to doublespeak is incongruity, the incongruity between what is said, or left unsaid, and what really is: between the word and the referent, between seem and be, between the essential function of language, communication, and what doublespeak does—mislead, distort, deceive, inflate, circumvent, obfuscate.

When shopping, we are asked to check our packages at the desk "for our convenience," when it's not for our convenience at all but for the store's "program to reduce inventory shrinkage." We see advertisements for "preowned," "experienced," or "previously distinguished" cars, for "genuine imitation leather," "virgin vinyl," or "real counterfeit diamonds." Television offers not reruns but "encore telecasts." There are no slums or ghettos, just the "inner city" or "substandard housing" where the "disadvantaged," "economically nonaffluent," or "fiscal underachievers" live. Nonprofit organizations don't make a profit, they have "negative deficits" or "revenue excesses." In the world of doublespeak dying is "terminal living."

We know that a toothbrush is still a toothbrush even if the advertisements on television call it a "home plaque removal instrument," and even that "nutritional avoidance therapy" means a diet. But who would guess that a "volume-related production schedule adjustment" means closing an entire factory in the doublespeak of General Motors, or that "advanced downward adjustments" means budget cuts in the doublespeak of Caspar Weinberger, or that "energetic disassembly" means an explosion in a nuclear power plant in the doublespeak of the nuclear power industry?

The euphemism, an inoffensive or positive word or phrase designed to avoid a harsh, unpleasant, or distasteful reality, can at times be doublespeak. But the euphemism can also be a tactful word or phrase; for example, "passed away" functions not just to protect the feelings of another person but also to express our concern for another's grief. This use of the euphemism is not doublespeak but the language of courtesy. A euphemism used to mislead or deceive, however, becomes doublespeak. In 1984, the U.S. State Department announced that in its annual reports on the status of human rights in countries around the world it would no longer use the word "killing." Instead, it would use the phrase "unlawful or arbitrary deprivation of life." Thus the State Department avoids discussing government-sanctioned killings in countries that the United States supports and has certified as respecting human rights.

The Pentagon also avoids unpleasant realities when it refers to bombs and artillery shells which fall on civilian targets as "incontinent ordnance," or killing the enemy as "servicing the target." In 1977 the Pentagon tried to slip funding for the neutron bomb unnoticed into an appropriations bill by calling it an "enhanced radiation device." And in 1971 the CIA gave us that most famous of examples of doublespeak when it used the phrase "eliminate with extreme prejudice" to refer to the execution of a suspected double agent in Vietnam.

Jargon, the specialized language of a trade or profession, allows colleagues to communicate with each other clearly, efficiently, and quickly. Indeed, it is a mark of membership to be able to use and understand the group's jargon. But it can also be doublespeak—pretentious, obscure, and esoteric terminology used to make the simple appear complex, and not to express but impress. In the doublespeak of jargon, smelling something becomes "organoleptic analysis," glass becomes "fused silicate," a crack in a metal support beam becomes a "discontinuity," conservative economic policies become "distributionally conservative notions."

Lawyers and tax accountants speak of an "involuntary conversion" of property when discussing the loss or destruction of property through theft, accident, or condemnation. So if your house burns down, or your car is stolen or destroyed in an accident, you have, in legal jargon, suffered an "involuntary conversion" of your property. This is a legal term with a specific meaning in law and all lawyers can be expected to understand it. But when it is used to communicate with a person outside the group who does not understand such language, it is doublespeak. In 1978 a National Airlines 727 airplane crashed while attempting to land at the Pensacola, Florida, airport, killing three passengers, injuring twenty-one others, and destroying the airplane. Since the insured value of the airplane was greater than its book value, National made an after-tax insurance benefit of $1.7 million on the destroyed airplane, or an extra eighteen cents a share. In its annual report, National reported that this $1.7 million was due to "the involuntary conversion of a 727," thus explaining the profit without even hinting at the crash and the deaths of three passengers.

Gobbledygook or bureaucratese is another kind of doublespeak. Such doublespeak is simply a matter of overwhelming the audience with technical, unfamiliar words. When asked why U.S. forces lacked intelligence information on Grenada before they invaded the island in 1983, Admiral Wesley L. McDonald told reporters that "We were not micromanaging Grenada intelligence-wise until about that time frame."

Some gobbledygook, however impressive it may sound, doesn't even make sense. During the 1988 presidential campaign, vice presidential candidate Senator Dan Quayle explained the need for a strategic defense initiative by saying: "Why wouldn't an enhanced deterrent, a more stable peace, a better prospect to denying the ones who enter conflict in the first place to have a reduction of offensive systems and an introduction to defensive capability. I believe this is the route the country will eventually go."

In 1974, Alan Greenspan, then chairman of the President's Council of Economic Advisors, was testifying before a Senate committee and was in the difficult position of trying to explain why President Nixon's economic policies weren't effective in fighting inflation: "It is a tricky problem to find the particular calibration in timing that would be appropriate to stem the acceleration in risk premiums created by falling incomes without prematurely aborting the decline in the inflation-generated risk premiums." In 1988, when speaking to a meeting of the Economic Club of New York, Mr. Greenspan, now Federal Reserve chairman, said, "I guess I should warn you, if I turn out to be particularly clear, you've probably misunderstood what I've said."

The investigation into the Challenger disaster in 1986 revealed the gobbledygook and bureaucratese used by many involved in the shuttle program. When Jesse Moore, NASA's associate administrator, was asked if the performance of the shuttle program had improved with each launch or if it had remained the same, he answered, "I think our performance in terms of the liftoff performance and in terms of the orbital performance, we knew more about the envelope we were operating under, and we have been pretty accurately staying in that. And so I would say the performance has not by design drastically improved. I think we have been able to characterize the performance more as a function of our launch experience as opposed to it improving as a function of time."

A final kind of doublespeak is simply inflated language. Car mechanics may be called "automotive internists," elevator operators "members of the vertical transportation corps," and grocery store checkout clerks "career associate scanning professionals," while television sets are proclaimed to have "nonmulticolor capability." When a company "initiates a career alternative enhancement program" it is really laying off five thousand workers; "negative patient care outcome" means that the patient died; and "rapid oxidation" means a fire in a nuclear power plant.

The doublespeak of inflated language can have serious consequences. The U.S. Navy didn't pay $2,043 a piece for steel nuts; it paid all that money for "hexiform rotatable surface compression units," which, by the way, "underwent catastrophic stress-related shaft detachment." Not to be outdone, the U.S. Air Force paid $214 a piece for Emergency Exit Lights, or flashlights. This doublespeak is in keeping with such military doublespeak as "preemptive counterattack" for first strike, "engage the enemy on all sides" for ambush, "tactical redeployment" for retreat, and "air support" for bombing. In the doublespeak of the military, the 1983 invasion of Grenada was conducted not by the U.S. Army, Navy, Air Force, and Marines but by the "Caribbean Peace Keeping Forces." But then according to the Pentagon it wasn't an invasion, it was a "predawn vertical insertion."

These last examples of doublespeak should make it clear that doublespeak is not the product of careless language or sloppy thinking. Indeed, serious doublespeak is the product of clear thinking and is carefully designed and constructed to appear to communicate but in fact to mislead. Thus, it's not a tax increase but "revenue enhancement," "tax base broadening," or "user fees," so how can you complain about higher taxes? It's not acid rain, it's just "poorly buffered precipitation," so don't worry about all those dead trees. That isn't the Mafia in Atlantic City, those are just "members of a career-offender cartel," so don't worry about the influence of organized crime in the city. The Supreme Court Justice wasn't addicted to the painkilling drug he was taking, it's just that the drug had simply "established an interrelationship with the body, such that if the drug is removed precipitously, there is a reaction," so don't worry that his decisions might have been influenced by his drug addiction. It's not a Titan II nuclear-armed, intercontinental, ballistic missile 630 times more powerful than the atomic bomb dropped on Hiroshima, it's just a "very large, potentially disruptive reentry system," so don't worry about the threat of nuclear destruction. Serious doublespeak is highly strategic, and it breeds suspicion, cynicism, distrust, and, ultimately, hostility.

In his famous and now-classic essay "Politics and the English Language," which was published in 1946, George Orwell wrote that the "great enemy of clear language is insincerity. When there is a gap between one's real and one's declared aims, one turns as it were instinctively to long words and exhausted idioms, like a cuttlefish squirting out ink." For Orwell, language was an instrument for "expressing and not for concealing or preventing thought." In his most biting comment, Orwell observes that "in our time, political speech and writing are largely the defense of the indefensible. . . . Political Language has to consist largely of euphemism, question-begging and sheer cloudy vagueness. . . . Political language . . . is designed to make lies sound truthful and murder respectable, and to give an appearance of solidity to pure wind."

Orwell understood well the power of language as both a tool and a weapon. In the nightmare world of his novel *1984*, he depicted language as one of the most important tools of the totalitarian state. Newspeak, the official state language in *1984*, was designed not to extend but to *diminish* the range of human thought, to make only "correct" thought possible and all other modes of thought impossible. It was, in short, a language designed to create a reality which the state wanted.

Newspeak had another important function in Orwell's world of *1984*. It provided the means of expression for doublethink, which Orwell described in his novel as "the power of holding two contradictory beliefs in one's mind simultaneously, and accepting both of them." The classic example of doublethink in Orwell's novel is the slogan "War is Peace." And lest you think doublethink is confined only to Orwell's novel, you need only recall the words of Secretary of State Alexander Haig when he testified before a Congressional Committee in 1982 that a continued weapons build-up by the United States is "absolutely essential to our hopes for meaningful arms reduction." Or the words of Senator Orrin Hatch in 1988: "Capital punishment is our society's recognition of the sanctity of human life."

The more sophisticated and powerful uses of doublespeak can at times be difficult to identify. On 27 July 1981, President Ronald Reagan said in a television speech: "I will not stand by and see those of you who are dependent on Social Security deprived of the benefits you've worked so hard to earn. You will continue to receive your checks in the full amount due you." This speech had been billed as President Reagan's position on Social Security, a subject of much debate at the time. After the speech, public opinion polls recorded the great majority of the public as believing that President Reagan had affirmed his support for Social Security and that he would not support cuts in benefits. Five days after the speech, however, White House spokesperson David Gergen was quoted in the press as saying that President Reagan's words had been "carefully chosen." What President Reagan did mean, according to Gergen, was that he was reserving the right to decide who was "dependent" on those benefits, who had "earned" them, and who, therefore, was "due" them.

During the 1982 Congressional election campaign, the Republican National Committee sponsored a television advertisement which pictured an elderly, folksy postman delivering Social Security checks "with the 7.4 percent cost-of-living raise that President Reagan promised." Looking directly at his audience, the postman then adds that Reagan "promised that raise and he kept his promise, in spite of those sticks-in-the-mud who tried to keep him from doing what we elected him to do."

The commercial was deliberately misleading. The cost-of-living increases had been provided automatically by law since 1975, and President Reagan had tried three times to roll them back or delay them but was overruled by congressional opposition. When these discrepancies were pointed out to an official of the Republican National Committee, he called the commercial "inoffensive" and added, "Since when is a commercial supposed to be accurate? Do women really smile when they clean their ovens?"

In 1986, with the Challenger tragedy and subsequent investigation, we discovered that doublespeak seemed to be the official language of NASA, the National Aeronautics and Space Administration, and of the contractors engaged in the space shuttle program. The first thing we learned is that the Challenger tragedy wasn't an accident. As Kay Parker of NASA said, experts were "working in the anomaly investigation." The "anomaly" was the explosion of the Challenger.

When NASA reported that it was having difficulty determining how or exactly when the Challenger astronauts died, Rear Admiral Richard Truly reported that "whether or not a cabin rupture occurred prior to water impact has not yet been determined by a superficial examination of the recovered components." The "recovered components" were the bodies of the astronauts. Admiral Truly also said that "extremely large forces were imposed on the vehicle as evidenced by the immediate breakup into many pieces." He went on to say that "once these forces have been accurately determined, if in fact they can be, the structural analysts will attempt to estimate the effect on the structural and pressure integrity of the crew module." NASA referred to the coffins of the astronauts as "crew transfer containers."

Arnold Aldrich, manager of the national space transportation systems program at Johnson Space Center, said that "the normal process during the countdown is that the countdown proceeds, assuming we are in a go posture, and at various points during the countdown we tag up on the operational loops and face to face in the firing room to ascertain the facts that project elements that are monitoring the data and that are understanding the situation as we proceed are still in the go condition."

In testimony before the commission investigating the Challenger accident, Allen McDonald, an engineer for Morton Thiokol (the maker of the rocket), said he had expressed concern about the possible effect of cold weather on the booster rocket's O-ring seals the night before the launch: "I made the comment that lower temperatures are in the direction of badness for both O-rings, because it slows down the timing function."

Larry Mulloy, manager of the space shuttle solid rocket booster program at Marshall Space Flight Center, responded to a question assessing whether problems with the O-rings or with the insulation of the liner of the nozzle posed a greater threat to the shuttle by saying, "The criticality in answering your question, sir, it would be a real foot race as to which one would be considered more critical, depending on the particular time that you looked at your experience with that."

After several executives of Rockwell International, the main contractor to build the shuttle, had testified that Rockwell had been opposed to launching the shuttle because of the danger posed by ice formation on the launch platform, Martin Cioffoletti, vice president for space transportation at Rockwell, said: "I felt that by telling them we did not have a sufficient data base and could not analyze the trajectory of the ice, I felt he understood that Rockwell was not giving a positive indication that we were for the launch."

Officials at Morton Thiokol, when asked why they reversed earlier decisions not to launch the shuttle, said the reversal was "based on the reevaluation of those discussions." The Presidential commission investigating the accident suggested that this statement could be translated to mean there was pressure from NASA.

One of the most chilling uses of doublespeak occurred in 1981 when then Secretary of State Alexander Haig was testifying before congressional committees about the murder of three American nuns and a Catholic lay worker in El Salvador. The four women had been raped and then shot at close range, and there was clear evidence that the crime had been committed by soldiers of the Salvadoran government. Before the House Foreign Affairs Committee, Secretary Haig said, "I'd like to suggest to you that some of the investigations would lead one to believe that perhaps the vehicle the nuns were riding in may have tried to run a roadblock, or may accidentally have been perceived to have been doing so, and there'd been an exchange of fire and then perhaps those who inflicted the casualties sought to cover it up. And this could have been at a very low level of both competence and motivation in the context of the issue itself. But the facts on this are not clear enough for anyone to draw a definitive conclusion."

The next day, before the Senate Foreign Relations Committee, Secretary Haig claimed that press reports on his previous testimony were inaccurate. When Senator Claiborne Pell asked whether Secretary Haig was suggesting the possibility that "the nuns may have run through a roadblock," Secretary Haig replied, "You mean that they tried to violate . . . ? Not at all, no, not at all. My heavens! The dear nuns who raised me in my parochial schooling would forever isolate me from their affections and respect." When Senator Pell asked Secretary Haig, "Did you mean that the nuns were firing at the people, or what did 'an exchange of fire' mean?" Secretary Haig replied, "I haven't met any pistol-packing nuns in my day, Senator. What I meant was that if one fellow starts shooting, then the next thing you know they all panic." Thus did the Secretary of State of the United States explain official government policy on the murder of four American citizens in a foreign land.

The congressional hearings for the Irancontra affair produced more doublespeak. During his second day of testimony before the Select Committee on Secret Military Assistance to Iran and the Nicaraguan Opposition, Oliver North admitted that he had on different occasions lied to the Iranians, his colleague Maj. Gen. Richard Secord, congressional investigators, and the Congress, and that he had destroyed evidence and created false documents. North then asserted to the committee that everything he was about to say would be the truth.

North used the words "residuals" and "diversions" to refer to the millions of dollars which were raised for the contras by overcharging Iran for arms. North also said that he "cleaned" and "fixed" things up, that he was "cleaning up the historical record," and that he "took steps to ensure" that things never "came out"—meaning he lied, destroyed official government documents, and created false documents. Some documents weren't destroyed; they were "non-log" or kept "out of the system so that outside knowledge would not necessarily be derived from having the documents themselves."

North was also careful not to "infect other people with unnecessary knowledge." He explained that the Nicaraguan Humanitarian Assistance Office provided humanitarian aid in "mixed loads," which, according to North, "meant . . . beans and Band-Aids and boots and bullets." For North, people in other countries who helped him were "assets." "Project Democracy" was a "euphemism" he used at the time to refer to the organization that was building an airfield for the contras.

In speaking of a false chronology of events which he helped construct, North said that he "was provided with additional input that was radically different from the truth. I assisted in furthering that version." He mentions "a different version from the facts" and calls the chronology "inaccurate." North also testified that he and William Casey, then head of the C.I.A., together falsified the testimony that Casey was to give to Congress. "Director Casey and I fixed that testimony and removed the offensive portions. We fixed it by omission. We left out—it wasn't made accurate, it wasn't made fulsome, it was fixed by omission." Official lies were "plausible deniability."

While North admitted that he had shredded documents after being informed that officials from the Attorney General's office wanted to inspect some of the documents in his office, he said, "I would prefer to say that I shredded documents that day like I did on all other days, but perhaps with increased intensity."

North also preferred to use the passive to avoid responsibility.

When asked, "Where are the non-logged documents?" he replied, "I think they were shredded." Again, when asked on what authority he agreed to allow Secord to make a personal profit off the arms sale to Iran, North replied with a long, wordy response filled with such passive constructions as "it was clearly indicated," "it was already known," and "it was recognized." But he never answered the question.

For North, the whole investigation by Congress was just an attempt "to criminalize policy differences between coequal branches of government and the Executive's conduct of foreign affairs." Lying to Congress, shredding official documents, violating laws, conducting unauthorized activities were all just "policy differences" to North. But North was generous with the committee: "I think there's fault to go on both sides. I've said that repeatedly throughout my testimony. And I have accepted the responsibility for my role in it." While North accepts responsibility, he does not accept accountability.

This final statement of North's bears close reading for it reveals the subtlety of his language. North states as fact that Congress was at fault, but at fault for what he doesn't specify. Furthermore, he does not accept responsibility for any specific action, only for his "role," whatever that may have been, in "it." In short, while he may be "responsible" (not guilty) for violating the law, Congress shares in that responsibility for having passed the law.

In Oliver North's doublespeak, then, defying a law is complying with it, noncompliance is compliance. North's doublespeak allowed him to help draft a letter to Congress saying that "we are complying with the letter and spirit" of the Boland Amendment, when what the letter really meant, North later admitted, was that "Boland doesn't apply to us and so we're complying with its letter and spirit."

Contrary to his claim that he was a "stand up guy" who would tell all and take whatever was coming to him, North disclaimed all responsibility for his actions: "I was authorized to do everything that I did." Yet when he was asked who gave him authorization, North replied, "My superiors." When asked which superior, he replied: "Well who—look who sign—I didn't sign those letters to the—to this body." And North's renowned steel-trap memory went vague or forgetful again.

After North had testified, Admiral John Poindexter, North's superior, testified before the committee. Once again, doublespeak flourished. In the world of Admiral John Poindexter, one does not lie but "misleads" or "withholds information." Likewise, one engages in "secret activities" which are not the same as covert actions. In Poindexter's world, one can "acquiesce" in a shipment of weapons while at the same time not authorize the shipment. One can transfer millions of dollars of government money as a "technical implementation" without making a "substantive decision." One can also send subordinates to lie to congressional committees if one does not "micromanage" them. In Poindexter's world, "outside interference" occurs when Congress attempts to fulfill its constitutional function of passing legislation.

For Poindexter, withholding information was not lying. When asked about Col. North's testimony that he had lied to a congressional committee and that Poindexter had known that North intended to lie, Poindexter replied, "there was a general understanding that he [North] was to withhold information. . . . I . . . did not expect him to lie to the committee. I expected him to be evasive. . . . I'm sure they [North's answers] were very carefully crafted, nuanced. The total impact, I am sure, was one of withholding information from the Congress, but I'm still not convinced . . . that he lied."

Yet Poindexter protested that it is not "fair to say that I have misinformed Congress or other Cabinet officers. I haven't testified to that. I've testified that I withheld information from Congress. And with regard to the Cabinet officers, I didn't withhold anything from them that they didn't want withheld from them." Poindexter did not explain how it is possible to withhold information that a person wants withheld.

The doublespeak of Alexander Haig, Oliver North, and John Poindexter occurred during their testimony before congressional committees. Perhaps their doublespeak was not premeditated but just happened to be the way they spoke, and thought. President Jimmy Carter in 1980 could call the aborted raid to free the American hostages in Tehran an "incomplete success" and really believe that he had made a statement that clearly communicated with the American public. So too could President Ronald Reagan say in 1985 that "ultimately our security and our hopes for success at the arms reduction talks hinge on the determination that we show here to continue our program to rebuild and refortify our defenses" and really believe that greatly increasing the amount of money spent building new weapons will lead to a reduction in the number of weapons in the world. If we really believe that we understand such language and that such language communicates and promotes clear thought, then the world of *1984* with its control of reality through language is upon us.

~ DAVID REID

Public Eloquence

"POETRY HAS EVERYTHING TO DO WITH SPEECHES—cadence, rhythm, imagery, sweep, a knowledge that words are magic, that words like children have this power to make dance the dullest beanbag of a heart." The speaker is Peggy Noonan; as the ghostwriter of Ronald Reagan and George Bush's most admired speeches, she is plainly an oracle on the subject of public eloquence. Knowing how to make the beanbags dance is a valuable skill in a democracy, especially one in which a quarter of the voters can elect a president (because half the electorate never bothers to turn up at the polls).

Noonan is a phenomenon, the most admired rhetorician in her specialized line of work since John F. Kennedy's ghost, Theodore Sorenson. She has been "profiled" in *Ms.* (December 1988) and in *Esquire* (December 1985). Christopher Thomas of the *Times* of London said the acceptance speech she wrote for George Bush to read at the Republicans' convention at New Orleans brought the vice president "bursting out of the shadows" and "made him real." His article spoke of "the sometimes graceful, sometimes poignant, sometimes slashing words that she pens for the great and the mighty who send them spinning into history."[1] The *New York Times* reported that Ronald Reagan's farewell to the nation (11 January 1988) "bore the stamp of the most gifted of his speechwriters, Peggy Noonan, who is also drafting the Inaugural Address that Bush will deliver." She was asked to write both speeches despite the fact that she had long since resigned from the former's staff and chosen not to serve on the latter's. At thirty-eight, she has written her memoirs.

Paradoxically, Noonan's reputation flourishes at a time when almost everybody complains that American political rhetoric has become vapid and mindless even by the republic's undemanding standards. But then, not everybody agrees about the quality of her public eloquence. During the 1988 campaign, for example, Michael Blumenthal wrote in the *New Republic* (10 September 1988): "During Bush's and Dukakis's lingering 'thousand points of light' exchange midway through their first debate, it was difficult to decide for whom to feel more sorry—Bush for having come up with such a sentimentally vacuous and insincere metaphor, or Dukakis for not having understood what he meant." Of course George Bush never pretended to "come up with" the figure that his dour and literal-minded opponent professed to find puzzling; the dread "thousand points of light" was Peggy Noonan groping for poetry.

Ghostwriting for presidents is as old as the republic (Alexander Hamilton wrote George Washington's farewell address), but what does it signify that Noonan's contributions to presidential eloquence are advertised as they are? What is the character of her rhetoric? What are her professional secrets? the sources of her style? What makes a speech "effective" in a time when politics is a spectacle on television? Contrarily, has Noonan been praised when the kudos belonged to presidential image-makers—to Michael Deaver, who was in charge of Reagan's totemization from 1981 to 1985, or to Roger Ailes, the media wizard who gave Vice President Bush lessons in deportment? (*Newsweek*, 22 September 1988: "There you go with that f---ing hand again. You look like a f---ing *pansy!*")

Noonan worked in the Reagan White House from 1984 to 1986. Before that, she was at CBS News, where she wrote "poetic bits" for Dan Rather. Noonan's politics are, in her description, "very conservative," but there was not much scope for their expression at CBS, from which she was plucked like a firebrand from the burning, or at the Aetna Insurance Co., where earlier she worked as a claims adjuster. In the White House she wrote some of Reagan's most combative speeches, but her nonpolitical efforts were regarded even more highly by the press, especially the president's address at Normandy on the fortieth anniversary of D-Day and his threnody to the crew of the space shuttle *Challenger*.

"In his speeches," says Fred Barnes in the *New Republic* (8 May 1989), "Reagan stressed soaring rhetoric." This is already tenacious myth, but "soaring" is exactly the wrong word. To the contrary, Reagan and his most gifted speechwriter had great trouble staying aloft. The farewell address presumably reflects much deliberation—here is how Noonan deals with the momentous renewal of détente with the Soviet Union: "we will continue to act in a certain way as long as they continue to act in a helpful manner. If and when they don't—at first pull your punches. If they persist, pull the plug."

With bathos came hyperbole—the latter, notoriously, in the president's address to the National Conservative Political Action Committee in 1985, the speech that described the contras as the "moral equal" of the Founding Fathers (and was in turn described by the *New Yorker* as "toxic waste"). Today, even Noonan regrets the comparison, which she says originated with the president. By his second term Reagan so rarely intervened in the speechwriting process that Noonan reportedly was "almost knocked off her chair" when he sent her a note offering a suggestion. Or as she explained later, "What I was trying to say was that the contras were like the Founding Fathers in the sense that they both faced a monolith. I didn't mean to imply that the Founding Fathers were rapists and murderers."[2]

For a professional writer, Noonan has a very careless way with words. Yet there were grace notes in the farewell, which she was called back to the White House to write; the structure was firm, though the tone was uneasy—it seemed to be an after-dinner speech with delusions of grandeur. The *New York Times* (12 January 1989) observed that the president sounded "almost puzzled as he enumerated the changes in the world" since he took office. No wonder.

What did it all mean, the last eight years? Well, "the image that comes to mind like a refrain is a nautical one—a small story about a big ship, and a refugee, and a sailor." In the South China Sea, a man on a boat "crammed" with refugees hails a Yankee tar on the carrier *Midway*: "Hello, American sailor—Hello, Freedom Man." It is an allegory. America is back! Mighty Grenada has been conquered, the Russians are coming around, and the deregulated market flourishes. Events have vindicated the political philosophy of Reaganism: "'We the people' are the driver—the Government is the car."

Other metaphors: the nation is a ship at sea, an army ("Reagan's Regiments," a group that evidently includes all the American people except for a few meddlesome "pundits"), and a shining city "built on rocks stronger than oceans, wind-swept, God blessed, and teeming with people of all kinds living in harmony and peace." Some figures are more apt than could have been intended, as in "The economy bloomed like a plant that had been cut back." The inflationary economy of the early 1980s was cooled by the highest unemployment since the Depression. From 1979 to 1987, the rich got richer, the poor got poorer, and the standard of living of working-class Americans fell.

"Wind-swept, God blessed, and teeming"—what a confection of clichés is this shining city! "High Noonan" conforms exactly to Sidney Blumenthal's description of the ruling aesthetic of Reaganism as "neokitsch."[3] In her exalted Stephen Vincent Benet mode, Noonan is very derivative—"retro," I should say—and very kitschy, reminiscent of 1940s war bond drives and Fox-Movietone newsreels. High Noonan does not consort easily with low demotic Noonan ("let 'em know it and nail 'em on it"), but her writing is swift, and the jumpy transitions evidently didn't bother audiences who grew up with the discontinuities of television. Or they were smoothed over by Reagan's superb delivery. Professional secrets: she is unafraid of clichés and she can epigrammatize: "And something else we learned: once you begin a great movement, there's no telling where it'll end. We meant to change a nation, and instead we changed a world."

The case has been made that Reagan's great communications marked an epoch. In *Eloquence in an Electronic Age* by Kathleen Hall Jamieson, we learn that from antiquity to the gray dawn of the cathode-ray tube, eloquence was defined as a *masculine* form of discourse. Ideally, eloquence was logical and factual—"grave, composed, luminous, compact," in Edward Channing's phrase. Happily, "the broadcast age has rendered the combative, data-driven, impersonal 'male' style obsolete." The new style, adapted to the electronic hearth, is "a self-disclosive, narrative, personal, 'womanly' style."[4]

Reagan's speeches certainly worked hard at the appearance of self-disclosure. From the farewell: "One of the things about the Presidency is that you're always somewhat apart. You spend a lot of time going by too fast in a car someone else is driving, and seeing the people through tinted glass . . . And so many times I wanted to stop, and reach out from behind the glass, and connect." Only connect! Still, Ronald Reagan has been riding in the back of limousines for fifty years. He is an elderly ex-movie star, who knows very well that for one in his station, distance is necessary to the preservation of mystique, not to mention life and limb (after all, one of the little people almost killed him). It is hard to imagine Jack Warner's protégé brooding about loneliness at the top. The tone is false, and the whole passage instinct with bad faith. What was Noonan thinking about?

Her grasp for what would play on television was usually sure. "'They had never had a speechwriter who'd come out of broadcasting before,'" she told Sheila Weller of *Ms.* "'I sat down and said, "Look, only eight seconds of the President's speech is going to wind up on the air. I know because my job was to cut them for Dan Rather. So either the network can pick those eight seconds that all America is going to hear tonight . . . or YOU can pick them, by embedding a colorful phrase (go ahead, make my day; we have nothing to fear but fear itself) into the text."' Noonan arches an eyebrow merrily. 'Amazing, isn't it? That they'd never figured that out before.'" Yes, it is, considering that twenty years ago Richard Nixon's courtiers devised the so-called HPS percept, by which presidential appearances were organized with a headline, photograph, and "sound bite" in mind.[5]

Does anybody really have to remind politicians about the value of a catchphrase? What Noonan obviously did learn at CBS was how to write in "broadcast style." It is odd how the illusion persists, even among professors of communications, that writing for radio and television calls for a terse, "abbreviated" style: news writing for these media is intentionally wordy. As Martin Mayer notes in *Making News*, broadcast style is "at once looser, more conversational than printed prose and yet more purposive and orotund in rhetoric."[6] Its swiftness and leanness is an auditory illusion, comparable to the laconism of Ernest Hemingway and Elmore Leonard, whose mannered dialogue looks so "lifelike" on the page. Paradoxically, the broadcaster must radiate sincerity, while speaking in a highly affected, singsong manner replete with unnatural pauses and emphases.

With her recent schooling in the medium and grasp of how a newsroom actually works, Noonan was a superb match for Reagan, who got his first job in radio in 1933 and was present at the creation of network television. Their collaborations got the best reviews of any of his speeches. Even so, the notion that he was a uniquely powerful "communicator" among presidents is simply mistaken. John F. Kennedy was at least as effective on television, and he was as mad for "facts" as Mr. Gradgrind; as cool in manner as Reagan was "warm." If Reagan's speeches reflected broadcast style, Kennedy's were self-consciously literary and pseudoclassical. Both were masters of the scripted performance, but Kennedy was superb at formal televised press conferences (the closest approximation in American politics to a prime minister answering the Opposition's questions in Parliament), while Reagan clearly regarded these occasions with a mixture of petulance and dread. I suspect both presidents realized, as academic observers sometimes forget, that television is a mysterious medium. Its light shines where it lists.

At any rate, her self-aggrandizing suggests why Noonan had a stormy tenure as a White House staffer. Unlike Sorenson, who was known as Kennedy's intellectual alter ego, she had no influence on policy matters at all and never approached what passed for Reagan's inner circle. Indeed, her folies des grandeurs irritated the hierarchs who ran the country while the president went about his ceremonial duties. "During the Beirut hostage crisis," according to *Esquire*, "she became so dissatisfied with the failure to take some action against terrorists that she fired off a memo embodying what she called her hurled-glass theory—that an irrational, violent retaliatory act, even if not surgically precise, was better than no response at all." Heads up, innocent bystanders of Beirut! Another time, she papered the West Wing with a doomsday memorandum, tagged "Darkness at Noonan" by her colleagues, about how apparatchiks at the National Security Council and the State Department were speeding the decline of the West. Patrick Buchanan, the right-wing columnist and scourge of Sodom who was then the White House director of communications, promoted her as head speechwriter, but chief-of-staff Donald Regan refused to make the appointment. Larry Speakes in his memoir *Speaking Out* (1988) explains, "Aside from being dogmatic, she insisted on taking credit in public for many of the speeches she wrote. She was always saying 'I wrote this' and 'I wrote that.' The best speechwriters," he adds severely, "are heard and never seen."[7]

After many triumphs, then, Noonan left the White House in the summer of 1986, but she was at George Bush's side in New Hampshire, when it looked as if Senator Robert Dole and the evangelicals might gang up on him and block the succession. There Bush adopted the "effeminate" style that worked so well for Reagan, except that he was forever confessing his inadequacies, something Reagan rarely felt obliged to do. Of course there were good reasons for this strategy. Reagan would never have been in serious trouble, political or rhetorical, if Peggy Noonan had run off to Peru and joined the Shining Path. George Bush, on the other hand, was a figure of fun for much of the electorate throughout the primaries in 1988 and up to his acceptance speech in New Orleans, when he was still seventeen points behind Michael Dukakis in the Gallup Poll.

Bush was a dreadful public speaker, always being surprised by syntax, and capable of bizarre utterances, which the newsmagazines gleefully collected. (One of the best was his description of how caribou in the far north were sexually aroused by the Alaska pipeline: "Now there are more caribou than you can shake a stick at!") To the learned, the apology Noonan wrote for him to deliver in New Hampshire might seem almost as bad. "As Abraham Lincoln said, 'Here I stand, warts and all.'" Of course it was Martin Luther who said, "Here I stand," and Oliver Cromwell who had the warts, but according to the

London *Times* the garbled quotations worked magic. "With her help, Bush has certainly found his voice, warts and all."

A professional, Noonan adheres to the ghostwriter's code. The pretense is always maintained that the prince *could* have written his own speeches except for his busy schedule, and anyway he did contribute to them. " 'I am a quiet man.' He really said that. And once we were in Jim Baker's office and he was sitting back—kind of scrunched up in his chair like a comma—and he had this little epiphany and said, 'I want a kinder, gentler nation.' (Have I typed that twenty-five times or WHAT?) Luckily, I was there with my pen." Yet once the election was safely past, she confided how, as the *New York Times* put it (21 January 1989), she "dissected Mr. Bush, and gave him a simpler, more self-deprecating style," sounding, in that moment at least, not unlike the woman in the Jules Feiffer cartoon who wanted "a strong, masterful man that I can mold."

And so to New Orleans: "I may not be the most eloquent. I may sometimes be a little awkward." A nice cadence describes a nexus: Bush's inarticulateness with the lives of the little people. "But there's nothing self-conscious in my love of country. I am a quiet man, but I hear the quiet people others don't—the ones who raise the family, pay the taxes, meet the mortgage. I hear them and I am moved, and their concerns are mine." This is the line that inspired the actor Albert Brooks to riposte, "I have a friend in Los Angeles who hears the quiet people others don't, and he has to take a lot of medication."

A forensic speech, the acceptance made liberal use of what rhetoricians call "antiparabole": the invidious comparison of his opponent's views to the speaker's. For example, Michael Dukakis "sees a long slow decline in our country," but "I see America as the leader, a unique nation with a special role in the world." Dukakis opposed the Pledge of Allegiance, prayer in public schools, the death penalty, the right to own firearms, and "the sanctity of life": all things Bush favored. Dukakis did champion the right of convicts to enjoy weekend furloughs on which to pursue their lives of crime, but Bush was opposed to that. In most published accounts, his campaign manager Lee Atwater and media advisor Roger Ailes are given credit for insisting that Bush pursue these matters, but presumably Noonan had the responsibility for phrasing them.

We approach the bravura passage, but here, perhaps, it ought to be noted that only since 1932, when Franklin D. Roosevelt flew to Chicago to accept his nomination, have presidential candidates addressed their party's conventions. Relatively few acceptance speeches have achieved eloquence: FDR in 1936 ("This generation has a rendezvous with destiny"), Adlai Stevenson in 1952 ("Let's talk sense to the American people"), Kennedy in 1960 announcing the New Frontier. George Bush and Peggy Noonan:

> And there is another tradition [in which he believes, along with "that there is a God" and "learning is good"]. And that's the idea of community—a beautiful word with a big meaning, though liberal Democrats have an odd view of it. They see "community" as a limited cluster of interest groups, locked in odd conformity. And in this view, the country waits passive while Washington sets its rules. But that's not what community means, not to me. . . .
>
> This is America: the Knights of Columbus, the Grange, Hadassah, the Disabled American Veterans, the Order of Ahepa, the Business and Professional Women of America, the union, the Bible study group, LULAC, Holy Name—a brilliant diversity spread like stars, like a thousand points of light in a broad and peaceful sky.

Well, that is what George F. Babbitt and his friends in Zenith thought too. Plainly, the lights are going out all over the Gutenberg galaxy, if the public eloquence of presidential candidates is evidence. In the November 1988 issue of *Interview* magazine, Alexander Cockburn argues that Kennedy's "truly awful oratory" at the Democratic convention in 1960 launched the iron age of unfeeling and unfelt "postmodernist" rhetoric. It's a thought. Still, what an ominous contraction of rhetorical resource and reach of allusion we have seen since then. There is something to be said for a politician who could quote Madame de Staël on "Meet the Press," as Kennedy once did. The quotations in George Bush's acceptance speech were from "Dragnet," Henry Luce ("American Century"), Clint Eastwood, and a sappy pop song ("Take a message to Michael").

In the epilogue at New Orleans he remembers "The Best Years of Our Lives" (to quote the title of an affecting Samuel Goldwyn movie of the time):

> And the war was over, and we wanted to get out and make it on our own. And those were exciting days. We lived in a little shotgun house, one for the three of us. Worked in the oil business and then started our own.

(Young George Bush's business start was underwritten by a $400,000 loan from a rich uncle who was a partner at Brown Brothers Harriman. In 1946 four thousand dollars a year was a decent income.)

> And in time we had six children. Moved from the shotgun to a duplex apartment to a house. And lived the dream—high school football on Friday nights, Little League, neighborhood barbeque.

People don't see their own experience as symbolic of an era, but of course we were. And so was everyone else who was taking a chance and pushing into unknown territory with kids and a dog and a car.

The same infusion of confessional bad faith we saw in the lonely-at-the-top business in Reagan's speech—not to mention bad prose in simple little thinly grammatical constructions. Belatedly, one sees another place where Noonan has found inspiration. For who are the "quiet" ones who George Bush claimed uniquely to hear, "who raise the family, pay the taxes, meet the mortgage," but our old friends the Silent Majority so memorably hymned by our lost leader Richard Nixon in 1968? ("They work and they save and they pay their taxes and they care.") There is something rather creepy about Bush (third-generation ruling class) being refashioned in the image of the lower-middle-class hustlers who were the front men of Republican party politics after the war, Richard Nixon being their archetype.

In her piece on the Republican convention for the *New York Review of Books*, Joan Didion contemptuously referred to the epilogue as "the famous no-pronoun sequence." Lance Morrow, the *Time* essayist, deplored Bush's vulgarity, using as examples phrases Noonan had crafted. Their reservations were very apparent. On the other hand, we know from *Newsweek* (21 November 1988) that Bush's handler Roger Ailes tested the acceptance speech on a "focus" group in Paramus, New Jersey, and they were particularly affected by George Bush's profound belief in the Pledge of Allegiance, and moved by the recital of his early struggles in Texas.

Is this simply a case of *vox populi* vs. self-important critics? Or more sinisterly, was Noonan's rhetoric, high and low, simply the faintly absurd libretto for a score composed by more accomplished political operatives, like Deaver and Atwater and Ailes?

La Bruyère says, "There are certain things in which mediocrity is intolerable: poetry, painting, music, public eloquence." Noonan plainly regards herself as a lord of language, but now that the tableaux vivants of the Reagan Era are fading, it's the catchphrases in her speeches that remain ("kinder, gentler nation"; the empty "thousand points of light"; the borrowed "read my lips"), and none, one suspects, for long. Her reputation is a far more interesting creation than her ghostwriting, which at best has the appeal of a clever television commercial. Leaving aside impressionable Paramus, New Jersey, I think it is entirely possible that Noonan's rhetoric appeals to nobody: that it has moved no one, exalted no one; that it pleasures nobody and edifies nobody; that her "eloquence" is a function of her reputation, and her reputation exists only in the gaze of the media with no other support.

Since the publication of Theodore H. White's *The Making of the President* (1960), not only have presidential campaigns become endless but reporting of them has been enveloped by what Alexander Cockburn very exactly calls "sycophantic knowingness." Print and television journalists train bright lights on the least courtiers, and few if any of them have any passion for anonymity. On the permanent campaign trail, standards of excellence tend to the pragmatic. Beyond her self-advertisements, the sufficient proof of Noonan's public eloquence for the boys on the bus was that she wrote for the winning side. Knowing how to make the beanbags jump is what it is all about, and having a reputation for knowing how is almost as good. In his unillusioned way, Jack Kennedy pointed the moral in 1961, when *Newsweek* described his New Frontiersmen as "coruscatingly brilliant." "Another 100,000 votes the other way, and we'd all be coruscatingly stupid," he said.

Fifty-six years ago, Franklin D. Roosevelt actually went to the trouble of copying out in long hand, late at night, Raymond Moley's draft of his inaugural address so that he, FDR, could gull historians into believing he had written it.[8] Reagan and Bush were above such an imposture because they never coveted the prestige of authorship in the first place. A writer possessing no influence at all in their inner councils was permitted virtual free play with their public characters and with what were represented as their deepest convictions and maturest reflections. The only contributions the then vice president is positively known to have made to "the speech of his lifetime" were its opening words:

> Thank you. Thank you very much. Thank you so much. Thank you so very much. Thank you ladies and gentlemen. Thank you very, very much. Thank you. Thank you all very much. Thank you so much. Thank you ladies and gentlemen. Thank you very, very much. Thank you. Thank you. Thank you ladies and gentlemen. Thank you very, very much.

Notes

Because I was interested in speeches by Ronald Reagan and George Bush as they were actually delivered, I have quoted the relevant texts as they appear in the *New York Times*: 19 August 1988 for Bush's acceptance speech at New Orleans and 12 December 1988 for Reagan's farewell address. I am grateful to Jayne L. Walker for reading and improving earlier drafts of this essay.

1. Christopher Thomas, "Behind Bush's Words," *The Times* (London), rpt. *San Francisco Chronicle*, 16 September 1988.

2. Jane Mayer and Doyle McManus, *Landslide: The Unmaking of the President, 1984–1988* (Boston, 1988), p. 86.

3. Sidney Blumenthal, *The Rise of the Counter-Establishment: From Conservative Ideology to Political Power* (New York, 1986), p. 284. I am greatly indebted to the chapter "Morning Again" in this book and to "Reaganism and the Neokitsch Aesthetic" in *The Reagan Legacy* (New York, 1988), which he coedited with Thomas Byrne Edsall. Ron Rosenbaum notes Noonan's fondness for the "incantational rhythms of Stephen Vincent Benet" (*Esquire*, December 1986).

4. Kathleen Hall Jamieson, *Eloquence in an Electronic Age: The Transformation of Political Speechmaking* (New York, 1988), pp. 118–19.

5. See Mayer and McManus, *Landslide*, p. 104.

6. Martin Mayer, *Making News* (New York, 1986), p. 152.

7. Larry Speakes, *Speaking Out* (New York, 1988).

8. It was not Moley, however, but Louis Howe who contributed "the only thing we have to fear is fear itself." See Jamieson, *Eloquence in an Electronic Age*, pp. 201–4.

Further Thoughts:
The Executives Take Over

IN THE LAST FEW YEARS, THERE HAVE BEEN undeniable, if scarcely un-foreseeable, changes in the hopes and purposes of television. These are reflected less notably, for the moment, in the finished product than in the processes which procure it. Gestation periods are very long, not least when ridiculous mice are being conceived. Vladimir Nabokov once spoke, with characteristic accuracy, of the fundamental law of evolution, "The Survival of the Frailest." I doubt whether his field-work was devoted to television. Recent developments in Europe have been, as so often, in belated imitation of American methods, not least those which Americans are, optimists suggest, beginning to find obsolete.

The French have long been in the habit of referring to television professionals as "*journalistes,*" not a wholly disparaging term but one which indicates the workaday *métier* in which, with possibly prophy-lactic modesty, the photogenically garrulous elect to place themselves. If cinema is sometimes called "The Seventh Art," few encomiasts have elected to find the eighth in television. It may excite pretentious discourse (usually of a scathing kind) among columnists—at least un-til, having auditioned with acid, they are coopted to sugary pur-poses—but who chooses to find in today's television those qualities of subtlety, either of montage or of narrative-management, which *ci-néastes* attribute (often willfully) to the silver screen? Television's

golden age is now held to have been synchronic with that 1950ish period when John Mason Brown, in an observation which renders
everything else he ever said forgettable, spoke of its being "chewing
gum for the eyes." Whatever the medium's subsequent achievements,
the *mot* sticks: there are, it can plausibly be maintained, systematic
trivialities, inescapably perishable ingredients, in television which
deny it the role of cultural composting traditional to Art. Even when
the latter's formal articulations decompose, layers of disintegrated imagery and collapsed elaboration continue to inform those who have no
systematic awareness of the past or of its religio-mythical subtleties.
(We do not need to know where the story of Sisyphus is to be found
in ancient literature for us to take the point when Camus insists that
we imagine him happy.) Can anyone even suggest what high form religion could take when transmitted on TV? Is it "accidental" that the
only massively successful "religious" programs are those which
broadcast ideas of emollient banality interspersed with appeals for
funds from the gullible? A creed of insolent imposture seems natural
to the now-you-see-it-and-now-you-see-it-again importunities of
those who seek to make anxious addicts of an audience afraid to miss
the news, afraid to miss the next episode, afraid to miss salvation: if
money can buy it, how can it be a good bet, salesman Pascal demands,
to miss it? The creation of appetite, not beauty, is the aesthetic of the
new executives. What might a television Chartres, or *Missa Solemnis*,
or *Four Quartets*, conceivably be like? No new-season-program conference is any more likely to be embarrassed by the question than it
will be disposed to attempt an answer. Who cares?

Television never seems likely to become classic in the basic sense of
being the subject of formal instruction, unless it is in those catch-all
institutions where literally anything may be regarded as teachable, unless it is difficult enough (like Latin and Greek) to require learning. If
we ask what it would be for a television program to become a "classic," we are constrained to answer that it would be the kind of program which those who hope to work in the business might be encouraged to copy: a good example will be an example of the bad. The
medium may have its serious practitioners, its driven perfectionists, its
eager polemicists (especially in the field of investigative journalism),
and its maverick originals (though not if the networks can help it,
which they almost always can), but it is largely designed to entertain
the masses (and to amass viewing figures to prove their recruitment)
and to enrich the professionals.

I suggested in my essay for the 1980 *State of the Language* that television was above all a syncretic activity: elements from radio, film, the
lecture hall, the stage all went into in a kind of cultural *paella*; the va-

riety of the ingredients and the range of flavors made up for the lack of finesse. Good news and bad news spiced the same recipe. The bad news was that vulgarity was always likely to hog prime time: the good news was that quality could still hope to find a quiet corner in which to remain available, whether through window-dressing insistence on the part of quasi-official bodies or through lazy monitoring by those so busy procuring trash that they had no time to prevent some good stuff slipping by. (The Hollywood studio system allowed good films to be made as often because there was a great need for "product" as because there was a craving for finesse.) Human appetite, even among executives, for awards (and the accompanying kudos) meant that some good programs had to be produced, however reluctant the resources granted to them, in order to justify hopeful black ties (and grateful, team-spirited speeches) at season's end.

The BBC was the exceptional institution that established the fundamental rule of variety—of which quality was at least an admitted, sometimes even a demanded, part—when television became one of the expected amenities of a civilized state. (The "cost of living" is now held to include the cost of access to TV, as if one literally could not live without it.) The primacy of the British was, as so often, soon obscured—and British pretensions debunked—in the commercial usage of the U.S., but certain traces of antique piety endured for a while: there was a vestigial sense of "public service," even in the American networks, as Ed Murrow's famous humiliation of Joe McCarthy so memorably demonstrates (for those who remember it).

The notion of a duty to the community, as well as to the shareholders, persisted in England even when the Independent—that is, commercial—Networks (companies) were established. Those who sought the franchises (renewable, and removable, at regular intervals) were, like the politicians who longed to control them, obliged to protestations of noble purpose. Humbug thus required them to give *some* space to what they had to pretend to respect. The need to show evidence of worthy plans for the future and worthy achievements in the immediate past induced a certain deference to "quality" during the first three decades or so of "commercial" TV in the U.K. Executive cant spoke regularly of educative and even elevating purpose. Notions of service deplored personal ambition (even if it was rampant) and justified uncommercial practices and purposes. The BBC—the training ground of the majority of all television professionals in the U.K.—initiated at least some of the "commercial" executives with virtuous catechisms.

The Thatcher government, for reasons which range from the spiteful to the ideological (no very great span is required to effect the bridge), decided to attack the BBC—not least because it was always regarded as a hive of Lefties—and in effect to denationalize it. The Corporation was promptly humiliated by the defenestration of its unwisely principled Director-General. Before he (a program-maker by trade) was replaced, by an accountant, the demoralized rump was threatened with the removal, or severe limitation, of the public funds with which its uncommercial programming had been subsidized. It was, in short, encouraged—with a bigger stick and a smaller carrot—to find real-world means of self-support.

To a degree, this blunt message was overdue. Its effect, however, in key areas, of which drama (including film) is certainly one, was to drive it into the international marketplace in the search for cofinancing. Well, why not? The answer is that the merits of the BBC's output lay, to a marked degree, in its quasi-"pastoral" parochialism: its best work (procured by payments in prestige and artistic liberty, rather than at the going rate) was protected from the generalizing, that is, vulgarizing, intrusion of those who, having paid the piper, thought themselves entitled to influence the tune. "Coproduction," the current method of most large-scale financing, minimizes specific quality—local colors—in order to maximize quantity and global sales. The British government's interest in distinguishing between babies and bathwater has proved considerably smaller than its determination to teach boobies of all ages a lesson, especially those of independent, élitist—a term of abuse from both ends of the vote-getting spectrum—or heterodox tendencies. Ruthlessness in executive decision, rather than creative originality or integrity, is licensed by a new morality which cares nothing for morals unless they make a profit. The Age of the Executive and the trumping force of front-office program-catering result from an ideological rupture with old consensual, antipolitical Establishment procedures. The élites were squeezed from all sides and the vocabulary of living along has been replaced by that of militant commercialism. The aesthetics of monetarism carry no ethical freight: what is beautiful and good is what most people like. Values are all very well, at a price. The new populism cares little for the preservation of "abstract" or traditional standards. In practice, these were found to reinforce the vanity of corporate officers and made them less easy to intimidate. The privatization of the BBC was, of course, said to be no part of the government's renovating purpose; such denials are a measure of its determination to reduce the bastions of those sarcastic barons to whom the central power was reluctant to pay further lip-service or cash. For clear instance, the BBC's failure to enthuse over Mrs. Thatcher's endorsement of Reagan's bombing of Libya did nothing to encourage the prime minister to geniality (a report from Tripoli by an "unpatriotic" reporter of undentable integrity exasperated her). By the same token, an "independent" company's brave decision to mount a documentary inquiry into the killing of three (as it proved) unarmed IRA persons on the rock of Gibraltar may have confirmed Mrs. Thatcher's determination to take the commercial stations down a peg or two. This she has done by threatening to marginalize considerations of "quality" when franchises are next allotted. Her declared intention is to sell the rights to broadcast by auction. The immediate effect of this has been to modify the tone of executive discourse, to put it mildly, though mildness is scarcely the new lingo. "Loadsamoney" is the immodest watchword.

Executives who had, with whatever enthusiasm or reluctance, to commission drama series (in particular) of the kind which had (almost without anyone noticing it) altered the perspectives of film narrative, sometimes resulting in genuine innovations in cinematic/dramatic styles, are now disencumbered of the (expensive) obligation to subsidize "quality." The new television is indeed an overt form of journalism, with circulation—viewing figures—the only certificate of success. The new brutalism in economic life finds nothing disreputable in quasi-monopolies, funded by literally rootless satellite-borne networks whose *raison d'être* is transnational profitability. The new executive "language" speaks, in particular, of "accessibility" as a necessary quality. This cant term refers not to any public or artistic access to the medium, in creative or critical terms, but of the need for the audience not to feel excluded; any form of discrimination, especially in the happiest sense, has become a warrant for program abortion. This, in turn, renders admirable the most craven concessions to vacuity of content: the cult of nonexclusion (accessibility's aim) means that no intellectual requirements can respectably be required, or even hoped for, from the audience, for whom open-armed disdain is the accepted executive sentiment. The esperanto of banality debars divisive nuance.

The aggressive dictation of program-content is the mark of the new executive class. There is, supposedly, a wish to see program-making farmed out to "independent" creative enterprises, but since there is small possibility of a "hit," in the theatrical or cinematic sense, in the television world, there is little incentive to take risks or to hope to recoup brave losses by virtue of one smashing success. In practice, independence is a form of dependence: the central authorities can dictate absolutely to their client-suppliers whose separation merely enables them to undercut others competing for the same narrow markets, and so keep production costs down. The humiliation of the creative, "irresponsible" personnel (directors, writers, musicians, designers) reduces the "critical" possibilities of the medium and impels it to concentrate on "entertainment." It could be argued that politicians themselves will finally pay the price of their demolition of "serious" television, since they too, dependent on TV for access to voters, will be obliged (if they have not already been) to eliminate all contentious or disagreeable matter from their "programs" and compete with vacuousness (saleable placebos) for the numb attention of an audience void of critical example. It is, of course, possible that such an obligation either to please or to vanish from the air-lanes will procure an era of unending bread and circuses, game-shows and sitcoms, which will rival the Age of the Antonines in its blissful blandness. We shall, if nothing else, see.

Note

Frederic Raphael's essay in the 1980 *State of the Language* was entitled "The Language of Television."

Editing and Its Discontents

A. R. ORAGE WAS THE EDITOR of the British weekly *The New Age* in the early part of the present century—a near-legendary figure, widely regarded (among the literati, at least) as one of the outstanding editors of his time. Long ago, reading about him in someone's memoirs, I was struck by one sentence in particular. Asked whether he regretted not having time to write his own books, he replied: "I don't write books; I write writers."

The remark has a fine ring to it, and when I first came across it I thought I knew what Orage meant—that in relation to his contributors a good editor should be a mixture of guide, sounding board, friendly critic, and impresario; that he saw his job as that of fostering new writers and steering established ones in profitable directions, making a suggestion here, opening up a possibility there.

Within a few years I had decided that he must have had something else in mind as well, something rather more elementary. Yes, editing had its inspired and inspiring moments; but it also involved long hours spent laboring over slovenly prose, trying to turn it into respectable English.

What had happened in the interval is that I had acquired some serious editorial experience myself, first as literary editor of one weekly, then as editor—"the" editor—of another. And no one can hold such positions, or comparable positions in publishing, without being reminded every day of the importance of humdrum copyediting.

Some of the contributors I dealt with during my years as an editor were dream contributors: you knew in advance that everything was going to run smoothly. Many more, the majority, were reasonably good: there would usually be a few knots in a piece that needed straightening out, often quite tricky ones—but only a few. And then there were the other contributors, a sizable minority, cheerfully serving up muddled syntax, fuzzy approximations to meaning, unlovely lumps of congealed verbal spaghetti.

Some of the worst offenders, moreover, were professional authors, historians, critics, full-time journalists (as opposed to economists, psychologists, and other nonliterary specialists, many of whom in fact wrote extremely well). I recall with mild chagrin, for example, the clotted prose of the eminent historian Professor X; I recall with mild amusement the dust jacket of one of his books on which he was commended by the no less eminent Professor Y for "writing like an angel."

Once you get over the shock of discovering how many esteemed writers can't write, you find that your colleagues have similar tales to tell. One friend of mine, the literary editor of a leading newspaper, managed to secure the regular services of a celebrated novelist, and rightly regarded it as a feather in his cap. The man was a "name"; he usually had something fresh and provocative to say.

It also turned out, alas, that his writing straggled aimlessly all over the page—when one of his reviews showed up, everything else had to be set aside for the rest of the day while it was pulled into shape. His most maddening trick (though he had plenty of others) was to use the same word three or four times in close, clumsy succession, and in contexts that made it impossible for an editor to find adequate synonyms.

The odd thing is that I had read his novels, and would have said that the best of them were not only well written, but positively incisive. Does this mean that he took more trouble with his fiction than he did with his journalism? Or that his books had been gone over by a particularly skillful editor? Or is one simply less sensitive to stylistic failings when they come armed with the authority of print? A mysterious business.

In spite of such mysteries, nothing could weaken my conviction that copyediting is an honorable and a necessary trade. Every author has reason to be grateful to editors for saving him from his blunders (and even dream contributors sometimes nod).

And yet gratitude isn't the only feeling that copyeditors can provoke. My first week in charge of a paper brought with it a warning of just how many mines there might be strewn across the field.

It wasn't possible for me to read everything that appeared in this paper when it arrived in the office. Many items I read only in proof; and it was one such piece that held me up, that first week, with its puzzling reference to "the soft Celtic mistiness of Yeats and Housman." Well, the early Yeats, perhaps; but Housman? I tried in vain to squeeze some kind of meaning out of the phrase; I reminded myself of Yeats's comment on *A Shropshire Lad*—"a mile further and all had been marsh." But that didn't seem to help much, either. Then I thought I had better take a look at the original typescript.

It was just as well that I did. The author of the article had in fact written "the soft Celtic mistiness of Yeats and A. E."—George William Russell, poet and mystic, leading associate of Yeats in the Irish Renaissance, the man whom Stephen Dedalus recalls borrowing money from in *Ulysses* ("A.E.I.O.U."). One subeditor, assuming that the name "Housman" must have been dropped, had silently "restored" it; then a second subeditor, no less alert, had decided that Housman was too well known to need his initials. Hey presto!

Editorial idiocies have doubtless been perpetrated since editing began: individual instances don't prove anything in themselves. But the past generation or two have seen the spread of far more systematic and insidious forms of editorial damage—of damage committed in the name of accuracy, clarity, and attention to detail.

I think it fair to say that the disease has made deeper inroads in the United States than in Britain. I think it fair to add that American editorial standards are generally more demanding than British ones; that a good deal of American editing is first-rate, and that a good deal of British editing is careless and lackadaisical.

But some kinds of attention are worse than inattention. In America an author is far more likely to find himself subjected to wanton interference, and it is only appropriate that it should be an American, Jacques Barzun, who has written the best short summing-up of current editorial misdeeds: the essay "Behind the Blue Pencil," which can be found in his collection *On Writing, Editing and Publishing* (the second, expanded edition, published in 1986 by the University of Chicago Press).

There are two broad tendencies of which Mr. Barzun complains. One is what he calls "creeping creativity." The editor sets himself up as a kind of invisible coauthor, emending, expanding, substituting, and deleting as his inner light guides him; the "improvements" that he produces are often unnecessary and quite often harmful.

The second bane of contemporary editing is rigidity. Fixed rules are mechanically enforced, without regard for tone, context, or even sense; trivial errors are slavishly corrected, even if it means generating large infelicities in the process. And although this conformism may seem at odds with "creativity," in practice the two impulses readily coexist. It is only the editorial department's style book that is sacred, not the author's style.

Mr. Barzun is mainly concerned in his essay with books, and it is book editing that offers the maximum scope for playing creative havoc. By contrast, copyeditors in journalism tend to be preoccupied with the rules and the facts (understandably, but often excessively, too).

My one reservation about "Behind the Blue Pencil" is that—for polemical purposes, no doubt—it underrates the problems created by authors themselves: there's not much hint of congealed spaghetti. In practice the problem is more complicated, and since many authors can't be relied on to put problems right even when they are pointed out, the most self-effacing editor frequently finds himself forced to be more inventive than he would ideally choose. But in other respects the situation seems to me exactly as Mr. Barzun describes it—and every bit as alarming.

True, I can't quite match his example of the novelist who submitted a manuscript in which one of his characters spoke about seeing a play starring the Lunts; it came back to him from his publisher with the marginal suggestion, "Wouldn't the Hunts be better?" But I have come across *Eminent Victorians* changed to *The Eminent Victorians*, and "adverse" substituted for a perfectly correct "averse," and a reference to the poet Horace circled with a query—Horace who?

Editors can be curiously stubborn, too. Someone I know had a book published by a famous university press: a controversial book, dealing with (among other things) German heavy industry. To his dismay, he found that references to "Dr. Schmidt," "Dr. Schultz," and so on had been uniformly changed to "Mr. Schmidt" and "Mr. Schultz." But "Dr." was the title these particular individuals used, he protested, and it was important to get the facts right. His editor dug her heels in: no, an industrialist wouldn't call himself "Dr." even if he had a doctorate. Eventually the author won the battle, but it frayed his nerves, and it took time.

The changes that rankle most are those that involve factual errors and incorrect titles and names. It is easier—somewhat easier—to shrug off the rewording that blunts the impact of a phrase than the last-minute alteration (too late for you to put right) that makes you look as though you thought there was a poet named Thomas Grey. But of course, one form of injury doesn't rule out another.

A particularly common form of editorial sabotage is the substitution of an indefinite article for a definite article. I write about someone meeting "the Czech communist Rudolf Slansky"; it comes back, in print, as a reference to "a Czech communist, Rudolf Slansky." If I'm cross, and I am, it is partly through amour propre. I don't want readers to suppose that I have never heard of the man who was the principal victim of one of the most infamous show trials in postwar Eastern Europe. But I'm also assuming that most of my readers don't want to be treated as though they had never heard of him either.

The editor who crossed out *the* and put in *a* retorts that I'm wrong to make such an assumption. I, of course, disagree, and the truth is that neither of us can know for sure—the Slansky trial isn't as famous as all that. But I'm relying on my sense of the kind of readers I'm writing for; and even if it could be shown that many of them can't identify Slansky, it would be misleading them to suggest that he was just any Czech communist. Either the editor (who, it turns out, has never heard of him) should have left *the*—it's vague, but it does at least convey Slansky's importance—or he should have substituted "a Czech communist who was later executed in a purge trial" or some similar descriptive phrase.

The problem with the latter course is that if you adopt it too often you are going to slow down the story and clutter the text. And if you pursue it indiscriminately, you are going to end up with references to "the novelist Jane Austen" and "the scientist Albert Einstein." Or even "novelist Jane Austen"—which certainly cuts through the difficulties—and "scientist Albert Einstein."

There are in fact no easy answers. A writer for a popular paper obviously couldn't afford to be as allusive as a mandarin literary critic, even if he wanted to be. But allusion, in one form or another, is a mark of civilization, and there is something barbarous about the urge to spell everything out, to equip everyone with an identity tag and leave no oblique reference unturned.

Nor do editors necessarily limit themselves to inserting facts for the simple purpose of clarification, or what they see as clarification. A spirit of exhaustiveness is abroad, and many editorial offices seem dominated by the fear of leaving anything out at all. Every place has to be pinpointed on the map, every name or date has to be supplied in full. It isn't enough to explain that Asquith was prime minister; he has to be "prime minister Herbert Henry Asquith," even in a casual aside.

The effect of piling on all this data is one of pedantry. Informal texts—"a man talking to men"—are reduced to the droning level of reference-book entries and legal documents. And you can't even rely on a pedantic editor knowing his own pedantic business. It might turn out to be a reference to "prime minister Herbert H. Asquith," if you are not careful. It might indeed. Only the day before writing this article I came across an editorially inspired reference to the literary critic "Ivor A. Richards."

Then there are the needless problems that can be thrown up when you quote something. American editors tend to be far more conscientious about checking quotations than their British counterparts—in itself, an unarguably good thing. But all too often this concern for accuracy becomes a determination to be accurate at all costs. There is no room for the tiny adjustments—changing a single pronoun from first person to third person, say—that sometimes have to be made if a quotation is going to be incorporated smoothly into the surrounding text.

There is also a corresponding insistence on giving the source of a quotation, no matter how obtrusive it may look when it is cited. You describe someone or something as "born to blush unseen"; an editor interpolates, "in the words of Thomas Gray." If you had known that you would have to bring Thomas Gray into it, you wouldn't have used the quotation in the first place.

Inflexible and insensitive rules for handling facts are all too often matched by inflexible and insensitive rules for handling usage. Editors pounce mercilessly on split infinitives, sentences that end with a preposition, and all the other supposed offenses that are often no offense at all; they prove their mettle by ruthlessly cutting out every *which* they can lay their hands on and replacing it with a *that*. (A desirable change, in moderation; but what Jacques Barzun calls "the great *which* hunt" can also serve as a way of keeping busy without having to grapple with the really tricky editorial problems, the kind for which the stylebook won't supply a ready-made solution.)

Once you start enforcing reasonable rules with too heavy a hand, you are likely to find quite arbitrary rules springing up alongside them. One American newspaper I know has taken the hitherto unheard-of step of banning the word *hitherto*. Another frowns on the use of the words *embark* and *launch* except in relation to boats, missiles, and so forth. The extended uses of these words is not something one wants to overdo, but the writer who isn't allowed to describe someone embarking on a new career or launching a new magazine is going to find himself in difficulties sooner or later.

So is the writer who isn't allowed to refer to "a woman doctor." At least one leading American publication, in an effort to placate feminists, has prohibited the use of *woman* as an adjective. But is the alternative that it proposes, *female*, really an improvement? On the contrary, "female doctor" strikes me as a fairly demeaning and unattractive phrase, in a way that "woman doctor" isn't. But a rule, however inept, is a rule. There are times when it is important to establish that the doctor you are referring to is a female/woman doctor—it would be confusing if you didn't; it would be inappropriate to refer to her by name; and if you don't like *female*, and you can't use *woman*, you are horribly hemmed in.

Most writers I know have tales to tell of being mangled by editors and mauled by fact-checkers, and naturally it is the flagrant instances that they choose to single out—absurdities, outright distortions of meaning, glaring errors. But most of the damage done is a good deal less spectacular. It consists of small changes (usually too boring to describe to anyone else) that flatten a writer's style, slow down his argument, neutralize his irony; that ruin the rhythm of a sentence or the balance of a paragraph; that deaden the tone that makes the music. I sometimes think of the process as one of "desophistication." When a good writer is subjected to it, everything tends to come out that little bit more dumb.

None of which is an argument against editing, and tough editing where necessary. Good writers have in fact sometimes proved to be among the toughest of editors themselves. When Dickens—the novelist Charles Dickens—was editing *Household Words*, for example, he was famous for the ruthless surgery he performed on contributors' prose. He once spoke of "the dreadful spectacle I have made of the proofs, which look like an inky fishing-net"—and who can doubt that his changes were improvements?

Dickenses may be in short supply, but there are still plenty of sound, workmanlike editors to be found at copy desks and in publishers' offices. They need to be encouraged (instead of being hobbled by the misguided policies of their superiors, as they so often are), while mediocre editors need to be resisted, and criticized, and persuaded that they might be happier in other jobs. All this is no doubt easier said than done; but unless writers keep protesting, they are liable to find more and more words being put into their mouths—uncongenial words, as often as not, inelegant words, sometimes even words that they wouldn't normally be seen dead with.

✑ ALISON LURIE

Notes on the Language of
Poststructuralism

INNOVATIONS IN LANGUAGE ARE ALWAYS interesting metaphorically. When the words used for familiar things change, or new words are introduced, they are usually not composed of nonsense syllables, but borrowed or adapted from stock. Assuming new roles, they drag their old meanings along behind them like flickering shadows. To the amateur observer this seems especially true of the language of the contemporary school of literary criticism that now prefers to describe itself simply and rather magisterially as "theory" but is still popularly referred to as poststructuralism or deconstruction.[1]

Many of the terms current in the field, like its ideas, originated in France, and their translation into English sometimes subtly alters the shadow-meaning. The earliest neologisms of the movement, Saussure's "signifiant" and "signifié," became *signifier* and *signified*, now employed to distinguish words (*signifiers*) from their meanings (*signifieds*) and emphasize the arbitrariness of the terms we chose. The use of these particular terms (rather than, say, *word* and *thing*) underlined the seriousness of the process and its claim on our attention. Since in English *to signify* can also mean "to portend" it was also possibly suggested that words predicted coming events—as indeed they did in this case.

With *deconstruction* we move into another and more complex realm of implication. The most common use of the terms *construction* and *de-*

construction in English is in the building trades, and their borrowing by literary theorists for a new type of criticism cannot help but have certain overtones to an outsider. First, it suggests that the creation and interpretation of literature are not organic but mechanical processes; that the author of a piece of writing or "text" (see below) is not an inspired, intuitive artist or interpreter, but merely a workman who cobbles existing materials (words) into more or less conventional structures.

The term *deconstruction* implies that the text has been put together like a building or a piece of machinery, and that it is in need of being taken apart again, not so much in order to repair it as to demonstrate its underlying inadequacies, false assumptions, and inherent contradictions. This process can be repeated many times and by many literary hard hats; it is expected that each deconstruction will reveal additional flaws.

The preference for the term *deconstruction* rather than *criticism* is also interesting etymologically. *Criticism* and *critic* derive from the Greek *kritikos*, "skilled in judging, decisive." *Deconstruction* (Latin *constructus*, "piled or put together"), on the other hand, has no overtones of skill or wisdom; it merely suggests the demolition of an existing building. In popular usage *criticism* suggests censure but not change. If we criticize someone or something we may condemn them but we do not carry out the sentence ourselves. The contemporary theorist, by implication, is both judge and executioner. When he or she is finished with a text it will have been totally dismantled, if not reduced to a pile of rubble.

Central to the new language of poststructuralism, and rich in association, is the word *text*, which now appears even in the discourse of critics who fear and detest the new theories. The notion of using a single word to designate every sort of written message was innovative and practical; what gives a neutral observer pause is the term (or, if you prefer, *signifier*) chosen. In the past critics spoke of stories, tales, novels, and poems: words that etymologically evoke a world of human lives and human creation. *Story* derives from the Greek and Latin *historia* ("narrative history"), *tale* from the Old English *talu* ("reckoning, speech") and the Old Norse *tala* ("talk, tale, number"). *Novel* comes from the Latin *novella narratio* ("new tale"), and *poem* from the Greek *poeima* ("something made").

Before deconstruction a *text* in common parlance was one of two things: a school textbook, or "a short passage from the Scriptures, especially one quoted . . . as the subject of an exposition or sermon." The expansion of the term to include all written works inevitably suggests to the uninitiated observer that literature is not intended to entertain but to instruct; a text is something we study under the direction of an authority. (The discussion by Roland Barthes of "the pleasures of the text" may at first suggest an attempt to restore enjoyment ["jouissance"] to reading. But in practice this enjoyment seems to be both dependent on critical interpretation and directly related to a disregard of the author's intentions; it is a kind of guided erotic tour.)

Etymologically the word *text* derives from the Latin *texere* ("to weave") and *textus* ("a web; texture, structure"). The suggestion is of something made by a spider or a human weaver for practical use. Appropriately, the texts studied by deconstructionist critics are approached without interest in their individual authors, as examples of the mumblings of the *zeitgeist*, as if they were the work of either an ignorant artisan or an anonymous arachnid. (And if you read the papers written by some members of this school, you will often get the impression that they are flies struggling in the sticky verbal strands of theoretical discourse.)

A text is also expected to be difficult of access. When we study Shakespeare, physics, or the Bible, we are not supposed to be able to understand what we read without the help of a teacher or preacher. Redefining poems and novels and stories as *texts* removes them from occasions of private appreciation and sets an interpreter between them and us. It elevates the works concerned, but at the same time diminishes them. In church and classroom the "text" is often only the jumping-off point for a sermon or lecture which may range far afield. So it has been with the texts of deconstruction, which more often than not give rise to amazingly intricate and far-fetched discourses. At times it seems that the briefer the text the more elaborate will be the critical structure built upon it. Contemporary critics often, like medieval churchmen, seem to prefer to stand between the text and the reader, blocking direct access and substituting their own commentaries or "metatexts" for the Gospel. The tendency of some modern theorists to "read" the whole world as a text—a notion reminiscent of the medieval idea of the world as God's book—expands the area of the layman's presumed ignorance.

Many people have pointed out the practical advantages of the term *text*, which embraces every sort of written document from an advertising slogan to a verse epic. The hidden implication of this apparently generous and inclusive term, however, is that all texts are equal: the difference between the advertising slogan and the epic is one of social context rather than of value or meaning.

In practice, texts are only equal until some of them are *privileged*. This term, most often used in a negative sense, has also passed into common academic—and even nonacademic—discourse. Outside the

university, though, it is still most often associated with matters of social class, and for literary critics to adopt the term suggests that there
is still rank among documents. But it is not popularity or traditional
acclaim (economic success or aristocratic lineage, so to speak) that
now determines the value of a text; it is the decision of the critic.

At first this might suggest that critics, like royal personages, assign
rank and title to selected members of the mob of texts suing for their
favors. This is true only to a certain extent. The contemporary critic,
like many sovereigns, tends to keep the highest honors for his own
practice. Today it is critical theory which is truly "privileged." As Jonathan Culler puts it in his lucid and thoughtful, if at times terrifying,
survey of current trends in the field, *Framing the Sign*, "formerly the
history of criticism was part of the history of literature . . . now the
history of literature is part of the history of criticism."[2] Paul de Man
has even suggested that critical or philosophical or linguistic texts are
fully as "literary" as poems and novels,[3] which may account for the
fact that many articles and books in the field seem, to an author, intended not so much to supplement as to compete with the works they
claim to discuss.

In some university courses today students read mainly critical theory, and class discussions revolve around such second-level texts. The
fact that these texts too are subject to deconstruction, and their decon-
structions to further deconstruction, has produced an exhausting series of commentaries on commentaries which recall nothing so much
as the productions of medieval scholasticism. To the unconverted this
mass of words resembles the infinitely retreating and dimming reflections in opposing mirrors.

While texts are privileged, characters and concepts within them are
more apt to be spoken of as "valorized," that is, valued highly. The
term is almost always used in a negative, debunking way, to expose
the hidden assumptions of a given text. But because most of us learnt
the word *valorize* ("to fix the value or price of a commodity") before
we read literary theory, the old meaning haunts the new usage, with
its implication that what writers are doing in presenting any character
or idea as admirable is equivalent to price-fixing. Echoes from the
word *valor* also hint that there is something illegitimate in attributing
"boldness or firmness; courage or bravery" to anyone or anything,
since a reputation for these qualities must usually be won rather than
assigned.

More recent developments in poststructuralist criticism, and more
recent verbal inventions, are too many and various for me to even attempt to cover. A thorough investigation, though, might look at the
metaphoric suggestions of Derrida's *différence* and *différance*, and the

daunting vocabulary of terms from classical rhetoric adopted by writers like Paul de Man and Harold Bloom, which suggest that literature is a form of political oratory, and that to write is essentially to pose or deceive.

Attention should also be paid to the emerging language of feminist criticism which, for example, sometimes speaks of women's writing as *fluant* ("flowing"), suggesting that it may be wet and transitory.[4] Equally interesting is the vocabulary of the New Historicists, who tend to use the term *subversion* in the place of *deconstruction*, calling up a Conradian world of plots and counterplots, revolution and ruin. Several recent writers, both feminist and historicist, have been accused of *recuperating* (reviving) Marxist vocabularies and works—a word choice which by association implies that these terms and works were seriously ill, or perhaps even that literature itself is an illness.

To the common reader all these new vocabularies are daunting and confusing. Perhaps that is one of the aims of their inventors and users: many new intellectual disciplines, like elementary school cliques, tend to adopt as fast as possible their own special version of pig latin in order to build morale and confuse outsiders. Among these confused outsiders, unfortunately, is often the author. Earlier schools of literary criticism have been either friendly and easily accessible, or if anything too intrusive—prying into writers' personal lives and their psychological and economic motivations. "Theory," by contrast, excludes authors from consideration. A writer and college professor I know recently learnt through the student grapevine that a junior colleague would be teaching one of his novels in her seminar on modern fiction. Assuming that she was too shy to ask, he volunteered to visit the class and answer questions about his text. "Oh, no thank you," she told him. "That won't be necessary."

Before the present time it is unlikely that many authors of poetry or fiction or drama ever sat down to create a text. But I suspect that some writers today are doing just that. They are deliberately producing work that is intended to be taken apart and studied rather than read and enjoyed. Some of these productions have been original and interesting; but most of them depress me and make me sorry for their authors, whom I see as trying in vain to run round the end of the new school of literary criticism and score some points for their own words. Even if what they say won't be taken seriously as a poem or story, or a statement of values, the hope is that it will qualify as a kind of criticism.

I am afraid these writers are in for a disappointment. Critics have never taken kindly to attempts to usurp their functions; and though the new theorists may claim that their own work is literature, they are unlikely to concede that any collection of words put together by an author, including the present one, could be taken seriously as criticism.

Notes

1. Deconstructionists themselves have also noted that words come bearing their "traces," though (as far as I can discover) without reference to the implications of their own language.

2. Jonathan Culler, *Framing the Sign* (Norman, Okla., 1988), p. 40.

3. Culler, *Framing the Sign*, p. 116.

4. Culler points out that Elaine Showalter's use of the term *gynocriticism* for the feminist study of women's writing seems to make the critic a gynecologist.

❧ MICHAEL ROGERS

Computers and Language:
An Optimistic View

ONE EVENING IN 1945, A LUCKLESS MOTH flew into a huge government computer in Virginia. Computers were then in large part mechanical, and the insect was crushed instantly between the metal blades of a relay, shutting down the machine and lending English its first widespread bit of computer slang: *bug*.

Since that lepidopteran's demise, computers have proliferated at an astounding rate, culminating in the past decade's barrage of bits and bytes, RAMs and ROMs. Yet thus far, the computer's influence on general language has remained slight, compared to the jargon of war, sports, or commerce. On the timeline of technology, however, computers are still embryonic. Their real impact on English will be far more than merely etymological: ultimately, computers will profoundly alter the way that language itself is written.

Before the flood tide of tiny computers, only engineers and scientists came into contact with computer terminology. Now, a large part of educated society is exposed to the jargon, either in the office, through schools, or in the media. Even polite conversation is not immune: anyone trapped at dinner with voluble new computer owners knows that the little machines can easily become an obsessive topic. At some gatherings in California, hosts and hostesses are known to ban computer language from the table altogether.

Discoursing on RAM and ROM at dinner, of course, is in the end no different from carrying on about horsepower or carburetors. More compelling is the way computer jargon is increasingly applied to other concerns. It is perhaps emblematic of an emerging technology that, as with *bug*, the most successful linguistic crossovers thus far are all inspired by computer failures. *Glitch*, meaning a small but serious error (usually in software) has gathered wider use—perhaps because it is common in aerospace engineering and thus in televised space-shots. *Crash*, which is a major system shutdown, has also found broad acceptance. *Crash* probably arose with the first student computer enthusiasts at the Massachusetts Institute of Technology, most of whom also belonged to the MIT model railroad club, where crashes were of the conventional variety.

Other computer borrowings aren't hard to find. Some, such as *programmed*, to describe behavior, have been enriched by their computer association but are ultimately not far from their precomputer meanings. The business world, eager to lend a high technology aura to mundane matters, has appropriated words like *network* and *interface*. Such borrowing simply replaces existing words with graceless jargon; because the motive is so transparent, both examples are already growing unfashionable. There is, however, a more intriguing class of computer-inspired language. This derives from the fact that some aspects of computers seem so similar to human thought that they provide new words with which to describe our own mental processes.

One such example, which briefly baffled the national press, occurred when John Sculley, an East Coast business executive, first became president of Apple Computer. In interviews, he described his conversations with young Apple cofounder Steve Jobs as "core dumps." The reference was to high-speed data transfer between the magnetic memory cores of large mainframe computers, and the implication was that Jobs and Sculley shared information in its most condensed form—a true meeting of minds, requiring little translation or explication. The expression is commonly used to indicate that a conversation will be short and to the point.

Computers also offer fresh meaning for the word *background*. When powerful computers are given more than one job to do, they relegate the lesser task to "background"—processing that problem only when the more important "foreground" task is momentarily at rest. Computerists have found *background* an attractive metaphor for a certain level of thought. Instead of "I'll sleep on it," one may say, "I'll keep that in background"—implying that the thought will not only be stored but some additional, probably subconscious, thinking will be done.

A new and exotic arrival linking thought and computers is *munge*.

Given a difficult task, such as processing realistic images, even a very powerful computer may take a few moments to come up with a result. Such delays are usually sources of great irritation to avid computerists. Performing these particularly difficult computations, however, is dubbed *munging*, implying the speaker's awareness that the computer is doing something so hard that the delay is forgivable. *Munge* is also applied to difficult human mental tasks, expressing at once regard for the difficulty of the task and sympathy for the thinker.

These usages remain mostly confined to technical communities, such as Silicon Valley or Boston's Route 128. In the long run, however, the mentation models may prove to be the computer's most original and vital contribution to general language. At the same time, some commentators are concerned that such metaphors are dangerous. In her book *The Second Self*, a study of computers and culture, MIT sociologist Sherry Turkle warns that when children take computers too literally as models of human thought, they may devalue the subtlety of their own minds. Though research has shown that conventional computers operate differently from the human brain, the newer "neural network" computers more closely imitate the brain's structure and may well someday offer even more enticing mental metaphors.

If the computer's influence on language as a whole remains small, its impact on literary language is smaller still. Poets or novelists may use jargon for effect, but most serious writers ignore the vocabulary as a matter of course. Motivations are several: unfamiliarity, combined with fear that new language may date one's work. A lingering class bias in liberal arts education may also be at work; at one time understanding the operation of, say, an internal combustion engine suggested a streak of grimy curiosity that wasn't entirely well bred. The class issue still lurks when essayists discourse on the impossibility of ever learning how to operate a word processor—when every day, in back offices from Secaucus to Sacramento, millions of Americans with high school educations use computers as a fact of life.

In the end, the very ubiquity of computers will bring far more profound changes to language than merely fresh vocabulary. By early next century, the computer will fundamentally alter the way people write, in a manner that most observers alive today will never fully embrace. While the current adult population may sooner or later largely adopt computers for writing, few will use the machines the same way as will their children, who have never known anything else.

For these new writers, the computer will be an active participant in writing itself. The now-ubiquitous spelling checkers are only a hint of what powerful artificial intelligence software will contribute two decades hence. Sophisticated parsers will analyze writing style, suggesting improvements, even criticizing word choice. Already, the possibilities are proliferating: one current style checker chides writers for sexist usages. Another scans for the characteristic errors made by native French speakers writing in English.

A new class of software called idea processors now permits writers to manipulate language in larger units than the single word. Someday, "intelligent" idea processors may actually suggest organization and structure based on the way the writer has taken notes. New York poet Michael Newman has already created a sophisticated poetry processor with which even the most unskilled poetaster can build a technically perfect sonnet or villanelle. The act of note-taking will change, as on-line information systems (or huge reference libraries encoded on optical disks) radically democratize access to library materials. New copyright questions will arise, as it becomes possible to load entire articles or books into one's own computer for digestion and regurgitation. To the horror of publishers, one influential computer programmer has already suggested "autoplagiarism" software.

For traditionalists, the prospect of computer-mediated writing may sound nightmarish, and such fears have rich precedents. Socrates warned that the very act of writing would destroy scholars' memories; German historian Trithemius argued that the printing press would ruin learning by eliminating the need to copy texts by hand. Word processing has already spawned similar concerns: if computers make writing physically easier, text more fluid, will the quality of writing degrade?

Certainly, new abuses become possible. Some editors have already learned to recognize word processor logorrhea—a characteristic wordiness and repetition that comes from editing on-screen. (For most writers, editing on paper, then transferring the changes to screen, quickly cures the condition.) Similarly, the ease of rearranging paragraphs with a computer can, if overdone, turn intellectual structure into mush. In a vaguely medieval prescription aimed at this pitfall, one critic recently insisted that word processors should be limited to documents less than one thousand words in length.

Fear of new writing technology may be inevitable, for physical process has a powerful subconscious significance. When an established writer meets with students, someone is almost certain to ask whether the visitor composes with pen, typewriter, or computer. The urge to elicit personal ritual is not misplaced: repetitive writing activities (sharpening a dozen pencils; aligning perfectly the day's sheets of paper) probably do help create a mental state conducive to creativity.

By destroying those old rituals, the transition to word-processing can seem very dangerous. I immediately adopted the computer for journalism; the advantage of quick revision without retyping overwhelmed any qualms I had about process. But at the same time, I was reluctant to entrust fiction to the new machine: if using the computer damaged the work, how long would it take to realize the loss, and how much would be ruined in the process?

Thus the new computer sat alongside an aging typewriter for nearly a year; journalism on the computer, fiction on the typewriter. Then one day, as I sat hopelessly stuck in the middle of a short story, a thought arose, entirely unbidden: why not retype the story on the computer and just see what happens? The idea was irresistible, and since then, the computer has served me well for fiction—and idea-processing software has become an additional aid for plotting longer stories.

Society is sure to manage a similar rapprochement with the new writing technology. In the end, computers far more sophisticated than today's machines will democratize access to language, diminishing the barriers of class and education by making clear writing easier to achieve. One may fear the rise of cookie-cutter, machine-processed prose stripped of flair and idiosyncrasy, but that undervalues the basic human desire to personalize expression. Certainly, the rise of the straight edge and French curve failed to rob the graphic arts of anything essential.

Broadening access to good prose will place an additional premium on the ability to create original thought and diminish the value of well-schooled but merely glib expression. The most elegant, evocative, and revolutionary creations of language will still spring directly from human inspiration—but new writing technology, by elevating the common denominator, will allow that inspiration to rise from higher ground than language today inhabits.

ᴄ MICHAEL HEIM

Infomania

WHAT IS THE STATE OF THE LANGUAGE? No state at all. It is in process. Our language is being word-processed. If languages have states of health, get sick or well, then ours is manic.

We face a tidal wave of written words. The wave of future shock swelled on the horizon. First came speed reading—a twentieth-century version of literacy. Next Xerox duplication, the word processor, and the fax machine. Now we drive a technology that drives our verbal life faster and faster. The word processor is computerizing our language.

Word-processed submissions have doubled the workload of editors at commercial and academic presses. Writers grow prolix, with manuscripts bloated to twice normal size. The prose is profuse, garbled, torturously disorganized—as if the difference between writing and revising were passé. Pages are becoming more difficult to read. Reams of paper pour out unedited streams of consciousness. The only writer who admits he is no faster than he was before computers is Isaac Asimov, who published 141 books in 138 months.

Before 1980 the microcomputer was a crude, costly kit for hobbyists and experimenters. Then Dan Bricklin and Dan Fylstra created software for an electronic spreadsheet (an accounting tool for figuring finances in rows and columns). *Visicalc* ran on the Apple II and opened the market for desktop computers. In 1981 International Business Machines (IBM) persuaded businesses that computerized spreadsheets would increase productivity. Once installed, computers could also run other software including word processing. The lure of greater productivity hooked professional writers too. By now most writers use word processing.

IBM first coined the term *word processing* in 1964 to describe a brand of typewriter. The MTST (Magnetic Tape "Selectric" Typewriter) boasted word-processing capabilities because it used magnetic tape to store pages of text. You could select pages for retrieval from electronic memory, which greatly streamlined the production of texts. Machines dedicated solely to word-processing, like the Wang, soon appeared. The quantum leap in writing technology, however, came with microcomputers. The broad base of micro users allowed word-processing software to flourish. A decade earlier, data processors had used text-editing software on mainframe computers to create programs for number crunching. Their editing programs applied information-processing techniques rather than allow direct human interaction with texts on video monitors. When video arrived, inventors like Doug Engelbart and Ted Nelson saw that computers could do more than aid mechanical typewriting. They believed word processing could amplify mental powers and increase our command over language. Word processing ceased being a typing gadget and became a cultural phenomenon. Over 80 percent of computer use is now word processing. Today computers spew out the major bulk of written English.

During the 1980s a new vocabulary established the computerization of English. To be initiated, you had to repeat buzzwords like *access*, *input*, and *output*. You learned to speak of *files* having no apparent physical dimensions, *menus* offering a selection of nonedibles, and *monitors* providing vigilance over your own words. You learned to navigate with *wraparound* and with a *cursor*—sometimes dubbed *cursee* as it became the recipient of your profanities. You may have even explored *mouse compatibility*, the *ASCII code*, and the difference between *RAM* and *ROM* memory. At the very least, you addressed yourself to *floppies* and *windows*, to *function keys* and program *documentation* (read: instruction manual). You had to take into account *block moves*, *hyphenation zones*, and *soft spaces* versus *hard*. The editorial *cut-and-paste* became yours electronically. You learned not only to *delete* but also to *unerase*, then to *search-and-replace*, and onward to *globally search-and-replace*. *Automatic formatting* and *reformatting* entered your writing routine.

Once initiated into the basics of word processing you sigh, this is bliss! No more cutting paper and pasting, no more anxiety about revisions. Now you can get to work without the nuisance of typing and retyping. Words dance on the screen. Sentences slide smoothly into place, making way for one another, while paragraphs ripple rhythmically. Words become highlighted, vanish and then reappear instantly at the push of a button. Digital writing is nearly frictionless. You formulate thoughts directly on screen. You don't have to consider whether you are writing the beginning, middle, or end of your text. You can snap any passage into any place with the push of a key. The flow of ideas flashes directly on screen. No need to ponder or sit on an idea—capture it on the fly!

But the honeymoon fades, and the dark side of computing descends upon you. The romance with computers shows its pathological aspects: mindless productivity and increased stress.

Your prose now reads, well, differently. You no longer formulate thoughts carefully before beginning to write. You think on screen. You edit more aggressively as you write, making changes without penalty of retyping. Possible changes occur to you rapidly and frequently, so that a leaning tower of printouts stretches from the wastebasket to the heights of perfection—almost. The power at your fingertips tempts you to believe that faster is better, that ease means instant quality.

Business in America embraced computers under the magic rubric of *productivity*. Yet company reports do not seem to get better after thirty drafts. Growth in economic productivity in the United States actually declined over the last decade, and so has the competitiveness of the U.S. economy. Feel productive, push more paper.

Universities and colleges also bought into computerization. Miles of fiber-optic cable make subterranean links between academic buildings, snaking under the tree-lined footpaths like invisible superhighways. Yet few believe that computer networks actually advance liberal learning or that a greater outpouring of scholarly research makes better readers. Push a button, fell a tree.

Before computers, newspaper editors had a mentor-apprentice relationship to reporters. Reporters would write a piece, show it to the editor, and after blue-pencilling it, the editor would discuss it with the reporters. The reporters would then take responsibility for making the changes. Now things are different. The editor gets the electronic text, makes the changes, then sends the reporters a copy. Reporters are not learning how to rewite. While the editors are becoming better writers, the reporters are becoming data entry clerks.

If your company had a computer network installed, you could conduct business without worrying about coordinating schedules or reserving conference rooms or flying on airplanes to meetings. Through electronic mail you can belong to a virtual (nonphysical) workgroup.

You exchange reports or PROF notes without the small talk of phone conversation and without the delay of paper mail. To prevent the accusation "You didn't tell me you were going to do that," you (and everyone else in the group) just hit a key and copies of your message fly off to everyone in the network.

On the receiving end, however, life is less rosy. Computer-generated notes, memoranda, and reports accumulate. Files clutter your workspace, daunting your mind with their sheer volume. You are working in an intellectual swamp. Since you do not know immediately which files are worth saving, you have to wade through each of them before deleting any. The paperless office has more, not less, junk mail.

Physical hazards also lurk on the dark side of computing. Phosphorescent words on the screen hold a hypnotic attraction. So intensely do they attract that human eyes blink less often when viewing computer texts. The cornea of the eye requires frequent fluid baths, and eyelids normally bathe and massage the eyeballs by blinking every five seconds. The stress of computer interaction tends to fix vision in a stare. As blinking decreases, the eye muscles have difficulty focusing. The resulting strain eventually leads to refractive error, most often myopia.[1]

The stress of digital writing breeds more than myopia. Because it is intensely interactive and yet nearly frictionless, computer work involves more prolonged strain than pencil or typewriter. You take fewer rest breaks. You have no paper file cabinets to visit, no corrections to make by hand, no variety of physical motions. Fingers just keep moving, repeating the same keystrokes. You hardly notice your unrelieved adaptation to the machine's specifications. The result is a workplace epidemic called Repetitive Motion Syndrome (RMS). The inflamed hand and arm tendons of RMS patients often require surgical operations; doctors are finding permanent damage to bodily movement in many RMS patients. The word processor is not merely a glorified typewriter.

I have yet to find a single writer who learned word processing and then abandoned it for pen or typewriter. Most writers and journalists share Stephen White's affection for word processing:

> A writer of any kind who does not work on a word processor is either dead broke or some kind of fool: it is as simple as that and we should not shilly-shally about it. He may be at the same time an absolutely first-rate writer, but although he may well dispute it, he gains nothing by his abnegation, and only makes life harder for himself and, to a limited extent, for others.[2]

Gore Vidal, neither broke nor a fool, would disagree. "The word processor is erasing literature," he says. Efficiency, speed, and networked communication are in our bones. Our life rhythm moves to the tempo of the computer.

Already in 1957 Heidegger noticed a shift in the felt sense of time. He saw the drive for technological mastery pushing into the human interior where thought and reality meet in language:

> The language machine regulates and adjusts in advance the mode of our possible usage of language through mechanical energies and functions. The language machine is—and above all, is still becoming—one way in which modern technology controls the mode and the world of language as such. Meanwhile, the impression is still maintained that man is the master of the language machine. But the truth of the matter might well be that the language machine takes language into its management, and thus masters the essence of the human being.[3]

Heidegger's philosophy was neither Luddite nor technophobic. He resisted every attempt to categorize his view of technology as either optimistic or pessimistic. Whether the glass was half-empty or half-full, Heidegger was interested in the substance of its contents. He was a soft determinist, accepting destiny while studying different ways to absorb its impact.

Heidegger correctly sensed that word processing is part of our destiny. Each epoch has its love affair, its grand passion, an enthusiasm that gives it distinction. Pyramids or cathedrals do not distinguish us and shopping malls will never last. Ours is not the age of faith or reason but the age of information. Madness, Plato reminds us, is ambivalent; it can be divine or insane, inspired or crackpot. Lovers, inventors, and artists are maniacs. So are computer enthusiasts. For infomaniacs, word processing is not merely a tool.

Language technology belongs to us more essentially than any tool. When a technology touches our language, it touches us where we live. The chief inventors of word processing were aware of this. These visionaries were not marketing a commercial product but seeking a revolution in the way we think. They wanted to radically alter the way we interact with language. Douglas Engelbart wrote "The Augmentation of Man's Intellect by Machine" as he put together the first text-processing hardware and software at the Augmentation Research Center (ARC) in the 1960s.[4] He balked at the inflexibility of the means we have for handling symbols. If we could manipulate symbols in tandem with computers, he argued, we could boost thought processes at least as much as handwriting boosted the powers of preliterate humans. Engelbart was not in fact trying to replace the mind with artificial intelligence. Instead, he conceived the computer as a symbol manipulator for supercharging thought processes at the language level. Computers could constitute a world network where the thoughts of countless individuals merge. Since Engelbart, many others have introduced software to affect our prose composition, our word choices, and even our logical processes.

Computer networks can be revolutionary. The 1989 prodemocracy student uprisings in China were supported by computer networks and fax machines connecting thousands of Chinese people around the world. Computer bulletin boards created a public forum for free expression. Government-suppressed news streamed into China from outside. In Beijing, calls for freedom and reform circulated in Tiananmen Square on computer printouts.

Literature too changes as the written word migrates to electronic text. On computers, literature presents an unlimited cross-reference system for all symbol creations. A text includes footnotes that open up onto symphonies, films, or mathematical demonstrations. Browsing means push-button access to the text of all texts, or "hypertext," as Ted Nelson called it. Hypertext, and its offspring HyperCard, are already evolving nonlinear ways of reading. Books like Joyce's *Finnegans Wake* deserve another look on hypertext.[5] Hypertext heightens nonlinear and associative styles. Background knowledge and commentary pop up at the touch of a button. Like fractal structures, a text can turn back on itself linguistically, and hypertext shows the turns, the links, the recurring motifs, and the playful self-references.

How will traditional books fare? When Heidegger looked again ten years later in 1967, he saw a rising crest of information which, he suspected, might soon swallow his own writings:

> Maybe history and tradition will fit smoothly into the information retrieval systems which will serve as resource for the inevitable planning needs of a cybernetically organized mankind. The question is whether thinking too will end in the business of information processing.[6]

He saw a growing obsession with data without a concern for significance.

Writing is the primary means we have for putting our thoughts before us, for opening mental contents to criticism and analysis. Using computers for writing, we experience language as electronic data, and the machines reinforce information over significance.

Information is a unit of knowledge which by itself has only a trace of significance. Information presupposes a significant context but does not deliver or guarantee one. Because context does not come built in, information can be handled and manipulated, stored and transmitted at computer speeds. Word processing makes us information virtuosos, as the computer automatically transforms all we write into information code. But human we remain. For us, significant language always depends on the felt context of our own limited experience. We are biologically finite in what we can attend to meaningfully. When we pay attention to the significance of something, we cannot proceed at the computer's breakneck pace. We have to ponder, reflect, contemplate.

Infomania erodes our capacity for significance. With a mindset fixed on information, the attention span shortens. We collect fragments. We become mentally poorer in overall meaning. We get into the habit of clinging to knowledge bits and lose our feel for the wisdom behind knowledge. In the Information Age some people even believe that literacy or culture is a matter of having the right facts at our fingertips.

We expect access to everything *now*, instantly and simultaneously. We suffer from a logic of total management where everything must be at our disposal. Eventually our madness will cost us. There is a law of diminishing returns: the more information accessed, the less significance is possible. We must not lose our appreciation for the expressive possibilities of our language in the service of thinking.

Notes

1. R. Anthony Hutchinson, *Computer Eye-Stress* (New York, 1985), gives useful exercises for alleviating focusing stress. Chinese Qi Gong exercises can heal and prevent the RMS syndrome. Industry should protect its people by providing the time and training for these exercises.

2. Stephen White, *The Written Word: And Associated Digressions Concerned with the Writer as Craftsman* (New York, 1984), p. 68.

3. Martin Heidegger, *Hebel—der Hausfreund* (Pfullingen, 1957); translated by Michael Heim and Bruce Foltz as "Hebel—Friend of the House," in *Contemporary German Philosophy*, vol. 3 (University Park, Penn., 1983), pp. 89–101.

4. Howard Rheingold gives a good account of Engelbart and Nelson in his *Tools for Thought: The People and Ideas behind the Next Computer Revolution* (New York, 1985).

5. Gerrit Schroeder and Tim Murphy began hypertext assembly of *Finnegans Wake* at the University of California, Los Angeles, in 1987.

6. Heidegger, from the preface to *Wegmarken* (Frankfurt, 1967), my translation. For more on Heidegger's critique of information, see chapter 3 of my *Electric Language: A Philosophical Study of Word Processing* (New Haven, 1987).

I'm Having Trouble
With My Relationship

THE WORD *RELATIONSHIP* APPEARS FOR THE FIRST TIME in the 1743 edition of *The Dunciad.*[1] Pope uses it in a way both funny and cruel to identify his enemy Cibber with the insane. Cibber is said to be related to famous heads, sculpted by his father, representing despondent and raving madness. The heads were affixed to the front of Bedlam. Pope calls them Cibber's "brothers." Cibber and the heads have the same father; they stand in a blood, brains, "brazen," family "Relationship." The word effects a contemptuous distance between Pope and Cibber, and makes Cibber one with the sculpted heads. Funny in its concreteness; cruel in the play of implications; luminous in genius. Before Pope, *relationship* may have been part of daily talk, but until he uses it nothing exists in this way, bearing the lineaments of his mind, the cultural affluence of his self and time.

After 1743, *relationship* appears with increasing frequency, with no joke intended, and it not only survives objections to its redundant structure (two abstract suffixes), but, in the 1940s, it begins to intrude into areas of thought and feeling where it never belonged, gathering a huge constituency of uncritical users and displacing words that once seemed more appropriate, precise, and pleasing: *romance, affair, lover, beau, fellow, girl, boyfriend, girlfriend, steady date,* and so on. People now find these words more or less quaint or embarrassingly innocent.

They use *relationship* to mean any of them when talking about the romantic-sexual connection between a man and a woman or man, or woman and woman. In this liberal respect, Pope's use of the word is uncannily reborn.

People say, "I'm having trouble with my relationship," as though the trouble were not with Penelope or Max but with an object, perhaps a BMW, a sort of container or psychological condition into which they enter and relate. By displacing the old words for romantic love, *relationship* indicates a new caution where human experience is extremely intense and ephemeral, or a distrust of concrete words in which our happiness might suffer any idea of limit, or perhaps a distrust of words in general. It could be argued that *relationship* is better than the old words since it makes abstraction palpable, generously distributing it among four syllables; a feeling of love in the actions of sex; or philosophy in desire; and, as love is various, so are the syllables of *relationship*, not one of them repeating another. Though intended to restrict reference to a single person, the word has the faint effect of suggesting many persons. In its palpableness, syllables bob like Bedlam heads. Strange images of mind.

People also say, "I can relate to that," where no person is intended or essentially involved, just an idea of some kind of experience. The expression is innocuous, and yet it is reminiscent of psychopathic thinking. In the same modern spirit, people say *mothering* to mean no particular person is essential to the action; that is, "mothering" does not flow from a mother as poetry flows only from a poet, or life from the sun god. *Fathering* has a sexual charge different from *mothering* and cannot be used like this. We talk, then, of *parenting*. The political necessity for *mothering* and *parenting*, which justifies the words, doesn't make them less grotesque. But this sort of judgment is precious. The antinomies of our culture cling to each other like breeders in a slow, violent divorce, and aesthetic considerations are irrelevant. We have no use, in our thinking, for the determining power of essences, or depths of soul, or ideas of value that inhere, like juice in grapes, in the quiddity of people. Mom is not by any means an inevitable source of love. She might well be a twisted bitch, and many vile creeps are Dad. The words no longer pack honorific content. Commitments built into blood are honored only by the Mafia. Philip Larkin writes: "They fuck you up, your mum and dad."

What conservatives, feminists, Marxists, and other contemporary thinkers have in common is the idea that value has fled the human particular. Larkin might agree. He might even say that, long ago, value went off someplace to vomit and it has not returned. If this is true, we have been abandoned to the allure of nonspecific possibility, or the thrill of infinite novelty. A lexical whorehouse shines in the darkness of the modern mind. (The "new," says Roland Barthes, is itself a value. No big surprise to the automobile industry.) To descend again to my theme: your hot lover has cooled into your *relationship*, which in another aspect you have with your grocer or your cat.

This large disposition in our thinking and speaking arises from impersonal democratic passions, the last refuge of supreme good. As Simone Weil says, thinking of God, "Only the impersonal is sacred." But it is a little crazy that *relationship*, an uppity version of *relation*, should be enormously privileged, lumbering across the landscape of English with prefix and two suffixes streaming from a tiny head of substance like ghostly remains of its Latin roots and Germanic ending (*referre*, n. *latus*, and *ship*).

To have survived the guns of our grammarians and displaced more pleasant words in the natural history of English, it must answer to an exceptionally strong need. The other words may seem impossibly quaint, but it isn't only the sophistication of *relationship* that is needed. It is the whole word, including the four syllable sound, which is a body stumbling down stairs, the last two—*shunship*—the flap of a shoe's loose sole, or loose lips and gossip. In fact, *relationship* flourished in the talky, psychological climate of the modern century as we carried it from the offices of our shrinks, and, like a forgotten umbrella, left *romance* behind.

Notice well how the syllabic tumble of *relationship* makes a sound like sheer talk, or talking about something, emphasis on *about*, not *something*. Exactly here, in the eternally mysterious relation of sound and sense, *relationship* confers the dignity of thought upon referential promiscuity, its objects graced with interestingness, a sound basis in indeterminacy for interminable talk.

Philosophers might complain that it is a word without much "cash value." Heidegger, on the other hand, might take it as an expression of "the groundlessness and nullity of inauthentic everydayness." He means the nonstop impetuous trivialization, in "idle talk," of *Dasein*, by which he means anything real, by which he means that thing of which anyone who "is genuinely 'on the scent of' [it] will not speak." Certainly, then, in regard to *relationship*, Heidegger might say:

> Being-with-one-another in the "they" is by no means an indifferent side-by-sideness in which everything has been settled, but rather an intent, ambiguous watching of another, a secret and reciprocal listening-in. Under the mask of "for-one-another," an "against-one-another" is in play.

By which he means, "I'm having trouble with my relationship."

"The secret king of thought," forerunner of deconstruction, who spoke of the Nazis as "manufacturing corpses," Heidegger had the deepest grasp of what is authentic and inauthentic in human relations. (His literary descendants—as too often noted—manufacture "texts" out of "works.") But to feel what has been lost in thought, consider this text from a letter by Kafka to Milena, the woman he loved:

> Today I saw a map of Vienna. For an instant it seemed incomprehensible to me that they had built such a big city when you need only one room.

The incomprehensible city is *relationship*, or what you have with everyone in the abstract and lonely vastness of our social reality. The room, all one needs, is romance, love, passionate intimacy, the unsophisticated irrational thing you have with someone; or what has long been considered a form of madness, if not the universal demonic of contemporary vision.

The city is also *relationship* in the movie *Last Tango In Paris*, where Marlon Brando texts to his lover, "Everything outside this room is bullshit." He makes the same point as Kafka, but the subtext of the movie is that, in our lust for relationship, we have shoveled all the bullshit into the room. This lust, which is basically for power, or control, or the illusion of possessing something that isn't there—*Dasein*, needless to say, but what the hell—makes us prefer Theory to novels, poems, and people, or flat surfaces in architecture to the various elaborations of material that once engaged our hearts.

Native speakers of Swedish say *förhållande* is close in meaning to *relationship*, which suggests the Swedes are in the same boat as speakers of English (native speakers of other European languages and of Asian languages say it is difficult to find a close equivalent to *relationship*). *Relationship*, then, shouldn't be taken as a mere tendency of English where any noun might lust for sublimity in the abstract extension of itself. It isn't just another polysyllabic fascist on the left or right, but rather something that bespeaks a deeper tendency, in the soul, like what one sees in Andy Warhol's disquieting portraits of Marilyn Monroe and Mao, their faces repeating and vanishing into the static quality of their "look."

Relationship has a similarly reductive force, ultimately even an air of death worship. The "aura of death," says Georges Bataille, "is what denotes passion." It also denotes its absence, one might suppose, but this old notion isn't likely to seize our imagination, which is why *relationship* has slipped unnoticed into astounding prominence and ubiquitous banality. The word is no less common than death, and no less pathetically private; it is used much as though, after being consigned to the grave, one had lingered to love the undertaker, having had no such exquisitely personal attention before, nothing so convincing that one is.

Note

1. The word appears in a footnote, book 2, line 3. Pope writes, "Mr. Cibber remonstrated that his Brothers at Bedlam . . . were not Brazen, but Blocks; yet our author let it pass unaltered, as a trifle, that in no way lessened the Relationship."

Art

The poet's role hinges on his ability to create that
inner tongue, that wondrous argot comprised
of only authentic names.

JOSÉ ORTEGA Y GASSET

In art it is as hard to say anything as
good as: saying nothing.

LUDWIG WITTGENSTEIN

A man may play the fool anywhere else
but not in poetry.

MONTAIGNE

~ MARGARET A. DOODY

Changing What We Sing

IN THE PAST TEN YEARS OR SO, various committees and groups have been engaged in altering the service books of various Protestant denominations. The Episcopalian Book of Common Prayer has been done in by some insistent authorities within the church, and survives only under difficulties. Other Protestant churches have altered traditional Christian prayers (including the Lord's Prayer) out of all recognition. Now the revising spirit is having its way with the standard Christian hymns of the Protestant tradition.

The use of hymns is perhaps always a somewhat uneasy subject within the Church in general. Some agnostics quite like hymns, and will attend church in hope of singing an old favorite; harvest festivals and Christmas celebrations are particularly apt to offer this inducement to occasional conformity. Some believers, on the other hand, dislike hymns; C. S. Lewis, for instance, had to force himself to tolerate them. Hymns have frequently been controversial, their very existence a cause of dispute. They have been a means of introducing secular music, popular tunes; the defensive question "Why should the devil have all the good tunes?" has been countered by "What do the devil's tunes have to do in a house of worship?" The Protestant movement at its inception inclined first to the belief that no hymns should be sung in church services save the Psalms of David, as these were divinely and directly inspired. As late as 1776, Augustus Toplady (author of "Rock of Ages") had to defend the use of hymns, or what he termed "spiritual Odes" (borrowing the term from St. Paul). Toplady points out that the hymns sung in the early Church were undoubtedly *"human Compositions,* as much so as the Hymns of PRUDENTIUS, . . . VIDA, Dr. WATTS, Miss STEELE, or Mr. HART." Such spiritual Odes are "written by spiritual Persons, under the impressions of spiritual Influence." "Some worthy persons," Toplady acknowledges, "have been of opinion (and what absurdity is there, for which some well-meaning people have not contended?) that it is *'unlawfull* to sing *Human Compositions* in the House of God.'" But if this were true, he argues, then "by the same rule, it must be equally unlawfull, to preach, or publicly to *pray*, except in the very words of Scripture. Not to observe, that many of the best and greatest Men, that ever lived, have, both in antient and modern times, been *Hymn-writers*; and that there is the strongest reason to believe, that the best *Christians*, in all ages, have been *Hymn-singers*."[1]

This short Preface to Toplady's anthology *Psalms and Hymns for Public and Private Worship* does not say directly what it strongly indicates— that the Psalms of David were also *"human Compositions"* not the less spiritual for that reason, and that hymn writers, including Toplady's own contemporaries like Anne Steele and Isaac Watts, could participate in divine inspiration no less than King David. Hymn writers have the gift of making something (humanly composed) which also serves the congregation as "one of the divinest Mediums of communication with God, which his gracious benignity has vouchsaf'd to his church below."[2] Hymns are human songs reaching to the divine, and also moments of the divine touching the human, and they are the product of individual human persons, men and women, who can be individually named as makers. Toplady himself was a real individual; "Rock of Ages" had its origin in an experience of his own, as he tells us, when he was sheltering from a storm. All poems are the "human Compositions" of human beings, and that includes the poems in our hymnbooks—the poems that are now being subjected to such wholesale and merciless revision.

I am fully aware that the revision of hymns seems a very local matter, of little interest save to those who expect to participate in worship at the churches which accept the new versions. What Christians sing or do not sing can hardly evoke much interest on the part of non-Christians. Yet perhaps it ought to do so. Because when we look closely at the revision of hymns, the changes being wrought in particular "human Compositions," then the whole nature of language and the status of a poet's work turn out to be involved.

It ought to be explained that the revisers' overt intention is always benevolent. I am using as the example of a revised hymnal the one that is most familiar to me, the one repeatedly used at Princeton University Chapel. This revision is at present a booklet called *Inclusive Language Hymns*, and it emanates from the First Congregational Church, Amherst, Massachusetts. The title is supposed to be self-explanatory, or nearly so, for the interior of the book provides only one short paragraph of explanation, and most of the explanation is found in the following sentence: "This collection of amended texts with music was prepared because we found no collection of hymns available to support our desire to offer the hymns of our tradition in inclusive language for worship in our services."[3] There is no definition of what "inclusive language" means, but there is plenty of evidence that a primary concern is the removal of language now regarded as "sexist." In the traditional hymns, God is referred to as "He," people are "men" and "brothers." The Amherst revisers have gone through the standard hymnal conscientiously removing all such references to God or Christ involving the words *He, His, Him. Mankind* and *men* become *People* or *all races*. These revisers (unlike the Prayer Book revisers) have not insisted on omitting all the *thees, thous,* and *thines,* so we have what looks like a traditional language enfolding a changed language.

There are other changes too, not so clearly explained by the phrase "inclusive language." The revisers apparently dislike anything that smacks of the Church Militant. All references to metaphors of soldiering have been expunged. Thus the "Negro Spiritual" (so labeled) known by its first line as "We Are Climbing Jacob's Ladder" has had the last line of the first verse altered from "Soldiers of the cross" to "Bearers of the cross" (a different statement). The revisers are also staunchly republican and antimonarchical in their views. All references to the Deity in monarchical metaphor are done away with. Thus the hymn well known to Protestants as "O Worship the King" by Robert Grant has undergone considerable change. The first verse looks thus in the first printed version of 1839:

> O worship the King
>   All glorious above,
> O gratefully sing
>   His power and his love—
> Our shield and defender,
>   The Ancient of days,
> Pavilion'd in splendour,
>   And girded with praise.[4]

That is essentially the version we have been singing for nearly one hundred and fifty years until the Amherst revisers gave us this:

> We worship thee, God,
>   all glorious above,
> And publish abroad
>   thy power and thy love . . . [5]

The second verse of Grant's hymn runs as follows:

> O tell of his might,
>   O sing of his grace,
> Whose robe is the light,
>   Whose canopy space.
> His chariots of wrath
>   Deep thunder-clouds form,
> And dark is his path
>   On the wings of the storm.

Moderns have put in "The deep thunder-clouds" as the extra syllable makes the verse easier to sing to the traditional melodies.[6] But otherwise the verse has survived undamaged—until now. The hymn, based on Psalm 104, stems from the tradition of singing the Psalms of David arranged in English verse and meter. Yet it is not Psalm 104 but a new human composition picking up various ideas and images from the Bible and from other poets. Robert Grant was born in 1779 and thus came poetically of age at a time when the poetry of Cowper was most well known. Sir Robert Grant was a real human individual, as Cowper was, with a local habitation and a name. He was a distinguished public servant—as judge advocate-general he supported and helped to push through the Jewish Emancipation resolution—who was also a modest but not negligible religious poet. "O worship the King" exhibits the influence of Cowper's poetry—its excitement, its bold metaphor—while lacking Cowper's foreboding sense of doom and his anxiety. Grant's is a stirring piece which has long been popular. It attaches itself to the sense of lyric immediacy which is a common theme in the book of Psalms: "O sing . . ." The speaker is a poet, a singer; he cannot forbear singing, and urges those about him—the public, the congregation—to *sing*, to sing the splendor of God.

The Amherst revisers, however, have an allergy to all monarchical reference, so "O Worship the King" has fallen severely under the knife. God is no longer King. Besides, "King" is masculine and thus must be "sexist." These aversions are at least readily explicable in political terms. What seems stranger is that the revisers—these exponents of clean hymnody—have an aversion to all exhortation. Nobody should order anyone to do anything—at least, one supposes that must be their reason for quietly banning exhortation and statements urging action. All imperatives (including those of the "let us" variety) seem to have been changed into calm statements of fact. "We worship"—so there's no need for anyone to *tell* anyone else what to do.

In this translation from English into another English, the sense has been truly altered. Lyric immediacy has gone with the removal of "O gratefully sing." There's no need for gratitude, or for the contact of the voice. *We* are now publishing (We publish abroad). This sounds like a remarkable late tribute to the supersession of oral culture by print culture, but it seems hardly necessary in reference to one of the few modern events (hymn-singing in church) in which everyone is involved in *oral* performance. The words "publish abroad" are by no means noticeably modern; they seem rather less modern, indeed, than "gratefully sing." "Publish abroad"—hmmm—like the *International Herald Tribune?* To make any sense of the line, an older sense of the words must be insisted on, a slightly archaic sense, not the modern primary meaning. Given a choice between archaism and wording now deemed ideologically incorrect, the revisers will opt for archaism. This is their version of the second verse of Grant's "O Worship the King":

> We tell of thy might,
>   we sing of thy grace,
> Whose robe is the light,
>   whose canopy space;
> Thy chariots of wrath
>   the deep thunderclouds form,
> And dark is thy path
>   on the wings of the storm.

After we have had to endure all the exhortation to get rid of every *thee* and *thou* and *thine* in the Prayer Books and in the Bible translations, we are to be given them by the plateful in the new and ultramodern hymnals. They serve for handy one-syllable equivalents to *him, he,* and *his*—and they *must* be poetical. It is very hard to make graceful grammatical sense out of the switch from *thy* to *whose,* a possessive pronoun more customarily and colloquially employed in reference to a third person than to an addressee. But never mind. Nobody can possibly think of God as male. Yet—those chariots of wrath are surely not feminine conveyances? And do not military and regal ideas still cling about the imagery? More rewriting is still necessary. There is obviously a crying need for a thorough overhaul of Psalm 104 itself. But nevertheless, our Amherst revisers may congratulate themselves on having performed the remarkable modernizing feat of getting rid of four instances of *his* and giving us four brand new, spandy-new *thys.*

The sense of an original statement is not evidently a criterion of paramount importance to these removers and changers. At least, one may judge this to be the case by looking at the results. Take, for instance, their revision of Charles Wesley's hymn (also well known and popular) "O for a Thousand Tongues." The first verse (old style) is this:

> O for a thousand tongues to sing
> My great Redeemer's praise,
> The glories of my God and King,
> The triumphs of his grace!
> (*Pilgrim Hymnal*, no. 223)[7]

The "inclusive language" version changes it to this:

> O for a thousand tongues to sing
> My great Redeemer's praise,
> The glories of my God to bring,
> Who wins our hearts by grace!
> (no. 223)

Now there is no vulgar triumph about God—no implied victories of grace, nor anything that might seem nasty-nasty military. And nothing as horrible (indeed unspeakable) as a King appears. Getting rid of "King" while keeping the first line must have cost these new-fledged rhymers considerable trouble and some headaches. Or perhaps it did not—they cannot surely have troubled themselves too long about it, because they came up (and were content) with the totally inane and meaningless line "The glories of my God to bring." This is an incomplete clause which as it stands is a nonsense. How do I "bring" the glories of God? Where do I bring them?—bring to notice, to book, to light, to the "bring and buy" sale? When sung, the expression comes off as "to bring who," which sounds not only ungrammatical but puzzling. The revisers evidently cannot see that the old—that is, Charles Wesley's—construction had "praise," "glories," and "triumphs" as a sequence of three noun objects of the verb "to sing." If these new rhymesters are not to be trusted with sentence construction, why must we trust them with our hymns? Their new fake line is a grammatical and linguistic disaster, and makes the hymn a parody of itself.

I have not yet found a publication in which the revisers of hymns defend their practices and clearly state their objectives and criteria, though surely somewhere some such essay on the subject must exist. I can, however, make some of their case for them. It is certainly true that hymns have been changed and altered and tampered with through the centuries. Isaac Watts's hymns were changed shortly after they began to be sung. There are a number of hellfire verses in eighteenth-century hymns that got eliminated in the nineteenth century. Members of the clergy (and sometimes choir directors too) could dictate which verses of a particular hymn were to be sung on any particular day; any churchgoer has attended services during which the pastor announces "Now we will sing Hymn Number Such-and-such, omitting verses 4, 5, and 9." New verses were often added to favorite hymns. When I was a child I was accustomed to seeing these added verses marked with an asterisk in the hymnbook, and the names of various authors and their dates given at the top of the page; I was thus offered an early education in historical changes of taste. It is true that the hymns of any period (like other poetry) reflect unconscious as well as conscious attitudes, and that the reiteration of "men," "brothers," and so on in some hymns is truly constricted by the attitudes we now call "sexist." Racism disfigured some hymns of the past, and there is also too much colonialism and imperialism in some hymns both British and American. Some British hymns in particular have expressed a class smugness that seems far from Christian. Mrs. Cecil Frances Alexander's hymn "All Things Bright and Beautiful" (first published in 1848), well known and loved by generations of children, was marred by its third verse:

> The rich man in his castle,
> The poor man at his gate,
> GOD made them, high or lowly,
> And ordered their estate.[8]

In defense of Cecil Frances Alexander (or Miss Humphreys as she was in 1848 when her enormously popular *Hymns for Little Children* was printed), some of the other hymns express a more appropriate sense of Christ's poverty and the vanity of worldly greatness. We can see in the lines about the rich man in his castle some of the ill effects of being a member of the Protestant ascendancy in 1848, that uneasy year of revolution and threatened revolt. Cecil Alexander was a poet of considerable influence in her humble volume for children whose proceeds went "to the support of a school for deaf and dumb children." Gounod admired "There is a Green Hill Far Away," which he set to music, and Alexander wins another star with "Once in Royal David's City."

For sheer consistent excellence in any one piece, one might rank C. F. Alexander above Christina Rossetti, and she has recently won a place in an anthology of the work of Irish women poets. Lines from her hymns continue to be quoted, and even to supply book titles (for example, *All Creatures Great and Small*, and *Without a City Wall*). "All Things Bright and Beautiful" has many excellencies. Like many Prot-

estant children, I loved the hymn, which expresses a sense of the freshness and joy in the world, and a delight in God's creation. It was one
of the very first works to point out to me the beauty of nature. But I
did not sing the verse about the high and lowly; that verse has long
been tacitly censored out. And I would not wish to sing it or to teach
anybody else to do so.

Given all these concessions to the revisers' position, and to the fact
of a history of hymn renovation, how should I object to the newly
amended hymnals? How can I object? When I am a liberal from way
back, a card-carrying feminist, and, if not a convinced republican, at
least an ardent democrat with socialist tendencies? Why can I not go
along and beat the drum for a new era? What, in short, is wrong with
me, that I feel so angry and defiant when a revised hymn is introduced
at a church service, and stubbornly sing along—and pretty loudly at
that—in the remembered "old" or "real" words? What is the matter
with Mary Jane when it's lovely rice pudding for dinner again? Why
can I not swallow this bland rice pudding hymnology without wry
faces and protest?

Let me try to put a case to the revisers. First, theirs is the most
wholesale and systematic attempt to rewrite a body of works that we
in the Western English Protestant churches have ever known. Other
revisions of hymnals have come about piecemeal and singly, a quiet
result of some consensus. The most radical rewriting hitherto has consisted of simple omission. We have never before been faced with the
rewriting of line after line, verse after verse. This is a systematic attempt by one group totally to rewrite the main body of our hymnody
on a very bold scale. For one thing, we are invited to forget that our
Christian forefathers and foremothers ever said anything that poses
problems. Thus, people in the congregations will be misled into believing that we always thought as we do now—and Protestants will
get assumed or imputed credit for having been always *bien-pensants*.
Such a rewriting of history encourages complacency and blindness,
even when it is carried out for the most benevolent purposes. But our
twentieth-century experience of tyrannies in the political world has
shown us that the rewriting of history for ideological purposes is
highly dangerous and always plays into the hands of one power group
at the expense of other people. The danger seems less that we will get
credit for having always thought "properly" (when we didn't) as that
there will be no voices from the past correcting our present (and of
course largely unconscious) modes of thinking ill—of being immoral
and imperfect. Everything that has come down to us is to be subjected
to drastic alteration, refurbished and tricked out to look unlike itself,
like antique furniture smartly enameled.

It seems peculiarly modern and self-complacent to assume that the past has nothing to say to us. The revisers of service books are, they will retort, extremely interested in the past; that is, they will point to some reconstruction of ancient worship in Palestine or Rome, not unsupplemented by imagination and speculation, but will decry the Middle Ages and the eras of the Renaissance and the Enlightenment as having nothing of value to offer. The doctrine of redemption, the new Canadian Anglican service book tells us with sweeping simplicity, is merely a medieval invention. Once such a doctrine is to be suppressed, it is of course true that hymns expressing that doctrine become inimical. But revisers of hymnbooks do not like trying to put their case clearly and philosophically before congregations. In this, they resemble the revisers of prayer books, who have successfully promoted large-scale doctrinal change without announcing their ideologies or their intentions to the humble (or humbled) churchgoers. Only the Canadians (so it seems to me, a Canadian) would have the requisite simple-mindedness to state their purpose so openly. Wholesale theological revision must of course be served by trimming the hymns to make them fit.

Of course it is true that we need hymns for the twentieth century!— or rather, we should now be saying, for the twenty-first. The simple answer is: Write them. Write more new hymns! Like the graffito once spotted in Oxford, "Down with Victorian Church Music!," "Write more new hymns!" is not a very stirring rallying cry. But still—that is the answer. Actually, America at this moment is enjoying an efflorescence of hymnody, though one would not know it from the revised hymnals of the decorously liberal churches. Gospel song is thriving. Like an oasis in a barren and dry land, where no water is, the occasional appearance of the Princeton Gospel Ensemble at the University Chapel rejoices the heart. A good rendition of gospel song—*soul* music indeed!—assures the worshipper that there are modern hymns of great value. Yet these hymns are (embarrassingly for the liberal revisers) written in a language which, modern and even colloquial as it often is, yet strongly relates itself to the language of the King James Version of the Bible. The lyrics of these hymns express doctrines which would be immediately comprehensible (and congenial) to Herbert or Wesley. There is also a good deal of the *agon* in Afro-American hymns, and their writers prefer exhortation and activity; these are not hymns of the passive voice. We do have a body of great new hymns which we should try to learn and incorporate into our services.

We can all have more hymns, too, if we write them. Let us have some new singable poems that genuinely reflect the way we feel and act in our spiritual lives now. These hymns will then join the body of hymns that has been accruing for nearly two thousand years, and the better of these will survive to give voice to our best spiritual feelings or insights. Our hymns will be sung by others in the future who will also be writing their new hymns . . . and so on. Meanwhile, let us all keep the body of our history, including the Psalms of David, without trying to pretend that there were no kings, majesties, dominions, and powers in the olden days. We may once again come to understand some positive aspects of kingship or of fighting the good fight, and may be less scared of these terms and less apt to misapply them than (in the revisers' eyes) we are at present. If a hymn for the old days really puts us off, either omit the offending verses if they can be omitted or just don't sing the thing at all.

We should not, I think, assume total control over a written work—even a bad work. There are ethical and philosophical issues at stake here, which the revisers refuse to notice in taking so for granted our—or rather, *their*—inalienable right to rewrite individual works. In terms of present-day philosophies affecting and molding literary criticism, the revisers can be termed "deconstructionists." There are varieties of deconstruction, but what the sects have in common is a repudiation of the notions (termed "*belle lettriste*" or "humanistic") of the value of the individual work and author, the sacredness, completeness, and meaning of any text whatever. History or the universe is a large perverse text, and individual works are merely continuations of the whole text of the era, and more significantly, of the language itself. The attempt at writing is absurd; literary "works" are like small fragile tents that are in rags and tatters, like our ozone layer, with great holes that let in the frightening vision of the cold dark sky and eternal wind. At least they are so in the vision of Jacques Derrida, greatest and least readable of deconstructionists, who resembles a prophet rather more than a literary critic of the old school; trying to read him is like encountering the Book of Ezekiel rewritten by Nietzsche.[9] Another version of deconstruction, more friendly to literary activities promoted in American departments of English, was propagated by Paul de Man and took root at Yale. The modern critic is reassured that there is no vestige of the sacred about the author—there is no such being, just as there is no Author of the universe. The culture writes the texts, and the individual does not matter. After de Man's recent death some disturbing facts came to light and the general academic public learned that his early published works (during World War II) cooperated with Nazi thought. He could not perhaps have published had he not cooperated; nobler souls had to give up the desire for fame during that period. De Man's view that the individual writer is merely the plaything of greater forces and has no responsibility for his words thus strikes some as too close to a convenient psychological alibi to let pass without question. Nevertheless, the fact that such views took root so well in America in the 1970s shows that they were congenial to a devaluation of the individual that was quite acceptable to smart and ambitious individuals.

If the revisers see the old hymns as merely (largely unfortunate) epiphenomena of a culture, and that culture happily extinct and deserving of no respect, then we too are entitled to look at the revisers not as independent moral agents but as symptoms of their times. Their revised hymnal offers a practical example of a deconstruction—or a postdeconstruction—at work. These revisers may be more modern than they themselves are aware. Their activities offer hints of a new attitude to language, an attitude which may profoundly affect authors in the future. The revisers' activities, too, be it noted, are not restricted to classroom philosophizing, but are a practical operation in the world. It is not out of place to ask whether the business and busy-ness of the Amherst committee signals a real ending to our idea of poetry, and of literary works in general.

Poets from antiquity have been considered "makers" and "seers." In modern times, particularly since the eighteenth century, we have developed a strong sense of individual poetic (and literary) style, regarding poets as original artists with a proprietary right over their creations. We see—or have seen—a work of "literature" as an independent entity emanating from a mind which we regard very highly when we call it "creative." (And universities where deconstruction is advanced from time to time in classes in the English and Modern Language departments still have programs in what is grandly termed "Creative Writing.") Plagiarism is a sin, then, whereas in earlier periods writers and musicians borrowed materials and even thematic expressions and traded back and forth without a starkly defined proprietary sense. It would, however, be carrying this matter much too far (although too far is where some wish to carry it) to assert that there is *no* concept of originality in antiquity and in the Middle Ages. It is in the interests of deconstructionists and some others to assert that the whole idea of originality is a recent invention and specifically the invention of capitalism arising from the sale of printed works as commodities in the modern marketplace. Yet Horace gives us quite another impression, and Juvenal claims that he is not like those other poets and that he's fed up with listening to their tired old stuff. Even Chaucer, with all his notable borrowings, expects the reader to have read Boccaccio, for instance, and to enjoy the places where Chaucer is like and where he is very different. Just so, the embedded quotations from Dante in Boccaccio's work are in no sense what we would now call a plagiarism but rather an unexpected and witty ornament which would lose its point could we not recognize a separate source. And Petrarch did not receive his laurel crown for just writing what the other fellows wrote. Still, we can with qualification assent to the notion that the eighteenth century gave peculiar credit to each individual writer (not just to the greatest) and began to allow individual literary artists a permanent claim upon their works. In a recent article in the academic magazine *Representations*, Mark Rose has argued very tellingly that the emergence of modern copyright law reflects the new idea of genius creating a property:

> the proponents of perpetual copyright asserted the author's natural right to a property in his creation. . . . the proponents [of copyright] responded that the property claimed was neither the physical book nor the ideas communicated by it, but something else entirely, something consisting of style and sentiment combined. What we here observe . . . is a twin birth, the simultaneous emergence in the discourse of the law of the proprietary author and the literary work. The two concepts are bound to each other. To assert one is to imply the other, and together, like the twin suns of a binary star locked in orbit about each other, they define the center of the modern literary system.[10]

Professor Alvin Kernan suggests that the emergence of new technologies of communication in our own day are probably more important than the mere words of the theorists in changing our attitude to the status of written works. "In the shifting sea of images and words that technology has created," Kernan says, "concepts like originality and creativity are becoming much less plausible and real." Recent legal cases involving copyright, Kernan argues, only point out the difficulty of sustaining a law based on a romantic notion of creativity combined with a Lockean or early capitalist notion of individual property: "In [Harold] Bloom's nightmare of ceaseless imitation, copyright is only a tragic assertion of freedom in the face of the human fate of plagiarism. . . . as relativism and skepticism increase, the fundamental ideas of romantic art theory, creativity and the unique work of art began to shimmer and disintegrate, while their legal expression—copyright—begins to take on the vagueness of metaphysics." Recent legal cases (and such incidents as the recent debate about *The White Hotel*), Kernan believes, "warn us of a deeper shift in consciousness, in which individuality, creativity, the possibility of the new and the distinct object—ideas that have been socially objectified in copyright law and in a poetic theory that is centered on creativity and an idealized work of art—appear to be giving way to concepts like indeterminacy and repetitiveness."[11]

It may be that the philosophical theorists, the deconstructionists and others, are simply owls of Minerva, hooting some wisdom at a change accomplished, a change visible in the cool undifferentiating screen of the computer. If all language and all arrangements of language reflect merely indeterminacy, then there is nothing that cannot be rewritten or recast, and no single piece of writing need remain. And what any "author" writes is, the deconstructionists assert, provisional and imperfect. An author is a kind of crippled magpie, beak open, picking up what the wind of the Zeitgeist blows in the poor bird's direction. An author is no longer the busy enlightening classical bee, or the romantic aggressive self-involved spider. Authorial activity is minimal. If we entertain the possibility that the age of "creativity" is at its end, then the hymn revisers exemplify—and impose—the new concept in all its strength.

The hymn revisers are not committing the old sin of plagiarism, to be sure. Rather, they are engaged in a new postdeconstructionist activity, which may be summed up as "unlimited rewriting"—erasing the original text and making it unquotable. They willingly and wilfully execute their own wills upon texts, without acknowledging any limitation. Their undifferentiating activity refuses to believe in any *difference* between a twentieth-century committee's words and those of an eighteenth-century writer. The poem (hymn) is simply a plastic thing, to take what shape they may please at any moment.

It is a matter of interest to Protestant hymn singers that the revisers are not tidying up obscure or gloomy or seldom-used hymns; they are tackling some of the best known, those often used in the highest festivals of the Christian Church (and with very singable and memorable tunes). Charles Wesley's Easter hymn "Christ the Lord is Risen Today," with its resounding "Alleluias," has undergone a number of changes. The Amherst revisers have radically altered the line "Lives again our glorious King" to "Jesus lives, eternal spring," thus modestly getting rid of all might, majesty, dominion, and glory, and turning the Lord into a season rather than a person. The third verse originally runs thus:

> Love's redeeming work is done
> Alleluia!
> Fought the fight, the battle won
> Alleluia!
> (*Pilgrim Hymnal*, no. 182)[12]

But in the new Amherst hymnal it is this:

> Love's redeeming work is done,
> Alleluia!

> Suffering ended, freedom won,
> Alleluia!
>
> (no. 182)

Whose suffering, what freedom, how? The new lines very nicely get rid of any touch of unwelcome pugnacity—also of struggle. Virtue is always sweetly passive. Nobody must be encouraged to think of a resistance, an energy, an effort, a self-conquest, an ardent and demanding activity against something and for something.

One wonders how truly innocent of metaphor the revisers may be. Do they *really* fundamentally believe that all references to "fight" or "battle" truly refer only and directly and most literally to taking up arms against our fellow human beings? (Indeed, what absurdity is there, for which some well-meaning people have not contended?) Do they really believe that all these metaphors must be got rid of, lest they lead astray the weak-minded? If so, what are Christians to do about Biblical examples? We not only have Jacob *wrestling* with the angel in the Old Testament, for instance, but in the New Testament verses such as *agonizou ton kalon agona tes pisteos* (1 Tim. 6:12), which the Revised Standard Version, like the King James Version, translates as "Fight the good fight of the faith." If *agonizein* does not mean to go to war with spears and swords, it does mean to enter into a conflict, to struggle forcefully against something, to contest with effort (like a wrestler or debater). Oh, but I forgot. In the past, texts (including the Bible) might be retranslated and reinterpreted. Now all texts (including the Bible) may be rewritten too—as has already happened in that popularizing and extraordinary text *The Good News Bible*. I can envisage the Amherst revisers' sort of Bible and its advertisement: *The Stress-Free Bible*. Very soothing. The Christ who never enters into an *agon* is no longer a prot*agon*ist; everything gets done by the wonderful magic of passive construction—of which these revisers are amazingly fond.

If Easter hymns and Biblical texts in hymns may be tampered with, there is no reason why national songs should not be similarly improved. The following example will be familiar to almost all Americans, for most people living in this country, Christian or not, know "America the Beautiful." It was written by a woman, Katharine Lee Bates, who was also a scholar and critic of American literature. Bates used the language available to her to express presumably what she meant, and what a number of Americans who sang and still sing this song have meant. The second half of the first verse goes thus:

> America! America!
> God shed his grace on thee,

> And crown thy good with brotherhood
> From sea to shining sea.
> (*Pilgrim Hymnal*, no. 440)

But in the new *Inclusive Language Hymnal* we are given this:

> America! America!
> God shed full grace on thee,
> Establish thee in unity
> From sea to shining sea.
> (no. 440)

This is of course very different. The expression "full grace" is annoying (what is partial grace?). Altogether lost is the idea contained in the word "brotherhood"—the word Bates wrote. The word may be inadequate, culturally flawed, but it expresses something of vital importance: that we should each think of all others in this nation as our brothers and sisters. That is, we have a familial and communal relation to each other—we don't have it yet, Bates says, but it is something to pray for, and thus to work for too. "Establish thee in unity" is a major change. The United States (which is what is meant throughout by "America") is already a unified nation from sea to shining sea, and that was established a long time ago. Many nations have political *unity* without very much *brotherhood*. The sense of responsibility, affection, and commitment has quite disappeared. This is a salient example of ostensibly "liberal" revision in a very illiberal direction. A very fine baby has been tossed out with some only very slightly impure bathwater.

Well—but—this is only a kind of popular song after all, not worth making much fuss about. And Katharine Lee Bates was not a *real* poet, was she? Who thinks of her, or of her words, in this flurry of ostensive feminism? Ah, well—Bates may not be a "great poet," nor Robert Grant a figure in anthologies. But Isaac Watts and Charles Wesley have been treated by many scholars of the eighteenth century as poets of some importance. Donald Davie has argued well for the "classicism" of Watts, and the "rhetorical splendour and intensity" of Wesley's treatment of paradox.[13] Still, are Watts and Wesley part of *the canon*? Worth making such a fuss about? If we insist that only authors found in textbook anthologies may count, then what shall we say of George Herbert? Herbert has long figured in the anthologies. He is an acknowledged poetical presence, one of the most important Metaphysicals, a seventeenth-century writer of classics of our lyric treasury. Why, people have written whole books on Herbert. He must be that important thing, a "real poet." Well he may be, to many general readers, and (deconstruction notwithstanding) to most modern English departments. But he is not anyone in particular to the revisers of the hymnals. It is especially ironic that Herbert, who made it into hymnals only rather recently, is already being retouched and radically "improved."

Yet it is possibly a sign of Herbert's importance, a symptom of some uneasy respect for him as a known poet, that the revisers do let him keep his wicked first line, "Teach me, my God and King." Surely, they would not have allowed that to any lesser light, but would have briskly altered it to "teach me my God and spring." And it is likely that elsewhere they would have got rid of the ugly concept of teaching, which implies superiority and activity. But now the revisers gain heart. They are perhaps encouraged by the fact that the hymnbook compilers who included this work by Herbert have always omitted the poet's second verse because they have thought it too difficult for a congregation either to sing or to grasp. What we have had as the second verse is really the third. In the original poem (entitled "The Elixir") as first published in the seventeenth century that verse is this:

> A man that lookes on glasse,
> On it may stay his eye;
> Or if he pleaseth, through it passe,
> And then the heav'n espie.[14]

With some trifling changes in spelling, this is exactly how this verse of 1633 has come down to us in modern verse anthologies and in hymnals—until now. According to the Amherst revisers, it is to be thus:

> Whoever looks on glass
> Thereon may stay the eye;
> Or if it pleases through it pass
> And then the heaven espy.
> (no. 401)

What a wonderful array of "it"'s! We have got rid of that old masculine pronoun, but only by garbling the lines and sacrificing (as so often in these revisers' work) immediacy and the concept of choice. There would be no use in the professed critic of poetry—or another poet—arguing with the revisers about the nice steps whereby Herbert relates man-glass-heaven—nor would these rewriters be interested in noticing the subordination and parallelism of "it," which in Herbert's verse means the glass in each of the two cases. But one cannot forbear ridiculing the clumsy ear and dull mind that can refuse to notice what a howler is perpetrated by the introduction of another kind of "it" in the desperate search for some inoffensive bland middle voice. "Or if it pleases through it pass"—you are to look at the glass first, stay your eye on it, and if it pleases you go through it? Not what Herbert said! Or does the glass please (like, want) to go through the glass?

If the revisers can do this sort of thing to one of our acknowledged "great" poets, I think it will be clear that they have got over any shamefacedness about altering any combination of words in our (or any other) language. Let readers outside the Protestant church and indeed outside the Christian churches take fair warning. The revising spirit is not confined to churches alone. If brazen-faced rewriting is considered advantageous in one sphere, it becomes less abhorrent in another. If Herbert should be rewritten for the church, then why not for the classroom? What is there to prevent a group of well-disposed academics on some occasion rewriting a number of popular and canonical poems to get rid of the embarrassments of some of their unacceptable ideas and wording? What objection can there be to an "inclusive language" Shakespeare? Many lines obviously cry out for a change:

> Journeys end in lovers' meeting
> Every wise man's son doth know.

Why, change it to "Every wise man's child does know." Autolycus's "For a quart of ale is a dish for a King" can be rid of its taint of monarchism by being rendered "For a quart of ale is a drink for Spring"— quite suitable to the season repeatedly referred to in the song.[15] And why should not all of the Metaphysicals' works be revised so that our students' minds will not be contaminated by limited language and hateful imagery and morally imperfect metaphors? Let John Donne really be made to forget the He and She, and change a number of his lines, such as

> Yesternight the Sunne went hence,
>   And yet is here today,
> He hath no desire nor sense,
>   Nor halfe so short a way.[16]

Change the third line to "It has no desire nor sense" and you don't even spoil the rhythm. And in the same poem the line "O how feeble is man's power" can readily be adapted to "O how feeble's human power." This sort of thing is certainly not difficult once you get the hang of it. I could undertake to rhyme you so eight years together. There are some more difficult passages, like the one in the *Divine Meditations* when Donne wonders at the Devil's power:

> Why doth he steale nay ravish that's thy right?
> Except thou rise and for thine own worke fight
> Oh I shall soone despaire.[17]

This is much too diabolical and militaristic and monarchical.

> Why does one steal what is not really right,
> Unless you come and bad is put to flight.

That gets rid of the Devil's being a "he" (I presume the same courtesy is being extended to Satan as to the Higher Powers). And at least it gets rid of God's *right* (possessiveness) in the speaker, and of too much activity, especially fighting; we have the passive voice to do all the dirty work. No, this is all doable, and therefore quite imaginable. We need not imagine that the canon—even enshrined in Oxford Books or Norton Anthologies—has any special sacredness. The ideology denies the sacred, any kind of sacred, in any kind of words.

Herbert's copyright has long run out, and here I think the copyright argument breaks down. Even before the proprietary era of capitalist copyright, we have had some sense of some combinations of words "belonging" ultimately to Virgil or Chaucer, say, no matter how often borrowed, paraphrased, imitated, or quoted. There is a kind of authorial possession which is not material possession, not related to cash benefit. There is a sense of *belongingness*, reflected in the classical story about Virgil on his deathbed wishing to destroy the *Aeneid* because it was not good enough.[18] His desire and anxiety reflect an idea that in some sense the poem was *his*, and he was responsible for it, with no sense of cash benefit intruding. Those of us who are authors, at however humble a level, may feel somewhat irate at the assumption that a poet's words may be taken from him—or her. It does not matter if he or she is dead and thus beyond personal injury, and it makes no difference that there are no heirs who suffer loss of material benefit. There is an original voice that is silenced when words are taken away. Nay, worse than silenced—perverted.

To think thus is to belong to the old Romantic (or Renaissance) world which believed in creative originality. This is the world to which Dorothy Sayers belonged when she argued (in 1947) that there can be a Christian aesthetic. Not only does she justify "creative writing" on the part of the Christian, she assumes that the creative power as an aspect of the divine is more than just a metaphor. She proposes that "this idea of art as creation" is "the one important contribution that Christianity has made to esthetics."[19] And she further suggests that the Christian doctrine which beholds in Christ the brightness of God's glory and the image of God's reality does endorse imagination and image-making. The soul itself, as the image of God, is like God in being able to *create* images, not merely being fettered to pagan copy, imitation, or representation. Such a concept is of course possible only to those who believe not only in God but also in the soul. That there

is any such imaging possible—any such creation of golden worlds—
is implicitly denied by many people today both within and without the
academy; we tend to be more interested in *representation*. I think Sayers
is on the right track, and that the ideas of poetic creation and *originality*
stem not from the printing press or from the early modern capitalism
of copyright, but from the idea of the soul itself. In the modern philosophies, not only does the Author not exist, but the Individual does
not exist as a subject; there is no true original or essential "I" but only
the "subject position" of "I," a poor patched thing composed of historical influences and cultural constraints, learned social strategies and
inevitable artifice. If "I" is only a construct, a feeble metaphor, then I
can do nothing, will nothing, and be responsible for nothing. (This
emptying out is a kind of reversal of the emptying out implicit in Sar-
trean existentialism, which imagined that the individual could newly
recreate the self at any moment—in a play of will practically unlimited
by historical conditioning and the experience of the past.) If there is no
subject (and the concept of subjectivity is currently derided as a kind
of offshoot of romanticism at best and mercantilism at worst), then
there is nothing but the group. My own detective sense tells me that
thus I have solved the mystery as to why revisers of the prayer books
have changed the Creed from "I believe" (originally "Credo") to "*We*
believe" in defiance of all history and usage. Hence, too, the exhortation to the individual (as well as the group) "O worship the King"
is changed to "*We* worship."

In the secular world, it was widely assumed even after the "death of
God" that the Individual could go on trading at the old stand. This is
what writers like George Eliot could assume. Nineteenth-century philosophies tried to fill in the gap with moralism, when they were not
busy looking (like Marx) at society as the saving phenomenon as well
as the locus of interest. (What makes human beings worthwhile,
worth "saving," is society.) Now all these chickens have come home
to roost, including the cocks and hens of Marxism, which are being
prettily plucked by Gorbachev in the downing of the Red Menace. Yet
Marxism rested its appeal on an evangelical interest in converting, and
assuring the individual of prophetic truths; the current philosophies
emanating chiefly from France are a bleak replaying of symphonies of
the nineteenth century, the harmonies of Marx or Freud, for they cannot assume the presence of the subject, and the emphases on the futile
processes of self-construction remind us to what lengths Freud went
in saving the soul, or at least saving appearances by calling it the "psy-
che" and loving it, despite its fragmented and partially experiential nature. Jung made heavy investments in the soul, but his doctrines can
be redrawn also as a formalist doctrine of merely cultural forms.

We are at last coming face-to-face with some weighty consequences of the denial of God or of the divine. The consequence newly visible is the death of the soul. Americans have conventionally accused the Marxists of being "soulless," but this was a turn of phrase which did not cause us to investigate what *soul-less-ness* would really feel like. (The absence of the soul is not the same thing as the absence of a belief in life after death.) Such an absence divides us sharply from much of the rest of mankind, past and present. The current surge of "New Age" beliefs, including reincarnation, represents an attempt by our contemporaries to accommodate the maximum amount of historic conditioning (the individual is conditioned and shaped by one life after another) while permitting and indeed insisting on the existence of the soul, as mobile, labile, and responsive, yet consistent and essential. New Age reincarnationism represents, paradoxically, what might be called a postmodern or deconstructionist soul. Such a belief is immensely attractive, for the individual thus avoids the plunge into *soul-less-ness*. This is not a belief (or set of beliefs) that is taken up by the uneducated, whatever academics or clergymen may wish to assume. Most proponents of New Age systems are knowledgeable about and in touch with their culture and its traditions; the New Age phenomenon is worth serious philosophical attention.

Such beliefs reinforce individualism, sometimes of a very callous kind. Yet the individualism (even frantically insisted on) may be felt to be necessary under the threat of the alternative—the loss of the soul. In revising their hymnals, the Protestant churches are now actively (if implicitly) encouraging just this alternative. All arguments about language at the present are circling about the major (but not stated) question, whether or not the soul exists. Without the soul, "I" is a mere form, a grace mark representing a position where nothing really is. "I" means little more than "God." "I" is dead. What we think of as the individual (or even sometimes as a "self") is merely a rather uninteresting passive receptor. Always being made, the so-called individual cannot really make anything at all. In the modern world, so we are assured, humankind has not only left off belief in God, but as a corollary, all belief in personal creation of any kind. In some high reaches of academe, this is now taken for granted. In the same issue of the significantly named periodical *Representations* in which Mark Rose (quoted above) argues the significance of copyright law, another essayist, Tomoko Masuzawa, in an article on Durkheim, can assume that we have already learned to reject the bundle of old notions:

> it is the prerogative of origin as such . . . that has come under suspicion in recent times, together with the assumption of the unity, simplicity,

and self-identity of absolute beginning—in short, all of the pristine metaphysics of presence/permanence/plenitude that the concept of origin is said to embody. In this connection we have also come to see that the sovereignty of the author/originator over his [*sic!*] text is as imaginary as any other assumption of a unitary origin.[20]

There is no God, there is no Author and no Creation. Therefore we are not authors, and no words abide. It might further follow that no words ought to abide. The deliberate naivete of the Amherst revisers means that they can proffer their tinkered and adulterated goods with smiles of pure reason and benevolence upon their faces. They—the faceless ones—have obliterated their originals as purely imaginary, erased the authors and their verses.

It is because I strongly object to this position on theological, philosophical, and political grounds that I have tried to sneak in some references to the individuals (Toplady, Grant, Alexander, Wesley, Bates) who wrote the hymns. Of course they were individual human beings; as Toplady argues, hymns are undoubtedly *"human Compositions."* And no one pretends that any human being exists outside time and cultural influences, including very distressing and negative cultural influences. But they are human beings, and Christians are certainly theologically entitled—whatever the Zeitgeist may say at present—to think that human beings have the power to create. In denying this power or rendering it of nothing worth, the Amherst revisers are smilingly repudiating the whole complex of doctrine that includes God the Creator and Author and the human being in the image of God. They do not spell out the implications of their actions, and probably would be better off not doing so. Yet it is one of the strengths of all poststructuralist and deconstructionist critical philosophies that any writer or critic is supposed to recognize and to articulate the philosophical positions personally espoused; the assumption of such pretenses as "common sense" or "objectivity" or "truths universally acknowledged" is frowned upon. In their adoption of naivete and philosophical taciturnity, if in nothing else, the revisers have defied the postmodernist theorists. One would certainly guess that many of these improvers are unaware (at least at the conscious level) of the theological and philosophical implications of what they are doing. Their defense will be that they did this work for the benefit of the community (of the Congregational church or of Protestantism, or of the Christian churches at large). It is fashionable nowadays to say that we put too much emphasis on the individual, and should stress the community, the group in general. This sounds good as a political reaction to a very nasty and narrow mercantilist individualism popular in the past decade, but in fact it holds great dangers. Terrible deeds have been done—and done in this century—in the name of the welfare of the group (as terrible things have been done in the name of the benefit to the individual). To pit individual and community against each other is to damage both. God's people are obliged to look to the welfare of both; the present tendency to play down the idea of individual salvation erodes the sense of inner worth which makes it possible for human beings to do what is vital for the welfare of the whole. Saints and martyrs and heroes (Mother Teresa, Martin Luther King, Nathan Sharansky) are not rooted in jelly.

The Amherst revisers would apparently be well content to get rid of such troublesome heroisms, for they have erased such ardent activity whenever they have met it. But they appear not to realize the inherent self-parody of their whole activity—that while they are still trying to praise God, they are denying God, and denying his presence, potential or actual, among real live human beings. Their denial of authorship, imagination, and individual creation spells a certain assent to the proposition that there is no Author of Creation. Therefore the word "God" they still use is meaningless. As in the third of the Ages imagined by Joachim da Flora, we are in the age of the Holy Ghost alone and the Holy Ghost's last name turns out to be the *Zeitgeist*. Everything is writ on water, or at least on windblown sands. There are no responsibilities, for there is no attribution and no point in attribution. The old writers' names may appear (in a mockery of convention) above the hymns, but no individual piece can be an author's any more. We rewrite the records or erase the tapes. We do not have to face the embarrassments of difficult theologies or inhumane sentiments in the older hymns, nor can we join in a discussion of various kinds of meaning in older verses. The *bien-pensants* can rewrite at any moment, making sure that all is well and all is modernized. (I can believe that when this essay is published I will get letters explaining that the extra instances—and indeed all instances—of *thee* and *thy* will be removed in the next round.)

The inclusive language hymnal is apparently produced for the benefit of the modern congregation. But whose benefit and how benefited? The revisers may base their largely implicit argument on the concept that the community needs take precedence over the value of individualism (such as authorial rights). Yet it should be noted that these abruptly appearing books are not the product of the community, and that church congregations are not supposed to argue about them. I know from experience that she who protests at the end of a service gets but cold looks and dusty answers for her pains. As to what would happen should anyone get up and protest in the middle of a service—

well, Heaven knows! We are supposed to be docile. We are to be fobbed off with bad and even ungrammatical language, but if we make a fuss then we are acting in a bad, naughty, uncharitable manner. As congregations, we are less than the dust.

Revisers would no doubt protest against my suggestion that it is a short step from their booklets to rewritten poetry anthologies; they would probably say that I indulged only in the most fanciful flight of satire, and that they of course trust that the universities will still produce appropriate original texts for the edification of university students. But if they think thus—why, their liberalism forms a bunch of chopped straw! And they are not more to be trusted with egalitarianism than with theology. For if that is what they think, then they are a bunch of snobs, and believe in a mental refection for the few which is to be quite different from the cold porridge with which they will comfort the faithful.

The theological implications of what these revisers are doing are very grave—if somewhat comical too. Many of these rewriters are clergymen, yet they are, by implicitly denying creation and the Creator, cutting off the comfortable branch on which they are sitting. Their anticreative actions speak louder than their rice-pudding words of their doubt about the being of God. Neither do they believe in the individual. No individual contribution matters. Words and wordsmiths are all the same—brought to one dead level every mind. A dead poet may be subjected to posthumous brainwashing, and made to utter from beyond the grave sentiments not his or her own. There is not much interest in individual sin, salvation, or moral action (indeed, the revisers consistently counteract these concepts whenever they can). And the individual leaves a service with a dull aching feeling of being of little consequence in a universe which is apparently made of cotton wool and very difficult to see or get about in.

The revisers' principles, as seen in their activity, have political implications. Their ostensible political principles are generous and liberal, and they pride themselves on them: they are nonsexist, nonracist, nonmilitaristic. I too am against racism, against sexism, against militaristic and nationalistic aggressive adventures. I consider war a great evil—though not the worst of evils. Yet I cannot accept what I see as the implicit principles beneath these announced views. No Christian is commanded to give way to the historical pressures (whether political or philosophical) of the moment. And no Christian can accept the principles of the paralysis of the will, the death of the soul, and the emptiness of creation. The revisers' principles of communication, of language more simply considered, introduce us to a world of undifferentiated rewriting, of indeterminate change. If all texts can be rewritten, and not just through interpretation, but by actively taking the old text away and putting a new version in its place—why then we are very unsafe. Not only the Bible may be rewritten, but the Constitution of the United States. After all, there are no permanent words. No statements are worth holding onto, and no "authors" or works should be privileged so as to permit them identity.

In this era of precarious civil rights and threatened human rights, it seems foolish to plead that a body of words like Herbert's poem—or the Constitution—should be considered as having some sort of "right" not to be absolutely *rewritten*, however variously all pieces of writing may be *interpreted*. But I believe that to take away a poem's "rights" is taking us a step towards taking away the political rights of individuals and groups of individuals. Despite lofty ideas about the community they are writing for, the Amherst revisers are after all themselves a small group of dictators, mental overlords who compel obedience without calling for discussion or entertaining protest.

The very liberal in me must and shall reject the rights of nameless groups to revise my hymnbook by arbitrarily rewriting words, lines, and verses when and as it suits them. The liberalism they pretend to espouse is betrayed by the principle of tyranny invigorating their actions. Tyrannies censor and rewrite texts to suit themselves—always for ends that quite genuinely seem good, just, and justifiable to some persons in control. It does not seem a mere historical mischance or accidental circumstance that Paul de Man, the critic who has done so much to popularize the "death of the author," himself contributed in his youth to a paper with strong ties to the Nazis. If the *Zeitgeist* does all the writing, the individual is blameless, and may simply be borne along by the wind of change. Such a passivity is inculcated in the new hymnbooks in the new words, including the abundant verbs in the passive voice. The revisers have got rid of conflict and struggle, of fight and *agon*, so there will be nothing to encourage the individual to protest against evil in high places. In apparently getting rid of our militarism for us, the revisers have got rid of conscience; they destroy the voice of conscience in eliminating all expressions of the spiritual necessity of discontent and opposition—including discontent with ourselves and opposition to our own baser desires.

The revision of the hymnbooks represents a battle over language—though it is a battle not waged, not announced. It is an undeclared onslaught which is presented (ah, how like imperialism) as a modern set of benefits conferred. These revisers have left us poorer than they found us, and, while they think they are making us progressive, they are suiting us for dictatorship. And it is one of the evils of dictatorship that one is forced to go along with ugly and ungracious words. "Or if it pleases through it pass." No, it does *not* please.

Notes

1. Augustus Toplady, preface to *Psalms and Hymns for Public and Private Worship* (London, 1776), a 1ʳ- a 1ᵛ.

2. Toplady, preface to *Psalms and Hymns*.

3. *Inclusive Language Hymns based on the Pilgrim Hymnal* (The First Congregational Church, Amherst, Massachusetts, 1984); the short preface here quoted is found on the inside of the front cover, and is signed Philip H. Ward.

4. Robert Grant, "Psalm CIV," in *Sacred Poems* (London, 1839), p. 33.

5. "We Worship Thee, God, All Glorious Above," hymn no. 6 in *Inclusive Language Hymnal*.

6. See, for example, *The Pilgrim Hymnal* (Boston, 1965), hymn no. 6; cf. the English *Hymns Ancient and Modern* (London, 1924), hymn no. 167.

7. *Hymns Ancient and Modern* has "my blest Redeemer's praise" in accordance with the 1738 version. Anybody who thinks Wesley himself at all militaristic should look at his hymn "On the Death of THOMAS BEARD, who was Imprest for a Soldier, and died in the Hospital at Newcastle," which rejoices that the poor man now lives "forever free" "From Man's oppressive Tyranny"; Charles Wesley, *Hymns and Sacred Poems*, 2 vols. (Bristol, 1749), 2:79.

8. [Cecil Frances Alexander], *Hymns for Little Children*, 5th ed. (London, 1852), p. 27. Cf. *Hymns Ancient and Modern*, no. 573. *Hymns for Little Children* is quite systematic, with hymns annotating or amplifying various statements in the Catechism and all the major phrases of the Creed and Lord's Prayer. "All Things Bright and Beautiful" has no title save for its epigraphic and referential phrase "Maker of Heaven and Earth." "Once in Royal David's City" annotates "Who was Conceived by the Holy Ghost, Born of the Virgin Mary," and "There is a Green Hill Far Away" comments on "Suffered under Pontius Pilate, was Crucified, Dead, and Buried." The entire anthology has structural rigor and intellectual intent, and the effect of the whole is far less "sentimental" than accords with our view of Victorian tendencies in writing for children. The clarity and depth of intellectual purpose doubtless helped Cecil Frances Humphreys (later Mrs. Alexander) to write with uncluttered simplicity and force. See the *Dictionary of National Biography* entry for Gounod's remark on "There is a Green Hill Far Away."

9. It is worth noting Derrida's statement: "The movements of deconstruction do not destroy structures from the outside. They are not possible and effective, nor can they take accurate aim, except by inhabiting those structures, inhabiting them *in a certain way*. . . . Operating necessarily from the inside, borrowing all the strategic and economic resources of subversion from the old structure, borrowing them structurally, that is to say without being able to isolate their elements and atoms, the enterprise of deconstruction always in a certain way falls prey to its own work." Jacques Derrida, *Of Grammatology*, trans. Gayatri Chakravorty Spivak (Baltimore, 1976), p. 24 (originally published as *De la Grammatologie*, 1967). (It occurs to me that our own era of virology and faltering immune systems will probably be particularly prone to employ images that reflect the metaphors used in discussing infection; intellectual movements may be tempted to identify themselves alternately as virus and virologist.) The hymnal revisers, in the most literal and practical way, seem to be enacting the subversive role

that Derrida suggests belongs to all deconstructive movements. In the light offered by Derrida, it would then very logically follow that such revisers cannot at heart "believe" in God in any of the traditional senses, or in such belief, but are instead burrowing into and borrowing the old resources without isolating their atoms.

10. Mark Rose, "The Author as Proprietor: *Donaldson v. Becket* and the Genealogy of Modern Authorship," *Representations* 23 (Summer 1988): 65.

11. Alvin B. Kernan, "Art and Law," *Princeton Alumni Weekly* 12 (October 1988): 34–36, 66–69. In D. M. Thomas's novel *The White Hotel* (1981) four or five pages are copied from Dina Pronicheva's testimony about the massacre at Babi Yar as recorded by Anatoli Kuznetsov in his book *Babi Yar*. There was some agitated correspondence in the press about this fact, but no court case, a fact that Kernan finds dismaying in itself.

12. Wesley himself adapted the ideas for this hymn from an older hymn (anonymous) published in *Lyra Davidica*, 1708. Both of the eighteenth-century hymns survive—or they have until now. Anglicans tend to prefer the hymn from *Lyra Davidica* (see *Hymns Ancient and Modern*, hymn no. 134), whereas Methodists and other Protestant churches are more likely to use Wesley's hymn.

13. Donald Davie, *A Gathered Church: The Literature of the English Dissenting Interest, 1700–1930* (London and New York, 1978), pp. 25–28, 51.

14. George Herbert, "The Elixir," in *The Temple. Sacred Poems and Private Ejaculations* (Cambridge, 1633), pp. 178–79. The second verse, the one that has been left out in the hymnals, is this:

> Not rudely, as a beast,
> To runne into an action;
> But still to make thee prepossest,
> And give it his perfection.

The distinction Herbert draws (between mere animal activity and *doing* out of thought and for God) seems valuable (I rather like the rude running beast).

15. William Shakespeare, *Twelfth Night* 2.3.44–45; *The Winter's Tale* 4.3.8. Both songs are often anthologized, and thus would constitute a suitable case for treatment.

16. John Donne, "Song" ("Sweetest love, I do not goe"), ll. 9–12, in *Donne*, ed. John Hayward (London, 1962), p. 12.

17. Donne, "Holy Sonnets," no. ii ("As due by many titles I resigne"), p. 280.

18. This story comes to us through Suetonius; according to this report, Virgil begged Varius, one of his executors, to burn the epic. It was not destroyed; the emperor Augustus ordered it to be published, and set the executors to editing it. Some passages are known to have been cut, but that may very well have been because his friends knew Virgil's opinion of them; no additions were made, and the editors notably resisted what may have been a very real temptation, to rewrite and amplify a most unsatisfactory and apparently incomplete ending. The poem has come down with Virgil's name upon it, and has not been the property of the executors and editors who saved it from erasure. Both Virgil's desire and the executors' opposing desire recognize the uniqueness of writer and work. That the story could be told shows that the ancients could see that Virgil thought of himself as the true maker and thus in some sense "proprietor" of the *Aeneid*.

19. Dorothy L. Sayers, "Toward a Christian Esthetic" (1947), in *The Whimsical Christian* (New York, 1978), p. 83.

20. Tomoko Masuzawa, "The Sacred Difference in the Elementary Forms: On Durkheim's Last Quest," *Representations* 23 (Summer 1988): 25.

~ ROBERT PINSKY

The Refinery

". . . our language, forged in the dark by centuries
of violent pressure, underground,
out of the stuff of dead life."

Thirsty and languorous after their long black sleep
The old gods crooned and shuffled and shook their heads.
Dry, dry. By railroad they set out
Across the desert of stars to drink the world
Our mouths had soaked
In the strange sentences we made
While they were asleep: a pollen-tinted
Slurry of passion and lapsed
Intention, whose imagined
Taste made the savage deities hiss and snort.

In the lightless carriages, a smell of snake
And coarse fur, glands of lymphless breath
And ichor, the avid stenches of
Immortal bodies.

Their long train clicked and sighed
Through the gulfs of night between the planets
And came down through the evening fog
Of redwood canyons. From the train
At sunset, fiery warehouse windows
Along a wharf. Then dusk, a gash of neon:
Bar. Black pinewoods, a junction crossing, glimpses

Of sluggish surf among the rocks, a moan
Of dreamy forgotten divinity calling and fading
Against the windows of a town. Inside
The train, a flash
Of dragonfly wings, an antlered brow.

Black night again, and then
After the bridge, a palace on the water:

The great Refinery—impossible city of lights,
A million bulbs tracing its turreted
Boulevards and mazes. The castle of a person
Pronounced alive, the Corporation: a fictional
Lord real in law.

Barbicans and torches
Along the siding where the engine slows
At the central tanks, a ward
Of steel palisades, valved and chandeliered.

The muttering gods
Greedily penetrate those bright pavilions—
Libation of Benzine, Napthalene, Asphalt,
Gasoline, Tar: syllables
Fractioned and cracked from unarticulated

Crude, the smeared keep of life that fed
On itself in pitchy darkness when the gods
Were new—inedible, volatile
And sublimated afresh to sting
Our tongues who use it, refined from oil of stone.

The gods batten on the vats, and drink up
Lovecries and memorized Chaucer, lines from movies
And songs hoarded in mortmain: exiles' charms,
The basal or desperate distillates of breath
Steeped, brewed and spent—
As though we were their aphids, or their bees,
That monstered up sweetness for them while they dozed.

✍ LORRIE GOLDENSOHN

Poets' Letters:
"The Mind alone,
without corporeal friend"

READING OTHER PEOPLE'S MAIL, especially famous people's mail, is
one of those satisfying occupations. Even more so when you have to
cross a security desk and be buzzed into a locked room in the breast of
a library to do it: in this space your vulgar curiosity has become Research. The older and dryer those discolored little papers are, dragged
out of their often stiff and resistant envelopes, the more the research
resembles a denial of death, a dismissal of the voiceless corpse, and a
resting of hands on spirit. "Today is parched and handsome, though
the Grass is the color of Statesman's Shoes, and only the Butterfly rises
to the situation," Emily Dickinson says; "His little Body glistens with
crispness—an ell of Rapture to an inch of wing," and her creature vi-
brates before you.

The very same letters published and pressed into a book are never
quite the same thing—the ink hasn't bleached, the hooks and arms of
the poet's alphabet don't draggle on bad, unhappy days, or go all tiny
with excitement, or flatten, with the typewriter lacking the same winning way of fattening *h*s, and no unknown tropical insects having
eaten their curlicues into the corners of the paper.

But it's nearly as good: a letter always announces itself as something
that a real person did on a real day in a real place. And for the poets of
the midtwentieth century we've begun to form that record, the um-

bilical link between life and art: although suicide truncated the lives of Sylvia Plath, John Berryman, Anne Sexton, and arguably Randall Jarrell, it has pushed up the date at which we have begun to retrieve their letters and notebooks, violently rushing the point at which the figure of the work can be understood in bewildering relation to the figure of the life.

Unlike Sylvia Plath and John Berryman, whose current published letters are mostly to their mothers, Randall Jarrell and Anne Sexton have had editors who have selected broadly, an arc of autobiography obviously intended.[1] Each book of letters marches a body of poetry from obscurity to renown, from youth to middle age; each book over time adds people and sheds them; each book traces a style for meeting and missing honors, and each fights the onslaught and withdrawal of love. In each collection the poets are seen to face lovers, spouses, friends, and family with unasked or unanswerable questions, and in a small, terminal flurry of editorial italics, they trail off-page into the silence of their deaths.

With the inevitably partial record of the personal letter in hand, we, the unintended audience, come as a kind of scavenging afterthought, to probe for instruction in the triggering interval between the living and the writing of a life. In the conversation of the poet's letter, we think to move within that mysterious, transformative junction in which, without fumbling, life as language reverberates hugely and memorably. Yet on the evidence of these quite disparate collections, the personal letter in the grand style, written in the full exuberance of a writer practicing the farthest reach of the craft, seems to be fading.

It hasn't always been this way. In Keats's letters the spill of language is all we can ask of a poet, the famous pages full of a conversation mad for definition and distinction-making. "I am certain of nothing but of the holiness of the Heart's affections and the truth of Imagination— What the imagination seizes as Beauty must be truth—whether it existed before or not," he trumpets to Benjamin Bailey. "O for a Life of Sensations rather than of Thoughts!" he is heard to think. An effortless maker of aphorism, totally unembarrassed by apostrophe, donning hypostasis like old socks, he pronounces at the fall of a comma, and in the style of his age strews capital letters about as if they were pins for fixing the spinning soul.

There is no self-consciousness in his address to Literature; the topic arises from a walk with friends, from the simple action of dining out, in a continuous and unforced narrative. At the mention of Kean's acting Company, Keats turns on his capital C and genuflects to the subject of Kean's art, Shakespeare:

at once it struck me, what quality went to form a Man of Achievement especially in Literature & which Shakespeare possessed so enormously— I mean *Negative Capability*, that is, when man is capable of being in uncertainties, Mysteries, doubts, without any irritable reaching after fact & reason—Coleridge, for instance, would let go by a fine isolated verisimilitude caught from the Penetralium of mystery, from being incapable of remaining content with half-knowledge. This pursued through volumes would perhaps take us no further than this, that with a great poet the sense of Beauty overcomes every other consideration, or rather obliterates all consideration.

All the sentences are part of one flow of language, one outpour, and the letter runs easily from one curve or freshet to the next. Literature, Poetry, Art, Beauty, and Men of Achievement are never very far from the surface of Keats's thought, and they press into articulation with the naturalness that we have come to take for granted as his signature.

Spontaneous in origin, improvisational in character, the words of Keats's letters have hardened over generations into Romantic doctrine; we roughly understand the paradoxical fraction of wholeness that Keats's "half-knowledge" has come to represent as the limit of reason within the desideratum of Beauty. Nor will the current Keats scholar chide the poet who had barely left adolescence for a firmer or sharper-colored explanation of what a fine isolated verisimilitude caught from a Penetralium of mystery might look like. To ask for more description might be to slip into some of that irritable reaching.

And yet the reach of these letters into abstract thinking about primary matters is enviable, even as Keats extols the Life of Sensations over the Life of Thoughts. In these letters there seems no miring in either an obsessive preoccupation with the character of the self which Keats called the egotistical sublime, the hand in the pocket groping too narrowly for Maxim: "We hate poetry that has a palpable design upon us—and if we do not agree, seems to put its hand in its breeches pocket. Poetry should be great & unobtrusive, a thing which enters into one's soul, and does not startle it or amaze it with itself but with its subject."

Full of literary advice as the letters are, though, narrative pulses through them, every prescription with its flashing kernel of event, lived or imagined, all of the letters shaded by dramatic urgencies. In mid-August, taking flight for Italy through Shelley's generosity, and sensing death a few months ahead of him, he writes to Shelley, "My nerves at present are the worst part of me, yet they feel soothed when I think that come what extreme may, I shall not be destined to remain in one spot long enough to take a hatred of any four particular bed-posts." Instinctive stylist that he is, mortal illness is something to be managed through the synecdoche of the vanishing bed-posts; at the last, there is still time for a parting shot wrapped as literary injunction, and ribboned with quotation: "You I am sure will forgive me for sincerely remarking that you might curb your magnanimity and be more of an artist, and 'load every rift' of your subject with ore." Without a break the passage rushes on to further metaphor, pride and despair alike governing: "The thought of such discipline must fall like cold chains upon you, who perhaps never sat with your wings furl'd for six Months together."

If we look in at Randall Jarrell at the close of his life, his estranged words to his wife of twelve years seem muted, schooled in a hopeless and wooden submission to the nonfigural speech of therapy:

> I want to say all over again how sorry I am that things have turned out this way for us—considering our earlier life and families, it just couldn't have turned out differently, I think, short of our both being analyzed and thoroughly changed.

In pain and confusion, the voice dulls; it isn't until we get to an editorial aside that we hear a different, more recognizable Jarrell speak about his mental illness; his wife remembers his saying: "It was so queer . . . as if the fairies had stolen me away and left a log in my place."

In a world done with both gods and high rhetoric there are no angel wings left even for furling and chaining; the fairies, Jarrell's potent, magical intercessors, have to be drawn from the world of childhood and then frisked for real weapons by irony.

What has happened to the language of the post-Romantic poet-correspondent? In letters that diet Sensation, is there also a certain deafness to the calling of Thoughts? When we turn to these letters, a kind of brief narrative is still in place, but it is the Maxim or the High Thought which is missing, and a more meager Sensation promptly, if irregularly, there in its place.

Only a couple of years older than Keats in the Negative Capability letter, Jarrell muses on allegiance to different forms of knowing, moving from science, which is "just description," into his poet's way:

> I think all in all I've got a poetic and semifeminine mind, I don't put any real faith in abstractions or systems; I never had any certainties, religious or metaphysical, to lose, so I don't feel their lack—I don't mean that I don't *show* their lack, I may very well. I think my mind is *really* unsystematic; along with that or perhaps because of it, I can't help thinking the world (as such little animals see it anyway because I can't help thinking that) is too. When you carry any analysis past a certain point things

get contradictory and incomprehensible, if you look at anything long
enough you stop moving and fall through the ice into the abyss.

Hiding out there as a little animal a few Thoughts away from the
abyss, the language struggles. *I don't put any real faith . . . I never had
. . . I don't feel . . . I can't help . . . things get contradictory and incomprehensible.* The postmodern style of manifesto perhaps: here Jarrell, one
of the most brilliant of the century's poet-critics, cannot be said to
present poetry as a strong player in the theater of ideas, which is possibly to have taken away from poetry more than Jarrell intended.

He defended his childlikeness: "I *am* childlike . . . and I'd like very
much to be in the other more important sense, that of the Gospels."
Yet the self-description as "childlike" and "semifeminine" points to
Jarrell's sense of his marginalization; a number of the metaphors in the
letters look out at the world through female eyes. He also describes
himself as "someone whose principal work-and-amusement is writing, and reading and thinking about things." Age and gender indeterminacy, fusion of life and work, all seem there to scale the troublesome body down, balancing the poet on the rim of physicality. Robert
Lowell called him "unworldly," placing him not in the diminished
world of fairies but up there with the angels:

> Randall *did* somehow give off an angelic impression. . . . His mind,
> unearthly in its quickness, was a little boyish, disembodied and brittle.
> His body was a little ghostly in its immunity to soil, entanglements, and
> rebellion. As one sat with him in oblivious absorption at the campus bar,
> sucking a fifteen-cent milkshake and talking eternal things, one felt, be-
> side him, too corrupt and companionable.[2]

A poet living the life of the mind; it's tempting to conclude that to sustain such a character a disreputable but potent Zeitgeist required the
poet's sidelining as a form of child and woman, flushing rhetoric from
him and narrowing the flow of his thinking to strengthen image over
discourse.

In the letters, images are high; language and rhetoric kneel in service
to them. In 1943, Randall Jarrell compares one of his U.S. Army posts
with the other:

> Chanute is on the outskirts of town; it's a *very* big field, twice as big as
> Sheppard . . . big brick administrative buildings, enormous concrete
> hangars, and mess halls made of concrete blocks—mess halls 125 or 150
> yards long. It was twilight last night and it rained today, so for me Chan-
> ute's strictly Whistler, a morbid mechanical one done for a soot-remover
> advertisement. It has lots of engine blocks where they run tests—when
> a couple of engines are going full power they sound like a terrific bel-
> lowing, something enormous in a tetanus of pain and anger.

In this description, the "enormous" thrusts forward twice, and each time the size and blown-up scale of building and machine efface the fragile soldier. The hangars that house the planes, the engine testing sites, show the habit of the army, where engulfing, mechanizing war hardens and diminishes the human. Buried in the language of the image, in its mechanics, the Thought gets taken over too: judgments are implicit in the workings of the sentences, but nowhere declared, or made axiom, paradox, or definition. Hemmed in by the reflexes of conventional patriotism as he felt himself to be, the uneasy soldier-poet records the stiffening and displacement of the personal in which it is the engines that bellow and not the invisible men purportedly running them. Art and the resources of language depart in the overruling conventional culture of war. As Whistler gives way to the ad campaign, war standardizes, stamps people and things *Government Issue*, puts them mentally and physically into uniform—a quite different process from art's universalizing.

Jarrell rejoiced over being transferred to Chanute, however, because the posting meant proximity to the library at the University of Illinois. And yet again the very language of Jarrell's delight at access to books reflects the infantilization and reduction to thing that he has elsewhere projected as the army's way of mastering men. In this section of his *Letters*, editor Mary Jarrell quotes from an unpublished address for the American Library Association. Safe from the army, but still in reaction to it, Jarrell says: "I rarely feel happier than when I'm in a library—very rarely feel more soothed and calm and secure. Sitting back there in the soft gloom of the stacks, a book among books, almost, I feel very much in my element—a fish come back to the sea, a baby come back to the womb." Much more sinisterly, this immobilized infantilization shows up in Jarrell's poem, "The Death of the Ball Turret Gunner":

> From my mother's sleep I fell into the State,
> And I hunched in its belly till my wet fur froze.
> Six miles from earth, loosed from its dream of life,
> I woke to black flak and the nightmare fighters.
> When I died they washed me out of the turret with a hose.

In his soldier letters Jarrell uses metaphor and narrative description as brilliantly as Keats. Using indirection, implication, and a diffused irony as his most effective tools, in these years, Jarrell's direct statements still run close to a familiar and platitudinous grousing. What Jarrell suffers most keenly is the dilemma of the intellectual, who pushed too near to others unlike himself can only lament, "If this world were cleverer I'd be happier." When he writes about the army to Allen Tate in March 1945, saying "the atmosphere was entirely one of lying, meaningless brutality and officiousness, stupidity not beyond belief but conception—the one word for everything in the army is *petty*," we can believe him. But the words don't take us into new territory conceptually or make his particular experience more memorable. Nothing grandly valedictory appears in the letters. The knottiness of Jarrell's syntax eases, while diction keeps its free mixture of allusive and colloquial in both his letters and his poems, essays, and novel, but in the sieve of his correspondence only the smaller, cooler fragments of the man's mind are left to glitter.

Is the picture the same for the incidental literary criticism in these letters, from the best poet-critic since Eliot and Pound? Yes and no. The hints we get from the exchanges that Mary Jarrell includes between Jarrell and Robert Lowell, the literary advice to Adrienne Rich, are interesting, the passages lively, but many of the comments fuss too much about rank and manufacture, with lots of workshoppy annotations for specific poems. Nonetheless, about being on the receiving end of these notes, Lowell wrote to Jarrell:

> I was just rummaging through a carton of old poems, envelopes, pictures, etc., and came on some of my poems all marked up, stabbed, puffed, and dissected by you. You had such wit and patience and such generosity and justice, at least in your jokes: "these divisions roll on square wheels"; "you generally have one line in a poem where the rhythm gets, not harsh, but tetanic like a muscle under too long tension." The times come back and I feel excited all over again.

Elsewhere, Lowell wrote about the depth and generosity of Jarrell's support, adding:

> What he did was to make others feel that their realizing themselves was as close to him as his own self-realization and that he cared as much about making the nature and goodness of someone else's work understood as he cared about making his own understood. I have never known anyone who so connected what his friends wrote with their lives, or their lives with what they wrote. This could be trying: whenever we turned out something Randall felt was unworthy or a falling off, there was a coolness in all one's relations with him. You felt that even your choice of neckties wounded him. Yet he always veered and returned, for he knew as well as anyone that the spark from heaven is beyond man's call and control.

This piety about the nature of poetic inspiration is echoed by Jarrell, the fervent tone a little doused, the melancholic rising, as he writes to Adrienne Rich, saying:

How hard it is to write a good poem! How few good poems there are! What strange things you and I are, if we are. To have written one good poem—*good* used seriously—is an unlikely and marvellous thing that only a couple of hundred writers of English, at the most, have done— it's like sitting out in the yard in the evening and having a meteorite fall in one's lap; and yet, one can't believe that, and tries so hard, by willing and working and wanting, to have the mail man deliver them—and feels so disappointed, even, when he doesn't.

What a discouraging distance the poet has trudged, to this passive domestic sitting in his yard, waiting for the mailman to deliver a meteorite, from Shelley's defense of poets as the unacknowledged legislators of the world. Perhaps a source of the difficulty for poets is registered in Jarrell's lament that "the gods who had taken away the poet's audience had given him students." More marginal than ever, poets have joined the caretakers of the adolescent mind, but without the didact's essential rhetoric, as haplessly they become professional rhetoricians. Yet the deepest sense of community and shared work that Jarrell seems to have experienced came from his teaching, which he also, contradictorily, welcomed: "If I were a rich man I would pay for the privilege of being able to teach."

If we are at a critical distance from the heroic labor of Thought, and must be content with Sensations, it is a further constriction we are looking at in Jarrell's letters, because the record for Sensation trained on anything but poetry is severely edited in his rather chaste world. For a different energy, one for sprawling over rather than clenching the sensate world, it is useful to turn to another poet, Anne Sexton.

Yet what we have is ultimately skeletal; even as her letters seem to flood us in their abundance of feeling, the greater precision and boldness of confessional energy deep in the work of her poetry makes them empty by comparison. The letters, a kind of submaintenance dosage for keeping language alive in her, merely confirm and back up, often in a desperate, garrulous prolixity, what we know with a larger intelligence, in firmer detail, and in subtler nuance, from the poems. Sexton knew this about her work. Again and again she repeats that poetry "saves" her; that her poems work harder. It is instructive, for instance, to look at the brief references to her hysterectomy in the letters, and then at her poem, "The Operation." In the letter of careful explanation she drafts for John Holmes about her manic expressivity, her confessional candor, she says soberly: "I do not know how to be what you would rather have me be." In her poem, "For John, Who Begs Me Not To Enquire Further," she is bolder, far less deferential; in "that narrow diary of my mind," in its glass, "inverted bowl," she pleads for the exposure of truths that are after all more than her own:

This is something I would never find
in a lovelier place, my dear,
although your fear is anyone's fear,
like an invisible veil between us all . . .
and sometimes in private,
my kitchen, your kitchen,
my face, your face.

Like Jarrell, Sexton often backs into speech in these letters behind a disguising persona of small ordinariness. To one correspondent she wrote, "I am actually a 'suburban housewife' only I write poems and sometimes I am a little crazy"; then, only a sentence later she takes that back, saying "I fear I am not myself here in my suburban housewife role." Unlike Jarrell, she finds her role a little frighteningly convenient.

Anne Sexton's daughter does provide a broad sampling of her mother as correspondent. While the editing is sensitive, tactful, and discreet, a balanced portrait surely drawn together by love and respect, there are only occasional or inadvertent peeps at the working artist, moving from speech to poetry, from act into art.

Such a progression can unfold in a single word. For a time there is the word *moralist*, which Sexton's psychiatrist has given her to describe herself. And a moralist bobs up in several letters. She takes the word in her mouth, and gives it a good shake, a flourish in every direction before she puts it down. Then the word *axe* is featured, when she anticipates rejection or disapproval as a poet. Anxiously she writes to W. D. Snodgrass: "I NEED communication from you because only YOU know if I axed myself with Fred Morgan in N.Y. . . . now I think that I must have and you don't know how to tell me. Please tell me, De. I must know if I'm axed or not." Again to Nolan Miller, about the "bastard form" of her manuscript resting at Knopf: "I feel it will axe me." But three years later, when she publishes *All My Pretty Ones*, the axe's edge is permanently blunted by her epigraph from Franz Kafka: "the books we need are the kind that act upon us like a misfortune, that make us suffer like the death of someone we love more than ourselves, that make us feel as though we were on the verge of suicide, or lost in a forest remote from all human habitation—a book should serve as the axe for the frozen sea within us."

All of Sexton's unacceptable feelings, the fear and suffering exploding from a self she felt to be deeply outrageous, acquire their legitimate home in poetry, as within it she finds authority to turn the threatening axe from weapon to tool. Fear, or grief—deep, lacerating grief—is something not to be put in a letter: if immediate and perishable, it's either mute, or goes on the telephone, or passes out of earshot. If it burns and twists deeply enough to swell into figure it's kept for a poem—in the interim between writing and publication a much more enticing and private, safer place for a feeling than a letter.

Speech in poetry asked something bigger or grander of Anne Sexton which she was careful not to confuse with speech in letters. She wrote to Brother Dennis Farrell, a man she knew only through letters:

> You see, I dare to write to you quickly, pouring forth, badly written, all misspelled, any old way the words come. Only in a poem is the emotion intensified, sharpened, made acute and sometimes more than I knew I knew. Too much verbiage in a letter by Anne Sexton . . . too many words, words all over the field like obstacles. Not meaning to, I get mixed up in them . . . and nothing remains defined except the gesture, the pouring forth, the friendship and the acknowledgement of love.

Nothing is better than this in the letters, and much is not as good. Later, however, a distraught Brother Dennis makes some effort to see her about his decision to leave the monastery, and what she goes on to say to him about the limits and benefits of the letter-writing relationship is equally interesting:

> Our letters . . . no matter how direct and human they may seem to you are not to be compared to a direct relationship. In a letter (no matter how quickly it is written or honestly or freely or lovingly) it is more possible to be loving and lovable, more possible to reach out and to take in . . . there are no walls in a letter, no objects—the words can fly out of your heart (via the fingers) and no one really need live up to them. I mean this seriously and coldly and (as always) lovingly. You tell me "suddenly I found myself within a human relationship that I had often dreamed of, but never realized existed" . . . Oh dear God. You must listen to me, for I feel I have somehow deceived you into thinking this is really a human relationship. It is a letter relationship between humans . . .

Poor Brother Dennis. Like the countryman unused to theater who flies down the aisle to rescue the stage heroine from the dire embrace of the villain, he has taken actress Anne's words "to him" as real. "(I talk to myself when I write to you)," she says in a quick and despairing parenthesis.

In this writing she is never other than Anne, the person who experiences what the poems, not the letters, are there to explain. Anne Sexton flooding the field of words rarely leaves room for a Keatsian large-souled talk. She is, however, inimitably shrewd about the function of letters as wish fulfillment, as fantasy about the selves that we would like to be, or meet, saying to Brother Dennis:

> I knew an "us" once and after many more letters and even quite a few phone calls the "us" met and it crumbled apart like a rotten cookie. It

was built on air and ghosts . . . it was truly beautiful but it died . . . because it tried to get real and it was never real.

As the letter moves towards closure she quotes Kafka again, and rises
to eloquence, having more to say about the genre of letters than Jarrell, our usually more theoretically sophisticated correspondent:
"writing letters . . . means to denude oneself before ghosts, something for which they greedily wait. Written kisses don't reach their
destination, rather they are drunk on the way by ghosts." We are here
an unhappy distance from Donne's verse letter to Sir Henry Wotton:
"more than kisses, letters mingle Soules."

In the free space of the letter, life can be imagined more purely as it
might be; as in a kind of dream, it can be held at arm's length, or rehearsed or revised. The last possibilities, however, seem the trickiest:
unlike other correspondents, as writers' private lives increasingly become the staging arena from which literature is extracted, life has to
be protected, and saved from incursion by letters. As literature swells
to take in more and more life, or outright biography, the prose of a
writer's letter shrinks to practical function, or fleshes out only minor
or miniature fantasy.

The distinction between provisional and finished work blurred by
the extensive publication of journals and diaries, those letters by the
writer to the writer, along with literature, will constitute the proper
place in which to work out what is to be said. For decades, we've seen
two effects of the thinning letter and the fattening journal: one, a novel
or poem increasingly self-conscious about its status as work of art;
two, an increasingly "artless," or provisional novel or poem, presumably coextensive with an unfinished, provisional "life." Letters, more
and more preempted by the telephone, are bewilderingly often reserved for the conventions writers haven't dropped, for the formal relations they haven't moved to alter or disturb: for an incomprehending
mama, for the friend too distant from the heart to telephone, for the
editor or committee member requiring a carefully monitored speech,
and so on. The deeper tests of a life are kept for novels, poems, or
stories, or for the half-light of a journal, in which speech for the self
becomes the purest form of trial speech for an other. While private life
steadily encroaches on literature, the letter, as actual conduit for the
American writer's life, seems dry of any vital exchange. Does this
mean that the ways in which we talk to ourselves grow in complexity
and freedom, but the ways in which we talk to others attenuate? Or
are writers a special case?

Planned for a single recipient, the mid-to-late twentieth-century
letter stops short of the writer's ideal audience for the deposition of

either Thoughts or Sensations. As Virginia Woolf described old letters in contrast to modern ones:

> A letter then was written to be read and not by one person only. It was a composition that did its best to deserve the expense it cost. The arrival of the post was an occasion. The sheets were not for the waste-paper basket in five minutes, but for handing round, and reading aloud and then for deposit in some family casket as a record. These undoubtedly were inducements to careful composition, to the finishing of sentences, the artful disposition of trifles, the polish of phrases, the elaboration of arguments and the arts of the writing master.[3]

In an earlier age, the Wordsworth scholar Beth Darlington reminds me, letters were charged to the receiver, and sold by the postman. Senders had to be confident that what they were writing, page for page, ounce for ounce, would be considered worth buying. Keats's spontaneity, all the more remarkable and endearing in that setting, nonetheless flowered in a slower, more deliberate, and less populated age than ours, one with a longer attention span and with less to claim it.

It seems that only in the indefinite, but elastic territory of literature, where the audience for the speaker is free to enlarge to the All, or in a lightning flash to shrink to the self, that Sexton or Jarrell, poet, is fully to be found. All the rest—letters, journals, notebooks—serve as varying data for the occasion of the poem. Even so, we can't seem to stop wanting to peer into the beginning, preliterary places from which the dross is finally swaled away, in which the living words take wing out of the body and become art: even when the word itself is only of the body's finality, and of the limit of literature.

For Jarrell, Sexton, and others, poems, novels, journals, notebooks, and aide-mémoires seem the preferred receptacle for meditation. Provisional, tentative, and yet open to all the twists of language that a writer may invent, they are the bulky yet supple containers for the generative secrets of our lives. Letters only reflect the incurably partial nature of our relations with others; they catch us in our stalled, repetitive maneuvering, as well as in the all-too-brief moments of what John Berryman called "the glory-hole." The reader, like an angler over troubled waters letting his line drop, fishes patiently for human nature and is duly, if occasionally dully, rewarded in this interim catch of poets' letters. If what we want is the fullest possible range of speech on their lives, and what they made of them, then there is no other place to turn to, but back to their most artful shapings, to the ones that made them the resourceful, visionary though tormented people we wish to read about in the first place.

Notes

1. *Randall Jarrell's Letters*, ed. Mary Jarrell (Boston, 1985). *Anne Sexton: A Self Portrait in Letters*, ed. Linda Gray Sexton and Lois Ames (Boston, 1977). All references to Jarrell's and Sexton's correspondence refer to these editions.

2. *Robert Lowell: Collected Prose*, ed. Robert Giroux (New York, 1987). All citations from Lowell in this essay are taken from "Randall Jarrell," pp. 87–98.

3. Virginia Woolf, "Modern Letters," in *The Captain's Death Bed and other Essays* (New York, 1950).

~ ROBERT BURCHFIELD

Two Kinds of English?
Jeffrey Archer and Anita Brookner

As part of the process of revising Fowler's *Modern English Usage* (1926) I am at present devoting a great deal of time to a reexamination of all the major areas of disputed English usage, and to the history of such disputes. It did not take long to discover that there is an unmistakable stagnancy about the pool of received wisdom. Sides taken and stances adopted at least a century ago (in some cases two centuries ago), and enshrined in the work of grammarians like Robert Lowth (1710–1787), Joseph Priestley (1733–1804), Lindley Murray (1745–1826), Henry Alford (1810–1871), and H. W. Fowler (1858–1933), continue to form the basis of popular belief.[1] More recent descriptive grammarians, on the other hand, like the editors of *A Comprehensive Grammar of the English Language* (1985), give only casual attention to debatable matters of English usage, insisting that the true nature of our language can be ascertained with more certainty by describing what "is" rather than what "should be."[2] Aging databases of varying degrees of worth have been pillaged and repillaged by the descriptivists, have been set alongside moderate-sized collections of privately assembled quotational evidence (spoken and written), and have then been puffed out with quantities of invented examples. The whole process of obtaining evidence has been severely democratized, with very low priority given to literary language.[3]

The battle between prescriptivists and descriptivists is far from over and looks likely to continue into the twenty-first century.

Meanwhile, as my own investigations proceeded, it occurred to me to wonder whether a reexamination of the works of a popular (now unread) writer like Marie Corelli (1855–1924) and of a near-contemporary like Thomas Hardy (1840–1928) might, in terms of their attitude to debatable matters of English usage, provide insights into the degree of public acceptance of linguistic change towards the end of the nineteenth century. Indeed, would the Corellis of any age tend to be more conservative and old-fashioned in matters of usage, and the higher-browed Hardys of any age the more forward-looking and innovative? Or the opposite? Or would both kinds of writer tend to stand in line with the broad conclusions of their contemporary prescriptive linguistic spokesmen? How would it all go?

A comparison of Corelli and Hardy was ruled out because both writers fell outside the time-frame of my work on *Modern English Usage*. I decided instead to apply some standard linguistic tests to the works of two equally contrasting writers of the present day, namely Jeffrey Archer (comparatively lowbrow, though brows do come lower) and Anita Brookner (highbrow).[4]

I started with two preconceptions, that in one of the authors I would find the language (like the style) as characterless—though as practical—as a relay baton, and that in the other the language would be richly evocative while remaining firmly within the boundaries of acceptable usage.[5] It seemed to me likely that the work of two writers with such different backgrounds and tastes—the one a man of the world, a financial swashbuckler, a playwright, a politician, the other a distinguished art historian, apparently a deeply reflective and reticent person—would be sharply distinguishable in the general area of linguistic "correctness."

Descriptive techniques

It hardly needs to be demonstrated that Archer's descriptive techniques are dramatically explicit and rumbustious, and that, by contrast, those of Brookner are quietly restrained and decorous. Just to clear the ground, observe the way in which sex and death are treated by the two authors. First, sex:

> In the constricted darkness Zaphia made some adjustments to her clothing that Wladek could not figure out, and pulled him gently on top of her. It took her very little time to bring Wladek to his earlier pitch of excitement through the few remaining layers of cloth between them. He

thrust his penis into the yielding softness between her legs and was on
the point of orgasm when she again drew her mouth away. "Undo your
trousers," she whispered.   (*Kane and Abel*, p. 186)

In Betty's flat, their eyes brilliant with the progress of the evening, they
finally turn to one another and take each other's measure. When they
kiss, they are passionate, knowing. Max has been passionate and knowing since he was fifteen years old but Betty has not. Sitting on the edge
of her bed, Max utters one last laugh, this time ruminative, reflective,
before pulling Betty down beside him, and silencing any protests she
might have been about to offer for the rest of the night.
                                                    (*Family and Friends*, p. 97)

And death:

The old man slowly raised his right arm, removed from his wrist the silver band and held it forward to a speechless Wladek, whom he clasped
on to firmly, running his fingers over the boy's chest as if to be sure that
it was he. "My son," he said, as he placed the silver band on the boy's
wrist.
   Wladek wept, and lay in the arms of the Baron all night until he could
no longer hear his heart, and could feel the fingers stiffening around
him.   (*Kane and Abel*, p. 67)

"Should we disturb her?" "I think not," he replies. "She will be sleeping
by now." But he slips out of the room to make sure. . . . When Lautner
returns he says nothing. This is a supremely painful moment for him.
His past, his incredible present, inhabit him to the exclusion of all those
assembled, of that family with whom he has only honorary kinship, like
a temporary visa. Mimi looks up, bright-faced, a little sleepy now. How
innocent she is still! Lautner finds that he cannot meet her eyes. "Sleeping?" she asks, her smile now a little anxious. . . . When he turns to face
them, they see that he is in fact an old man. "Oh, Joseph," whispers
Mimi, suddenly not daring to raise her voice. "Do you think we should
send for Frederick?" "No," says Lautner. "There is no need now."
                                                    (*Family and Friends*, p. 176)

Vocabulary

Archer's fictional world is largely concerned with banking and stock
exchange deals, conducted by scheming men dressed in modish
clothes. They spend a lot of time in restaurants and often visit gambling dens:

Moreover, the chairman of Lester's had continued to own fifty-one per
cent of Kane and Cabot, making the merger simply a matter of
convenience.   (*Kane and Abel*, p. 379)

His suit revealed that he went to Chester Barrie. His shoes were Loeb's.
His tie Ted Lapidus. (*Shall We Tell the President?*, p. 78)

"I recommend the shrimp marinara . . ." Mark took his advice and
added a *piccata al limone* and half a carafe of Chianti. Stampouzis drank
Colt 45. (Ibid., p. 124)

Jean-Pierre stuck at eighteen, two nines which he chose not to split as the
dealer had an ace. Harvey stuck on eighteen, an eight and a jack, and the
young man on the left bust again.
  (*Not a Penny Less, Not a Penny More*, p. 160)

Archer draws on the workaday world of words to describe his heroes
and heroines and their activities: adjectives like *callous, nervous, startled*
are frequently put to work, as is the resigned phrase *So be it* (see below). Millions of dollars are won or lost in turn. The financial wizards
fight deadly silent battles by means of secret deals that are so arranged
that they cannot easily be traced back to the originator. The vocabulary used to describe these goings-on is fairly characterless and unsur-
prising. But in the plot astonishing coincidences are more frequent
than they are in *The Comedy of Errors*. General Mark Clark happens to
be in the corridor of the recruitment office as Abel tries to enlist. And,
of course, why not?

By contrast, the scholarly art historian's vocabulary is shown at its
best and most varied in descriptions of works of art, domestic furniture, closely observed female attire, and literary concepts:

In old prints melancholy is usually portrayed as a woman, dishevelled,
deranged, surrounded by broken pitchers, leaning casks, torn books.
  (*Look at Me*, p. 6)

Sideboards, in the Louis XIII style, fumed and contorted, with breaks
and returns in their brooding silhouettes, supported épergnes, silver
cake stands [etc.]. (*A Start in Life*, p. 12)

The bales of satin, taffeta, and organza, the buckram for the hip padding
and the whalebones for the strapless bodices of the ball dresses were suddenly obsolete. (*Providence*, p. 12)

She wears a beautiful beaded dress and an egret feather in her hair. It
must have been attached to a hat but the hat is hidden by her coiffure,
which is in itself hat-shaped. (*Family and Friends*, p. 7)

There are no objective correlatives [in Benjamin Constant's *Adolphe*].
  (*Providence*, p. 81)

Brookner's characters move in a fastidious academic world: words (seemingly unknown to Archer) like *authorial, claustration, diapason, discarnate, exigence, ineluctably, libation, palliate, sybaritic, vatic,* and *vetiver* fall like soft snowflakes on almost every page. So, from time to time, does the word *rebarbative,* a well-known linguistic signpost towards the advanced literariness of novelists like herself and Iris Murdoch. Slang forms no part of Brookner's vocabulary. Unmarked standard English is the norm both in dialogue and in the intervening prose. The unexpectedness of "I took a pull at myself" (*Look at Me,* pp. 135, 155), a slang expression of comparatively recent vintage, brings a sharp reminder that Brookner's characters generally live in a slangless world.

Reticent about slang Archer isn't, though his choice of slang is fairly conventional:

> He's a first-generation American who's had his fingers in more dubious deals in Boston than you've had hot dinners.
>
> (*Not a Penny More,* p. 62)

> There was one hell of a lot of things he was going to do next week.
>
> (*Shall We Tell the President?,* p. 155)

> If you had minded your own fucking business . . .
>
> (*Kane and Abel,* p. 175)

His dependence on clichés is legendary:

> The ambulance shot off like a scalded cat.   (*Not a Penny More,* p. 164)

> Wladek leaped on him, hitting him in places the boy would never have thought of.   (*Kane and Abel,* p. 111)

Archer's foreigners show their foreignness by speaking in broken English. Thus Angelo Casefikis, an illegal Greek immigrant in *Shall We Tell the President?*:

> I am illegal immigrant and so is wife. We both Greek nationals, we came in Baltimore on ship and we been working there two years.   (p. 26)

Xan Tho Huc, a Vietnamese, "tended like so many educated Orientals, to omit the definite article, giving his speech a curious staccato effect":

> I was in car with Tony whole evening when we got your orders to eliminate two men in Ford sedan.   (*Shall We Tell the President?,* p. 81)

Brookner is untroubled by the foreignness of many of her characters: she simply allows them to be fluent in whatever language they are speaking, especially English and French.

Literary references

Brookner's books are studded with references to the works of European writers of the present day and of the past, whereas Archer's signally are not. The plot of Brookner's *Providence* largely hinges on the characters' study of the contents of Benjamin Constant's *Adolphe* (1816). The *douleur profonde* of the Romantic movement is expressed in a classical manner in *Adolphe* and also in *Providence*. There are frequent references in Brookner's works (but especially in *Providence*) to the works or sentiments of Balzac, Racine, Molière, Camus, Chekhov, Dante, Ariosto, and others. Ruth Weiss, the heroine of *A Start in Life*, is writing a thesis on "Vice and Virtue in Balzac's Novels."

By contrast, Archer's characters move in houses and buildings where there are no bookshelves. It is true that a minor part of the plot of *Shall We Tell the President?* depends upon the recognition of a line or two of Shakespeare's Sonnet 29 ("Haply I think on thee") and its relation to Cole Porter's "Is it at long last love?" (or so it would appear: I am not *au fait* with the songs of Cole Porter). In Archerese it is a far-stretching miraculous achievement to make such connections. In the "real world," that is the unbookish world of real people, Florentyna Rosnovski is seen in Scribner's, New York, but like the good businesswoman that she is, she is acquiring copies of John Kenneth Galbraith's *The Affluent Society* and John Gunther's *Inside Russia Today*. Otherwise strategic business planning seems to require the main characters to concentrate on reading reports (especially those of rival companies) and gazing in a meaningful way at friends and enemies alike.

Foreign languages

Archer's only foray into foreign languages takes him into Polish in *Kane and Abel*. Baron Abel Rosnovski, alias Wladek Koskiewicz, spends the first part of his life in terrifying circumstances of war, deprivation, and torture in the vicinity of the Polish city of Slonim (now in Byelorussia). Inevitably a few Polish words creep into the text—words like *barszcz* (borsch), *bigos* (sauerkraut stew), and *Kum* (godparent). Elsewhere he remains steadfastly monolingual.

Brookner, by contrast, is thoroughly and pedantically at home with her continental languages, especially French. Her novels are dotted with words and phrases like *amende honorable, comme il faut, en gelée, mauvais genre, petite nature,* and *pièces d'eau.* Sentences of untranslated French are introduced at regular intervals (for example, *A Start in Life,* pp. 8, 9, 46; *Hotel du Lac,* p. 37) just as they are in many nineteenth-century classics like *Villette.*

English usage

In the matters discussed so far there is no doubt which of the two writers is the more sophisticated. When I turned to an examination of matters of English usage I expected to find the same Grand Canyon of difference between them. It did not quite turn out like that. I considered in turn the unstable linguistic areas of the subjunctive mood, certain pronouns, and numerous matters that are treated in Fowler's *Modern English Usage* and similar manuals. The gap between the two turned out to be more like a small trench.

The subjunctive mood

After *if* (including *even if, only if, if only*), *as if,* and *as though,* there are seventy-nine clear examples of subjunctive constructions in Brookner (*If I were to be afflicted; as if she were indeed a servant; as though it were no longer autumn*). There are three examples of the formulaic phrase *as it were,* two of *were* at the head of a clause (*Were I to think of two living human beings*), one after *lest* (*jealous lest a fact of his life escape her*), one after *supposing,* and one in the set phrase *bless him.* The subjunctive occurs nine times in all in subordinate clauses after the verbs *demand, dictate, insist, suggest,* and *wish.* Expressed in terms of frequency, there are ninety-six examples of the subjunctive mood in 928 pages, that is, one example every 9.7 pages.

In Archer the subjunctive and the indicative moods tend to alternate in similar circumstances (*a truly stunning creature who looked as if she was alone; and began to pace around the room as if it were a cage*).[6] Archer's world is predominantly an indicative world—perhaps this is true of the writings of other "popular" authors? *Be* and *were* are used very occasionally, and somewhat stiltedly, at the head of clauses (*in such situations any man prays to any god, be it Allah or the Ave Maria; Were I required to leave Boston*). The fossilized formula *So be it* turns up five times, and *come what may* once. The subjunctive mood is used once each after *unless* (*unless it be the wish of the majority of its directors*) and after the verbs *desire, insist, order, request,* and *wish.* There are only thirty-two examples of the subjunctive mood in 1,060 pages, that is, one example every 33.1 pages.

The employment of the subjunctive is clearly not a matter of principle for the two writers but one of frequency.

Pronouns

After *it is / it was*, Archer uses subjective and objective forms with about equal frequency, like most other writers (*as if to be sure that it was* he; *it's* I *who am going to need your help*; *it's* me *who's been dumb*). The evidence is sparse, but he seems to restrict *one another* to contexts referring to two people, and *each other* to contexts referring to more than two people. By so doing he goes against traditional grammar, but he is far from being the only writer to merge, or to fail clearly to distinguish, the functions of these two pronominal phrases. The indefinite pronoun *none* normally governs a singular verb in his work, and *neither of us* a plural (*neither of us intend to return to New York*). There is nothing to get excited about in these. So too in his use of *me too, not me, silly me, Me, sir?* (in answer to a question), all of them idiomatic uses of the objective form of the pronoun *I* in standard English. Loose pronominal uses in his work (like his occasional lapses about collegiate matters in Oxford) are agreeably rare: *If you find either of them are free for any reason, perhaps you would ring me* (*Not a Penny More*, p. 91); *I only found out by sheer accident that you, Alan Lloyd and Milly Preston are all trustees, and each have a vote* (*Kane and Abel*, p. 147); *Us Texans have a reputation for speaking our mind* (ibid., p. 251). And contextually even these have possibly been brought into use as typifying the speech of the persons concerned.

As one would expect, Brookner's assurance in the use of subjective and objective forms of the first and third personal pronouns is complete: *Why don't you come to the pub with Brian and me?* (*A Start in Life*, p. 31); *it was always I who called the doctor* (*Look at Me*, p. 86); *it was she who was hungry* (*Providence*, p. 126). The indefinite pronouns *none* and *neither* govern singular verbs in her work. *Who* and *whom* are used with grammatical precision, as they are in Archer. Like half the world now, Brookner is uncertain of the separate roles of *each other* and *one another*: in her work *each other* is used both of two people and of more than two people (*But Mrs Bentley and Kitty were delighted with each other*—*Providence*, p. 84; *Everybody knew each other or about each other*—*Look at Me*, p. 60), and so too is *one another* (*there is no such thing as complete harmony between two people, however much they profess to love one another*—*Hotel du Lac*, p. 95; *Women share their sadness, thought Edith. Their joy they like to show off to one another*—ibid., p. 149). Somewhat surprisingly Brookner falls in line with many other modern writers by using the pronouns *them* and *their* after *anybody, someone,* and *a person*:

She . . . seemed able to dispose of anybody's *random or unfinished business,* their *previous contracts, . . . (Look at Me,* p. 72); *I might stay there until* someone *came along and then I might summon up the courage to follow* them *down those steps* (ibid., p. 170); *Supposing that you were* a person *who was simply bored with living* their *own life (Hotel du Lac,* p. 96). I found no such constructions in Archer.

Miscellaneous points of usage

Both writers use *all right* (never *alright*) and *anticipate* in the sense of "to expect." Both keep *on to* (in prepositional use) as two words except that Brookner, against her practice elsewhere, uses *onto* five times between pages 27 and 141 of *Hotel du Lac* before reverting to *on to*. Both writers occasionally (and idiomatically) place a word or words between the particle *to* and its infinitive (the so-called split infinitive): *It suited her looks* to never quite get *dressed (A Start in Life,* p. 81); to once again see *his castle in Poland (Kane and Abel,* p. 446). Both occasionally use *like* as a conjunction: *Then I would shed my surroundings* like *a butterfly sheds a chrysalis (Look at Me,* p. 55); *It's* like *Aristotle Onassis said (Not a Penny More,* p. 126).

Brookner pedantically prefers *an hotel,* and frequently uses double possessives (*that blouse of my grandmother's—A Start in Life,* p. 45). Archer prefers *a hotel,* and occasionally uses double possessives (*a close friend of Harvey's—Not a Penny More,* p. 247).

Archer enters debatable territory, unknown to Brookner, by using *sunk* (as the past tense of *sink*), *hopefully* as a sentence adverb, *advisors* (for *advisers*), and *less* with count nouns (*less bandages*). Both writers misplace *only* from time to time (like virtually everyone else). I found *hopefully* used only once in Brookner, and then in a traditional manner: *"I hate you," she shouted, hopefully (Hotel du Lac,* p. 102). In both writers participial clauses are usually correctly attached to the clauses they qualify. I found only one serious lapse, in Archer as it happened: *A small electric shock when you touched a light switch caused by nylon carpets (Kane and Abel,* p. 490).

Both writers use the bare infinitive and also the *to* + infinitive after the verb *help: As he helped to dry her (A Start in Life,* p. 82); *I was all ready to help him shop for them (Look at Me,* p. 117); *Covering your ass will not help me to locate Mr Stames (Shall We Tell the President?,* p. 46); *which could help us reduce the number of suspects* (ibid., p. 131).

Brookner almost always uses the notionally correct form of concord in constructions of the type *one of those who/that* + verb: *one of those unsettling spring days that induce bad temper (A Start in Life,* p. 124). I found only one seemingly aberrant example: *She is well aware that*

Betty is one of those women, rather like herself, in fact, who is the instinctive ally of men (Family and Friends, p. 41). This use of the singular is, however, often defended by modern grammarians. I did not find the construction in Archer.

Of the two, only Archer falls into the familiar redundancy net by using *reason* and *because* in the same sentence: *he assumed the reason was because of Diana Parfitt's presence (Kane and Abel*, p. 351). Regrettably, too, Archer lets the erroneous form *lay* stand in *I'll keep you informed on the lay of the land (Kane and Abel*, p. 350). He also fails to distinguish *disinterested* from *uninterested*, and uses *disassociate* instead of *dissociate*. Brookner makes the necessary (and traditional) distinctions. The usage trench between the two writers fractionally widens.

Of the two writers, Brookner is distinctively more fond of the possessive gerund. There are some eighteen examples of the two main types in Brookner's five novels: (pronoun) *there was not much point in* his *doing the shopping (A Start in Life*, p. 63); (name) *Perhaps this feeling dates from* Frederick's *having chosen Evie (Family and Friends*, p. 113). The possessive gerund is avoided in her work, and generally in modern English, when the word immediately before the gerund is an ordinary noun: *there wasn't the slightest chance of the* timetable *being changed (Providence*, p. 39). I found only five examples of possessive gerunds in Archer, all of them after a pronoun: *I don't remember* your *booking a table (Shall We Tell the President?*, p. 236). Almost always the possessive gerund is pointedly avoided in his work: *I don't think he would approve of* me *being drunk (Kane and Abel*, p. 165).

Conclusion

There are indeed two kinds of English in the two sets of novels, and it must be said that both authors, as far as one can tell, give satisfaction to their target audiences. The fact that the audiences are different can be said to account for the contrast of subject matter, vocabulary, and narrative style, but hardly for the differences of English usage. In Pattern A the sentences are simply, paratactically, and triumphantly shaped to please a mass-market readership. The vocabulary is plain, whipped in, unfancy, narrow-gauged. The flame burns low in the ring of words. In Pattern B, on the other hand, the sentences are fashioned with fastidious care, with all the joinings and couplings in perfect running order. A foreigner confronted with just these two sets of works as paradigms of the English language in the last quarter of the twentieth century would note that certain matters are markedly optional, others more firmly fixed. Changes in standard usage may be foreshadowed in some of the optional areas. The well-taught foreigner will also notice that the edge of Pattern A is more ragged than that of Pattern B—*disassociate, less bandages, the lay of the land* stalk its landscape. At the spectral edge of the unknowable linguistic moors and meadows of the future it is impossible to judge whether the rule-breaking irregularities of Pattern A—including the use of *disinterested* to mean "uninterested"—will form part of the normal core language of the twenty-first century, or whether Pattern B will broadly prevail. Time will tell.

Notes

1. Classically represented in the House of Lords on 4 March 1987 when the quirks and oddities of the English language (*rubbish* used as a verb, *data* treated as a singular, "vulgar" Americanisms like *meet with*, and so on) were formally debated by the noble lords.

2. Randolph Quirk, Sidney Greenbaum, Geoffrey Leech, and Jan Svartvik, eds., *A Comprehensive Grammar of the English Language* (London, 1985).

3. In *CGEL*, references to specific sources are exceedingly rare. I have so far noticed only two—one each to works by Margaret Drabble and Kurt Vonnegut—both on p. 661. The quotational evidence presented is overwhelmingly anonymous.

4. For practical reasons I have based this essay on three novels by Jeffrey Archer: *Not a Penny More, Not a Penny Less* (1976), *Shall We Tell the President?* (revised version of 1986), and *Kane and Abel* (1979); and five novels by Anita Brookner: *A Start in Life* (1981), *Providence* (1982), *Look at Me* (1983), *Hotel du Lac* (1984), and *Family and Friends* (1985). As Brookner's novels are much shorter than Archer's, the amount of text examined is approximately the same for each author: 1,060 pages of Archer and 928 pages of Brookner. For Archer's works I used the Coronet paperback versions; for Brookner I read the first three in the Triad paperback versions and *Hotel du Lac* and *Family and Friends* in the Jonathan Cape hardback editions.

5. Reviewers of Brookner characterize her style in various ways: "rich and interesting" (Frank Kermode); "I am no devotee of the lace doily and the silver cream jug; I prefer something gamy, spicy" (Anthony Burgess); "Miss Brookner's earlier novels have included poignantly unsentimental scenes of pain, age, and the only end of age, and their presence . . . gives a weight to what might otherwise seem a too unwounded epigrammatism of style" (Stephen Wall). Journalists who review Archer's work (academic reviewers ignore him) speak in more down-to-earth terms: "a series of flat statements" (Byron Rogers); "written entirely in clichés" (Andrew Gimson); "If Jeffrey's books are all ill-written and boring as I think they are, why do so many people enjoy them?" (Tim Heald).

6. The indicative would have been appropriate had the "truly stunning creature" been alone. But she was not: "The only other person in the carriage was a middle-aged lady reading *Vogue*" (*Not a Penny More*, p. 84). The context depends on the coincidence that a picture of the "truly stunning creature" appears on the front cover of this issue of *Vogue*, a circumstance noticed, and immediately taken advantage of, by Viscount Brigsley, one of the heroes of the novel.

~ LEON BOTSTEIN

Language, Music, and Politics

IN 1911, IN AN "UNWRITTEN POSTSCRIPT to *Der Rosenkavalier*," the poet Hugo von Hofmannsthal observed that in truly unified operatic dramas (*Der Rosenkavalier* in particular) "groups oppose groups; those who are connected become separated, and the separated come together. They all belong to one another, and what is best lies between them: it is immediate and eternal, and here is the place for music."[1]

Why music? The "immediate and eternal" are, after all, categories which cover everything that exists in time. Hofmannsthal identifies music as an instrument through which truths otherwise hidden from us, not only on stage but in life, can be revealed. Among the truths affirmed by music is the sense of an implicit community; music renders human solidarity concrete. Although the operatic stage is admittedly artificial, by demarcating shared space and linkages among individuals music assumes, in Hofmannsthal's view, political significance: "Music is endlessly affectionate and unifies everything," he concluded.[2]

Ironically, music, the art form most tied to the logic of time, can permit the timeless to be conjured up—that which in our imaginations is not contingent on time but is deemed immortal. The immortal, the timeless, is in turn assumed to be the best, the highest that can emerge from human action and speech. A human act, the creation of music, can become the language of immortality and transcend the fixed boundaries of the human condition.

Yet in the narrative of the book of *Genesis* it was the word (as the *Gospel According to St. John* reminds the reader, "In the beginning was the word . . .") that was with God from the start. Speech (as perhaps a consequent sign of some silent thinking that may have gone on, even unconsciously) has been construed in the Western religious tradition as the essential noble action, the instrument of creation, undertaken by man in God's image. It has remained a sign for the link assumed by ordinary mortals between interior mental processes and external reality.

In Aeschylus and the various versions of the myth of Prometheus, language is the instrument that renders the fire—symbol of godly power—effective. Language enables humans to defend themselves against the consciousness of the inexorable fact of death and the envy of the gods. In modern political thought the idea that speech is the quintessential form of action, the alternative to violence and therefore crucial to freedom and peace, has remained fundamental to conceptions of democracy, civility, and justice.[3]

Hofmannsthal's observation reminds us that despite this weighty legacy, at the start of the twentieth century considerable doubt as to the truthfulness, benign power, or aesthetic merit of ordinary speech and literary language was rampant. Even if Hofmannsthal's effusive assertion falls short by the standards of logic and clarity, the idea that music communicates the immediate and the eternal—the real truths that speech and action cannot—betrayed a passionate rejection of the power of ordinary language. What was substituted (not only by Hofmannsthal but by nineteenth-century writers and theorists from Jean Paul and Arthur Schopenhauer to Richard Wagner) was, curiously, music, the most un-natural of the arts.

There is no music (in Hofmannsthal's sense) in nature, or in the act of creation (despite Haydn's glorious approximation in *The Creation*), and none in the teachings of Christ. In the Jewish tradition, musicians stand behind speaking priests and written law. Moses was no musician, as Arnold Schoenberg well understood: in *Moses und Aron*, written in 1932, Moses expresses himself more in speech (using *Sprechstimme*) than music. His brother Aron sings but without conveying the law and ways of God to his people. At the end of the second act, the last Schoenberg would complete, the curtain falls after Moses has the last word on the failure of speech to communicate truth: "O word, you word that I lack."[4]

The crisis of language at the *fin de siècle* was decisive in the career of twentieth-century aesthetic modernism. The search for a refuge within the world of music was paradoxical since music is a mode of expression marked by a self-contained logic, the absence of descriptive or denotative power, and a detachment from any ordinary sense of the real and the natural. That music, an artificial creation of men and in some cultures also gods (as in the Greek Pantheon), may be more the medium of the essential and truthful in life than speech, and at a minimum may be a necessary complement to ordinary language— which itself has come to be viewed as a crippled and limited instrument—is a provocative basis for evaluating the career of language in our century.

The crucial proposition, exemplified by Hofmannsthal's observation, was that music can best communicate that which is unsaid and perhaps unsayable on the dramatic stage where action assists the comprehensibility of speech. In this context music required language and language required music to permit the space to be created in which music could communicate the "immediate and the eternal." Theater without music, although purportedly less divorced from the illusion of realism (we don't, after all, sing to one another in real life), could never be as penetrating or powerful in the sense of the truly real and the psychologically significant. Neither could pure instrumental music. For example, when Count Almaviva in *The Marriage of Figaro* begs for forgiveness at the end of the opera, the musical exchange between him and the Countess communicates ambivalence, the pain of memory, skepticism, and ethical superiority—all true, unspoken psychological subtexts that fail to be communicated by either Beaumarchais's original text or Da Ponte's libretto. This is why the model of Mozart, amplified by the example of Wagner, inspired Hofmannsthal to turn from writing drama and lyric poetry to writing texts for music. He saw in music a way to restore to literary language and ordinary speech the power which the Biblical narratives and the political theorists of Anglo-American democratic schemes reserved for words alone.

Hofmannsthal's contemporary Ludwig Wittgenstein noted that music might be understandable, much like a sentence of words or possibly like "a play of sounds, without vocabulary and grammar." Music communicates, in either case, in the sense of meaning, but without precise narrative or explicit content. But with any paradigm of meaning in music, to explain what music "says," whether by itself or in combination with words, one is forced to employ linguistic comparisons which, owing to the limitations of language, in the end always fail to replace or approximate the special communication of music.[5]

Wittgenstein, after all, bequeathed to the twentieth century the barrage of closely argued observations that the world of knowledge in the ordinary sense is tied to language, which, in turn, is a sort of game, albeit a deadly and serious one. Despite Wittgenstein's later reconsiderations, the closing propositions of his 1918 *Tractatus*—again a beginning for twentieth-century traditions of thinking—argue, without reference to music, what Hofmannsthal suggested in more overtly poetic terms. Consider Wittgenstein's conclusions that "those who have found after a long period of doubt that the sense of life became clear to them then have been unable to say what constituted that sense"; that "there are, indeed, things that cannot be put into words." Philosophy was a "ladder" which needed to be thrown away after being used so that the individual might "see the world aright," which meant recognizing that "what we cannot speak about we must consign to silence."[6]

The suggestion that what might be truly at stake in life and therefore in culture cannot be talked about has terrifying consequences, primarily in the effort to create a community through a politics based on language; to resolve conflict; to negotiate through differences; and to translate and to communicate. The cynical tenor of this twentieth-century line of thought was articulated precisely by Elias Canetti, who asserted in 1965 that "there is no greater illusion than thinking that language is a means of communication between people. One speaks to another person but in such a way that he does not understand. One keeps talking and one understands even less. . . . Seldom does anything penetrate the other person, and if it does, it is usually twisted awry."[7]

Given this damaged confidence in language, the state of music, viewed as a sort of alternative medium of communication in twentieth-century culture, might assist our grasp of what has become of our use of ordinary language. Following Hofmannsthal's suggestion, the space occupied by the musical environment of the late twentieth century—our artificial aural world—is, as in the theater of opera, reflective of significant meanings in our life. There is little doubt that in popular culture in particular the place and prestige of music have grown dramatically since 1900, in part as a result of technology. Its evolution has influenced the direction of language; filled vacuums left by other modes of discourse; created surrogates for—and possibly imprisoned efforts to reclaim—the sacred place occupied by language in religious thought and the pivotal secular place occupied by language in the traditional political process to which we still avow allegiance in the name of freedom and democracy.

Language has, in fact, become closely tied both to patterns of music and to habits of physical mobility in our contemporary culture, much like the setting of words on the artificial stage of opera. Music, in turn, reveals equally well our sense and use of time, for it, like language, functions in time. Among the most controversial aspects of contemporary culture is the near universal spread of forms of rock music. Jeremiads against the influence of rock on young people have become commonplace events since the 1950s.[8] Indeed, the rock song is among the most widespread forms of music-listening and music-making. Attachment to the music is intense and is accompanied by an eagerness to regard the lyrics as invested with serious meaning and insight. Intimate issues—love, abandonment, loneliness—are not rock music's only subjects. Politics and social criticism are packed into the same formulas and clichés as desire and remorse. Adherents of rock songs listen to the songs over and over again, convinced that in the repeated hearings, voice is being given to fundamental political beliefs shared by them and other listeners.

This ubiquitous and decisive musical form of the late twentieth century has peculiar characteristics. The rock song rarely lasts more than six minutes, sometimes less. Its musical form depends on easily grasped units of repeated music. The foreground is the song, the background an instrumental sound framed by an insistent and regular rhythmic pulse. Repetition and simplicity create a special intensity designed to survive endless rehearings by the customer. The adolescent enthusiast appropriates the song as an autobiographical symbol and invests (and sometimes decorates) it with personal meaning through the integration (through repetition) of the simple song into the flow of his or her daily life. That meaning is rehearsed through easy recollection by interior silent repetition. Ease of comprehension of short units impervious to serious variation or elaboration is the design formula common to all songs. This formula is, in turn, dependent on a short attention span, so that the music and text can easily be imprinted and reinforced.

Simplicity and regularity—both deceptive qualities—in rock music are constructed to permit no extended and complex dramatic or narrative invention or response. This effectively discourages the listener from any extended linguistic or musical thinking that might come nearer to either reality or the limits of the imagination. Complexity remains unacknowledged. In contrast to the operas Hofmannsthal helped to create, the rock song's text and music are not developed into a web of multiple meanings, conflicts, or temporal cross-references and contradictions, often displayed simultaneously on stage. The rock song is in every sense monothematic and direct.[9]

The texts conform to the musical formula. But here music does not "set" text. The procedure common to nineteenth-century art-song writing or the musical settings of operatic libretti—adapting a pre-existing text to music—is not followed. When Strauss first read the translation of Oscar Wilde's *Salome*, musical ideas came to him throughout his reading of the text. Wagner wrote his texts first, before composing the music. In contrast, a symbiosis of dependence in which text is subordinate to music in the act of creation is essential to rock music. The music dominates. Not only do the texts have little meaning apart from the music, but any claims to logic or profundity become contingent on (and often compromised by) the music's overpowering presence.

The simplicity, dominance, and sheer sonic power of the music release verbal language from any obligation to render sense independently. The subordination of text to the demand for simple regularity and symmetry adequate to the rock music form is masked from the listener by the consistent focus on the music. Music inspires text, and in turn text reveals no obligation to justify itself as language. It is shaped to fit musical formula and gesture.

The rock enthusiast never hears (and rarely reads) the words apart from the music. But he or she senses profundity and meaning through the musical stimulation, thereby emancipating himself or herself from making sense through language alone. In earlier examples of text-music interactions, a senseless text (with the exception of the use of words as mere sounds as in Ernst Toch's *Geographical Fugue* for chorus) was at most a rarity.

The listener and the performer of rock music, however, assert that the text does possess serious meaning. That meaning is often expressly political, with the result of the appearance of politics in language. But the language, tragically, is deracinated. The discourse conducted is one of language in music, or just as music, and the meaning of linguistic propositions becomes marginal. Often the language of the song even celebrates the evident impotence of commonplace political language, such as slogans. In contrast to the world of intimate concerns dealt with in rock music—love and sex—in matters political a young listener of these songs may never transcend the evident exploitation of his or her honest and intense desire to understand and express frustration about a world that could be so much better than it seems. For individuals the chances for authenticity in intimacy are after all somewhat greater than in politics.

Consider, for example, when Tracy Chapman sings "Love is Hate, War is Peace; / No is Yes, and we're all free. / But somebody's gonna have to answer; / The time is coming soon; / Amidst all the questions and contradictions, there're some who seek the truth; / But somebody's gonna have to answer; / The time is coming soon; / When the blind remove their blinders and the speechless speak the truth."[10]

Apart from the displacement of political responsibility in the text (to "somebody . . ."), the seemingly prophetic allusion to utopia is trivialized by the idea, dictated merely by musical considerations, that blindness is the result of blinders. The irony of the reference to freedom in the midst of the wide deceit displayed through the abuse of language ("war is peace," and so on) is likewise trivialized by the singer's claim to know "questions and contradictions," which implies that the truth being sought is actually known or discoverable. Chapman's text implies that the truth is known not by the "speechless" but the opposite; in fact, it might be known by the singer. Such knowledge and the actions it might demand are a reflection of real freedom and efficacy, but freedom that demands both language and knowledge. Chapman assumes a posture of ignorance and powerlessness to the listener belied by her own text.

Chapman's texts are models of philosophical discourse in comparison to the texts of the popular group The Police, who sing, again for explicit metrical reasons, the following in a song entitled "De do do do de da da da": "Poets, Priests and Politicians have words to thank for their positions; / words that scream for your suppression, and no one's jamming their transmission; / 'cos when their eloquence escapes you, their logic ties you up and rapes you."[11] The conclusion, that the governing "logic" in society—presumably force, not language (for it is violence that rapes and is used when "eloquence" fails)—is material power and not words and ideas stands in contradiction with the song's initial premise, which is that it is to words that politicians, poets, and priests owe their power, their "positions." That would indeed reflect either a rational political process or a peculiar world of power politics in which economic or military might was subordinate to talk, in which the holding on to power was merely a function of rhetoric.

The facile use in the song of poets as the moral equivalents of priests and politicians in the history of oppression is, I suspect, a matter of thoughtlessness and alliterative musical convenience rather than the outgrowth of a study of Plato or the role of poets in Nazi Germany. The nearly criminal aspect of these lyrics is, finally, not the simplification itself, but the pretentious abuse of verbal fragments of ideas and historical allusions. Meaning in language is at once alleged and destroyed, leaving the sound of thought without its content.

In the context of rock music, meaning in language is not expanded by music, but rendered nearly impossible. Meaninglessness and thoughtlessness are secured by the most primitive and successful of teaching and learning techniques: exact, tireless repetition of simple formulas. The formal logic of rock music replaces the grammar of logic in language. The result is a false ideology of powerlessness and oppression reflected in lyrics that fraudulently allude to meaning. A pseudopolitical statement of helplessness to which there is no exit is offered. And this all succeeds in enriching the record companies and the rock stars who exploit their image as rebellious and socially concerned. They, after all, periodically participate in grand hands-across-the-seas benefit concerts ("live aid" for example), which only enhance the sales of future albums. There is perhaps no better expression of this central characteristic of rock music than the Police's own lyrics: "Don't think me unkind, words are hard to find;/they're only cheques I've left unsigned from the banks of chaos of my mind /. . . De do do do de da da da is all I want to say to you; / de do do do de da da da, their innocence will pull me through; / de do do do de da da da, is all I want to say to you, they're meaningless and all that's true." Apart from the appropriation of a bad metaphor (until recently, at least) for chaos and emptiness, laziness of mind and the impotence of language become conflated. The latter seems to justify the former and is written off and celebrated in the ears of the literate and affluent young listener as a justifiable "innocence." What, finally, becomes of any notion of truth if words are meaningless? Yet truth is still alleged.

The prevalent types of music in our culture, the mode of their consumption, and role they play not only influence ordinary language and thought. They reveal incomplete meanings only suggested by music. In the case of rock music, linguistic incompleteness and nonsense, brevity, and high volume act as a screen against political thought, either manifest indirectly by music, expressed in language, or displayed in the integration of the two. The decline in participation in democratic politics is the appropriate corollary from our daily life. The brief and formulaic character—the absence of extended argument—of the language employed in political news broadcasts and newspapers such as USA Today mirrors the function of language in rock music.

Rock music, in text and song, requires from its listeners neither extended memory nor concentration, skills that demand patience and the devotion of time to listening, learning, and ultimately arguing in the public arena. In this way it projects an image of the way in which we use time in daily life: whether in conversation or in the act of shopping or waiting for someone, our attention span is limited. If one contrasts the dialogue in recent films and television programs to earlier examples, one will notice a similar constricted periodicity. Brevity, staccato exchanges, and the inability to maintain, in dramatic dialogue, extended sentence structure or sustained argument are commonplace qualities that parallel our own patterns of personal interaction. Except for in rare adaptations of classic novels, literary language has vanished from the screen. In film and television, the action, aided by complex visual effects, dictates the shape of language, just as in rock music, music shapes the text.

II

In the world of so-called classical music, the most widespread and successful phenomenon is the advent of minimalism. The works of Philip Glass, Steve Reich, and John Adams are among the most popular and acclaimed new contributions to music since 1960. The habits of listening associated with the rock form have become appropriated in the concert hall. New long forms of musical expression are created by the repetition of simple formulas heard over and over with minimal variation. Memory and concentration are easily induced in the listener because the units of musical logic are, as in rock music, easy to grasp at first hearing and are never camouflaged or transformed in the context of a complex multifaceted discourse. This minimalism is not provocative, cast against decorative habits of overstuffed art-making. Contemporary musical minimalism is itself the appropriate decoration for the thoughtless and silent habits of contemporary life and listening.

The one exception, John Adams's opera *Nixon in China*, is compelling musically only insofar as it resists minimalist formulas. But there too the text is confused, contradictory, and only inadvertently political, despite the obviously political subject. In fact, the opera ends by setting aside and trivializing, through the display of Nixon's and Mao's personal intimacies, the overt historical political content.

The success of the work as theater has depended upon the audience's delight in the unintended comical and farcical appearances of a figure—Nixon—who carries sharply delineated connotations for all American adults. Once the independent audience memory of Nixon the historical figure fades, the work may well lose its power and appeal. A corollary to formal brevity—impermanence in meaning—the transient character of the text, whose effect is wholly contingent on forces external to the use of language on stage, becomes a key to theatrical success. The music of Adams may survive as the most inventive sound produced within the minimalist movement. But, more than in traditional opera (no matter how poor the libretto), the music's success is entirely divorced from the meaning of the linguistic text or any interaction between text and music.

In contrast to the world of the early twentieth century, we are surrounded by musical sounds. Not only is silence at a premium, but we are inclined to resist it, using walkman gadgets with earphones as we travel and exercise. We demand aural distractions. We do not travel to hear music or create it at home by singing or playing. Rather, we immerse ourselves in recorded music, created in studios, often with effects unreproducible by live music-making.

Yet we reject the call of silence for introspection and welcome sound in our cars and on telephone lines, even if it is Muzak. We see the musicians only rarely; they are as hidden in the music video and the film as they are on the CD. In Ingmar Bergman's memorable film of *The Magic Flute*, which shows props, dressing rooms, and stagehands, the only participants not made visible are the orchestral musicians. The music in films has always been a magical, unseen, and crucial dimension in the illusion. Whether in rock music or in the so-called classical world, audiences at live performances listen with memories of repeated hearings of recorded performances. They bond less with the performer than with the recollection of their own past hearing of recorded sound.

Neither musical literacy based on the ability to read a printed text nor the imitative literacy that enables us to hear, reproduce, and improvise constitutes the contemporary foundation of the way in which we receive musical communication. So completely ubiquitous is musical sound that we expect it as a background accompaniment to the tasks of daily life: working, traveling, shopping, sleeping, and waking up. We no longer sense the need to be actively literate in music, for music's presence in our lives has become entirely separate from our individual capacities to make or use music. The passivity of listening parallels the absence of resistance within the musical forms we encounter. The shattering of the meaning of language within musical forms is the consequence of the debasement of music into an unremarkable dimension of the background of daily life.

Our absence of literacy is appropriate, since the music we consume demands no active response in terms of music-making. The most striking exception is the home-grown rock band among young people where the precise formulas of commercial rock are mimicked. Furthermore, our encounter with music has been rendered a primarily solitary activity, not a social act such as playing and singing with others or gathering in concerts or assemblies to listen in public with others. The loss of the social aspect of musical culture robs music of its potential to activate a sustained sense of solidarity and mirrors the domination of text by music.

Hofmannsthal's vision of the collaboration of music and language is rendered anachronistic. The contemporary music that permeates life and entertainment—rock and classical—has been stripped of its power to illuminate either the immediate or the eternal. Expression, in both music and speech, becomes forgettable, brief, formulaic, and, upon closer scrutiny, meaningless.

III

Film and television, arguably the most widespread and influential cultural mediums that employ both music and language, are, in historical perspective, the heirs and modern equivalents of the opera of the nineteenth century. As Hermann Broch observed in the 1940s, the opera was the nineteenth century's quintessential form, the medium that permitted historicism to take on a living shape and function in what he called the "value-vacuum" of mid-nineteenth-century urban culture.[12]

It was the vision of a "total work of art" (*Gesamtkunstwerk*) that triumphed in the arena of opera by the end of the century. Originally associated with Wagner, the idea that text—either poetic, dramatic, narrative, or epic—was both less adequate to and less reflective of the human condition than an artistic form that unified text, music, and the visual influenced the late Verdi (*Falstaff* and *Otello*), Richard Strauss (*Salome* and *Elektra*), Debussy (*Pelleas et Melisande*), and Berg (*Wozzeck*). The use of great autonomous texts in music—adaptations of Shakespeare, Oscar Wilde, Maeterlinck, Büchner, and the Greek tragedians—were outgrowths of an ideology best articulated in Nietzsche's 1872 tract *The Birth of Tragedy*, which argued that the modern equivalent of Greek tragedy in terms of its potential to reach and transform the public was the integration of music and language evident in Wagner's *Tristan und Isolde*.

The notion of the total work of art as an expressive unity also influenced the direction of *fin de siècle* symphonic writing in which poetic and literary programs, if not actual texts, became integrated in the work of Mahler and the early Schoenberg, for example. The fusion of the visual, the musical, the dramatic, and the verbal had been a characteristic of all opera, including the Verisimo movement of Puccini and Mascagni, where opera sought to convey real time and emotion using music as self-consciously illustrative and psychologically suggestive. The lure of opera—and its sibling outgrowths, the operetta in Europe and the musical theater in America—for audiences remained greater than that of concert music and even ordinary theater until the advent of the sound film. Not surprisingly, one of the first aspirations for the sound film in Europe was the filming of opera.

Given the heritage of the idea of the *Gesamtkunstwerk* and the damaged confidence in language with which the twentieth century opened, it is not surprising that the dominant cultural forms with which we now live continue to subordinate language and integrate it with other forms of expression. In rock music language is subordinated to music, and in film and television it is subject to the visual and dramatic and is surrounded by a musical soundtrack whose function is to anticipate and underscore the narrative and plot.

As we contemplate the poverty of both music and language as effective instruments of intimate expression and political discourse, it makes some sense to consciously work to discard the traditions of the *Gesamtkunstwerk* that have been carried forward by films and television. By separating speech from music, language from pictures, and music from both language and the visual, we might accelerate the expansion of language as an autonomous vehicle so that it begins to approximate the demands and difficulties of contemporary politics and life. The separation of text from the visual and from music—both popular and self-consciously high-art music—can become one route for music out of minimalism or the so-called musical postmodernism whose vocabulary is more historicist in character than original.

This is both a literary and a political task and has little to do with the conservative call to restoration of earlier conceptions of literacy. Rather, it rests on the assumption that if individuals are asked, both in speaking and in writing, to express private and public concerns without the crutch of visual and musical accompaniment, we can once again learn to tolerate subtlety and duration in thinking and in the use of language. Patience and complexity are crucial to argument and debate, the essential language-based components of a functioning free society and democracy.

Cultivating the autonomy of language can inspire a new generation of oral storytelling, just as jazz in its heyday revived the essential art of musical improvisation. Written forms of language require cultivation, primarily in the schools. The influence of the oral forms on the written forms can once again be crucial, providing them with the essential frameworks in which to develop. The Homeric tales, for example, when committed to writing framed the Western tradition in which the epic and prose novel emerged, just as the transfer of Aeschylus's oral poetry to versions that could be read shaped the character of the tragic drama.

The sense of exhaustion and pessimism regarding language inherited by the twentieth century needs to be cast aside. Language, particularly in the democratic context of America, must be liberated from its dependence on musical and visual frameworks within popular culture. At stake is not only the future of a complex and vital linguistic tradition but the instrument on which our political future rests. It was in the age of Samuel Johnson, an era of high romance with potentialities of language and literacy, that the optimistic credos of rational politics and democracy saw practical realizations. The *fin de siècle* frustration with language and the resultant culture of doubt—formed, admittedly, in response to the compromised realities that emerged from the ideologies of democracy, freedom, and literacy during the nineteenth century—became part of a world that either embraced or failed to resist fascism.

Therefore, at the heart of the task to emancipate language and music from the routines of false simplicity, formula, and a mutual dependency that is equally destructive to both forms of expression is more than art; there are also truth and justice—civilization in its widest sense. We must cultivate the independent powers of language, used in an elaborated fashion to achieve meaning and communication in the public arena, our philosophical doubts notwithstanding. We must cultivate music as a parallel form of extended expression, independent of language. We should hesitate to bring them together until we have generated new levels of literacy and active discourse in both language and music. Above all, we should defend ourselves against the crippling patterns of their integration into the routine and ineffective daily life to which we have become accustomed.

Notes

1. Hugo von Hofmannsthal, "Ungeschgriebenes Nachwort zum Rosenkavalier," in *Gesammelte Werke. Dramen Vol. V Operndichtungen* (Fischer Verlag Frankfurt am Main, 1979), p. 146.
2. Hofmannsthal, "Ungeschgriebenes Nachwort," p. 147.
3. See in particular Hannah Arendt's *The Human Condition* (Chicago, 1958).
4. Arnold Schoenberg, *Moses und Aron* (London, 1984), p. 502.
5. Ludwig Wittgenstein, *Philosophical Investigations*, 2d ed. (New York, 1958), p. 143e.
6. Ludwig Wittgenstein, *Tractatus Logico-Philosophicus* (London, 1961) pp. 149–51. On Wittgenstein's musical attitudes, see Brian McGuinness, *Wittgenstein: A Life: Young Ludwig 1889–1921* (Berkeley and Los Angeles, 1988).
7. Elias Canetti, "Karl Kraus: The School of Resistance," in *The Conscience of Words* (New York, 1965), pp. 34–35.
8. The most popular and least convincing conservative critique can be found in Allan Bloom's bestselling book *The Closing of the American Mind* (New York, 1987). Bloom conveniently forgets that the severest critique of the popular hit tunes and popular music in general (from the perspective of politics and art) came from a Marxist tradition and can be found in the writings of Theodor W. Adorno as early as the mid 1930s.
9. In this analysis the common critique of rock's commercialism is avoided. The comparison with opera is made with operas, and, for that matter, light operetta or musical theater, that were, like *Der Rosenkavalier*, immensely popular in their own time.

Therefore, a discussion of underground rock does not affect the argument since successful forms are contrasted with equally successful earlier art forms.

10. Tracy Chapman, "Why?," *Album No. 9-60774-4* (Elektra/Asylum Records, New York, 1988). In another song in the same album, "For You," Tracy Chapman refers to "intellect and reason" as "guards" against intimate feeling which leave her "at a loss for words." The apparent ideal is the transmission of feeling without words, rendering language an enemy of personal authenticity.

11. The Police and Nigel Gray, "De do do do de da da da" (text by Sting), in *Album: Every Breath You Take* (A and M Records, USA, 1981).

12. See Hermann Broch's *Hugo von Hofmannsthal und seine Zeit* (1950), now in a fine translation by Michael Steinberg entitled *Hugo von Hofmannsthal and His Time* (Chicago, 1984).

~ MICHAEL BAWTREE

No Opera Please—We're British

THE ITALIAN ORIGINATORS OF THE FORM of artistic activity known as "opera" claimed they were attempting to recreate ancient Greek tragedy by restoring to it the lost element they believed had been essential to the form: music. Thus the goal of an integrated dramatic presentation in which music and words both serve the whole has since the late sixteenth century always stood as the "idea" of serious opera. In the beginning, the music of opera served as a more or less humble handmaiden to the words: seventeenth-century composers were preoccupied with trying to develop its expressive power to match that of language. But they were so successful that within another century the emotionally expressive power of music was the marvel, and the composer and his company of technically adept singers and instrumentalists were the new heroes. Text took on the more modest role of pretext.

From time to time then and since, some composers sought to "return" to an even balance of words and music in opera, claiming to want to pull back the virtuosity of musical and specifically vocal elements in order to let music serve effectively both the precision of language (and therefore of ideas and emotional nuance) and the intensity of dramatic action. But the pressures placed on the art by singers who wished to show their paces and by fashionable and courtly audiences who prized virtuosity over dramatic wholeness worked against a balanced integration. The opera, after all, was more entertainment than instruction—was attended often enough not for the doctrine but for the music and social intercourse there. Even the French Revolution, which saw an end to the old "opera seria" and the development of a new and more vigorous breed of music-drama based on the "opera comique," could not resist the sheer force of music, now bursting into full romantic flower. Opera was the ideal vehicle for the emotional extremes of the romantic novel, but the general lines of the story were all the composer needed: the actual lines of the text were infinitely adjustable. The job of adapting such works did not often attract writers who valued their literary skills as much as the composers valued their music.

Librettists after all have had to accept that the words they have toiled over may no longer be themselves once the composer has finished with them, but may be changed, cut, repeatedly repeated, or at the very least rearranged. And then, even if the words survive intact, their referential function will be carried out only if they can be heard enough to do their job of referring. The degree to which this referential function is performed depends on a number of variables, none of which is in the control of the writer: the pitch that the composer has set to certain vowel sounds and consonants (generally, particularly with women's voices, the higher the fewer), the speed of the setting, the volume of the accompanying instrumentation, the competence of the conductor in achieving balance, the technical skill of the singer, the actual staging of the scene, and the acoustics of the house can each separately or all together conspire to make the words an unintelligible mush.

All this is dispiriting enough to the librettist. But even if the composer has cared sufficiently about the words to ensure that they remain there along with the music, and that (given adequate performance) they can be heard, the librettist must still give up control over many things which are the very stuff of an accomplished writer's voice and craft. For a writer, intention not only inheres in individual words and images or in sentences: it lies too in the precise control of tone, color, rhythm, emphasis, pauses, and variety of pace, and, on a larger scale, of the setting up of situations, the motivations for the actions of characters, and the overall shape and balance of the material. These things too must be handed over to the often rough mercies of the composer and his music.

From the composer's point of view, the words—and the situations they depict—are satisfactory only if they initiate music. But as the music starts to form, it will in turn suggest structures and thematic resonances and repetitions and rhythmic figures of its own, which will mold the original text to its own purposes. Composers who are too polite to writers and their words will end up decorating a text rather than transmuting it. But the composer who wrestles a good text into submission beneath the imperious needs of the music can miss the mark too—if the mark is an equal partnership of words and music.

The development of opera, as outlined here with impertinent brevity, took place without the English language being more than marginally involved. For this, Shakespeare and his contemporaries are considerably to blame. Their multiple theatrical achievements—their control of plot and dramatic structure, variation of pace and mood, and maintenance of dramatic urgency; their delineation of character and their capacity to reflect nuances of emotion and ethical choice; their development of a dramatic vernacular language and a poetry which combined beauty with freedom; and their building of a popular as well as aristocratic audience—set a standard which continued to separate the British stage from the rest of Europe for two hundred years. Their influence survived the closing of the theaters by the Puritans and cast a spell over subsequent attempts to create native musical drama.

Ben Jonson had hopes of the Jacobean Court masque, pronouncing with somewhat shaky determination that they "either have been, or ought to be, the mirror of mans life." But by the time the masque fell away with the monarchy it had long since been shanghaied by its design department: Inigo Jones regarded masques as "nothing else but pictures with Light and Motion."[1] After the Restoration (and even a little before) there were some serious attempts to establish a native operatic activity—significantly dominated by musical versions of Shakespeare's plays. The enterprise reached its high point in the work of Purcell, who made a musico-dramatic work drawn from Spenser's "The Faerie Queene," coaxed an indifferent libretto from Nahum Tate for his masterpiece "Dido and Aeneas," and collaborated with the foremost poet of the day, John Dryden, on the Dramatick Opera "King Arthur." Purcell's early death in 1695 put an end to the English operatic initiative, and the way was open for the Italians.

When Italian opera—with Italian language, Italian musicians, Italian castrati, and soon the Italian-opera-writing of Handel—settled in London at the beginning of the eighteenth century, English men of letters, still aware of what language alone could achieve in the theater, were contemptuous of the constraints placed on it by music, and of the Italian solution to the problem of combining words and music on the stage. Swift castigated the "Italian effeminacy and Italian nonsense" of the opera, which he described as "wholly unsuitable to our Northern Climate, and to the Genius of the People." He talked of "the

Composer, who in setting a Song, changes the Words and Order so often, that he is forced to make it Nonsense before he can make it Musick." Addison echoed Swift: "Nothing is capable of being well set to Musick, that is not Nonsense." For Dr. Johnson, later in the century, opera was "an exotic and irrational entertainment."[2]

These carpings against Italian opera, and against the effect of music on words in general, can be dismissed as the ignorant response of largely unmusical literary men. But it was natural for them to see the modish passion of London society for the antics of the Italians as a betrayal of the English tongue—and therefore of the English writers themselves. Gay to Swift (1722): "There's nobody allow'd to say I sing but an Eunuch or an Italian Woman. Every body is grown now as great a judge of Musick as they were in your time of Poetry." Gay seems to have felt that there had been an actual displacement of the written word as a medium of emotional expression, and a wavering of confidence in native musical skill as a result of the florid vocal artistry of the Italians. The success of Gay's "The Beggar's Opera" in 1728 was due as much to its parody of Italian opera's formulae and its reliance on native singer-actors as to its political satire. The production is reputed to have put Handel temporarily out of business, and thenceforward the native bent for music theater in Britain found its expression in pieces which continued to be comedic or sentimental rather than dramatic or tragic, to feature actors who sang rather than singers who acted, and to tend towards parody and satire of the manners, acting and singing styles, standard plots, and repetitive conventions of Italian opera and its descendants.

The line of music theater development in English led from John Gay to Gilbert and Sullivan, and eventually to the contemporary Anglo-American musical. And through all these evolutions there has run a common thread: musical numbers alternate with spoken dialogue, and the sung words are as important as those that are spoken. The "Genius of the People," as reflected in their language, seems to have been unable to give up the dramatic gains that Shakespeare had won for it in the field of "lifelikeness" and in the entente that had been forged between sound and sense: the conventions of through-composed Italian opera (in which the music is continuous from beginning to end), with its characters singing their thoughts and intentions and feelings rather than speaking them, and with the demands of the music dominating the text and the plausibility of the dramatic action, were to the commonsense bulk of English audiences, as they were to Addison, an "absurdity." It made them laugh. Between Purcell's death and the beginning of the twentieth century, not a single serious work of opera by an English-speaking partnership achieved more than momentary fame, nor do any from that period feature now in the traditional repertoire of opera companies. Serious musicians took the lead from Handel's transfer of energies from opera to oratorio, and it was in these religious concert works, and in church music generally, that the most able British composers henceforward concentrated their vocal writing. The writer of Holy Writ is a generous furnisher of texts and untroublesome as a collaborator. Poets and novelists moved in other worlds.

The English language itself was frequently made the scapegoat for the aridity of British opera development. Its lack of pure open vowels in comparison with Italian, its strong plosives, its bunching of unvoiced consonants, and its lack of liquidity in *l* and *r* led to its being described as an unmusical language, a language ungrateful for the singer. It has even been said that the clear expression of the language actually gets in the way of the music: that English does not have the capacity of Italian to become a mere set of beautiful sounds because its sounds keep reflecting an emotional involvement in the meaning. The response of many singers trained in the Italian manner has been to make English sound like Italian: "Ah-ee weesh to ween yourr hearrt."

But the twentieth century has seen a remarkable change, which needs no documentation. The late Victorian revival of the theater as a vehicle for serious artistic activity, coupled with the gradual breakdown of Britain's musical insularity—caused to some extent by the phenomenon of Richard Wagner—set British composers once again dreaming of a native opera. There were two parallel processes at work. The primary goal was the development of the infrastructure necessary if Great Britain was belatedly to join the European operatic family—the building of financial support, the training of singers for the European repertoire, and the education of audiences. The secondary goal, believed by an impresario like Thomas Beecham (though not by any means by everyone) to be fundamental to the reaching of the first, was the creation of new English operas. As the pool of accomplished English operatic singers began to grow, and as the climate for subsidy slowly improved, there were occasional performances of new English works. Charles Stanford, Ethel Smyth, Frederick Delius, Rutland Boughton, Ralph Vaughan Williams, Gustav Holst, Arthur Benjamin, and Arthur Bliss all turned to the operatic form.

Now the old problem of opera's relationship with the English language began to reassert itself. Some composers, like Stanford and Boughton, brought to their work a post-Wagnerian perspective and aspired to cultural parity with the great operatic nations—in Boughton's case substituting Arthurian myth for Wagner's "Ring of the Nibelungs" and attempting to establish an English Bayreuth at Glastonbury in Dorset. Others, particularly Vaughan Williams, reopened the search for a British solution to the problem of words and music. Cecil Sharp's recent researches into British folksong had resurrected the idea that there was no fundamental reason why serious works of music theater could not be created from the English language, with the music of folksong as a base.

But it was finally in Benjamin Britten that for the first time since Henry Purcell a British composer emerged who systematically sought out the riches of English (and now American) literature—not only Shakespeare but John Donne, Wilfred Owen, George Crabbe, Herman Melville, Henry James, and many others—as a primary source. Britten inherited Vaughan Williams's regard for the English folksong, in which music and English words had evolved together; and in all his vocal settings he sought to find the same proper marriage of musical form with comprehensible language—language which was not merely an excuse for the music but which the music sought to reflect, interpret, and amplify.

But Britten went further. At the end of World War II, after the unexpected success at Sadler's Wells of his first full-scale opera "Peter Grimes" (based on an episode from George Crabbe's "The Borough"), the young composer combined with the dramatist and poet Ronald Duncan and the painter John Piper to bring together a select company of singers dedicated to the development of small-scale operas. Britten's experience during the protracted and unsatisfactory rehearsals of "Peter Grimes" had made him realize that the scale of such an opera, as of the great French, Italian, and German operas of the nineteenth century, was a powerful obstacle to the growth of national operatic activity in the twentieth. The lack of audience familiarity with new work and with modern musical idiom put producers at considerable financial risk, and the demands of a heavy production schedule constrained the careful development of new work. But Britten also believed in the creative possibilities of small-scale opera, with its opportunities for greater aural clarity of the text and for more intimate psychological revelation of character. He was reaching back, in fact, to the scale of seventeenth- and eighteenth-century opera, finding inspiration from Monteverdi and Purcell as much as from Verdi. The group's first production, "The Rape of Lucretia" (1946), with eight singers and twelve musicians, was an intense experiment—conceived, written, and rehearsed at Glyndebourne within the space of eight months. But its method of creation was of historic significance, suggesting a unique closeness of collaboration between librettist and composer.

Britten and librettist Ronald Duncan have both written about their work collaboration:

> With "The Rape of Lucretia" Britten and I worked at the same desk. We first discussed the shape of the whole drama and spent several days working over this in order to reduce it to its essential simplicity. . . . This done, we then divided the drama into two acts, each of two scenes. . . . Next, we made a synopsis of each scene and then proceeded to break this up into its appropriate musical forms: recitative, accompanied recitative, arias, and ensembles. . . .
>
> First we decided to write a vocal overture to be sung by the chorus. As soon as I had written this, Britten set it and played it over to me several times. Then we would pull it to pieces, cutting out two or three lines of verse here and putting in two or three there in order to improve the flow and coherence of the whole. . . . I found that he would rethink a phrase or a setting as willingly as I would rewrite a line.

So Ronald Duncan, engaged in his first libretto. And Britten:

> This "working together" of the poet and composer . . . seems to be one of the secrets of writing a good opera. . . . The composer and poet should at all stages be working in the closest contact, from the most preliminary stages right up to the first night. It was thus in the case of "The Rape of Lucretia."[3]

Duncan's libretto came in for heavy criticism, its particularities attracting attention partly because he was the first librettist for many years whose words could actually be heard in their entirety. But the quality of the work is not the issue here. It was Britten's intense interest in the power of language and in the interrelationship of words with music—in their equal weight and in the effects of their appropriate combination—that had established a whole new order of collaboration, in which writer and composer sat down together and worked as equal partners. At this time Britten still composed within the conventions of the Italian opera, making use of distinct recitative, arioso, and aria in the style of late Verdi, and balancing his solos, duets, and ensembles in the approved manner. But the logical consequence of his interest in language was a continued search, during the next quarter century, for new ways of shaping music to fit the words and the meaning of the words; and more and more he chose subjects for libretti which were not obviously "operatic" material in the Italian sense. The crowning surprise was his final full-scale opera (1973), which was based on an English translation of Thomas Mann's "Death In Venice"—a story larded with ambiguity, full of inner musing rather than external action, and entirely devoid of sharp dramatic confrontations.

The text was not adjusted in order to provide these traditional operatic requirements. On the contrary, it was the music which held back, reaching a different kind of entente with the subtleties of the text. Though resonant with emotion (suppressed and infertile within the character of Dr. Aschenbach but none the less ravaging for that), it is also perhaps the most profoundly intelligent musical score ever written for an opera: "he feels at each thread, and lives along the line." It is, among other things, about the struggle between ordered reason and uncontrollable feeling: the same relation, it could be said, as that of words to music.

What Britten did, in fact, was to search for a unified verbal-musical language which could reflect complexity, ambiguity, and nuance in thought and feeling. The direct expressive force of the Italian (and later French and German) operatic tradition, and of the flood of musical and artistic forms which sprang from it (among them the symphony and the concerto, the string quartet, the vocal concert, the oratorio, and even the ballet), is so commanding that it has not merely dominated Western musical practice but has been to some extent the very definition of it. In face of this it has been the tendency of other European and American national cultures to aspire to its qualities rather than to move in a different direction. Britten, brought up within the English culture and language with its behavioral mix of reason and feeling weighted quite differently, went his own way.

W. H. Auden was perhaps the first major English-writing poet since Dryden to have turned some of his attention to writing for the "serious" singing theater, and he had an opportunity to make a special contribution to the search for an "English solution." He translated several operas, and wrote a number of original libretti, most notably that of "The Rake's Progress" for Igor Stravinsky (1951). But Auden's espousal of opera was unabashed in its acceptance of music's predominance over text. He discovered opera late, he tells us, and it seems to have provided for him, in its music and spectacle, the kind of simple emotional release that the times did not encourage within his poetry, or indeed within the middle-class English society into which he was born. It was as though the genre rested his intellect, sanctified the final powerlessness of reason in the grip of passion. "The librettist need never bother his head, as the dramatist must, about probability. A credible situation in opera means a situation in which it is credible that someone should sing. . . . No good opera plot can be sensible, for people do not sing when they are feeling sensible."[4] This embracing of the implausible is common to many lovers of traditional opera, and—like the faith of religionists—it can be affirmed, not argued.

Gary Schmidgall, in his sharp and engaging study *Literature as Opera*, suggests that the world is divided "into two classes of people: those 'poor, passionless, blunt-minded creatures' (Stendhal's words) who dislike opera, and those to whom it comes naturally and who subject themselves as willingly to its absurdities as to its compelling expressive powers."[5] Auden belonged to this second class.

But those who feel antipathy to traditional opera late in our century are not always running away from its primal emotions or dismissing its uncertain logic. They react too, some of them, to the social context that traditional opera seems to require, to a scale of presentation they find too obtrusively lavish to convey the intimacy of psychological truth; to the egos of prima donnas, to the wearying talk of aficionados comparing Miss A's B flat to Miss M's, and to the assumption that the grandness of grand opera is an inalienable element of the form. Opera in the late twentieth century, not only on the continent of Europe but now also in Great Britain and North America, is a fine old party for the opera aesthete. And the excitement of new creation, of fresh insights expressed in new ways, is rarely a part of the operatic experience.

Auden in his happy espousal of all things operatic seems to have been able to thrust this context aside. His creating and translating of libretti gave him the opportunity to exercise his poetic craftsmanship: exceptional rhythmic gifts and linguistic erudition, but also considerable powers of parody in both style and language. There was always an element of pastime, of playfulness, even of pastiche, in this area of his work, as though his vocation as a poet were taking a holiday. The main purpose of verses composed by a librettist, he wrote, is to suggest a melody to the composer: "once that is over, they are as expendable as infantry to a Chinese general."[6] No grudges against such fun, but it is hard not to see it very much in the tradition of libretto-writing as I described it at the outset, and very much estranged from the possibilities opened up by Benjamin Britten. When asked once why he wrote libretti, Auden replied that he did so because they were "the last refuge of the High style."[7] But when high style is whimsically adopted—in any field—it may not be pitching itself so very far from Isherwood's High Camp. And the old operatic warhorses, with their gorgeousness, strained credibility, and gestured emotion, tend to wear similar colors.

Auden defined opera as "an imitation of human willfulness": "it is rooted in the fact that we not only have feelings, but insist upon having them at whatever cost to ourselves."[8] But the emotional directness of opera, I would maintain, is not so much endemic to its form as it is the result of its Mediterranean origin, where dramatic gesture is a part of speech, and where the habit of full-throated, unconsidered emotional response is deeply engrained. The Italian temperament seems to slide easily from tragedy to comedy, and the display of emotional stress tends to drive nuances of feeling underground. Auden maintains that "opera cannot present character in the novelist's sense of the word, namely people who are good *and* bad, active *and* passive."[9] But why not? Opera's emotionally one-dimensional characters derive as much from the uniquely Italian melodrama of emotional display, from the commedia dell'arte tradition with its wagonload of familiar archetypal characters, and from the propagandist courtly origins of Italian opera as from the essential effect of music upon them.

Auden, one of the most gifted English-writing poets of midcentury, and with a foot in both Britain and America, had the chance to make a new path for the singing theater: to take advantage of the twentieth century's developments in both poetry and music, and to rethink the potential relationship between them in "serious"—intellectually as well as emotionally challenging—works of singing theater. In the war years he actually collaborated with Britten on the operetta "Paul Bunyan," a strange but vigorous piece of British-Americanism written for Columbia University and performed there in 1941. But Britten withdrew the work from circulation until late in his life: the partnership was not a happy one. A pity, because in the enterprise of making a new concordat between music and the English language, which has spluttered along in the postwar years, this supremely talented team could have made a spectacular contribution.

Unlike Auden, Britten for all his musical conservatism was stimulated by the fresh creative possibilities in "serious" music theater, readily adjusting musical structure to the implications of language while still calling for virtuoso gifts from his singers and working within the operatic tradition and infrastructure. Since before his death in 1976, British and American composers in increasing numbers and with growing skill have pursued the form of singing theater, taking advantage of the freedom that has come both from a lack of national tradition as well as from the general break-up of musical conventions in form and tonality. As early as 1928 (and again in 1947) Virgil Thomson brought his highly individual musical gifts to bear on texts by his friend Gertrude Stein. Some composers, like the complexly intelligent Michael Tippett and (in a more simplistically theatrical vein) Gian-Carlo Menotti, have created their own libretti; while the majority, like so many composers before them, continue despairingly to seek out the services of writers who will provide them with words.

At the commercial end of the spectrum, the American musical, especially in the early work of Leonard Bernstein and more recently in the creations of composer-librettist Stephen Sondheim, is occasionally bursting out of its Broadway conventions, presenting works which in form and intensity, if not in disinterested seriousness of intention, are close to through-composed opera: Sondheim's "Sweeney Todd" and "Sunday in the Park With George" are prime examples. Britain's highly successful commercial musicals, on the other hand, seem to have reverted to the world of Inigo Jones, offering high-decibel "pictures with Light and Motion." Leading subsidized theaters in Britain are also embracing the form of music theater with productions of large scale and dramatic power like "Les Misérables." Nonetheless, the gap between the opera world, with its virtuoso singers who are increasingly being required to act, and the world of the theater, with its actors whose vocal skills are sometimes defiantly unmusical, remains to be bridged. And stage directors who straddle both worlds are not able to make them one.

The last years of the century will show whether these various English-speaking and English-singing initiatives will be able to bring their forces together to create a genuinely new beginning for the art of the singing theater. Their capacity to do so will depend on the interest of operatically trained singers in becoming contemporary and thinking artists. But it will also depend on the readiness of writers of great gifts to join with similarly endowed composers in the pursuit of that elusive collaborative language of expression, English words and music working together, which might yet reflect the "Genius of the People."

Notes

1. These comments by Jonson and Jones were first put illuminatingly side by side by Stephen Orgel in his book *The Jonsonian Masque* (Cambridge, Mass., 1967), p. 3.

2. These more or less celebrated remarks by Johnson, Swift, and Addison are quoted by Gary Schmidgall in his chapter on Handel in *Literature as Opera* (Oxford, 1977).

3. "The Rape of Lucretia," a symposium by Benjamin Britten, Ronald Duncan, John Piper, Henry Boys, Eric Crozier, and Angus McBean (London, 1948) pp. 64–65, 8.

4. W. H. Auden, "Notes on Music and Opera," in *The Dyer's Hand* (London, 1963), p. 471.

5. Schmidgall, *Literature as Opera*, p. 10.

6. Auden, *The Dyer's Hand*, p. 473.

7. Auden was quoting himself; see his lecture "The World of Opera," in *Secondary Worlds* (London, 1968), p. 102.

8. Auden, *The Dyer's Hand*, p. 470.

9. Auden, *The Dyer's Hand*, p. 470.

～ PAUL MULDOON

The Key
A Prose Poem

I RAN INTO FOLEY SIX MONTHS AGO in a dubbing-suite in Los Angeles. He was halfway through postproduction on a remake of *The Hoodlum Priest*, a film for which I've a special affection since my cousin, Marina McCall, was an extra in the first version. She worked as a nanny for various movie stars, including Tippi Hedren, and seemed to spend half her time in the sky between New York and L.A. Though I sat through three or four showings of *The Hoodlum Priest* in the Olympic Cinema, Moy, and carefully scrutinized the crowd-scenes, I was never able to point to Marina with anything like conviction.

Foley was working on a sequence involving a police lineup, in which the victim shuffled along, stopped with each suspect in turn, then shuffled on. At a critical moment, she dropped a key on the floor. Foley was having trouble matching sound to picture on this last effect. I was struck by the fact that, just as early radio announcers had worn dinner jackets, he was wearing an ultramarine tuxedo. After half a dozen attempts, he decided to call it quits, and emerged from his sound-booth like a diver from a bathyscope. He offered me a tidbit that tasted only of mesquite.

I wanted to say something about Marina, something about an "identity-parade" in which I once took part, something about the etymology of "tuxedo," but I found myself savoring the play between "booth" and "bathy-," "quits" and "mesquite," and I began to "mis-quote" myself;

> *When he sookied a calf down a boreen*
> *it was through Indo-European.*
> *When he clicked at a donkey carting dung*
> *your grandfather had an African tongue.*
> *You seem content to ventriloquize the surf.*

Foley swallowed whatever it was;

> *Still defending the same old patch of turf?*
> *Have you forgotten that "hoodlum" is back-slang*
> *for the leader of a San Francisco street gang?*

He flounced off into his cubicle. Though this, our only exchange, was remarkable for its banality, Foley has had some profound effect on me. These past six months I've had occasion to run a little ahead of myself, but mostly I lag behind, my footfalls already preempted by their echoes.

ↄ PAUL LENTI

Boffo Goes International

WHEN THE STOCK MARKET PLUMMETED in October 1987, a headline on Variety's front page brought a nostalgic smile to most readers: "WALL STREET LAYS AN EGG: THE SEQUEL."

Reading like a title from one of the many motion picture sequels chronicled on the inside pages, the words recall the paper's most w.k. and oft-quoted banners, penned during Variety's linguistic heyday when it was rife with slanguage and original coinages. The other most quoted head in Variety appeared in 1935: "STICKS NIX HICK PIX," noting that rural audiences disdained corny country films.

Variety's lex appeal and raffish prose proved as natural to the showbiz industry as the lifestyle of those who worked in it. But to keep in step with the indomitable march of time, one must follow the changes of its rhythm and tempo.

Bowing to the current global crossover of the entertainment industry, Variety editors now tell their reporters to write copy "so every reader, including those for whom English may not be the first language, will have no trouble understanding it." Such advice seems a drastic change from when legiter George Bernard Shaw confided to Bennett Cerf in 1938: "I thought I knew the English language, until one day I saw Variety in a friend's home. Upon my soul, I didn't understand a word of it. I subscribed at once."

In his classic study "The American Language," H. L. Mencken

wrote that the "barbaric (but thoroughly American) jargon of Variety
. . . developed a dialect all its own" whose vocabulary and syntax
were "so bizarre" that they "attracted much attention from students
of national language." But those days were numbered.

When I began writing as a foreign correspondent for Variety in
1983, the rampant use of Varietyese was already in decline. Although
accepted Variety terms and abbreviations still peppered periodical
pages, a Variety stylebook of the time stressed that "clarity is the first
law" and further added: "There is positively no objection to proper
English." The latest stylebook even allows use of the long-taboo word
movie, a perennial no-no for staffers and space stringers. Indeed, vet-
eran reporter/critic Joe Cohen (Jose.) noted in the 1988 82d Variety
anni: "A regretful step (I think) was the decision to make the paper
more readable to foreigners by toning down on Varietyese. But then
some of the newer staff members would have to take a course on the
language used in the paper. It wouldn't have been the same so Varietyese will be confined to treatises written by scholars, based on ancient issues."

This is not one of those treatises. Rather, its backward glance is a
chance to probe some of the verbal shorthand and special buzzwords
and terms that comprise the currently accepted Variety style.

Since its founding in 1905, so many terms coined or made popular
in the pages of Variety have been incorporated into the native American vocab that most people are unaware of their origins. The unof-
ficial rule went: whenever a Variety reporter didn't know how to spell
a word, he invented a new one. Just consider a list of common words
or expressions that first saw print in Variety: platter (for record), big
time, vamp, payola, payoff, pushover, blockbuster, freeloader, disc
jockey, deejay, emcee, cliffhanger, whodunit, soap opera, demo, inside stuff, looker (for beauty), corny, hick, oldie, passion pit, belly-
laff, hoofer.

Bad spellers, indeed! It was a fun showbiz approach to otherwise
serious and at times tedious tasks. It eschewed the cuteness and rave
of fanzines. When film p.r. reps puffed their product, Variety let out
the air.

You need to catch only one of the many tv, mag, or newspaper film
critics today to hear how many Variety terms perk their copy. Variety's slightly cynical edge created a reviewing style that set the mode
for tube and type.

Founder Sime Silverman (Sime.) believed that the paper should be
written in the colorful language that showbiz people spoke. He was
joined by other like-minded reporters such as Jack Conway (Con.), a
former streetcar conductor, who brought with him an earthy par-

lance. He introduced palooka, scram, click, bimbo, gams, and s.a. (sex appeal).

Paper's 2d editor Abel Green (Abel.) also had a flair for his own vox pop. In one of the paper's anni editions he penned his guide to Varietyese:

> Modified simplified spelling is Style, viz., cigaret, brunet, soubret, but not thru, tho, nor even $15-Mil., or Time-style $2 million; all ciphers are preferred in $15,000,000 and $2,000,000, excepting where headwriting sometimes compels the contractions. Autobiog, prez, veepee are run-of-the-mine usages.

Although necessity may be the mother of invention, per Green, "convenience coins many words."

In Variety, verbs are given new functions. Editors and writers frequently make verbs out of nouns: to ink, to bankroll, to premier (or preem), to showcase, to pact, to lens, to opinion, and to unspool (to screen a film). Verb phrases become simple verbs: to ready, to siesta, and to plane (at times "to TWA").

Nouns are contracted, stretched, abbreviated, synonyms invented: distribs, exhibs, b.o. (box office), vaulties (films kept off tv), pics (and its variations vidpic, biopic, telepic, etc.). Coin replaces money. The same rule that produced eatery, nitery, and scripter (scriptwriter), sparks diskery (record company), distribbery (distribution firm), and cabler (tv cable franchise owner).

Some Variety terms have come and gone. Seldom seen in print these days are: whisperlow (speakeasy), out-fronters (audience), hand-to-hand music (applause), hoofologist (dancer), silo circuit (vaudeville farm circuit), 88er (pianist), and the long-outlawed "megger" for director (from megaphone), which went out of style with talkies, circa 1927.

Other terms are in active use but seldom seen outside Variety pages: ozoner (drive-in movie) vs. hardtop (indoor cinema), to ankle (depart), chopsocky (martial arts pic), oats opera or oater (western), mitting (applause), bird (satellite), web or net (tv network), kidvid or kideo (children's videos), nsg (not so good), w.k. (well-known), o.o. (once over).

Some famous heads include: BLIZ BOFFS BUFF (about a sudden snowstorm in Buffalo), PITT CAUGHT WITH ITS PLANTS DOWN (when unseasonal heat caught Pittsburgh exhibs without their cooling systems), MOOLA FOLLOWS HULA AS 50TH STATE JUMPS (about the tourism influx following Hawaii's statehood), and HIP NIP IN HUB (concerning a Japanese pianist in Boston, in a less racially sensitive period). One Variety

head is so w.k. that when former Soviet rep to the UN Andrei Gro-
myko met a Variety correspondent, he is reported to have asked: "Is
it true that rural audiences continue to spurn pictures about country
life?"

At times, Variety practices a reverse showmanship, its tongue in its
cheek. When every major Yank newspaper carried banner headlines
about the marriage of Monaco's Prince Rainier to Grace Kelly, Variety
buried the item in its back pages in a list of other marriages: "Married:
Grace Kelly, actress, to Prince Rainier III, non-pro." Likewise, when
Kelly's daughter Princess Caroline got married, the item simply mentioned that her mother was an actress and her father operated a gambling casino. The marriage of President Reagan's and Jane Wyman's
son prompted: "Parents are former film actors."

Showbiz took delight in Variety's pop prose. Joe Cohen noted that
"many have the suspicion that some of the most outrageous typos that
found their way into Variety were deliberately devised by some impish
printers. One of the worst came when a vital letter was left out of
Count Basie's first name. But probably the most eyebrow-raising and
causing the most laughter was the one which had Bing Crosby stop-
ping off in Pittsburgh 'for a few lays.'"

Variety writers (formerly muggs) are proudly conscious of the paper's slanguage tradition and its trickle-down effect on the entertainment community. Besides linguists, many staffers have written their
own reflections on Variety lingo. Both Conway and Green authored
pieces. Madrid bureau chief Peter Besas (Besa.) even penned a frequently reprinted Variety glossary, which was later made into an in-
house promo poster. It still proves to be a valuable guide to both readers and new staffers.

With a current emphasis on corporate ownership of major studios,
showbiz has gone bigbiz: its fortunes and misadventures are now
charted on the financial pages of the Wall Street Journal along with the
Dow Jones Industrial Average. Millions are spent in anticipation of
more millions to be made. International and industry crossover is the
name of the game. In the motion picture industry alone, even before
the first foot of celluloid is exposed, the ink is already dry on a plethora
of contracts: an original soundtrack disk and CD are in preparation
and accords concerning foreign distrib rights, licensing of spinoff
merchandise including perhaps a novelization, t-shirts, toys, coffee
mugs, etc., and followup sales for homevid, cable, and broadcast tv
are all in the works.

But this was not the world that greeted Sime Silverman back in
1905, when Variety preemed at Gotham newsstands with a sixteen-

page tabloid that cost a nickel. It boasted an editorial staff of four, headed by Sime, who founded the paper with a $1,500 loan from his father-in-law. His own dad disapproved of vaudevillians.

As a vaude critic for the New York Morning Telegraph, Sime had been fired when he panned an act that later withdrew its holiday ad. The paper he founded would not yield to ad interests. Even today a display ad touting some pic's global appeal can be found facing a review stating that said film stinks like last week's fish. It took many a legit battle and lost ad coin to maintain this independence.

The name itself has proven adaptable. When the paper was founded, it originally covered the then-booming vaudeville circuit. Sime shrewdly chose the British moniker "variety" as the title, which Stateside incorporated most other forms of entertainment. His wife Hattie, known to readers as "The Skirt," drew up the present logo with its characteristic "V" on a nightclub tablecloth, and little has changed in the format since.

As the paper is proud of noting, at that time "radio as a form of entertainment did not yet exist, tv hadn't been invented and film had just begun its commercial life." In fact, Broadway in 1905 referred to the area in Gotham somewhere between Union Square and 28th Street, and the chief West Coast venue was San Francisco.

When Hollywood later became the base of the motion picture industry, Sime founded Variety's Tinseltown sister publication, Daily Variety.

Besides Variety's special lingo, many of its other inventions have also become standards. The world's first film review appeared in Variety on 19 January 1907. Variety also printed the first gossip column, first radio review, first tv criticism, etc. Sime himself discovered such pre-star figures as Charlie Chaplin, Jimmy Durante, and Buster Keaton.

Variety staffers and stringers are expected to write for all sections, from reporting to obits. No one has ever come on the staff as a critic. Reviewing is always on the side, which accounts for the wide range of styles and quality. Reviews are geared as to how well a pic is expected to clean up at world wickets, either bullish or offish. Instead of bylines, reviewers use signatures, three- or four-letter coded initials, referred to by former managing editor Robert J. Landry (Land.) as "the dogtags of the critical troops." The tradition began with Sime (Sime.) and continues today.

After moving to New York, I discovered Variety's former Gotham digs were as ancient as its layout—the antique typewriters would have been more at home in the Smithsonian. Going to the cramped quarters of the sixteen-foot-wide five-story walkup, located on West 46th

Street in the heart of the Theater District, was like visiting the newsroom in the original (1931) version of "The Front Page." On the top floor was Sime's former legendary "whisperlow," where the booze flowed freely during the prohibition era.

It was a family biz in the old sense. Every writer cut his own deal with Syd, Sime's grandson and current publisher, in terms of salary and raises. The paper was owned and operated by the Silverman family for over eighty years.

In July 1987 staffers learned through the morning papers that Variety had been sold. The new owners, Cahners Publishing Co., noted that even though the paper would undergo changes, the spirit would always remain the same, which would have pleased Sime. Variety has become an American showbiz tradition, after all.

The old Variety haunt with all its legends and memories was left to the wrecking ball, succumbing to the Times Square renovation project, while the office moved into a new glass-skinned tower on P.A.S. (Park Ave. S.).

Syd and former managing editor Frank Meyer summed up the move simply and succinctly: "Variety Ankles Great White Way."

The weekly tabloid received a new look at the end of 1988 that included color, pix, and previously unheard of white space. Even the size had changed. The spellcheck on staffers' new word processors had to be reprogrammed to accept wammo, powwow, and prexy. Boffo had not only gone international but thoroughly modern as well.

Lent.

~ WALTER J. ONG

Subway Graffiti
and the Design of the Self

AS AN ACTIVITY AND AN IDEOLOGY, writing tangles itself through our conscious and unconscious life. In high-technology society writing is so necessary that minimum skills in its use are enforced on all by public law. However, although writing is thus democratized by statute, it also provides a route to elite standing. Writing improves you, makes you upwardly mobile in all sorts of occupations. Being a more or less professional writer gives you a certain distinction. Association with writing is validated and strengthened by writers' clubs and writers' guilds and by complementary associations of readers in all sorts of book clubs. Our chronic bemoaning of inadequate writing skills in society at large attests to our pervasive writing ideology.

Subway graffiti artists are not commonly thought of as a group caught up in writing ideology. And yet, in curious ways, they are, as is evident from Craig Castleman's book of a few years ago, *Getting Up: Subway Graffiti in New York.*[1]

The reflections I here set down (in writing) are based on the con-

---

Editors' note: On 12 May 1989, after this essay was written, the New York City Transit Authority took its last graffiti-covered train out of service. The city's massive effort to clean up its subway system curiously confirms the points made in this essay: by wiping away graffiti almost as soon as they appear, the Transit Authority has thwarted the very motivation behind graffiti art that Professor Ong describes—that is, the persistent testimony to the graffiti artist's existence.

ditions in the period on which Castleman so thoroughly reports, a period which produced the overwhelmingly marked-up trains that climaxed the graffiti work familiar to millions. Though the graffiti artists are not quite so omnipresent as they were a few years ago, they are still around.

All who have ridden the subways know that the graffiti artists can paint a lot of pictures. They have to do their work mostly at night in the yards and lay-ups where subway trains are stored, which they enter by climbing over walls or through holes in fences, or by vaulting over gates. Castleman notes that the graffiti artists come "from every race, nationality, and economic group in New York City" (p. 67). Almost all of them male and between eleven and sixteen years of age, they are engaged in a form of puberty rite, courting danger to prove their emergent adulthood.[2]

Commoner than their pictures and designs, but less specialized, is the writing of the graffiti artists. Even though they produce the cartoonlike and sometimes surrealistic paintings that can cover the outside of whole cars and even whole trains, they refer to themselves, surprisingly, not as artists or painters but as "writers." The origins of this term appear clear enough: the graffiti of these young New Yorkers were at first simply their written names (normally pseudonyms). But the name "writers" persists even for those who do mostly painting.

Speaking of the work he composed with four others, which included massive amounts of creative pictures and designs "to make this train beautiful," Bama (his pseudonym) states, "It was fun . . . that's the beauty of the writing" (p. 51). Both the writers themselves and others associate the graffiti work with art, and some "writers" also paint on canvas and seek recognition as "serious" artists (p. 71). Occasionally more formal organizations have sprung up with names such as United Graffiti Artists (p. 117). All the more striking that the term "writers," at least through the time that Castleman reports on, has kept firm possession of the field. The writers have set up what they call "writers' corners" in subway stations, strategic points at which they can gather to check their own and other writers' work on trains roaring by. Writers use politico-social or merely trendy mottoes or messages and at times work with themes (Christmas, for example), but their basic aim is to get their own names or "tags" up in public as often and as spectacularly as possible (hence Castleman's title, *Getting Up*). A work is done in order to make known who did it.

Naming is pivotal to the writer's identity. Writers' names have "meant something to them," Bama states. "Tabu, he liked the name Tabu, like it meant danger. . . . Sweet Duke. His nickname was Duke and he thought he was sweet. . . . Lee, his name was Lee" (p. 72)—a real name but common enough to serve the purposes of a pseudonym. If the name is associated with a gorgeous painting the writer has done, all the better. Writers may switch names from time to time for various reasons, even using long names for larger paintings or "pieces" (p. 75) and reserving their short names for "throw-ups," their relatively unadorned pseudonymic signatures. But the painter is still a "writer," no matter what, and it is the individual's inscribed name in one form or another that is crucial to the graffiti work.

What counts most is the number of times a writer gets his (or, more rarely, her) tag up. Often the name may be accompanied by a message, such as "I'm Lover Lee, Can't You See" (p. 90), but the name alone suffices. The work done by these writers is obviously a means of achieving some sort of sense of self in a mass, high-technology society that uses lettered words in public displays for all sorts of purposes. The writers really want to call public attention to themselves individually. Style is desirable because of what it does for names: it is a way of "making your name sing" (p. 53).

But usually not your real name, for this could bring a call from the police. The true reference of the pseudonyms the writers use is known throughout their own world but seldom elsewhere. Most New Yorkers I have quizzed seem not to know even of the existence of the writers' culture. The distinctive art styles and the ubiquity of the graffiti simply leave them puzzled. "Work of crazy kids," they mutter.

Writers' activity puts them in danger with the law, not only because they deface property on a heroic scale but also because most writers operate on the principle that all markers and paint they use in writing must be stolen or, as they put it, "racked up" (pp. 46–48, 110). One reason writers retire around the age of sixteen is that they fear being charged as adults with criminal activity (p. 67). Racking up can become a large-scale operation—in fact, for many projects it must become large-scale. The most spectacular operation of a writer, his highest achievement, is unbelievably elaborate: doing a "whole train," covering the outside of every car end to end and top to bottom with diagrams and cartoonlike portraits and scenes, the writer's name in letters peeping out here and there or blaring out in huge and decorative designs. All this work writers manage furtively, at night, in a lay-up lighted only by their hand lamps.

For less prolific writers, racking up paint and color markers is more restrained. There is a certain drive to keep one's pseudonym short, for a short name can be "got up" more quickly. But you must not go too far, lest your work be derided as a "toy," a term which is the common designation of anything inconsequential—including crude performers. Apparently to get up more quickly, one writer adopted the pseud-

onym "IN"—four strokes which could be got through in four light-
ninglike continuous movements. IN was so phenomenally successful
in getting his name up that his initially "toy" name was redeemed by
his tremendous industry, and he earned the respect of other writers by
his sheer quantitative achievement (pp. 20, 61–64). Few names could
match his for ubiquity.

Except for "Pray." Pray, it was commonly believed among writers
interviewed by Castleman, was a woman, possibly an eighty-eight-
year-old woman (pp. 77, 82–83). She got up her name (in this case the
exhortation "Pray" or, alternatively, at times "Worship God") typically not in subways but in telephone booths. Although other writers
are vague about her identity, they agree she is no "toy." With her name
appearing in thousands of telephone booths, Pray is in competition
with those doing whole trains. The name is the bottom line.

II

The social and psychological significance of the subway writers' behavior is of course manifold, as Castleman and the authors in his bib-
liography have demonstrated. Here I should like to consider how that
behavior reveals a sense of self that is related to writing (and print).
The public display of one's picture or statue or bust as a means of making one's presence felt goes back to antiquity. One thinks of the Cae-
sars, of Hitler or Mussolini or Stalin, of any number of political figures today, even of Colonel Sanders. But the public display of one's
pseudonymic signature in multiple copies is something else and, in the
dimensions which it has reached in the case of the subway writers,
something new.

Individuals have of course long scratched all sorts of markings on
boulders, cliffs, tree trunks, public monuments, and other objects as a
way of asserting or memorializing themselves publicly. The term
"graffiti" itself has long been used to refer to such "scratchings" (the
Italian *graffiare* means to scratch or, in drawing, to hatch or cross-
hatch—it does not refer exclusively or directly to writing as such).
Graffiti consisting of all sorts of things from mysterious symbolic designs or human or animal figures to lettered words are known from
prehistoric times. But the use of lettered names for public street identification even of one's place of business—for example, "F. W. Wool-
worth Company"—dates only from the eighteenth century.[3] Before
that, emblematic symbols (of which our barber's pole and pawnbro-
kers' three balls are relics) had been the common public identifying
marks for locales of particular activities or for particular materials or
objects. In addition, alchemists, who were generally literate, used

iconographic signs rather than lettered words for marking their phar-
macopoeia, as astrologers or astronomers did in identifying celestial
bodies.[4]

Now this old symbolic world has gone, or has gone underground.
When a logo is used today, its meaning is usually indicated in lettered
words (for example, by the company's or product's name). The power
is largely in the alphabetic letter rather than in the iconographic symbol. With the growth of display advertising in print, letters have been
exhibited more and more as pictures; and with the more precipitate
rise of television advertising they have ultimately been made into mobile performers and put through all sorts of contortions. A new kind
of visual rhetoric has been created out of text, treating letters of the
alphabet themselves as physical entities, even mobile physical entities.
Identifying themselves with lettered names rather than with iconographic symbols, the subway writers belong in the modern public textual world.

And of course they also belong in the world of display advertising:
they want to display and advertise themselves individually; their tags
are like merchandise labels. A writer will say, "Look at my name," one
of them reports. "It's like they've got their own TV show" (p. 79).
The subway writers' work—like advertising—is also a contest, a game
that is won by "getting up" the most. But it is also a game that involves the real-life danger of getting caught by the police. Subway
writers must disguise themselves at the same time that they advertise
themselves—and they add to the danger by doing so in *writing*. In the
best Heideggerian tradition, writing here both reveals and conceals. A
portrait of oneself would reveal too much—to the police and perhaps
to others.

These writers are indeed writers, despite their often evident expertise in designing and painting. What they want to get up is letters of
the alphabet identified with themselves. Personal literate identity is
crucial in this youthful writers' world. As a writer known as Wicked
Gary put it: "Writing your name identifies who you are. The more
you write your name [in public, conspicuously], the more you begin
to think about and the more you begin to be about who you are. Once
you start doing that, you start to assert your individualism and when
you do that, you have an identity" (p. 76). In earlier cultures, no ideology such as this initiated the identity quests of heroes or of any
others.

III

In a way, insofar as it is a marking system, there is nothing new about
the subway writers' activity, even at the biological level.[5] Many ani-

mals mark their territory, not to perpetuate their memory for future generations but rather to establish operational proprietary rights. Human beings, on the other hand, have long wished to commemorate themselves in permanent public display, to preserve their identity in some way against the ravages of time and death. The subway writers undoubtedly participate in this common human urge. But for them the urge is filtered through the patterns of mass communications: lots of copies of the same thing everywhere to gain a foothold with the "public."

What is interesting here is the persistence of the term "writers," even for those who paint whole trains. Fame is achieved by text. The stability of this term gives curious and valuable evidence of the way literacy has soaked through our culture—more directly and widely and deeply, I am convinced, in the United States than in any other part of the world ever. (Chinese character writing has certainly as deeply penetrated Chinese culture, but not so widely or directly in the sense that only a relatively small fraction of the people have ever had the leisure to learn the intricacies of this system, conspicuously elitist as compared to the alphabet.) If I am a subway writer, my lettered tag, written by me, is my identity as even a self-portrait is not. My writing can actually represent my own inner self, my person, my free action, as no portrait can. Signatures, not pictures, certify personal identity on checks, forms, and legal documents. The lettered name on the container of a product tells what the product truly is. The contents often cannot be seen (as the interior self cannot) or, even if they can be seen, you may well learn more from the tag than from looking at the product.

The value our culture puts on literacy has subtly, if not always very effectively, penetrated the sensibility even of those who are not personally committed to literacy, such as the subway writers. These writers are much more than simply writers and individually may or may not be literate in any programmatic sense. In saying that the literate mindset has penetrated them and our entire culture, I do not mean to deny that in many ways (not in all ways) lack of adequate literacy is a problem in the United States as elsewhere and that we must intensify the teaching of reading and writing. I am speaking of the mindset, largely subconscious or unconscious, that feels writing as a very personal expression, connected not merely with conveying information but also intimately with the revelation of one's self. "Me Tarzan, you Jane." A spoken word is a cry. For the subway writer the self is no longer represented directly this way, by a personal voice, a cry, but through a secondary coding system which is visual—that is, through writing. I do not mean to deplore this situation—literacy does not destroy but raises oral consciousness—but merely to point it out.

What kind of self emerges in these tags? The question is discouragingly complicated—it involves the entire history of consciousness, personal and social—and cannot be answered here in any fullness at all. Here we can note simply that it is a self seeking recognition, as all selves do. But it is not always an entirely moral or responsible self. Many graffiti writers consider their writing a public service, beautifying the city. Yet they also consider themselves to be "master outlaws" (p. 76). In 1973, cleaning up the defaced cars cost the Metropolitan Transit Authority (ultimately the riders of subways) $2.7 million (p. 149). Certainly at one level defacing property and "racking up" color markers and paint relate to the risk-taking and condoned outlawry that puberty rites involve. But they also relate to the public advertising world, which seems to be a model universe for subway writers and which appears to many people generally as morally unconcerned. With their tags, the writers are thinking of and advertising themselves, willy-nilly, as amoral merchandise. Achievement of personal identity is assimilated to sales promotion.

Something psychologically very complex is going on in the world of these writers, merging the self and public writing (goodbye to the private writing found in diaries) and mingling writing with massive and spectacular drawings and paintings. Here realization of the self is pursued through the hype externalism of much public advertising. Seeking to break through the kind of impersonality that our high-tech culture creates (other cultures all have their own ways of depersonalizing), the writers find themselves using high-tech methods. 'Twas ever thus. In the *Phaedrus* Plato denounced writing in writing.

Writing, as we all know, both reveals and conceals (as, indeed, spoken verbalization does in its different ways). But the dialectic of revealing and concealing here has special accents because of the need for anonymity enforced by the illegal cast of the "writers'" activity. Furthermore, the advertising hype in which the writers' world is caught up and which can entail the use of assertive visual illustration, enforces a peculiar mix of revealing and concealing—a mix that has yet to be properly examined.

Deep within ourselves, we all know this world in which the subway writers live, or we should. Their problems are our problems writ large. We live in the same high-tech culture and must use high-tech methods, too. We can sense the urges at work in them and can enter empathetically into the writers' world even without fully analyzing it or understanding it. Perhaps a little more historical reflection about the psychic and social universe underlying this curiously conditioned cult of self might help us all to discern better the human forces at play and the issues at stake in our whole culture.

Notes

1. Craig Castleman, *Getting Up: Subway Graffiti in New York* (Cambridge, Mass., 1982). References are included in the text.

2. Like many male puberty-rite participants, the graffiti artists display a certain misogyny to counter their own sexual insecurity. See Castleman, pp. 69, 121, and my *Fighting for Life: Contest, Sexuality, and Consciousness* (Ithaca, 1981).

3. See Jacob Larwood and John Camden Hotten, *The History of Signboards: From the Earliest Times to the Present Day* (London, 1900), pp. 30–31.

4. See Frances Yates, *The Art of Memory* (Chicago, 1966).

5. See Ong, *Fighting*, pp. 55–61.

ᔧ JOHN HOLLANDER

Now and Then

Then, we were our originals, and then
We will be whatever it is to be:
Now is the moment of our mirror when
Our own seeing is part of what we see.

The middle of our moment plays both ends
Until that symmetry must be undone
And the old game of those opposing *thens*
           Now is won.

Rectitudes

Wheresoever manners and fashions are corrupted,
language is. It imitates the public riot.
BEN JONSON

The English (it must be owned) are rather
a foul-mouthed nation.
WILLIAM HAZLITT

What a difficult language the English (said an Italian to
Capt. Pasley)—4 words all pronounced the same /
Ship, Sheep, Chip, Cheap.
SAMUEL TAYLOR COLERIDGE

First the adjectives wither, then the verbs.
ELIAS CANETTI

ᕙ ROY HARRIS

Lars Porsena Revisited

FUTURE HISTORIANS OF THE ENGLISH LANGUAGE will undoubtedly look back on the 1980s as a notable decade, if only for its lively contributions to the longest-lived sociolinguistic controversy in the history of the British Isles: the vexed question of "bad language."

This perennial debate has now been running nonstop as a colorful feature of the British way of life at least since the days of Chaucer. It shows no signs of flagging. On the contrary, during the past ten years bad language has made the headlines in the United Kingdom with increasing frequency. The decade began promisingly with the first "swearing strike" in the annals of industry (when, in 1982, the workforce at the British Leyland factory in Oxford downed tools as a protest against swearwords used by the management staff) and in the same year there was the official banning of the verb *fuck* as "unparliamentary language" in the House of Commons. But its two most momentous landmarks were certainly the attempt to prevent the broadcasting of Tony Harrison's poem *v.* on Channel 4 television in 1987, and the swearing which, a month later, brought a Test match to a halt for the first time in the history of cricket.

Poetry and cricket are both litmus-paper areas of British culture, and episodes of this significance deserve more detailed documentation both by lexicologists and by sociologists than can be attempted here. What was of particular relevance in both cases, as an indication of the state of the language, was the form the arguments took. It is this aspect of these controversies which will be singled out for attention below.

Some preliminary terminological questions must first be addressed. The fact—and it is a very relevant fact for the issues under discussion—is that current British metalinguistic usage is here in a state of considerable confusion. Nowadays terms such as *swearword, taboo word, oath, obscenity, profanity,* and *expletive* are often used as if they were synonymous. Furthermore, although there is much talk of *four-letter words* it takes little investigation to discover that people disagree as to which words these are, and even whether they all have four letters. (For American readers it may be relevant to note that although the published text of the Nixon Watergate tapes contains many examples of the phrase "expletive deleted" the editors did not think it incumbent upon them to delete the four-letter words *damn* and *hell*, which occur frequently.)

One factor in this confusion is probably the well-known British tendency to resort to vagueness when confronted by embarrassing topics. The upshot is that the class of English expressions the use of which may count as "bad language" in the U.K. is not well defined. It is not even clear that there is a nucleus of such expressions on which all speakers of any single variety of British English would agree. This state of affairs is complicated by the fact that degrees of badness are acknowledged. One dictionary of contemporary usage distinguishes no less than five degrees of swearing "strength." Euphemisms, which may not always be recognized as such, abound. (*Good gad!, Great pip!, My hat!,* and *Crikey!* were perfectly familiar in print to schoolboy readers of *The Magnet* in the 1930s, even though some of these expressions might have been frowned upon by their parents.) Consequently, anyone who wishes to take seriously the injunction "Don't use bad language" faces a considerable sociolinguistic problem in ascertaining exactly what is forbidden and to whom. For a variety of reasons this problem is probably more intractable at the present day than at any previous time in the history of English.

Worse still, as far as the descriptive linguist is concerned, is that some of these metalinguistic usages come with garbled bits of sociolinguistic theory already attached to them. Take, for instance, the two commonest applications of the term *swearing*. In one of these, swearing is the solemn undertaking of a binding commitment in a court of law or in a religious ceremony, or on some similar formal occasion. Swearing in this sense pledges you, under pain of certain penalties, either to a future course of action or to the truth of certain propositions. But swearing in the sense we are principally concerned with here does not commit anybody to anything: it would perhaps be less problematic as a linguistic practice if it did. Because both activities are called *swearing*, many people regard the latter as an abusive or degenerate variety of the former, and to be condemned *for that reason*. Now there is no doubt that these two uses of the word *swearing* are etymologically connected. Nor that one particular range of swearing behavior widely condemned in British culture borrows its vocabulary from swearing of the solemn and respectable kind. But if we are to approach such a contentious topic with due academic caution, it cannot be overemphasized that etymology is not to be confused with explanation. To treat everyday vituperative swearing as a corrupt form of oath-taking or misinvocation of solemn procedures is already to adopt a theory *about* it (albeit a popular one, which has at various times in history been invoked by authorities in order to condemn or suppress "bad language").

Against this theory it can be—and has been—argued that it gets the essential relationship the wrong way round. In other words, oath-taking may be merely a special institutionalized form of the more primitive and general practice of swearing. The psychological and anthropological evidence relevant to this argument would take us too far afield to be discussed here. But the whole subject of bad language is such a minefield that it would be irresponsible not to sound this note of caution before venturing into it. We may argue about bad language endlessly: but it is far from clear that anyone has any adequate theory about it as a form of linguistic behavior.

Whatever doubts may be entertained about what actually constitutes bad language, or why it is bad, it seems clear that during the 1980s many observers felt it was on the increase in Britain. A widely read report to that effect appeared in the *Sunday Times* in 1982. It cited as one witness, among others, the then vice-chancellor of London University, himself a distinguished scholar in the field of English studies.

A reported increase in British swearing, however, is not verifiable in the way that one can check the annual rainfall in the British Isles. Occasionally summers perceived by the general public to be "poor" are pronounced by meteorologists to be "good." But precisely because no one can produce statistics for the annual incidence of British bad language, the perception itself becomes the (only) significant sociolinguistic fact. What lies or may lie behind such perceptions are the questions that will interest the linguist.

To begin with, the perception can at least be put in its historical context. For there is no doubt that there is a twentieth-century history of such perceptions. For instance, between the first and second world wars a perceived diminution in the amount of British bad language prompted Robert Graves to write a worried monograph on its de-cline. *Lars Porsena, or The Future of Swearing and Improper Language* was published in 1927 and begins with the matter-of-fact statement: "Of recent years in England there has been a noticeable decline in swearing and foul language." Furthermore, we may note that there is a history of such perceptions being associated with the notion that the incidence of swearing is a kind of thermometer of social health. (Diagnostic readings may be taken as welcome or deplorable, depending on the so-cial analyst's own view of how alarming the current situation is.)

Graves noted that in the 1920s an exception to the general decline in British swearing was to be found in "centres of industrial depression." In turn, that perceived connection between bad language and indus-trialization can be traced well back into the previous century. Disraeli's novel *Sybil*, for example, makes it quite explicit. All this is part of a lay sociolinguistics which sees bad language as a generalized response to bad living conditions. Graves predicted that the decline of swearing in England would continue until something happened to give a "new shock to our national nervous system." The kinds of shock he had in mind were evidently war or revolution.

This is one version of what we may term the "social thermometer" view. On this view one seeks explanations of rises and falls in the prev-alence of bad language by looking for factors relating to the state of the nation and its social well-being. For the current crescendo of foul-mouthedness in Britain the explanation would presumably have to lie in the economic plight of the country, unprecedentedly high levels of unemployment, and so on. Nor would one predict a reversal of the trend until better times or better policies bring prosperity.

A rather different social thermometer view has, however, been more fashionable in Britain throughout the past decade. This relates changes in the incidence of bad language not directly to socioeco-nomic conditions but to resultant changes in social attitudes. Accord-ing to this version, bad language can be expected to increase in the course of social change as old shibboleths are swept away and certain sections of the community liberate themselves from traditional verbal constraints (dubbed "oppression"). This in turn will provoke a con-servative backlash, in which outspoken condemnations of bad lan-guage are to be interpreted as indirect disapproval of the new social trends (dubbed "permissiveness").

Unfortunately, neither of the two most notorious four-letter fu-rores of the 1980s can straightforwardly be explained on either version of the simplistic social thermometer theory.

The facts pertaining to the Channel 4 broadcast on 4 November 1987 can be simply and uncontroversially stated. The poem by Tony

Harrison at the center of the row had already appeared in print some time previously. It is a long poem, concerned with the poet's outrage at the desecration of his parents' grave in a public cemetery by football fans who had sprayed aerosol obscenities on the headstones and monuments. Of the words in question the poem contains numerous examples, and this led to the *Daily Mail* publicizing in advance a protest against the impending broadcast. The decision to broadcast the poem was defended by Bernard Levin in an article in the *Times* on 19 October. This provoked a letter to the *Times* from Mrs. Mary Whitehouse, President of the National Viewers' and Listeners' Association, calling in question the judgment of the members of the Independent Broadcasting Authority. The chairman of the I.B.A., Lord Thomson, replied in a letter to the *Times* on 29 November, and the broadcast duly took place.

The first point of importance is that the poem in question, far from celebrating or even condoning the spraying of obscenities on gravestones, is an unequivocal, heartfelt and powerful lament at the verbal vandalism involved. This fact in itself calls in question the logic of any theory which construes current debates about bad language simply in terms of stereotyped clashes between permissive progressives and reactionary moralists. The fault found with the poem by those who found it objectionable was not its moral standpoint or its message, but the fact that it reported publicly and verbatim, albeit in poetic form, the vandalism it condemned. Nor can it be denied that an unsuspecting bookshop browser who happened to take the Penguin edition of Tony Harrison's *Selected Poems* from the shelf might well replace it rather hastily if by chance the volume opened at a page where CUNT, PISS, SHIT, "and (mostly) FUCK" leap in stark capitals from the printed text.

Undeniable also, however, is the fact that the poem exposes exactly the kind of sociolinguistic reasoning which one version of the social thermometer theory appeals to. In an imaginary dialogue, the poet puts into the mouth of one of his skinheads the following implied defense of this type of linguistic misconduct:

> folk on t'fucking dole
> 'ave got about as much scope to aspire
> above the shit they're dumped in, cunt, as coal
> aspires to be chucked on t'fucking fire.

But it would be a gross misreading to suppose that the poet *accepts* this philosophy: on the contrary, the entire poem rejects it.

More interesting still is that when Bernard Levin quoted the above lines in his article on the controversy, he was himself immediately taken to task by his fellow columnist in the *Times*, Ronald Butt, for choosing "to reproduce a verse of unmitigated obscenity to illustrate an argument" (*Times*, 22 October 1987). This criticism is illuminating in that it reveals that what the rumpus was about is indeed a metalinguistic issue: quotation is deemed to be not merely as objectionable as, but even more objectionable than, the original. For it does not have the excuse of the poet's original wrath. Butt was quite specific on this point. Mr. Levin, he said, had gratuitously outraged the readers of the *Times*, just as the poet had been outraged by the words on his parents' grave. "It is the same offence committed against many more—and for what purpose?" (There are many more readers of the *Times* than readers of Tony Harrison's poetry, and more readers of Tony Harrison's poetry than visitors to his parents' grave. Society is society, and heads count.)

Although she did not put it as eloquently as Ronald Butt, Mrs. Whitehouse was making the same proliferation point in her complaint about the I.B.A.; but it was a point Lord Thomson's reply seems to have missed. What is relevant for purposes of the present discussion is that the Butt-Whitehouse doctrine, if we may for convenience so call it (that is, "it is the same offence . . ."), is one which no social thermometer theory of bad language gets any purchase on at all.

Why it fails to do so is a question better dealt with by considering in tandem the (almost contemporaneous) cricketing fracas. Here the details are not so uncontroversial. However, the following might pass, one hopes, as an impartial linguist's summary.

Shortly before the scheduled close of the second day's play in the Test match at Faisalabad between England and Pakistan on 8 December 1987, while Pakistan were batting and England fielding, the Pakistani umpire at square leg interrupted play on the ground that the England captain had illegitimately altered his field placing while the bowler was in the process of bowling to the Pakistani batsman at the wicket. In the immediately ensuing verbal interchange, in which the captain denied the allegation, both captain and umpire lapsed (in English) into what would currently be described (in English) as "bad language," and was, at least in part, later so described by both participants. The umpire refused to continue with the match on the next day unless he received an apology. The England captain refused to give an apology unless he in turn was given an apology by the umpire. This stalemate resulted in no play on the third day of the Faisalabad Test match. This had never happened before in a first-class cricket match of any kind, let alone an international match.

If the England captain had ever read *Lars Porsena*, which is doubtful, one military lesson seems to have escaped him. Graves has an apposite story about the soldier accused in the orderly room of calling someone a dreadful name. The worst possible defense in such circumstances is to allege that the individual thus insulted had previously used equally insulting language. Regardless of the scoreboard, anyone who attempts this strategy is bound to lose (as many a schoolmaster could confirm). In the end, officials were flown from London to mediate in the verbal cricket being played in Pakistan, and the captain of England was obliged to sign a humiliating retraction. The game eventually resumed. But the more interesting bone of contention was the complaint subsequently lodged with the British Press Council against the *Independent*. The complaint was that the *Independent*, alone among British newspapers, had spelled out the actual words allegedly (according to the England cricketers involved) uttered in the fateful altercation on the field.

This objection came not from a source in Pakistan but from the editor of another British newspaper, the *Sun*. His allegation was not that the *Independent* had failed to give the Pakistani version of what happened, but simply that the words in question should not have been reported verbatim in *any* British newspaper. What the *Independent*'s cricket correspondent had reported on 10 December was that the umpire had allegedly called the England captain a "fucking cheating cunt." (Philologists may be interested to note that according to the England captain he was called not a "cunt" but a "bastard.") In his letter to the Press Council the editor of the *Sun* complained that "all newspapers in fact had this quote, but declined to use it as they were family newspapers." He described the *Independent* as "a new member of the gutter press." The editor of the *Independent* replied: "Where obscene language is necessary for the understanding of an important story we will always publish it. Our readers are adults." (By implication, one presumes, readers of newspapers like the *Sun*, which try to boost their circulation by featuring photographs of nude models, are not.)

The case presented by the editor of the *Sun* at the Press Council hearing was noteworthy on various counts. He maintained that the interests of full and accurate reporting of the foul language at Faisalabad could have been served by a judicious use of typographical resources: for example, instead of printing the word *cunt* in full, substituting for it the letter *c* followed by three dots. This substitution, he claimed, would not have prevented any intelligent adult from understanding the facts of the story. Furthermore, he argued, the printing of socially unacceptable language in supposedly reputable sources bestowed a legitimacy upon it, especially among the young and gullible. And the back page of the *Independent*, he added, was undoubtedly seen and read by a very large number of children and young people.

Here we have an intriguing variant of the Butt-Whitehouse doctrine. According to this version, the offense caused by quoting bad language is mitigated if the quoted words, although identifiable, are disguised. The traditional practice of partial expurgation by dots or asterisks had already attracted comment from Bernard Levin in connection with the controversy over the broadcasting of Tony Harrison's poem. Levin professed to find the expurgatory practice even dottier than the taboo on printing the words in full, being unable to understand how offensive words, by wearing this thin typographical veil, become "at once and entirely robbed of their dreadful power, and may be read by the most sensitive souls without harm or danger" (*Times*, 19 October 1987). Dottier still, on the face of it, was the belief evidently subscribed to by the editor of the *Sun* that the hypothetically innocent children of parents who take the *Independent* would be devoid of the intellectual curiosity which might prompt questions like "Why did the umpire call him a f...ing cheating c..., daddy? What was the umpire trying to say?" Or is the assumption that even though children who read the back page of the *Independent* know what *c* followed by three dots stands for just as well as their parents do, nevertheless this typological subterfuge acts as a public warning to them that they should feign ignorance?

It would be muddled thinking to suppose that dots and asterisks can somehow transform a swearword into something which is not a swearword, or cancel an obscenity. If a skinhead with a queer sense of humor sprays *F...* on the headstone instead of *FUCK* the grave is desecrated none the less. Dots and asterisks are essentially metalinguistic devices. One of their functions is to mark out words as unfit for public use, and this they do in a curiously literal way by indicating their "unsayability" (for dots and asterisks have no pronunciation). This is doubtless the underlying educational reason why the editor of the *Sun* would prefer children to see *cunt* spelled *c...*, but whether children need the metalinguistic reminder is another question.

According to the Oxford University Press's *Practical English Usage*, "children usually avoid swearing in front of adults, so as not to shock or annoy them, and adults avoid swearing in front of children for similar reasons."[1] This shrewd comment gets us nearer to—although not quite to—the heart of the matter; but at least far enough to explain why Lord Thomson in his reply to Mrs. Whitehouse laid stress on the decision by the I.B.A. to broadcast Tony Harrison's controversial poem "late at night" (in fact at 11 P.M., by which time, presumably, all good children are expected to be asleep in bed). The I.B.A.'s "late at night" defense is manifestly an attempt to reach a compromise with the Butt–Whitehouse doctrine. In effect, this defense concedes that a poem including four-letter words should be broadcast only to a restricted section of the public (that is, that self-selected section comprising viewers who choose to switch on Channel 4 late at night). But it does not deal with the core of the Butt–Whitehouse argument, which is that *any* repetition of bad language is *ipso facto* objectionable since it repeats "the same offence." On Mrs. Whitehouse's view, although it may have been the poet who was originally at fault in composing this "work of singular nastiness," as she called it, the I.B.A. was even more at fault in compounding his offense. Gratuitously to broadcast a "work of singular nastiness" when one has a statutory custodial obligation not to offend against "good taste or decency" is outright sinning against the light. Whatever we think of the poet's original misjudgment in thus giving vent to his personal feelings about the desecration of his parents' grave, at least he had no formal public obligation of the kind the I.B.A. had.

There is an umbilical cord tying this line of argument to the excuse which those accused of bad language in the international cricket arena have tended to offer, which puts the blame on the modern media's technology. Commenting on the Faisalabad episode in his autobiography, the England captain complained that the Pakistani authorities had violated "the unwritten code of practice concerning mikes on cricket pitches." Instead of being used simply to pick up the sound of ball hitting bat, and then being turned off, the microphone had in his view been used "to highlight and broadcast private conversations and comments from the players."[2] This complaint was echoed officially during the subsequent England tour of New Zealand, when for the first time an England bowler was fined for swearing on the field of play. The formal apologia issued by the England management included what one cricket correspondent described as "a rambling statement condemning the use of the pitch microphones that had transported the offending words into thousands of living rooms. The offence, apparently, was not the offence itself, but the fact that it had been made public" (Martin Johnson writing in the *Independent*, 10 June 1988).

In the event, the Press Council rejected the complaint against the *Independent*, just as the I.B.A. turned down objections to the Channel 4 broadcast. The reasons given were similar in at least one respect. The Press Council absolved the *Independent* of any intention "to shock." Lord Thomson similarly absolved Tony Harrison. The bad language in the poem, he said, was "used neither to shock nor to titillate"

(*Times*, 29 October 1987). The exculpation which is unexceptionable
in one case sits uneasily, to say the least, on the other. No titillation,
granted. But a reader whose grasp of contemporary English is so weak
as to result in failure to recognize verbal shock as one of the central
mechanisms of Tony Harrison's poem immediately forfeits any credibility as a literary judge.

So much for the evidence. What are future historians of English to
make of it? That may in part depend on whether, to their twenty-first-
century ears, saying "Fuck!" sounds as quaint as saying "Gadzooks!"
does to ours. One question they may well ask is whether our generation did not mistakenly construe *less inhibited* swearing as *more* swearing (a confusion of quantity with distribution). They may well ask,
too, why we tended constantly to conflate the question of why bad
language is bad with the question of why reporting bad language
is bad.

Perhaps, on the other hand, it will seem to them quite clear in retrospect that the four-letter furores of the 1980s were merely symptomatic of a much deeper sociolinguistic malaise in Britain; and that
what at the time was perceived as a rising tide of bad language was in
reality something different and more alarming. Perhaps they will see
it as a failure to adjust to living in a linguistic community dominated
by its own reflection in the great magnifying mirror held up by the
media to modern verbal behavior.

Gazing constantly and collectively into that mirror could be predicted to have, sooner or later, one inevitable consequence: a breakdown of the distinction between private English and public English.
English society had pinned so much on that distinction, and for so
long, that its rapid erosion, whether by journalists or by poets, could
not be expected to be other than traumatic.

The trauma would inevitably be twofold. Without a clear distinction between private and public language, all kinds of behavioral
guidelines suddenly vanish, and all kinds of disconcerting questions
about British culture suddenly emerge. Not merely "What is cricket
coming to?" Nor even "What are British poets at?" But a different order of questions, which go for the cultural jugular: "Who are the educated?" "Who are the uneducated?" "Who are the children?" "Who
are the adults?"

The second aspect of the trauma is no less predictable but even less
amenable to social therapy. An erosion of the distinction between private English and public English automatically threatens the sacrosanct
distinction in British culture between the rights of the individual and
the rights of the community. The ultimate irony about the lesson

which the swearing disputes of the 1980s teach us is that we live in a society where bad language can become worrying *not* because it is getting worse but, paradoxically, because it is no longer bad enough. (Bad enough, that is, to be banned from open inspection and discussion.) For the British, communal life is bearable only on the understanding that one may withdraw from it, temporarily or permanently, into another world of inviolable, timeless privacy. The English language is itself the guarantor of that inviolability and its swearwords the boundary stones which it would be folly to displace.

Protesting against its public proliferation is one way of trying to preserve the cultural value of bad language. That value is symbolic of society's recognition that there are some things which can neither be said in public nor repeated in public. The double prohibition is the essential point, the criterial assurance that in the English-speaking community we have not crossed the Rubicon which divides sociolinguistic order from sociolinguistic anarchy. The epitaph on the tomb of British bad language in the 1980s should read: "Valued most by those who most vehemently condemned it." Although *Lars Porsena* did not envisage communication in the post-McLuhan era, Robert Graves was right to be concerned about the future of English swearing. The four-letter words had in the 1980s more than one sterling curator among their detractors. But those curators understood neither what they were preserving nor what they were consigning to history's midden.

Notes

1. M. Swan, *Practical English Usage* (Oxford, 1980), p. 589.
2. M. Gatting, *Leading From the Front* (London, 1988).

Censorship

The BBC does not like certain words.
Dildoes and buggery are always out.
"Cocks are OK, as long as they aren't sucked"—
a young researcher telephoned me back.

Latin's polite. *Vagina* just meant *sheath*.
What doctors use, of course, must be alright.
(But *penis* was a *penis*—nothing else.
The Romans like to call a prick a prick.)

The BBC's *De-effer* bleeps things out
or else suggests a synonym instead.
A poet I know was told he should use *screw*—
his line—"There's fuck-all fucking in the grave."

I got away with using bugger once.
I tried to be demure at first and said
it rhymed with Rum Tum Tugger, but the host
coerced me to recite it at the end.

In Wales, I said a simple "prick" and "piss"—
the show's producer had okayed both words—

But when the bosses' switchboard jammed with calls,
her earphone buzzed "For God's sake, get her off!"

These days, when on the air, I just conform
and skirt around like the professionals,
so audiences can play a crossword game—
"Four letters, sounds like duck, begins with F."

~ LIZ HASSE

Violent Acts and Prurient Thoughts

I HAD LUNCH WITH MY FAVORITE LAWYER, and he asked me what I thought of the new rule proposed and, apparently, widely supported on the Stanford campus. Anyone who used the words *nigger, kyke,* or *faggot,* among a few others, would be subjected to sanction. The Stanford law school's constitutional law professor had written a letter to the *New York Times* explaining how such a law did not infringe basic free speech rights. I was surprised that my lawyer friend was not decidedly against the proposal. Just a few weeks earlier, in Berkeley, he had published his name among a very few others willing to pay a reward for information leading to the arrest of whoever had bombed Berkeley bookstores selling Salman Rushdie's *Satanic Verses* (probably the least read of the most bought books of the decade). My friend said he would modify the Stanford rule: those who used the racist words but identified themselves would not be punished, but they must be prepared to take the consequences of being immediately punched out by the object of the slur who, in turn, would not be disciplined for physically attacking the person who said those insulting words.

Some advocates of the Stanford rule argued that if the quite reasonable response to one of these insults was to punch out the blasphemer, then the offensive words fell neatly within the category of "fighting words," the use of which U.S. "free speech" doctrine permits the state to punish. In fact, the tendency or likelihood that the public use of certain words will lead to violence is not sufficient to strip them of their protection under the First Amendment to the Constitution. Instead, First Amendment free speech doctrine allows censorship of "fighting words" only when the speaker *intended* to provoke an *immediately* violent response. So it looked like the Stanford proposal, if it did not require, in each instance, an inquiry into the intent of the speaker and the likely immediacy of an actual violent reaction, contemplated more censorship than the constitutional doctrine in its current state would tolerate.

Jesse Jackson said the word *hymietown* in public. Maybe that is one of the words the Stanford rule would outlaw. If uttering the word had been against the law, and, as a result, Jackson was more careful and never used it, wouldn't my friend know less about Jackson than he does now? Does outlawing such words change the people who might otherwise use them? Surely, one assumption behind all laws limiting speech, and behind constitutional limitations on those laws, is that they affect the way people talk. A further assumption and worry is that limitations on speech can determine whether or not certain facts will emerge in a linguistic media.

According to doctrinal statements repeated in numerous American legal decisions, the fundamental value of free speech protection is that it creates a free marketplace of ideas in which a search for truth can genuinely take place: "The best test of truth is the power of the thought to get itself accepted in the competition of the market," Justice Holmes said in 1919. The more language there is out there bumping around in the world, the more likely it will be that the truth is bumped up to the surface. It looks a little like Brownian motion.

The constitutionality of some restrictions on speech is, however, well established; that is, despite the absolute wording of the First Amendment—"no law abridging the freedom of speech or of the press"—the doctrine permits prohibitions on the publication of pornography, libelous statements, "fighting words," government secrets. As formulated, these permitted restrictions are not necessarily abandonments of the free marketplace theory. Instead, there are some (maybe of little faith) who advocate the free marketplace theory and would, at the same time, insure that the correctness of the theory—that truth will eventually "out"—is realized by fine-tuning or controlling the marketplace so that it will not be skewed by something overwhelmingly or disruptively false, offensive, or provocative.

In permitting some restrictions, free speech doctrine also arranges categories of speech in a hierarchy according to which kind of speech should be most protected from the allowable restrictions and, consequently, which kind of truth should be most encouraged to emerge.

The kind of truth that the courts are most concerned to promote is "political" truth. Arguing from history, from precedent, from the function of a constitution, and from the "essence" of democracy, the courts have decided that "the central meaning of the First Amendment" is to prohibit persecution for the "criticism of government and public officials."

In 1968, a young man named Cohen was convicted of disturbing the peace by wearing a jacket bearing the plainly visible words "Fuck the Draft" in a Los Angeles courthouse corridor. He claimed that his conduct was "political" speech, since he intended to inform people of his feelings about the Vietnam War and the draft. In 1971 the U.S. Supreme Court, deciding that the conviction should be reversed, identified the issue of the case as follows:

> It is whether California can excise, as offensive conduct, one particular scurrilous epithet from the public discourse, either upon the theory of the [California] court that its use is inherently likely to cause violent reaction or upon a more general assertion that the States, acting as guardians of public morality, may properly remove this word from the public vocabulary.

In finding that Cohen's conviction had amounted to unconstitutional censorship, the Supreme Court emphasized that no one in the courthouse had taken extreme offense, there had been no violent reactions, and no intention to provoke violence. What the California court had done was to affirm the state government's aggressive attempt to "maintain a suitable level of discourse within the body politic." In Justice Harlan's view, Cohen's message did not amount to "fighting words":

> While the particular four letter word being litigated here is perhaps more distasteful than most others of its genre, it is nevertheless often true that one man's vulgarity is another's lyric. Indeed, we think it is largely because governmental officials cannot make principled distinctions in this area that the Constitution leaves matters of taste and style so largely to the individual.

Given the U.S. Supreme Court's announcement of its sensitivity to "one man's vulgarity [as] another's lyric," one might expect generally to find no lack of protection within constitutional free speech doctrine for differences in style, for the value of differences in taste, and for artistic speech in general. In fact, the opposite may be the case.

There is no express recognition in the doctrine for the special value of the literary or the poetic, the artistic, the fictive, the lyrical, or the aesthetic, in general. Because there isn't and because the rationales underlying First Amendment protections are so expressly connected to the discovery and spread of political truth, speech not explicitly related to exposition about or advocacy for or against some public good is, in fact, often more likely to be subject to censorship. This means that any language which a judge puts into the category of the literary, stylistic, or artistic may end up particularly vulnerable to censorship, unless the language is so artful as to be "meaningless," in which case it is harmless and protected.

Take as an example a recent California case in which the opposing parties contested the value of the lyrics of a popular rock song. The factual basis of the case was a suicide. In October 1984 a Los Angeles teenager, John McCollum, shot and killed himself while lying in bed listening to a recording of Ozzy Osbourne, also known as "the madman of rock and roll." John's parents sued Osbourne and his producers on the grounds that Osbourne and the rest of them should have foreseen that the lyrics and "hemisync" sound of Osbourne's music might influence listeners such as John who, because of their emotional instability and "special relationship of kinship" with Osbourne, were particularly susceptible and might react in a self-destructive manner. The parents alleged that the defendants: (Count I) negligently aided, advised, or encouraged John to commit suicide; (Count II) created an uncontrollable urge in John to commit suicide; (Count III) incited John to commit suicide; or (Count IV) intentionally aided, advised, or encouraged John to commit suicide in violation of the California Penal Code.

The California Court of Appeals agreed with the defendants that the parents could state no claims against Osbourne at all because guarantees of freedom of speech and expression which "extend to all artistic and literary expression, whether in music, concerts, plays . . ." protected Osbourne from punishment for the content of his lyrics and also protected the audience's freedom to hear them:

> [The First Amendment] protects a free flow from creator to audience of whatever message a film or book [or song] might convey . . . [and recognizes] the need to maintain free access of the public to the expression.

As we know, "access," the "flow," the "marketplace of ideas," and so on, are not necessarily unregulated in order to be "free," but may, without violating the U.S. Constitution, be constrained by laws restricting certain disturbing categories of expression. Obscenity has no constitutional protection; indecent speech is given a little; the defamatory or libelous is more or less subject to restrictions depending on the status of the publisher and the object of the defamatory speech; commercial speech is less protected than the political. John's parents contended that Osbourne's lyrics fell within the unprotected category of "speech which is directed to inciting or producing imminent lawless action and which is likely to produce such action," sometimes called "fighting words," of which the cry of "fire" in the crowded theater is the prototype.

The court, unsure about just which Osbourne song John had been listening to, focused on one with a suicidal theme:

> *Suicide Solution*
> Wine is fine but whiskey's quicker
> Suicide is slow with liquor
> Take a bottle drown your sorrows
> Then it floods away tomorrows
> Evil thoughts and evil songs
> Cold, alone you hand in ruins
> Thought that you'd escape the Master Keeper
> Cause you feel life's unreal and you're living a lie
> Such a shame who's to blame and you're wondering why
> Then you ask from your cask is there life after birth
> What you sow can mean hell on this earth
> Now you live inside a bottle
> The reaper's traveling at full throttle
> It's catching you but you don't see
> The reaper is you and the reaper is me
> Breaking law, knocking doors
> But there's no one at home
> Made your bed, rest your head
> But you lie there and moan
> Where to hide, suicide is the only way out
> Don't you know what it's really about.

John McCollum's parents claimed that the song preached that "suicide is the only way out" for someone who drinks too much. They claimed that this song and a sequence of songs leading up to it on Osbourne's *Blizzard of Oz* album had the cumulative impact of taking the susceptible listener "down the path of emptiness to suicide."

The producer, CBS, argued for a different analysis: "the vocalist casts his remarks to a hypothetical alcohol abuser. The song expresses the abuser's anxiety, discordant thoughts and self-destructive behavior. He is alienated and despondent; he drinks to 'drown [his] sorrows' and now is given over to alcohol. . . . the abuser will not help himself and only feels hopeless. . . . The alcohol abuser uses alcohol (a liquid solution) as a 'solution' to his anxiety; because it will kill him in the end, it is a 'suicide solution.'"

Lest its own reading not be absolutely convincing, CBS also advanced the argument that advocacy of suicide as an alternative to an intolerable life has a long philosophical tradition, showing up in such illustrious literature as Hamlet's "to be or not to be" soliloquy, Tolstoy's Anna Karenina, and Willy Loman's plans in *Death of a Salesman*.

So, the plaintiffs and the defendants approached the lyrics in the same manner. The question for each was whether or not the song's message conformed to, or deviated from, established or conventional values attached to life, suicide, and alcoholism. CBS argued for the conventionality of the sentiment; the parents, that the lyrics were and promoted dangerous deviations. The questions from each side were the same: did the songs praise and encourage suicide and social deviance while condemning more positive efforts to "cope" with the difficulties of adolescence, alienation, substance-abuse? Or did they criticize the deviant and in the portrayal of suicide as a miserable alternative actually condemn it?

The court was not convinced by either of the readings of the values, positive or negative, of Osbourne's lyrics. Rather, in a high-minded way, it found that the words were "unintelligible"; at best, a "poetic device." Thus, the court held that no rational person would mistake such "unintelligible" lyrics or poetry for literal commands or directives to immediate action. Because the parents failed to show that the putatively offending speech met the standard for "immediate incitement to lawless or violent action," Osbourne's lyrics were found to be speech protected by the Constitution.

This case might be read as a victory for artistic freedom, another of the court's recognitions that "one man's lyric is another's vulgarity" and that both are equally deserving of protection. In fact, the Osbourne analysis was quite different from the one finding the antidraft jacket deserving of the same protection. The jacket was meaningful and value-laden. Indeed, it was "political" and therefore fell within that category to which free speech doctrine is most sensitive. Osbourne's speech was "unintelligible" and valueless and, simply by virtue of that assessment, immune to the "incitement" charge. In deciding that criminal sanctions could not be imposed for uttering an offensive word in a public place, the Supreme Court remarked that no one who saw the jacket "was in fact violently aroused" and no one "powerless to avoid [it] . . . did in fact object to it."

Was the lack of a violent reaction actually germane to the Court's decision? Should it be? The McCollum (Osbourne) court said no. Faced with the suicide of a vulnerable young man described by the parents as a typical Ozzy Osbourne listener, the California court emphasized that Osbourne had no reason to anticipate the tragic response. "It may in fact be quite difficult to predict what particular expression will cause such a reaction and under what circumstances." "The circumstances and conditions under which the listener might receive [the Osbourne recording] are infinitely variable and totally beyond both the control and the anticipation of the artist . . . who cannot be penalized for disseminating work to the general public which allegedly has an adverse emotional impact on some listeners who thereafter take their own lives."

But, in another case where restrictions on the public utterance of words like Cohen's were at stake, the U.S. Supreme Court (seven years after the Cohen decision) was quite solicitous of one individual's response to the allegedly offensive language in question. The case, *FCC v. Pacifica Foundation*, involved a twelve-minute radio broadcast called "Filthy Words" from a comedic album by satirist George Carlin. The piece was aired during a program about attitudes towards the use of language. Prior to playing the selection, the station advised listeners that the next fifteen minutes of broadcast would include language some of them might find offensive and that they might consider changing the station for that period of time. The Carlin recording then began with the remark that there are seven words you can't say over the airwaves, "the ones you definitely wouldn't say ever." He listed the words: "shit, piss, fuck, motherfucker, cocksucker, cunt, and tits . . . the ones that curve your spine, grow hair on your hands and maybe even bring us, God help us, peace without honor." Carlin repeated the words over and over in various popular expressions. A man called the FCC and said that he and his young son had heard the broadcast over the car radio and that it had offended them.

The U.S. Supreme Court upheld an FCC "Declaratory Order" that the radio station could be subject to sanctions for broadcasting the Carlin monologue. Justice Stevens, writing the opinion, distinguished the court's *Cohen* reversal from the Carlin affirmation by noting that while no one reacted adversely to Cohen, "in this case, the [Federal Communications] Commission was responding to *a* listener's strenuous complaint, and Pacifica does not question its determination that the afternoon broadcast was likely to offend listeners." The *Cohen* court was worried that laws forbidding the use of offensive words in public places might silence particular speakers and sterilize particular messages: "we cannot indulge the facile assumption that one can forbid particular words without a substantial risk of suppressing ideas in the process." In contrast, Justice Stevens said of "Filthy Words":

A requirement that indecent language be avoided will have its primary effect on the form, rather than the content, of serious communication. There are few, if any, thoughts that cannot be expressed by the use of less offensive language.

Unlike Cohen's filthy word (and Osbourne's "unintelligible" words), Carlin's seven filthy words were not evaluated under the "immediate incitement to lawless action" standard. Along with Cohen's word and Osbourne's lyrics, Carlin's monologue too would have remained protected under the test for language promoting violence. Instead, the U.S. Supreme Court decided that the standard applicable to obscenity was appropriate for Carlin's words.

Justice Stevens first decided that the FCC was not out to ban anything of a political nature:

> If there were any reason to believe that the Commission's characterization of the Carlin monologue as offensive could be traced to its political content—or even to the fact that it satirized contemporary attitudes about four letter words—First Amendment protection might be required. But that is simply not the case.

The court then subjected the Carlin monologue to the test it applies to language banned as obscene and concluded:

> These words offend for the same reasons that obscenity offends. Their place in the hierarchy of First Amendment values was aptly sketched by Mr. Justice Murphy when he said, "such utterances are of no essential part of any exposition of ideas, and are of such slight social value as a step to truth that any benefit derived from them is clearly outweighed by the social interest in order and morality."

The obscenity test, developed in part in a case that upheld the constitutionality of a law criminalizing the sale of books which "tend to stir sexual impulses and lead to sexually impure thoughts," allows a state to prohibit offensive depictions or descriptions of sexual conduct when, "applying contemporary community standards, the dominant theme of the work as a whole appeals to the prurient interest of the average person and the work as a whole lacks serious literary, artistic, political or scientific value."

In the comparison of the Cohen and Carlin decisions and of the incitement and obscenity tests, the double standard that American constitutional law applies to the language of sex on the one hand and the language of violence on the other becomes apparent. That the potential reaction (an aroused "prurient interest") is remote or the author's intention innocent is no excuse under the obscenity standard. Joyce's

Ulysses and Aristophanes' *Lysistrata* were subjected to the Postmaster General's restraints long after their first publication and with no inquiry into the authors' intentions. Nor did any court ever suggest that *Lady Chatterley's Lover* or *Memoirs of Hecate County* or *Fanny Hill* should not be banned for the lascivious thoughts it aroused in some readers because, as the court said in protecting Osbourne's lyrics, "the circumstances and conditions under which the [audience] might receive [the works] are infinitely variable and totally beyond the control and anticipation of the . . . artist."

The obscenity standard holds the author responsible for anticipating not (as the incitement to violence standard) that the language with which that author intended to provoke immediate violent acts is likely to provoke such acts, but that the language with which that author may have intended to communicate love or disgust, to amuse, satirize, or even abuse, may at any time incite a prurient (defined by *Webster's* as lustful, lewd, morbid, or lascivious) interest in the mind of another. In other words, where the sexually explicit work has no redeeming social value—and lyrics like Osbourne's had no value because they were "unintelligible" to the court, and dirty words like Carlin's had no value simply because the court said that less offensive words could have been found—it may be banned for the possibility that it may instill impure thoughts in the mind of a reader. Nothing in the standard requires the censor to demonstrate that impure thoughts lead to any kind of deplorable or lawless actions. Established doctrine simply allows the state to punish an author because a jury may think that the words are likely to have an undesirable effect on the thoughts of another. Provided, that is, that the words are about sex. If the work depicts or describes or promotes violence, its effects must be visible and physical and lawless and violent and immediate and intended and foreseeable before the state is permitted to intervene.

Consider just one consequence of this constitutional double standard. The project of some feminists to redefine pornography away from the sexual, where rules against it also threaten to suppress feminist and sex education books, and instead within the violent, as violence and the provocation of violence against women, might have the effect of affording pornography far more protection from state censorship than it receives under a sexual obscenity standard. Similarly, those who would cleanse the vocabulary of a student body might have more success if they began by trying to excise not words that provoke violence and racial hatred, but words that a jury might consider obscene. For it is only in the expression of the sexual that American constitutional law allows the state to punish someone for the thoughts his language instills in another.

Dirty Words

I JUST READ AN ARTICLE ABOUT RISK-TAKING by a freelance writer whose name I can't mention because she used a pseudonym. Daredevils will only go so far. I say "she" because it was written from a woman's perspective but its author may be a lying man—a laying lying man. It is a confession that despite her own warnings in numerous columns about unsafe sex she has been sleeping around without condoms and has found out that a man she trusted has been sleeping around without her. The moral, she tells us, is that you can't trust anyone. But there's no reason we should trust what she tells us. She doesn't take her own advice and we don't even know who she is. I, however, have some advice about sex and you can trust me because I'm a virgin. It is something I discovered when a man with whom I did not intend to go to bed asked for my sexual history. He wanted to know if I had been with a lot of men during the past year. I told him fifty not knowing if that was a lot. He was so agitated about the possibility of his catching a disease (not considering the impossibility of his having me) that I figured out he didn't have one. So my advice is that when coming clean about your history you should make it sound dangerous. If you find anyone willing to sleep with you it's a safe bet that he or she is unsafe. I don't pretend to be a risk taker, but pseudonyms are made of thin rubber and are bound to tear.

I have another method of protection. When in doubt I avoid the En-

glish language. In the film *Prick Up Your Ears*, Joe Orton (Gary Old-
man) presses Kenneth Halliwell (Alfred Molina) on whether he has
read Orton's diaries. When Halliwell denies, Orton tells him that he
should: "My mum did. I used to have to put the dirty bits in shorthand." In order to transcribe the diaries, Anthea Lahr asks her mother
to decipher the words. Somebody's mother read them. I translate my
dirty stuff into French.

In spite of their reputation for being unclean people, the French
make acceptable that which might otherwise be deemed dirty and
merely dirty. In *Prick Up Your Ears*, French Morocco is a nice backdrop
for Orton and Halliwell's sexual excursion because it is so visually
clean. The white walls of buildings and Halliwell's white trousers are
a dramatic contrast to the dark flat in England and his usual brown
clothes. The setting makes the sex less offensive. But even more necessary to the film's acceptability is that after Orton and Halliwell have
had theirs (and plenty of it) they get theirs. If not for their brutal end,
which is used in the first scene, the film would most likely have been
rejected in England and America. The heated-up remake of *The Postman Always Rings Twice* and the more recent *Dangerous Liaisons*, an
English-speaking version, required their punishing ends to get seen.
The film *Betty Blue* by Jean-Jacques Beineix, based on the novel by
Philippe Djian, opens with a scene between lovers Betty (Beatrice
Dalle) and Zorg (Jean-Hugues Anglade) that no English-speaking
filmmaker would get off with. Americans are better with props. The
British are better with clothes on. But this was a scene without language because sex is an activity without language, and without language barriers. The basic activities and inactivities of human existence—sex, sleep, nourishment, and excretion—are languageless. We
are taught not to talk with our mouths full and not to read on the toilet.
But we may acknowledge a language which is made up of squeals,
grunts, guttural sounds, bowel sounds, burps, and piss noise. This is
the common language. It is a dirty language because it is common but
a clean language because it is pure.

The French speak the common language well because they are not
overly concerned with being clean and, therefore, not overly concerned with being dirty. This is why they are able to use erotic language gracefully without deeroticizing it. The same is true for their
performance of erotic acts—even naked and without props. English-
speaking people are concerned. We are concerned with being clean,
concerned with being dirty, and we are concerned with words. In the
David Leland film *Wish You Were Here*, Lynda, played by Emily Lloyd,
is asked by a psychiatrist to recite all of the dirty words she knows be-

ginning with each letter of the alphabet. She gets through A and B without trouble, then stops on C.

SHE: Că—No.
HE: Take your time.
SHE: Can't think of nothing.
HE: Think really hard now. The letter C. Something very filthy. Very, very dirty.
SHE: Ca ca?
HE: Ca ca?
SHE: Ca ca. Poo poo.
HE: Are you feeling ashamed?
SHE: What of?
HE: Of what you're really thinking.
SHE: I'm not thinking of anything.
HE: Yes you are.

When she protests that they skipped from D to F he tells her to take his word that there isn't one beginning with E and ignores her suggestion to "give it a try."

HE: F. Can you think of a filthy, dirty, smutty word beginning with F? Not too hard I should think, Lynda.
SHE: No.
HE: Come on. Come on. Of course you can. I can. Anybody can.
SHE: Well what then? You tell me.
HE: You must be one of the last people on God's earth who doesn't know. Everybody knows a swear word beginning with F.
SHE: Well then what are you asking me for?
HE: Because I want to hear you say it.
SHE: You dirty old bugger.

The way Emily Lloyd delivers "up your bum" is purely vulgar. But it is the purity of Lynda's vulgarity that has her psychiatrist frustrated. He needs to hear the words *cunt* and *fuck* to be sure of his case. Although English-speaking people have used clean those very, very dirty words, we are unable to recognize vulgarity without them. We are hung up on the words. *Wish You Were Here* is set in postwar England where prophylactics and psychiatrists were a novelty. But those have prevailed. Certainly these days both are bigger than ever—more common anyway. Everyone on God's earth, at least the English-speaking sectors, knows what a psychiatrist is. But to distinguish one from counselors, social workers, therapists, psychotherapists, psychoanalysts, and psychopaths, shrink is needed.

Most everyone knows what plunkers, "what the yanks call condoms," are, too. The word *condom* has had a recent comeback because of AIDS. Prophylactics have had to be reidentified in order to encourage people to use them. *Rubber* or *plunker* would not do. They're not serious enough. Neither would words like *Durex*, what Lynda used (or didn't), or *Trojan*. In order to popularize the word *condom*, in order to popularize condoms, people like the U.S. Surgeon-General C. Everett Koop have had to overcome a particular word hang-up that has to do with brand names. Brand names have become generic names. Nobody knows what a cotton swab is. Call it a Q-tip. And all adhesive bandages are Band-Aids.

The trouble with that sort of object identification, aside from what the competitive trademarks might suffer, is that words take the place of the things they identify. The things lose significance. This is nothing to worry about when cotton swabs are in question. But the problem is not isolated. It is as prevalent as prophylactics and psychiatrists. *Cunt* and *fuck* are the brand names of vulgarity. It would do little good to look for a swear word beginning with E. No one would use it. It wouldn't be for lack of understanding of the word itself, which may be defined and taught, but for lack of understanding of what the word represents. *Coke* represents America and it represents dark brown carbonated soft drinks. *Cunt* represents vulgarity and, well, we all know what *cunt* is. Or do we? If in your typical college English class the really old word *queynte* comes up, which is quite probable, the professor will almost certainly ask, "You all know what that means, don't you?" If not everyone does, the question will tip off those in the dark. Still, no one will be satisfied, not students, not teacher, until the word *cunt*, not pudendum, is used. Explication of the other word by its own vulgar context is insufficient. *Queynte* is lost and so are any variances on its meaning.

It may be said that the word *cunt* is in full possession of its meaning and is therefore more effective than other like words. But while being possessed the meaning is also repressed. The word becomes the meaning and without the word the meaning is lost. It is as if the thing itself, that which should be represented by the word, does not exist. The word that takes over its own meaning is no longer in possession of itself. It becomes a nonword or worse a bad word. *Cunt* had its day in court when women writers discovered they could use it and nothing happened. I still call *cunt* "the C word." Maybe because I'm prudish, or maybe because it's more vulgar that way—Lynda had her psychiatrist titillated by what she was thinking, or what he hoped she was thinking, more than if she had said the word—or maybe because *cunt* is so bad. There is no worse word in the English language. It is too graphic, too physical, too occlusive, too onomatopoeic, too obvious, too exclusive, too violent, too specific. But sometimes there is no better word.

Cunt's counterpart, *prick*, is at least more useful. *Prick Up Your Ears* works so well as the title of John Lahr's biography (1978) of Joe Orton because of the many applications of *prick*. It is suggestive of Orton's fascination with his prick and with The Prick. And also of the way in which his life was a prick in time or a series of pricks, every one conspicuously conscious of a preceding prick and a posterior prick. His coming up was a prick. Kenneth Halliwell harped on that prick during the time he pricked Orton—told him what to wear, how to act—and pricked him on. His fame was a prick. His success was a prick. According to John Lahr, Orton wasn't even sure if it had happened. He said of *Entertaining Mr. Sloane*, "It wasn't the overall critical success people think it was. I had to hack my way in." As Halliwell would have it, Orton's cranium, or its content, wasn't what people think it was and he had to hack his way in. Joe Orton's death was a prick. And he died by pricking, albeit hacking or hammering. Then Halliwell pricked his suicide note. It may be incidental, though not to Halliwell, but Halliwell's mother died by the prick of a wasp—in her mouth.

Prick Up Your Ears is masterful as a title not only because of *prick* and its associations with Orton but because of what *prick* does to your ears in their association with Orton. The ear is just another bodily orifice. In the title, "Prick" comes full circle and inserts itself into "Ears"—in one ear and out the other—(and also into rears which we hear in "Your Ears"). It says, "Drop your pants and bend over. You'll get an earful," and wants the response, "Come again? Did you say 'Prick up your ears?'" A man from the gallery calls out "In your ear!" It is the ghost of Kenneth Halliwell but nobody recognizes him. Not because he is any more invisible than he was alive but because he isn't wearing his wig. Besides, no one is listening. They're too busy laughing at the Joe Orton play being performed. Then the curtain comes down and the ghost of Orton says, "Thank you all. Come again." And everyone thinks he means that literally.

Names matter to us. In *Wish You Were Here*, Lynda mocks the significance of names when her psychiatrist asks, "Do you mind if I call you Lynda?" and she tells him "I prefer that to Beryl" which is not her second name as he supposes. But even she retorts when her name is overfamiliarized by the ex-lover who calls her Lyndie when begging her back: "Lyndie. Oh, I say, never called me Lyndie before. Must be after something. Ha Bloody Ha." In *Prick Up Your Ears*, Joe Orton tells his psychiatrist that he is an orphan. His parents called him John. What we are called by our parents has more to do with their ideas about themselves and each other, and later our ideas about ourselves and them, than with their ideas about us. We are not easily identifiable when we are born because we have no identities except by our relationships to our parents. Orphans are called orphans before they are called Joe or John. Children with parents are called anything their parents like. Name changes made by those who decide to choose their own are like little deaths. They don't deny history, they duplicate it. Bob Dylan and Robert Zimmerman have the same face but separate histories. The first is ongoing (and older) and the second is over.

Joe Orton was not John Orton. Peggy Ramsey, who in the film later tells Orton that "Americans are so sensitive about their names," knew what she was doing by suggesting that he pick another name. When John became Joe a new history began. Unless they are gotten rid of, we become our names whether or not they are unbecoming. In *Prick Up Your Ears*, Joe, like Lyndie, in turn becomes a dirty word. The name was a barrier for Orton and Halliwell. It was the first of the many words that came between them.

The trouble with barriers is not word stoppage but word inundation: condoms give us safe sex, the oxymoron that is more purgative than love. In the 1980s AIDS, AmFAR, and AZT superseded S&M and MDA. The English language is padded with and its barriers built on the evidence of its purges. We suspect that our language, especially written, gives confirmation of our existence. But history wants our bodies. And we can't feed our bodies with words. They're not digestible and not easily eliminated—even with names (which are in league with condoms: messy means to make things clean). An African poet says, "Void gives shape to substance," and the creation of void requires elimination—of self, of language, of others or their language.

Historically, disease has been a tool for elimination. Malaria eased the white man's burden. Louise Erdrich and Michael Dorris tell of how smallpox-infected blankets were used by settlers to clear American Indians from the white frontier.[1] Disease keeps the missionaries in business. AIDS was a godsend to religious leaders. When the gods or goads of the heathen are rendered ineffective, converts are more easily won from among those who have not already been eliminated. Allen Ginsberg, who has had to eliminate some of the pleasures from his life, reasons the process of eliminating: "So I'm *already* having all these little deaths . . . Funny explorations that I've been making—is death so bad? Is saying goodbye to matzo balls, is that so bad? Or bagels— or sucking semen directly into my gut?[2]

Ginsberg thinks he's been saved from death by AIDS because of his preference for straight boys, though he unhappily admits that boys aren't so willing to experimentally cross over anymore. But while converts of that kind aren't on the rise, it is the time for crossing over.

Ginsberg has taken seriously to photography, the art of most immediate gratification. David Mamet, who did *House of Games* and *Things
Change* for screen, and Sam Shepard, playwright turned actor and
screenwriter, both directed films in the 1980s. Bob Dylan took a role
in a Hollywood-style movie. Harry Dean Stanton toured the United
States with his guitar, harmonica, and voice backed by "The Call,"
whose member Michael Been acted with Stanton in *The Last Temptation of Christ*. The once somewhat obscure director Barry Levinson not
only had a small acting part in his film (one of the more convincing
performances) but was tempted to cross the bridge to box office bucks
with *Rain Man*. The film used autism, the ultimate symbolic disorder
for the submission of language to mechanics. The language of Raymond Babbit (Dustin Hoffman) is part mystery, part memory, and
part mimicry, mostly of television game shows and top forty songs.
But the language of younger brother Charlie Babbit (Tom Cruise) is
even more limited. This was a crossover for Cruise to a serious dramatic role, but it seems that the writers thought *fuck* was the only
word he could deliver effectively. It was also a crossover for Dustin
Hoffman. This time he played the subject of a custody suit. Harvey
Fierstein took his *Torch Song Trilogy* off Broadway and into the cinema. Matthew Broderick, who on stage played the boy adopted by a
cross-dressing performer (Fierstein), was cast as the transvestite's
lover in the film. And gay writers have crossed over the mainstream
and into the gully of American publishing.

With AIDS came a surge of gay writing and unprecedented interest in it. Publishers caught on to new gay writers with crossover appeal to heterosexual readers. *Newsweek* told us that AIDS "galva-
nized" gay writers, but Edmund White revealed what AIDS has done
to their art:

> Most of all the body is unloved. Onanism—alone or in groups—has re-
> placed intercourse. This solitude is precisely a recollection of adoles-
> cence. Unloved, the body releases its old sad song, but it also builds fan-
> tasies, rerunning idealized movies of past realities, fashioning new
> images out of thin air.[3]

While gay writers engage in onanism, publishers continue to court
them. White says that for gay men the "force of history has been made
to come clean." Along with history, commercialism has come clean.
Publishers are coming clean by allowing gay people to have their final
say. And does the Whitney Circle really approve of Robert Mapplethorpe's social as well as his societal photographs, or was it seeking
reparation by way of testament to S&M (which to Mapplethorpe
"means sex and magic, not sadomasochism")?[4]

The closing of the St. Marks Baths because of AIDS indicates the irony of this quest for cleanliness on the part of observers. "The smart society that has accepted [Mapplethorpe's] work has done so because it is so far removed from their own lives," and "they thought it was so wonderful the Whitney was hanging this show" because certainly pictures hung on the walls of the Whitney were a safe see for curious patrons. But then artists don't get their due until after they are dead. Those with AIDS are the living dead. Gay people are being given the opportunity to write their own histories, their own epitaphs, so that the rest of the world might stop to read them and seek explanation of itself. And gay artists themselves are coming clean in other ways. Part of the process has been the elimination of terms. They are no longer *gay*. *Homosexual* is the word of choice and even that is being called obsolete. White reminds us that Foucault said that there are homosexual acts but not homosexual people. Harvey Fierstein says

> At this time in history, when the media cover gay people and AIDS in the same breath, it's important that we don't lose our humanity. We must portray ourselves as loving people with self-respect.[5]

In other words, we are humans not homosexuals. And Mapplethorpe's alter boy ego calls S&M sex and magic.

Even Allen Ginsberg is wearing a white shroud. He's been spending much of his time "framing things" and coming clean about his past. With the annotated *Howl* came a confession of revision.

> I perhaps *over*-emphasized the nonrevised aspect of it—lied about it outright and bald-faced to John Ciardi when he called me up in Paterson in 1958 and said did I revise it and I said, "No—not at all." It certainly was cleaned up a lot.

Now Ginsberg alleges that the point is refinement. In telling what kind of advice he could offer with the new *Howl* he says:

> I guess the best lesson is seeing the quality of the things that I included and the vulgarity of the things that I excluded—'cause a lot of people write vulgar *Howls*. There's not enough refinement. Thinking that the *freedom* is the whole point and not the refinement part also.

This advice is harder to swallow than semen into the gut coming from Allen Ginsberg. The trouble is in determining what is refined and what to refine, and what is coarse and what to eliminate. Would Ginsberg recommend the elimination of vulgar words such as *cunt* and *cocksuckers* or the refinement of those words or neither? The translation of *Howl* to mainland Chinese has "suckers of corks" for "cocksuckers." Is that profane or refined?

It is a good response to the admonition that Lynda received from her younger sister in *Wish You Were Here*: "Language. If you can't watch your own language, watch someone else's." AIDS itself is a vulgarity because it is common, or vernacular. And it is refined because it is a reduction from Acquired Immune Deficiency Syndrome, although people with AIDS are thought to be given a more dignified and refined death when it is cited that they died of "complications relating to Acquired Immune Deficiency Syndrome" rather than of AIDS. The elimination of terms may be considered refinement. But with all this elimination going on what becomes of the waste? Men like to pass the dirty things, like responsibility, off on women. Sperm may not become women but it becomes women's. And it is lately overemphasized that women do their own dirty things like produce semen and ejaculate too. They've even given us a new term, *spurt*, for ejaculation because, according to J. Kenneth Davidson, Ph.D., who came up with the term, it's more feminine. Isn't that lovely? A feminine ejaculation. Women can't be given the responsibility for AIDS, though, so the Africans took the heat for a while, and gay people are given the blame as if they created the disease.

In *Betty Blue*, Zorg, the closet artist whose novel is typed by his lover, Betty, and mailed to every publisher in Paris, is told by one that his art is in the worst possible taste and shows all "les signes . . . de SIDA." We get the idea, as soon as he opens the door to Betty and Zorg (who thinks they are at the gynecologist's to check on her IUD) wearing a zebra skin smoking jacket, that this particular publisher is no judge of good taste. But though his comment that the work showed the signs of AIDS may not have been an accurate assessment of Zorg's novel, it does describe the condition of art today—moreover, of art that attempts to confront AIDS. When White advises that such art "must begin in tact, avoid humour, and end in anger," he is mapping the progress of the disease—the way that *Rain Man* showed the signs of autism.

If Joe Orton were alive today, he'd be dying of AIDS. But, still, death would take him the same way—by surprise. Orton would live his life up until the day he died. And he would die laughing. Orton's life was testimony to the fact that it is impossible to separate tact from tactic—so he avoided tact—and impossible to separate the joke from anger. John Lahr tells us:

> As late as 1961, in his novel *Head to Toe*, Orton contemplated a new kind of writing "that would create a seismic disturbance" whose "shock waves were capable of killing centuries afterwards." In farce, Orton found a way of turning his aggression into glory. "To be destructive," he wrote, "words have to be irrefutable."

To be irrefutable, words have to be, like history, self-destructive. They must be able to come back upon themselves and devour the trappings of their own meanings, as well as the contextual trappings of tactic and tact. The punitive pun, the refined vulgarity, and the acronym that is a heteronym—AIDS—are irrefutable, destructive. Prick up your ears and if you are assaulted through them "by words only," the artist is a success. White is right, "it is only sane to rage against the dying of the light." But it is improper to rage with propriety. John Lahr quotes Penelope Gilliatt on Orton in his introduction to the *Diaries*, "He'd suffered an awful lot of ribaldry about camp. He was furious. He lived his life in a state of cold, marvellous, funny fury." Orton's Gombold has this prayer:

> Cleanse my heart, give me the ability to rage correctly.

After all is said and done, it has all been said and done before. All we can do is refine and revise. Even our sexual histories are shared. No one is safe. The joke is on us. History has the last laugh. The sentiment in this hour of "the dying of the light" is to come clean now or don't come at all. To come clean is to be infertile. I say, come clean if you must but by all means come. We can't beat history so we may as well join it. Make your own history irrefutable. If you can't take my advice, take your mother's. Don't read on the toilet because you'll get hemorrhoids; don't talk about sex, not because it's tactless but because it's pointless. And don't talk with your mouth full, especially if it is full of words. The English language needs to come closer to the common language. This doesn't necessitate the elimination of words or the invention of new words but a cooling of our concern for banal, anal, inconsequential words. Irrefutable words should be the rage of the 1990s; because as we enter the next decade, our artists having been left by the last both prolific and inactive and their art prophylactic, the moral is this: it is to do and die for the English language.

Notes

1. Interviewed by Bill Moyers on "A World of Ideas," PBS, 29 October 1988.

2. This and subsequent quotations are from an interview with Allen Ginsberg by Steve Silberman, "No More Bagels," *Whole Earth Review* 56 (Fall 1987).

3. "Out of the Closet Onto the Shelves," *Newsweek*, 21 March 1988; Edmund White, "The Artist and AIDS," *Harper's Magazine*, May 1987. See also *Artforum*, January 1987.

4. Quoted in Dominick Dunne, "Robert Mapplethorpe's Proud Finale," *Vanity Fair*, February 1989, p. 186.

5. Harvey Fierstein, *Harper's Bazaar*, December 1988, p. 174.

꼭 JOHN ALGEO

It's a Myth, Innit?
Politeness and the English Tag Question

ENGLAND IS A LAND THAT LIVES BY MYTHS. And one of the greatest of the national myths is that the English are a polite race. They are nothing of the kind. Indeed, the English, never known to do anything by halves, have developed impoliteness into an art form of great sophistication and complexity.[1]

Not that all English impoliteness is sophisticated. Much of it is merely Englishly stolid. But even the stolid variety has been honed to near perfection. For example, when a subway (anglice "underground" or "tube") train arrives in a station, the pride of the English nation waiting on the platform crowd around, effectively preventing would-be detrainers from leaving the car. Deaf to repeated pleas over the loud-speaker system (anglice "Tannoy") that they should "stand back to let the passengers off first," the would-be entrainers press forward en masse against the contrary mass of would-be detrainers. The result: the English tube scrum, only marginally less violent than that of the Millwall supporters on the playing fields of Luton.

Between the would-be entrainers and the would-be detrainers is a tertium quid: the doorway blockers. The English are mystically drawn to the doorways of subway trains. There is an English gene that impels its carriers to gravitate to the door of a train and there take their stand with immobile British stolidity. By spiritual magnetism the English find their proper place in a train door and will not leave it short of the application of force majeure. There can be an abundance of clear standing space down the aisle between doors; there can even be empty seats on the train. True English persons know that their proper place in life is in front of the subway train doors.

Another form of the myth of politeness is that the English cheerfully and willingly form lines (or "queues") whenever they are in a group waiting for the same service. Because in present-day England there are far more persons who want service than there are those willing to give it, there is indeed intense demand for almost everything—and consequently hordes of people waiting. The famous English queue, however, is not a line but an illusion.

It is true that the waiting hordes, at a post office, for example, do tend to form themselves into a thinnish mob that creates the impression of a line. But it is here that the true genius of the English appears. The queue is really a decoy to get those who don't know any better away from the window where they sell stamps so that the knowledgeable and deserving, that is, real Englishmen or more often Englishwomen, can do their business undisturbed by the masses.

Your little old English lady has developed queue-busting into an art of great refinement. Hunched down to make herself nearly as invisible as one of the Irish good people, the little old English lady comes dithering along sideways like a crab so that it isn't clear where she's bound. Head bobbing, her lips set in a cherubic smile that blazons forth innocence, she mutters some syllables that might be a greeting to her next of kin but are in fact directed to a stranger. In this fashion she makes her way by a dignified but steady progress to the front of the queue. Then she pops in directly before the window, where she prefaces her request for an 18p stamp by a protracted exchange with the postal clerk about their arthritis and the beastly state of the weather.

Modeling themselves on their little old ladies, the English are the world's most skilled people in giving an illusion of politeness. An American who steps on another's foot will say "Excuse me" or "Pardon me." Your true Englishman has no truck with such servile behavior. He proffers no excuses and sues for no pardons. Indeed, having stepped on another, he says nothing at all. If he, however, is stepped on, he will say "Sorry!" It is invariably said in a tone of voice indicating that the person addressed is an unmannerly clod and probably an American.

In no aspect of English national life is the myth of politeness more ingeniously worked out than in the British elaboration of tag questions. A tag question is a bob at the end of a sentence that changes a statement into a question—for example, "It's not so hot, *is it?*" and "I'm right, *aren't I?*" Tag questions are tricky grammatically (witness "aren't I" where there is no "I are"), but they are useful pragmatically. They are devices by which people relate to one another in the process of a conversation.

Since they are questions in form, one might suppose that tag questions are used to elicit information. But function and form do not always go together. There are at least five uses of tag questions, some of them characteristically British, showing a progressive decline in politeness and in the degree to which they draw the addressed person into the conversation:

1. *Informational Tags.* To ask for information was probably the original purpose of tag questions, but today this purpose is the least important of their uses. Yet some tags still serve that end:

> Q: You haven't got the ages of these other guys, *have you?*
> A: Which other guys? $(S2/6.1053-54)^2$

> Q: You don't have to wear any sort of glasses or anything, *do you?*
> A: Well, I wear glasses for reading sometimes.   (S1/9.1246–47)

As genuine requests for information, these tag questions value the person to whom they are addressed more highly than do any of the others. The speaker has an idea about something (the statement preceding the tag), but asks for information without presuming to know what the answerer will say. The tune of the tag is a rising intonation, characteristic of open questions. The responder to an informational tag may quite appropriately either agree or disagree with the speaker or seek clarification. The person speaking and the person spoken to are thus on equal footing.

2. *Confirmatory Tags.* A more frequent use of tag questions is not to seek information but to draw the person addressed into the conversation—to evoke agreement and thereby to forward the conversation. These tags ask for confirmation of what the speaker has said:

> Q: Yeah, I'd just finished my thesis, *hadn't I?*
> A: That's right.   (S2/4.229–31)

> Q: So we don't know whether they taste nice or not, *do we?*
> A: No.   (S2/10.1447–49)

> Q: Well, we all understand the circumstances, why it has to be surreptitious, *don't we?*
> A: Of course.   (S2/5.697–99)

> Q: But you don't have Swindon on your little map, *do you?*
> A: No, I don't have Swindon on my map.   (S1/11.1262–64)

> Q: You have some pull with the management, *do you?*
> A: [laugh]   (S2/10.776–77)

In such questions, the speaker assumes that the person addressed will agree with the truth of the statement. The question is thus not a request for information, but an invitation to express agreement, to confirm the opinion of the speaker. The person addressed is asked to participate in the conversation, albeit more passively than actively. The intonation of these tags may be a rising tune, but is more likely to be a falling one, such as characterizes statements. Typical responses to a confirmatory tag are "Of course," "Yes, certainly," and "That's right," or simply an "umm" or a nod of the head.

3. *Punctuational Tags.* Some tags are used to elicit neither information nor confirmation but merely to point up what the speaker has said. These tags are the vocal equivalent of an exclamation point or of underlining for emphasis:

> You classicists, you've probably not done Old English, *have you?* Course you haven't.   (S1/6.929–31)

> So, you've managed to ring up, *have you?* [laughs] You did manage to pick up the phone, *did you?*   (S1/12.1199–1201)

> And as for the idea of working the market to their advantage: "We all three of us applied for TSB shares when they were privatised," said the lecturer gloomily. "Two of us got some. But we didn't cash in on them when they were quoted on the market. Well, it was too much trouble, *wasn't it?*"   (*Sunday Telegraph Magazine*, 21 August 1988)

> "He's shot a fucking policeman. That little wimp, didn't know he had it in him, *did I?*"   (Antonia Fraser, *Your Royal Hostage*)[3]

Such tags do not ask of the persons spoken to that they share either actively or passively in a conversation, but only that they pay attention to the speaker and note well the important points. These tags treat addressees as audience rather than participants. Such a tag is not uncommunicative, or even unfriendly. It is merely self-centered. It emphasizes the point that the speaker wishes to make under the guise of asking a question.

4. *Peremptory Tags.* The peremptory tag is typically used in response to a statement speakers do not want to hear or a question they do not want to answer. A peremptory tag immediately follows a statement of obvious or universal truth, with which it is practically impossible to disagree. In asking a question about an obvious truth, the peremptory tag may be condescending or impatient. The implication of the peremptory tag is that everyone knows the truth of the preceding statement, and therefore even someone of the limited intelligence of the addressee must be presumed to recognize it:

I wasn't born yesterday, *was I?*
(*Home Front*, BBC2, 24 August 1988)

A: Do you know why I gave that money to Barry?
Q: No, I wasn't there, *was I?*
(*Brookside*, Channel 4, 6 August 1988)

Miss Kirkwood [an actress] got to know Prince Philip during her relationship with Baron. So are there royal bombshells in the star-spangled manuscript she is now penning?

"You'll have to wait and see, *won't you?*" she said teasingly from her Yorkshire fastness. (*Evening Standard*, 6 September 1988)

WIFE: Haven't you even started [papering the walls] yet?
HUSBAND: Yeah, well pet, it's all preparation, *innit?*
(Heineken Beer commercial, Channel 4, 4 September 1988)

The intent—and often the effect—of the peremptory tag is to leave speechless the person to whom it is directed. Rather than seek information, encourage agreement, or ask for attention, the peremptory tag is a signal that the speaker prefers to avoid the subject and considers the conversation about it at an end. The intonational tune is always a falling one. The tag is sometimes a tease but more often a put-down of the addressee.

5. *Aggressive Tags.* The aggressive tag is superficially similar to the peremptory one but with a crucial difference. Whereas a peremptory tag follows an obvious truth, an aggressive tag follows a statement that is by no means obvious and that the addressee cannot be reasonably expected to know. Yet it treats that unobvious statement as one every person, however limited in intelligence, should recognize as fact. By implying that addressees ought to know what they actually cannot know, the aggressive tag is insulting and provocative:

A: I rang you up this morning, but you didn't answer.
Q: Well, I was having a bath, *wasn't I?*

A: You need to go to your local police.
Q: I've done all that, *haven't I?*
(*Bergerac*, WGTV-8, Athens, Georgia, 20 December 1986)

A: Is that your brother? [question addressed to a young man talking on the telephone]
Q: It's my dad, *innit?* (*EastEnders*, BBC1, 5 February 1987)

A: What are we going to do with them? [spoiled merchandise]
Q: We're going to sell them, *aren't we?*
(*Coronation Street*, ITV, 9 February 1987)

A peremptory or aggressive tag is frequently part of a response to a question, as in the last two examples; or to an implied question, as in the first example; or to a suggestion for action, as in the second. Peremptory and aggressive tags are both antagonistic, the former mildly and the latter more vigorously so. Both tags oppose cooperative communication, the former terminating a discussion and the latter in addition expressing an impatient or hostile reaction.

Americans often think tag questions to be feminine and British. They are half right. Robin Lakoff has argued that tag questions are more characteristic of women's than of men's speech and are perceived as tentative or subordinating since they seek and defer to the opinions of others.[4] Whether the conventional wisdom that tags are more feminine than masculine is correct (and it has been challenged), the peremptory and aggressive tags are by no means deferential or uncertain. On the contrary, they are antagonistic and assertive. They do, however, seem to be characteristically British.

The following is an American comment on the use of tag questions in early twentieth-century England. It covers both confirmatory and peremptory tags:

> English people end almost every sentence with a question. Your grand lady says: "It looks like rain, *doesn't it?* We shall have a muddy ride, *sha'n't we?*" You say to the girl in the shop, "These gloves are hard to get on"; and she replies: "But all gloves are hard to get on at first, *aren't they?* And they soon wear easier, *don't they?*"[5]

Your grand lady ends her sentences with polite confirmatory tags. The girl in the shop, however, replies with quite a different sort, tags intended to obviate the shopper's objection to ill-fitting gloves and therefore peremptory in effect.

Punctuational, peremptory, and aggressive tags all seem to have begun with the lower orders. But they have not remained there. During a tour of China, the Duke of Edinburgh issued a joking warning to British students resident in the Far East that they should be wary of staying too long in those parts lest their eyes grow slant. The Duke was, to be sure, merely expressing in his own jolly way the long-established xenophobia of the British ("The wogs begin at Calais"). But as his remark was reported by the press, it was made to seem a tad racially invidious. So the Royal handlers put a word in the Royal ear, and the Duke sought to cover his trail:

> . . . the Duke gathered a group of ocularly-suitable girls around him at a cultural performance in Kunming, demanded that the Fleet Street photographers record the event and barked to the . . . reporters . . . that "I've got to do something right, *haven't I?*"
>
> (*Sunday Times*, 19 October 1986)

The Duke's photo opportunity and tag question were both clearly intended to end, not open, discourse. It is notable, however, that the Duke used a rhetorical device redolent of *EastEnders* and *Coronation Street*. Nowadays, the Crown's consort and the shop girl are brother and sister under the skin.

To look at tag questions as signals of politeness and deference, as American grammarians have tended to do, is not right by half. Their older uses, common to all varieties of English, may have been that. But the newer British tag questions serve vigorously antagonistic ends. If anything they are signals of impoliteness.

The five uses of tags move from including the addressee as an equal in the conversation to antagonistically rejecting the addressee as a participant in discourse. They form a series of decreasing politeness and increasing Britishness:

1. The informational tag seeks a substantial answer from the addressee, and does not predict what that answer may be. This tag asks the person to whom it is directed to become a full partner in the discourse by providing independent information.

2. The confirmatory tag invites the addressee to agree with the speaker, perhaps only by some sound of encouragement for the speaker to go on. Such tags assume a community of views, in which the speaker is the leading player and the addressee has a supporting role.

3. A punctuational tag asks only that the addressee pay attention and follow what the speaker is saying. From the standpoint of audience participation, this tag is the most neutral of all. It treats the addressee not as a participant but as an auditor in the communication.

4. A peremptory tag seeks to end the discussion of the subject by closing off communication. This tag seeks not to encourage communication, even passively, but instead to abort it.

5. An aggressive tag is openly hostile and expresses antagonism. It accuses the addressed person of a lack of common sense, consideration, or good will. It is the retort scurrilous.

Whether the politer types of tag question are distinctively feminine is debatable. It is clear that the impoliter types are distinctively British. The notion that tag questions, like the British, are on the whole a polite species is linguistic mythology.

Notes

1. I am grateful to Charles Clay Doyle for his help and to Sheila Bailey for her critique of this piece, which she found mean-spirited. Though I tried to sweeten the tone, either the subject is intractable or I am. I have treated tag questions at greater length but with fewer types of use in "The Tag Question in British English: It's Different, I'n'it?," *English World-Wide* 9 (1988): 171–91.

2. Examples identified with these cryptic numbers are from the corpus of the Survey of English Usage, University College London. The Survey, founded by Professor, now Sir, Randolph Quirk and today directed by Professor Sidney Greenbaum, is the richest store of grammatically analyzed texts of British English in existence. Examples whose identifications begin with an S are from the spoken half of the corpus, but are here transcribed in conventional orthography.

3. Antonia Fraser, *Your Royal Hostage* (1987; London, 1988), p. 143.

4. Robin Lakoff, *Language and Woman's Place* (New York, 1975), pp. 14–18.

5. Julian Ralph, "The English of the English," *Harper's Magazine* 103 (1901): 448.

❧ KEITH THOMAS

Yours

How SHOULD ONE END A LETTER? As a child in the 1940s, I was taught that the subscription was largely determined by the opening and that both depended upon the nature of the relationship and degree of acquaintance between writer and recipient. A formal business letter began "Dear Sir" and ended "Yours faithfully." A slightly more archaic variant, reserved, I was told, for correspondence with a bank manager, was "Yours truly." A letter addressed by name to an individual with whom one was not closely acquainted ("Dear Mr. Ricks") would be signed "Yours sincerely." To a colleague, friend, or intimate ("Dear Ricks" or, on closer acquaintance, "Dear Christopher") one would sign "Yours ever," or, more casually and informally, "Yours." A jauntier form, popular among military men and kilt-wearing Scots, was "Yours aye." For letters to editors of newspapers "Yours, etc." was appropriate, while in the armed Services there were stiffer forms such as "I have the honour, Sir, to remain your most humble and obedient servant" (or something like that). "Love" was to be bestowed very sparingly, particularly by men writing to men, though it was in order for them to send love to their friends' wives. "Yours affectionately," by contrast, was an acceptable form for women to use.

This was the state of affairs which was briefly codified in 1954 by Alan S. C. Ross during the course of his celebrated article "Linguistic Class Indicators in Present-Day English."[1] He added some interesting nuances, allowing that "Yours very truly" might be used in place of "Yours faithfully" in cases where the writer hoped to meet the recipient, and pointing out that "Yours very sincerely" was, perversely, a less cordial ending than "Yours sincerely" (in the same way, perhaps, that "Very fair" is a less reassuring entry on a school report than "Fair"). Ross described the ending "Yours" as "one often used by gentlemen if they are in doubt as to which ending is appropriate." He also observed that "intellectuals, of any class" (!), often began letters, even when the acquaintance was slight, with a boldly undeferential combination of first name and surname ("Dear Christopher Ricks").

Thirty-five years later, it is only the elderly who still respect these carefully graduated distinctions. Many university students, for example, appear to be barely aware of them. If they begin a letter with "Dear Professor Ricks" they are equally likely to end it with "Yours faithfully" or "Love XXX." For them the subtle (or not so subtle) gradations of relationship expressed by the ascent from "Dear Mr. Ricks" via "Dear Ricks" to "Dear Christopher" have collapsed into the instant intimacy of "Dear Chris"; and the upward progress from "Yours faithfully" via "Yours sincerely" to "Yours ever" has given way to the ubiquitous "Best wishes," a greeting so indiscriminately bestowed upon friends and strangers alike that anyone who really wants to send best wishes to a friend has at the very least to up the bidding to "*Very* best wishes."

The old conventions which are now in disarray were themselves the fossilized survivals of an earlier and more flexible practice in which forms were less stereotyped and more freely adapted to fit particular circumstances. What united the different forms employed in written English over most of the past five hundred years was that they all reasserted the essential relationship of the writer to the subject: "Your humble orator and most bounden beadsman"; "Your sincere wellwisher"; "Your most assured and loving brother"; "Your obedient servant"; "Your true lover"; "Once thy friend." Formulae like these affirmed the attitudes appropriate to different social and personal relationships. Servants were humble and obedient. Husbands and brothers were loving. Friends were affectionate.

Of course, there were numerous changes in fashion between the fifteenth and twentieth centuries. In Tudor and Stuart times the emphasis in subscriptions in letters tended to be on the writer's love, fidelity, constancy, and obedience: "Your lordship's most bounden during life"; "Your own to command"; "Your very assured loving friend and faithful ally." In the Romantic era, by contrast, letter-writers were more likely to stress their truthfulness and authenticity. Hence the rise of "Yours sincerely" at the end of the eighteenth century and the wider currency of such associated forms as "Yours truly" or "Believe me, dear sir." The transition from the old to the new can be seen in 1787, when the Prime Minister signed himself "Most sincerely and faithfully yours, W. Pitt."

Out of these successive protestations of obedience, fidelity, truthfulness, and sincerity there emerged the stereotyped forms which would constitute the standard usage of the midtwentieth century. In themselves they were not necessarily new: the *OED* cites "Yowres, Will Paston" (1430), "Yours ever, T. Heywood" (1611), and "With my best wishes, J. Taylor" (1627). But it is only during the last hundred years or so that they became so dominant. It took time for them to settle; the inversion of "Yours sincerely" into "Sincerely yours" which is nowadays predominantly North American was a common form in the late eighteenth and early nineteenth centuries: "Truly yours, W. Cowper"; "Ever yours, Sydney Smith." They were also originally much stronger in force. In 1792 "Most truly yours, Wm. Cowper" meant what it said; in the 1880s Thomas Hardy used "Yours ever" and "Yours" when writing to his wife. It was only with the passage of time that such expressions became mere formulae, indicative of the degree of previous acquaintance between writer and recipient but otherwise largely devoid of content.

When a phrase once vibrant in meaning has degenerated into an empty formula, it will soon find its detractors. In the Elizabethan period a tendency to undue obsequiousness by courtly letter-writers produced an inevitable reaction. John Smyth of Nibley, Gloucestershire, the Jacobean steward of the Berkeley family, lamented that "Your humble servant" in subscription of letters "hath almost driven 'Your loving friend' quite out of England," while in 1629 Sir Francis Hubert concluded the dedicatory epistle to his poem *The Historie of Edward the Second*, addressed to his brother ("Worthy Sir"): "And so . . . I rest, not 'Your servant,' according to the new and fine but false phrase of the time, but in honest old English 'Your loving brother and true friend for ever.'" Despite such protests, however, "Your humble [or "obedient"] servant" would long be used by those whose relationship to the recipient was anything but servile.

In the midseventeenth century the Quakers reduced the flattering plurality of "Yours" to the literal singularity of "Thine." In the later eighteenth century the reaction against formality expressed itself in the employment of abbreviations: "Yours &c" or, more impressively, "Yours &c, &c." In modern times this would survive as a ponderously old-fashioned way of signing a letter to *The Times*, but originally the *et cetera* formula was used between intimates. Dr. Johnson often signed himself "I am &c" when writing to Mrs. Thrale, while in *Pride and Prejudice et ceteras* are used between brothers and close friends, though Darcy, writing to Mr. Collins, signs himself more ambiguously as "Your's sincerely, &c."[2]

How are we to explain the virtual demise in recent years of the letter-writing formulae which were so universal a few decades ago? Partly, no doubt, it is a matter of the ever-continuing tendency to abbreviation, stemming to some extent from a desire to save time, as in the old style "Yrs" for "Yours," but primarily from a reluctance to spell out the full formula in all its precision. Thus "Yours sincerely" is reduced to "Sincerely" or "Yours" and "Yours ever" to "Ever." "All Best wishes" becomes "Best" or "All Best." I have even seen "All good wishes" rendered as "All good."

This is not just the embarrassed gruffness of middle-aged males, reluctant, for fear of misunderstanding, to bestow tokens of affection upon those who are not their spouses, lovers, parents, or children. The decline of the old subscriptions to letters is better understood as part of that much larger revulsion against formality in personal relationships which has been such a feature of late twentieth-century-life. The distaste for forms of greeting associated with social hierarchy is everywhere evident in contemporary speech and social intercourse. There was a time when British visitors to the United States were startled or even affronted to find themselves addressed by their first names by bank clerks or shop assistants whom they had not previously met and with whom they were doing casual business. But nowadays it is usual in British National Health Service hospitals for patients to be so addressed by their nurses; clergymen seek to break down barriers by asking to be addressed not as "Vicar" or "My Lord" but as "Steve" or "Bishop Derek"; and in professional and business life the use of first names has become universal. In correspondence, the opening formula "Dear Ricks," though standard in the 1950s, has now almost totally disappeared; younger people would certainly find it offensive. An academic writing to a colleague whom he does not know will therefore say "Dear Mr. Ricks," while a journalist or television producer will say "Dear Christopher Ricks." Both of them will dislike the element of distance implicit in these intermediate forms and move to "Dear Christopher" as soon as possible. Similarly, "Esq." has virtually vanished from envelopes, which are as likely as not to be addressed to "Christopher Ricks," without a title of any sort.

In the early twentieth century "Dear Ricks" had been an intimate form of address between professional men and it was only in the last period of its history that it became a mere staging-post on the road to the greater intimacy of "Dear Christopher." With the collapsing of the old-style gradation of relationships it became redundant. Its de-

mise symbolizes the acceptance on equal terms of women in professional life, for it had always been a masculine form, unavailable to fe-
males, and the conversion of "Miss Austen" into "Austen" came too
late to save it. Its disappearance also indicates a greater sense of social
equality. For "Dear Ricks" was essentially an appellation used between those who were deemed to be social equals; and it excluded
those who were not, unless they were at an unambiguously lower social level, in which case it was equally appropriate.[3] Thirty years ago,
when I was a Fellow of All Souls College, Oxford, I received a note
addressed to "Mr. Thomas" from my then colleague, the eminent Socialist writer G. D. H. Cole. It began "Dear Thomas" and turned out
to have been intended for one of the College servants with the same
surname. Cole subsequently reproached me for having opened it,
pointing out that if the letter had been meant for me it would have
been addressed to "K. V. Thomas, Esq.," not "Mr. Thomas," although it would still have begun "Dear Thomas."

In his article of 1954, A. S. C. Ross stressed that the rules for ending
letters were very strict and that, in the eyes of the upper classes, departure from them constituted a serious solecism. It is easy to see why
this was so, for the slackening of these ways of expressing different
kinds of hierarchical relationship parallels and symbolizes the slackening of the relationships themselves, or at least the change in their nature. A child who calls his parents by their first names will not sign his
letters "Your loving son"; and an employee who regards himself as as
good as his employer will not describe himself as "Your obedient servant." Formal subscriptions to letters cannot be expected to survive in
a world where informality has become a public value. Informality is
thought to represent unpretentiousness, ease of access, consideration,
amiability; and it is symptomatic of current attitudes that virtually
every Oxford college feels obliged to describe itself in its admissions
brochure as "friendly and informal." Whether friendliness and informality are necessarily the same thing may be doubted. Certainly it is
possible to applaud the decline of manifest social distinctions while re-
gretting the parallel decay of forms indicating the degree and closeness
of acquaintance between social equals. It is one thing to rejoice that
letter-writers no longer pull their forelocks. It is another to be pleased
that a letter from a stranger is indistinguishable in format from one
from a lifelong friend.

Notes

1. Alan S. C. Ross, "Linguistic Class Indicators in Present-Day English," *Neuphilo-
logische Mitteilungen* 55 (1945).

2. The use of the apostrophe in the possessive pronoun is another subject altogether. The modern ubiquity of intrusive apostrophes in advertisements and other public notices (Breakfast's, Dinner's, Tea's) gives it some topicality.

3. In his *Names, Designations and Appellations* (Society for Pure English Tract 47, Oxford, 1936), R. W. Chapman says that its use was "regulated by class distinctions fairly well defined" (p. 239).

Further Thoughts:
They Can't Even Say It Properly Now

I WILL RESTRICT MYSELF TO JUST ONE newish instance of fashionable malapropism, though it is a very fine one, before switching to another approach.

The *OED* defines *infamy* as "evil fame or reputation, public disgrace, shameful vileness," a word conveying the strongest moral disapprobation. It was this of course that F. D. Roosevelt had in mind when he called that of Pearl Harbor "a day that will live in infamy." Quite suddenly the meaning of the word withered to something like the weaker sense of "notorious," famous for being naughty, disreputable, shocking to those of old-fashioned morality or sensibilities, embarrassing; famous, in fact, for being conventionally unrespectable, nothing worse. So in an official biography we read that

> Evelyn Waugh's career as an Oxford undergraduate is now *infamous*. It wasn't while he was there; it was naughty, etc., but nothing more, because very few people knew about it. Now we all know and so it's become infamous. [I wonder how many others did what I did and stopped reading the book at that point.]

A year or two ago a female novelist who until then would have been described in the press as possessing nothing more disgraceful than a "stormy" or "turbulent" love life, with a liberal garnishing of terms like "unconventional," "offbeat," etc., got a large press interview under the headline, "The Infamous Edna." Oho, I thought, there are still plenty of older people around, especially in places like the law, where *infamous* is still taken to mean what it used to mean; I estimated the average age of those likely to be concerned in a libel action in this country as about fifty. Edna darling, I thought, you've just come in for something like half a million quid. But not a bloody word was said, at any rate in public, and all that had happened was that we had finally lost one more word from the English language. In future we must speak of evil, shameful, vile, etc., behavior, not infamous, or we run the risk of seeming no more than mildly disapproving.

To switch completely now: the most effective and insidious attack on the language is coming now probably from the spoken, not the written, word, from actors and broadcasters. An evening's TV in the U.K. (I cannot believe it is any better in the U.S.) will show that a large number of people who make their living from the speaking of the language have lost interest in the meaning of what is said. If the program looks good, it's good; who cares what it says, because—and here we have a vicious circle already in full swing—a lot of those watching or half-watching aren't listening in any sense, and a lot of the rest are only half-listening. Because the reader is too lazy to go over his material beforehand, he keeps stressing the wrong words and pausing in the wrong places. It would take somebody really quite interested *already* in the subject to make out by listening hard more about the situation wherever it may be—Washington? Syria?—than that there was a hell of a fuss going on there, and who's that interested?

It's even clearer and more comic and awful with drama. I have room for just three examples of the stress falling in the lamentably wrong place. The first I suspect of being apocryphal, but here goes. A small-scale robbery is planned. One of the gang says, "No guns on this trip, fellows—we can get all we want without hurting anyone." And the leader sneers. "What's the matter with you, Scruples?"—taking the last word as, presumably, some exotic nickname. And nobody said Cut, because nobody was listening and it looked all right.

In a wartime escapade a small band of desperadoes is going in to blow up something vital. While the paras are waiting for the drop, the leader says, "Oh, and sorry, guys, there's no return ticket on this one, so say your good-byes now." And a young malcontent bawls, very distinctly, "They *told* me there was a way out!" And nobody said Cut, because, etc.

And most shameful of all, from an internationally famous actress playing Isabella in a prestige production, facing up to Angelo in *Measure for Measure*:

> O! it is excellent
> To have a giant's strength, but it is tyrannous
> To use it like a *giant*.

Nobody could have said Cut then, or not as loudly as it deserved, because this was happening on the stage of a London theater, but I do very much wonder how many in the audience noticed. Certainly there was not the deserved howl of execration.

Honestly, when you get that at what is presumably the top, what are the rest of us to do? We seem to be moving on two fronts, one being the kind of printed atrocity I discussed (along with other writers) in the original volume, the other provided chiefly by television and the habits it brings in its train, towards a social and linguistic situation in which nobody says or writes or probably knows anything more than an approximation to what he or she means and on the hearer's or reader's part nothing more is expected or could be recognized.

Now of course most human discourse has always been like that, if not as much, but we seem to have arranged things, with the powerful back-up of an incomprehension-fostering educational system, to make any approach to precision more difficult, rarer, and *less apparently important* than ever before and at an increasing rate. I can imagine no general solutions. My two private partial ones are to switch to the tabloid press—everything's over sooner—and keep the sound turned down on the television. Yes, and possibly read a book. It would be good if the title page had by law to carry the author's date of birth, so you could avoid anyone born after about 1945. Now *there*'s a practical suggestion.

Note

Kingsley Amis's essay in the 1980 *State of the Language* was entitled "Getting It Wrong."

CHRISTOPHER RICKS

Word Making and Mistaking

I HAD BEHAVED BADLY. (It was getting on for twenty years ago, with marital misery in full swing.) Furied by the revelation that certain revelations had been made to the young ones—when it had been understood, had it not?, that they should be left out of all this for the unforeseeable future—I had gone by myself and had punched the windowpanes alongside the petite conservatory across from our bedroom. It was worse than foolish of me. The breaking glass lacerated my hands much less than I had assumed it would, sanguine as I had been of demonstrating melodramatically how I had been cut to the knuckled quick. Added to which, the panes, duly, later, cost me much more than I had imagined they would, to repair. Worse, it irreparably alarmed my then wife, the crashing tinkling, though less (I continue to believe) than it suited her to incarnate. She 'phoned for the police.

I had judged myself the one the more in danger. But she now felt able to assure herself, not unreasonably, that the looming danger (mine) of being left by her was less than the immediate danger (hers) of *not* being left by me and of being left with me, her being left in the company of someone who was now, what with what, and what with what used to be called cuckoldry, violent to the point of pane-crazing. Anyway, she 'phoned for the police.

They came, two British bobbies, with commendable promptitude given that though the hours were not quite the small ones, it was pretty late at night. It dawned on me later, from something they straightway said, that, seeing me in my dressing-gown, they had detected—wrongly—that here was a husband who had been denied his conjugal rights. This was doubly or even quadrupally a misprision of the state of affairs, but let it pass. I didn't at first understand their male solidarity of solicitude; it took me more than a moment to twig. But the one who spoke, of the two, was altogether understanding. "Well, sir," he rumbled, he was a caution, "Well, sir, we sympathize with you, sir" (how come? my mind whirled, bent rather upon conjugal wrongs)—"but then, sir, you must sympathize with us, sir." Pause. "We get a 'phone-call, sir, telling us that someone has gone beresk."

Beresk! My heart leapt up when I beheld this rainbow in the night sky. What a covenant. All shall be well, and all manner of thing shall be well. On a night like this, even on a night like this, it was good to be alive. Beresk! Bereft, burlesque, grotesque, and berserk as I had become, beresk was exactly what I had gone. He said it. Lips parted, the hope: "beresk." I felt better at once.

Not, naturally, that this stopped things from taking their course. But I haven't forgotten the adrenalin-leap in sympathy with the salmon-leap of the language. I haven't forgotten how hope suddenly took wing, like Marvell's very bird of a soul in "The Garden," or like the Beatles' very soul of a bird (it taking off from a flatfoot pedestrian phrase), a bird which was, the singer sings, only waiting for this moment to arise.

I breathed again. The policeman's breathmaking word deserved to be welcomed, first, with a comic-strip punctuation, beresk!*?!*, and then with a more savoring one: beresk . . .

II

Set aside the old unhappy far-off things, those marriage rights and wrongs; the linguistic-cum-social rights and wrongs remain. For did I have the right to smile, to more than smile, to feel my heart lift? So somebody made a mistake with a word. Word making and mistaking.

What is the nature of the happiness which I (or such as I) feel in the inspired inadvertence, the ignorant bliss, which precipitates such a bizarrerie as "beresk"? I might put it comfortably to myself that a triumph like "beresk" is the higher dyslexia of inspiration, but is dyslexia of any form ever good for a smile? Perhaps all such pleasure is smutched with condescension and snobbery. With, here, the comic stereotype of the British constable, a figure who centuries ago was on

secondment to Messina, much-ado-ing as Constable Dogberry, saying "odorous" when he meant "odious" and "vigitant" when he
meant "vigilant." A modern Dogberry might mean by *vigitant*—or
his creator might suggest by the word—some combination of fidg-
eting and vigilant, but *fidget* wasn't to hand in Shakespeare's day
(though *fidge* was, to move about restlessly or uneasily).

The slithy toves? "Well, *slithy* means 'lithe' and 'slimy,'" explained
the egg-head Humpty Dumpty, doing the unpacking (and he fated to
be soon beyond any repacking), "You see it's like a portmanteau—
there are two meanings packed up into one word." No mistake about
that. So it has to be acknowledged that at the policeman's moment my
happiness (piercingly unexpected, in the circumstances) was different
in kind from any which I could have been given even by Lewis Carroll
or James Joyce with their portmanteau powers and their wordsmith's
artistry.

The point doesn't turn on "*conscious* artistry," since the artist imaginatively takes advantage of the unbeknownst, and the greatest writers
are those who have the most cooperative subconscious, not those who
presume that by taking thought they can add a cubit to the stature of
the language. Art not only can but does—and not only does but does
well to—tap subterranean workings which are concealed from the
light of its day, from its conscious deliberations. Art finds worth in
what began as accident. Art has its *felicities*, to use the good old word
which once resisted the exacerbations of the will by acknowledging
the part played by hap and happiness in any creative enterprise. (How
infelicitous the cagey dicey word *aleatory* feels in comparison.) The
Muse takes you unawares, she

> dictates to me slumb'ring, or inspires
> Easy my unpremeditated verse.

Art is allowed to be not only unpremeditated, but unpostmeditated.

The nub, then, is not simply that the policeman was unaware
whereas Lewis Carroll was aware, for Carroll had divinations at a
depth well below anything like conscious awareness.

> *mantology*: *Obs. rare.* The art or practice of divination. 1774. "That re-
> markable mantology, or gift of prophecy, which distinguishes the in-
> habitants of the Hebrides under the name of second sight." So *mantolo-*
> *gist*, "one skilled in mantology or divination; a diviner, a prophet."

Carroll, like Joyce with his second hearing as well as second sight, was
a portmantologist.

Some part of Carroll, as of Joyce, knew what he was doing, even
if he did not know all that he was doing. A distinction therefore re-

mains, a crucial difference between an artist's felicity and a blunderer's fluke, and therefore a crucial difference in the nature of the delight we might take or make in a mistake or a "mistake."

By *beresk* the policeman may well have meant no more than "berserk" after all. I was in no position to divine from our brief encounter whether he had much by way of a cooperative subconscious. If *beresk* looked like a portmanteau word, that is probably because I packed it. If the word struck me, that may be because it was I who stood within striking range. I just happened to be there, that's all. If there was a joke, it was probably I who made it or who made a joke of it. But I haven't made up the policeman or his word; you must please take my word for it. At this date I cannot produce any witnesses.

> I see no indecency, said the policeman.
> We arrive too late, said Mr. Hackett. What a shame.
> Do you take me for a fool? said the policeman.
> Mr. Hackett recoiled a step, forced back his head until he thought his throatskin would burst, and saw at last, afar, bent angrily upon him, the red violent face.
> Officer, he cried, as God is my witness, he had his hand upon it.
> God is a witness that cannot be sworn.
> If I interrupted your beat, said Mr. Hackett, a thousand pardons. I did so with the best intentions, for you, for me, for the community at large.
> The policeman replied briefly to this.

Samuel Beckett's policeman, there at the beginning of *Watt* (and exemplary he is too), is a living figment. My policeman was—as God is my witness—a living fact and an arresting mistaker of the language. Did I take him for a fool?

He was unwitting, and that was a great part of why his word recovered my spirits (as no crafty crafted word-work could have done), but this is not to judge him witless or half-witted. T. S. Eliot once tried to bring back the concept of "holy mirth"—if holy, then close to the fool or the Fool or the Holy Fool. Could the policeman have made such fun for me without my being charged with making fun of him? A deep phrase, *make fun of* (we are brazed to it, as we are to the surprise of *make love*). The *Oxford English Dictionary* too curtly defines *to make fun of* as "to ridicule." Fun is a more genial or generous thing than that, even more genial than sport (making sport of), and far more genial than mockery (making a mock of).

III

There is no glee but could give offense, and there is no joke but could give offense because of a prejudicial *-ism*. It is not that the charge would necessarily stick, but that if no such charge were conceivable, no true joke would have happened. Analogously, erotic art must expect to be deemed pornographic by some, and religious art blasphemous by some; if the art's even being questioned on this score were to be manifestly out of the question, the art would be culpably unimpeachable. Art must say, with Mrs. Malaprop, "I own the soft impeachment."

Is the creation that is Mrs. Malaprop sexist? If it is not, this will be largely because of the handsomeness with which Richard Brinsley Sheridan has her partake of his creativity. Among the many pairs in *The Rivals* who can be thought of as the Rivals, there figure Mrs. Malaprop and her creator, glowingly contestant. For Mrs. Malaprop has a scarcely less wonderful sense of the life of language than he has, and you can feel Sheridan's sheer gratitude to her. She lends him her supremely cooperative subconscious. It was a stroke of collaborative genius by her maker that gave her this first idiosyncrasy at her first entrance: "But the point we would request of you is, that you will promise to forget this fellow—to illiterate him, I say, quite from your memory." Nothing will obliterate that from one's memory. If Mrs. Malaprop says "contagious" when she means "contiguous," this is because something in her has divined an unexpected relation between the two. Her practice is not to pack portmanteaux or to telescope words' forms exactly, but in unerringly choosing the wrong word she is a great one for hitting on a right relation. She is mistress of the household misappliances.

In the circumstances which condition her utterances (and not only there, since like all the rich mythological figures in literature she lives beyond her means) she is right to choose not to "wish a daughter of mine to be a progeny of learning." She feels acutely that the "intrinsic" of which she wishes to speak is intrinsically and intricately involved with the "intricate" (the word she comes up and out with). She unmisgivingly grasps that the "meritorious" is often no more and no other than what she says it is, "meretricious." She wings the thought that the "velocity" she urgently advises would be a "felicity," as she felicitously puts it: "Why, fly with the utmost felicity to be sure, to prevent mischief."

"Ah! few gentlemen, now a days, know how to value the ineffectual qualities in a woman!" A decision on political grounds to have no truck whatsoever with any disreputable *-ism* would be tantamount to the decision to ban jokes. All jokes depend on stereotypes, upon generalizations, and upon typicalities or representativenesses which can easily—as we now easily know—constitute an abuse as well as be abusive. But the benignity of jokes is inseparable from, though not indistinguishable from, the possibility of their malignity. When would-be jokes cry simply Avaunt! at racism, sexism, classism, ethnicism, or élitism, the old want is supplied instead by speciesism, fattism, baldism, heightism, smokerism, or whatever. If a joke is in touch with no -*ism*, it is out of touch and is no joke.

Even to speak of a linguistic mistake as a "solecism" is, after all, to risk representations from the citizens of Soloi. They insist that they are not philistines; which prompts the people of Philistia . . . The entry under *Philistine* in the *Oxford English Dictionary* ("A person deficient in liberal culture and enlightenment, whose interests are chiefly bounded by material and commonplace things") is moved to a caveat at once salty and genuinely liberal: "But often applied contemptuously by connoisseurs of any art or department of learning to one who has no knowledge or appreciation of it; sometimes a mere term of dislike for those whom the speaker considers 'bourgeois.'"

To browse in the second edition of the *OED* (1989's supreme book) is to see that lexicography, no less than literature, is news that stays news—including the news of that which has not stayed. One reason why we need so capacious a dictionary—twenty volumes—is that only on such a scale can there be recorded all those words which died, which were let die. The *OED* records the death of many opprobrious terms under *woman, women, female, feminine,* and their cognates. The life of a language is at one with its *not* persisting in the sneers and fleers of injustice, even though it be the dictionary's duty to preserve their traces. Many ugly, graceless, bigoted, irresponsible, and unworthy usages came to nothing. A good thing too. All is not lost.

All is not won, either. A delicate humane vigilance about -*isms*, sexism for instance, is not everybody's desire, and some (from all flanks) who propose it in theory oppose it in practice. Even those who genuinely seek it are not always able to achieve it, so *nuancé* and *nuancée* can a word be. The second edition of the *OED* defines *wimmin*: "A semi-phonetic spelling of 'women,' recently adopted by some feminists as a form not containing the ending -*men*. Also, at an earlier date, occasionally used ironically in other contexts." Whether one likes the word or not (I do, because of its being a retort, turning contempt back upon the contemptuous: Grumpy in *Snow White and the Seven Dwarfs*, "Wimmin! Pah!"), "wimmin" is more than *semi*-phonetic; I'd have said it was phonetic. And when "s/he" is defined as "written representation of 'he or she,'" I'd say rather "of 'she or he.'"

Even the entries for the suffixes -*ism* and -*ist* themselves lack something. The definitions of *racism* (*racialism*), *sexism,* and *speciesism* are all persuasive:

Belief in the superiority of a particular race leading to prejudice and antagonism towards people of other races, esp. those in close proximity who may be felt as a threat to one's cultural and racial integrity or economic well-being.

The assumption that one sex is superior to the other and the resultant discrimination practised against members of the supposed inferior sex, esp. by men against women; also conformity with the traditional stereotyping of social roles on the basis of sex.

Discrimination against or exploitation of certain animal species by human beings, based on an assumption of mankind's superiority.

The etymology of *racism*, *sexism*, and *speciesism* is given simply and rightly as the root noun plus the suffix *-ism*. But the entries under the suffixes *-ism* and *-ist* don't then catch these touchy cases. For *-ism* in *racism* carries the charge of prejudicial discrimination, an animus not manifest in the suffix entries:

1. Forming a simple noun of action [as *baptism*]
    b. the action or conduct of a class of persons [as *heroism*]
2. Forming the name of a system of theory or practice,
    religious, ecclesiastical, philosophical, political, social, etc. [as *Buddhism*]
    b. More of the nature of class-names or descriptive terms, for doctrines or principles [as *feminism*]
3. Forming a term denoting a peculiarity or characteristic,
    esp. of language [as *Scotticism*, *solecism*]

None of these covers the case of what is imputed by *-ism* in *racism*, *sexism*, and *speciesism*; the nearest is 2b, but in being near it is also in some ways the opposite. Those who subscribe to feminism would not accept that their *-ism* is of a piece with the *-ism* of *sexism*. For such pejorative words as are instanced under 2b are indicted by their root ("libertinism"), not—as with *speciesism*—by a pejorative imputation in the suffix itself.

Here even the great dictionary, which is right to take words as it finds them, mistakes its findings. It is a mild mistake, but with something as powerful as words the consequences might not be mild. Not that we should expect of a team of lexicographers what every single one of us ordinarily lacks, a perfectly balanced mind, so we should not be fuming or furious when a dictionary comes short of it. "If you have that rarest of gifts," said Lewis Carroll, "a perfectly balanced mind, you will say 'frumious,' instead of 'fuming furious.'"

~ GEOFFREY NUNBERG

What the Usage Panel Thinks

IN EVERY AGE, LANGUAGE CRITICISM HAS BEEN concerned with issues that in retrospect often seem incomprehensibly trivial. Swift and Addison railed at the contemporary abbreviations of *mobile vulgus* to *mob* and *positive* to *pozz*. Benjamin Franklin wrote to ask Noah Webster whether the lexicographer might not in some future publication "set a discountenancing mark" upon the verb *to notice* and the use of *improve* in place of *ameliorate*—even as Webster was dedicating his own efforts to purging the American language of British spellings like *honour* and *theatre*. Matthew Arnold berated the *Times* for its "orthographical antics" spelling *diocese* as *diocess*. And just a few years ago, critics were describing the verb *to contact* as an "abomination" and a "lubricious barbarism."

If we take all these complaints at face value, we can only conclude that language criticism is a vain and futile exercise, as many linguists have claimed. One way or another, the language sorts itself out: either the offending usages become wholly respectable, as with *mob* or the verb *to notice*; or, like *pozz* and *diocess*, they are discarded without need of outside prompting.

But it is a mistake to read the critical tradition too literally, or to assess its importance in terms of its material effects on the language itself. Language criticism is concerned with language only as it reflects the values and models that determine the shape of public discourse.

For Swift, the use of abbreviations like *mob* typified the spoken language of court fops, and by extension the indifference of the aristocracy to literary authority. For Webster, the spelling *honour* signaled obsequious deference to British cultural models, in an age when it was still up for grabs whether Americans would continue to think of themselves as speaking "English" at all.

Changes in the language itself have played very little part in determining the form of these critical questions, and vice versa. It is true that Swift's reservations about *mob* were obviated when that particular word passed from fashionable cant into general usage, but it is more important that once Johnson and his contemporaries established the undisputed authority of literary precedent, subsequent generations of critics and grammarians no longer shared Swift's concern about the spoken language. The main effect of language change is epiphenomenal, since it often obscures from us the significance that a usage had for its contemporaries. A generation from now, most people will find it puzzling that critics should have objected to the verb *to impact*. That will not show that the objections were without substance, but only that *impact* has lost the connotations that make it for us the perfect example of pretentious jargon.

Linguists are therefore right in observing that the debates over usage in recent years have very little to do with the current "state of the language," whatever that is. English takes care of itself. But the controversies do signal important changes in critical attitudes about language, which in turn reflect tacit changes in the conception of the public discourse. It is misleading to describe these changes in terms of the abstract debate between "traditionalist" and "permissivist" views of usage. The dichotomy does not do justice to the subtleties of the changes in actual critical attitudes, and is itself a purely modern formulation. The very description "traditional values" is an anachronism that would have meant nothing to Arnold or Fowler. What lends the critical discourse its particular meaning is not the substantive points of usage that critics seize upon, but the kinds of arguments they bring to bear, and the kinds of social questions that are symbolically at stake. In fact I will suggest here that the line of traditional language criticism is now carried on not in discussions of those usage rules that are commonly described as "traditional," but in debates about the sorts of usage questions that feminists have raised.

To document some of these changes in critical attitudes, I will be drawing on the results of a survey that I designed with Kristin Hanson and the editors of the *American Heritage Dictionary*. The survey was administered in 1988 to the members of the dictionary's "usage panel," a group of about 175 well-known writers, scholars, broadcasters, and public figures who are periodically polled for their opinions on sensitive questions of usage.[1] The surveys serve primarily to obtain information about the acceptability of particular items that might be helpful to users of the dictionary; thus in the usage note at *finalize*, a user can learn that although the word is in widespread general use, it is unacceptable to 90 percent of a panel of writers and scholars. But the survey also enabled us to get an overview of the linguistic concerns of the literary and cultural elite that is traditionally vested with authority over the public discourse. And by comparing our results with those of earlier surveys, we were able in many cases to trace changes in the critical evaluation of particular usages.

The most recent set of questionnaires covered more than 250 different items, ranging over new-age coinages like *wellness* and the verb *to parent*, canonical grammatical questions like the distinction between *who* and *whom*, and many of the usage problems that feminists have raised. Obviously the panelists' reactions to different items reflected different preoccupations; as the linguist Antoine Meillet once put it, "every word has its story." But interesting tendencies did emerge, many of which signaled changes in the panelists' attitudes, not just toward particular words, but about the importance of usage questions in general.

We were struck, for example, by the panel's turnabout on a set of traditional rules of diction that involve arguments from etymology: "*aggravate* should not be used to mean 'irritate,' since its etymological meaning is 'make worse' "; "*anxious* should not be used to mean 'eager' "; and so on. Here are the relevant example sentences (in all of the following, the percentage indicates the proportion of panelists who found the highlighted usage "acceptable"):

Anxious for "eager": *We are anxious to see the new sculpture show.*
　　1969: 23%
　　1988: 52%

Aggravating for "irritating": *It's aggravating to have to ask Michelle twice whenever you want something done.*
　　1969: 43%
　　1988: 71%

Transpire for "occur": *All of these events transpired after last week's announcement.*
　　1969: 38%
　　1988: 58%

Transpire for "become public" (etymologically correct): *Despite efforts to hush the matter up, it soon* transpired *that the Colonel had in fact met with the rebel leaders.*

    1988: 50% (not asked in previous surveys)

Cohort as an individual term: *The cashiered dictator and his* cohorts *have all written their memoirs.*

    1969: 31%
    1988: 71%

Cohort as a collective noun (etymologically correct): *The gangster walked into the room surrounded by his* cohort.

    1988: 44% (not asked in previous surveys)

Decimate for "slaughter the majority of": *The Jewish population of Germany was* decimated *by the war.*

    1973: 26%[2]
    1988: 66%

Dilemma for "choice among three or more": *Students who haven't finished their dissertations by the time their fellowships expire face a difficult* dilemma: *whether to take out loans to support themselves, to try to work part-time at both a job and their research, or to give up on the dissertation entirely.*

    1988: 65% (not asked in previous surveys)

Celibate for "unmarried" (etymologically correct): *He remained* celibate, *although he engaged in sexual intercourse.*

    1988: 32% (not asked in previous surveys)

It is clear that these shifts in opinion don't reflect any abrupt changes in general use.[3] The unetymological uses of *anxious, aggravating,* and *transpire* all have respectable nineteenth-century literary precedents; the extended uses of *cohort* to refer to an individual, and of *decimate* to mean "kill a large proportion," are more recent, but these too have been well established for years. Certainly none of these usages were any less common twenty years ago than now.

On the other hand, the shifts don't reflect any broad tendency for panelists to be more liberal or permissive than they were on previous ballots. In fact the panel remained adamant in rejecting other usages that have the weight of general acceptance on their side. For example, 89 percent of the panel refused to accept *disinterested* for "uninterested" (the figure was 93 percent in 1969); and in the notorious case of *hopefully* as a sentence adverb, the panel has actually become progressively more conservative over the course of several surveys:

Hopefully, *neither side will insist on a complete cease-fire as a precondition for opening negotiations.*

1969: 44%
1975: 37%
1988: 27%

So the changes of heart with respect to *aggravate, decimate, transpire*, and the rest signal a reevaluation of these particular usages. It is not simply that they are now perceived as lost causes—that has been clear for years, and might as easily be said of *hopefully* and *disinterested*—but that the panelists have come to regard them as "trivial," and "not worth fighting about," as several of them remarked in their comments.

What distinguishes the arguments for the "correct" uses of words like *aggravate* and *decimate* is that they call for a deference to the senses of the Greek and Latin elements that the words are composed of. (Apart from the odd remark on "shamefaced," I can think of no cases where critics have based an argument for correctness on an Anglo-Saxon etymology.) The panel's discounting of these rules indicates the diminished relevance and authority of those languages, and of a classical formation in general. In an age when a knowledge of Latin and Greek could be presumed of anyone who might participate in the public sphere, the unetymological uses of *aggravate* or *transpire* might have seemed genuine illiteracies (in the sense in which Chesterfield in 1748 could define an *illiterate* as "a man who is ignorant of" Greek and Latin). But it has been a hundred years since a writer could insert an untranslated Latin tag into a text without appearing pedantic or pretentious. As the Hellenist G. S. Kirk noted several years ago: "We no longer need to do Latin and Greek in order to become philosophers, priests, historians, or artists—or just to become educated."[4] It is true that you do not have to be a classicist to recognize the scraps of Latin concealed in words like *aggravate* or *decimate*. But whatever the practical arguments for acquiring a little Latin, the accomplishment no longer has any symbolic importance. Etymology can sometimes still tell you what a word actually means, but it can no longer dictate what it ought to mean.

These usage questions rehearse in miniature the debates surrounding the perception of a precipitate decline in the importance of humanist classicism, and the efforts to reconstitute its program in the name of "cultural literacy." There too, many advocates have had qualms about making the case for the Great Tradition on moral grounds and have fallen back on pragmatic arguments: just as you may be able to figure out what *decimate* means (or used to mean) if you know that *deci-* means "tenth" and *-mate* means "kill," so you may be helped to recognize a textual allusion in a text if you know who dragged whom around the walls of what. But this sort of reasoning can't restore the place of the classics as prescriptive models. Like etymology, literature itself may be a useful thing to know about, but it no longer has any privileged moral authority in the wider public sphere. The responses to these questions indicate the panelists' acknowledgement of the marginalization and professionalization of literature—indicate it more decisively, perhaps, than anything they might have said about the question directly.

This sense of the etiolation of the critical tradition also played a role in the panel's attitudes toward those canonical rules of usage based on arguments from grammatical consistency: matters like the choice of *who* or *whom*, the split infinitive, the rules of pronoun agreement, and the qualification of absolute adjectives like *unique*. On first consideration, the panel appeared to take a more conservative line on these rules than on rules based on etymology. For example:

> *Her designs are* quite unique *in today's fashion scene.*
> Acceptable to 16%
> (1969: 6% accept the phrase "the most unique"; no context given)

> *Even if he* was/were *elected, he would be unable to form a majority.* (Choose one or both)
> *was:* 4%
> *were:* 84%
> both: 12%

> *Anyone who isn't happy with the decision can take* their *grievance to the arbitrator.* (Queried for acceptability in informal speech)
> Acceptable to 33%

> *The move allowed the company* to legally pay *severance payments to the workers.*
> Acceptable to 50%

> *Since that day, none of the conspirators* has/have *been brought to trial.* (Choose one or both)
> *has:* 79%
> *have:* 10%
> both: 10%
> (1969: 28% say that *none* must always take a singular verb; no context given)

But the conservatism of these figures is not especially informative: the bare percentages don't indicate what importance the panelists attach to these rules. Did the responses reflect a commitment to grammatical principle, or simply a don't-make-trouble accommodation of traditional norms? The suggestion of an answer came from the panelists' responses to some additional queries, which called for more careful reflection on the grammatical points at issue. In addition to asking the panel about the phrase *quite unique*, for example, we included other examples involving modification of *unique*, and got some revealing results:

> *The American Constitution is still* nearly unique *in that it allows no self-destruct mechanism.*
> Acceptable to 28%

> *Los Angeles is* no less unique *a city than New York or Paris.*
> Acceptable to 31%

Even allowing that *unique* is unequivocally an absolute term, these constructions ought to be acceptable. Grammarians have always noted that the absolutes can be freely modified by qualifiers like *nearly, almost,* or *surely*; there is nothing illogical in saying "The wound was nearly fatal," or "Hamlet's wound was no less fatal than Laertes'." Yet in their comments on these examples, many of the panelists indicated that they had interpreted the traditional rule as prohibiting any modification of *unique* whatsoever: "*Unique* by definition does not mix with qualifiers"; "Something either is unique or it isn't"; and so forth. It appears that most of the panelists were applying an overgeneralized rule that keeps *unique* at arm's length from any adverb. Such a rule ensures that you will never commit any egregious solecism, but it is unrelated to the logical principle that originally motivated the censure of phrases like *quite unique* and *most unique* in the first place.

We found similar patterns in the panelists' approach to usage problems involving *each other* and *one another, further* and *farther,* and the subjunctive and indicative moods. The split infinitive was an interesting case in point. To be sure, about half the panelists judged split infinitives acceptable: this has always been one rule that even many purists call puristic. But among those who do adhere to the rule, there was a tendency to overgeneralize the rule to constructions that did not in fact involve an infinitive, but rather a prepositional phrase:

> *It appears that much of my life as a journalist has been devoted* to sedulously setting off *firecrackers.*
> Acceptable to 49%

Thus a large proportion of the panelists appeared to be flagging any construction where an adverb occurs between the word *to* and any form of a verb.

Admittedly, these were trick questions. It's fair to assume that most

of the panelists would have accepted *nearly unique* if they had given the
construction any serious reflection, and that they would have realized
on consideration that the phrase *devoted to sedulously setting off firecrack-
ers* does not contain a split infinitive. Their responses on these items
betray not ignorance but inattentiveness: they appear to be mainly
concerned with avoiding the sorts of grammatical pitfalls which got
them into trouble in high school English, or which might provoke objections from overzealous copy editors who took *their* high school English seriously. As one panelist wrote in explaining why he had insisted that *none* must always be treated as singular (a notion dismissed
by both Fowler and the *OED*): "The shade of Sister Petra sits watch
over this one."

Of course there has always been a tendency toward grammatical
overgeneralization and hypercorrection. Sixty years ago, Fowler cited
numerous examples of adverb misplacements that had obviously resulted from an unwarranted fear of splitting an infinitive. And the
rules of grammatical correctness have always done double duty as social shibboleths, particularly in the Victorian era. ("A little youth, a little beauty, a little good sense and pretty behavior—one musn't object
to those things; and they go just as well with money as without it. And
I suppose I should like her people to be rather grammatical"—William
Dean Howells, *The Rise of Silas Lapham*.) Yet it is clear that earlier ages
took grammar more seriously—which is also to say, less fetishisti-
cally—than it is taken now.

It is tempting to see the decline of general interest in grammar as a
casualty of the success of modern linguistics in establishing its authority. In recent years, the academic growth of the field and the spate
of popular writing about the "Chomskian revolution" have succeeded
in persuading a large portion of the intellectual community that the
study of grammar is a dauntingly technical discipline, with closer connections to logic and mathematics than to the study of literary texts.
It is no longer commonly assumed that the logic of grammar is accessible to the reflection of ordinary folk.

But in its rarified form the study of grammar has always been
somewhat arcane; what is new is the sense that it is also irrelevant. The
original canonization of grammar was based on the doctrine that the
structure of language recapitulated the form of human reason, so that,
as Mill put it, "the structure of every sentence is a lesson in logic." The
study of grammar could therefore offer a model for the organization
and acquisition of all knowledge, or in Hegel's words, as "the single
letters or rather the vowels of the spiritual realm, with which we begin
in order to spell it out and then learn to read it."

Thus grammar provided a metaphysics of criticism, and its rules were the schemas for all the rules that regimented the conduct of public discourse. Cobbett made this rationale explicit in 1823 in his *Grammar of the English Language:*

> as to knowledge connected with books, there is a step to be taken before you can fairly enter upon any path. In the immense field of this kind of knowledge, innumerable are the paths, and GRAMMAR is the gate of entrance to them all. And, if grammar is so useful in the attaining of knowledge, it is absolutely necessary in order to enable the possessor to communicate, by writing, that knowledge to others.[5]

Given this understanding of the importance of grammar, it is natural that the eighteenth- and nineteenth-century writers should have made usages like the *who/whom* distinction the canonical issues of language criticism, or that they should have taken the rules as matters of serious controversy—for example, Webster held that *Whom did you speak to?* was an absurdity. It is only in the present century that the rules have been ossified as a body of traditional lore.

Now we hold that the logic of grammar is peculiar to itself. That is the doctrine that distinguishes modern theories of grammar from their predecessors; for many linguists, in fact, the underlying principles of grammar are determined by an innate, language-specific mechanism that has not even a biological connection to the general principles of human reasoning. But technical arguments have had less effect on general attitudes toward grammar than the erosion of its symbolic importance. Textual criticism and exegesis is no longer the model for public discourse, and the organization and communication of knowledge—or as we now say, information—need not obey specifically linguistic laws.

This trivialization of grammar explains why the panelists, like most writers, should tend to conform uncritically to the traditional rules. If there is no larger issue at stake in the question of whether *none* can be treated as a plural, then there is no point in defying the dictates of Sister Petra. The usage has become a matter of simple etiquette, and in such matters, precisely because they are unimportant, we submit to arbitrary precedent.[6] That is why we now think of an insistence on grammatical correctness as a "conservative" position, and why it is hard for us to understand how these same principles could have been part of the radical political program of writers as diverse as Cobbett and Gramsci. Yet this shows only that rules of usage count for nothing in themselves, and acquire meaning only in a cultural setting.

The declining importance of these traditional canons reflects a new conception of the function of public discourse. The line of language criticism that stretches from Addison to Fowler was part of the larger critical enterprise of articulating a body of cultural values within a relatively homogeneous public sphere. It is a view that can still exercise a nostalgic appeal on writers and intellectuals, particularly where the proprietary language of cultural criticism is at stake; hence the panelists' resistance to the change in meaning of words like *disinterested*. But the modern view of the importance of language owes more to writers like Orwell, whose language criticism was concerned with maintaining a coherent political discourse in a culturally and ideologically fragmented community. In the modern critical discussion, the most sensitive and interesting points of disputed usage involve the claims of various political, professional, and social constituencies.

The ideology of pluralism has had a profound effect on language criticism—so much so that we did not feel ourselves entitled to repeat some items that had appeared on earlier surveys, where panelists were asked to rule on the acceptability of expressions like *gay*, *pro-choice*, and *Native American*. Over the last twenty years, it has become a widely accepted principle of usage that every political or social group has the right to name itself and its own, unless the changes have collateral linguistic effects.[7]

Such effects abound in the linguistic program that feminists have proposed, which is one reason why it has become the paramount issue in modern language criticism. Sex differences have such extensive linguistic reflexes, and are so intricately woven into the whole of English grammar, that the problems cannot be resolved by fiat, in the way that the name *Oriental* can be unproblematically replaced by *Asian*, or *Negro* by *black*. But the debate over feminist linguistic concerns has also taken a different form from discussions of other usage questions, because in this case the relevant interests largely transcend distinctions of class, ethnicity, and cultural and professional background, so that the problem is one of adjudicating claims that arise within the cultural elite itself. With questions of diction or grammatical correctness, the panelists tended to see their task as prescribing standards for the larger community; here they approached the problems as matters of common concern.

In this survey, we asked the panelists about several dozen words and constructions that have been implicated in feminist discussions of language.[8] In one set of questions, for example, we asked the panelists to judge the acceptability of sentences containing a variety of words with the suffix -*ess* (for these items, I have broken down the responses according to the sex of the panelists):[9]

When the ambassadress *arrives, please show her directly to my office.*
women: 13%
men: 28%
total: 23%

Georgia O'Keeffe is not as well known as a sculptress *as she is as a painter.*
women: 15%
men: 42%
total: 34%

Mary Ann is such a charming hostess *that her parties always go off smoothly.*
women: 74%
men: 92%
total: 86%

Mata Hari used her ability as a seductress *to spy for the Germans.*
women: 69%
men: 70%
total: 69%

His only hope now is to marry an heiress.
women: 92%
men: 95%
total: 94%

Mr. Bhutto's daughter and political heiress, *Benazir Bhutto, returned to Pakistan in April.*
women: 28%
men: 37%
total: 34%

There are not very many good parts available for older actresses.
women: 92%
men: 98%
total: 96%

He coaches British actors and actresses *in the pronunciation of American English.*
women: 73%
men: 83%
total: 80%

The feminist objection to suffixes like *-ess* is that they imply invidiously that there is a difference in social and occupational roles as they are performed by a man or a woman.[10] Clearly the great majority of the panelists have found this sort of argument persuasive in at least some cases, as witness the large proportion of panelists who reject *sculptress* and *ambassadress*. (The numbers for men are particularly striking when you consider that the average age of men on the panel is over sixty.) On the other hand, very few of the panelists appear to have dropped the suffix categorically: more than 90 percent accept some uses of words like *actress* and *heiress*, for example. Instead, they evaluated these words on a case-by-case basis. The suffix is generally less acceptable when used in occupational terms like *sculptress* and *ambassadress* than it is with the names of social roles, such as *seductress* and *hostess*, presumably because the occupational distinctions might have pernicious economic consequences. But the distinction between *actor* and *actress* is allowed, since that is one profession in which the jobs one can take obviously depend on one's sex. Note also that the acceptability of a particular word may depend on the context. *Heiress* was acceptable to 94 percent of the panel when used literally, but to only 34 percent when used metaphorically to refer to a political relationship. In the same way, the acceptability of *actress* varied according to the point under discussion.

We found a similar pattern in the panelists' reaction to the use of *-man* in compound words like *statesman* and *businessman*. Here again, the acceptability varied greatly according to both the particular item and the context. As with *-ess*, the forms with *-man* were generally less acceptable with words that denoted occupational roles (*spokesman, businessman*) than with more general social roles (*layman, freshman*). The *-man* forms were also less acceptable when applied to a particular woman than when used generically. Here are some of the responses (these are not broken down according to the sex of respondents, but the proportions here were much the same as with *-ess*):

> The chairman *will be appointed by the Faculty Senate.*
>   acceptable to 67%

> *Emily Owen,* chairman *of the Mayor's Task Force, issued a statement assuring residents that their views would be solicited.*
>   acceptable to 48%

> *The antitrust laws are intended not only to promote economic efficiency, but also to protect consumers and small* businessmen.
>   acceptable to 61%

> *The real reason for the success of her law practice is that she's such a good* businessman.
>   acceptable to 19%

> *To the* layman, *the field sounds more recondite than it actually is.*
>   acceptable to 85%

> *To the* layman, *a negative result on a Pap test seems to offer complete reassurance of freedom from cervical cancer.*
> acceptable to 70%

> *Sally has lived off campus since she was a* freshman.
> acceptable to 90%

Finally, we asked the panel about the problem of the "generic" use of masculine pronouns with singular antecedents referring to groups of mixed or unspecified sex; that is, antecedents like *a taxpayer, every student,* and so on. In fact it is doubtful whether these pronouns are really grammatically gender-neutral (if they were, we would not be made uneasy by sentences like *Each of the stars of "It Happened One Night" won an Oscar for his performance* or *A ballet dancer must be prepared to switch to character parts when he reaches his forties*). Rather, the traditional convention should be understood as allowing that when speaking of a group of people of mixed or unspecified sex, we may take the representative member to be a male. The feminist objections to this presumption are well known, but there are complications to all of the alternatives to using the masculine pronoun—adopting disjoint forms like *his or her* or *his/her*, going to the plural *their*, alternating automatically between masculine and feminine forms, or introducing a wholly novel pronoun like *s/he*.

For these items, we asked the panelists to fill in the blanks in a number of sentences where a pronoun would normally be required. We tabulated the responses according to whether the panelists used *he* or some other form, such as *his or her, his/her, their,* and so forth. (The panelists often indicated that they would have preferred to rewrite the sentence so as to provide a plural antecedent like *parents* or *all patients.* This is doubtless the most common strategy for avoiding the pronoun problem, but we did not permit the panelists this option; we wanted to know whether they would use the masculine form when their backs were against the grammatical wall.) Here are some of the results:

> *A writer who draws on personal experience for* _____ *material should not be surprised if the reviewers seize on that fact.*
> his: 50%
> other singular (*his or her, her or his, his/her, her,*[11] etc.): 48%
> their: 2%

> *A taxpayer who fails to disclose the source of* _____ *income can be prosecuted under the new law.*
> his: 46%
> other singular: 53%
> their: 1%

A patient who doesn't accurately report _____ *sexual history to the physician*
runs a risk of misdiagnosis.
    his: 37%
    other singular: 61%
    their: 2%

A child who wants to become a doctor should be encouraged by _____ *parents*
and teachers.
    his: 36%
    other singular: 60%
    their: 2%

Several tendencies are evident here. First, almost none of the panelists were willing to violate the traditional requirement that a singular pronoun be used, even though every speaker uses *they*, *their*, and *them* as singular pronouns in unmonitored conversation.[12] Faced with a choice between a masculine and a disjoint form like *his or her*, the panelists chose one of three strategies. About 35 percent stuck with the masculine in all contexts, and another 50 percent used only the disjoint forms. The remaining 15 percent made their choices sentence-by-sentence. They allowed the masculine where the sex of the subject would be irrelevant, as when talking about a writer's use of personal material or a taxpayer's disclosure of income. But they insisted on a more explicit form where the sex might be contextually important, as when talking about a child's career plans.

The immediate conclusion from these responses is that the feminist program has had a considerable effect on what people say (or at least on what they report they say). The overwhelming majority of panelists, male and female, have abandoned at least some of the usages that feminists have objected to. Of course there is no way to know how many of them are sincere in this (or even what it would mean to be "sincere" about using a certain pronoun, say) and how many are chiefly concerned to avoid raising feminist hackles. Often, the disavowal of sexist language is simply the tribute that vice pays to versa. But in any event, the panelists' approach to these issues is markedly different from their categorical acquiescence to traditional grammatical strictures, where there seem to be no larger issues at stake. In the feminist cases they have obviously given considerable thought to the problems; they evaluate each case in the light of the conflicting claims of syntax, precedent, and social justice. Even the minority of panelists who still cleave unequivocally to unreconstructed usages were able to present closely reasoned rationales for their choices.

In an important way, then, the feminist linguistic program has already succeeded, in that it has forced most literate speakers to reflect

on the ways in which usage might imply or reinforce gender stereotypes. Of course the panel was split in its opinions more often than
not, and it is a certainty that most of these issues will be controversial
for some time to come. But it is neither important nor even desirable
that the public should arrive at a consensus about all of the words and
constructions that might be seen as embodying presuppositions about
gender roles. If it were possible to eliminate every gender-related English expression by magic, there is no reason to suppose that the cause
of sexual equality would be advanced, but only that we would be deprived of some excellent occasions for talking about the problem, in
all of the complexity with which it presents itself in language.

Terry Eagleton has suggested that in feminist discourse we can see
a resurgence of the eighteenth-century conception of the public
sphere, in which class differences and partisanship are subordinated to
common cultural concerns: "As with the classical public sphere, 'culture' is once more a vital nexus between politics and personal experience, mediating human needs and desires into publicly discussable
form."[13] Contemporary discussions of feminist linguistic issues evoke
the kind of critical solicitude that the eighteenth-century writers accorded to questions of grammar, even as grammar itself has been de-
preciated to a purely ceremonial role. What matters is the substance of
the discussion; forms, it has been said, are merely the *disjecta membra*
of history. If we keep our eye on the social function of language criticism, rather than on the particular usages it takes as occasions, we will
take the discussions of issues like those that feminists have raised as the
legitimate successors of the critical tradition.

Notes

1. The panel used in this survey was 64 percent male, and the estimated average age
of its members was sixty-one—not exactly youthful, but not wildly out of line for
what the eighteenth-century critics might have referred to as "authors of reputation."
On the average, more than 65 percent of the panelists returned each of the mail ballots
they were sent—an extremely high figure for this sort of survey, and an indication of
how seriously the panelists took the enterprise. Taken together, the panelists were a distinguished group; here is a sample of the membership:

Critics and journalists: Roger Angell, William F. Buckley, Alistair Cooke, Norman
Cousins, Frances Fitzgerald, Roger Kahn, Mary McGrory, Jessica Mitford, Edwin
Newman, John Simon, Susan Stamberg, Nina Totenberg, Tom Wicker.

Bellettrists: Margaret Atwood, Louis Auchincloss, Annie Dillard, Garrison Keillor,
Galway Kinnell, Mark Helprin, Maxine Hong Kingston, Maxine Kumin, Leonard
Michaels, Cynthia Ozick, Paul Theroux, Anne Tyler, Fay Weldon, Eudora Welty.

Academics and intellectuals: Jacques Barzun, Harold Bloom, Daniel Boorstin, Leo
Braudy, Rachel Brownstein, John Kenneth Galbraith, A. Bartlett Giamatti, Alfred Ka-
zin, Elaine Showalter, Susan Sontag, Helen Vendler.

Politics and public life: William Bradley, Mark Hatfield, S. I. Hayakawa, Shirley M.

Hufstedler, Barbara Jordan, Jeanne Kirkpatrick, Eugene McCarthy, Theodore Sorenson.

Science and medicine: Isaac Asimov, Robin Cook, Freeman Dyson, Douglas Hofstadter, Alvin Poussaint, Carl Sagan, Glenn T. Seaborg.

Linguistics and language study: Dwight Bolinger, Claire Cook, Ellen Prince, Carlotta Smith, Elizabeth Traugott, Calvert Watkins.

2. This figure was drawn from a survey conducted with a panel containing most of the same members, which was reported in the *Harper Dictionary of Contemporary English* (New York, 1975).

3. Nor is it likely that these changes in evaluation are due simply to changes in the composition of the panel. For one thing, we have seen that old and new panelists were uniformly conservative on other issues. What is more, the panelists' comments suggested that a number of them had changed their minds about these issues: "I've given in on this," and so forth.

4. G. S. Kirk, "The Future of Classics," *The American Scholar* 45 (1976): 536.

5. William Cobbett, *A Grammar of the English Language* (Oxford, 1984), p. 4.

6. Nor is it surprising that in the schools the study of grammar should have been demoted to the status of a low-level skill that figures as part of the "mechanics" of writing, while the intellectual faculties that the study of grammar was once supposed to enhance are now taught as "critical thinking," an independent subject concerned with argument in the abstract, without regard for the mode of its expression.

7. Thus general usage was obliged to replace *Negro* with *black* in deference to the preferences of that group, but the question of whether *black* should be capitalized is not so easily resolved, since it has consequences for the spelling of *white* as well.

8. In addition to the examples discussed here, we asked about the distinction between *sex* and *gender*, about the word *feminist* itself (can it be applied to a man?), and about the use of generic *man* and its derivatives, such as *man-made, mankind*, and *man-eating*.

9. Care should be taken in interpreting the differences in the responses of men and women, since some part of this variation may have been due to age differences; on the average, the men on the panel were older than the women. I have no good explanation for the fact that men and women were more in agreement as to the acceptability of some items, such as *seductress*, than on others, such as *sculptress*.

10. Casey Miller and Kate Swift put the argument against all such words more strongly in their *Handbook of Nonsexist Writing* (New York, 1981): "When . . . suffixes like *-ess* and *-trix* are attached to these words to designate women, even if the addition is intended as a courtesy, the basic form [i.e., *actor, host, sculptor*] acquires a predominantly masculine sense with the unavoidable implication that the feminine gender form represents a substandard variation" (p. 109).

11. Two of the panelists (out of 125 who responded to these items) apparently adopted the strategy of alternating masculine and feminine forms in successive sentences.

12. Some linguists have argued that *they, them*, and so on can in fact be singulars, as evidenced by the fact that the form *themself* (analogous to the singular form *yourself*) is commonly used in speech in sentences like "Anyone who tries to get themself a job at the plant should have no trouble." The argument is ingenious, but it is worth noting that *their* was offered as an alternative by only one of the eight linguists on the panel.

13. Terry Eagleton, *The Functions of Criticism* (London, 1984), p. 118.

~ J. ENOCH POWELL

Further Thoughts: Grammar and Syntax

IN 1989, WE CELEBRATED—SOME OF US—in the Church of England the fifth centenary of the birth of Thomas Cranmer, to whom, no doubt rightly but without absolutely cogent evidence, is attributed the principal hand in the language of the Book of Common Prayer. The current form of that Book is that authorized in 1662 after the restoration of the monarchy; but substantially the text is that of the Elizabethan Book of 1558, which, after the Roman Catholic interlude under Mary (1553–1558), reverted to the Edwardian Book of 1552, a slightly more Protestant edition of "Cranmer's" original English Prayer Book of 1548.

The struggle now going on in England to preserve the traditional sixteenth-century text against supersession by the twentieth-century "Alternative Service Book" is part of a wider contemporary struggle within English education. Government and the political parties have awoken with horror to the inroads made into schooling by two combined influences: the view of education as a universal right rather than the privilege of an elite; and the rising proportion in the school population—it was already 8 percent nationally by 1985—of what are gingerly called "ethnic minorities." Under the present government an endeavor is being made to stem those inroads through central prescription of curriculum and standards.

In that prescription there is a notable preoccupation with the English language, and in particular with reviving the grammatical study and analysis of it. What those at the center know, but dare not say, is that the great disaster has been the loss of Latin as an obligatory element in school education. From Cranmer's time until the very recent past, English was a language written by those who knew Latin, who self-consciously analyzed it as they wrote, and who understood and exploited the resources of an essentially Latin syntax for the enrichment and enlargement of human thought and expression. This was something made possible by the widespread knowledge of Latin, despite the fundamental linguistic difference between English which is lightly inflected and Latin which is strongly inflected.

Written—and spoken—English is rapidly becoming today the tongue of those who do *not* know Latin. We are for instance losing— as transatlantic English has already lost—the expressive resource of the difference in English (uniquely among European languages) between the aorist (*I saw*) and the perfect (*I have seen*). "What is your judgement of George Eliot as a writer of English? I ask because I have just reread *The Mill on the Floss*." As likely as not, the wording today would be: "I just reread *The Mill on the Floss*," spoken without the least consciousness—grammatical consciousness—of what has been sacrificed by degrading the perfect *have read* into the aorist *read*. The result is English impoverished because it is English ungrammatical.

Another powerful asset of English—including (what is by no means irrelevant to ordinary speech and writing) a rhetorical asset—is the peculiarly flexible English relative pronoun. How brilliantly Cranmer exploited this and how ruthlessly his revisers have dispensed with it is strikingly illustrated by the prayer of consecration in the Holy Communion ("commonly called the Mass," 1548), which in Common Prayer consists of one continuous vast sentence, made possible by the relative pronoun: "Almighty God, our heavenly father, *who* of thy tender mercy . . . *who* made there by his one oblation . . . HEAR US and GRANT . . . *who* in the same night that he was betrayed . . . Amen." Quite deliberately the revisers have destroyed this architectural structure and replaced it with a series of separate independent sentences, in the belief presumably that English speakers and hearers no longer understand and appreciate relative pronouns—have, in other words, become de-Latinized and linguistically uneducated. Only draftsmen who were themselves in that condition could have dared in the *Te Deum* to replace the correct English equivalent "we praise thee, O God" with the horrific mistranslation "You are God, and we praise you."

Much of the discussion on the changes in a language tends to concentrate upon vocabulary. My contention is that a language, especially one like English, which can legitimately make a verb out of any noun from anywhere in the world, can cope with no end of damage to its vocabulary. What it cannot survive is assault upon its structure—its grammar and its syntax. That after all is the process which barbarized classical Greek into modern Greek and the process (though it turned out to be wonderfully fruitful) which debased Latin into the Romance languages. The protection for the structure of English, which it is doubtful can now be restored even by the edict of a more reactionary government than Britain is likely to elect, is a cultural elite which has absorbed its English while being educated in Latin grammar and the Latin classics.

And yet that ship is still no farther off than hull down on the horizon. When the Jewish refugee professors of Classical Philology turned up in England in the 1930s what astonished them most was the linguistic standard of public school boys who not only translated unseen passages which (as one of them put it to me) "I should have been lynched for setting to doctoral candidates," but—what is far more to the point—translated superb examples of their own English tongue into passable Latin and Greek prose and verse. For that no substitute will be found.

Note

J. Enoch Powell's essay in the 1980 *State of the Language* was entitled "The Language of Politics."

From *Wordstruck*

THIS IS A TIME OF WIDESPREAD ANXIETY about the language. Some Americans fear that English will be engulfed or diluted by Spanish and want to make it the official language. There is anxiety about a crisis of illiteracy, or a crisis of semiliteracy among high school, even college, graduates.

Anxiety, however, may have a perverse side effect: experts who wish to "save" the language may only discourage pleasure in it. Some are good-humored and tolerant of change, others intolerant and snobbish. Language reinforces feelings of social superiority or inferiority; it creates insiders and outsiders; it is a prop to vanity or a source of anxiety, and on both emotions the language snobs play. Yet the changes and the errors that irritate them are no different in kind from those which have shaped our language for centuries. As Hugh Kenner wrote of certain British critics in *The Sinking Island*, "They took note of language only when it annoyed them." Such people are killjoys: they turn others away from an interest in the language, inhibit their use of it, and turn pleasure off.

Change is inevitable in a living language and is responsible for much of the vitality of English; it has prospered and grown because it was able to accept and absorb change.

As people evolve and do new things, their language will evolve too. They will find ways to describe the new things and their changed perspective will give them new ways of talking about the old things. For example, electric light switches created a brilliant metaphor for the oldest of human experiences, being *turned on* or *turned off.* To language conservatives those expressions still have a slangy, low ring to them; to others they are vivid, fresh-minted currency, very spendable, very "with it."

That tolerance for change represents not only the dynamism of the English-speaking peoples since the Elizabethans, but their deeply rooted ideas of freedom as well. This was the idea of the Danish scholar Otto Jespersen, one of the great authorities on English. Writing in 1905, Jespersen said in his *Growth and Structure of the English Language*:

> The French language is like the stiff French garden of Louis XIV, while the English is like an English park, which is laid out seemingly without any definite plan, and in which you are allowed to walk everywhere according to your own fancy without having to fear a stern keeper enforcing rigorous regulations. The English language would not have been what it is if the English had not been for centuries great respecters of the liberties of each individual and if everybody had not been free to strike out new paths for himself.

I like that idea and do not think it just coincidence. Consider that the same cultural soil, the Celtic-Roman-Saxon-Danish-Norman amalgam, which produced the English language also nourished the great principles of freedom and rights of man in the modern world. The first shoots sprang up in England and they grew stronger in America. Churchill called them "the joint inheritance of the English-speaking world." At the very core of those principles are popular consent and resistance to arbitrary authority; both are fundamental characteristics of our language. The English-speaking peoples have defeated all efforts to build fences around their language, to defer to an academy on what was permissible English and what not. They'll decide for themselves, thanks just the same.

Nothing better expresses resistance to arbitrary authority than the persistence of what grammarians have denounced for centuries as "errors." In the common speech of English-speaking peoples—Americans, Englishmen, Canadians, Australians, New Zealanders, and others—these usages persist, despite rising literacy and wider education. We hear them every day:

Double negative: "I don't want none of that."

Double comparative: "Don't make that any more heavier!"
Wrong verb: "Will you learn me to read?"

These "errors" have been with us for at least four hundred years, because you can find each of them in Shakespeare.

Double negative: In *Hamlet*, the King says:

> Nor what he spake, though it lack'd form a little,
> Was not like madness.

Double comparative: In *Othello*, the Duke says:

> Yet opinion . . . throws a more safer voice on you.

Wrong verb: In *Othello*, Desdemona says:

> My life and education both do learn me how to respect you.

I find it very interesting that these forms will not go away and lie down. They were vigorous and acceptable in Shakespeare's time; they are far more vigorous today, although not acceptable as standard English. Regarded as error by grammarians, they are nevertheless in daily use all over the world by a hundred times the number of people who lived in Shakespeare's England.

It fascinates me that *axe*, meaning "ask," so common in black American English, is standard in Chaucer in all forms—*axe, axen, axed*: "and *axed* him if Troilus were there." Was that transmitted across six hundred years or simply reinvented?

English grew without a formal grammar. After the enormous creativity of Shakespeare and the other Elizabethans, seventeenth- and eighteenth-century critics thought the language was a mess, like an overgrown garden. They weeded it by imposing grammatical rules derived from tidier languages, chiefly Latin, whose precision and predictability they trusted. For three centuries, with some slippage here and there, their rules have held. Educators taught them and written English conformed. Today, English-language newspapers, magazines, and books everywhere broadly agree that correct English obeys these rules. Yet the wild varieties continue to threaten the garden of cultivated English and, by their numbers, actually dominate everyday usage.

Nonstandard English formerly knew its place in the social order. Characters in fiction were allowed to speak it occasionally. Hemingway believed that American literature really did not begin until Mark Twain, who outraged critics by reproducing the vernacular of characters like Huck Finn. Newspapers still clean up the grammar when they quote the ungrammatical, including politicians. The printed word, like Victorian morality, has often constituted a conspiracy of respectability.

People who spoke grammatically could be excused the illusion that their writ held sway, perhaps the way the Normans thought that French had conquered the language of the vanquished Anglo-Saxons. A generation ago, people who considered themselves educated and well-spoken might have had only glancing contact with nonstandard English, usually in a well-understood class, regional, or rural context.

It fascinates me how differently we all speak in different circumstances. We have levels of formality, as in our clothing. There are very formal occasions, often requiring written English: the job application or the letter to the editor—the dark-suit, serious-tie language, with everything pressed and the lint brushed off. There is our less formal out-in-the-world language—a more comfortable suit, but still respectable. There is language for close friends in the evenings, on weekends—blue-jeans-and-sweat-shirt language, when it's good to get the tie off. There is family language, even more relaxed, full of grammatical short cuts, family slang, echoes of old jokes that have become intimate shorthand—the language of pajamas and uncombed hair. Finally, there is the language with no clothes on; the talk of couples—murmurs, sighs, grunts—language at its least self-conscious, open, vulnerable, and primitive.

Broadcasting has democratized the publication of language, often at its most informal, even undressed. Now the ears of the educated cannot escape the language of the masses. It surrounds them on the news, weather, sports, commercials, and the ever-proliferating talk and call-in shows.

This wider dissemination of popular speech may easily give purists the idea that the language is suddenly going to hell in this generation, and may explain the new paranoia about it.

It might also be argued that more Americans hear more correct, even beautiful, English on television than was ever heard before. Through television more models of good usage reach more American homes than was ever possible in other times. Television gives them lots of colloquial English, too, some awful, some creative, but that is not new.

Hidden in this is a simple fact: our language is not the special private property of the language police, or grammarians, or teachers, or even great writers. The genius of English is that it has always been the on-gue of the common people, literate or not.

English belongs to everybody: the funny turn of phrase that pops into the mind of a farmer telling a story; or the traveling salesman's dirty joke; or the teenager saying, "Gag me with a spoon"; or the pop lyric—all contribute, are all as valid as the tortured image of the academic, or the line the poet sweats over for a week.

Through our collective language sense, some may be thought beautiful and some ugly, some may live and some may die; but it is all English and it belongs to everyone—to those of us who wish to be careful with it and those who don't care.

✍ ELIZABETH REES

Hard Characters

The words spade arrows.
They fork fondue
and hammer horseshoes.
The words paste holes,
the words are spatulas.
Words won't be domestic,
will not be worlds. The words
climb over each other and
sit on top of words
in the overstuffed trunk.
The words won't shovel,
the words want more words.
Words so small they fit
in the palm of the hand,
the words that blow
at the first hard lie.

E. S. C. WEINER

The Federation of English

THE FIRST EDITION OF THE *OXFORD ENGLISH DICTIONARY* was completed in 1928. Its aim was to register the entire vocabulary of English from the early Middle Ages to the present. The present was, of course, a moving target, for the *OED* was published in serial parts between 1884 and 1928. Since most of the work was done before the outbreak of the First World War (nearly half was published before 1900), the *OED* can be fairly regarded as covering the English language down to the end of the nineteenth century. R. W. Burchfield's *Supplement* was begun in 1957, and published (in four parts) between 1972 and 1986: its essential purpose was to bring the record up to date by registering the new vocabulary of the major part of the twentieth century (though it added much else). The second edition of the *OED* appeared early in 1989. Its primary function is to combine these two mighty works of lexicography into one integrated sequence.

The atmosphere of many parts of the *Supplement* certainly contrasts with that of the first edition of the main *OED*. Opening a volume at random, one can encounter a series of severely scientific terms, such as *spirogyra, spiroidal, spirolactone, spironolactone,* rubbing shoulders with pungently demotic phrases: *spit and sawdust, to go for the big spit, the dead spit of;* alongside them, clusters of markedly foreign terms: *Sprechgesang, spreite, sprezzatura, springar; ephemeral,* rather ludicrous expressions, like *Spock-marked, squalorology, Squaresville, squattez-vous;*

names of artifacts, many proprietary: *Staybrite, Stechkin, Steinway, Steinwein, Stelazine, Sten*; and words, or meanings of words, that until recently were unprintable: *shit, slit, slot, spunk, suck off,* and so on. It is difficult to imagine some of these (whether in existence or not at the time of its compilation) appearing in the original *OED*. What has changed—the English language, or lexicography, or something else?

In the "General Explanations" which preface the *Oxford English Dictionary* James Murray introduces his model of the English vocabulary by comparing it to "one of those nebulous masses familiar to the astronomer," in which a well-defined nucleus shades gradually off on all sides into darkness:

> The English Vocabulary contains a . . . central mass of many thousand words whose "Anglicity" is unquestioned; some of them only literary, some of them only colloquial, the great majority at once literary and colloquial—they are the *Common Words* of the language. But they are linked on every side with other words . . . which pertain ever more and more distinctly to the domain of local dialect, of the slang and cant of "sets" and classes, of the peculiar technicalities of trades and processes, of the scientific terminology common to all civilized nations, of the actual languages of other lands and peoples. And there is absolutely no defining line in any direction: the circle of the English language has a well-defined centre but no discernible circumference.[1]

Murray provides a diagram which shows how these fields of vocabulary interrelate. The literary component of the common central mass shades off in one direction into scientific terminology and in another into foreign words. The colloquial component shades off a third way into slang. Slang is flanked on one side by technical language, which borders scientific terminology, and on the other by dialect, which has affinities with foreign loanwords; technical and dialectal words enter the common core through both speech and literature. Murray set a clear-cut aim for the Dictionary. The lexicographer

> must include all the "Common Words" of literature and conversation, and such of the scientific, technical, slang, dialectal, and foreign words as are passing into common use, and approach the position or standing of "common words", well knowing that the line which he draws will not satisfy all his critics. For to every man the domain of "common words" widens out in the direction of his own reading, research, business, provincial or foreign residence, and contracts in the direction with which he has no practical connexion: no one man's English is *all* English. The lexicographer must be satisfied to exhibit the greater part of the vocabulary of *each* one, which will be immensely more than the whole vocabulary of *any* one.[2]

We may visualize Murray's approach in terms of a Venn diagram. The *universal set*, the English vocabulary as a whole, is for practical purposes boundless. Murray's "one man's English" is a *subset*. If it were possible to plot every English speaker's vocabulary on the diagram, we should arrive at a diagram with three characteristics: the *union* of all the vocabulary sets should be virtually coterminous with the *universal set* (the total vocabulary); there should be a common *intersection* of all the sets (the "greater part of the vocabulary of each one"); and there should be a zone around this where many, but not all, sets overlapped, gradually merging into an outlying region in which only a very small minority of vocabulary sets overlapped.

Murray's view implies a set of English speakers with a shared cultural base. They read a common literature written in a homogeneous literary dialect, which they also write. Cultural factors explain why it seemed to Murray relatively easy to mark the boundaries of this common core. The vast cloud of linguistic data was as complex then as now; but between it and the observing lexicographer we should imagine cultural "filters," focusing and magnifying some phenomena, obscuring and suppressing others.

Much the most important filter was the lexicographer's reliance on written evidence. This filter was a cultural phenomenon of Murray's time. Only certain kinds of language reached print or were used with a view to publication in print. There were, firstly, particular ways of writing when publication was intended, knowledge of which was imparted largely by the educational system. This shaped the "literary" component of the "central mass" in Murray's diagram. It also screened out all that was unacceptable for printed publication. This filter was not merely a way of censoring taboo words, it was a reflection of the whole range of ethical and aesthetic tastes of the nineteenth century. Society subscribed to the convenient fiction that "English" was *written* English.

Murray largely adheres to the criterion of "writtenness" in his handling of modern dialectal vocabulary. Dialect words from after 1500 he will admit only in exceptional circumstances.[3] But we can sense his discomfort, as an accomplished dialectologist, in drawing this line.

A second filter was the criterion of cultural intelligibility. The predicament is best exemplified in the field of scientific vocabulary, which was already expanding rapidly. Discussing pronunciation, Murray had written of "words such as *acetamine*, which have no popular currency, and which indeed were made, not primarily to be spoken, but to be used in books."[4] The existence of vocabulary created by the learned largely for print qualifies Murray's dictum that "speech comes first, and writing is only its symbolization." If all scientific language was printed language, should it all be counted as part of the core of English? Certainly not. He drew the line like this:

> The aim has been to include *all words English in form*, except those of which an explanation would be unintelligible to any but the specialist; and such words, not English in form, as either are in general use, like *Hippopotamus, Geranium, Aluminium*, . . . or belong to the more familiar language of science, as *Mammalia, Lepidoptera, Invertebrata*.[5]

Victorian society was undergirded by science (to an extent hitherto unknown). An educated member of that society was familiar with, and able to comprehend, the essentials of the science which played such an important part in its life. To the extent that a department of science was relevant to contemporary social existence, its terminology was, as it were, socially acceptable, and could be regarded as part of the common core of vocabulary.

In the realm of slang the filter of print must have operated at its most efficient. Slang is either the specialized jargon of subgroups within a community, a quasi-secret language, or a set of highly colloquial words and senses which are generally known and used, but which are felt to be somehow substandard.[6] The second kind of slang is a linguistic register that enables sensitive subjects (bodily functions, bodily extinction, spiritual matters, emotions, and so on) to be handled in a flippant and irreverent way. Victorian taste did not permit such linguistic behavior in public; therefore it could not be expressed in print; therefore it was not there to be collected by the lexicographer. It is significant that the living taboo words which did attain the OED were generally exemplified from pre-nineteenth-century literary sources.

Murray discusses foreign loanwords in some detail. He accords them a threefold classification into (1) "denizens": "words fully naturalized as to use, but not as to *form, inflexion*, or *pronunciation*, as *aide-de-camp, locus,* [etc.]"; (2) "aliens": "names of foreign objects, titles, etc., which we require often to use, and for which we have no native equivalents, as *shah, geyser,* [etc.]"; and (3) "casuals": "foreign words . . . not in habitual use, which for special and temporary purposes occur in books.'"[7] He recognizes that there are no fixed limits between these classes, and that words continually "pass upwards" from the category of "casual" into that of "natural" (that is, native and naturalized words forming the common core).

The OED's cultural borderland, then, had an outer perimeter, determined by the limits of what was printable, and an inner, determined by what was perceived to be culturally familiar and comprehensible, in contrast to what was alien and obscure.

Can we still discern, as Murray did, a common core of vocabulary which gives the English language its unity? The determining factors were cultural rather than purely linguistic. If our model is different, is this due to changes in the linguistic data themselves or—as I believe—in the cultural filters through which the data reach the student of the lexicon today?

The first edition of the OED relied mainly on printed evidence. This policy has been maintained by the editorial staff of the OED. It has not ignored the significant work during the present century to collect purely spoken forms of English: the Survey of English Dialects, the materials of the American Dialect Society, and the researches underlying the *Dictionary of American Regional English*; the huge number of separate collections of oral slang assembled mainly by independent scholars; and the various recordings and transcriptions of unselfconscious spoken English. Most of this research has culminated in printed publications.

That Oxford lexicographers continue to view the English language through the filter of print might be a cause for disquiet, if it were not for the radical change in the function of print during the past century. Not only is English-language publishing now on a scale unimaginable in Murray's time, it is carried on in every part of the world, and (most importantly) handles every conceivable interest, pastime, entertainment, and subject of study. Print can scarcely be said to act as a filter any more.

The net of print potentially covers the whole vocabulary of English, right out to its nebulous edges. Each of the five peripheral realms of Murray's diagram is fully represented in printed sources. In addition (and perhaps as a result) the distinction between the literary and the colloquial vocabularies has become less straightforward. It is no longer true that society reserves special styles of language for print, and permits only a certain range of language to be published. Many varieties are used for writing as they are for speaking, and no variety is debarred from publication on the basis of ethics or taste. The elaborate stylistic tribunal, maintained by the nineteenth-century social code and an education system based on the classics, has been bypassed by social change. Any variety of English is permitted to appear in print, and many different varieties do. As the lexicographer faces the huge array of printed sources, he finds that the language is no longer prefiltered for him. If a boundary line is to be drawn he must draw it himself, since society has abandoned that role.

In registering the vocabulary of the last hundred years it would have been utterly inadequate to select only a range of published works comparable in literary standing to the nineteenth-century works excerpted for the first edition of the *OED*: the equivalents of George Eliot, Tennyson, Darwin, Huxley, the *Times, The Athenaeum,* and so on. The language of Joyce, Lawrence, Shaw, Dylan Thomas, T. S. Eliot, and their contemporaries, whose writings were read and excerpted for the *Supplement,* does not fit into the mold of a homogeneous literary dialect, but spills over in a wildly heterogeneous mixture of coarseness, archaism, jargon, technicality, dialect, conscious high style, and deliberate low style.

The *Lady Chatterley* trial, which permitted a few four-letter words to appear in print, is a rather obvious symbol of a greater change. This becomes clearer when it is appreciated that, in the early 1970s, lexicographers still had to scour rather disreputable underground publications with names like *Oz* and *Screw* to find examples of vocabulary which was in widespread everyday use but still not quite acceptable written down. Today, this kind of language can be heard on the street one day and read in a quality daily newspaper the next, and will certainly occur in almost any contemporary novel. This is not a linguistic change. A cultural filter has simply been dismantled.

Murray wrote that the limits of the Dictionary had not been extended as far in the domain of slang or cant as in those of science and philosophy. This may or may not still be true in terms of absolute numbers. What is much more important is that Murray's boundary on this side has collapsed. Any slang, any cant, any colloquialism may appear in print. Whereas in the first edition of the *OED* one can find examples only of "literary" language even from a newspaper published "by office boys for office boys," the *Daily Mail*—"The sex of future man will be predeterminable. For a time one sex will predominate, then another" (31 December 1901)—in the *Supplement* one encounters colloquialisms such as this from the former "top people's" paper, the *Times*: "The Duke of Edinburgh had adopted a new 'limp' handshake . . . Expecting something flabby and wimpish, the men got royal bonecrushers" (11 February 1985).[8] Language that would once have been debarred for its grammatical sloppiness or incoherence is permitted in any newspaper or broadcast news bulletin. Unless lexicographers are prepared to live in the past, they can rely on no cultural yardstick to determine the limits in this area.

When we turn to technical language we find another kind of cultural change at work, but tending in the same direction. The spheres of life where technical vocabulary is forged could be treated for the most part as isolated subcultures in Murray's day. Terms from the industrial processes which kept Victorian society running received their due recognition in little subsenses labeled "Soapmaking" (12 occurrences), "Mining" (850), "Calico-printing" (20), and so on. Even the sports could be tucked away in corners, with the terminology of different games often lumped together.

The mass leisure pursuits of the present era have swung the balance of publication in a new direction. While all these pursuits involve skill and require a considerable measure of self-education for the practitioner to become proficient, they are not, as the old crafts were, the preserves of isolated and sometimes hereditary subsections of the community but are open to anyone. Alongside the many sports and games played or watched by thousands, there are numerous pursuits which can also have a utilitarian function, or share the technology of workaday activities, such as photography, carpentry, and other do-it-yourself skills, fishing, hang-gliding, gardening, and so on. Each of these pursuits comes with a sizable vocabulary of its own. This terminology cannot be said to be common to the entire English-speaking community, but neither can it be relegated to the periphery of the language. The lexicographer who wishes to sample the range of language with which the ordinary English speaker comes in daily contact has only to visit the local newsagent's and collect from the shelves the dozens of magazines dedicated to leisure pursuits. Our reading program takes in titles like *Caves & Caving, Racing Pigeon, Runner's World, Hairflair, Tool World, Bus Times*. Each is well stocked with the technical terminology of its field. Here again, society no longer exercises cultural censorship by relegating such language to a few technical handbooks or the dictionaries of arts and crafts which Murray so often cited (there are, for example, 2,396 quotations from E. H. Knight's *Practical Dictionary of Mechanics* in the first edition of the *OED*). A whole realm of technical vocabulary lays claim to admission to the common core.

In the scientific sphere, the last hundred years have seen an explosion of activity that has taken specialization to the limits. It goes without saying that no scientist can be acquainted with all the branches of his own discipline, let alone other disciplines. Each of these vast autonomous areas of research is continually generating quantities of terminology. This vocabulary is certainly not everyone's English. How does the lexicographer draw the line? The scientific enterprise is far too deeply entrenched in the fabric of our culture for its terminology to be treated as peripheral; but it is far too complex for Murray's criteria of familiarity and comprehensibility to be useful any longer.

Furthermore, if Murray in his day could instance *acetamine* as an example of words "made, not primarily to be spoken, but to be used in books," how much more can lexicographers today puzzle over the enormous proliferation of sesquipedalian chemical names, such as *sulphinpyrazone, tetrachlorodibenzo-paradioxin,* or *tetraethylpyrophosphate,* which are entered in the *Supplement*—not to mention the expressions required to define many of them, like "10 [3 (4-methyl piperazin-1-yl)propyl]-2-trifluoromethylphenothiazine"? No one, of course, would expect terms of the latter type to be accorded dictionary entries, but they bring home sharply the fact that much of the language of science is a symbolic written code not in parallel relationship with the spoken word.

Especially in the fields of scientific and technical language the lexicographer today runs up against another lexical boundary resolutely fenced by Murray, the frontier of proper names. Pharmaceutical endeavor has generated thousands of drug names, generic and proprietary. Twentieth-century technology has given rise to thousands of appliances, commodities, conveyances, weapons, and the like, which are usually referred to only by their brand names: from aircraft and motor cars down to detergents, sandwich fillings, and toys. Most are proprietary. The first edition of the *OED* contained perhaps twenty-five, the best known being *Kodak, Pianola, Plasticine, Tabloid, Tarmac, Thermos*, and *Vaseline*. A sample of twenty pages of the *Supplement*, volume 4, 1139–1159, contains ten such terms: on that basis there could be two to three thousand in the whole work. Their huge concentration in present-day communication presents the lexicographer with a severe problem. They seem to belong to a lexical no-man's-land, having at once the characteristic of specificity which should relegate them to the realm of proper names, and the lack of substitutability which puts them back into the common language.

The physical frontiers of Murray's world gave substance to the fine distinctions he drew among foreign words. Either a common notion came in with, or acquired, a foreign name (usually from one of the most familiar foreign languages) as *genus* or *table d'hôte*, or a foreign one brought with it its foreign name. Somehow, foreignness is not as foreign now as it was. The all-too-familiar facts that the world is increasingly a single political and economic community, that foreign travel has become commonplace, that immigrant and expatriate communities from all parts of the world are sprinkled throughout the English-speaking community, and that cultural exchange at all levels is fashionable mean that, again, the boundary that Murray could draw fairly firmly has become very vague. Hence the enormous variety of foreign words brought into the second edition by way of the *Supplement*. Some, no doubt, are "casuals" which do not deserve the recognition of *OED* status. Drawing the line is fiendishly difficult.

This tour of the peripheral areas of vocabulary brings us back to dialect. Many of the literary works of the twentieth century have drawn heavily on dialect: Lawrence, the great Irish writers, Faulkner, for example. Nevertheless the vocabularies of minority communities, rural or urban, in their own context, have probably remained as peripheral as they were in Murray's day. But what Murray entirely omitted from a place in his diagram, and from any extended discussion in his General Explanations, was the regional variation of English.

Murray's model is unblushingly Britocentric. Words and senses not used in Britain are labeled "U.S.," "Austral.," and so on. Words used in Britain but not used in other regions are almost never labeled "U.K." Vocabulary occurring in North American, Australasian, South African, and Caribbean English, but not in British English, would probably have been classified as "dialect," "technical," or "slang." The implicit assumption was that Standard British English was identical with the standard version of English overseas. And this was probably correct in the 1880s. Britain's linguistic hegemony had not been questioned: good English, the English that all English-speakers had in common, was probably believed to be British English (the Queen's/King's English) in all communities, both in Murray's day and for many years afterwards.

This is an impossible view for the contemporary lexicographer. We now talk in terms of "Englishes" (unknown until very recently).[9] It is recognized that each region has its own dialects and its own standard language. Sir William Craigie, in the 1920s and 1930s, pioneered the idea of dictionaries for the major regional varieties of English, and since then American, Canadian, Australian, Caribbean, and Scottish English have all received some kind of treatment on the OED model.[10] Equivalent treatment was imported into the OED by R. W. Burchfield: the varieties of overseas English "have been accorded the kind of treatment that lexicographers of a former generation might have reserved for the English of Britain alone."[11] Moreover, it has become increasingly clear that the preponderant English-speaking community, that of North America, is now the chief center from which most of the linguistic innovations radiate to the other communities.

If several regional Englishes are to be recognized, what becomes of the concept of the common core? It remains true that a vast quantity of vocabulary is shared by all Englishes, but it also has to be realized that many central concepts are no longer conveyed by the same expressions in all regions, and standard expressions used in some regions may well be unknown in others. Again, it is an untidy picture. We cannot push the term "Englishes" to its logical extreme and try to make out that the common core has broken up into global dialects. There are forces working against that: for instance, the internationalizing forces that import such quantities of foreign words into the language. But we do seem to have to accept a picture of a number of overlapping subsets. The monolithic arbitrating culture that once filtered out the peripheral varieties of vocabulary before many of them even reached the lexicographer's attention has been replaced by a loose federation of subcultures which may have lingering emotional loyalties to old patterns of language but yield dominion to no other group.

Let us return to our Venn diagram. Print now spreads its net over a far greater proportion of the universal set than it ever did. It no longer functions as the major filter, screening out the coarse and the abstruse. An overlay of each individual speaker's vocabulary set no longer results in a clean intersection which can be labeled the common core. If there is a single intersection, it is almost certainly too small to make a complete and viable vocabulary. Instead, there are a number of important intersections which represent the main regional forms of English. Finally, there are many zones of partial overlapping which represent the areas of specialization that have attained a new cultural importance.

The English vocabulary is now federated rather than centralized. No one person's English is all English, but each English speaker is to some extent "multilingual" within English. We are competent in varieties of English in which we do not perform. Where, then, does the lexicographer draw the boundary? The problem is not yet resolved. To be sure of including a complete common core, all the major world Englishes must be covered; the common core cannot be less than the sum of their cores. Outside that, the only certain limiting factor is the size of the lexicographer's resources. Accommodating the vocabulary is no problem in a computerized database such as the *OED* now is. Collecting, researching, defining, and editing each vocabulary item, however, will remain a skilled and labor-intensive occupation. This means that priorities must be assigned: the vocabulary that receives immediate attention must be that which is perceived to have the greatest cultural "importance." Judgments have to be made, and lexicographers cannot look to a homogeneous cultural tradition for guidance; they have to rely on their collective sense, as participators in contemporary social life, of what is significant. They run the risk, if they do not do their job with sufficient thoroughness, of selecting the ephemeral and trendy at the expense of the permanent but unspectacular. Murray's description of the lexicographer "well knowing that the line which he draws will not satisfy all his critics" is truer than ever.

Notes

1. James Murray, "General Explanations," in *The Oxford English Dictionary* (1933) 1:xxvii (originally published in fascicle 1 [1884]). The second edition of the *Oxford English Dictionary* retains this explanatory introduction with minimal alterations and some additions.

2. "General Explanations," p. xxvii.

3. "General Explanations," p. xxviii.

4. "Preface to Volume I," in *A New English Dictionary* (Oxford, 1888) 1:xi (not reprinted in the 1933 edition of the *OED*).

5. "General Explanations," p. xxviii.

6. Following J. A. Simpson's classification: see "Slang" in I. C. B. Dear, *Oxford English* (1986), p. 308.

7. "General Explanations," p. xxix.

8. Cited s.v. *predeterminable* a, *wimpish* a. The description of the *Daily Mail* is Lord Salisbury's, in H. Hamilton Fyfe, *Northcliffe, an Intimate Biography* (cited in *Oxford Minidictionary of Quotations*).

9. It is common in linguistic journals such as *English World-Wide* (e.g. in 5 [1984]: 248).

10. See W. A. Craigie, "New dictionary schemes presented to the Philological Society, 4th April 1919," *Transactions of the Philological Society* (1925–1930): 8.

11. *Supplement* 1:xv.

❧ SYLVIA ADAMSON

The What of the Language?

MILTON'S ADAM, SO ROBERT BRIDGES TELLS US, shows the first symptoms of his fallen state in lust, anger, and a slipshod use of the relative
pronoun. Later prescriptive grammarians might lack Milton's confidence in equating moral and grammatical error, but the metaphor of
the Fall still dominates their conception of "the state of the language."
They are apt to contrast its present state—typically represented as a
state of "decline" or "corruption and decay"—with an original or
ideal state, where it exists as a transparent medium for fact and reason;
and they blame the loss of this linguistic innocence on human perver-
sity, specifically the "folly, vanity, and affectation" of speakers, or
their "lazy and defiant" flouting of rules. Adam's descendants are all
around us, "distorting" the sense of *hopefully*, "irredeemably tarnish-
ing" *refute*, and making "improper" uses of *while*.

In the 1970s, a different conception of "the state of the language"
became fashionable under the influence of structuralist linguistics. The
phrase provides a rough translational equivalent of Saussure's *état de
langue*, and it takes its force from structuralist definitions of language
as a static "self-sustaining system," or "a deft tracery of prepared
forms from which there is no escape." As the last clause implies, this
vision of the relation between speaker and language is hardly less pessimistic than that of the prescriptivists, but here the villain is not the
speaker but the language-system, commonly depicted, in imagery

drawn from totalitarian tyrannies, as an "arbitrary and inexorable" power, or a "prison-house," whose inmates are deprived of all rights to free speech and self-expression.[1]

A state of lawlessness and degeneration? or a state of perpetual imprisonment? At least these depressing alternatives can't *both* be true. We may even suspect that the darkness of the imagery in each case results from a one-eyed perspective, from seeing language as governed *only* by speaker or *only* by system. If we could put the viewpoints together, we might see the possibility of a state in-between, where language—like English case-law or American jazz—is simultaneously improvised and orderly. Saussure himself, unlike his poststructuralist successors, seems to have had some such state in mind. His famous distinction between *langue* and *parole* attempts to capture its paradoxical qualities: "The language-system [*langue*] is not a function of the speaker; it is a product that is passively assimilated by the individual. . . . Speaking [*parole*], on the contrary, is an individual act. It is wilful and intellectual. . . . It is in speaking that the germ of all change is found."[2] But to imagine the paradox of a voluntarist-determinist state is one thing, to find a methodology for investigating it is more difficult, and, in the event, Saussure resolved the difficulty by driving a wedge between speaker and language, putting the awkward, unsystematic facts of usage, innovation, and change outside the domain of linguistic inquiry. Half a century later, and equally influentially, Chomsky took a similar decision when he divorced the study of grammar from the study of actual linguistic "performance," where factors like "memory limitations, distractions, shifts of attention and interest, and errors" blur the outlines of the ideal system that exists in the mind prior to speech.[3]

The most striking feature of the linguistics of the 1980s has been the degree to which these orthodoxies have been attacked or abandoned as linguists have redirected their energies from *langue* to *parole*. Publishers' lists of the last ten years show a boom in those disciplines which study the language-system in a state of formation (child language acquisition, creolistics), or in a state of variability (dialectology, sociolinguistics), or in a state of spontaneous, informal performance (pragmatics, conversation analysis). And at the end of the decade, these separate studies are beginning to come together to foster a revitalized historical linguistics which aims to establish the relation between language as a system and language as an activity of speakers. In effect, Saussure's paradox is now the site of investigation, and the results of that investigation promise to revise our notions of "the state of the language" as a concept as well as enrich our understanding of the current state of English.[4]

II

In the 1980 edition of *The State of the Language,* Josephine Miles traced a shift in poetic vocabulary corresponding to a historical shift in poets' perceptions of where truth and value are located, from the conceptual world of the Renaissance, through the natural world of the late eighteenth century, to the world of human consciousness in the nineteenth century—a world which, in the poetry of our own time, shows an increasing "interiority and self-isolation."[5]

One hypothesis to be drawn from the new historical linguistics is that the language itself is following the same pathway. Many of the individual solecisms that offend prescriptivists turn out to be fragments of a larger pattern of change which has already worked itself through and become accepted elsewhere in the language-system. And the pattern is one of deepening subjectivity. Terms grounded in the conceptual and physical world—that is, serving logical or descriptive functions—are converted through a protracted but apparently inexorable development into terms grounded in the internal world of the speaker—that is, serving the function of expressing emotions, attitudes, and beliefs. The history of those notorious perverts, *hopefully,* *refute,* and *while,* shows the effects of this process of subjectivization on three very different aspects of our grammar.

Hopefully has changed both its syntax and its meaning since the *OED* illustrated its "modern" usage with "he set to work hopefully." In current popular practice, it is more commonly found in a parenthetic or sentence-initial position—"he set to work, hopefully" or "hopefully, he set to work"—and it is used to describe not the manner of the person reported but the state of mind of the reporter. It means "I hope that he set to work," not "he set to work full of hope." This change is one of the favorite targets for British prescriptivists, who normally blame it on the corrupting influence of American English (itself said to be a victim of German-speaking immigrants). But there is no need to look abroad for scapegoats, or to regard *hopefully* as aberrant. It is, rather, the latest recruit to a growing class of adverbs which give speakers the resources to qualify their statements by expressing increasingly refined degrees of certainty or diffidence:

Probably/evidently/certainly/surely he set to work.

No one complains of a solecism in any of these alternatives, yet, like *hopefully,* all of them originally performed a descriptive function. Some members of the group, like *obviously,* retain both subjective and objective senses ("I confidently infer" versus "in a clearly perceptible manner"). Others have shed their original meaning altogether, so that earlier usage may sound strange: "you wrote so *probably* that it put me in a fear of dangers to come." Or it may sound deceptively familiar. The revisers of the Authorized Version of the Bible detected a problem in the following text: "O foolish Galatians . . . before whose eyes Jesus Christ hath been evidently set forth." Their decision to revise *evidently* to *openly* suggests that the subjective sense of *evidently*, unknown in 1611, had become so dominant by the late nineteenth century as to make the revelation of Christ to the Galatians appear, dangerously, a matter of inference rather than a historical fact.

Refute, for Dr. Johnson and his contemporaries, meant "to prove erroneous," preferably by physical demonstration, as in Johnson's own famous claim that he could "refute" Berkeleyan idealism by kicking a stone. In the modern language, it more commonly refers to the world of speech than to the world of action and, in the usage that provokes complaint, it has lost all connections with public processes of proof, whether empirical or logical. In effect, it is used as an emphatic or emotionally charged variant of *deny*. This change, too, has precedents: many of the verbs we use to characterize acts of mind or speech started life as verbs of physical action, for example, *assume, observe, remark, discuss*. The closest parallel to *refute* is *insist*. In 1616, *insist* was defined by John Bullokar in exclusively physical terms: "rest or abide"; by 1755, when it was defined by Johnson, it had acquired the sense of "to dwell upon in discourse"; and before the end of the eighteenth century, it had added its current meaning of "assert emphatically." This development not only sets a pattern for the current subjectivization of *refute*, but almost entails it, by creating the need for an adequate balancing term. *Deny* would be too weak for contexts like "the Chancellor *insisted* that his policy was working well and *refuted* suggestions that the economy was in difficulties."

While has been the subject of complaint for at least fifty years. It is attacked as "perverted," "improper," or "illogical" when used as a marker of contrast or shift of focus in contexts that make its original meaning of temporal simultaneity implausible or impossible:

> The Dean read the Lessons *while* the Bishop preached the Sermon.

> *While* the team lost heavily last year, they should do better in the coming season.

Although the *OED* charts the development of contrastive overtones in *while* from the time of Shakespeare, it appears to have cut loose from its temporal anchoring only in this century. But the same drift of meaning began much earlier in other conjunctions: *since* widened its meaning from temporal to causal relations, and *whereas*, which originally referred to spatial proximity, became an expression of contrast— and so specialized in this function that it vigorously resists William Morris's attempt to revive the earlier meaning: "and quickly too he gat / Unto the place whereas the lady sat." In the case of conjunctions, then, the general pattern of subjectivization takes the form of a shift from meanings based on relations in the external world of space and time to meanings dependent primarily on the speaker's judgment or attitude: causal relations may or may not be empirically verifiable, and contrastive relations run the gamut from logical incompatibility to private prejudice. A critic who concludes that "Browning was a poet, *whereas* Tennyson was a gentleman" may be telling us less about Browning or Tennyson than about himself.[6]

III

When we look for an explanation for these changes, or at least for a mechanism by which they came about, we are thrown back on Saussure's paradox of the passive yet innovative speaker. But here the paradox appears not as a problem but as a solution. The solution depends on the existence of two kinds of meaning—on the one hand, meanings that are encoded in the vocabulary and grammar of the language and, on the other, meanings that arise contingently and by improvisation in particular contexts of speaking. Because speakers are helpless prisoners of the *état de langue* which they inherit, they cannot say more than the language gives them means to encode. But they may well mean more than they can say, or the conversational context may give their hearers warrant to infer more meaning than is formally declared. So, for example, in an imaginary state of the language in which there were no connectives such as *if*, *since*, *whereas*, and *while*, speakers would still be able to imply (or hearers infer) temporal, conditional, or causal links in such apparently disconnected sequences as: "I came, I saw, I conquered," or "more haste, less speed," or "Luigi Infortunato died on Tuesday. On Monday he had supper with the Borgias."

And in a state of the language which provided only temporal connectives, speakers and hearers would bring into play the same processes of implication and inference, this time enriching the words with meanings beyond those they explicitly encode. So a speaker might specify a relation of temporal simultaneity between events precisely because he wanted to suggest that their conjunction was incongruous: "can he imagine that God sends forth an irresistible strength against some sins *while* in others he permits men a power of repelling his grace?" Or he might use a stated relation of temporal succession to imply an unstated causal relation, like the anonymous Knight in *King Lear*:

> Since my young lady's going into France, sir, the Fool hath much pined
> away.   (1.4.73)

As a courtier, this speaker dare not directly criticize the king for rejecting his daughter, so he contents himself with placing two events—Cordelia's departure and the Fool's malaise—side by side as a temporal sequence; Lear's consciousness of the causal connection lurking in that *since*, with all the rebuke it implies, appears in his hasty and repressive response: "No more of that."

As the final stage in this not altogether imaginary history, we may posit a state of the language in which these contingent interpretations and nonce meanings become so firmly established that the connectives can be transplanted to new contexts where the original temporal interpretation would be quite out of place: "*since* I won't be here tomorrow, I'll type that letter now"; "*while* the team lost last year, they should do better in the coming season."

Once usages like these go unchallenged, we have reached the stage at which speaker-meanings and context-meanings have been converted into system-meanings, or, in Saussurean terms, *parole* has become *langue*. The popular solecism marks the point of transition, the moment when language as an *activity* begins to impress itself upon language as a *system*, changing the code to accommodate the needs of its speakers.[7]

IV

If the mechanism of change in these cases is indeed the pressure of unstated private meanings on an insufficiently expressive public code, it is hardly surprising that the direction of change should be towards an ever intensifying subjectivity. But what does this imply? Should we infer that twentieth-century language is in danger of becoming so irrevocably subjectivized that it can no longer exercise its descriptive and logical functions and will have to cede them to the new formal languages created by mathematicians, philosophers, and computer scientists? Must we project from our imaginary history a future state of the language in which all descriptions of the world are "ringed round with that thick wall of personality," the prison-house of solipsism which Pater predicted as the final achievement of the subjective forces released by the Renaissance?

Negative adjectives provide a case history that partially confirms but significantly modifies the pattern I have described so far. To negate is a basic logical function, but it is also something that people do for other than logical reasons, and here, as elsewhere, these more expressive functions have left their impress on the history of forms. The prefix *in-*, borrowed from Latin, had wide currency in the Renaissance, when it was used freely, alongside the native prefix *un-*, to form the negative of Latin-derived adjectives. As far as we can tell, the two forms were at that stage semantically identical: so Shakespeare uses pairs like *ingrateful/ungrateful, insubstantial/unsubstantial* more or less interchangeably, and this equivalence persists in later doublets such as the nineteenth-century coinages *insanitary/unsanitary*. But increasingly over the last three centuries the forms have diverged in meaning, with the *in-* prefix acquiring implications beyond straightforward logical negation. *Insubordinate* does not mean "not subordinate," just as *infamous* does not mean "not famous," and *inhuman* does not mean "not human" (King Kong might be classed as *not human*, but Hitler is more likely to be called *inhuman*). In many cases, what the *in-* form expresses is a hyperbole of simple negation, whereby the negative inverts, rather than merely excludes, the sense of its positive counterpart: so an *insubordinate* officer overturns hierarchy, *immoral* or *irreligious* acts are those which flout rather than just fail to conform to standards of morality or religion. At the same time, the *un-* form has also been losing some of its neutrality; often it has a markedly evaluative role, implying something like "departure from a norm." This departure can be viewed with either approval or disapproval, depending on the feelings aroused by the norm itself: hence the twist in the tail of Edward Fitzgerald's "Alfred [de Musset] is a fine fellow, very un-French," or Gavin Lyall's "Tyler and a party of the second part did something Unspeakably UnBritish together. Or Unspeakably British even." But much of the effect of these examples depends on the fact that the norm is something we normally endorse. In the absence of contrary directives, therefore, we are likely to assume that speakers intend to criticize a person or activity they describe as *unsocial* or *unprofessional*.

Negative adjectives, then, follow the predicted pathway into subjectivity, logical negation giving way to expressive and evaluative negation. But in this case at least, the logical function of language has not been lost. Instead, it has been transferred to two alternative forms, the prefixes *a-* and *non-*. Used only sporadically in earlier stages of the language, they have become increasingly productive as a source of new adjectives in the last hundred years, with *a-* replacing *in-* in the formal register and *non-* challenging *un-* everywhere else. Most of the *a-* adjectives occur in scientific discourse, but a few have wider currency: *amoral* and *alogical* were both coined in the 1880s, specifically, it appears, to provide neutral alternatives to *immoral* and *illogical*, and the same refusal to pass judgment characterizes more recent terms such as *atonal, apolitical, atheoretical.* The massive expansion in *non-* adjectives in this century is due, at least in part, to the way they have reduplicated existing *un-* forms, and the creation of so many doublets is due in turn to a systematic distinction between evaluative and unevaluative—or rather nonevaluative—forms of negation. To avoid the pejorative overtones of *unsocial* and *unprofessional,* we can now turn to *nonsocial* and *nonprofessional.* The difference may be crucial, as John Algeo points out: "A Moslem is a *non-Christian* but only a Christian can be *un-Christian* in behavior; a *nonrealistic* novel is one whose goal is other than a realistic view of the world, but an *unrealistic* novel is likely to be one that aims at, and fails to achieve realism."[8] Or, to add another example, cricket is a non-American activity but not, hopefully, an un-American activity.

But the present subjective-objective equilibrium may be less stable than it appears. In the case of negative nouns, where the *non-* prefix has a longer history of productivity than among the adjectives, there have been signs in the last twenty years or so of a shift in meaning from neutral negation to pejorative evaluation. Algeo glosses the new meaning as "possessing the superficial form but not the value of": a *nonevent* is not something that does not take place, but an event that disappoints expectations, and *nonfood* is certainly eaten, if only at cocktail parties. And this shift into pejorative evaluation affects not only new coinages but the meanings of existing terms: so *nonstarter* is now ambiguous, referring either to a competitor who does not take part in the race (say a horse) or to one who does but shouldn't have (say a presidential candidate). Although the fashion for this usage dates from the 1960s, an early precedent is to be found in the history of *nonentity,* which began life in seventeenth-century philosophy with the meaning of "nonbeing" but by the early nineteenth century had come to mean "worthless being," as in this very unphilosophical analysis by Lytton: "he was an atom, a nonentity, a very worm and no man." There may be a similar prognostic of the fate of *non-* adjectives in the history of one of the few words of this class formed before the nineteenth century. *Nondescript* was coined in the seventeenth century with the definition "not hitherto described" but is now used exclusively to mean "not worth describing"; so that an eighteenth-century writer appears to contradict himself in referring to "this fine nondescript owl." As for *a-* adjectives, there are signs that those in common use may be following *in-* adjectives towards a charged rather than a neutral negation. For some speakers, *amoral* and *alogical* have already collapsed into *immoral* and *illogical,* and in an informal poll of young speakers of British English, I found that a majority interpreted *apolitical* as "consciously refusing political alignment," in contrast with "nonpolitical," which they understood as a term of logical exclusion: "falling outside the category of political."

What we can infer from this case study (which could be repeated for other sets of forms) is that there is no irrevocable slide into subjectivity. Just as certainly as forms become subjectivized over time, their descriptive or logical functions find expression through other forms, so that the overall functional ecology of the system remains in balance. Language, we might conclude, is a set of relatively stable functions distributed across a set of constantly shifting forms. The only drawback to this conclusion is that it requires us to find a way of talking about language as something simultaneously at rest and in motion.[9]

V

Perhaps the first step towards revising the concept of "the state of the language" is to replace the word "state." With its connotations of stable and determinate structures, it too readily promotes the structuralist fallacy of believing that there is fixity in language and the prescriptivist fallacy of believing that there has been or should be fixity. To speak instead of "the flux of the language" might lead us to appreciate the centrality of *change* among the facts of language. But while it captures the notion of dynamic instability, "flux" fails to do justice to the small- and large-scale *patterning* of change which I illustrated in section II. It was this very perception—that change itself might be systematic—which led Sapir to coin the term "drift"; but this brings with it the suggestion of a cumulative directionality and ignores the possibility, illustrated in section IV, that change might take the form of cyclical alternations and renewals. A better choice, if the editors of this volume will permit a solecism, would be the term "between." Graceless though it is, "the between of the language" at least captures the insight that a language exists always in transitions and tensions: it is always found somewhere *between* states, swinging in the arc of a seesaw between descriptive and expressive functions, between public code and private implication.

"Between" is also appropriate because it represents a class of items—the spatial particles—that are particularly unstable in the present between of the language. One well-documented development in American English is the Californian slang, satirized by Cyra McFadden, which converts spatial terms (both particles and verbs) into psychological descriptors: *get behind* ("identify with"), *get to* ("affect"), *where you're coming from* ("what you mean").[10] Once again, the pattern is one of subjectivization and, in a less striking and systematic way, it is affecting other dialects. In British English over the last few years a number of such idioms have established themselves quite widely and with none of the flamboyance of conscious in-group slang: for example, "I don't *go on* Christmas," where *go on* means "enjoy," or "that's *down to* me," meaning "that's my responsibility/ achievement."

In the last edition of *The State of the Language*, David Lodge undertook the defense of "Californian psychobabble."[11] Where its detractors claimed that the idiom was a "vicious" perversion of denotative meaning, which threatened the accurate communication of ideas, he argued that it should be seen as a "metaphorical type of discourse" which "presents experience primarily in terms of the movement and organization of matter in space." Lodge's argument is persuasive, but what he overlooks is the extent to which prescriptivist outrage may be a necessary ingredient in his own response. The domain of physical space has always been a common source of metaphors for the domain of consciousness, but hardly anyone now notices the metaphor in a word such as "understand," or detects a spatial narrative in the sequence "I took in the idea, turned it over, thought it through, and kept it in the back of my mind." As soon as a metaphor is conventionalized within the language it is bleached of its original color. *Down to* is no different in origin from its predecessor and partial synonym *up to*, but we have been anesthetized to the latter's spatial force. It is perhaps only while such metaphors are also felt as solecisms that they can renew the tension between physical and psychological meanings.[12]

The contemporary between of spatial particles is activated in a poem of Gary Snyder's which begins:

> To be in
> to the land
> where croppt-out rock
> can hardly see
> the swiftly passing trees[13]

The typography breaks the flow of the opening phrase, *to be into*, making us pause long enough to wonder whether the most relevant meaning is psychological ("to be keen on") or physical ("to occupy a place in")—a self-questioning designed to discomfit all those of us who are merely armchair ecologists (like Cyra McFadden's Kate, who "didn't actually jog yet but . . . was reading *The Ultimate Athlete*"). The same ambiguity shapes the last stanza:

> Up here
> out back

> drink deep
> that black light

The act proposed by the imperative—"drink deep"—is one of ingestion, in which, by a triumph of modern subjectivism, the external world is to be absorbed into the inner space of the perceiving subject. Yet the opening line maintains the opposite possibility, shrinking and localizing the act and the subject into a small corner—"up here"—of a larger geographical site. The second line intensifies the subject-object debate. *Outback*, whose spatial origins have been bleached by conventional usage, is revitalized by being typographically splintered into its component particles, each of which offers a double reading: "out" may be spatial (a successful exodus from domestic and mental interiority), or it may have the psychological meaning that Lodge says it carries in psychobabble forms like *spaced out* ("the breaking of some conventional limit or boundary, a dangerous but exhilarating excess"); "back" may be spatial (the hinterland behind the city), or temporal (a return to the primeval rocks of stanza 1) or, again, psychological (a reversion to a simpler state of consciousness). Whatever our final interpretation of the poem, the act of trying to understand it is bound to engage us in the interplay between some at least of these possibilities.

This kind of creative ambiguity is perhaps no more than we expect from poetic language. But within ordinary language, the solecism performs exactly the same function, by hovering indeterminately between two automatized states. The utterance, as the speaker intends it, may fall unambiguously within the categories of an emerging state of the language, in which, for example, *while* means "whereas" or *to come from* means "to mean"; by resisting the innovation, the prescriptivist reimposes or at least reawakens the categories of the receding state. As a result, we see, momentarily, both states together, sometimes with disconcerting effects, as in A. P. Herbert's "The Dean read the Lessons while the Bishop preached the Sermon," or Cyra McFadden's "Listen, I know where you're coming from. I just wondered where you're going." Accompanied by the ghosts of its past and future senses, the banal form of words becomes, like Balla's Futurist dachshund, at once dynamic and surreal, reminding us that every act of *parole* both subverts and creates a rule of *langue*; language is in process and between is what we speak.

Notes

1. The words and phrases in quotation marks in the opening two paragraphs (as elsewhere in the essay) are all real quotations; they are unattributed because, torn from context and blended together, they are intended to represent the vocabulary and atti-

tudes of a school rather than the statements of any of its individual members. Readers may recognize the tone of voice of Johnson, Fowler, Partridge, Kingsley Amis, or Basil Cottle among the prescriptivists and Meillet, Sapir, Paul de Man, and Fredric Jameson among the (post)structuralists.

2. F. de Saussure, *Course in General Linguistics*, trans. W. Baskin (New York, 1966), pp. 14, 98.

3. N. Chomsky, *Aspects of the Theory of Syntax* (Cambridge, Mass., 1965), p. 3.

4. The book that set the tone and the agenda for the linguistics of the 1980s is T. Givon, *On Understanding Grammar* (New York, 1979). Less comprehensive in scope but more accessible in style is J. Haiman, *Natural Syntax* (Cambridge, Eng., 1985). For a textbook incorporating many of the insights of the decade, see P. Hopper and E. C. Traugott, *Grammaticalization* (Cambridge, Eng., forthcoming in 1990).

5. Josephine Miles, "Values in Language; or, Where Have *Goodness, Truth, and Beauty* Gone?," in *The State of the Language*, ed. Leonard Michaels and Christopher Ricks (Berkeley and Los Angeles, 1980), pp. 362–76.

6. The study of subjectivity in language, primarily associated with the work of Saussure's successor, Emile Benveniste, gained a foothold in the linguistics of the English-speaking world largely through the efforts of John Lyons. See J. Lyons, "Deixis and Subjectivity. Loquor ergo sum?," in *Speech, Place, and Action: Studies in Deixis and Related Topics*, ed. R. J. Jarvella and W. Klein (Chichester, 1982), pp. 102–24. The role of subjectivity in language change has been discussed in specialist conference papers through the 1980s, many of them, like this essay, indebted to E. C. Traugott, "From Propositional to Textual and Expressive Meanings: Some Semantic-Pragmatic Aspects of Grammaticalization," in *Perspectives on Historical Linguistics*, ed. W. P. Lehmann and Y. Malkiel (Amsterdam, 1982), pp. 245–71.

7. There are close parallels and precedents for my imaginary history in accounts of current developments in creoles and past events in other established languages. See S. Romaine, *Pidgin and Creole Languages* (London, 1988), J. Haiman and S. Thompson, eds., *Clause Combining in Grammar and Discourse* (Amsterdam, 1988).

8. John Algeo, "The Voguish Uses of *Non*," *American Speech* 46 (1971): 87–105.

9. Parts of this section draw on Peter Matthews's discussion of productivity in negative adjectives in *Morphology*, 2d ed. (Cambridge, Eng., 1990). I am grateful to him for the loan of his manuscript. For a fuller discussion of negative nouns, see John Algeo's article (reference above). The "voguish uses" that he describes seem to be more widespread in American than in British English.

10. Cyra McFadden, *The Serial* (New York, 1977).

11. David Lodge, "Where It's At: California Language," in *The State of the Language* (1980), pp. 503–13.

12. For a fuller discussion of the role of spatial metaphors in our descriptions of consciousness, see G. Lakoff and M. Johnson, *Metaphors We Live By* (Chicago, 1980).

13. Gary Snyder, "Source," from the collection *Turtle Island* (New York, 1974).

SYLVIA ADAMSON holds the Lectureship in English Language in the Faculty of English, University of Cambridge.

JOHN ALGEO is Alumni Foundation Distinguished Professor of English at the University of Georgia. In 1986–1987, he was a Guggenheim Fellow and Fulbright Research Scholar at the Survey of English Usage, University College London. He is the coauthor of *Origins and Development of the English Language* and author of *On Defining the Proper Name*, and for ten years was editor of *American Speech* (to which he currently contributes "Among the New Words"). He is preparing a *Dictionary of Briticisms*.

KINGSLEY AMIS is a poet, novelist, essayist, honorary fellow of St. John's College, Oxford, and former teacher of English literature at two British and two American universities. He has published many articles on the language, and in 1974 gave a series of talks on the subject on BBC radio.

RICHARD W. BAILEY is Professor of English Language and Literature at the University of Michigan and former president of the American Dialect Society. With Manfred Görlach, he edited *English as a World Language* (1982). He is the author of a volume tentatively entitled *The Reputation of the English Language*.

MICHAEL BAWTREE is a Canadian director, writer, and educator. A former associate director of the Stratford Festival, Ontario, and a founder of one of North America's first music theater companies, COMUS Music Theatre (1975–87), he also established in Banff (Canada) an integrated music theater training program for performers, composers, writers, and designers. He has lectured on music theater throughout North America and Europe, and has recently completed a book called *The New Singing Theatre*.

LEON BOTSTEIN is president and professor of music history and history at Bard College and Simon's Rock. As a conductor, he has performed with the London Philharmonic, the Boston Pro Arte Orchestra, and the Hudson Valley Philharmonic, and has premiered and recorded the works of numerous American composers. His articles have appeared in *The New Republic, Partisan Review, Harper's, New York Times Magazine, Nineteenth-Century Music*, and other journals and collections.

ROBERT BURCHFIELD, formerly chief editor of the Oxford English dictionaries and editor of *A Supplement to the Oxford English Dictionary*, 4 vols., 1972–86, is now revising H. W. Fowler's *Modern English Usage*. His books include *The English Language* (1985) and *Unlocking the English Language* (1989). He has been a tutor of English language at the University of Oxford for nearly forty years.

MICHAEL CALLEN is a gay man who was diagnosed as having AIDS in 1982. Deeply involved in AIDS activist politics, he is cofounder of the People with AIDS Coalition in New York, president of the Community Research Initiative, and editor of *Surviving and Thriving with AIDS: Collected Wisdom* (1987, 1988) and the *PWA Coalition Newsline*. He is also a singer and songwriter.

SEYMOUR CHATMAN, Professor of Rhetoric and Film at the University of California, Berkeley, is the author of *Story and Discourse* (1978) and *Antonioni: The Surface of the World* (1985). He has just completed a book entitled *Coming to Terms: Narrative Among the Text-Types*.

DAVID DABYDEEN won the Commonwealth Poetry Prize and Cambridge University Quiller-Couch Prize with his first collection of poems, *Slave Song*. His second collection, *Coolie Odyssey*, was published in 1988. He is currently Lecturer in Caribbean Studies at the University of Warwick.

DONALD DAVIE, the English poet, Professor Emeritus at Vanderbilt, has retired to his native country after twenty years in the United States. His latest book of poems is *To Scorch Or Freeze*.

ARTHUR DELBRIDGE is Emeritus Professor of Linguistics and Honorary Director of the Dictionary Research Centre, Macquarie University. He is editor-in-chief of the *Macquarie Dictionary*, and has published books and articles on linguistics and on English in Australia.

MARGARET ANNE DOODY is Andrew W. Mellon Professor in Humanities and Professor of English at Vanderbilt University. She is the author of two published novels and coauthor (with Florian Stuber) of a play, *Clarissa: A Theater Work. Part I*, performed in New York in 1984. Her works of criticism include *A Natural Passion: A Study of the Novels of Samuel Richardson* (1974); *The Daring Muse: Augustan Poetry Reconsidered* (1985), for which she was cowinner of the Rose Mary Crawshay Prize awarded by the British Academy; and *Frances Burney: The Life in the Works* (1988).

M. F. K. FISHER has published some twenty books since *Serve it Forth* in 1937 and has written regularly for the *New Yorker*. She still consults the dictionary and enjoys writing too much to be stopped by the supposed hazards of aging. Her next book is about French landladies, with Kathleen Hill, and is her first collaboration.

BRYAN A. GARNER, both as a practicing lawyer and as an academic, has written widely on legal style, the English language, and Shakespearean philology. Known for *A Dictionary of Modern Legal Usage* (1987), he currently serves as the chief editor of the *Oxford Law Dictionary* and teaches at the University of Texas School of Law, where he is the director of the Texas/Oxford Center for Legal Lexicography.

HENRY LOUIS GATES, JR., is W. E. B. Du Bois Professor of Literature at Cornell University. A MacArthur Prize Fellow, he is the author of *Figures in Black* and *The Signifying Monkey*, general editor of the *Norton Anthology of Afro-American Literature*, and editor of the thirty-volume series *The Schomburg Library of Nineteenth Century Black Women Writers*.

SANDRA M. GILBERT is Professor of English at the University of California, Davis. She is the author of *Acts of Attention: The Poems of D. H. Lawrence* (1973), and the coauthor with Susan Gubar of *The Madwoman in the Attic: The Woman Writer and the Nineteenth-Century Literary Imagination* (1979) and *No Man's Land: The Place of the Woman Writer in the Twentieth Century*, vols. 1 and 2 (1988, 1989). She has also published several volumes of poetry, most recently *Blood Pressure*.

LORRIE GOLDENSOHN, a poet and critic who teaches at Vassar, is working on a book on Elizabeth Bishop. Her last collection of poems was *The Tether* (1984).

SIDNEY GREENBAUM is Quain Professor of English Language and Literature at University College London. He is coauthor of *A Comprehensive Grammar of the English Language* (1985). His most recent books include *Good English and the Grammarian* (1988), a coauthored *Guide to English Usage* (1988), and *A College Grammar of English* (1989).

JOHN GROSS was editor of the *Times Literary Supplement* from 1974 to 1981 and worked as a staff reviewer for the *New York Times* from 1983 to 1988. He is the author of *The Rise and Fall of the Man of Letters*.

JAN ZITA GROVER, a historian and critic living in California, has written extensively on AIDS. Her work has been published in the United States, Great Britain, and Canada.

ROY HARRIS is Emeritus Professor of General Linguistics at Oxford University and an Honorary Fellow of St Edmund Hall, Oxford. His books include *The Language-Makers* (1980), *The Language Myth* (1981), *The Origin of Writing* (1986), and *The Language Machine* (1987). He is the editor of the interdisciplinary journal *Language & Communication*.

LIZ HASSE, a California attorney and film producer, frequently writes and lectures on constitutional, media, and arts law.

ANTHONY HECHT is a University Professor at Georgetown University.

MICHAEL HEIM wrote the first book on computerized writing, *Electric Language: A Philosophical Study of Word Processing* (1987). He has finished another book, *Feedback: Philosophy for the Computer Age*, and was the translator of Heidegger's *The Metaphysical Foundations of Logic* (1984). He lectures in Philosophy at California State University, Long Beach.

JOHN HOLLANDER's most recent book of poetry is *Harp Lake*. He is also the author of *The Figure of Echo* and *Melodious Guile: Fictive Pattern in Poetry*. He is A. Bartlett Giamatti Professor of English at Yale University.

TED HUGHES has been Poet Laureate since 1984. His first book of poems, *The Hawk in the Rain* (1957), established him as one of the foremost poets of his generation. Since then he has published more than twenty volumes of poetry, some of them for children. He lives in Devon.

ROBERT ILSON is an Honorary Research Fellow of University College London, associate director of The Survey of English Usage, and editor of the *International Journal of Lexicography*.

HUGH KENNER is Andrew W. Mellon Professor in the Humanities at The Johns Hopkins University. His books include *The Pound Era* (1971), *The Stoic Comedians: Flaubert, Joyce, and Beckett* (1975), *A Homemade World: The American Modernist Writers* (1975), *Geodesic Math and How to Use It* (1976), *Joyce's Voices* (1978), *The Mechanic Muse* (1986), and *A Sinking Island: The Modern English Writers* (1988).

WAYNE KOESTENBAUM teaches English at Yale University, and is the author of *Double Talk*, a study on the erotics of male literary collaboration. As a poet, he was a cowinner of the 1989 *The Nation*/"Discovery" contest.

HERMIONE LEE is Senior Lecturer in the Department of English and Related Literature at the University of York. She reviews regularly for the London *Observer* and is the author of books on Virginia Woolf, Elizabeth Bowen, and Philip Roth. Her study of Willa Cather and her anthology of Cather's stories were published in 1989.

PAUL LENTI is an entertainment writer. He began working with *Variety* in 1984 as the Mexico City correspondent and currently runs the paper's Latin Desk in New York.

WENDY LESSER, the founding editor of *The Threepenny Review*, is the author of *The Life Below the Ground: A Study of the Subterranean in Literature and History*. She is currently working on *The Severed Self*, a study of male artists looking at women.

DAVID LODGE is Honorary Professor of Modern English Literature at the University of Birmingham, where he taught from 1960 to 1987. He has published several works of criticism, including *The Modes of Modern Writing* (1977) and *Working with Structuralism* (1981), and eight novels, of which the most recent are *Small World* (1984) and *Nice Work* (1988).

ALISON LURIE is a novelist and Professor of English at Cornell University. In 1985 she won the Pulitzer prize in fiction for *Foreign Affairs*. Her most recent novel is *The Truth About Lorin Jones*.

WILLIAM LUTZ teaches at Rutgers University, Camden, and serves as the chair of the Committee on Public Doublespeak for the National Council of Teachers of English and as editor of the *Quarterly Review of Doublespeak*. He is the author of *Doublespeak, From Revenue Enhancement to Terminal Living* (1989) and *Beyond Nineteen Eighty-Four* (1989), and the editor of the revised *Webster's New World Thesaurus* (1985).

ROBERT MACNEIL is executive editor of the MacNeil/Lehrer NewsHour. His most recent book, *Wordstruck*, was published in 1989 by Viking.

MEDBH MCGUCKIAN, recently writer-in-residence at Queen's University, Belfast, is the author of three books of poetry, *The Flower Master* (1982), *Venus and the Rain* (1986), and *On Ballycastle Beach* (1988).

LEONARD MICHAELS, Professor of English at the University of California, Berkeley, is the author of two collections of stories, *Going*

Places and *I Would Have Saved Them If I Could*, and the novel and screenplay *The Men's Club*. In 1980 he edited *The State of the Language* with Christopher Ricks.

MARTHA MINOW is a professor at Harvard Law School where she teaches Civil Procedure, Family Law, and Jurisprudence. She was a law clerk to Judge David Bazelon and Justice Thurgood Marshall. Her forthcoming book is entitled *Making All the Difference: Problems of Distinction in Legal Thought*.

PAUL MULDOON was born in Northern Ireland in 1951. He now lives in the United States. His most recent book was *Selected Poems 1968–1986*.

LISA NEMROW is a screenwriter.

GEOFFREY NUNBERG is a linguist associated with the Xerox Palo Alto Research Center and The Center for the Study of Language and Information at Stanford University. In addition to technical work in semantics, sociolinguistics, and linguistic technology, he has published popular articles on usage, and is the usage editor of the *American Heritage Dictionary*. His commentaries on language are heard regularly on the National Public Radio program "Fresh Air."

KATHLEEN ODEAN is the author of *High Steppers, Fallen Angels and Lollipops: Wall Street Slang* (1988).

WALTER J. ONG, S.J., is Emeritus University Professor of Humanities, William E. Haren Professor of English, and Professor of Humanities in Psychiatry at St. Louis University. Among his recent books are *Fighting for Life: Contest, Sexuality, and Consciousness* (1981), *Orality and Literacy: The Technologizing of the Word* (1982), and *Hopkins, the Self, and God* (1986).

ROBERT PINSKY's most recent books are *Poetry and the World*, a volume of essays, and *History of My Heart*, awarded the William Carlos Williams Prize for poetry by the Poetry Society of America. A new collection of his poems will be published in 1990. He lives in Boston and teaches at Boston University.

FIONA PITT-KETHLEY is the author of several collections of poetry, including *The Perfect Man* (1989), and a travel book, *Journey to the Underworld*. She lives in East Sussex, and is currently working on novels, more poetry, journalism, and an anthology of erotic literature.

THE RT HON. J. ENOCH POWELL was a Member of Parliament from 1950 to 1987 and served as Minister of Health in a Conservative Government. He was Professor of Greek at the University of Sydney 1938–39. Among his recent books are *No Easy Answers* (1973) and *Wrestling with the Angel* (1977).

SIR RANDOLPH QUIRK is the President of the British Academy. Among his numerous books on the English language is *Words at Work* (1986), based on lectures in Singapore as Lee Kwan Yen Fellow. During 1988, he traveled widely in Asia and the Pacific on a project funded by the Leverhulme Trust to examine standards of English in education and the media.

FREDERIC RAPHAEL is the author of sixteen novels, among them *The Limits of Love, Lindmann, Like Men Betrayed, California Time, Heaven and Earth*, and *After the War*, from which a ten-part Granada television series has been made. His collections of stories include *Think of England*, and he has written a number of screenplays. For his sequence of six television plays, *The Glittering Prizes*, he received the Royal Television Society's award as Writer of the Year in 1976.

ELIZABETH REES teaches at the Writer's Center in Washington, D.C. Her poems have been published in *The Partisan Review, Ironwood, Northwest Review, The Berkeley Review*, and *The Christian Science Monitor*, and her first collection of poems was a 1988 finalist in the Wesleyan University Press New Poets Series.

DAVID REID has written for *Vanity Fair, Ploughshares, Threepenny Review*, and other magazines. With Leonard Michaels and Raquel Scherr, he edited *West of the West*. He is working on a book about New York City after the war.

CHRISTOPHER RICKS teaches English at Boston University, which he joined in 1986, having formerly taught at the universities of Oxford, Bristol, and Cambridge. He is a Fellow of the British Academy, and the author of *Milton's Grand Style; Tennyson; Keats and Embarrassment; The Force of Poetry*; and *T. S. Eliot and Prejudice*. He has edited *The Poems of Tennyson; The New Oxford Book of Victorian Verse*; and *A. E Housman: Collected Poems and Selected Prose*. With Leonard Michaels, he edited in 1980 *The State of the Language*.

MICHAEL ROGERS is the author of three novels, *Mindfogger* (1973), *Silicon Valley* (1982), and *Forbidden Sequence* (1988), and a collection of short stories, *Do Not Worry About the Bear* (1979). He often writes and lectures about high technology, and is a senior writer for *Newsweek* magazine.

SUZANNE ROMAINE is Merton Professor of English Language at the University of Oxford. She is the author of *The Language of Children and Adolescents* (1984), *Pidgin and Creole Languages* (1988), and *Bilingualism* (1989).

ROGER SCRUTON is a philosopher, novelist, and critic, editor of the *Salisbury Review*, and Professor of Aesthetics at Birkbeck College, University of London. His books include *Art and Imagination* (1974),

The Aesthetics of Architecture (1979), *Fortnight's Anger* (1981), *The Meaning of Conservatism* (1980), and *Sexual Desire* (1986).

NIKKI STILLER, Associate Professor of English at the New Jersey Institute of Technology, is the author of *Eve's Orphans* (1980) and the forthcoming *The Figure of Cressida in British and American Literature*. Her essays, poems, and stories have appeared in *The Hudson Review*, *Response*, *Midstream*, and other journals.

AMY TAN is the author of the novel *The Joy Luck Club* (1989). Her work has been translated into French, German, Italian, Dutch, and Chinese. She is the American-born daughter of Chinese immigrants.

SIR KEITH THOMAS is President of Corpus Christi College, Oxford. He has written extensively on the social and intellectual history of early modern England, and is the author of *Religion and the Decline of Magic* (1971) and *Man and the Natural World* (1983).

CHRIS WALLACE-CRABBE is a Melbourne poet and director of The Australian Centre at The University of Melbourne. His most recent book of poems is *I'm Deadly Serious* (1988), and his critical study of autobiography, *Falling into Language*, is due out in 1990.

MARINA WARNER is the author of *Alone of All Her Sex: The Myth and the Cult of the Virgin Mary* (1976), *Monuments & Maidens: The Allegory of the Female Form* (1985), and, most recently, *The Lost Father*, a novel. In 1987–88 she was a Visiting Scholar at the Getty Center for the History of Art and the Humanities. She lives in London.

EDMUND WEINER has been coeditor of the *Oxford English Dictionary* since 1984. He previously worked for seven years on the *OED Supplement*.

DESIGNER:	Eric Jungerman
COMPOSITOR:	Wilsted & Taylor
PRINTER:	Arcata Graphics
BINDER:	Arcata Graphics
TEXT:	Linotron 202 Bembo
CLOTH:	Holliston Roxite A
	Permalin Antique
PAPER:	50 lb. Glatfelter Offset

The English language
Is there such a thing, *the* English language worldwide?
ENGLISHES [Greenbaum, Quirk]

since the close of the 'Anglo-Saxon' or fully inflected stage
How does the dictionary constitute English, and now that people no longer know an inflected language (Latin), can they truly grasp their uninflected one?
RECTITUDES [Weiner, Powell]
ENGLISHES [Kenner]

as distinguished from U.S.
But aren't there two distinguishings to be done: as distinguished from the U.K., and as containing distinctions within the U.S. itself, ethnically and culturally, black, Chinese, Jewish . . . ?
ENGLISHES [Ilson, Gates, Tan, Stiller]

etc.
Don't immense areas of the world get tucked into this little *etc.*, as if the U.K. and the U.S. ruled the roost of English, with God on their side, whereas Africa, India, the Caribbean, Australia . . . ?
ENGLISHES [Bailey, Hecht, Dabydeen, Delbridge, Wallace-Crabbe]

illiterate or ungrammatical
But does anyone still believe in these prescriptions, in abuses, in mistakes, in incorrectness?
RECTITUDES [Amis, Ricks, Nunberg, MacNeil, Rees, Adamson]

From the
Oxford English Dictionary

ENGLISH

B. *substantive.*
1.a. **The English language**. First in the adverbial phrase, † *on* (now *in*) *English*. Also in phrase **the King's, the Queen's English**, apparently suggested by phrases like 'to deface **the king's coin**.' In 9th century, and probably much earlier, *Englisc* was the name applied to all the Angle and Saxon dialects spoken in Britain. The name *English* for the language is thus older than the name *England* for the country. In its most comprehensive use, it includes all the dialects descended from the language of the early Teutonic conquerors of Britain; but it is sometimes popularly restricted to the language **since the close of the 'Anglo-Saxon' or fully inflected stage**; sometimes to the language and dialects of **England proper**, **as distinguished from** those of Scotland, **Ireland, U.S.**, etc.; and sometimes to **the literary** or **standard form** of the language as distinct from **illiterate or ungrammatical** speech, etc.